EVOLUTION OF ENVIRONMENTAL JURISPRUDENCE IN INDIA

The great Indian economic growth story is intricately linked to, and dependent on, the story of India's natural environment. The development of Indian environmental jurisprudence, since India's independence, has been an effort to make sense of this dependence. This effort, by no means, has been easy. It has been fraught with challenges of a different order. Significant competing interests of uplifting millions out of extreme poverty, while heavily relying on an already plundered environmental inheritance, has made the legal and regulatory landscape tremendously challenging.

Accordingly, the evolution of Indian environmental jurisprudence, essentially, is an evolution of the legal response of the Indian judiciary while navigating these complex and competing rights and interests, within the larger context of the India Story. The Indian judiciary, led by the Supreme Court of India, has time and again espoused novel environmental principles and has modified the application of legal precedents in response to various competing considerations. This has included the creation of dedicated environmental law courts in the country.

The aim of this work is to explore the impact of legal trends and inconsistencies, and highlight different dominant considerations at play within the evolution of Indian environmental jurisprudence. In doing so, it seeks to contextualize and situate the recent adjudicatory trends, particularly of the National Green Tribunal, within the larger adjudicatory framework carved out over the decades by the Supreme Court of India.

The reader will find this work useful in understanding not only where we presently are in the larger scheme of Indian environmental law, but also where we are headed.

Raghuveer Nath is an Adjunct Faculty at the Jindal Global Law School, O.P. Jindal Global University, Sonipat.

Armin Rosencranz is the Founding Dean of Jindal School of Environment and Sustainability, and a Professor of Law at Jindal Global Law School, O.P. Jindal Global University, Sonipat.

EVOLUTION OF ENVIRONMENTAL JURISPRUDENCE IN INDIA

THE NATIONAL GREEN TRIBUNAL

RAGHUVEER NATH
ARMIN ROSENCRANZ

CAMBRIDGE
UNIVERSITY PRESS

Shaftesbury Road, Cambridge CB2 8EA, United Kingdom

One Liberty Plaza, 20th Floor, New York, NY 10006, USA

477 Williamstown Road, Port Melbourne, VIC 3207, Australia

314–321, 3rd Floor, Plot 3, Splendor Forum, Jasola District Centre, New Delhi – 110025, India

103 Penang Road, #05–06/07, Visioncrest Commercial, Singapore 238467

Cambridge University Press is part of Cambridge University Press & Assessment, a department of the University of Cambridge.

We share the University's mission to contribute to society through the pursuit of education, learning and research at the highest international levels of excellence.

www.cambridge.org
Information on this title: www.cambridge.org/9781009379199

© Raghuveer Nath and Armin Rosencranz 2024

First published 2024

A catalogue record for this publication is available from the British Library

ISBN 978-1-009-37919-9 Hardback
ISBN 978-1-009-37921-2 Paperback

To the silent champions of environmental justice who, knowingly or unknowingly, have helped shape India's environmental jurisprudence and whose tireless efforts, both inside and outside the courtroom, give hope for a brighter and greener future for generations to come

CONTENTS

IMAGES

FOREWORD

In the annals of India's legal history, the journey of environmental jurisprudence stands as a testament to the country's evolving consciousness and commitment towards preserving its natural heritage. Tracing its evolution through the decades, thus, becomes vitally important in not just understanding the pulse of India's evolving environmental paradigm but also in assessing the direction in which it is heading.

My own journey in environmental law, marked by relentless legal battles, has been driven by a deep-seated belief in the power of jurisprudence to safeguard our natural world. The establishment of environmental tribunals in India, a direct consequence of these legal battles, symbolizes a shift in the Indian judicial paradigm – a shift aimed at moving from reactive measures to proactive environmental governance. The National Green Tribunal (NGT), in particular, was established to be an embodiment of this transformation, serving as a specialized body to address the complex and urgent environmental challenges facing our nation. However, even after more than a decade of the Tribunal's establishment, the general dearth of comprehensive literature on the NGT has often hindered a deeper understanding of its functions, challenges, and impacts.

The authors, Raghuveer Nath and Armin Rosencranz, have done commendable work in filling this significant void in the literature on environmental jurisprudence in India. Their book, *Evolution of Environmental Jurisprudence in India: The National Green Tribunal*, provides nuanced insights into the NGT's formation, functioning, and the challenges it is yet to overcome. In a country where environmental issues are as diverse as its ecology, the need for such comprehensive academic work cannot be overstated. It offers a reservoir of knowledge for practitioners, academicians, policymakers, and students alike.

Perhaps, one of the most important aspects of this work is that it allows the reader to situate the present environmental legal trends within the larger context of India's environmental jurisprudence. For instance, the three most important environmental law principles – polluter pays, precautionary principle, and sustainable development – have undergone significant changes over the last few decades. The book highlights how these principles have been historically evolved and deployed with varying standards depending on the circumstances of different cases. In doing so, it allows the reader to navigate through internal legal contradictions and helps them to contrast the NGT's adjudication with that of the Indian Supreme Court and international environmental law. Such an analysis is very useful for any environmental legal practitioner or student.

Another striking aspect of this book is its candid exploration of the challenges facing the NGT. As highlighted, these challenges are not hypothetical but real and pressing. They range from infrastructural constraints and bureaucratic hurdles to deeper issues of legal interpretation and enforcement. The effective functioning of the NGT is imperative for the safeguarding of India's environmental future. Hence, addressing these challenges is not just an institutional necessity but a national imperative.

The journey of environmental jurisprudence in India, as illustrated in this book, is a narrative of struggle, resilience, and hope. It mirrors the country's aspirations of sustainable development, balancing economic growth with ecological preservation. The NGT's role in this journey is pivotal. As an institution, it embodies the spirit of our constitutional promise – to protect and improve the environment for present and future generations.

In conclusion, *Evolution of Environmental Jurisprudence in India* is a significant contribution to the field of environmental law. It offers a comprehensive understanding of the NGT's role in India's environmental landscape. I commend the authors for their thorough research and insightful writing. This book is a valuable resource for anyone interested in the intersection of law, policy, and environmental protection in India.

M.C. Mehta
Padma Shri (2016)
Ramon Magsaysay Award (1997)
Goldman Environmental Prize (1996)

PREFACE

The 'India Story' – in all the multitude of senses and contradictions that it is perceived – is largely a story of collective amnesia coupled with the thirst to regain a lost glory. To put this into perspective, India's share of global gross domestic product (GDP) went from around 24.2 per cent in the early 1700s to about 2.3 per cent around the time of its independence – a reduction of over 90 per cent after more than two centuries of colonialism.[1] At the same time, India's population more than doubled. Thus, in addition to the extreme economic depredation, poverty, and burden there was a deep-seated sense of injustice and the need to regain the lost economic and political glory India enjoyed a few centuries ago.

This India Story has fashioned, and continues to fashion, most political and socio-economic narratives, discourses, and policies in India.

However, this India Story is intricately linked to, and dependent on, the story of India's natural environment. The development of Indian environmental jurisprudence, since India's independence, has been an effort to make sense of this dependence. This effort by no means has been easy. It has been fraught with challenges of a different order. Significant competing interests of uplifting millions out of extreme poverty, while heavily relying on an already plundered environmental inheritance, has made the legal and regulatory landscape tremendously challenging.

Accordingly, the evolution of Indian environmental jurisprudence, essentially, is an evolution of the legal response of the Indian judiciary while navigating these complex and competing rights and interests, within the larger context of the India Story. The Indian judiciary, led by the Supreme Court of India, has time and again espoused novel environmental principles and has modified the application of legal precedents in response to various competing considerations. This has included the creation of dedicated environmental law courts in the country.

The aim of this work is to explore the impact of legal trends and inconsistencies, and highlight different dominant considerations at play within the evolution of Indian environmental jurisprudence. In doing so, it seeks to contextualize and situate the recent adjudicatory trends, particularly of the National Green Tribunal (NGT), within the larger adjudicatory framework carved out over the decades by the Supreme Court of India.

We hope that the reader finds this work useful in not only understanding where we are presently in the larger scheme of Indian environmental law, but also where we are headed. It is written keeping in mind the different needs of academics, law students, and practitioners.

Academics might find the comparative analysis of adjudicatory trends of international law, the Indian Supreme Court, and the NGT useful in furthering their research. We have employed the case-book method to highlight the relevant portions of several landmark environmental judgments followed by notes and questions. This direct interface with case law and legal reasoning is likely to assist the reader, especially law students, in formulating their own legal opinion and critically analysing the case. Furthermore, the book explores the socio-enviro impact of environmental policy and adjudication that might assist a legal practitioner in making a more cogent case.

NOTE

1. Aditya Mukherjee, 'Empire: How Colonial India Made Modern Britain', *Economic and Political Weekly* 45, no. 50 (December 2010): 73–82,75.

ACKNOWLEDGEMENTS

We are indebted to several remarkable individuals who have provided us with their invaluable guidance, support, and encouragement. Their expertise, dedication, and insights have enriched this project, and we remain deeply grateful for their assistance.

We extend our heartfelt appreciation to Prof. (Dr.) C. Raj Kumar, Vice Chancellor and Dean, O.P. Jindal Global University, without whose remarkable vision and leadership the authors would not have met. His foresight has not only ensured the creation of one of Asia's leading law schools, but has also yielded academics and scholars that have contributed significantly in shaping India's evolving jurisprudence.

We express our deep gratitude to Prof. (Dr.) S.G. Sreejith, Executive Dean, Jindal Global Law School, for his encouragement and support. His work on transcendental jurisprudence provides a unique and important paradigm to understand Indian environmental jurisprudence. It has been very valuable to the authors and any student of law would greatly benefit from it.

Our sincere gratitude also extends to Prof. (Dr.) Lavanya Rajamani, Professor of International Law, University of Oxford, whose extensive knowledge of international environmental law has been invaluable in providing a global perspective to this work. Her work has been deeply inspirational and has provided several inputs that have allowed us to compare the interpretation and application of international environmental principles within Indian environmental jurisprudence.

We are also indebted to Prof. (Dr.) Elizabeth Fisher, Professor of Environmental Law, University of Oxford, whose expertise in environmental policy and law has contributed significantly to the inclusivity and equity of this book. Her insights into the intersectionality of environmental law with social justice have been instrumental in broadening the scope of the discussion.

We are very thankful to Sudhanshu Kalla, Sehal Cheema, and Prathik Karthikeyan for their invaluable assistance in researching and compiling the legal precedents and case studies featured in this book. Their meticulous attention to detail and comprehensive analysis have enhanced the depth and relevance of the material.

We are deeply grateful to Cambridge University Press (CUP) and the entire CUP team for their relentless support, guidance, and encouragement. Despite the challenges posed by the pandemic they have been exceptional and it has been a privilege to work with them. We would like to especially thank Qudsiya Ahmed and Anwesha Rana for their commitment to academic excellence. Without their support, this work would not be complete. We are also very thankful to Aniruddha De and Anandadeep Roy for their patience, thoroughness, and care. They ensured that the book was presented in its best light.

Finally, we are profoundly indebted to the several anonymous reviewers that were enrolled by CUP to peer review the book. Their meticulous insights, comments, and feedback have elevated the quality of the material and ensured its accuracy and relevance.

We acknowledge with heartfelt gratitude the contributions of each individual mentioned above, as well as the countless others who have supported and inspired us along this journey. This book stands as a testament to the collective effort and dedication of all those who strive to protect and preserve our environment through the rule of law.

Any omissions or errors remain our own.

ABBREVIATIONS

AAQ	ambient air quality
BIRSA	Bindrai Institute for Research and Action
CBR	California bearing ratio
CNG	compressed natural gas
CPCB	Central Pollution Control Board
CSE	Centre for Science and Environment
CSR	corporate social responsibility
DDA	Delhi Development Authority
DDMA	Delhi Disaster Management Authority
DDT	dichloro-diphenyl-trichloroethane
DPCC	Delhi Pollution Control Committee
EC	environmental clearance
EIA	environmental impact assessment
ELD	environmental liability directive
ERF	Environmental Relief Fund
EU	European Union
GDP	gross domestic product
GIS	gas-insulated sub-station
GPI	grossly polluting industries

ICJ	International Court of Justice
ICMR	Indian Council of Medical Research
IFCD	Irrigation and Flood Control Department of Delhi
IIT	Indian Institute of Technology
INR	Indian Rupees
LCI	Law Commission of India
ML	mining leases
MoEF/MoEFCC	Ministry of Environment and Forests/Ministry of Environment, Forests, and Climate Change
MPPCB	Madhya Pradesh Pollution Control Board
NEAA	National Environment Appellate Authority
NEAA Act	National Environment Appellate Authority Act, 1997
NEERI	National Environment Engineering Research Institute
NET Act	National Environmental Tribunal Act, 1995
NGT	National Green Tribunal
NGT Act	National Green Tribunal Act, 2010
OCEMS	online continuous emission/effluent monitoring systems
OECD	Organization for Economic Co-operation and Development
OHSC	occupation health and safety centre
PIL	public interest litigation
PMC	Pune Municipal Corporation
REA	resource equivalency analysis
REIA	regional environmental impact assessment
SDM	subdivisional magistrate
SOR	statement of objects and reasons
SPCB	State(s) Pollution Control Board
UN	United Nations
UPIC	Uttar Pradesh Irrigation Committee
UPPCB	Uttar Pradesh Pollution Control Board
US	United States
USD	United States Dollars
WCF	World Cultural Festival
WTO	World Trade Organization

1

INTRODUCTION TO THE NATIONAL GREEN TRIBUNAL

THE NEED FOR A "GREEN COURT"

1.1   INTRODUCTION TO ENVIRONMENTAL PROBLEMS AND HISTORICAL CONTEXT

If metaphors are an essential part of legal imagination, Bruno Latour's metaphor of the "fabric of law" aptly captures law's incessant endeavour to cover "everything completely and seamlessly".[1] Well-established doctrines, principles, and procedures provide a predetermined framework that seeks to regulate social interactions.[2] To keep the legal fabric warm and ironed, law exudes a homeostatic quality that is manufactured by the obligation to keep the fragile tissue of rules and texts intact.[3] As a result, a premium is put on legal stability and coherence. This premium is expressed in many ways: the significance accorded to the rule of law and legal certainty, the run of precedent in common law, the emphasis on legal formalism and reasoning, and circumscribing of the role of courts.[4]

However, environmental law is the law relating to environmental problems.[5] The nature of environmental problems, thus, has a significant influence throughout the creation and operation of environmental law. It moulds the latter's structure and asks questions that tend to stretch the legal imagination of courts and lawyers. Being polycentric, normatively complex, interdisciplinary, socio-politically charged, and scientifically uncertain, environmental problems produce legal heat that tends to expand the contours of the legal fabric.[6] Hence, understanding the nature of environmental problems is crucial to understanding and evaluating the role courts have played in adjudicating such problems.

Environmental problems come in many shapes and sizes, and each is embedded in its own political and cultural context.[7] Despite this diversity, however, environmental problems seem to have a common structure.[8] This structure is highlighted in a short story that Elizabeth Fisher narrates in relation to car parking in East Oxford.[9] When she moved to East Oxford in the early 1990s, there was plenty of parking space on the streets.

However, by the early 2000s, due to a rapid increase in the number of cars parking, there was a lack of free parking spaces. Due to this, ambulances, fire engines, and pedestrians found it increasingly difficult to access the roads in East Oxford. Moreover, taxis refused to drop residents at their homes, often complaining that it would be too difficult to manoeuvre around the badly parked cars. The local authority finally took notice and proposed a permit system whereby two permits would be issued per house. This, however, resulted in a mixed public reaction.

Some saw no parking problem, some did not want to pay for the permit, some had diverging views on the number of permits per house, and others were concerned about the economic impact on local shops. As Fisher highlights, no one gave much attention to the finite capacity of parking spaces. Rather, the focus of the discussion was on the right to park, the need to park, and the desire to park. The issue soon snowballed into larger questions of the proper role and legitimacy of the government. In the end, after several rounds of consultations and heated public meetings, the residents' permit scheme was finally introduced in 2012, with effect only in a small number of streets.

This problem of parking is a quintessential example of an environmental problem.[10] It is a tragedy of the commons.[11] This tragedy arises as everyone exploits public resources for their own benefit, due to a lack of direct incentive to moderate their usage as someone else might take a larger share. Thus, as Fisher highlights, while this story of parking spaces in East Oxford is a story of many things, it is primarily a story about the finite capacity of the physical environment.[12] Similar to how irrespective of the varying hopes and expectations of the residents, the reality was that there were limited parking spaces, the Earth's environment has a finite carrying capacity. This carrying capacity, however, is often invisible and comes to the fore only after proper scientific inquiry.

Thus, in contrast to other fields of law, environmental problems are "hot" as there is an absence of a stabilized knowledge base to identify overflows, multiplicity of actors, sociopolitical conflict, and scientific uncertainty. This is evident from the fact that tragedies of the commons and externalities are not quietly sitting out in the word with a label on them.[13] The legal heat inherent in environmental problems is primarily characterized by polycentricity.[14] As Justice Brian Preston, Chief Judge of the Land and Environment Court of New South Wales, highlights, a polycentric problem involves "a complex network of relationships, with interacting points of influence".[15] In other words, each decision made communicates itself to other centres of decision in a way that a new basis must be found for the next decision. Lon Fuller helps visualize this legal polycentricity through an analogy of a spider's web.[16] A pull of one strand of the web will distribute the tension across the whole web in a complex manner. Moreover, doubling the initial pull does not necessarily result in doubling the tension across the web, but rather creates different and complicated patterns each time.

This is aptly exemplified in the *Huaraz Case*, which involved a farmer in Peru suing a German multinational energy company for the potential destruction from flooding that was likely to be caused due to rising water levels from climate change.[17] Interestingly, even though the company did not have any operations in Peru, the claim was based on a scientific calculation of the company's overall contribution to global climate change (measured at 0.57 per cent). As expected, the district court rejected the claim due to a lack of causation and the lack of scientific evidence linking the emissions from the company to the exact rise in water levels near the farmer. Accordingly, though it is clear that the flooding resulted due to climate change and that the defendant company contributes to this, there is no way of ascertaining whether the particular emissions of the company were responsible for the flooding in a different continent. Thus, the cold application of traditional legal doctrines is not well equipped to deal with the legal heat inherent in environmental problems.

Accordingly, it is not surprising that environmental protection is increasingly viewed as not being effectively dealt with by traditional domestic law. Indian environmental jurisprudence has evolved over the years to tackle this issue. One of the aims of this book is to analyse this evolution from the initial years of the Supreme Court after independence up to the National Green Tribunal.

1.1.1 HISTORICAL CONTEXT TO INDIA AND ITS ENVIRONMENT

The enactment of the National Green Tribunal Act, 2010 (hereinafter, "NGT Act"), on 2 June 2010 marked a historic moment in Indian environmental adjudication. It was the first time that a properly functional adjudicatory body dedicated to environmental issues, staffed with both judicial and expert members, and with wide-ranging powers was established in India. However, viewing this in isolation betrays the significance of this moment. To fully appreciate why it was necessary to establish the National Green Tribunal (NGT), we need to understand the historical and legal context.

For the most part of Indian history, people in India have had a direct symbiotic relationship with the environment.[18] The environment has been revered due to its significance in the lives of people, and the environmental condition has had a direct impact on the quality of people's lives. Due to this, sustainable use of natural resources was historically ingrained in the people of India. For instance, a team of geotechnical engineers from the Indian Institute of Technology, Gandhinagar, and archaeologists from the Archaeological Survey of India recently discovered a water harvesting system in the Harappan city of Dholavira.[19] This revealed an intricate system of water reservoirs, channels, drains, and dams that were used to sustainably divert water from rivers into large reservoirs by the Indus Valley Civilization.[20]

The *Manusmriti*, or the *Laws of Manu*, though criticized for its misogynistic treatment of women,[21] placed considerable emphasis on developing a comprehensive and sustainable system of water laws.[22] It required kings to protect public waters and commons and imposed a system of punitive actions for those who polluted water.[23] Similarly, environmental protection has been emphasized in Kautilya's *Arthashastra*. It recognized commons and water resources as common property, akin to the modern-day concept of the public trust doctrine.[24] Further, numerous public officials were appointed to oversee sustainable exploitation of natural resources, and overexploitation was punished.[25] The environment was intricately linked to the lives of people and even in the Mughal period, most traditional enterprises such as crafts, textiles, and spices were grown in sustainable ways.[26]

However, with the advent of colonialism and the Industrial Revolution in Europe, this symbiotic relationship between the environment and the people of India was permanently ruptured. Massive systematic de-industrialization of India's traditional enterprises forced people to produce cash crops such as indigo to feed the growing demand in Europe.[27] Innumerable forests were cleared to supply wood for the growing British Empire and the creation of the Indian railways (which were primarily meant for ensuring a steady supply of British soldiers and resources).

Michael H. Fisher, discussing the effect of British rule on India's ecology, notes:[28]

> The systemic scope and level of technology of state intervention into the environment and into the lives of local people, was unprecedented in Indian history … each kilometer of track initially used about 1,000 sleepers, about 200 large trees, with periodic replacement as they decayed…. Much of the more than a million tons of railway fuel burned annually was extracted from Indian forests. All this caused major deforestation, in addition to expanding commercial timbering made profitable by railway transportation.

In 1947, at the dawn of independence, we inherited an India that had been economically and socially ravaged for nearly two hundred years by colonialism. Not only was India systematically de-industrialized, it was also deprived of the opportunity to partake in the process of modern industrial transformation that occurred elsewhere in the world. To add some factual perspective, India's share of world gross domestic product (GDP), which accounted for about 25 per cent till as late as the beginning of the eighteenth century, was reduced to an abysmal 4.2 per cent when India gained independence, while India's population more than doubled during this time.[29]

The growth of per capita income in India during the colonial period, between 1820 and 1913, was either zero or negligible. In fact, the per capita GDP declined at an annual rate of −0.22 per cent during the period between 1913 and 1950.[30] Even more astonishingly, the level of industrialization fell from 93 (taking 100 to be the industrial level in England in 1900) in 1750 to 60 in 1900![31] In other words, the Indian economy, at least statistically, was worse off than it was about two centuries ago.

It is no surprise, therefore, that Indian political leaders at independence were aware that extreme mass poverty, widespread illiteracy (both educational and cultural), a ruined agricultural system and industry, and structural distortions caused by colonialism made the transition to self-sustained growth a difficult task.[32] It is in this context that we need to appreciate the political, social, and economic trajectories undertaken by them.

After the end of the Second World War, it was not only Jawaharlal Nehru in India but also Kwame Nkrumah in Ghana, Julius Nyerere in Tanzania, and several other developing world leaders who tried to prioritize inclusive economic development. However, in most cases, these efforts were not sustainable. Military coups and the lust for power made democracy collapse in many nations. If one were to look at the map of democracy in 1985, one would see the bleak landscape that it had in almost all developing and emerging nations. India was an exception.

This is because shortly after independence, the Indian political design in terms of regular elections, a progressive Constitution, and an empowered Supreme Court made India resemble an advanced nation. In this respect, it had very few peers in the developing world.[33] Nevertheless, India was largely abysmally poor due to colonial exploitation. Accordingly, the central political narrative in the first few decades after independence was self-sufficiency through aggressive economic growth.

This economic growth, invariably, came at the cost of the environment. However, in response, the first environmental legislation came only in the 1970s. Given this context, let us explore how the Indian Supreme Court dealt with increasing environmental degradation. In doing so, we will be able to better appreciate the need for a dedicated environmental court in India.

1.2   PUBLIC INTEREST LITIGATION AND ENVIRONMENTAL ADJUDICATION IN INDIA: THE NEED FOR A "GREEN COURT"

Given this historical context and independent India's natural predisposition towards aggressive developmental policies, large-scale public projects were initiated by the Indian government in the first few decades following independence.[34] The Nehruvian developmental model focused on a socialist form of development through the introduction of large hydroelectric dams and infrastructural projects.[35] The central narrative behind the pursuit of aggressive economic growth was to make India economically independent and attain its former glory.[36] This development, however, invariably came at the cost of the environment.

As noted, the Indian environment had already suffered at the hands of colonial debauchery. Added to this, the new capitalist class in India wanted to create wealth, though under the name of development, with no regard for environmental concerns. To tackle these issues, the Indian legislature enacted several laws to protect the environment, such as the Wildlife Protection Act, 1972, the Water (Prevention and Control of Pollution) Act, 1974, the Forest (Conservation) Act, 1980, and the Air (Prevention and Control of Pollution) Act, 1981. These laws were enacted immediately following the Declaration of the United Nations Conference on the Human Environment, Stockholm (1972), which symbolized the international consensus regarding the need to preserve the environment.

Shortly after the Stockholm Conference, the legislature, in 1976, through the forty-second amendment to the Constitution, added Articles 48A and 51A(g) with an aim to advance environmental protection. Article 48A, though not enforceable, directs the government to protect and improve the environment and to safeguard the forests and wildlife of India. Further, Article 51A(g) prescribes it a fundamental duty of every citizen to promote and improve the natural environment, including forests, lakes, rivers, and wildlife.

While these environmental legislative enactments crystalized India's international commitments to safeguarding the environment, their application on the ground was limited. This is because the aforementioned overarching environmental laws required the enactment of rules, regulations, and notifications at the local level to be effective. In the absence of local legislation, the Supreme Court felt forced to intervene.

The Court, throughout the 1980s, responded to governmental inaction towards environmental degradation through the process of public interest litigation (PIL). This allowed it to provide wider remedies by way of procedural innovations such as the expansion of *locus standi* and the introduction of a non-adversarial procedure.[37] For instance, through the introduction of epistolary jurisdiction, a simple handwritten letter to the Court explaining grievances could be treated as a writ petition filed under Article 32 of the Constitution.[38] This ensured that the people at large had access to justice.

It is during this period that contemporary Indian environmental jurisprudence was created. Most landmark environmental cases adjudicated by the Supreme Court during this time were trailblazing as the field of environmental regulation in India was previously unexplored at the highest levels of the judiciary. This allowed the Court to considerably balance environmental concerns with developmental interests. The Court adopted international best practices and upheld India's international commitment towards safeguarding the environment by applying international environmental principles such as sustainable development,[39] precautionary principle,[40] and polluter pays principle[41] in the domestic context (discussed in detail in Chapter 3).

Further, based on these international principles and the constitutional directives contained in Articles 48A and 51A(g), the Court held that the right to a clean and safe environment is a subset of the fundamental right to life guaranteed under Article 21 of the Indian Constitution. This ensured that the otherwise unenforceable mandates contained under Articles 48A and 51A(g) could be made enforceable through the fundamental right to life.

Not surprisingly, Upendra Baxi, in 1985, stated that the Supreme Court of India had, after thirty-two years of the republic, become the "Supreme Court *for* Indians" (emphasis supplied).[42] Further, he stated:[43]

> For too long, the apex constitutional court had become "an arena of legal quibbling for men with long purses." Now, increasingly, the Court is being identified by justices as well as people as the "last resort for the oppressed and the bewildered." The transition from a traditional captive agency with a low social visibility into a liberated agency with a high socio-political visibility is a remarkable development in the career of the Indian appellate judiciary.

Baxi highlights that this transformation of the Supreme Court from a traditional captive agency, which was largely seen as being out of reach for the masses, to the last resort of the oppressed was necessitated by governmental inaction. The re-characterization of the Court had tangible social impacts. Baxi highlights:[44]

> People now know that the Court has constitutional power of intervention, which can be invoked to ameliorate their miseries arising from repression, governmental lawlessness and administrative deviance. Under-trial as well as convicted prisoners, women in protective custody, children in juvenile institutions, bonded and migrant labourers, unorganized labourers, untouchables and scheduled tribes, landless agricultural labourers who fall prey to faulty mechanization, women who are bought and sold, slum-dwellers and pavement dwellers, kins of victims of extra judicial executions – these and many more groups now flock to the Supreme Court seeking justice.

> They come with *unusual problems*, never before so directly confronted by the Supreme Court. They seek *extraordinary remedies*, transcending the received notions of separation of powers and the inherited distinctions between adjudication and legislation on the one hand and administration and adjudication on the other. They bring, too, a *new kind of lawyering and a novel kind of judging*.

The problems brought to the Court's notice were indeed "unusual" as the Court had not previously dealt with issues at the grassroots level as directly as it did during the PIL period. It was an extraordinary period when the Court took up issues on its own as well as empowered the masses in an unprecedented manner. Due to this, the Indian Supreme Court was regarded as one of the most powerful courts in the world.[45] While Baxi, in 1985, rightly commended the creation of extraordinary remedies and the use of novel procedural innovations to further justice, he also foresaw some of the issues that were likely to come with this "novel kind of judging".

First, invariably, the Court had to frequently overstep its constitutional boundaries and enter into regulatory, administrative, and policymaking domains to meet the ends of justice. Second, being primarily an appellate court[46] (though being vested with original jurisdiction), the Supreme Court had to conduct fact-finding and evidence collection akin to a trial court. Third, not being equipped with technical and scientific expertise on the bench, judges of the Supreme Court sometimes found it difficult to adjudicate complex environmental matters when they were presented with equally compelling scientific evidence from both parties. Let us explore a few cases that exemplify these issues.

One of the most celebrated cases of the Supreme Court was *M.C. Mehta v. Union of India* (popularly known as the *Taj Trapezium Case*).[47] The Taj Trapezium is the 10,400 square kilometre area around the Taj Mahal – one of the greatest architectural marvels in India – that underwent rapid industrialization over the past few decades. Several factories were set up in the area. These factories were powered by coal, which produced toxic fumes that resulted in acid rain. It was alleged that this acid rain was responsible for causing the discoloration of the Taj Mahal's pristine white exterior.

For almost three years, the Court monitored the situation by collecting facts and assessing the validity of different scientific reports. This was necessary to ascertain the propensity of damage to the environment and the monument on account of the industrial emissions. Once enough evidence was gathered, the Court recommended changes to the functioning of the industries situated within the Taj Trapezium. It ordered the industries to switch from coal to cleaner fuels such as natural gas and mandated the closure of industries that did not comply.

While the Court played an important role in safeguarding the environment and the Taj Mahal from the excesses of industrialization, it had to invariably conduct fact-finding and monitor the situation on the ground for several years. Moreover, there were concerns that the Court's provocativeness in terms of playing a monitoring and regulatory role would make the concerned governmental authorities even more complacent.

One of the defining moments of the PIL regime was the Supreme Court's unprecedented expansion of *locus standi*. In fact, as we will discuss in the next chapter, the NGT has been able to expand access to environmental justice due to the Court's holdings in this period. In *M.C. Mehta v. Union of India* (popularly known as the *Oleum Gas Leak Case*),[48] the Supreme Court ruled that even a letter addressed to an individual judge of the Court ought to be entertained. The Court held:[49]

> [L]etters addressed to individual justices of the court should not be rejected merely because they fail to conform to the preferred form of address. Nor should the court adopt a rigid stance that no letters will be entertained unless they are supported by an affidavit.

The case dealt with a petition praying for the closure of Shriram Industries, which was engaged in the manufacturing of hazardous substances and was located in a densely populated area. On 4 December 1985, Oleum gas leaked from the premises of Shriram Industries and killed an advocate while gravely injuring others. In response, Justice Bhagwati created the doctrine of absolute liability. He held that the previous tortious standard of strict liability derived from *Rylands v. Fletcher*[50] was outdated as it was made in the early nineteenth century when industrial developments were at a nascent stage. Accordingly, the Court held:[51]

> [W]here an enterprise is engaged in a hazardous or inherently dangerous activity and harm results to anyone on account of an accident in the operation of such hazardous or inherently dangerous activity resulting, for example, in escape of toxic gas the enterprise is strictly and absolutely liable to compensate all those who are affected by the accident and such liability is not subject to any of the exceptions which operate vis-à-vis the tortious principle of strict liability under the rule in *Rylands v. Fletcher*.

This emphatic reinterpretation of a liability standard derived from tort law was the Court's way of reclaiming its image just a year after the infamous Bhopal Gas Tragedy (discussed in Chapter 3). However, the frequent invocation of epistolary jurisdiction had its own challenges. Cases taken up through letters or newspaper articles often lacked evidence and did not properly identify the wrongdoers. This effectively meant that the Court would take on the burden of collecting data by engaging in fact-finding and evidence collection. In several environmental cases, the Court set up fact-finding commissions that would report to the Court every few weeks.[52] Thus, the Court, in many ways, took to doing trial work that was ideally supposed to be done by lower courts as they were better equipped.

This is, perhaps, best exemplified in *T.N. Godavarman Thirumulpad v. Union of India*.[53] The case initially involved the illegal felling of trees in the Nilgiri Hills. What came to the fore, however, was a striking deficiency in basic environmental regulations attributable to legislative inaction. The Court took note of this inaction and started a long legal battle that resulted in the Court virtually crafting the entire forest policy of India. Thus, what started as a local petition involving the illegal felling of trees in the Gudalur area of Nilgiris in Tamil Nadu had far-reaching consequences due to the Court's intervention. Even though the petitioner, T.N. Godavraman Thirumulpad, passed away in June 2016, the case has been going on for more than a quarter of a century since September 1995. Hundreds of orders have been passed by the Court in an attempt to provide environmental justice.

The Court, in this case, embarked on an unprecedented fact-finding exercise. It set up several committees such as the High-Powered Committee and the Central Empowered Committee to investigate, gather evidence, and oversee the implementation of the Court's directions. Due to this role, these committees became involved with the implementation and regulation of forest policy in India. This was done through a procedural innovation developed by the Court called "continuing mandamus", whereby the Court retained control over the situation on the ground through a continuous monitoring and feedback process. Though the changes brought forth by the Court were much needed, the Court effectively stepped into the shoes of the legislature and the executive.

Similarly, in the *M.C. Mehta v. Union of India* (popularly known as the *Delhi Air Pollution Case*),[54] the proceedings lasted for more than a decade, starting in 1985. The catena of orders passed in the case set up various fact-finding committees that gathered evidence and helped implement the Court's orders. The results of the Court's intervention were extremely positive as it led to the introduction of the compressed natural gas (CNG) regime in Delhi. However, akin to the *T.N. Godavarman Case*, the Court had essentially made a policy decision to introduce CNG after a decade of oversight and factual inquiry.

These cases demonstrate that while the trend of establishing fact-finding committees and creating an oversight mechanism by the Court helped further environmental justice in India, it involved the Court transgressing its constitutional boundaries. The Court, in several instances, promulgated regulatory frameworks, executed its own orders, and made environmental policies. The extensive durations of the aforementioned environmental cases are partly attributable to the lack of compatibility between conventional court procedures and the particular requirements of environmental adjudication.

In particular, since environmental cases often involve complex scientific and technical questions that have a strong bearing on the final outcome, both parties try to provide equally compelling scientific arguments. However, since judges usually do not have formal scientific training, arriving at a conclusive decision based on all facts and scientific knowledge takes time. This issue is compounded by the problem of scientific uncertainty. Many times, due to competing scientific data, there is no scientific consensus. For instance, despite many scientific studies conducted, there are still some scientists that believe that global warming is a hoax. Further, the present scientific consensus is often fluid and keeps changing as and when new scientific discoveries are made. A chemical that is scientifically declared as safe for use can be banned later due to environmental and health impacts that were not previously known. Thus, it is important to have a feedback mechanism in place whereby decisions can be revisited based on new scientific developments.

For instance, the history of the use of dichloro-diphenyl-trichloroethane (DDT) provides an illustration of the scientific complexities that courts have to deal with. Paul Hermann Müller discovered DDT's insecticidal uses in 1939, and it was used to control malaria and typhus among soldiers and civilians during the Second World War.[55] In acknowledgement of this contribution, Müller was awarded the Nobel Prize in Physiology or Medicine in 1948, and his discovery was widely acclaimed in the scientific community.

By October 1945, DDT was publicly sold in the United States and was widely promoted by the government and corporations for its use as an agricultural pesticide.[56] However, from the beginning, there were environmental and health-related concerns with respect to the use of DDT. In her book titled *Silent Spring* (1962), Rachel Carson put forth arguments that highlighted the problems with the uninhibited use of pesticides.[57] While she cited specific instances of harm to the environment and human health from the use of DDT, she mainly questioned the logic behind the governmental support and broadcasting of the chemical without proper scientific investigation into its potentially harmful effects.

Carson highlighted how the research budget allocated to governmental labs was abysmally low and that due to the pesticide corporate lobby's influence, not much research had been done. Given that most of the research on the possible harms caused by certain pesticides was done in small private labs, the book helped uncover several stories of people and farmers who had been adversely affected. However, it was too late, and it was later found that many people had lost their lives and the environment had suffered great damage.[58] Though her book did not specifically call for banning the use of DDT, it triggered a public movement against the use of the chemical.

Due to the public movement, more scientific studies were conducted, and the United States finally banned the chemical in 1972 – a decade after Carson's book. Subsequently, a worldwide ban on DDT's agricultural use was crystalized through the Stockholm Convention on Persistent Organic Pollutants in 2001. The story of DDT demonstrates how the scientific consensus can take time to change (it took almost sixty years to ban the chemical internationally after its first public use) and how this can have a material bearing on the environment and human health. Thus, in addition to being equipped with scientific expertise, a court needs to have a continuous redressal mechanism whereby it can review its decision based on new scientific data.

Given the need for development in India, the higher Indian judiciary has an important role to play by ensuring that both developmental needs and environmental concerns are balanced. However, achieving this balance requires judges to weigh intricate scientific evidence to take appropriate measures. Due to this, the scientific and technical aspects of environmental adjudication – which are central to the final outcome of a case – are outsourced to ad hoc technical committees in most environmental cases. The function of these ad hoc committees is not limited to fact-finding and involves converting complex scientific data into simple conclusions for adjudicators. These conclusions invariably help in arriving at the final decision in a case.

This is aptly exemplified in the *Oleum Gas Leak Case*, where the Court stated:[59]

> In most of these cases there is need for neutral scientific expertise as an essential input to inform judicial decision making. These cases require expertise at a high level of scientific and technical sophistication. We felt the need for such expertise in this very case and we had to appoint several expert committees to inform the court as to what measures were required to be adopted by the management of Shriram to safeguard against the hazard or possibility of leaks, explosion, pollution of air and water etc. and how many of the safety devices against this hazard or possibility existed in the plant and which of them, though necessary, were not installed. *We had great difficulty in finding out independent experts who would be able to advise the court on these issues. Since there is at present no independent and competent machinery to generate, gather and make available the necessary scientific and technical information, we had to make an effort on our own to identify experts who would provide reliable scientific and technical input necessary for the decision of the case and this was obviously a difficult and by its very nature, unsatisfactory exercise.* (Emphasis supplied)

This highlights the difficulty that the Court had in finding independent experts who would be able to provide reliable and scientific information that was essential to enabling the judges to make the correct decision in the case. Additionally, it is an acknowledgement by the Court of the integral role that experts play in environmental adjudication. Further, acknowledging the issues we have been discussing with respect to how the higher judiciary is underequipped to deal with complex scientific issues involved in environmental cases, the Supreme Court made its first recommendation to the Central government for the establishment of a dedicated environmental court:[60]

> We would also suggest to the Government of India that since cases involving issues of environmental pollution, ecological destruction and conflicts over natural resources are increasingly coming up for adjudication and these cases involve assessment and

evolution of scientific and technical data, it might be desirable to set up Environment Courts on the regional basis with one professional Judge and two experts drawn from the Ecological Sciences Research Group keeping in view the nature of the case and the expertise required for its adjudication.

This marked the first of many recommendations that the Supreme Court gave to the Central government to create an adjudicatory body solely dedicated to environmental matters. As we will see later in this chapter, the creation of the NGT was primarily driven by the Supreme Court. This recommendation highlights the need for having independent expert members to aid the judges. In the cases we have discussed so far, the Court had initially set up its own ad hoc committees for fact-finding rather than directing the State Pollution Control Boards to do the same. This fact points towards the need for having a readily accessible pool of experts that aids the judges in their decision-making.

The significance of scientific expertise was duly recognized by the Court in *Goa Foundation v. Konkan Railway Corporation.*[61] In this case, the Court was required to adjudicate on a railway development project that would have considerably harmed the environment. The project had proceeded without any environmental clearance or compliance process. However, the Court refused to interfere with the project primarily due to the scale of the project and the involvement of substantial public funds. In doing so, it held:[62]

> No development is possible without adverse effects on the ecology and environment but projects of public utility cannot be abandoned and it is necessary to adjust the interests of the people as well as the necessity to maintain the environment. The balance has to be struck between the two interests and *this exercise must be left to the persons who are familiar and specialized in the field.* (Emphasis supplied)

These comments by the Court reveal the extent to which judges are dependent on expert members. Not only is scientific expertise required to weigh competing evidence and ascertain the real potential of environmental harm from a proposed activity, the Court also seems to defer to scientific expertise in matters of balancing developmental needs and environmental concerns.

In *Indian Council for Enviro-Legal Action v. Union of India,*[63] one of the suggestions put forth to the Court was that environmental courts should be constituted all over India. It was suggested that proceedings through writ petitions under Articles 32 and 226 of the Constitution were not appropriate to deal with environmental matters as they involved "several disputed questions of fact and technical issues".[64] Thus, it was suggested that the dedicated environmental courts, once set up, should alone be empowered to deal with environmental cases and should be vested with powers to give appropriate directions, initiate technical and scientific investigations, and oversee the implementation of their orders whenever necessary.

The Court replied positively to this suggestion and also referred to the problem of increasing pendency of environmental cases in ordinary courts.[65] The Court stated:[66]

The suggestion for establishment of environment courts is a commendable one. The experience shows that the prosecutions launched in ordinary criminal courts under the provisions of the Water Act, Air Act and Environment Act never reach their conclusion either because of the workload in those courts or because there is no proper appreciation of the significance of the environment matters on the part of those in charge of conducting of those cases.... Very often, interim orders are granted meanwhile which effectively disable the authorities from ensuring the implementation of their orders. All this points to the need for creating environment courts which alone should be empowered to deal with all matters, civil and criminal, relating to environment. These courts should be manned by legally trained persons/judicial officers and should be allowed to adopt summary procedures. This issue, no doubt, requires to be studied and examined in depth from all angles before taking any action.

This highlights the issues with the environmental adjudication regime that existed prior to the NGT. Since lower courts were already heavily burdened[67] with other matters, they were unable to devote adequate time and attention required for environmental cases. Further, due to the lack of scientific expertise for appreciation of intricate technical details involved in environmental adjudication, lower courts were often unable to appreciate the significance of environmental concerns. The governmental authorities constituted under several environmental legislations such as the Water Act, 1974, and the Air Act, 1981, were unable to hold polluters adequately accountable due to this. As the Court highlights, because of the lack of appreciation of environmental concerns, very often interim orders passed by lower courts would effectively disable the governmental authorities from implementing their orders and preventing environmental degradation.

Just a few years later, in *A.P. Pollution Control Board v. Prof. M.V. Nayudu (I)*,[68] the Court dealt with issues relating to the environmental damage by a vegetable oil factory to the drinking water supply in the vicinity of the factory. In particular, the validity of the clearance given to the factory by the Andhra Pradesh Pollution Control Board was under question. To ascertain the validity of this clearance, the Court invariably had to delve into scientific and technical questions of the potential environmental harm from the alleged emissions. It was called upon to assess the correctness of a scientific report submitted by the respondent industry wherein the industry provided evidence to support its claims. Due to the lack of scientific training, the judges faced "considerable difficulty" in ascertaining the merit of the submissions put forth by both parties. The Court unequivocally stated that such exercises[69]

involve the correctness of opinions on technological aspects expressed by the Pollution Control Boards or other bodies whose opinions are placed before the courts. In such a situation, *considerable difficulty is experienced by this Court or the High Courts in adjudicating upon the correctness of the technological and scientific opinions presented to the courts* or in regard to the efficacy of the technology proposed to be adopted by the industry or in regard to the need for alternative technology or modifications as suggested by the Pollution Control Board or other bodies. (Emphasis supplied)

The selection of an alternative and less polluting technology as well as the efficacy of the technology under challenge are important considerations that have a significant bearing on the final decision of the Court. In no uncertain terms, the Court expresses the difficulty that the higher judiciary faces while judging the merit of technological and scientific opinions. Given these issues, the Court – for the third time – recommended the establishment of a dedicated environmental adjudicatory body:[70]

Of paramount importance in the establishment of environmental courts, authorities and tribunals is the need for providing adequate judicial and scientific inputs rather than leave complicated disputes regarding environmental pollution to officers drawn only from the executive.

The Court raised an important point by stating that complicated environmental matters must not be left solely to executive officials. This relates back to the trend of the Court to not order the establishment of ad hoc fact-finding committees under the State Pollution Control Boards in the first instance. This is because independent scientific expertise was necessary to provide useful insights and further environmental justice. However, as we will discuss shortly, this caveat would go unheeded, and a decade later this problem would go on to become the main reason behind the failure of the National Environment Appellate Authority (NEEA).

Further, in *A.P. Pollution Control Board v. Prof. M.V. Nayudu (II)*,[71] the Supreme Court again referred to the need for instituting effective environmental courts with overarching jurisdiction over environmental matters. The Court referred to relevant literature, such as the "Environmental Court Project" published by the University of Cambridge,[72] and suggested important features that were ideal for the formation of an environmental court. These were:[73]

a) a specialist and exclusive jurisdiction;
b) a power to determine merit appeals;
c) vertical and horizontal integration – by this is meant a wide environmental jurisdiction which integrates both subject matter and different types of legal proceedings;
d) hallmarks of a court or tribunal;
e) dispute resolution powers – it is pointed out that this court's powers extend to disputes over the formulation of policy as well as more traditional adjudication;
f) expertise – the members would be specialists in environmental matters;

g) access – there would be broad rights of access to the court;

h) informality of procedures – such as the use of alternative dispute resolution procedures;

i) costs – this is linked to the need for access and involves means of overcoming the problem of high costs inhibiting access; or

j) capacity for innovation.

Interestingly, these points were given by the Court after the legislature had already established the National Environment Tribunal (NET, 1995) and the NEEA (1997). These were the predecessors of the NGT and, as we will discuss shortly, became dysfunctional and ineffective due to the lack of governmental will. Through these points, the Court heavily emphasized the need to enact appropriate legislation to ensure that environmental authorities were accorded broad powers and included scientific and technical experts who were well versed in environmental laws. Further, the Court undertook a high-level analysis of the provisions of the National Environment Appellate Authority Act, 1997 (NEAA Act), and concluded that the statutory framework of the Authority came "very near to the ideals set by this Court". However, as subsequent years would go on to show, the practice would be far less ideal than the text of the legislation.

1.3 FAILURE OF THE NGT'S PREDECESSORS: THE NET AND THE NEAA

The PIL regime ushered in a new era of environmental justice by providing procedural innovations such as the unprecedented expansion of *locus standi*, establishing a non-adversarial procedure, and ensuring continued monitoring through continuing mandamus. Equipped with these new procedural tools in its arsenal, coupled with the international environmental principles discussed, the Supreme Court created Indian environmental jurisprudence. However, as the previous discussion highlights, this manner of environmental adjudication was inherently unsustainable.

Frequently, the Court had to overstep its constitutional boundaries and enter into regulatory, administrative, and policymaking domains. Being primarily an appellate court, the Supreme Court had to conduct fact-finding and evidence collection akin to a trial court. Additionally, judges were underequipped to deal with complex technical and scientific issues contained in environmental matters when they were presented with equally compelling scientific evidence from both parties. Finally, lower courts were unable to appreciate the significance of environmental matters as they were already overburdened with the pendency of other cases. Due to these shortcomings, the Supreme Court, through various cases, called for the establishment of a dedicated environmental court that would have broad powers and would be staffed with both judicial and expert members.

About six years after the Supreme Court made its first recommendation to the Central government for establishing an environmental adjudicatory body in the *Oleum Gas Leak*

Case, the international community recognized the need for the same. In August 1992, the United Nations General Assembly passed the Rio Declaration on Environment and Development, which under Principle 10 stated:

> States shall facilitate and encourage public awareness and participation by making information widely available. Effective access to judicial and administrative proceedings, including redress and remedy, shall be provided.

Further, Principle 13 of the Rio Declaration stated that states shall develop national laws regarding liability and compensation for victims of environmental pollution and damage. This added international impetus finally resulted in the legislature enacting the National Environment Tribunal Act, 1995 (NET Act). In fact, the preamble to this Act specifically recognized that it was in furtherance of India's commitments under the Rio Declaration. In particular, it recognized the obligations contained under Principle 13 and stated that the primary aim of the Act was to provide strict liability, compensation, and relief against harm arising out of any accident occurring while handling hazardous substances.[74]

The overwhelming emphasis on providing compensation to victims of hazardous waste accidents can be partly ascribed to the apathetic handling of compensation claims put forth by the victims of the Bhopal Gas Tragedy (1984) by the government and the judiciary (discussed in detail in Chapter 3). Thus, from the outset, the NET Act had a very limited scope with respect to the environmental matters it could adjudicate. However, due to a complete lack of governmental will, despite its enactment, the NET Act was never notified, and the tribunal envisaged therein was never actually constituted. In essence, the Act remained purely on paper, with absolutely no practical manifestation.

Faced with repeated calls for the establishment of an environmental court from the Supreme Court, the legislature enacted the NEAA Act. The preamble to the Act indicated a shift away from the previous overemphasis on accident-based compensatory adjudication. However, the scope of the NEAA still remained narrow, and its powers were not near the environmental court that the Supreme Court was recommending.

The preamble to the NEAA Act clarified that it was established for the purpose of only hearing appeals in a limited class of cases. These cases involved the operation of industries or industrial processes in restricted areas subject to certain safeguards provided under the Environment (Protection) Act, 1986. The NEAA became functional on 30 January 1997.[75] Justice N. Venkatachala was appointed as the first chairperson of the Authority. Even the members appointed alongside the chairperson and vice-chairperson did not actually possess the qualifications or the scientific expertise that was expected of the tribunal.[76]

The organization of the NEAA was, for the most part, dismal. It remained understaffed, and after the first chairperson's retirement in 2000, the post of the chairperson remained vacant. All applications were heard by a bench of former bureaucrats who did not possess the necessary technical skills and expertise. In fact, within a few years, it became obvious that the posts of technical members of the NEAA had primarily become retirement jobs for superannuated officers from the Ministry of Environment and Forests (MoEF) and state governments.[77]

Perhaps the only significant decision in the NEAA's tenure was in *A.P. Pollution Control Board v. M.V. Nayudu.*[78] As noted previously, the case involved a vegetable oil industry being set up in the vicinity of a city. Even though the waste discharged from the industry was apparently toxic and was contaminating the groundwater in its vicinity, the project proponent provided a scientific expert report evidencing that there was no environmental damage. The appellate authority, constituted under Section 28 of the Water Act, 1974, and the concerned High Court accepted this report and gave their consent to operate.

On appeal, however, the Supreme Court noted that the scientific report was based on a single scientific expert who had been brought forward by the project proponent. The Court held that the report required scrutiny by independent experts and sought expert advice from the NEAA. Taking assistance from other scientific institutions, the NEAA went through several scientific reports and concluded that there was considerable risk posed to the water supply in the region by the industrial discharge. On the basis of these findings, the Court finally refused the permission to operate granted to the industry by the High Court.

Apart from the aforementioned instance, the NEAA contributed little to dispensing environmental justice. Due to the narrow scope and jurisdiction conferred on the Authority, it had a minimal workload and could not make an impact on environmental adjudication in India. Ravleen Kaur, in her article published in *Down to Earth*, describes the abysmal situation of the NEAA:[79]

> It is the forum for redressing grievances of people affected by environmental clearances, given by the government, to dams, infrastructure projects, mines and industrial activities. But a visit to the office of the National Environment Appellate Authority (NEAA) at Bhikaji Cama Place, Delhi, would make one think one got the address wrong.
>
> There is no board to indicate the office. Nor is there any activity in the office seen in other courts and consumer forums. Set up 11 years ago, the NEAA is without a chairperson or vice-chairperson and is understaffed. Former Supreme Court judge, Justice N Venkatachala, was its first chairperson. He retired in 2000 and the post has remained vacant since. The vice-chairperson's post fell vacant in 2006. Three technical members, a court master, a section officer and a few peons comprise the NEAA staff.

In fact, even the 186th Report of the Law Commission, while assessing the NEAA, noted the lack of work due to the narrow scope and jurisdiction. It remarked:[80]

> It is understood that the Appellate Tribunal did not have much work in view of the narrow scope of its jurisdiction as per notification issued. It dealt with very few cases.

Even in the cases that the NEAA did hear, it was heavily criticized for rendering unsound decisions. Activists and lawyers, in the overwhelming majority, castigated the bureaucrat-occupied authority for serving the developmental ends of the government.[81] Appeals were usually heard by three retired bureaucrats and were rejected on technical and procedural grounds such as delay in filing or lack of *locus standi*.[82]

For instance, in 2005, an appeal was filed by Vimal Bhai, an environmental activist, against the environmental clearance granted to the Loharinag Pala Hydroelectric Project in Uttarkashi (an interview with Vimal Bhai highlighting his experiences in challenging clearances is featured in Chapter 4). Rejecting the appeal preliminarily, the NEAA reasoned that the application had been filed after a delay of twenty-three days beyond the thirty-day period stipulated for challenging clearances. Despite the wide-ranging environmental concerns that the project had raised, the NEAA refused to examine the appeal on merits.[83]

Subsequently, Vimal Bhai approached the Delhi High Court where, in addition to praying for the NEAA to be directed to reconsider its decision, he brought on record the dysfunctional nature of the NEAA. The Delhi High Court accepted the petitioners' arguments and ruled:[84]

> The Appellate Authority has also overlooked that these petitioners deserve to be heard on merits as the order of clearance and setting up of the project was bound to affect a sizeable population in the area. As against this the Authority has adopted a very hyper-technical approach in rejecting the petitioners' application for condonation of 23 days delay instead of dealing with their plea on merit. This order in our view is unsustainable and is quashed. The petitioners' appeal shall revive. The Appellate Authority should now consider their appeal on merits and pass appropriate orders in accordance with law.

In addition to quashing the NEAA's order and asking it to hear the case on merit, the High Court directed the Central government to take appropriate measures to ensure the effective functioning of the NEAA. However, in 2009, the petitioners again approached the Delhi High Court seeking the enforcement of its previous orders as the Central government had not taken any measures in furtherance of the Court's directions.[85] The High Court noticed serious lapses on the government's part in organizing the NEAA. The Court noted:[86]

> [T]he pay, allowances and conditions of service of the Chairperson of the NEAA is no different from that of the Vice-Chairperson and a Secretary to the Government of India. This is not the position in many other Tribunals and quasi-judicial bodies headed by former judges of the Supreme Court. Not surprisingly therefore no retired judge of the Supreme Court or retired Chief Justice of a High Court was willing to accept the offer of the post of Chairperson NEAA.

Significantly, it held:[87]

> [T]he Court *cannot be expected to remain a mute witness to the unfortunate rendering of a statutory body ineffective by an unwilling executive* … [the] failure of the government to appoint a Chairperson for over eight years *inexcusable. A headless NEAA has thus been rendered ineffective by the act of omission of the government.* The intention of Parliament in requiring the government to constitute an independent body for quick redressal of public grievances in relation to grant of environmental clearances has thus been *defeated.* (Emphasis supplied)

Thus, the High Court strongly called out the governmental inaction and apathy in relation to establishing an environmental court. It held that the fact that the Central government had not appointed a chairperson for over eight years was inexcusable. It noted the unwillingness of the executive to cooperate had rendered the NEAA ineffective. The High Court imposed a penalty of INR 20,000 on the Central government while issuing detailed directions pertaining to the appointment of future members to the NEAA. Though the amount was meagre, it was a symbolic penalty that was intended to embarrass the executive. Nevertheless, the aforementioned observations by the High Court judgment are a testament to the failure of the NEAA in dispensing environmental justice.[88]

Apart from the *Loharinag Pala Case*, the NEAA also came under criticism in other cases where it displayed a similar hyper-technical approach. For instance, in 2007, an environmental activist in Orissa appealed against the environmental clearance granted by the MoEF to Vedanta Corporation for setting up its aluminium smelter plant.[89] The appeal was dismissed preliminarily by the NEAA on the ground that the petitioner did not qualify as a "person aggrieved" under Section 11 of the NEAA Act.

The NEAA reached this conclusion because it held that the environmental activist was not "personally affected" by the prospective project and thus lacked *locus standi*. This conclusion was reached despite the credentials of the appellant evincing a bona fide concern for the environment. In many ways, this decision of the NEAA considerably narrowed the expansive *locus standi* that the Supreme Court had created over several years in the PIL regime. It was a regressive decision.

Not surprisingly, the Delhi High Court reversed the NEAA's judgment on appeal. However, it is noteworthy that it was argued, on behalf of the respondents, that the petitioner could only be considered as a "person aggrieved" if he could establish that he was a member of a local community or a non-governmental organization in the affected area.[90] The High Court rejected this argument after comprehensively interpreting and explaining the concerned sections of the NEAA Act. It held that if the respondent's contention was accepted, it would defeat the objectives behind the establishment of the NEAA and would curtail access to justice. It further stated:[91]

India, even today, lives largely in its villages. A project or scheme, which is likely to affect or impact a remote community, that may comprise even a cluster of villages, may or may not have an "association of persons" who work in the field of environment. The villagers, like most others, are unlikely to know about the project clearance, or possess the wherewithal to question it, through an appeal. If the third respondent's contention, and the authority's impugned order were to be accepted, and upheld, such community's right to appeal, meaningfully, would be rendered a chimera, an illusion.

Thus, where the NEAA failed to uphold access to environmental justice, the Delhi High Court dispensed justice. Finally, the High Court ordered the respondents to pay a penalty amounting to INR 50,000, quashed the impugned order, and directed the appeal to be heard again.

Similarly, in 2008, an appeal was filed before the NEAA against the clearance granted to the Monnet Ispat and Energy Limited plant in Raigarh.[92] Despite the aforementioned verdict of the Delhi High Court, the NEAA again applied an unduly narrow interpretation of the phrase "aggrieved person". It held that the appellant organization, despite having shown a consistent involvement in the environmental impact assessment (EIA) consultation and hearing process, did not possess the *locus standi* to challenge the clearance granted by MoEF. On appeal, the Delhi High Court overturned this order citing its earlier verdict.[93]

In *Ramesh Gauns v. Ministry of Environment and Forests*,[94] the appellant, an environmental activist, challenged the environmental clearance granted to a mining project in Sarvona, Goa. The major grievance put forth by the appellant was that the EIA report was faulty and was based on inadequate information. He contended that during the public hearing process, nearly all villagers raised objections, to which no response was given by the project proponent. The NEAA, with unwarranted optimism, simply stated:[95]

> The authority is convinced the Expert Appraisal Committee and the ministry duly considered the objections before issuing environmental clearance.

Like the earlier cases discussed, this decision was challenged before the Delhi High Court. Accepting the appellant's submissions, the High Court finally held that the Expert Appraisal Committee of the MoEF had failed to take into account the objections raised during the public hearing process and invalidated the clearance.

These cases demonstrate the failure of the NEAA and the need for an independent expert panel. As discussed, the story of the NGT's predecessors – the NET and the NEAA – is one filled with governmental apathy and disregard towards environmental concerns. While on paper the Supreme Court's recommendations and India's commitments under the Rio Declaration (1992) were upheld, the dysfunctional nature of the two environmental tribunals proved otherwise. Due to governmental inaction, the NET was never established and the NEAA was without a chairperson for almost a decade. The lack of appointments, strategic curtailment of jurisdiction, and the bureaucratic nature of these tribunals did little to further environmental justice in India.

1.4 THE 186TH LAW COMMISSION REPORT AND THE NATIONAL GREEN TRIBUNAL BILL, 2009

Through the four judgments we have discussed,[96] the Supreme Court had recommended the creation of a dedicated environmental court. In response, the Law Commission of India (LCI), through its 186th report titled *Proposal to Constitute Environmental Courts*, undertook a detailed study on the subject and made several recommendations. In particular, the LCI looked at, inter alia, the proposal for a multifaceted environmental court by Lord Woolf in England[97] and international legislation establishing environmental courts in Australia and New Zealand.[98]

At the outset, the LCI highlighted the need to create an effective environmental tribunal given the dismal state of the NET and the NEAA. It reiterated that the NET was yet to be established as the NET Act, 1995, had not been notified by parliament despite the expiry of eight years. Further, the NEAA had very little work due to the narrow jurisdiction accorded to it, and no judicial member had been appointed since the year 2000.[99] Due to these shortcomings, the LCI unequivocally stated that "these two Tribunals are non-functional and remain only on paper".[100]

The report dealt extensively with the existing scheme of appeals under various environmental laws such as the Water Act, 1974,[101] the Air Act, 1981,[102] and the Environment (Protection) Act, 1986.[103] Since the mechanism for appeals under most of these pieces of legislation was directed to state-level authorities, the LCI proposed that all appellate powers conferred under these laws must be accorded to the proposed environmental court. This would ensure a unified system of appeals.[104]

The report also suggested that such an environmental court should be set up in each state or should be responsible for a group of states in India. It was suggested that each such court should consist of three judicial members, who are[105]

a) either sitting or retired judges of a High Court; or
b) experienced members of the bar (with not less than twenty years' standing).

Further, the LCI recommended that these three judicial members should be assisted by three environmental experts (to be called "Commissioners") in each environmental court.[106]

As noted previously, one of the reasons that the NEAA did not have enough work was its limited jurisdiction and powers. Accordingly, to tackle this issue, the LCI proposed that the new environmental court should be accorded broad jurisdiction, including cases involving the Public Liability Insurance Act, to ensure easy access to environmental justice. Further, to guide this court in decision-making, the LCI recommended the express incorporation of certain international environmental principles such as the precautionary principle, the polluter pays principle, the principle of sustainable development, the new burden of proof principle, the principle of strict liability, the public trust doctrine, and the principle of intergenerational equity.[107]

The LCI also stressed the need for effective implementation of the proposed court's orders. To achieve this, it recommended that the environmental court should be endowed with the power to frame and monitor comprehensive environmental schemes and issue directions to various government authorities. It further suggested that to ensure effective implementation, the proposed court should be conferred with all the powers of a civil court. Thus, it recommended that while such a court would not ordinarily be granted jurisdiction for criminal and judicial review, it was necessary to accord this environmental court with contempt jurisdiction. It was felt that this would enable the court to hold non-complying parties accountable through summary proceedings, without involving the tardy processes of criminal law.[108] However, the final NGT Act did not incorporate this suggestion.

The LCI report also suggested that the environmental court should interpret *locus standi* broadly and that appeals against such court's decisions should only lie with the Supreme Court. Accordingly, it suggested that after the establishment of the court, High Courts should not invoke their writ jurisdiction with respect to environmental matters as there would be an equally efficacious alternative remedy. Further, this would help streamline the process of appeals.[109] However, counterintuitively, the report suggested that the jurisdiction of ordinary civil courts over environmental matters should be maintained. This suggestion did not find its way into the NGT Act.

Overall, this report formed an integral part of the Supreme Court–led movement for the establishment of a dedicated green court in India. Many of the LCI's recommendations in relation to appellate jurisdiction, power to frame schemes, broad *locus standi*, and incorporation of general environmental principles were adopted while framing the NGT Act. As we will discuss in subsequent chapters, these have become important facets of the NGT's present functioning.

The LCI's report was published in 2003. As discussed previously, the following years saw the NEAA come under extensive scrutiny and criticism by lawyers and environmental activists for a number of reasons. These included the Authority's tendency to consistently deny justice on technical grounds and the bureaucratic nature of members who did not possess the requisite scientific or technical expertise. These issues effectively rendered the Authority defunct as a forum for environmental litigation.

Simultaneously, the pressure to put the LCI's recommendations into effect was increasing. Extensive debates took place about the NEAA's role and the need for a new tribunal.[110] The NEAA's apathetic attitude towards genuine environmental concerns added fuel to fire. Finally, the National Green Tribunal Bill was introduced in the Lok Sabha on 31 July 2009.

The Bill was referred to the Standing Committee on Science and Technology, Environment and Forests, which submitted its 203rd report on "The National Green Tribunal Bill, 2009".[111] This reference played a critical role in highlighting some important points that the Bill had missed or had not clarified. First, the Standing Committee highlighted that there was likely to be ambiguity surrounding the NGT's jurisdiction due to the use of an open-ended phrase giving the Tribunal jurisdiction over any "substantial question relating to environment".[112] As we will discuss in the next chapter, the NGT has been able to use this broad definition to exercise jurisdiction in a manner that expands access to environmental justice.

Second, another concern voiced by the Standing Committee was in relation to the lack of details regarding the appointment of members.[113] The Bill did not specify the number of members in the Tribunal and simply stated that the Central government would notify the number of members from time to time. Realizing that this could effectively lead to a situation similar to the NEAA, which became dysfunctional due to a lack of appointments, the Standing Committee highlighted the need for specifying a minimum number of judicial and expert members who must occupy the Tribunal at all times. It recommended that the NGT must have a minimum of five and a maximum of ten judicial members, and a minimum of ten and a minimum of twenty expert members.

Third, the Standing Committee expressed particular concern for the lack of access to justice. Since the Bill proposed to accord the NGT exclusive jurisdiction over all civil cases where a substantial question relating to the environment was involved, the Standing Committee opined that this would seriously hamper access to justice:[114]

> The Committee feels that the National Green Tribunal which claims itself to be a mechanism aimed at effective and expeditious disposal of civil cases relating to environmental protection and conservation of forests does not exude much confidence given its infrastructural framework, particularly in view of the geographical vastness of our country.... Thus, the poor and the tribal people living in remote areas will be deprived of the opportunity to approach civil courts for redressal of their grievances on substantial question relating to environment.

These concerns were extremely valid and, as will be discussed in Chapter 4, just a decade later, even the regional benches of the NGT would be closed due to a lack of appointments by the Central government,[115] thereby turning the Standing Committee's concerns into reality. Fourth, despite the LCI's recommendation to provide an appeal to the Supreme Court from the NGT's decision, the Bill did not provide such a mechanism. It simply stated that the NGT's decision would be final. The Standing Committee again reemphasized the need for having such a provision to streamline the appeal process and to avoid multiplicity of proceedings.

Another important point highlighted by the Standing Committee was the exclusion of the Wildlife (Protection) Act, 1972, from Schedule I of the Bill. This effectively meant that the NGT would not have jurisdiction over issues related to wildlife. Explaining the exclusion, the MoEF stated:[116]

> [T]he tribunal has been consciously provided with a jurisdiction limited to cases of civil nature because criminal adjudication requires a hierarchy of courts and the tribunal system does not fit into the architecture of criminal courts. Most of the violations of the Wildlife Act, 1972 are criminal offences and the Act has specific chapters incorporating provisions for prosecution and trial, seizure and confiscation and the creation of the Wildlife Crime Control Bureau.

Nevertheless, as will be discussed in the next chapter, the NGT broadly construed "substantial issues relating to the environment" to include issues relating to wildlife.[117] This ensured that the NGT could exercise jurisdiction on cases involving wildlife. Finally, the Standing Committee, reiterating the LCI's recommendation, suggested that international environmental principles such as the principle of sustainable development, the precautionary principle, and the polluter pays principle should be expressly incorporated in the Bill. This suggestion was accepted and presently forms the basis of Section 20 of the NGT Act.

The Bill was finally passed on 5 May 2010, and the Central government, by notification, declared 18 October 2010 as the date for enforcement of the NGT Act. Justice L. S. Panta, a retired judge of the Supreme Court, was appointed as the first chairperson of the Tribunal. However, this appointment was made only notionally as the Tribunal had not yet become functional as of then. As we will discuss shortly in the next chapter, there were several infrastructural issues that the NGT faced during its initial years that delayed its functioning.

Therefore, the passing of the National Green Tribunal Bill should not be seen as an isolated event. It was the culmination of several factors operating simultaneously to further environmental justice in India. The establishment of the NGT should be seen in the historical and legal context we have discussed over the course of this chapter.

Through the next three chapters, we aim to provide an in-depth analysis of the NGT's functioning, its contribution to Indian environmental jurisprudence, and the challenges it needs to overcome. Chapter 2 is a commentary on the NGT Act and analyses the broad themes contained therein. These themes are, inter alia, the Tribunal's composition, jurisdiction, trends in awarding compensation, and general powers. Subsequently, Chapter 3 analyses the NGT's interpretation and application of three international environmental principles. These principles are sustainable development, the precautionary principle, and the polluter pays principle.

In doing so, we provide an introduction to the international evolution of these principles and their domestic application by the Indian Supreme Court prior to the establishment of the NGT. This enables us to compare the NGT's use of these principles with the international standard and the domestic precedents set by the Court. Finally, Chapter 4 reviews the NGT's performance in the first decade of its existence and highlights ten challenges that the NGT needs to overcome.

NOTES

1. Bruno Latour, *The Making of Law: An Ethnography of the Conseil d'Etat* (Cambridge, UK: Polity Press, 2010), 243.
2. Elizabeth Fisher, Eloise Scotford, and Emily Barritt, 'Why Understanding the Legally Disruptive Nature of Climate Change Matters', *OUP Blog* (22 April 2015), https://blog.oup.com/2015/04/legally-disruptive-nature-of-climate-change/ (accessed 15 March 2021).
3. Latour, *The Making of Law*.
4. Elizabeth Fisher, Eloise Scotford, and Emily Barritt, 'The Legally Disruptive Nature of Climate Change', *MLR* 80, no. 2 (2017): 173–201.
5. Elizabeth Fisher, *Environmental Law: A Very Short Introduction* (Oxford: Oxford University Press, 2017), 6–10.
6. Elizabeth Fisher, "Environmental Law as 'Hot' Law", *Journal of Environmental Law* 25, no. 3 (2013): 347–58.
7. Fisher, *Environmental Law*.
8. Ibid.
9. Ibid.
10. Ibid).
11. Garrett Hardin, "The Tragedy of the Commons", *Science* 162, no. 3859 (1968): 1243–48.
12. Fisher, *Environmental Law*.
13. Fisher, "Environmental Law as 'Hot' Law".
14. Ibid.
15. *Bulga Milbrodale Progress Association Inc v. Minister for Planning and Infrastructure and Warkworth Mining Limited*, [2013] NSWLEC 48 (NSW Land and Environment Court, Australia).
16. Lon L. Fuller and Kenneth I. Winston, "The Forms and Limits of Adjudication", *HLR* 92, no. 2 (1978): 353–409, 395.
17. *Saul Luciano Lliuya v. RWE*, Case No. 2 O 285/15 Essen Regional Court (2015).
18. Michael H. Fisher, *An Environmental History of India: From Earliest Times to the Twenty-First Century* (New Approaches to Asian History Series) (Cambridge, UK: Cambridge University Press, 2018).
19. Paul John, "Dholavira's Water Conservation Secret Is an Engineering Marvel", *Times of India* (Ahmedabad, 19 May 2018), https://timesofindia.indiatimes.com/city/ahmedabad/dholaviras-water-conservation-secret-is-an-engineering-marvel/articleshow/64228386.cms (accessed 17 December 2021).

20. Ibid.

21. Soha Kala, "By Burning Manusmriti, We Are Burning Discrimination: 10 Shocking Verses about Women from the Ancient Text", *Newsgram* (New Delhi, August 2017), https://www. newsgram.com/10-shocking-verses-about-women-from-manusmriti/ (accessed 17 December 2021).

22. Philippe Cullet and Joyeeta Gupta, "India: Evolution of Water Law and Policy", in *The Evolution of the Law and Politics of Water*, ed. Joseph W. Dellapenna and Joyeeta Gupta, 157–73 (New Delhi: Springer Academic Publishers, 2009), 159, https://www.uvm.edu/~pbierman/classes/ gradsem/2014/India_Water_Compiled.pdf (accessed 17 December 2021).

23. *Manusmriti*, ch. XI, §174; ch. VIII, §309; ch. IX, §281.

24. Kautilya and L. N. Rangarajan, *The Arthashastra* (New Delhi: Penguin Books India, 1992).

25. Ibid., Topic 35.

26. Amirthalingam Murugesan, "Perspectives of Environmental Studies during the Mughal Period", *Journal of Indian History and Culture* 22 (September 2016): 178–85.

27. P. Parthasarathi and I. Wendt, "Indian Cotton Manufacturing", in *The Spinning World: A Global History of Cotton Textiles, 1200–1850,* ed. G. Riello and P. Parthasarathi, 397–407 (New York: Oxford University Press, 2009).

28. Fisher, *An Environmental History of India,* 135.

29. Aditya Mukherjee, "Empire: How Colonial India Made Modern Britain", *Economic and Political Weekly* 45, no. 50 (December 2010): 73–82,75.

30. Ibid.

31. Paul Bairoch, "International Industrial Levels from 1750–1980", *Journal of European Economic History* 11, no. 2 (Fall, 1982): 268–333.

32. Bipin Chandra, Mridula Mukherjee, and Aditya Mukherjee, *India Since Independence* (New Delhi: Penguin Books, 2008).

33. Kaushik Basu, "A Short History of India's Economy", (UNU-WIDER Working Paper 124/2018. 3, 2018), https://www.wider.unu.edu/publication/short-history-indias-economy (accessed 17 December 2021).

34. *DNA India*, "PSU's: Modern Industrial Temples of India" (19 November 2013), https://www. dnaindia.com/special-features/report-psus-modern-industrial-temples-of-india-1296571 (accessed 17 December 2021).

35. *The Hindu*, "When the Big Dams Came Up" (New Delhi, 20 March 2015), https://www. thehindu.com/news/national/when-the-big-dams-came-up/article7012590.ece (accessed 17 December 2021).

36. Ibid.

37. *Municipal Council, Ratlam v. Vardhichand*, AIR 1980 SC 1622; *Indian Council for Enviro-Legal Action v. Union of India*, AIR 1996 SC 1446; *Deepak Nitrite v. State of Gujarat*, (2004) 6 SCC 402 (Supreme Court of India); *M.C. Mehta v. Kamal Nath*, AIR 2000 SC 1997.

38. *Bandhua Mukti Morcha v. Union of India*, AIR 1984 SC 802.

39. *State of Himachal Pradesh v. Ganesh Wood Products*, (1995) 6 SCC 363 (Supreme Court of India)*; Vellore Citizens Welfare Forum v. Union of India*, (1996) 5 SCC 647 (Supreme Court of India); Delhi Transport Department Case 1998 9 SCC 250 (Supreme Court of India).

40. *Vellore Citizen's Welfare Forum v. Union of India*; *M.C. Mehta v. Union of India*, (1997) 2 SCC 353 (Taj Trapezium Case) (Supreme Court of India); *A.P. Pollution Control Board v. M.V. Nayudu (I)*, (1999) 2 SCC 718 (Supreme Court of India).

41. *M.C. Mehta v. Union of India* (1987) 1 SCC 395 (Supreme Court of India); *Indian Council for Enviro-Legal Action v. Union of India*, (1996) 3 SCC 212 (Supreme Court of India); *S. Jagannath v. Union of India*, (1997) 2 SCC 87 (Supreme Court of India).

42. Upendra Baxi, "Taking Suffering Seriously: Social Action Litigation in the Supreme Court of India", *Third World Legal Studies* 4, no. 1 (1985): Art. 6, 107–32, https://scholar.valpo.edu/cgi/viewcontent.cgi?article=1125&context=twls (accessed 17 December 2021).

43. Ibid.

44. Ibid., 108.

45. S. P. Sathe, "Judicial Activism: The Indian Experience", *Washington. University Journal of Law & Policy* 6, no. 1 (2001): 30–107, 43, https://openscholarship.wustl.edu/law_journal_law_policy/vol6/iss1/3 (accessed on 17 December 2021).

46. Prakhar Chauhan and Raghuveer Nath, "The Dilution of Article 32: Convenience over Right", *GNLU Law Review* 7, no. 1 (2020): 71–93.

47. *M.C. Mehta v. Union of India* (1997) 3 SCC 715 (Taj Trapezium Case) (Supreme Court of India).

48. *M.C. Mehta v. Union of India*, 1987 SCR (1) 819 (Oleum Leak Case) (Supreme Court of India).

49. Ibid., para 5.

50. *Rylands v. Fletcher*, [1868] L.R. 3 H.L. 330.

51. Ibid.

52. *N.D. Jayal v. Union of India*, (2004) 9 SCC 362 (Supreme Court of India).

53. *T.N. Godavarman Thirumulpad v. Union of India*, (1997) 2 SCC 267 (Supreme Court of India).

54. *M.C. Mehta v. Union of India*, 1991 SCR (1) 866 (Delhi Air Pollution Case) (Supreme Court of India).

55. World Health Organization, International Programme on Chemical Safety and WHO Task Group on Environmental Health Criteria for DDT and Its Derivatives: Environmental Aspects, *DDT and Its Derivatives: Environmental Aspects/Published under the Joint Sponsorship of the United Nations Environment Programme, the International Labour Organization, and the World Health Organization* (Geneva, Switzerland: World Health Organization Environmental Health Criteria, 1989), vol. 9.

56. Samuel P. Hays, *Beauty, Health, and Permanence: Environmental Politics in the United States, 1955–1985* (Cambridge, UK: Cambridge University Press, 1987).

57. Rachel Carson, *Silent Spring* (Boston, MA: Houghton Mifflin, 1962).

58. Hays, *Beauty, Health, and Permanence.*

59. *Oleum Leak Case*, para 22.

60. Ibid., para 22.

61. *Goa Foundation v. Konkan Railway Corporation*, AIR 1992 Bom 471 (Bombay High Court, India).

62. Ibid., para 6.

63. *Indian Council for Enviro-Legal Action v. Union of India.*

64. Ibid.

   65. Ibid., para 70(6).

66. Ibid., para 70(6).

67. Roshini Sinha, "Pendency of Cases in Judiciary", *PRS Legislative* (August 2019), https://www.prsindia.org/theprsblog/examining-pendency-cases-judiciary (accessed 17 December 2021).

68. *A.P. Pollution Control Board v. M.V. Nayudu (II)*, (2001) 2 SCC 62 (Supreme Court of India).

69. Ibid., para 23.

70. Ibid., para 42.

71. *A.P. Pollution Control Board v. Prof. M.V. Nayudu (II).*

72. Malcoum Grant, "The Use for Environmental Courts", *Journal of Planning and Environment* (2000): 452–59, 453.

73. Ibid., para 72.

74. Preamble, National Environmental Tribunal Act, 1995 (Act 27 of 1995) (India).

75. Armin Rosencranz, Geetanjoy Sahu, and Vyom Raghuvanshi, "Whither the National Environment Appellate Authority?", *Economic and Political Weekly* 44, no. 35 (29 August 2009–4 September 2009): 10–14.

76. Ibid.

77. Ibid.

78. *A.P. Pollution Control Board v. Prof. M.V. Nayudu (II).*

79. Ravleen Kaur, "No Judge to Hear", *Down To Earth* (31 March 2009),   https://www.downtoearth.org.in/news/environment/no-judge-to-hear-3161 (accessed on 17 December 2021).

80. Law Commission of India, "Proposal to Constitute Environmental Courts" (17th Law Commission, 186th Report, 2003).

81. Kaur, "No Judge to Hear".

82. Ibid.

83. *Vimal Bhai v. Union of India*, 2009 SCC OnLine Del 289 (High Court of Delhi, India).

84. *Vimal Bhai v. Union of India*, Order dated 29 September 2005 in W.P. I 17682 of 2005.

85. *Vimal Bhai v. Union of India*, 2009.

86. Ibid., para 14.

87. Ibid., para 20.

88. Zee News, "Green Tribunal a Defunct Organization: Delhi HC" (New Delhi, 16 October 2009), https://zeenews.india.com/news/eco-news/green-tribunal-a-defunct-organisation-delhi-hc_571401.html (accessed 17 December 2021).

89. *Prafulla Samantra v. Ministry of Environment and Forests*, 2009 SCC OnLine Del 1333 (High Court of Delhi, India).

90. Ibid.

91. Ibid., para 13.

92. *Jan Chetna v. Ministry of Environment and Forests*, 2012 SCC OnLine Del 2778 (High Court of Delhi, India).

93. Ibid.

94. *Ramesh Gauns v. Union of India*, Judgment in W.P. 3208 of 2010 (Delhi High Court).

95. Ibid.

96. *M.C. Mehta vs. Union of India*, (1986) 2 SCC 176 (Supreme Court of India); *Indian Council for Enviro-Legal Action v. Union of India*; *A.P. Pollution Control Board v. M.V. Nayudu (I)* and *A.P. Pollution Control Board v. Prof. M.V. Nayudu (II)* .

97. Law Commission of India, "Proposal to Constitute Environmental Courts".

98. Ibid., ch. 4.

99. Ibid., 6.

100. Ibid., 6.

101. The Water (Prevention and Control of Pollution) Act, 1974 (Act 6 of 1974) (India).

102. The Air (Prevention and Control of Pollution) Act, 1981 (Act 14 of 1981) (India).

103. The Environment (Protection) Act, 1986 (Act 29 of 1986) (India).

104. Law Commission of India, "Proposal to Constitute Environmental Courts", 143.

105. Ibid., 142.

106. Ibid., 142.

107. Ibid., 148–49.

108. Ibid., 151.

109. Ibid., 21.

110. Meena Menon, "How Green Is My Tribunal", *The Hindu* (7 July 2010), https://www.thehindu.com/opinion/op-ed/How-green-is-my-tribunal/article16187122.ece (accessed on 18 December 2021); Rosencranz, Sahu, and Raghuvanshi, "Whither the National Environment Appellate Authority?"

111. Department-Related Parliamentary Standing Committee on Science and Technology, Environment and Forests, "Report on the National Green Tribunal Bill, 2009 Presented in Parliament of India – Rajya Sabha" (203rd Report, November 2009), http://164.100.47.5/newcommittee/reports/EnglishCommittees/Committee%20on%20S%20and%20T,%20Env.%20and%20Forests/For%20Net.htm (accessed on 18 December 2021).

112. Ibid.

113. Department-Related Parliamentary Standing Committee on Science and Technology, Environment and Forests, "Report on the National Green Tribunal Bill".

114. Ibid.

115. Raghuveer Nath and Armin Rosencranz, "Evaluating the National Green Tribunal after Nearly a Decade: Ten Challenges to Overcome", *NLIU Law Review* 9, no. 1 (2019): 1–39, 26.

116. Department-Related Parliamentary Standing Committee on Science and Technology, Environment and Forests, "Report on the National Green Tribunal Bill".

117. *Tribunal on Its Own Motion v. Ministry of Environment and Forests*, Judgment dated 4 April 2014 in Appeal No 16 of 2013 (National Green Tribunal, India).

2

THE NATIONAL GREEN TRIBUNAL ACT, 2010

ANALYSIS AND INTERPRETATION

The powers and functioning of the NGT are governed by the NGT Act, 2010.[1] Accordingly, this chapter deals with the broad themes covered in the various sections of the NGT Act and highlights how the NGT has interpreted and expanded on various provisions contained therein.

2.1 PURPOSE AND OBJECTS OF THE NGT

As discussed in Chapter 1, the predecessors of the NGT – the NET[2] and the NEAA[3] – were dysfunctional and ineffective due to a lack of legislative will. Furthermore, the call for the need for environmental courts by the Supreme Court[4] was augmented by the recommendations of the Law Commission of India.[5] This has been specifically recognized in the Statement of Objects and Reasons (SOR) contained in the preamble to the NGT Act 2010.[6] The SOR further recognized the need for expeditious disposal of environmental cases in light of the increasing number of pending cases in the higher judiciary requiring technical expertise. Accordingly, the long title of the NGT Act, 2010, provides the following purpose behind the establishment of the Tribunal:

> An Act to provide for the establishment of a National Green Tribunal for the effective and expeditious disposal of cases relating to environmental protection and conservation of forests and other natural resources including enforcement of any legal right relating to environment and giving relief and compensation for damages to persons and property and for matters connected therewith or incidental thereto.[7]

The SOR further states that the NGT Act, 2010, was enacted to uphold India's commitments under international conventions, such as the UN Conference on the Human Environment (1972)[8] and the UN Conference on Environment and Development (1992),[9] to take appropriate measures for enhancing environmental protection and access to judicial and administrative proceedings.[10] This involves developing national laws regarding liability and compensation for victims of pollution and environmental damage.[11]

Additionally, the SOR recognizes the judicial pronouncements declaring the right to a healthy environment as a part of the right to life under Article 21 of the Indian Constitution[12] and emphasizes the need to adopt a multidisciplinary approach for upholding it.

Given this context, it is apparent from the preamble and the SOR that the NGT has been primarily envisaged as an adjudicatory vehicle, which can effectively and expeditiously give effect to the constitutional obligations contained under Article 21 of the Indian Constitution relating to the right to a healthy environment. This involves providing the NGT with scientific and multidisciplinary expertise to enable it to award appropriate compensation and expand access to environmental justice. In this chapter, we will see whether the provisions of the NGT Act, 2010, their interpretation by the Tribunal, and other subsequent factors have allowed the fulfilment of these obligations.

2.2   ESTABLISHMENT AND CONSTITUTION OF THE TRIBUNAL

The NGT was notified by the Central government on 18 October 2010.[13] However, the Tribunal has to date not operated at full capacity. Nearly a decade later in 2020, all four regional benches of the NGT have been shut down, and the Tribunal solely operates from the Principal Bench in New Delhi.[14] The primary reason for this is the lack of governmental will and infrastructural support.[15]

Since its inception, the NGT has faced several hurdles in its functioning due to a lack of basic amenities and infrastructure. In fact, upon establishment, the Principal Bench of the NGT had to start operating from a temporary office and a makeshift courtroom in Van Vigyan Bhavan – a building used for housing governmental guests of the MoEF.[16] Further, despite the stipulated entitlements, the members of the Tribunal – who were retired High Court judges – were not provided basic amenities such as a kitchen and could not afford to rent a house due to the meagre allowance.

Due to these abysmal conditions, three judicial members resigned from their office.[17] Further, while a statutory minimum of ten judicial and ten expert members are necessary for the operation of the Tribunal (discussed later), the Principal Bench was made functional with only three judicial and three expert members due to poor response when applications were invited.[18] There was a period when four benches of the NGT were being operated by a total of five members.[19]

The Pune Bench was inaugurated on 17 March 2012 but was made operational only a year later due to a lack of governmental support.[20] The case with the Kolkata Bench was worse, and a report submitted by the Tribunal to the Supreme Court stated that the accommodation for the chairperson was without basic amenities.[21] Accordingly, the Supreme Court requested the Central government to consider shifting the bench to Guwahati from Kolkata due to the inaction of the state government of West Bengal.

Akin to how the process of establishing the NGT was spearheaded by the Supreme Court rather than the legislature, the Supreme Court led the push for providing basic facilities to the NGT. The Court expressed its displeasure at the fact that judicial members had resigned due to lack of residential accommodation[22] and issued directions to operationalize the Tribunal.[23] These included directions to appoint members and provide basic facilities to enable the functioning of the Tribunal and its regional benches (see below).[24]

Supreme Court of India

UNION OF INDIA v. VIMAL BHAI[25]

[Special Leave to Appeal (Civil) No. 12065 of 2009, Order Dated 13 July 2012]

G.S. Singhvi, J.;
A.K. Ganguly, J.

*   *   *

Relevant Extracts:

During the pendency of the special leave petition filed against order dated 11.2.2009 passed by the Division Bench of the Delhi High Court in Writ Petition No.17682 of 2005, this Court passed as many as 18 orders to facilitate the establishment of the National Green Tribunal, Principal Bench at Delhi and its four Benches at Chennai, Bhopal, Kolkata and Pune. These orders relate to appointment of Chairperson, Judicial and Expert Members, sanction of posts in different cadres, creation of infrastructure and deputation of officers from Higher Judicial Services of Delhi, Madhya Pradesh and Maharashtra to work as Registrars of the Principal Bench as well as Bhopal and Pune Benches.

The record of the case shows that at every stage the officers of the Ministry of Environment and Forests have created obstacle in the effective functioning of the Tribunal, Principal Bench at Delhi as well as its Benches at Bhopal and Pune and they had to be reminded time and again that it is the duty of the Central Government to provide infrastructure, manpower, etc. for effective functioning of the Tribunal…. [Learned senior counsel appearing for NGT] also pointed out that salary was not paid to the Registrar of the Principal Bench for many months and the amount was provisionally released on the intervention of the Chairman, NGT.

These and other communications filed from time to time are clearly indicative of the attitude of total non-cooperation of the Department of Environment and Forests. It gives an impression that the department is making all out efforts to ensure that the NGT does not function effectively so that the Court may be compelled to pass an order for restoration of jurisdiction of the High Courts and other Courts in matters which are presently dealt with by NGT.

*   *   *

2.2.1   COMPOSITION OF THE NGT

The NGT operates through five benches situated across different cities. The Principal Bench is in New Delhi. The four other regional benches are located in Pune, Bhopal, Chennai, and Kolkata.[26]

In furtherance of the need for scientific and multidisciplinary expertise, the NGT Act, 2010, equips the Tribunal with both judicial and expert members. Accordingly, the Tribunal comprises a chairperson, judicial members, and expert members. A minimum of ten judicial and ten expert members with a maximum cap of twenty members in both categories constitute the Tribunal.[27] Additionally, the chairperson is empowered to invite one or more persons having specialized knowledge and expertise in a particular case to assist the Tribunal when considered necessary.[28]

The chairperson and all the members are appointed by the Central government.[29] The Central government appoints the chairperson after consultation with the Chief Justice of India (CJI).[30] The judicial and expert members are appointed based on the recommendations of a Selection Committee constituted under the prescribed rules.[31] This Committee comprises the chairperson of the NGT, the director of an Indian Institute of Technology (IIT), an expert in environmental policy, an expert in forest policy, a secretary to the Government of India in the MoEF, and is chaired by a sitting judge of the Supreme Court nominated by the CJI in consultation with the Minister of Law and Justice.[32]

To qualify for appointment as the chairperson of the NGT, a person must be a serving or retired judge of the Supreme Court or a Chief Justice of a High Court.[33] Serving or retired judges of the High Courts are eligible for appointment as judicial members of the Tribunal.[34] To be eligible for qualification as an expert member, a person must have an advanced degree (that is, Master of Science) in physical sciences or life sciences coupled with a doctorate degree or a master-level degree in engineering or technology.[35] Additionally, this person must have experience of at least fifteen years in the relevant field, including five years of practical experience in environment and forests in a reputed national-level institute.[36] A person can also be eligible for appointment as an expert member if she has administrative experience of fifteen years, including five years of experience in dealing with environmental matters in the Central or state government or a reputed national- or state-level institution.[37]

Further, the NGT Act, 2010, provides for a cooling-off period of two years for a chairperson, judicial member, and expert member after her term has ended, wherein she is not allowed to accept any employment in, or connected with, the management or administration of any person who has been a part to the proceedings before the Tribunal.[38] The only exception provided is for any employment with the Central or state government or any statutory body.[39]

The salary and allowances of the chairperson of the NGT are the same as a serving judge of the Supreme Court.[40] Likewise, the judicial members are entitled to a salary and allowance equivalent to that received by a serving judge of a High Court.[41] The entitlements of an expert member correspond to the entitlements received by a secretary to the Government of India.[42]

The chairperson and members of the NGT hold their office for a term of five years and are not eligible for reappointment.[43] Additionally, different retirement ages are provided for members. The retirement age of a chairperson or a judicial member who has served as a judge on the Supreme Court is seventy years.[44] The retirement age is sixty-seven years for a chairperson or judicial member who has served as a judge of a High Court.[45] The retirement age for an expert member is sixty-five years.[46]

The NGT Act, 2010, provides for the removal of the chairperson and the members by the Central government. The Central government may, in consultation with the CJI, remove the chairperson or any judicial member of the Tribunal who[47]

a) has been judged insolvent; or
b) has been convicted of an offence which involves moral turpitude in the opinion of the Central government; or
c) has become physically or mentally incapable; or
d) has acquired such financial or other interest which is likely to prejudicially affect her functions; or
e) has abused her position as to render her continuance in the office as prejudicial to public interest.

Such a chairperson or judicial member can only be removed from office after an order is made by the Central government. This order has to be only after an inquiry has been conducted by a serving judge of the Supreme Court, wherein such chairperson or judicial member has been informed of her charges and has been accorded a reasonable opportunity of being heard in respect of these charges.[48] Nevertheless, the Central government can suspend such a chairperson or judicial member after a reference for conducting such an inquiry has been made against her, until the Central government passes an order post the receipt of the inquiry report.[49]

NOTES AND QUESTIONS

1. The SOR and the preamble to the NGT Act, 2010, highlight the need for a multidisciplinary approach to environmental adjudication. However, the provisions of the NGT Act, 2010, focus on expert members having scientific backgrounds and do not place an emphasis on expertise in social sciences. Given that most environmental concerns have a significant social impact, do you think the present scheme allows for multidisciplinary adjudication?

2. The eligibility for expert members is divided into two parts. Either a person should have the advanced educational qualifications in science specified coupled with fifteen years of work experience in the relevant fields or have fifteen years of administrative experience including five years of experience in dealing with environmental matters. Is the latter eligibility criterion comparable with the former? Do you think that bureaucrats working with the Central or state government for fifteen years, with only five years of environmental experience, can provide the multidisciplinary or scientific expertise needed? What do you think is the rationale behind such a distinction?

3. Further, in addition to the SOR and preamble to the NGT Act, 2010, the Environmental Impact Assessment Act, 2006, demonstrates the importance of a multidisciplinary approach. In addition to environmental impact, it specifically takes into account the social impact of environmental damage and has a separate screening process for it.[50] This is also evident from the fact that it requires a public consultation to be conducted prior to undertaking certain projects to assimilate the potential social impact of the activity. Given this context, what do you think can be done to ensure a more diverse and multidisciplinary composition of the Tribunal that caters to the social impacts of environmental degradation?

4. The NGT Act, 2010, provides that a minimum of ten judicial members and ten expert members are needed to constitute the Tribunal. Given the apathetic treatment provided to the NGT by the government, the Tribunal was forced to commence operations without the minimum strength necessary. Even after almost a decade, the NGT has mostly operated below the minimum threshold stipulated. What do you think is required to ensure that the Central government performs its statutory obligations under the NGT Act, 2010? Given that the Tribunal is responsible for most, if not all, environmental adjudication in India, do you think that the minimum number of members needed is sufficient?

5. The retirement age provided for expert members (sixty-five years) is less than the retirement age provided for judicial members (sixty-seven or seventy years). Do you think this distinction is justified? Further, there is a difference between the retirement age of judicial members who have served on a High Court (sixty-seven years) and those who have served on the Supreme Court (seventy years). Do you think this distinction bears a rational nexus and an intelligible differentiation with the purpose of the NGT Act, 2010?

2.2.2   THE TRIBUNALS REFORMS ACT, 2021

The parliament enacted the Tribunal Reforms Act during the monsoon session in late 2021. Though the constitutional validity of the Act has already been challenged, the Act seeks to govern and regulate, inter alia, the process of appointment, tenure, and eligibility of all tribunals that are listed in its Schedule I. Since the NGT Act, 2010, is mentioned under Schedule I, Table 2.1 lists the main changes that the Act seeks to introduce into the NGT's composition and functioning.

The constitutional validity of the Tribunals Reform Act, 2021, has been challenged on several grounds. First, Section 3(1) has been challenged on the grounds that it bars persons below the age of fifty from appointment and is, hence, in violation of the principle of separation of powers. Interestingly, in *Madras Bar Association (IV)*,[51] the Supreme Court had set aside a similar provision contained in the proviso to Section 184(1) of the Finance Act, 2017.

Section 3(7), which provides for a panel of two names to be recommended to the Central government, has been challenged on grounds of violating judicial independence. An identical provision contained in Section 184(7) of the Finance Act, 2017, was struck down by the Supreme Court in *Madras Bar Association (IV)*, on the grounds that executive influence on appointments in Tribunals should be minimized. The section has also been challenged for allowing the Central government to "preferably" take a decision on the recommendations of the Search-cum-Selection Committee within three months, if possible. It has been argued that this goes against the Supreme Court's holding in *Madras Bar Association III*,[52] wherein the Court held that appointments must be mandatorily made within three months of the recommendation.

Section 5 has been challenged for impinging judicial independence by providing for a "manifestly short tenure" of four years, which is in violation of the Court's directive in *Rojer Mathew*,[53] wherein it was held that appointees should have a minimum tenure of five years. Finally, Section 7(1) of the Tribunals Reform Act, 2021, has been challenged for providing the government with excess discretion to determine the housing rental allowance of members of the Tribunal, well beyond the guidelines and parameters laid down by the Court in *Madras Bar Association (IV)*. It has been argued that such a provision greatly curtails judicial independence and violates the security of the service conditions of members of the Tribunal, thereby violating Article 14 of the Constitution.[54]

Similar to the Tribunal Reforms Act, 2021, which has sought to shorten the tenure of members to four years in an attempt to circumvent the directions of the Supreme Court and weaken the functioning of the Tribunal, a more direct attempt to weaken the Tribunal had been made through the Finance Act, 2017. The Central government, under Section 184 of this Act, notified the Tribunal, Appellate Tribunal, and other Authorities (Qualification, Experience, and Other Conditions of Service of Members) Rules, 2017. These Rules were an attempt by the government to severely curtail the powers of the NGT. They provided, inter alia, a shorter tenure for members of only three years and

Table 2.1   Key divergences between the NGT Act, 2010, and the Tribunals Reforms Act in relation to the functioning of the NGT

Particulars	NGT Act, 2010	Tribunals Reforms Act, 2021
Minimum age for eligibility	None	Fifty years (for Chairperson and Members) **(Section 3(1))**
Appointment of Chairperson and Members	*For chairperson:* Centre in consultation with CJI **(Section 6(2))** *For members:* a Committee consisting of a) a sitting SC judge nominated by CJI and law minister in consultation (Chair of Committee); b) chairperson of Tribunal c) director of any Indian Institute of Technology (by rotation); d) expert in environmental policy nominated by MoEF; e) expert in forest policy nominated by MoEF; f) secretary to the Central government in MoEF (Member Secretary of the Committee) **(Section 6(3) and the NGT Rules (Amendment), 2012)**	*For both chairperson and members:* Centre in consultation with a Search-cum-Selection Committee, which includes: CJI/sitting judge of SC, two secretaries from the Central government, and chairperson of the Tribunal (when not seeking re-appointment) *If chairperson is being re-appointed:* a retired judge of SC or a retired CJ of HC replaces chairperson in the committee when re-appointing chairperson **(Sections 3(2) and (3))** Chairperson of Committee has a casting vote; Member Secretary does not **(Sections 3(4) and (5))** The Search-cum-Selection Committee shall recommend a panel of two names for appointment to the post of chairperson or member, as the case may be, and the Central government shall take a decision on the recommendations made by that Committee, preferably within three months from the date of such recommendation **(Sections 3(7))**
Appointment of Advocates for Membership	No provision	Advocate for at least ten years with substantial experience in litigation related to environment for judicial membership **(Rule 3(15)(iii) of Tribunal (Conditions of Service) Rules, 2021)**
Tenure of Chairperson and Members	Fixed at five years or age of seventy years for chairperson or former SC judge Age of sixty-seven years for chairperson or member who was former HC judge (whichever is earlier) Expert members must retire at sixty-five years **(Section 7)**	Fixed at four years for chairperson and members, irrespective of whether the member is judicial or expert Retirement age is seventy for chairperson and sixty-seven for members Between tenure of four years and retirement age, whichever is earlier **(Sections 5(1) and (2))**

(Contd)

Table 2.1   *(Contd)*

Particulars	NGT Act, 2010	Tribunals Reforms Act, 2021
Re-appointment of the Chairperson and Members	Not eligible for re-appointment	Eligible (take into account the service or tenure in the Tribunal) **(Section 6)**
Appointment criterion/ qualifications	As per **Section 5** of the NGT Act	As per the NGT Act, the only additions are: also allows for additional district judges and district Judges with ten years of experience to be appointed **(Rule 3(15)(ii) (Conditions of Service) Rules, 2021)**
Removal of the Chairperson and Members	Centre in consultation with CJI after following set procedure in **Section 10**	Same procedure as Section 10 of the NGT Act, subject to the change in the constitution of the Search-cum-Selection Committee, discussed earlier **(Section 4)**

diluted the qualifications necessary to be appointed as a chairperson or a member to an extent that even a person who was not a lawyer could head the NGT. Moreover, the Rules effectively equipped the Central government to remove the chairperson and sought to curtail the independence of the Tribunal by excluding the earlier requirement of a sitting judge of the Supreme Court and the chairperson from the appointment process of expert members in the Tribunal. Fortunately, this attempt was struck down by the Court in *Rojer Mathew v. South India Bank Limited*, which held these Rules to be unconstitutional.

2.3 JURISDICTION

In accordance with the PIL regime that preceded the establishment of the Tribunal, the NGT has been accorded vast jurisdiction by the NGT Act. It has both original and appellate jurisdiction. According to Section 14 of the Act, the Tribunal has jurisdiction over all civil cases where a substantial question relating to the environment is involved and such a question arises out of the implementation of statutes specified under Schedule I. Schedule I of the NGT Act consists of the following seven statutes:

a) The Water Act, 1974
b) The Water Cess Act, 1977
c) The Forest (Conservation) Act, 1980
d) The Air Act, 1981

e) The Environment (Protection) Act, 1986
f) The Public Liability Insurance Act, 1991
g) The Biological Diversity Act, 2002

Notably, the Wildlife Act, 1972, the Indian Forest Act, 1927, and the Forest Rights Act, 2006, are missing from Schedule I. This is surprising given that questions relating to wildlife and forests are integral to the environmental adjudication. As we have discussed in Chapter 1, through the PIL regime, the Supreme Court determined significant questions relating to forest policy and rights and wildlife.[55] Nevertheless, as we will discuss in detail later in the chapter, the NGT has held that issues relating to wildlife are within its jurisdiction:[56]

> As defined under the Act of 1986 "Environment" includes water, air and land and the inter relationship which exists among and between water, air and land and human beings, other living creatures, plants, microorganisms and property. We are of the opinion that occurrence of Wildlife in a particular ecosystem having relation with the environment has to be considered as a part of environment and therefore the matters related to wildlife are liable for adjudication and can be definitely brought under the environmental jurisprudence more so in cases pertaining to ESZs and therefore the matter being dealt in this OA is not just a Wildlife issue par se to be adjudicated under the Wildlife (Protection) Act 1972…. *Wildlife is a part of environment and any action that is causing damage to the wildlife or that may likely to lead to damage to the cause of wildlife, cannot be excluded from the purview of this Tribunal.* (Emphasis supplied)

Thus, the NGT has unequivocally held that it has jurisdiction to hear environmental matters relating to wildlife. This is because wildlife invariably forms an integral part of the environment, as defined under the Environmental (Protection) Act, 1986. In other words, wildlife is a part of the interrelationships that exist between living creatures, plants, and microorganisms, which form a part of the definition of the "environment" under the Environmental (Protection) Act, 1986. Thus, according to the Tribunal's interpretation of its jurisdiction, even though a matter may squarely fall within the purview of the Wildlife Act, 1972 – which is excluded from the NGT's jurisdiction – the Tribunal will still have jurisdiction over the matter under the Environmental (Protection) Act, 1986. The same logic can be applied to issues relating to forests as these issues invariably affect the environment. As we will see in the course of this book, the NGT has decided many cases that come within the domain of the Indian Forest Act, 1927, and the Forest Rights Act, 2006.

An application for adjudication of a dispute must be made within a period of six months from the date on which the first cause of action arose. However, the Tribunal can extend this period by sixty days if it is satisfied that the applicant was prevented by sufficient cause.[57] As we will see later in this section, to ensure that procedural impediments do not come in the way of substantive environmental justice, the NGT has interpreted the term "sufficient cause" very broadly. Further, we will highlight that in cases involving continuing offences, the NGT has held that each day constitutes a fresh cause of action, thereby eliminating the impediments that arise from the phrase "cause of action for such dispute first arose".

Under Section 15, the NGT can grant relief and compensation to victims of environmental pollution and damage arising out of the statutes mentioned under Schedule I. This includes accidents that happen while handling hazardous substances. Further, the NGT can order restitution of any damaged property and the environment. These reliefs are in addition to any compensation payable under the Public Liability Insurance Act, 1991. However, the claimant must inform the Tribunal about the compensation or relief received from any other court or authority.[58]

A distinct limitation period of five years is applicable for the grant of any compensation, relief, or restitution of property from the date on which the cause of action for such relief or compensation first arose. This period can be extended by sixty days as well if the NGT is satisfied that the applicant was prevented by sufficient cause from filing the application within the stipulated period.[59]

The heads under which the NGT can grant compensation are specified under Schedule II of the Act. These heads are:

a) Death
b) Permanent, temporary, total or partial disability or other injury or sickness
c) Loss of wages due to total or partial disability or permanent or temporary disability
d) Medical expenses incurred for treatment of injuries or sickness
e) Damages to private property
f) Expenses incurred by the government or any local authority in providing relief, aid, and rehabilitation to the affected persons
g) Expenses incurred by the government for any administrative or legal action or to cope with any harm or damage, including compensation for environmental degradation and restoration of the quality of environment
h) Loss to the government or local authority arising out of, or connected with, the activity causing any damage
i) Claims on account of any harm, damage, or destruction to the fauna including milch and draught animals and aquatic fauna
j) Claims on account of any harm, damage, or destruction to flora including aquatic flora, crops, vegetables, trees, and orchards
k) Claims including cost of restoration on account of any harm or damage to environment, including pollution of soil, air, water, land, and eco-systems
l) Loss and destruction of any property other than private property

m) Loss of business or employment or both
n) Any other claim arising out of, or connected with, any activity of handling of hazardous substance

In cases where there has been death, or injury caused to any person (other than a workman), or environmental damage on account of an accident or an activity under any statute specified under Schedule I, the person responsible shall provide relief or compensation under any or all of the aforementioned heads specified under Schedule II.[60] In such cases, if the damage caused is a combined effect of several activities, then the Tribunal may apportion the liability on an equitable basis. Further, in such cases, the NGT is required to apply the principle of no fault.[61] Effectively, this means that in such cases, the NGT has to apply the absolute liability doctrine developed by the Supreme Court in the *Oleum Gas Leaks Case* (refer to the discussion in Chapter 1).[62]

Original applications under Sections 14 or 15 can be filed by the following class of persons:[63]

a) Any person who has sustained the injury
b) The owner of damaged property
c) Legal representatives of the deceased
d) An agent duly appointed by any of the aforementioned persons
e) Any aggrieved person (including any representative body or organization)
f) The Central or state government, Union Territory administration, Central or State Pollution Control Boards, Pollution Control Committee, local authority, or any environmental authority established under the Environment Protection Act, 1986

In the next section, we will discuss how the NGT has expansively interpreted the aforementioned provision. In particular, in line with the expansion of *locus standi* by the Supreme Court during the environmental PIL regime, the NGT has broadly interpreted the term "aggrieved person". As we will discuss, the interpretation of the Tribunal effectively allows any citizen to file a case as he or she can be deemed to be aggrieved by any environmental harm. This is a recognition of the global and transboundary nature of environmental degradation.

The appellate jurisdiction of the Tribunal is conferred by Section 16 of the Act. An appeal to the NGT can be filed against the following class of orders:

a) Orders passed by the appellate authority under Section 28, or by the state government under Section 29, or by a Pollution Control Board under Section 33A of the Water Act, 1974
b) Orders passed by the appellate authority under Section 13 of the Water Cess Act, 1977

c) Orders passed by the state government or other authority under Section 2 of the Forest (Conservation) Act, 1980

d) Orders passed by the appellate authority under Section 31 of the Air Act, 1981

e) Any orders granting environmental clearance or directions issued under Section 5 of the Environment (Protection) Act, 1986

f) Any determination of benefit sharing made or order passed under the National Biodiversity Authority or a State Biodiversity Board under the Biological Diversity Act, 2002

Appeals under this section must be filed within thirty days from the date of communication of the order. Similar to Section 15, the NGT can extend this limitation period by sixty days if it is satisfied that there is sufficient case for delay. Appeals under Section 16 can be filed by any person who is aggrieved by any aforementioned order and has suffered a detriment from such a decision.

There is a bar on the jurisdiction of civil courts under Section 29 to entertain any appeal that the Tribunal is empowered to determine. Similarly, civil courts are also barred from entertaining any dispute or question relating to any claim that may be adjudicated upon by the NGT. This bar extends to filing any injunction by a civil court in relation to the settlement of any dispute or claim falling within the jurisdiction of the Tribunal.

As will be discussed in Chapter 4, the ouster of jurisdiction from 13,000 civil courts in the country has seriously impacted the access to justice in remote rural areas, which are the most vulnerable to environmental degradation. Adding to this, all zonal benches of the NGT have been shut down due to a lack of appointments in the past two years.[64] Moreover, due to a lack of appointments, even the Principal Bench at New Delhi is operating below the minimum required quorum. Thus, we are presently in a situation wherein all environmental cases in India are being heard by seven members (including the chairperson) of the NGT at New Delhi.[65]

To prevent any conflict between the provisions of the NGT Act and any other law, Section 33 provides that the NGT Act will have an overriding effect if there is any inconsistency in any other law. Further, the NGT Act repeals the NET Act, 1995, and the NEAA Act, 1997.[66]

Let us now analyse the major themes in relation to the NGT's jurisdiction.

2.3.1   INTERPRETATION OF AN "AGGRIEVED PERSON"

As noted in Chapter 1, the PIL regime that preceded the NGT expanded the *locus standi*[67] for instituting environmental claims through writ petitions. This was primarily done through the introduction of procedural innovations such as epistolary jurisdiction and placing emphasis on a non-adjudicatory process.[68] This was deemed necessary to enable public-spirited persons and non-governmental organizations to bring matters to the Court's attention, which would otherwise be unlikely due to low education and income levels in rural areas.[69] This legacy has been carried forward by the NGT. In addition to several enabling provisions of the NGT Act, 2010, discussed earlier, the Tribunal has interpreted the term "aggrieved person", contained in Section 18(2), in an expansive manner.

As per Section 18(2)(f), an application to the NGT for grant of relief, compensation, or settlement of a dispute can be made by an "aggrieved person, including any representative body or organization". Given that this provision is preceded by provisions that enable applications by, or on behalf of, persons who have sustained direct injury to their body or property, it follows that this provision is intended to cover people who are indirectly aggrieved. This interpretation follows from the statutory rule of interpretation that the legislature is deemed to not waste its words, convey anything in vain, or write anything that has already been conveyed or is redundant.[70]

Accordingly, the provision makes room for the institution of environmental adjudication by people who have not sustained any direct injury to their body or property. The NGT, however, has further expanded on the interpretation of the term and has included foreign nationals[71] and has unequivocally held that persons who may not be aggrieved per se will be allowed to institute proceedings in the Tribunal.

This is necessary due to three reasons. First, most projects that lead to environmental degradation are situated away from cities in rural areas and the countryside. People living in these areas may not be able to fully appreciate the extent of environmental degradation that has been caused on account of a project. Further, given the low level of education generally, they are unlikely to be able to appreciate the scientific details associated with the degradation and, hence, understand the potential impact that it is likely to have on their lives and surroundings.

Second, as noted previously, presently the NGT is operating only through its Principal Bench in New Delhi.[72] This effectively means that all environmental matters in India are being heard by the Principal Bench. Due to this, there is a lack of access to environmental justice. Many people living in remote and rural parts of the country are unable to travel to the capital for effective adjudication of their claims due to a lack of resources. While the option of videoconferencing exists, it remains under-effective.[73]

Third, there exists a fundamental duty for every citizen of India to protect and improve the environment. Article 51(A)(g) of the Directive Principles of State Policy contained in the Constitution of India confers a duty on every Indian citizen "to protect and improve the natural environment including forests, lakes, rivers and wildlife, and to have compassion for living creatures".

Thus, due to these three reasons coupled with the Supreme Court's precedent of expanding *locus standi*, it is necessary to have a liberal and expansive interpretation of the term "aggrieved person" to enable effective environmental adjudication. Let us now discuss a few illustrative judgments of the NGT that help us understand the contours of the term as interpreted by the Tribunal.

National Green Tribunal

(Principal Bench, New Delhi)

JAN CHETNA & ANR. v. MOEF

[Appeal No. 22 of 2011, Judgment Dated 9 February 2012]

A.S. Naidu, J. (Acting Chairperson);

Dr. G.K. Pandey (Expert Member)

* * *

Relevant Extracts:

1. M/s. Scania Steels & Power Ltd. (formerly known as Sidhi Vinayak Sponge Iron Ltd.) was operating a Sponge Iron Plant in Village Punjipatra, Tehsil Gharghoda, District Raigarh in the State of Chhattisgarh, before 2004 i.e. prior to issuance of EIA Notification, 2006.... The rules which governed at the relevant time did not mandate any need for seeking environment clearance for establishing Sponge Iron Units and as such, no environmental clearance was obtained, for installation of the said unit.... In the year, 2008, M/s Scania Steels & Power Ltd. (hereinafter called as Scania for the sake of brevity) applied to the MoEF for expansion of the existing project.... The proposal was considered by the MoEF and environment clearance (EC) was granted by letter dated 5th November, 2008 for the proposed expansion.

2. Jan Chetna (Appellant No.1) claiming to be a social and environmental group formed with the objective of working for the welfare of the local communities and creating awareness on social and environmental issues, represented through one or its Member Shri Ramesh Agrawal, and Shri Rajesh Tripathi claiming to be a Project affected person, having agriculture land adjacent to the project site and also claiming to be a social activist and a member of Jan Chetna, assailed the order dated 5th November, 2008, passed by the Ministry of Environment and Forests (MoEF) granting EC for expansion of the project in question before the then National Environment Appellate Authority (NEAA).... While NEAA was in session of the case, The NGT Act was promulgated and in consonance with the provisions of the said Act, the Appeal stood transferred to this Tribunal.

3. The main grievances of the Appellants are two-fold:

    a) That the Environment Clearance was granted to the project without Public Hearing, required under Clause-7 of EIA Notification, 2006.

b) The EAC in its meeting held on 15th April, 2008 erroneously exempted the proposal for Public Hearing under Clause-7(ii) of EIA Notification, 2006, construing the proposal to be an expansion project.

7.   … In its reply Scania raised preliminary objection with regard to the *locus-standi* of the Appellants and contended that the present Appeal having been filed under the National Environment Appellate Authority Act, 1997, the mandatory requirement of the said Act has to be considered. Under the said Act, it is averred, an Appeal can be filed only by a person who is: a) Either affected by the grant of Environment Clearance; b) xxx; c) Any association of persons (whether incorporated or not) likely to be affected by such order and functioning in the field of environment. According to Scania the Appellants do not satisfy either of the clauses, and as such they have no *locus-standi* to prefer this Appeal, and the same may be dismissed, *in limine*, on that ground alone.

18. We propose to deal with the question of locus-standi at the first instance. Admittedly, this Appeal was filed in the year 2009 invoking jurisdiction under NEAA Act, 1997. Though the said Act has been repealed and National Green Tribunal Act, 2010 has come into force, the Appeal having been filed under the NEAA Act, 2009, has to be disposed of under the provisions of the said Act.

20. … [We] may now proceed to examine the provisions of the NEAA Act. Section 11 of the Act which is material for the purpose of this appeal, is reproduced herein below:-

> "11. (1) Any person aggrieved by an order granting environmental clearance in the areas in which any industries, operations or processes or class of industries, operations and processes shall not be carried out or shall be carried out subject to certain safeguards may, within thirty days from the date of such order, prefer an appeal to the Authority in such form as may be prescribed.
>
> Provided that Authority may entertain any appeal after the expiry of the said period of thirty days but not after ninety days from the date aforesaid if it is satisfied that the appellant was prevented by sufficient cause from filing the appeal in time.
>
> (2) For the purposes of sub-section (1) "Persons" means –
>
> a) any person who is likely to be affected by the grant of environmental clearance.
> b) any person who owns or has control over the project with respect to which an application has been submitted for environmental

clearance; c) any association of persons (whether incorporated or not) likely to be affected by such order and functioning in the field of environment;

d) the Central Government, where the environmental clearance is granted by the State Government and the State Government, where the environmental clearance is granted by the Central Government; or

e) any local authority, any part of whose local limits is within the neighbourhood of the area wherein the project is proposed to be located".

21. On a plain reading of Section 11, it is seen that any person aggrieved by an order granting environmental clearance has a right to prefer an appeal to the Authority. The definition of 'person' as contained in sub-section (2) of Section 11 (a), provides that any person who is likely to be affected by the grant of environmental clearance has an undoubted *locus standi* to file an appeal. Section 11(2)(c) is worded differently and is wider in scope than sub-clause (a). Sub-clause (c) speaks of "association of persons" (whether incorporated or not) who are likely to be affected by the impugned action and who work in the field of environment. In other words, subclause (a) talks of those who are affected or are likely to be affected and the emphasis is on the impact on an individual, though the subclause, does not rule out more than one person likely to be affected and/or actually aggrieved. In contrast, sub-clause (c) refers to an association of persons, incorporated one. Such association of persons, (incorporated association), cannot be said to be affected in the manner traditionally understood. Moreover, in environmental cases the damage is not necessarily confined to the local area where the industry is set up. The effect of environmental pollution or environmental degradation might have far-reaching effects going beyond the local area and create national or global effects. For example, the destruction of forests is said to be one of the causes leading to global warming. Therefore, the aggrieved person need not be resident of the local area. Such an interpretation would also result in defeating the very objective of this enactment in terms of access to justice. (see Judgment of High Court of Delhi passed in LPA No. 277/2009 dated 14th September 2009 in the case of Vedanta Alumina Ltd. Vs Prafulla Samantra & Ors.).

22. The expression "aggrieved persons" cannot be considered in a restricted manner. Its scope and meaning depends on variable factors i.e. the aims and objectives and the intent of the Statute out of which the controversy arises. In the case of Gulam Qadir Vs Special Tribunal and other 2002 (1) SCC 33, the Supreme Court observed that an orthodox rule of interpretation regarding the locus-standi of a person to reach the Court has undergone a sea change and

the constitutional courts have been adopting a liberal approach in dealing with the cases or the claims of litigants. It is well settled that in construing remedial statute the courts ought to give to it widest operation which its language will permit. The words of such a statute must be so construed as to give the most complete remedy which the phraseology will permit, so as to secure the relief contemplated by the Statute is not denied to the class intended to be relieved. The statute being remedial in nature is given liberal construction to promote the beneficent object behind it.

23. In so far as, the present case is concerned, it appears from the records, that the first Appellant a social Environment activist had in several occasions in past, made representations before Competent Authority. The organization of the first Appellant is working in the area in question and as it appears from the deliberations made in the court, was following the issue of the project in question, during various stages of the project, it had complained about the impact of the project on ecology and environment and prayed to direct Respondent No.3 not to go ahead with the project. The second Appellant is a resident of the locality and is the owner of agriculture land situate in the vicinity. In the above circumstances, it is not right to say that the Appellants are not aggrieved persons within the meaning of Section 11 of NEAA Act. Denial of the right to file an appeal to the Appellants would virtually defeat the legislative intentions of granting access to justice.

24. A dispute involving similar controversy arose earlier in the case of 'Prafulla Samantra Vs MoEF & Ors.' Prafulla claiming to be a social and environmental activist challenged an order granting EC by the MoEF for setting up of an Alumina Smelter Plant, before the NEAA, by filing an appeal. The said appeal was resisted on the ground that he is not a "person aggrieved" and is not covered under Section 11 of the NEAA Act. The Authority dismissed the Appeal holding that he is not a "person aggrieved". Being aggrieved by the said order, Prafulla Samantra approached the Hon'ble High Court of Delhi in WP(C) No. 3126/2008. After hearing parties Hon'ble single judge of the High Court of Delhi by a well discussed judgment dated 6.5.2009 allowed the writ petition. The Hon'ble Judge observed as follows:-

> "India, even today, lives largely in its villages. A project or scheme, which is likely to affect or impact a remote community, that may comprise even a cluster of villages, may or may not have an "association of persons" who work in the field of environment. The villagers, like most others, are unlikely to know about the project clearance, or possess the wherewithal to question it, through an appeal. If the third respondent's contention, and the authority's impugned order were to be accepted, and upheld, such

community's right to appeal, meaningfully, would be rendered a chimera, an illusion. In their case, the Act would be a crude joke, paying lip service, while promising access to justice, but in reality depriving such a right...."

The Hon'ble Single Judge came to the conclusion that Prafulla Samantra satisfies the expression "Person aggrieved" and set aside the order passed by the NEAA. The said judgment was assailed by Vedanta Alumina Ltd., Respondent in the said case, before the High Court of Delhi in LPA No. 277 of 2009. The Divisional Bench of High Court of Delhi, by judgment dated 14th September, 2009, confirmed the finding of the Hon'ble single Judge, and held that Prafulla can be construed to a be a "Person aggrieved" in consonance with Section 11 of NEAA Act and dismissed the LPA. The findings arrived at by the Division Bench of Delhi High Court are squarely applicable to the case in hand, and we have no hesitation to hold that the Appellants satisfy the definition of "Person aggrieved" and they have *locus standi* to file this Appeal.

* * *

NOTES AND QUESTIONS

1. The case involves a matter that was initially filed with the NEAA and was later transferred to the NGT. Accordingly, the provisions of the NEAA Act, 1997, were made applicable. On the question of *locus standi*, Section 11(2) of the Act states that any person who is aggrieved and is "likely to be affected" or any association of persons who is aggrieved and is "likely to be affected" by the impugned action will have *locus standi* to file an appeal with the NEAA. In accordance with the relevant interpretative precedents of the Supreme Court cited, the NGT rightly holds that environmental damage is not confined to any particular area. Rather, it is likely to have far-reaching effects at a national and global scale (for example, global warming from deforestation). Accordingly, the NGT holds that a narrow interpretation of an aggrieved person will defeat the objective of the enactment by reducing access to environmental justice.

2. The NGT places emphasis on the fact that Jan Chetna was an environmental activist group, and it had several antecedents of making relevant representations in the case before relevant authorities. Do you think if Jan Chetna had not made any representations in the case and was also not involved in environmental activities, it would still have *locus standi*? From the NGT's analysis, can you infer any *de minimus* threshold that is required for a person to qualify as an "aggrieved person" under Section 18(2)(f) of the NGT Act 2010?

* * *

National Green Tribunal

(Western Zonal Bench, Pune)

BETTY C. ALVARES v. STATE OF GOA

[Application No. 63 of 2012, Judgment Dated 14 February 2014]

V.R. Kingaonkar, J. (Judicial Member);
Dr. Ajay A. Deshpande (Expert Member)

*   *   *

Relevant Extracts:

1. … The objections raised in these Applications are twofold. The first objection is that Applicant – Betty Alvares, has no *locus standi* to file the main Application. Secondly, the main Application is barred by limitation and as such, is liable to be dismissed *in limine*. The objections are raised by contesting Respondents Nos. 8 and 9 in the Writ Petition No. 1 of 2012, Public Interest Litigation (PIL) before the Hon'ble High Court of Bombay Bench at Goa. By order dated October 23, 2012, the Writ Petition came to be transferred to this Tribunal.

3. … We also may discern that the Hon'ble Bench of the High Court of Bombay at Goa expressed the view that it was not open to consider the said objection of *Locus* relating to maintainability of the Writ Petition. Needless to say, such objections were left open for consideration by the NGT. What appears from the record is that the Respondent Nos. 8 and 9, challenged *locus standi* of Betty Alvares to maintain a PIL Writ Petition mainly on the ground that she is not a citizen of India. There was no other reason ascribed to challenge her *locus standi* to file the Writ Petition. The Respondent Nos. 8 and 9, in their affidavit in reply raised such objection, alleging that only a citizen of India can file Writ Petition in the interest of public and that Betty Alvares being not a citizen of India, she is legally incompetent to file the petition in the garb of Article 21, because there is no guarantee of any right in her favour under the Constitution of India.

4. As regards the first objection, we may mention here that Article 21 of the Constitution gives guarantee of life to a person. It is not restricted to guarantee of life only to a citizen of India. We cannot take narrow view, so as to restrict applicability of Article 21 only to a citizen of India. Even assuming that Applicant–Betty Alvares, is not the citizen of India. Yes, the Application is maintainable. In fact, the Writ Petition reveals that she had filed other Writ

Petitions and Contempt Applications prior to filling of the present Application. The averments in the Application go to show that her complaints were duly inquired and the Authorities had found substance in the complaints, but had not taken affirmative action and therefore, she approached to Hon'ble High Court, inasmuch as the Respondents were found to have committed blatant violation of the CRZ Regulations. She asserted that the Respondents raised illegal constructions and encroached upon part of sea-beaches, as well as on government properties. She sought demolition of illegal constructions raised by the Respondent Nos. 8 to 21, which allegedly were hood-winked by the first seven (7) Respondents.

5. Nobody will deny that right to have pollution free air, good environment and proper enforcement of the CRZ Regulation, for such purpose, is a part of guarantee for maintaining dignified life in the society. Article 21 covers the guarantee to enjoy 'dignified life' and as such, Betty Alvares was entitled to file the Writ Petition before the Hon'ble High Court of Bombay, Bench at Goa and as such is entitled to maintain the Application before the NGT.

6. The learned Counsel for contesting Respondents argued that Betty Alvares is not 'an aggrieved person', nor she has sustained any injury due to alleged constructions raised by the Respondents and, therefore, the present Application is untenable for want of locus standi. It is contended that she cannot file the Application, because she is not owner of any property to which damage has been caused on account of construction activity carried out by the Respondents. It is further argued that the Application does not fall within ambit of Section 14 or Section 18 of the National Green Tribunal Act, 2010. We may take note of definition of word 'person' as enumerated in Section 2 (j) of the National Green Tribunal Act, 2010. Section 2(j) reads as follows:

"**2. Definitions**–(1) In this Act, unless the context otherwise requires,—

(j) "person" includes—

(i)   An individual,
(ii)   A Hindu undivided family,
(iii)   A company,
(iv)   A firm,
(v)   An association of persons or a body of individuals, whether incorporated or not,
(vi)   Trustee of a trust,
(vii)   A local authority, and

(viii) Every artificial juridical person, not falling within any of the preceding sub-clauses."

7.   A plain reading of Section 2(j) will make it manifest that the word 'person' has to be construed in broad sense. It includes 'an individual', whether a national or a person who is not a citizen of India. We need not, therefore, go into details of nationality of Betty Alvares. Once it is found that any person can file the proceeding relating to environment dispute, it goes without saying that the Application of Betty Alvares is maintainable, irrespective of the question of her nationality. It is not necessary to see whether she has personally suffered any loss on account of damage caused to environment or violation of CRZ Regulation by the acts of Respondents. It is not necessary to see whether she has suffered any injury. It suffices to see whether there is substantial question relating to environment and such question arises out of implementation of enactments specified in Schedule-I, appended to the National Green Tribunal Act, 2010. In our opinion, therefore, the Application cannot be dismissed for the reason that Betty Alvares has no *locus standi*, inasmuch as she falls within the definition of word 'person' as defined in Section 2(j) of the National Green Tribunal Act, 2010. The first objection is, therefore, overruled.

8.   Coming to the second objection raised by the contesting Respondents, learned Counsel appearing for Respondents contended that Betty Alvares ought to have filed the Application under Section 14 of the National Green Tribunal Act, 2010, within period of six (6) months from the date on which 'cause of action' had first arisen, for the first time, somewhere in 2009. The Application could be filed at least within six (6) months after the NGT Act, is enforced. The Application is hopelessly time barred, as the Writ Petition was filed in 2012. It is further argued that the Application cannot be considered under Section 18 of the National Green Tribunal Act, 2010, inasmuch as Betty Alvares has not sustained any injury or loss of property and is not entitled to compensation. It is contended that the Application is outside the scope of Section 15 of the National Green Tribunal Act, 2010, because Betty Alvares cannot claim any compensation under sub-clause (a) of Section 15(1), nor restitution under sub-clause (b) of Section 15(1) or restitution under sub-clause (c), when the Application is not filed within period of five (5) years from the date of cause of action. It is contended that Betty Alvares is well-versed in Court work and ought to have known the difficulties about the hurdle of limitation, under the National Green Tribunal Act, 2010, and therefore, played a trick by filing Writ Petition (PIL) No.1 of 2012 in the Hon'ble High Court of Bombay Bench at Goa. It

is argued that mere transfer of that Writ Petition to the NGT, will not save limitation period and it cannot be condoned only because the Writ Petition has been transferred.

9. We find it rather difficult to entertain the argument advanced by the learned Counsel for contesting Respondents. For, the original Writ Petition was not dismissed by the Hon'ble High Court of Bombay, Bench at Goa, on the ground of limitation. Nor it was dismissed at the stage of admission for the reason that alternate remedy to approach the NGT was available. Contesting Respondents also did not pin-point that such alternate remedy was available to Applicant–Betty Alvares and, therefore, the Writ Petition was not maintainable. It was only after the Judgment of the Apex Court in "Bhopal Gas Pideet Mahila Udhyog Sanghatn vs Union of India" (2012) 8, SCC 326 that by agreement of parties the Hon'ble Bench of High Court rendered the transfer order. It is obvious that Betty Alvares did not play any trick to avoid impediment of limitation in filing of the Application under Section 14 of the National Green Tribunal Act, 2010, which was not in contemplation at the relevant time. We cannot overlook that Writ jurisdiction under Article 226 of the Constitution, is available, irrespective of other remedies under the specified enactments. It is discretion of the Hon'ble High Court to consider whether the Writ Petition should be entertained even though any other remedy is available to the Petitioner. The learned Counsel for the Respondents submit that Section 5(A) of the Environment (Protection) Act, 1986, provides for an Appeal against the orders under the CRZ Notification. But in absence of directions under Section 5, Applicant – Betty Alvares cannot file any Appeal or Application. We do not find any substance in this argument, inasmuch as the Application is covered by Section 14, since it involves "substantial question relating to environment." ... Consequently we do not find any substance in both the objections raised on behalf of the contesting Respondents.

*   *   *

NOTES AND QUESTIONS

1. The NGT, through this case, clarifies that an "aggrieved person" under Section 18(2)(f) of the NGT Act, 2010, can be a person who is not a citizen of India. It is a welcome judgment as it carries forward the Supreme Court's approach to environmental adjudication during the PIL regime. However, the manner in which

the NGT arrives at this conclusion is also noteworthy. While the NGT correctly holds that a writ under Article 21 of the Constitution is maintainable by Ms Alvares as she does not need to be a citizen of India, the Tribunal holds that "Betty Alvares was entitled to file the Writ Petition before the Hon'ble High Court of Bombay, Bench at Goa *and as such is entitled to maintain the Application before the NGT*" (emphasis supplied).

Further, the NGT does not analyse the import of the term "aggrieved person" under Section 18(2)(f) and its jurisprudence as determined by the Tribunal in the past. Instead of interpreting the term "aggrieved", as the Tribunal did in *Jan Chetna & Anr. v. MoEF*, the Tribunal focuses on the term "persons" as defined under Section 2(1)(j) of the Act. On the basis of its analysis of Section 2(1)(j) – which, inter alia, defines a person as an individual – the Tribunal concludes that it is broad enough to include individuals who are not citizens of India. Do you think such a conclusion is valid solely on the basis of an interpretation of Section 2(1)(j)?

Rather, do you think the Tribunal should have arrived at the same conclusion by furthering its previous expansive interpretation of an "aggrieved person" under Section 18(2)(f) by demonstrating how a foreign citizen can also be aggrieved by environmental degradation? (Think about the NGT's analysis of deforestation leading to global warming in *Jan Chetna & Anr. v. MoEF*.)

2. Section 14(3) of the NGT Act, 2010, provides for a limitation period of six months from the date when the cause of action first arose. It further gives the Tribunal grant a sixty-day extension to the limitation period due to sufficient cause. One of the objections raised in the present case relates to the fact that the first cause of action arose in 2009 (prior to the enactment of NGT Act 2010) and that even if the limitation period was assessed from the date of enactment of the Act, the petition was still time barred as per Section 14(3). The NGT responds to this contention by stating that the High Court of Bombay (which transferred the case to the NGT) did not dismiss the application on the ground of limitation and that the respondents did not make Ms Alvares aware of the alternative remedy that existed in the form of the Tribunal. It further states that the High Court had transferred the case to the Tribunal on the direction of the Supreme Court and that Ms Alvares had not played "any trick" to avoid limitation.

While the NGT's decision provides the necessary procedural innovation to allow a smooth transfer of cases from High Courts to the Tribunal in the light of the directions of the Supreme Court, do you think the reasoning is sound? Do you think that simply because the High Court did not dismiss the application on the ground of limitation it would be sufficient to pass the test of Section 14(3)? Further, do you think it was the responsibility of the respondents to inform the appellant about the limitation period with reference to the NGT?

* * *

National Green Tribunal

(Principal Bench, New Delhi)

RANA SEN GUPTA v. UNION OF INDIA & ORS.

[Appeal No. 54 of 2012, Judgment Dated 22 March 2013]

V.R. Kingaonkar, J. (Judicial Member);
U.D. Salvi, J. (Judicial Member);
P.S. Rao (Expert Member);
Bikram Singh Sajwan (Expert Member)

*   *   *

Relevant Extracts:

1.   … This Appeal is filed by one Rana Sen Gupta, who claims to be a public spirited citizen–working for welfare of people, particularly for those whose concerns might otherwise would remain un-represented. He challenges the order of Environmental Clearance (EC) granted by the Respondent No. 1 (MoEF) … in favour of Respondent No. 3 (M/s. Rashmi Metaliks Ltd.). The EC is granted for expansion of existing Steel Plant by… the Respondent No. 3 (M/s. Rashmi Metaliks Ltd.,) referred to hereinafter as "Project Proponent".

5.   The Appellant has come out with a case that the Project Proponent concealed information regarding the Ductile Iron Pipe Plant that was being operated prior to the proposed expansion. The Respondent No. 1 (MoEF) failed to consider that the Project Proponent had omitted to include the pre-existing Ductile Iron Pipe Plant in the EIA Report which was presented before granting the impugned EC. The MoEF also failed to consider the fact that the Project Proponent did not submit Environmental Impact Assessment (EIA) report, taking into account the impact of pre-existing Ductile Iron Pipe Plant, and therefore, the proposal for the expansion of project in question, was improper. The information furnished by the Project Proponent was misleading and incorrect. The Appellant further alleges … he enhanced emission of carbon-di-oxide due to the proposed expansion of the industrial activity would cause irreparable damage to the eco-system and the environment of adjoining area and adversely affect the health of public. But these aspects are overlooked by the Respondent No. 1. The previous EC granted by the SEIAA to the Project Proponent also was illegal and improper. The Appellant further states that the Project Proponent has not provided for adequate green belt as per the conditions enumerated in the EC granted in the past and, therefore,

the proposed expansion of the project should not have been allowed by the Respondent No. 1.

6.   Respondents resisted the Appeal…. They submitted that the grant of EC for manufacturing project of 2 lakh T.P.A. capacity on 09.10.2009 cannot be challenged by the Appellant. They submitted that dismissal of Appeal No. 32/2011 filed by the Appellant has now sealed the issue regarding grant of said EC for the Ductile Iron Pipe Plant…. They further submitted that there was no concealment of any fact by the Project Proponent. They submitted that the expansion of the industrial activity falls within the project/activity item 3(a) of the Schedule appended to the MoEF Notification dated 14.09.2006 and as such the assessment/appraisal was done as required under the relevant regulations. They further submitted that the expansion of the project is legal and proper. They denied truth into the allegation that the conditions of the previous EC were violated by the Project Proponent. Consequently, they sought dismissal of the Appeal.

7.   In addition, the Project Proponent alleges that the Appellant has no *locus standi* to file the present Appeal. It is alleged that the Appellant cannot be treated as "aggrieved person". It is also submitted that the Appellant is unconcerned with the environmental impact of the project in question. It is pointed out that the Appellant is inhabitant of Dhakuria, Kolkata whereas the project is situated at village Gokulpur (District Paschim Mednipur). According to the Project Proponent, the Appellant is a busybody and has filed the Appeal without there being any element of so called public interest or alleged concern for environmental damage or public welfare. On these premises, the Project Proponent and other respondents sought dismissal of the Appeal.

12.   Having heard Learned Counsel for the parties, in our opinion, the following points arise for the purpose of deciding the appeal. They are:-

       (i). Whether the Appellant is "aggrieved person" and has locus-standi to prefer the appeal?

       … So far as *locus standi* of the Appellant is concerned, it would be appropriate to examine what he has pleaded in the Memorandum of Appeal. He alleged that although he has no personal interest in the matter, yet because he is working for the welfare of the people, particularly for those whose concern might have otherwise remained unrepresented, he is aggrieved. Secondly, he states that he has been raising the issue of non-compliance of environmental norms by the Project Proponent and had filed earlier Appeal No. 32/2011 with a view to stall installation of Ductile Iron Pipe Plant Project. He says that he is a public spirited citizen with working experience in steel and iron industry and has full knowledge of the impact of these industries on ecology, environment and human lives. These are the reasons given by him to demonstrate that he is competent to file the appeal.

Section 16 of the NGT Act, 2010 provides appellate jurisdiction to the Tribunal. The opening words of Section 16 go to show that "any person aggrieved" by order made granting EC can prefer appeal under Section 16(h) of the NGT Act, 2010. The expression "person aggrieved by" imply some or other reason which might have aggravated the person to undertake the legal remedy. Such a person must demonstrate that he is directly or indirectly concerned with the adverse environmental impact which is likely to be caused due to granting of EC by the competent authority. The Appellant, admittedly, resides at Babu Bagan, Dhakuria area of Kolkata. The main project and expansion area of the subsequent project is situated at Shyamraipur (District Paschim Medinipur). It is not the case of the Appellant that he has any property in the adjoining area of village Shyamraipur. It is not his case that he is personally adversely affected due to the installation of the expansion project in question. He vaguely states that he is a public spirited citizen with experience of working with steel and iron industries and has full knowledge of the impact of these industries on ecology, environment and human lives. He vaguely proclaims that he is working for the welfare of the people and particularly who have remained unrepresented.

14. We do not find any tangible material which would plausibly show that the Appellant has credentials as expert in the field of steel and iron industries and we are at a loss to know in what manner he is working for the welfare of unrepresented members of the public. It is not his case that he represents any NGO. His self-proclaimed status as "public spirited citizen" is of no much avail. There is absolutely no record to show that he participated in the public consultation process and raised any issue regarding the environment or socio-economic adverse impact on account of establishment of the proposed project. The only reason that he has unsuccessfully preferred Appeal No. 32/2011 against granting of earlier EC for production of Ductile Iron Pipe Plant is of no much significance and is irrelevant. Moreover, that appeal came to be dismissed and there is no finding of this Tribunal that the Appellant is to be treated as "an aggrieved person". Considering forgoing discussion, we have come to the conclusion that the Appellant has no *locus standi* to prefer the present appeal. He cannot be treated as an aggrieved person and the appeal filed by him cannot be entertained.

27. Considering totality of the foregoing discussion, we have no hesitation in holding that the Appellant failed to prove that the proposed expansion of the project is detrimental to the cause of environment. We hold that expansion of the industrial activity as approved by the MoEF is within the permissible limits of sustainable development. This answers the point no. (iii).

28. The net result of the findings recorded on the points no. (i) to (iii) is that the Appeal is destitute of merits. Therefore, it fails. We have noticed that the Appellant indulged in the litigation without proper cause, though he is not an aggrieved party as such. It is high time to discourage such practice of fuelling the litigation without any substantial reason. Hence the Appeal is dismissed with direction that the Appellant shall deposit a cost of Rs. 15,000/- into the Legal Aid Fund of National Green Tribunal Bar Association. The Appeal is accordingly disposed of as dismissed. In case the cost is not deposited by the Appellant within a period of four (4) weeks, the Registrar to take proper action for recovery of the said amount as provided under Order XXI R 30 of the C.P. Code or any other provision envisaged under Order XXI or the provisions of the National Green Tribunal Act, 2010.

* * *

NOTES AND QUESTIONS

1. This case involves an appeal from a governmental order granting an environmental clearance in favour of expanding a project and is primarily governed by Section 16(h) of the NGT Act, 2010. The appellant is a person who, though not directly aggrieved by the project, states that he is a public-spirited person and has been working for the welfare of those who remain unrepresented. He has working experience in the iron and steel industry and states that he is well versed in the ecological impact of the project. Further, he has previously raised the issue of non-compliance with environmental norms by the project. The NGT, however, holds that the appellant lacks *locus standi* to initiate the proceedings.

   Gitanjali Nain Gill, in her commentary on the NGT, has argued that this case demonstrates the NGT's strict ruling on how frivolous petitions filed by litigious persons who are a "busy body and their motives ulterior" should not be entertained.[74] However, when we compare the two reasons on which the NGT based its decision with the NGT's reasoning in *Jan Chetna & Anr. v. MOEF* (discussed earlier), a different understanding emerges. Let us discuss these two reasons and compare them with *Jan Chetna*.

First, the NGT holds that the appellant lacks *locus standi* since the place of residence of the appellant is not proximate to the impugned project (Dhakuria – where the appellant resides – is only 77.1 kilometres away from Shyamraipur, where the project is located). Further, the Tribunal states that it is not the case that the appellant has some property adjoining the village Shyamraipur and is not personally affected by the project. However, as previously held by the Tribunal in *Jan Chetna*, environmental damage is not confined to the local area where the industry is situated. In fact, it can have national and even global consequences, as seen from deforestation and global warming. Considering this reasoning, do you think that the NGT was justified in holding that the appellant does not have *locus standi* due to his lack of physical proximity to the impugned project? Do you think it is necessary that the appellant or his property must be personally affected to qualify him to initiate the present appeal?

Second, the NGT holds that the appellant lacks *locus standi* since mere self-proclamations of the appellant – that he is working for the benefit of the public – are not enough. There needs to be some evidence to demonstrate that he is an "expert" in the iron and steel industry and that there is no evidence that he has been working for the welfare of people. In addition, the NGT states, "It is not his case that he represents any NGO." Do you think, given the reasoning in *Jan Chetna*, an aggrieved person has to have expertise in the concerned subject? Further, how would the appellant being a part of an NGO grant him *locus standi* in the present case? Why do you think that the appellant's prior work experience in the industry and his antecedents in the case (filing a similar petition before to stop the project's expansion) are not enough?

2. The NGT holds that under Section 16(h) of the NGT Act, 2010, a "person aggrieved" must have "some or other reason which might have aggravated the person to undertake the legal remedy" and that "such a person must demonstrate that he is directly or *indirectly concerned with the adverse environmental impact* which is likely to be caused due to granting of EC by the competent authority" (emphasis supplied). The cases that we have discussed, technically, expand the meaning of an "aggrieved person" under Section 18(2)(f) of the Act and not of a "person aggrieved" under Section 16 of the Act. Moreover, Section 18 begins by stating that it applies without prejudice to the provisions of Section 16. Do you think there are two distinct standards between an "aggrieved person" under Section 18 and a "person aggrieved" under Section 16 of the Act that the Tribunal intends to outline? In other words, do you think the expanded *locus standi* under Section 18(2)(f) is also available to a person approaching the Tribunal under Section 16?

Ideally, the same standard of *locus standi* should be made applicable under both sections. In fact, even though the Tribunal, in this case, holds that the appellant lacks *locus standi*, its reasoning can be interpreted to make the same standards applicable in both cases. For instance, it holds that there should be some reason that has aggravated the appellant and that he should be able to demonstrate that he is directly or indirectly concerned with the adverse environmental impact. As noted in *Jan Chetna*, the environmental impact of the project is likely to have far-reaching consequences which indirectly affect everyone in the country, including the appellant. Accordingly, this reason is enough to qualify as an aggravating circumstance to enable the appellant to initiate the present appeal as he is indirectly affected.

Further, as held by the Supreme Court, the words of a statute must be construed in a manner that provides the most complete remedy which the phraseology permits so as to ensure that the relief is not denied to the class of persons intended to be relieved.[75] Accordingly, the standard of *locus standi* for a "person aggrieved" under Section 16 should be the same as the expanded standard under Section 18(2)(f) of the Act.

3. Despite holding that the appellant does not have *locus standi* to file the appeal, the NGT goes into the merits of the case. Accordingly, it holds that the appellant has failed to demonstrate any serious detriment to the environment that will be caused on account of the expansion of the project and rejects the appeal. The Tribunal, however, goes further and holds that the present appeal amounts to frivolous litigation and awards a penalty on account of initiating proceedings without proper cause. Do you think this is justified from the facts available in the judgment?

4. The NGT has, following this judgment, abandoned the narrow construction of an aggrieved person for the purposes of *locus standi*.[76] As seen in *Betty C. Alvares v. State of Goa*,[77] it has expanded the scope of an aggrieved person to even include persons who are not citizens of India. As noted in Chapter 1, this is in line with the approach adopted by the Supreme Court of India prior to the enactment of the NGT.

*   *   *

2.3.2   SUO MOTU JURISDICTION

As noted in Chapter 1, the exercise of suo motu jurisdiction has played an integral part in developing environmental jurisdiction in India. The Supreme Court would often take up cases on its own motion based on information contained in newspaper and magazine articles that reported environmental degradation.[78] Given that the NGT adjudicates on important environmental matters that were previously decided by a constitutional bench of the Supreme Court, it seems only natural for the NGT to have suo motu jurisdiction. However, such a power has not been specified in the NGT Act, 2010. The provisions of the Act neither expressly grant nor bar the exercise of suo motu jurisdiction.

Whether the NGT has such jurisdiction has been a contentious issue that has only recently been settled by the Supreme Court. In fact, the Tribunal's own stance on the issue has changed over the years. During its early years of inception (up until late 2012), the NGT was of the view that it lacked such powers. The Tribunal unequivocally held in *Baijnath Prajapati v. MoEF* that the NGT Act, 2010, did not confer suo motu jurisdiction on the Tribunal and that any exercise of it by the Tribunal would amount to an excess of jurisdiction.[79]

Nevertheless, it was widely felt that such jurisdiction was necessary to enable the NGT to effectively adjudicate. In fact, just a year after the establishment of the NGT, in September 2011, Justice L. S. Panta – then the chairperson of the Tribunal – wrote to the government requesting for the NGT Act, 2010, to be amended to expressly accord the NGT with suo motu jurisdiction.[80] Subsequently, in January 2012, Justice A. S. Naidu – then the acting chairperson of the NGT – again wrote to the government requesting the same. Both times, the MoEF refused the Tribunal by stating that the latter did not have such powers within the mandate of the NGT Act, 2010, and underscored that the government did not intend to provide it with suo moto jurisdiction. Accordingly, in a response to a parliamentary query, the MoEF stated:[81]

> The government of India has not agreed to confer *suo motu* powers on the tribunal ... it is for the NGT, an adjudicatory body, to follow provisions of the NGT Act, 2010.

In fact, the MoEF went on to state that the NGT was causing "embarrassment" by not adjudicating as per the NGT Act, 2010.[82] The NGT, however, disregarded these clarifications from the MoEF and began adjudicating on several important environmental matters on its own motion.[83] Shortly thereafter, in 2013, the MoEF challenged the exercise of suo motu jurisdiction by the NGT before the Supreme Court.[84] However, the focus of the proceedings quickly changed to the lack of infrastructural support provided by the government to the Tribunal (as noted at the beginning of this chapter, this was the period when there were significant infrastructural impediments to the functioning of the NGT due to lack of governmental will and support). Accordingly, the Supreme Court stated:[85]

> The [Environment and Forests] department is taking all-out efforts to ensure that the NGT does not function effectively so that the court may be compelled to pass an order for restoration of jurisdiction of the High Courts and other courts in matters which are presently dealt with by the NGT.

Thus, the Supreme Court stressed the need to make the Tribunal properly functional and did not conclusively address the issue of whether the exercise of suo motu jurisdiction by the NGT was valid. Nevertheless, the NGT continued to effectively use this jurisdiction to take up several important issues relating to, inter alia, pollution,[86] illegal mining,[87] deforestation,[88] and groundwater contamination.[89]

The rivalry between the MoEF and the NGT in this regard seems to highlight the tussle between development and environmental protection. The NGT is increasingly viewed as an obstacle to development by the MoEF due to several environmental clearances that it has invalidated. Thus, in addition to suffocating the Tribunal through a lack of infrastructure and basic amenities, the denial of suo motu jurisdiction was seen as a method of containing the Tribunal. However, generally speaking, there are several important reasons to accord such power to the NGT.

First, as noted previously, the NGT now adjudicates on environmental matters that were earlier decided by the Supreme Court. The Court had taken cognizance of many such cases on its own motion.[90] The rationale behind the exercise of suo motu jurisdiction by the Court was that environmental issues affected several people and it did not need to wait for any particular petitioner to file the case. Moreover, while the impact of an environmental issue may be large, the incentive for any person to pursue it and bring it before the Court may be relatively less direct.

Accordingly, given that the NGT's mandate requires it to adjudicate upon any case involving a substantial question relating to the environment, it should inherently have such a power to enable it to effectively adjudicate. Further, this is a move away from an anthropocentric approach to an eco-centric approach wherein the NGT should be able to protect the environment for its own sake. In other words, the Tribunal should not wait for any person to file a case for the protection of the environment. Rather, it should be able to take cognizance of the matter on its own for the sake of the environment per se. This is necessary to enable the NGT to uphold the right to a healthy environment under Article 21 of the Constitution, as stated in the SOR and the preamble to the NGT Act, 2010.

Second, given the complex and technical nature of environmental issues, it is possible that the petitioner may not be able to perceive the extent of the environmental harm caused or the remediation measures required. Thus, to enable effective adjudication of environmental issues, it is necessary to equip the Tribunal to look beyond what is prayed for by the petitioner.

Third, those who are most affected by environmental degradation usually live in the vicinity of projects in rural areas. These people are less likely to be able to afford filing a petition, hiring a lawyer, and travelling to and from their village to the Tribunal premises on each date of hearing (or to a place where video conferencing is available). To address this concern, it is necessary that the NGT has the power to initiate proceedings on its own.

Fourth, it may be possible that an aggrieved person may not be in a position to initiate proceedings before the Tribunal due to political or economic pressure from the polluter. Further, it is possible that the aggrieved person may compromise or settle the case outside the Tribunal. Having the inherent power to initiate suo motu proceedings will enable the NGT to have the necessary agency to address environmental degradation independent of the aggrieved person.

Fifth, if the NGT does not have suo motu jurisdiction, it will give rise to a peculiar procedural contradiction wherein an issue, though involving a substantial question relating to the environment, will be capable of adjudication by a High Court suo motu but not by the NGT despite its expertise. Since the raison d'être of the NGT is to scientifically adjudicate on complex environmental issues that the higher judiciary was not equipped to deal with, it follows that such a contradiction was not intended.

Sixth, according to Section 19 of the NGT Act, 2010, the Tribunal is allowed to regulate its own procedure while being guided by the principles of natural justice. When this is interpreted in the light of the expansion of *locus standi* by the Tribunal, it follows that the Tribunal can exercise suo motu jurisdiction as this amounts to a regulation of its procedure.

These reasons, however, were overlooked by the Madras High Court in 2014, wherein the High Court restrained the Southern Bench of the NGT from exercising suo motu jurisdiction.[91] The High Court stated:[92]

> There is no indication in the National Green Tribunal Act, 2010 or the rules made thereunder with regard to the power of NGT to initiate *suo motu* proceedings against anyone including the statutory authorities.... The tribunal is not a substitute for the high court in all respects. The tribunal should act within the four corners of the statute.

When asked about his thoughts on this holding of the Madras High Court, Justice Swatanter Kumar – then the chairperson of the NGT – in an interview, said:[93]

> *Suo motu* jurisdiction has to be an integral feature of NGT for better and effective functioning of the institution. In the Constitution of India, the high courts also have not been exclusively conferred *suo motu* jurisdiction. However, the high courts have been exercising the same. There are some inherent powers which are vital for effective functioning and *suo motu* jurisdiction is one such power.

Subsequently, in 2015, the Supreme Court provided guidance with respect to the scope of judicial review of tribunals in *Union of India and others v. Major General Shri Kant Sharma and Anr.*[94] (a more detailed analysis of the scope of judicial review of the NGT is discussed in section 2.3.4). Consequently, based on this, the Madras High Court dismissed the writ petition that challenged the exercise of suo motu jurisdiction by the Southern Bench of the NGT.[95]

In late 2021, however, in *Municipal Corporation of Greater Mumbai v. Ankita Sinha & Ors.*, the Supreme Court finally settled the controversy and held that the NGT had the power to take up a matter on its own motion, even though such power is not expressly mentioned in the NGT Act, 2010.[96]

There were two main arguments raised by the government against the grant of such jurisdiction. First, it argued that the Tribunal was a creature of the statute and lacked any inherent power similar to the one found in Articles 32 and 226 of the Indian Constitution for higher judiciary. By citing precedents which held that the powers of statutory tribunals are limited to what can be inferred from the statute, it argued that the NGT lacked such power as there was nothing in the NGT Act that accorded the same. Second, it argued that the jurisdiction of the Tribunal was limited to adjudicating "disputes", which must be necessarily interpreted as requiring "a lis" between two parties and, therefore, requiring an applicant. This was supported by the amicus curiae in the case, who lent support to the contention that Section 14 of the NGT Act empowered the NGT to hear only adversarial disputes.

The Supreme Court countered these arguments effectively by relying on a purposive interpretation of the NGT Act. After highlighting the scheme of the Act by looking at, inter alia, the wide discretion accorded in areas of jurisdiction and procedure, the Court examined Rule 24 of the National Green Tribunal (Practice and Procedure) Rule, 2011. This rule empowers the NGT to pass such orders as may be necessary to prevent the abuse of, and give effect to, its orders and to "secure the ends of justice". Accordingly, the Court held that the requirement to secure the ends of justice conferred a very wide mandate to the Tribunal, which necessarily involved looking beyond adversarial disputes that required an applicant.

The Court supported this interpretation of the legislative intent by further highlighting India's international commitments under the Stockholm Conference (1972) and the Rio Declaration (1992), coupled with the constitutional commitment to uphold the right to life under Article 21, by protecting the right to a clean and healthy environment. Further, it reasoned that parliament had intended to equip the Tribunal with wide jurisdiction to enable it to deal with environmental matters that were earlier being dealt with by the High Courts and the Supreme Court under Articles 226 and 32 of the Constitution, respectively. This was evident from the 186th Law Commission Report, which called for the establishment of a "green tribunal" that would provide an "environmental solution" to the problems faced by the higher judiciary and echoed the reasoning given by the Supreme Court in *Andhra Pradesh Pollution Control Board v. Prof. M. V. Nayudu (Retd.) and Ors.* (refer to Chapter 1 for more detail), wherein the Court had called for the creation of the NGT. Additionally, the Court highlighted Schedule 1 of the NGT Act which empowered the Tribunal to implement, inter alia, the Water Act, 1974, the Air Act, 1981, and the Environment (Protection) Act, 1986. To fully implement these laws and protect the environment, the Supreme Court reasoned, the NGT had to invariably look beyond the restrictive requirement of a "lis" between two parties and play a preventive, ameliorative, or remedial role when required by the situation. This is because many "non-human inflicted situations" of environmental damage might warrant the Tribunal's intervention for the formulation of decisions and guidelines, without requiring the adjudication of a dispute.

Importantly, the Court differentiated between four categories of statutory tribunals, which were categorized as administrative tribunals under Article 323A, tribunals under 323B, specialized sector tribunals, and tribunals that were created to safeguard the fundamental rights under Article 21 of the Constitution. Based on its functions the NGT, the Court observed, fell under the last category. Accordingly, in line with its sui generis characteristic, it held that the Tribunal not only acts as an appellate authority but also embodies a supervisory role to determine environmental matters. In particular, the Court observed that Section 14(1) of the NGT Act, which provides for the jurisdiction of the Tribunal, omits any specific requirement to trigger the NGT's mechanism. The only requirements mentioned are the presence of a civil case, the involvement of a substantial question relating to the environment, and the implementation of regulations contained in Schedule 1. The requirements, the Court held, do not envisage the need to be triggered by a specific party, and subsections 2 and 3 of Section 14 only came into play where there is an adjudication. Thus, it held, any restrictions imposed would be artificial and would curtail the effective functioning of the NGT, given the multifaceted role envisaged in the Act.

Finally, the Court looked at the mandate under Section 20 of the Act. Since the Tribunal was required to use the principle of sustainable development, the precautionary principle, and the polluter pays principle, the implementation of these principles would necessarily entail cases that are not advocated by any specific party. In particular, the Court held that to give effect to the precautionary principle, the Tribunal would need to be accorded the widest amplitude and discretion. Referring to Principle 10 of the Rio Declaration, which requires ensuring access to justice, the Court held that illiteracy, lack of mobility, poverty, or lack of knowledge should not hinder justice. Moreover, the Court opined that the ability of the Tribunal to take up cases on its own motion would deter potential polluters. Thus, in light of the aforementioned reasons, the Supreme Court unequivocally held that the NGT has suo motu jurisdiction:

34. In circumstances where adverse environmental impact may be egregious, but the community affected is unable to effectively get the machinery into action, a forum created specifically to address such concerns should surely be expected to move with expediency, and of its own accord. The potentiality of disproportionate harm imposes a higher obligation on authorities to preserve rights which may be waylaid due to such restrictive access. It is also noteworthy that the "global impacts of climate change will fall disproportionately on minority and low-income communities". Thus, an affirmative role, beyond mere adjudication at the instance of applicant, is certainly required for serving the ends of environmental justice, as the statute itself requires of the NGT. We cannot validate an argument which furthers uncertainty to justify the role of a spectator, if not inaction, and would most assuredly result in injustice.

35. The NGT, with the distinct role envisaged for it, can hardly afford to remain a mute spectator when no-one knocks on its door. The forum itself has correctly identified the need for collective stratagem for addressing environmental concerns. Such a society centric approach must be allowed to work within the established safety valves of the principles of natural justice and appeal to the Supreme Court. The hands-off mode for the NGT, when faced with exigencies requiring immediate and effective response, would debilitate the forum from discharging its responsibility and this must be ruled out in the interest of justice.

38. One could admit to the argument of danger of suo motu jurisdiction, if the NGT was acting outside its domain. But when it is legitimately working within the contours of its statutory mandate and with procedurals safeguards clarified above in play, the nature of the trigger itself viz. a letter or a "suo motu" initiation, cannot be the basis to curtail the role and responsibility of the specialized forum.

The concerns raised by the Supreme Court are very important. The lack of suo motu jurisdiction would certainly have serious negative consequences by stifling the Tribunal's functioning and rendering environmental justice incomplete due to procedural hurdles. Let us understand the practical need for suo motu jurisdiction by comparing two cases in detail. The first case deals with a situation wherein the NGT holds that it lacks suo motu jurisdiction, while the second case demonstrates an instance wherein the NGT exercises such power.

National Green Tribunal

(Principal Bench, New Delhi)

BAIJNATH PRAJAPATI v. MOEF & ORS.

[Appeal No. 18 of 2011, Judgment Dated 20 January 2012]

A.S. Naidu, J. (Judicial Member);
Vijai Sharma (Expert Member)

*   *   *

Relevant Extracts:

1.   Baijnath Prajapati, a resident of village Guwari, district Anuppur, Madhya Pradesh, while asserting that "he is involved in issues concerning the social development as well as the environment", has filed the present Appeal assailing the order dated May 28, 2010, and the corrigendum dated 1st September 2010 and the office memorandum dated 23rd November, 2010, granting environmental clearance in favour of M/s Moser Baer Power & Infrastructure Ltd (Respondent – 3) for a coal based thermal power plant. The environmental clearance was challenged on several grounds enumerated in the Memorandum of Appeal. The Appellant has enclosed a verification with his Appeal Memorandum affirming that the contents of different paragraphs were true to his personal knowledge.

3.   An application dated January 13th, 2012 was filed by the Appellant seeking withdrawal of the Appeal on the following ground:-

"That, the Appellant-Applicant begs this Hon'ble Tribunal for permission to withdraw this Appeal as the Appellant has come to the conclusion, after careful consideration, that this developmental project is required for development of the region and that he cannot oppose this project. It is submitted that this decision to withdraw the appeal is a personal one taken by the Appellant voluntarily without any pressure, coercion and undue influence from any person interested in this case."

4. Today when the matter was taken up, the Appellant was present in person along with his Counsel in court. A prayer was made on behalf of the Appellant to permit him to withdraw the case unconditionally.

5. Heard Learned Counsel for the parties and perused the documents filed before us. The Appeal was filed on September 15th, 2011. We fail to understand as to what transpired between then and now, which led the Appellant to realise and hold that the project was required for the development of the region. Neither is there any averment with regard to change of circumstances. Nor, is any reason being indicated that changed the mind of the Appellant.

6. The National Green Tribunal has been constituted for strengthening environmental protection and the conservation of forests and other natural resources. The Statement of Objects and Reasons of the National Green Tribunal Act, 2010 states that "the rapid expansion in industrial, infrastructure and transportation sectors and increasing urbanisation in recent years have given rise to new pressures on our natural resources and environment. There is a commensurate increase in environment related litigation pending in various Courts and other authorities. The risk to human health and environment arising out of hazardous activities has also become a matter of concern."

7. This Tribunal is expected to ensure effective environmental management and conservation, give relief and compensation for damages to persons and property and connected matters, and at the same time ensure sustainable development. In this regard, the jurisdiction of this Tribunal should not be invoked for frivolous litigation that unnecessarily consumes the time of the Tribunal without serving the purpose for which the Tribunal was constituted.

8. This Tribunal has to see that it does not engage in adjudication that is motivated by frivolous considerations or reasons not connected with environmental protection and conservation. It appears that the Appellant has dragged the project proponent, the Ministry of Environment & Forests and other State Government departments into litigation in a flippant manner amounting to abuse of the Tribunal process.

9. We cannot stop the Appellant from withdrawing the case filed by him. At the same time, it is mentionable that we are not conferred with suo moto powers to proceed with the case. Therefore, we allow the Appellant to withdraw this Appeal. But, to avoid such frivolous cases in future we intend to award some costs. In this regard, we enquired from the Appellant who was present in Court in presence of Mr. Aagney Sail, Learned Counsel. The Appellant agreed to pay Rs. 50,000/- towards costs.

10. We award the said amount, i.e., Rs. 50,000/- towards costs and direct that the same should be paid to Respondent – 4, i.e., Chief Conservator of Forests, within a period of six weeks to promote afforestation with appropriate species suitable for the area. We make it clear that if the aforesaid amount is not deposited within the time fixed, the same shall be treated as a Public Demand and recovered under the Public Demand Recovery Act.

* * *

NOTES AND QUESTIONS

1. The case demonstrates the serious challenges posed by the lack of exercise of suo motu jurisdiction by the NGT. The appellant challenged the environmental clearance granted for a coal-based thermal power plant on several grounds. He confirmed through an affidavit that the contents of the averments were true to his personal knowledge. However, shortly thereafter, he filed an application to withdraw the case on the ground that "this developmental project is required for development of the region". The NGT notes that there was no overt reason for such a sudden change in position of the appellant as he did not plead any change in circumstances. Further, the appellant does not adduce any reasons that led him to believe that the developmental needs outweighed the need to protect the environment. Do you think this situation is compatible with the mandate of the NGT conspicuous from the preamble and SOR of the NGT Act, 2010? Do you think the appellant should have the sole agency in determining whether an environmental issue is fit to be adjudicated?

2. The case exemplifies the anthropocentrism inherent in not exercising suo motu jurisdiction by the Tribunal. Even if the appellant suddenly felt that the project was needed for local development, this does not reduce the gravity of the environmental degradation alleged. Thus, by leaving the decision to withdraw the case in the hands of the appellant, the Tribunal is unable to provide environmental justice. Further, considerations of the environment per se do not feature in such a scenario as the environmental considerations lack agency in determining whether to proceed with

the case. This is exactly the situation that the Supreme Court, during the PIL regime, intended to avoid through the use of suo motu jurisdiction and the expansion of *locus standi.*

* * *

National Green Tribunal

(Central Zonal Bench, Bhopal)

TRIBUNAL ON ITS OWN MOTION v. MOEF & ORS.

[Appeal No. 16 of 2013, Judgment Dated 4 April 2014]

Dalip Singh, J. (Judicial Member);
P.S. Rao (Expert Member)

* * *

Relevant Extracts:

1. In the Bhopal edition of daily newspaper "Times of India" dated 10th April, 2013 a news item was published on the front page under the caption "Dolomite mining a threat to Tiger corridor in Kanha-Foresters want ban on mining in Mandla District". Considering the gravity of the news item *suo motu* cognizance was taken by this Tribunal and notice was issued to the Respondent Nos. 1 to 6 on 10th April, 2013 with a direction to place on record the particulars of Mining Leases (in short "ML") mentioned in the news item. In response to the above notice, the Respondent No. 5, Madhya Pradesh State Pollution Control Board (in short "MPPCB") submitted reply dated 29th April, 2013 stating that the officials of the MPPCB inspected the Dolomite mines in Mandla District and monitored the Ambient Air Quality (in short "AAQ") in different locations where Consent to Operate the mines was granted to 36 ML holders. Out of 36 mines, 26 mines are having valid Consent to Operate and during the inspection they were found to be under operation.... However, not satisfied with the above reply of the MPPCB, during the hearing of the case on 1st May, 2013 this Tribunal directed the MPPCB to furnish full particulars of all the Dolomite mines in Mandla District ... after verification of the record obtained from the Asst. Mining Officer, Mandla District it was found that there are 8 more Mining Leases granted in the area making a total of 43 mines. These 8 Mining lease holders have not sought any consent so far from the MPPCB and therefore being unaware of their existence, the MPPCB had submitted their earlier reply dated 29th April, 2013 listing only 36 mines.

7. It was further stated in the reply that as per the Forest Department Circular No. F-5/16/81/10-3 Bhopal dated 7th October, 2002 in ordinary course ML will not be sanctioned within 250 mt. from the forest area/boundary. In that event if the District Collector, considering the importance of the mining, decides that it is necessary to sanction the ML, the matter will be referred for consideration of Panchayat Level Committee consisting President, Zila Panchayat, District Collector and the Divisional Forest Officer.... The Respondent No. 1, Ministry of Environment and Forests (for short "MoEF") filed their reply on 3rd August, 2013 enclosing a copy of the field inspection report on the inspection of mines carried out by the officers of the Regional Office, MoEF, Bhopal from 2nd to 4th July, 2013 wherein all the 43 mines located in the villages noted below, were inspected.

11. The reply of the MoEF further says that during the site inspection it was observed that the mining operations are going on without any scientific and technical inputs. Overburden is dumped in the mining area without marking any designated place and without any sloping and terracing leading to loss of valuable top soil. The mine water is being pumped without any treatment and allowed to settle in the nearby natural water bodies. It was also stated that during the field visit wild animals such as wild boar, deer, jackal etc. were found in the area. It was also suggested that for the violation of the conditions by the ML holders, the MPPCB may be directed to enquire and necessary action may be ordered to be initiated.

12. ...[Under] the chairmanship of the Chief Secretary, Govt. of Madhya Pradesh a meeting was called with the Senior Officers of the Forest Department ... the minutes of the meeting ... stated that the area in question where the mines are located, is more than 10 km. from the Kanha National Park and 200 Km. from the Pench and Bandhavgarh National Parks. The mining sites in question do not fall in the corridor between Kanha, Pench and Bandhavgarh National Parks.... Therefore there is no possibility of notifying the area in question as a Tiger Reserve in future. It was further stated that Eco Sensitive Zone (for short "ESZ") has not yet been notified around these Protected Areas in the State of Madhya Pradesh and even if the deemed ESZ is considered to be 10 km. from the boundary of the above stated Protected Areas, the Dolomite mines in question are situated away from the aforesaid Protected Areas and hence beyond any possible declaration of the areas under the ESZ.

17. ... It was stated in the affidavit that the following remarks were received on 11th February, 2014 from the Wildlife Institute of India, Dehradun:

    "....the proposed mines are in close proximity to a very important source population of Tigers in Central India though they do not lie in any important connecting corridor, they do occur within the forested landscape that has Tiger occupancy and which serves to host dispersing aged individuals from the Kanha source. In this context, the disturbance and habitat loss caused by the mines and its associated infrastructure development would be detrimental for the source value of Kanha. If the communication route to and fro from these mines is from the south or south-west, then it can have disastrous effects of reducing the corridor connectivity between Kanha and Pench Tiger sources. Therefore, all caution needs to be used before granting approval if at all it is to be given."

19. Having gone through the record placed before us and having heard the Learned Counsel for the parties at length it is required to examine and discuss the issues to arrive at a conclusion whether any environmental laws are violated while granting MLs and whether any ecologically sensitive areas were subjected to illegal activities resulting damage to the environment in general and wildlife habitat in particular more so in case of Tiger.

20. We are conscious of the fact that under Schedule-I of the National Green Tribunal Act, 2010 Wildlife (Protection) Act, 1972 is not listed and therefore this Tribunal has no jurisdiction to adjudicate the matters related to Wildlife. But in this particular case the issue to be examined is whether these mines are sanctioned and allowed to operate in violation of provisions of the Environment (Protection) Act, 1986 (for short "Act of 1986") and Rules made thereunder.

21. As defined under the Act of 1986 "Environment" includes water, air and land and the inter relationship which exists among and between water, air and land and human beings, other living creatures, plants, microorganisms and property. We are of the opinion that occurrence of Wildlife in a particular ecosystem having relation with the environment has to be considered as a part of environment and therefore the matters related to wildlife are liable for adjudication and can be definitely brought under the environmental jurisprudence more so in cases pertaining to ESZs and therefore the matter being dealt in this OA is not just a Wildlife issue par se to be adjudicated under the Wildlife (Protection) Act 1972…. Wildlife is a part of environment and any action that is causing damage to the wildlife or that may likely to lead to damage to the cause of wildlife, cannot be excluded from the purview of this Tribunal.

23. … The population of Tigers is increasing in the wild whereas their habitat is shrinking and is under severe threat because of various anthropogenic activities. Mining is one of the most disturbing activities in these sensitive

areas…. The recent reports further reveal that due to increase in their population, because of good management practices, it is not only leading to increase of incidents of human animal conflict but the Tigers are trying to migrate/disburse to the nearest Protected Area/wildlife habitats by establishing corridor even in non-forest tracts crossing human habitations and criss-cross road network. The best example is the recent news report wherein it was stated that one male Tiger is moving from Panna Tiger Reserve and heading towards Bandhavgarh Tiger Reserve which is about 120 km. distance crossing the fragmented habitat. It is reported that earlier the corridor from Panna to Bandhavgarh was freely accessible for movement of wildlife but of late, increase the anthropogenic activity caused its discontinuity. This incident gives an indication how even the areas well beyond 10 km. from the boundaries of the Protected Areas and restoration of lost corridors connecting the habitat of this magnificent animal are critical and there is urgent need to minimize the human interference in these areas particularly from the activities such as mining.

25. Forest corridors play an important role in movement of Tigers from one locality to the other and thus help avoid inbreeding and maintain genetic variation among the Tigers. Therefore there is every need to restore the corridors wherever possible and increase the size of buffer areas around the Protected Areas if scientific management of the Tigers has to be sustained keeping pace with their increase in numbers in the wild.

28. In case of 8 mines among the total list 43 mines, it is reported by the Regional Office, MoEF, Bhopal that the distance from the mines to the notified forest boundary is "zero" indicating that the mines are touching the forest boundary. It was clear in the report of the MPPCB & Regional Office, MoEF, Bhopal that some of the ML holders have resorted to irregularities including encroachment of forest land and it appears that so far no concrete action has been taken against the erring ML holders as per the record placed before us.

29. It is reported that the Dolomite mined from these mines in Mandla District is of superior quality, highly valued and is in good demand in the market. It is also reported that this superior quality mineral is not found elsewhere in the country. However mining is required to be taken up only if it is compatible with the objective of protecting the environment, more so in the context of location of Dolomite mines relatively in close proximity to Kanha National Park. While the objective of granting ML forms part of the development process of the country, it is the duty of the Central Government and the State Government to take steps to protect the environment which includes wildlife

and maintain the ecological balance and prevent damage that may be caused by mining operations.

33. Considering the above, we direct that a meeting may be convened immediately at the highest level under the chairmanship of the Chief Secretary to the Government of Madhya Pradesh involving the officials of the State Forest Department, National Tiger Conservation Authority ... [to] examine and take following actions in accordance with law duly fixing a time limit for each of the issues to be taken up and completed with promptitude by the authorities concerned....

The reply filed on behalf of the State Govt. functionaries reveal that there is no coordination between the Mining and Forest Departments at least in case of those mines which are located in the Forest Area and which are in close proximity to the forest boundary. In the reply filed on behalf of the Respondents No. 2, 3, 4 and 6 it was stated that the local Forest officials have expressed their deep concern pertaining to the mines sanctioned in the Reserved Forest and mine operators are required to obtain transit passes from the Forest Department. It was also stated that the ML conditions are not informed to the Forest Department and the ML holders are also reluctant to provide the information to the Forest Department. There is a need to put full stop to this state of affairs and streamline the entire procedure of sanctioning & operating the mines. The Government should evolve a suitable mechanism to avoid such conflicting situation and ensure coordination among all the law enforcing authorities in the state.

The irregularities pointed in the reply filed by the Regional Office, MoEF shall be taken up seriously and all the mines found violating the provisions & ML conditions as well as Environmental laws shall be dealt with seriously in accordance with law.

Even though the mines are under operation for a long period, it is surprising to note that such grave irregularities have been noticed only during the inspection of mines by the officials of the Regional Office, MoEF that too after the case was taken up *suo motu* by this Tribunal and no record was placed before us to the effect that any severe action has been taken against the defaulting ML holders. The Chief Secretary shall get the whole issue enquired and initiate action against the erring officials if it is found that they indulged in dereliction of duty by allowing the mines to continue to operate violating the law.

* * *

NOTES AND QUESTIONS

1. The case exemplifies the need for the Tribunal to have suo motu jurisdiction. The government's dereliction of its duty to protect the environment is evident from several instances across the judgment. For instance, after the initial inspection, the MPPCB states that there are thirty-six mines operating in the concerned area. However, once the NGT asks for further investigation, a total of forty-three mines come to the fore which are operating in the concerned area. The MPPCB and other related governmental bodies claim that they did not know of the existence of these eight new mines as they had not sought their consent before operating. This seems incredulous given that each mine physically requires a significant area to operate, and it is difficult to believe that all the governmental agencies were not aware of the existence of eight mines within 10 kilometres of the Kanha National Park.

   Further, the NGT highlights that there is no communication or cooperation between the governmental departments. According to the Forest Department, the mining licenses have been granted without informing the Forest Department of the conditions stipulated therein. Further, the mine operators are unwilling to cooperate by providing relevant information.

   In addition, the NGT highlights that out of forty-three mines, eight mines are operating at a distance of less than a kilometre from the notified forest boundary without permission for several years, and the governmental agencies have not done anything to regulate them.

   Considering the gravity of the dereliction of duty by the governmental agencies coupled with the fact that no action has been taken against the defaulting mine operators, the Tribunal remarks that it is surprising that the MoEF noticed the grave irregularities only after the NGT took up the case suo motu. Do you think environmental justice would have prevailed had the Tribunal not taken suo motu jurisdiction? Do you think the matter would have likely reached the Tribunal given the deep mining mafia network at play?

2. As discussed earlier in this chapter, the NGT Act, 2010, does not confer jurisdiction on the Tribunal to hear cases involving the Wildlife (Protection) Act, 1972, as it is not mentioned in Schedule I of the Act. While the present case falls within the purview of the said Act, the NGT rightly holds that the environment also includes the interrelations created out of an ecosystem between wildlife and human beings. Accordingly, it holds that it has jurisdiction under the Environment (Protection) Act, 1986. Do you think it follows from this reasoning of the NGT that all cases involving any harm to wildlife come within the jurisdiction of the Tribunal?

3. The Supreme Court, in *Goa Foundation v. Union of* India,[97] allowed mining – despite severe environmental degradation – on account of its economic benefit to the state of Goa in the form of employment and revenue generation. However, the NGT in this

case upholds the tenets of sustainable development more seriously. It highlights that while the dolomite mined from the concerned mines is of superior quality and not found anywhere else in the country, mining is to be allowed only if it is in accordance with environmental protection. Do you think if the mining activity generated significant employment in the concerned area, the approach of the NGT would have been different?

4. It has been argued that some species are more charismatic than others, and hence get more funding for their protection.[98] For instance, the tiger, in addition to being India's national animal, is widely regarded as a symbol of wildlife. Accordingly, almost 50 per cent of all conservation funds in India are directed to Project Tiger, while other more endangered species do not get funding at all.[99] Do you think that if the animal in consideration was less prone to media attention, the outcome of the case would have changed?

*   *   *

2.3.3   JURISDICTIONAL RELATIONSHIP BETWEEN THE NGT AND THE HIGH COURTS

Before delving into the jurisdictional relationship between the NGT and High Courts, it is necessary to appreciate how the doctrine of exhaustion of alternative remedies has been evolved by the Supreme Court. According to this doctrine, the Supreme Court should not entertain a petition under Article 32 of the Indian Constitution if there exists an equally efficacious alternative legal remedy.[100] However, this doctrine is based on considerations extraneous to the law. This is reflected in *State of Uttar Pradesh v. Mohammad Nooh*, wherein the Supreme Court, with respect to the doctrine, held:[101]

> But this rule requiring the exhaustion of statutory remedies before the writ will be granted is a *rule of policy, convenience,* and *discretion* rather than a *rule of law.* (Emphasis supplied)

Thus, the Supreme Court has unequivocally admitted that the doctrine of exhaustion of alternative remedies is essentially a doctrine of "convenience" and is based on the discretion of the Supreme Court rather than the rule of law. Article 32 contains a fundamental right that "guarantees" the right to move the Supreme Court for the enforcement of other fundamental rights.[102] One of the co-authors of this book has argued elsewhere that the doctrine lacks a legal basis, which is evident from the Constitutional Assembly Debates and a comparative analysis of the development of the doctrine in the common law.[103]

Further, there seems to be a dichotomy in the way in which the Supreme Court has interpreted the doctrine. While the Supreme Court frequently uses the doctrine to dismiss petitions under Article 32 which have not been heard in an equally efficacious alternative forum, it has also held:[104]

> It is *wholly erroneous* to assume that before the jurisdiction of this Court under Art. 32 can be invoked, the applicant must either establish that he has no other remedy adequate or otherwise or that he has exhausted such remedies as the law affords and has yet not obtained proper redress, for when once it is proved to the satisfaction of this Court that by State action the fundamental right of the petitioner under Art. 32 has been infringed, it is *not only the right but the duty* of this Court to afford relief to him by passing appropriate orders in this behalf. (Emphasis supplied)

Accordingly, while it is desirable that all environmental cases be tried at the NGT first before the Supreme Court – as the former is equipped with experts to adjudicate on scientifically complex environmental issues – at present, the constitutional scheme does not mandate such a scenario. For instance, a person's right to life under Article 21 is infringed due to air pollution. However, technically, such a person can approach the Supreme Court under Article 32 by filing a writ petition for the enforcement of her fundamental rights. Hence, the doctrine of exhaustion of alternative remedies, in the context of the NGT, though lacking a firm legal basis, is necessary to enable effective environmental justice by directing the petitioner to the NGT.

Nevertheless, it can be argued that the application of the doctrine to High Courts under Article 226 of the Indian Constitution stands on a different footing. This is due to the fact that the provision is not a fundamental right. The Supreme Court, through several judgments, has tried to find a balance between the jurisdiction of the High Courts and specialized statutory tribunals.[105] It has held that while the existence of an equally efficacious remedy is not a complete bar on the High Court's jurisdiction, the High Courts are advised to not entertain a writ petition under Article 226 of the Constitution so as to respect the statutory remedy available.[106] In furtherance of this reasoning, the Supreme Court has held:[107]

> [W]here it is open to the aggrieved petitioner to move another tribunal, or even itself in another jurisdiction for obtaining redress in the manner provided by a statute, the High Court normally will not permit, by entertaining a petition under Art. 226 of the Constitution, the machinery created under the statute to be by-passed, and will leave the party applying to it to seek resort to the machinery so set up.

Thus, the Supreme Court has urged that the High Courts should respect this self-imposed limitation on their jurisdiction by not bypassing the statutory remedies available.

Accordingly, in *Cicily Kallarackal v. Vehicle Factory*, the Supreme Court restrained the Kerala High Court from entertaining a writ petition against an order passed by the National Consumer Disputes Redressal Commission.[108] The Supreme Court held that the High Court was required to respect the appellate machinery provided by the National Consumer Protection Act, 1986, and that the High Court's order amounted to a nullity for want of jurisdiction.[109]

Likewise, in *Union of India v. Major General Shri Kant Sharma*, the Supreme Court held that the Delhi High Court erred in exercising jurisdiction by entertaining a writ petition under Article 226 as this amounted to bypassing the statutory machinery provided under the Armed Forces Tribunal Act, 2007.[110] As noted previously in the section relating to suo motu jurisdiction, the Madras High Court reversed its earlier order against the NGT (Southern Bench) based on the Supreme Court's directions in this case.[111]

Nevertheless, the application of the doctrine of exhaustion of alternative remedies is not absolute. Through various judgments, the Supreme Court has formulated the following exceptions to the doctrine:

a) Where the lower court or tribunal acts wholly without jurisdiction or patently exceeds its jurisdiction[112]
b) Where the proceedings in the lower court or tribunal have been conducted in a manner that violates principles of natural justice, or violates accepted rules of procedure, or offends the superior court's sense of fair play[113]
c) Where the tribunal hearing the original trial or appeal was merely departmental in nature, lacking adequate legal training and background[114]
d) Where the constitutionality of the statute under which the relevant authority acted has been challenged[115]

While the cases and exceptions discussed thus far pertain to the jurisdictional relationship between High Courts and tribunals in general, they are applicable to the NGT and High Courts as well. Nevertheless, the Supreme Court has particularly addressed the jurisdictional relationship between the NGT and High Courts. In August 2012 – just about three months short of Justice Swatanter Kumar's appointment as the chairperson of NGT – the Supreme Court, through a single bench consisting of Justice Swatanter Kumar, transferred environmental cases from the High Courts to the NGT.[116] The case dealt with a writ petition filed by Bhopal Gas Mahila Udyog Sangathan as a PIL under Article 32 of the Constitution. The petitioner was led by a group of indigent victims of the infamous Bhopal Gas Tragedy in 1984, and they prayed for free medical assistance from the government. Let us look at the relevant excerpts from the judgment below:

Supreme Court of India

BHOPAL GAS PEEDITH MAHILA SANGATHAN v. UNION OF INDIA

[Writ Petition (Civil) No. 50 of 1998, Order Dated 9 August 2012]

Swatanter Kumar, J.

*   *   *

Relevant Extracts:

38. Keeping in view the provisions and scheme of the National Green Tribunal Act, 2010 (for short the "NGT Act") particularly Sections 14, 29, 30 and 38(5), it can safely be concluded that the environmental issues and matters covered under the NGT Act, Schedule 1 should be instituted and litigated before the National Green Tribunal (for short "NGT"). Such approach may be necessary to avoid likelihood of conflict of orders between the High Courts and the NGT. Thus, in unambiguous terms, we direct that all the matters instituted after coming into force of the NGT Act and which are covered under the provisions of the NGT Act and/or in Schedule I to the NGT Act shall stand transferred and can be instituted only before the NGT. This will help in rendering expeditious and specialized justice in the field of environment to all concerned.

39. We find it imperative to place on record a caution for consideration of the courts of competent jurisdiction that the cases filed and pending prior to coming into force of the NGT Act, involving questions of environmental laws and/or relating to any of the seven statutes specified in Schedule I of the NGT Act, should also be dealt with by the specialized tribunal, that is the NGT, created under the provisions of the NGT Act. The Courts may be well advised to direct transfer of such cases to the NGT in its discretion, as it will be in the fitness of administration of justice.

40. Normally, we would have even transferred this case to NGT. However, as it does not involve any complex or other environmental issues and primarily requires administrative supervision for proper execution of the orders of the Courts, we have considered it appropriate to transfer this case to the High Court of Madhya Pradesh. We may notice that the supervisory work concerns itself with regard to the proper functioning of the various Committees, which were constituted under the orders of the Court, to ensure proper running of the hospital established by the government and health care facilities available to the Bhopal Gas victims. Thus, the matter should be heard and supervisory jurisdiction be exercised by the High Court to better serve the ends of justice.

*   *   *

NOTES AND QUESTIONS

1. The aforementioned order to transfer all cases to the NGT was delivered on 9 August 2012 by Justice Swatanter Kumar, and he was subsequently appointed as the second chairperson of the NGT on 20 December 2012. Further, the relief prayed for by the petitioner – victims of the Bhopal Gas Tragedy – was very specific in nature and related to directing the state to provide them adequate and free medical assistance. On what basis do you think the Supreme Court could have made such blanket directions for transferring all environmental cases to the NGT within the purview of the impugned case?

* * *

Through this order, the Supreme Court addressed the jurisdictional friction between High Courts and the NGT. There are three relevant points from this order for our discussion.[117] First, the Supreme Court holds that High Courts will have to transfer all new cases, filed after the NGT Act, 2010, came into effect, involving a substantial question relating to the environment. Second, with respect to ongoing cases filed prior to the coming into effect of the NGT Act, 2010, the High Courts will have discretion regarding whether to transfer the cases to the Tribunal. Nevertheless, the Supreme Court opines that the High Courts are advised to transfer the cases to benefit from the NGT's specialized adjudication. Third, while this order does not take away the jurisdiction of the High Courts under Article 226 of the Constitution, the doctrine of exhaustion of alternative remedies, as discussed earlier, will continue to apply and the High Courts would normally ask litigants to approach the NGT for a speedy and efficacious disposal of their cases.

These directions of the Supreme Court have been subsequently followed by High Courts in many cases. For instance, the Delhi High Court, in a case involving water and air pollution on account of illegal industrial activity, transferred the petition to the NGT.[118] Similarly, in a case involving construction of a jetty over a marine sanctuary, the Gujarat High Court, based on the aforementioned order of the Supreme Court, transferred the case to the Tribunal.[119] Furthermore, the Madras High Court transferred a petition involving illegal road construction material to the NGT by stating:[120]

The environmental issues and matters covered under the NGT Act, Schedule I should be instituted and litigated before the National Green Tribunal only and not before this Court under Article 226 of the Constitution of India.

Thus, the High Courts have followed the Supreme Court's directions. However, on 10 March 2014, the Supreme Court, in *Adarsh Coop. Housing Society Ltd. v. Union of India*, gave the following directions in relation to the precedent set by the *Bhopal Case*:[121]

> In our considered opinion, the directions in [*the Bhopal Case*] that all matters instituted after coming into force of the National Green Tribunal Act, 2010 and which are covered under the said Act and / or [in Schedule I to] the said Act shall stand transferred and can be instituted only before the National Green Tribunal requires reconsideration by this Court.…. Till we pass final orders on such reconsideration the direction for transferring the pending matters before the High Court to the Green Tribunal … will not be given effect to. A copy of this order be circulated to all High Courts in the country.

However, the *Adarsh Case* was later withdrawn without re-examining the correctness of the directions of the Supreme Court in the *Bhopal Case*. This left the question open as to whether the directions of the *Bhopal Case* were still in force. Nevertheless, on 7 May 2015, Justice Swatanter Kumar – through the NGT – held that the directions given by him in the *Bhopal Case* were "fully in force and operative".[122] Therefore, presently, though the Supreme Court has not re-examined the correctness of the transfer of all environmental cases to NGT, in the light of the doctrine of exhaustion of alternative remedies it seems to be the appropriate procedure for the time being.

2.3.4   NGT'S SCOPE OF JUDICIAL REVIEW

Judicial review refers to the power of the judiciary to review any executive or legislative action in the light of constitutional principles. The judiciary, while exercising judicial review, can invalidate an executive order or legislation if it is in conflict with the provisions of the Constitution. This forms an integral part of the system of checks and balances between the three limbs of government – executive, judiciary, and legislature – and facilitates the separation of powers between them. Thus, it forms a part of the basic structure of the Constitution.[123]

Article 13 of the Constitution states that all laws or executive orders made in contravention of the fundamental rights enshrined in Part III of the Constitution shall be void. Accordingly, the Supreme Court and the High Courts have the power of judicial review which can be derived from Articles 32 and 226 of the Constitution, respectively. Further, these courts can invalidate a piece of legislation or order suo motu if it contravenes the constitutional scheme. While the power of judicial review for the higher judiciary is established, there remains controversy regarding the extent of judicial review that tribunals can exercise.

The Supreme Court addressed the issue in *S.P. Sampath Kumar v. Union of India & Ors.*, wherein it held:[124]

> The basic and essential feature of judicial review cannot be dispensed with but it would be within the competence of Parliament to amend the Constitution so as to substitute in place of the High Court, another alternative institutional mechanism or arrangement for judicial review, provided it is no less efficacious than the High

Court. Then, instead of the High Court, it would be another institutional mechanism or authority which would be exercising the power of judicial review with a view to enforcing the constitutional limitations and maintaining the rule of law. Therefore, if any constitutional amendment made by Parliament takes away from the High Court the power of judicial review in any particular area and vests it in any other institutional mechanism or authority, it would not be violative of the basic structure doctrine, so long as the essential condition is fulfilled, namely that the alternative institutional mechanism or authority set up by the parliamentary amendment is no less effective than the High Court.

Thus, the Court held that parliament had the power to create alternative mechanisms for judicial review as long as these mechanisms were not less efficacious than the High Courts. However, the judgment led to divergent views regarding whether tribunals could test the constitutional validity of statutes.[125] This concern, as well as the issue relating to whether the tribunals could be deemed as equally efficacious as High Courts, was addressed by the Supreme Court in *L. Chandra Kumar v Union of India*.[126] The relevant conclusions drawn by the Court are as follows:

1) Judicial review of legislative action by tribunals cannot be to the exclusion of the Supreme Court and the High Courts. This is because the power of judicial review under Article 32 for the Supreme Court and Article 226 for the High Courts is part of the basic structure of the Constitution.
2) Tribunals can, nevertheless, exercise judicial review in a supplemental capacity, rather than as a substitute for the High Courts or the Supreme Court. Further, any interpretation of a statutory provision or rule shall be heard by a bench consisting of at least one judicial member.
3) Tribunals have the power to test the constitutionality of subordinate legislation except for their parent statute. In cases wherein the *vires* of the parent statute is questioned, the relevant High Courts must be approached directly.
4) All decisions of tribunals will be subject to the scrutiny of High Courts under Articles 226 and 227 of the Constitution. The division bench of the relevant High Court under whose territorial jurisdiction the impugned tribunal comes will hear the matter.

However, the Supreme Court's decision to subject a tribunal's decision to the scrutiny of High Courts led to a proliferation of decisions being challenged. The Law Commission took note of this and recommended that the *L. Chandra Kumar Case* be referred to a larger bench of the Supreme Court.[127]

The Law Commission opined that there is a difference between the power of judicial review vested in the Supreme Court and a High Court. It stated that the latter is not as inviolable as the former. Furthermore, it stated that administrative tribunals were conceived as effective and real substitutes for High Courts in relation to the matters that they governed.[128]

Moreover, the objective behind the establishment of these tribunals would be defeated if the cases adjudicated by tribunals would have to pass the scrutiny of High Courts. It recommended that a more viable way, after exhausting intra-tribunal appeals, would be to approach the Supreme Court by way of a Special Leave Petition under Article 136 of the Constitution.[129]

L. Chandra Kumar dealt with the vires of the Administrative Tribunals Act, 1985, which under Section 28 excluded the jurisdiction of High Courts. The NGT Act, 2010, lacks such a provision. Section 29 of the Act excludes the jurisdiction of all civil courts on matters that can be heard by the NGT, and Section 22 states that an order of the NGT may be appealed to the Supreme Court. It is evident that the holding of the Supreme Court, in *L. Chandra Kumar*, had a significant influence in the drafting of NGT Act 2010.

The influence of *L. Chandra Kumar* is seen in subsequent decisions by High Courts. The Madras High Court has held that the Supreme Court's decision declared all clauses excluding the jurisdiction of the High Courts as unconstitutional.[130] Accordingly, this is the reason why the NGT Act, 2010, does not expressly take away the jurisdiction of High Courts, and the legislative intent is to allow High Courts to supervise the decisions of the NGT.[131]

In 2014, the NGT held in *Wilfred J. & Anr. v. MoEF* that the scheme of the NGT Act, 2010, accords the power of limited judicial review to the Tribunal to enable it to effectively adjudicate on environmental issues.[132] We will discuss the Tribunal's reasoning below.

National Green Tribunal

(Principal Bench, New Delhi)

WILFRED J. & ANR. v. MOEF & ORS.

[Appeal No. 14 of 2014, Judgment Dated 17 July 2014]

Swatanter Kumar, J. (Chairperson);
U.D. Salvi, J. (Judicial Member);
Dr. D.K. Agrawal (Expert Member);
B.S. Sajwan (Expert Member);
Dr. R.C. Trivedi (Expert Member)

* * *

Relevant Extracts:

Discussion on issue (A) i.e. "*The NGT being a creation of a statute is not vested with the powers of judicial review so as to examine the constitutional validity/vires or legality of a legislation – whether subordinate or delegated (in the present case, the CRZ Notification,*

2011). Exercise of such jurisdiction would tantamount to enlarging its own jurisdiction by the Tribunal":

20. In order to effectively and meaningfully deliberate upon this issue, the first and the foremost concern would be the legislative scheme under the NGT Act…. The essence of the Statement of Objects and Reasons of the Act found their trace in the Preamble of the statute. Besides reiterating that this Tribunal was being established for effective and expeditious disposals of cases relating to environmental protection and conservation of forests and other natural resources including enforcement of any legal right relating to environment and with a view to give relief and compensation for damages to persons, property and for matters connected therewith or incidental thereto, it was also due to the fact that in the [Stockholm (1972) and Rio De Janeiro (1992) Conferences] aforestated, all States were required to provide for effective access to judicial and administrative proceedings, including redressal and remedy and to develop national laws in relation to liability and compensation for the victims of pollution and other environmental damage. The States were also required to take appropriate steps for the protection and improvement of human environment. This is the essence of the Statement of Objects and Reasons and the Preamble that precedes the NGT Act.

32. Next, we are expected to deal with the question as to the impact of the provisions relating to the jurisdiction of the Tribunal under this welfare legislation. From the Statement of Objects and Reasons as well as the Preamble of the NGT Act, it is clear that the framers of the law intended to give a very wide and unrestricted jurisdiction to the Tribunal in the matters of environment. Be it original, appellate or special jurisdiction, the dimensions and areas of exercise of jurisdiction of the Tribunal are very wide. The various provisions of the NGT Act do not, by use of specific language or by necessary implication mention any restriction on the exercise of jurisdiction by the Tribunal so far it relates to a substantial question of environment and any or all of the Acts specified in Schedule I. Sections 15 and 16 of the Act do not enumerate any restriction as to the scope of jurisdiction that the Tribunal may exercise. There is no indication in the entire NGT Act that the legislature intended to divest the Tribunal of the power of judicial review. It is the settled cannon of statutory interpretation that such exclusion has to be specific or absolutely implied from the language of the provisions governing the jurisdiction of the Tribunal.

Another relevant consideration which the Tribunal should keep in mind is in regard to independence of judicial functioning of the Tribunal … [which is part of the] basic feature of the Constitution…. Let us examine if the

National Green Tribunal, has the complete trappings of Original as well as Appellate Court while dealing with all civil cases, does have complete judicial independence.

In terms of Section 5 of the NGT Act, a person is not qualified for appointment as the Chairperson or Judicial Member, unless he is or has been a Judge of the Supreme Court of India or a Chief Justice of a High Court, or is or has been a Judge of the High Court for being eligible to be appointed as Judicial Member.… The Selection Committee, particularly for selection of Judicial Members is to be chaired by a sitting Judge of the Supreme Court of India, along with the Chairperson of the Tribunal (who is or has been a judge of the Supreme Court) and other Members as nominated under Rule 3 of the said Rules. The Chairperson, Judicial Members and Expert Members can be removed … only after a regular enquiry is conducted by a Judge of the Supreme Court, after receiving the preliminary finding of a Committee constituted by the Government in terms of Rule 21 of the Rules.

35.   … There is nothing in the provisions of the NGT Act that directly or even by necessary implication is indicative of any external control over the National Green Tribunal in discharge of its judicial functions. MoEF is merely an administrative Ministry for the National Green Tribunal to provide for means and finances. Once budget is provided, the Ministry cannot have any interference in the functioning of the National Green Tribunal.… The Act is comprehensive enough to provide a complete mechanism for approaching the National Green Tribunal, adjudication of disputes in accordance with law and the appeals that would be preferred against the orders of the Tribunal.… The legislature under the Act has therefore, provided effective and efficient alternative institutional mechanism in relation to environmental cases.

36.   [As held by the Supreme Court in *Union of India v. Madras Bar Association* (2010) 11 SCC 1].… If the Tribunals are to be vested with judicial powers exercised by Courts, such Tribunals should possess independence, security and capacity associated with Courts. All the three stated features are satisfied in the present case. The scheme of the NGT Act clearly gives the Tribunal complete independence to discharge its judicial functions, have security of tenure and conditions of service and is possessed of complete capacity associated with Courts. A complete mechanism is provided for adjudication process before the Tribunal as well as the method and procedures under which the orders of the Tribunal could be assailed before the higher courts. Thus, this Tribunal has the complete trappings of a civil court and satisfies all the stated features for acting as an independent judicial Tribunal with complete and comprehensive powers.

39. Having dealt with the constitution of the Tribunal and having established its independence, now let us proceed to examine the scope of power of the Tribunal, with particular reference to examining a subordinate or delegated legislation as being ultra vires, unconstitutional or illegal. Judicial review is the power of the court to review statutes or administrative acts or determine their constitutionality or validity according to a written constitution. In a wider sense, judicial review is not only concerned with the merits of the decision but also the decision making process. It tends to protect individuals against the misuse or abuse of power by a wide range of authorities. Judicial review is a protection to the individual and not a weapon. It is the doctrine under which legislative and/or executive actions are subject to review (and possible invalidation) by the judiciary. A specific court with the power of judicial review may annul the acts of the State, when it finds them incompatible with a higher authority (such as the terms of a written constitution).

Judicial review is an example of checks and balances in a modern governmental system, where the judiciary checks the other branches of government. This principle is interpreted differently in different jurisdictions, which also have differing views on the different hierarchy of governmental norms. As a result, the procedure and scope of judicial review may differ from country to country and State to State. Unlike in England, where the judiciary has no power to review the statutes/Acts made by the Parliament, the United States Supreme Court in terms of Article III and Article VI exercises the power of judicial review of the Acts passed by the Congress and has struck down several statutes as unconstitutional. In India, the Supreme Court and the High Courts have frequently exercised the power of judicial review keeping intact the 'doctrine of separation of power'. Challenge to legislation before the Courts in India has primarily been permitted on a very limited ground. The legislation in question should either be unconstitutional, or should lack legislative competence. Challenge to such legislation as being unreasonable has also been permitted, if it violates or unreasonably restricts the fundamental rights, particularly under Article 14 and 19 adumbrated in our Constitution.

40. The Courts are vested with the power of judicial review in relation to legislative acts and even in relation to judgments of the Courts. The power of judicial review has been exercised by the Courts in India sparingly and within the prescribed constitutional limitations. The Courts have also taken a view that functions of the Tribunal being judicial in nature, the public have a major stake in its functioning, for effective and orderly administration of justice. A Tribunal should have judicial autonomy and its administration relating to

dispensation of justice should be free of opinions. (Ajay Gandhi v. B. Singh, (2004) 2 SCC 120). The National Green Tribunal has complete control over its functioning and all the administrative powers, including transfer of cases, constitution of benches and other administrative control over the functioning of the Tribunal, are vested in the Chairperson of the NGT under the provisions of the NGT Act.

41. The Principle that the Courts have inherent powers to do justice between the parties is equally applicable to administration of justice by the Tribunals.... From these stated principles it is clear that the Tribunal has to exercise powers which are necessary to administer the justice in accordance with law. Certainly the Tribunal cannot have contrary to the powers prescribed or the law in force but it certainly would have to expand its powers and determine the various controversies in relation to fact and law arising before it. This Tribunal has the inherent powers not only by implied application of the above enunciated principles of law but the provisions of the NGT Act particularly Section 19 of the NGT Act which empowers the Tribunal to regulate its own procedure and to be guided by the Principles of natural justice.

46. In the case of *S.P. Sampath Kumar v. Union of India* (1987) 1 SCC 124, the Apex Court ... took the view that the alternative institutional mechanism or arrangement for judicial review could be framed by the legislature, provided it is not less efficacious than the High Court but the jurisdiction of the High Court under Article 226 and that of the Supreme Court under Article 32 of the Constitution of India could not be ousted.

52. ... [It] can precisely be stated that the Tribunal can exercise the power of judicial review but not in relation to the law that constituted it. Even this limited power of judicial review is to ensure that the powers of the High Courts and the Supreme Court in terms of article 226 and 32 respectively, are not entirely excluded. The Tribunal functions to supplement and not supplant the powers of the High Courts or the Supreme Court of India. There has to be judicial independence of the Tribunal. It must inspire confidence and public esteem. It should be manned by expert minds and persons of judicial acumen and experts from the relevant field with capacity to decide cases with the judicial Members. With such judicial powers and functions, the Tribunals can also exercise limited power of judicial review, of course it would not substitute the High Courts and or the Supreme Court. The Tribunal should have effective and efficacious mechanism.

54. [In] L Chandra Kumar's case ... in paragraph 90 of the judgment while rejecting the contention that the Tribunals should not be allowed to

adjudicate upon matters where the vires of the legislation is questioned and that they should restrict themselves to handling matters where constitutional issues are not raised. The Supreme Court said we cannot bring ourselves to agree to this proposition as that may result in splitting up proceedings and may cause avoidable delay. If such a view were to be adopted, it would be open for the litigants to raise constitutional issues, many of which may be quite frivolous, to directly approach the High Courts and thus subvert the jurisdiction of the Tribunals. Moreover, in these special branches of law, some areas do involve the consideration of constitutional questions on a regular basis; for instance, in service law matter, a large majority of cases involve an interpretation of Articles 14, 15 and 16 of the Constitution. To hold that the Tribunals have no power to handle matters involving constitutional issues would not serve the purpose for which they were constituted.

55. The above declaration of law by the highest Court of the land unambiguously support the view that the Tribunal within the framework of the NGT Act would be entitled to exercise power of the judicial review within its prescribed limitations. As already noticed, the questions of interpretation of law, examination of Notifications, their correctness or otherwise is being raised before the Tribunal every day. The questions of law had environmental issues are so closely linked that it would hardly be possible to fully and finally decide the cases by segregating the jurisdiction which is neither the purport of the Act. These questions can squarely be heard and decide by the Tribunal keeping in view the constitution of the Bench which is always presided by judicial Member as per the constitution of the Benches prescribed under the Rules.

59. The courts have drawn a fine distinction between a 'court' and a 'tribunal'. However, this fine distinction is going thinner by the day. The word 'Tribunal' is a word of wide import and the words 'courts and tribunals' embrace within them the exercise of judicial power in all its forms.... The word 'Court' is used to designate those tribunals which are set up in an organized state for the administration of justice. When a *lis* is pending between the parties and is adjudicated upon by the Tribunal, following the procedure in accordance with the rules of law and when it administers justice, the Tribunal dealing with such *lis* will have the trappings of a Court.... Finally, the Supreme Court took the view that all Tribunals are not courts though all Courts are tribunals. This view has been reiterated by the Court, more particularly in relation to drawing a distinction between the two terms. A 'Tribunal' may be termed as a 'Court' if it has all the trappings of a court and satisfies the essential parameters.

64. Under the NGT Act, as already noticed, this Tribunal performs all judicial functions and determines the disputes between the parties in accordance with the provisions of the Act. It evolves its own procedure in consonance with the principles of natural justice and is not strictly bound by the provisions of the CPC. But, at the same time, for discharging its functions under the NGT Act, the Tribunal is vested with the powers as are vested in a civil court under the CPC. Furthermore, all the proceedings before the Tribunal shall be deemed to be judicial proceedings within the meaning of Sections 193, 219 and 228 for the purposes of Section 196 of the Indian Penal Code, 1860 and the Tribunal shall be deemed to be a civil court for the purposes of Section 195 and Chapter 26 of the Code of Criminal Procedure, 1973 in terms of Sections 19(4) and (5) of the NGT Act. Jurisdiction of the Civil Court is barred under Section 29 of the NGT Act. Thus, in our considered view, the National Green Tribunal has all the trappings of a court and is vested with original, appellate and special jurisdiction, performing exclusively judicial functions and hence is a Court.

65. Having come to the conclusion that National Green Tribunal has all the trappings of a Court and is, thus, a Court and further that within the framework of the NGT Act, the Tribunal is vested with the power of judicial review.....

*   *   *

NOTES AND QUESTIONS

1. Through this 142-page judgment, the NGT unequivocally holds that it has the trappings of a court and has the power to exercise judicial review in a limited manner as prescribed by the Supreme Court. While it bases this decision on several factors such as, inter alia, the scheme of the NGT Act, 2010, and precedents set by the Supreme Court, a major underlying factor remains the independence of the NGT. In other words, one of the main reasons that the Tribunal holds that it has all the trappings of a court is due to its independent functioning. It minutely details the selection and removal processes for the chairperson and members, explores the influence of the MoEF on the functioning of the Tribunal, and analyses the provisions of the NGT Act, 2010, that demonstrate its independent functioning. Given the recent introduction of the Tribunals Reforms Act, 2021 (discussed earlier in this chapter), and the consequent curtailment of the Tribunal's independence, do you think this reasoning is still valid?

2. The NGT holds that the test for determining whether a Tribunal is an equally efficacious and efficient alternative to a High Court is to analyse its independence,

security, and capacity associated with High Courts. Do you think the NGT's reasoning is applicable to other tribunals as well? Given that different tribunals have differing degrees of independence, security, and capacity due to their parent statutes, do you think that some statutory tribunals can be said to be worthy of exercising judicial review while others cannot?

3. The scheme of the NGT Act, 2010, as discussed by the NGT, requires the Tribunal to exercise judicial review for its effective functioning. Several executive orders and subordinate legislations are at the heart of challenges brought to the Tribunal on a daily basis. If the NGT lacks the power to test their constitutional validity, it will impair the Tribunal's ability to deliver environmental justice.

4. The Supreme Court's ruling in *L. Chandra Kumar* is applicable to administrative tribunals created under Article 323A of the Constitution. Article 323A(2)(d) states that the administrative tribunal set up under Article 323A will be able to exercise jurisdiction of all courts except the Supreme Court under Article 136 of the Constitution. Nevertheless, the NGT holds that the directions of the Supreme Court are applicable to tribunals such as the NGT as well. Do you think this reasoning of the NGT is valid? Do you think it can be termed an administrative tribunal under Article 323A? If not, on what other grounds do you think the NGT can base its power of judicial review?

* * *

The NGT in *Wilfred J.* unequivocally holds that it has the power of judicial review. In addition to basing this power on the scheme of the NGT Act, 2010, and its interpretation of precedents of the Supreme Court, it highlights that such power is needed for the efficient functioning of the Tribunal. This is due to the fact that there are several executive and legislative orders that are challenged before it in due course of proceedings which have a direct bearing on the environment as well as on the outcome of a case. Thus, it holds that it possesses the power of exercising limited judicial review, without ousting the jurisdiction of the High Courts or the Supreme Court under Articles 226 and 32, respectively. However, shortly after the NGT's decision, the High Court of Bombay came to a different conclusion.

In *Central India Ayush Drugs v. State of Maharashtra*, the constitutionality of Rule 17 of the Biological Diversity Rules, 2004, was challenged before the High Court of Bombay.[133] A preliminary objection was raised stating that in the light of the Supreme Court's holding in the *Bhopal Case* – whereby all cases involving a substantial question relating to the environment instituted after the enactment of the NGT Act, 2010, were transferred from High Courts to the NGT – the present case ought to be transferred to the NGT. Furthermore, it was argued that since the Biological Diversity Act, 2002, was mentioned in Schedule I of the NGT Act, 2010, and the impugned Rules were enacted under it, the NGT clearly had jurisdiction over the matter.

The High Court of Bombay, while addressing this objection, discussed the scheme of the NGT Act, 2010, in the light of the Supreme Court's decision in *L. Chandra Kumar* as well as the *Bhopal Case*. It held that while the *Bhopal Case* had directed High Courts to transfer cases involving a substantial question relating to the environment to the NGT, the present objections dealt with the *vires* of a rule which was on a different footing. Further, it held:[134]

> Here, considering the jurisdiction given to the National Green Tribunal is only to decide civil cases, where substantial question involved is in relation to environment, it is apparent that the NGT cannot be said to be conferred with the absolute jurisdiction to adjudicate all types of disputes or even all civil disputes. A limited jurisdiction to deal with specific type of civil disputes is only made available to it. Bare reading of Section 28 of the N.G.T. Act prescribing the bar of jurisdiction also substantiates this. Thus, power to pronounce upon the *vires* of any statutory provision or of any subordinate legislation cannot be read into any of the provisions which confer either appellate or original jurisdiction upon National Green Tribunal. The Parliament which has deliberately employed wide or liberal words while laying down the compass or the scheme of N.G.T. Act, has not used such words while phrasing Section 14 of that Act or conferring jurisdiction upon National Green Tribunal. On the contrary, its intention to limit the power to decide certain specified nature of disputes is apparent. We find that the scheme of N.G.T. Act does not permit National Green Tribunal to decide upon the vires of any of the enactments which confer appellate or other jurisdiction upon it and find mention in Schedule-I of N.G.T. Act. It also does not empower it to examine validity of any Rules or Regulations made under these enactments.

This decision of the High Court of Bombay is an exercise of the High Court's power of judicial review under Article 226 of the Constitution. Nevertheless, one may argue that it overlooks the combined effect of the directions of the Supreme Court in the *Bhopal Case* and *L. Chandra Kumar* as interpreted by the NGT in *Wilfred J.* As discussed, as per the Supreme Court's decision in *L. Chandra Kumar*, the NGT has the power to exercise judicial review, albeit limited in scope. Accordingly, it has the power to judicially review the *vires* of the Biological Diversity Rules, 2004, in a manner that supplements the High Courts and the Supreme Court.

Further, in the light of the *Bhopal Case*, it can be argued that the present case ought to have been transferred to the NGT given that an issue relating to the *vires* of a statute dealing with biodiversity can be deemed to be a question relating to the environment. Moreover, the Rules are made under a statute which is clearly mentioned under Schedule I of the NGT Act, 2010.

However, in 2019, the Supreme Court clarified the position with respect to the NGT's power of judicial review conclusively.[135] Through a two-bench judgment, the Supreme

Court held that the NGT does not possess a general power of judicial review akin to the High Courts under Article 226.[136]

In brief, the facts of the case were that the residents near a copper smelting plant in Thoothukudi, in Tamil Nadu, complained of breathing difficulties and nausea on account of emissions from the plant. The Tamil Nadu Pollution Control Board directed the closure of the plant under Sections 31A and 33A of the Air (Prevention and Control of Pollution) Act, 1981, and Water (Prevention and Control of Pollution) Act, 1974, respectively. Subsequently, the state government of Tamil Nadu reinforced this order by directing the closure of the same plant under Section 18(1)(b) of the Water Act, 1974. The NGT heard an appeal challenging these orders and reversed them by directing the reopening of the plant on account of a lack of evidence of health issues.

Accordingly, this order of the NGT was challenged before the Supreme Court. The Court ruled that the Tribunal should not have heard the case on appeal as this amounted to exercising a leapfrog jurisdiction and bypassing the appropriate authority which should have heard the appeal (we will discuss this aspect in greater detail in a later section dealing with appeals). Further, the Court held that the government order under Section 18 of the Water Act, 1974, could only be overturned in a suit or in an exercise of judicial review by a High Court under Article 226 of the Constitution. Hence, the Court set aside the NGT's order on grounds of maintainability and allowed the respondent – Sterlite Industries – to file a writ petition before the appropriate High Court. Let us examine the Court's reasoning in further detail below.

Supreme Court of India

TAMIL NADU POLLUTION CONTROL BOARD v. STERLITE INDUSTRIES LTD. & ORS.

[Civil Appeal Nos. 4763-4764 of 2013, Judgment Dated 18 February 2019]

R.F. Nariman, J.;
Navin Sinha, J.

*   *   *

Relevant Extracts:

40. Shri Sundaram [counsel for the Respondent] then argued that this Court in *L. Chandra Kumar* (supra) made it clear that Tribunals that are set up, generally have the power of judicial review, save and except a challenge to the vires of the legislation under which such Tribunals are themselves set up. For this, he relied strongly upon paragraphs 90 and 93 of the judgment in *L. Chandra Kumar* (supra). It is important to notice that *L. Chandra Kumar* (supra) pertained to a Tribunal that was set up under Article 323A of the

Constitution of India. Under Article 323A(2)(d), the Administrative Tribunal so set up would be able to exercise the jurisdiction of all courts except the jurisdiction of the Supreme Court under Article 136 of the Constitution. This would mean that the Administrative Tribunal so set up could exercise the jurisdiction of all High Courts when it came to the matters specified in Article 323A. This is further made clear by a conjoint reading of Section 14 and Section 28 of the Administrative Tribunals Act, 1985....

Article 323B of the Constitution of India also provides for Tribunals for certain other matters which are specified by sub-clause (2) thereof. Suffice it to say that the NGT is not a Tribunal set up either under Article 323A or Article 323B of the Constitution, but is a statutory Tribunal set up under the NGT Act. That such a Tribunal does not exercise the jurisdiction of all courts except the Supreme Court is clear from a reading of Section 29 of the NGT Act (supra). Thus, a conjoint reading of Section 14 and Section 29 of the NGT Act must be contrasted with a conjoint reading of Section 14 and Section 28 of the Administrative Tribunals Act, 1985.

41. It is in the context of Article 323A and the Administrative Tribunals Act, 1985 that this Court in *L. Chandra Kumar* (supra) has observed in paragraph 93 as follows:

> "93. Before moving on to other aspects, we may summarize our conclusions on the jurisdictional powers of these Tribunals. The Tribunals are competent to hear matters where the vires of statutory provisions are questioned. However, in discharging this duty, they cannot act as substitutes for the High Courts and the Supreme Court which have, under our constitutional set-up, been specifically entrusted with such an obligation. Their function in this respect is only supplementary and all such decisions of the Tribunals will be subject to scrutiny before a Division Bench of the respective High Courts. The Tribunals will consequently also have the power to test the vires of subordinate legislations and rules. However, this power of the Tribunals will be subject to one important exception. The Tribunals shall not entertain any question regarding the vires of their parent statutes following the settled principle that a Tribunal which is a creature of an Act cannot declare that very Act to be unconstitutional. In such cases alone, the High Court concerned may be approached directly. All other decisions of these Tribunals, rendered in cases that they are specifically empowered to adjudicate upon by virtue of their parent statutes, will also be subject to scrutiny before a Division Bench of their respective High Courts. We may add that the Tribunals will, however, continue to act as the only courts of first instance in respect

of the areas of law for which they have been constituted. By this, we mean that it will not be open for litigants to directly approach the High Courts even in cases where they question the vires of statutory legislations (except, as mentioned, where the legislation which creates the particular Tribunal is challenged) by overlooking the jurisdiction of the Tribunal concerned."

42. In *Bharat Sanchar Nigam Limited v. Telecom Regulatory Authority of India and Ors.*, (2014) 3 SCC 222 ["BSNL"], this Court had to construe the appellate power that is contained in Section 14 of the Telecom Regulatory Authority of India Act, 1997, by which, the TDSAT was conferred with the power to hear and dispose of appeals against any direction, decision, or order of the TRAI. In this context, after distinguishing the judgment in *L. Chandra Kumar* (supra), this Court held:

> "108. Before the 2000 Amendment, the applications were required to be filed under Section 15 which also contained detailed procedure for deciding the same. While sub-section (2) of Section 15 used the word "orders", sub-sections (3) and (4) thereof used the word "decision". In terms of sub-section (5), the orders and directions of TRAI were treated as binding on the service providers, Government and all other persons concerned. Section 18 provided for an appeal against any decision or order of TRAI. Such an appeal could be filed before the High Court. The Amendment made in 2000 is intended to vest the original jurisdiction of TRAI in TDSAT and the same is achieved by Section 14(a). The appellate jurisdiction exercisable by the High Court is also vested in TDSAT by virtue of Section 14(b) but this does not include decision made by TRAI. Section 14-N provides for transfer to all appeals pending before the High Court to TDSAT and in terms of clause (b) of sub-section (2), TDSAT was required to proceed to deal with the appeal from the stage which was reached before such transfer or from any earlier stage or de novo as considered appropriate by it. Since the High Court while hearing appeal did not have the power of judicial review of subordinate legislation, the transferee adjudicatory forum i.e. TDSAT cannot exercise that power under Section 14(b)."

> "114. ... From the above-extracted portion of the order it is evident that the Bench, which decided the matter, felt that the view taken by TDSAT would encourage rampant violation of the orders without any penal consequence and the entire scheme of the TRAI Act would become unworkable. The word "directions" used in Section 29 of the TRAI Act was interpreted to include orders and regulations in the

context of the factual matrix of that case and the apprehension of the Court that Section 29 would otherwise become unworkable, but the same cannot be read as laying down a proposition of law that the words "direction", "decision" or "order" used in Section 14(b) would include regulations framed under Section 36, which are in the nature of subordinate legislation."

"123. In *Union of India v. Madras Bar Assn.* [(2010) 11 SCC 1] and *State of Gujarat v. Gujarat Revenue Tribunal Bar Assn.* [(2012) 10 SCC 353 : (2012) 4 SCC (Civ) 1229 : (2013) 1 SCC (Cri) 35 : (2013) 1 SCC (L&S) 56 : (2012) 10 Scale 285], this Court applied the principles laid down in *L. Chandra Kumar case* [*L. Chandra Kumar v. Union of India*, (1997) 3 SCC 261 : 1997 SCC (L&S) 577] and reiterated the importance of tribunals created for resolution of disputes but these judgments too have no bearing on the decision of the question formulated before us."

"124. In the result, the question framed by the Court is answered in the following terms: in exercise of the power vested in it under Section 14(b) of the TRAI Act, TDSAT does not have the jurisdiction to entertain the challenge to the regulations framed by TRAI under Section 36 of the TRAI Act."

In the present case, it is clear that Section 16 of the NGT Act is cast in terms that are similar to Section 14(b) of the Telecom Regulatory Authority of India Act, 1997, in that appeals are against the orders, decisions, directions, or determinations made under the various Acts mentioned in Section 16. It is clear, therefore, that under the NGT Act, the Tribunal exercising appellate jurisdiction cannot strike down rules or regulations made under this Act. Therefore, it would be fallacious to state that the Tribunal has powers of judicial review akin to that of a High Court exercising constitutional powers under Article 226 of the Constitution of India. We must never forget the distinction between a superior court of record and courts of limited jurisdiction that was, in the felicitous language of Gajendragadkar, C.J., in *Re: Special Reference*, (1965) 1 SCR 413, made in the following words:

"We ought to make it clear that we are dealing with the question of jurisdiction and are not concerned with the propriety or reasonableness of the exercise of such jurisdiction. Besides, in the case of a superior Court of Record, it is for the court to consider whether any matter falls within its jurisdiction or not. Unlike a Court of limited jurisdiction, the superior Court is entitled to determine for itself questions about its own jurisdiction. "Prima facie", says Halsbury, "no matter is deemed to be beyond the jurisdiction of a superior court unless it is expressly shown to be so, while nothing is within the jurisdiction of an inferior court unless it is expressly shown on the face of the proceedings that the particular matter is within the cognizance of the particular court [Halsbury's Laws of England, vol. 9, p. 349]".

For this reason also, we are of the view that the State Government order made under Section 18 of the Water Act, not being the subject matter of any appeal under Section 16 of the NGT Act, cannot be "judicially reviewed" by the NGT. Following the judgment in *BSNL* (supra), we are of the view that the NGT has no general power of judicial review akin to that vested under Article 226 of the Constitution of India possessed by the High Courts of this country. Shri Sundaram's strong reliance on the NGT judgment dated 17.07.2014 in *Wilfred v. MoEF* must also be rejected as this NGT judgment does not state the law on this aspect correctly. This contention is also without merit, and therefore, rejected.

*   *   *

Through this case, the Supreme Court has clarified the scope and applicability of its directions in *L. Chandra Kumar*. While the NGT, in *Wilfred J.*, held that the directions of the Court in *L. Chandra Kumar* allowed it to exercise limited judicial review without ousting the jurisdiction of the High Courts and the Supreme Court, the Court clarified that these directions were applicable only to administrative tribunals constituted under Article 323A of the Constitution. Moreover, these administrative tribunals had the power of judicial review only in respect of the matters specified in Article 323A. Thus, given that the NGT is a statutory tribunal (that is, it is constituted under a statute), these directions were not applicable to it.

In the light of this judgment, the ruling of the High Court of Bombay in *Central India Ayush Drugs* seems technically sound. Article 323A(2)(d) of the Constitution unequivocally gives the administrative tribunal, constituted therein, the jurisdiction of all courts except the Supreme Court. Given that there is no corollary provision in the NGT Act, 2010, the Supreme Court's ratio in *L. Chandra Kumar* seems less applicable to the NGT.

It is necessary to contrast the Supreme Court's reasoning in relation to the distinction between a court and a tribunal with the NGT's reasoning in *Wilfred J.* As discussed previously, the NGT, in *Wilfred J.*, held that the distinction between a tribunal and a court was growing thinner by the day. It held that the term "court" is used to designate a tribunal which is set up in an organized state for the administration of justice. It reiterated the Supreme Court's view that while all tribunals are not courts, all courts are tribunals. Thus, it held that if a tribunal, after careful examination of the scheme of its parent statute, can be deemed to have all the "trappings of a court", it would be able to exercise all the powers of a court for practical purposes.

The Supreme Court, however, highlights the distinction between a court of superior record and an inferior court. Citing Halsbury, it holds that a superior court of record (such as the Supreme Court and the High Courts) normally has jurisdiction over all matters unless expressly prohibited. Inferior courts, on the other hand, have limited jurisdiction, and a matter has to be prima facie within their purview to enable them to exercise jurisdiction.

Thus, while the NGT has held that it has all the trappings of a court, the Supreme Court seems to have interpreted this as the trappings of an inferior court. Accordingly, it has held that it would be "fallacious" to state that the NGT has powers of judicial review akin to a High Court exercising constitutional powers under Article 226 of the Constitution. Therefore, as the law stands today, the NGT does not have any general power of judicial review.

However, it is desirable that the NGT be accorded such power. As noted by the Tribunal in *Wilfred J.*, judicial review is necessary to enable the effective functioning of the NGT. The Tribunal, in its first nine years of existence, disposed of over 28,000 cases.[137] Thus, on average it disposes of around 3,100 cases per year. According to the NGT, many of these cases involve challenges to several executive orders and subordinate legislation.[138] Accordingly, if the NGT is not allowed to test the validity of such orders and legislations, it is likely that the NGT will not be able to deliver environmental justice.

It must be borne in mind that the NGT adjudicates on environmental matters that were earlier decided by a constitutional bench of the Supreme Court. Given that the NGT was supposed to be the heir of the environmental movement based on PILs, it is necessary to equip the Tribunal with the power of judicial review. If this is not done, potential litigants are likely to prefer approaching a High Court under Article 226 instead of the NGT, irrespective of the latter's technical expertise. This is likely to defeat the purpose for which the NGT was established in the long run.

2.3.5   INTERPRETATION OF LIMITATION PERIOD

As noted earlier in this chapter, Sections 14 and 16 of the NGT Act, 2010, provide for a limitation period beyond which the NGT shall not entertain a petition. Section 14(3) states that an application for adjudication of a dispute has to be made within six months from the date on which the cause of action first arose. The proviso to the section provides that this period can be extended by sixty days if the Tribunal is satisfied that the applicant was prevented by a sufficient cause from filing the application.

Likewise, Section 16 provides that the Tribunal can exercise appellate jurisdiction within thirty days from the date on which the impugned order or decision was "communicated" to the appellant. The proviso to this section is identical to the proviso under Section 14(3) and states that this period can be extended by sixty days upon demonstration of sufficient cause.

In this section, we will analyse how the NGT has interpreted this limitation period and the requirement of "sufficient cause". Further, we will discuss the threshold of communication required under Section 16.

2.3.5.1 NGT's Interpretation of the Limitation Period and "Sufficient Cause"

Before delving into the NGT's interpretation of the limitation period provided under Sections 14 and 16 of the NGT Act, 2010, let us examine the position of the Supreme Court in this regard. In *Vimal Bhai v. Union of India*,[139] a few social activists had challenged an environmental clearanceenvironmental clearance granted to a hydroelectric power plant before the NEAA (the NGT's predecessor). As per the provisions of the NEAA Act, 1997, the appeal was supposed to be filed within thirty days of the grant of the environmental clearance. However, it was filed with a delay of twenty-three days, and the NEAA dismissed the appeal on account of delay. The Delhi High Court held that the NEAA had adopted a "very hyper-technical approach" in rejecting the petitioner's application for condonation of delay. It held that the NEAA should have dealt with the matter on merit rather than rejecting it on procedural grounds.[140]

Accordingly, in *Ram Nath Sao v. Gobardhan Sao & Ors.*, the Supreme Court held that a liberal interpretation has to be accorded to "sufficient cause" to advance substantial justice when no negligence, inaction, or want of bona fide is imputable to a party.[141]

In *Collector, Land Acquisition, Anantnag & Anr. v. Mst. Katiji & Ors.*,[142] an appeal by the state against a decision enhancing compensation payable for acquisition of land in public interest by the government was dismissed by the High Court of Jammu and Kashmir. Despite the fact that the case involved important questions of valuation (the challenged order had increased the compensation by 800 per cent), the reason for dismissal was that the appeal was time barred due to a delay of mere four days. The Supreme Court reversed the order of the High Court and held:

> The legislature has conferred the power to condone delay by enacting Section 51 of the Indian Limitation Act of 1963 in order to enable the Courts to do substantial justice to parties by disposing of matters on 'merits'. The expression "sufficient cause" employed by the legislature is adequately elastic to enable the courts to apply the law in a meaningful manner which sub-serves the ends of justice – that being the life-purpose for the existence of the institution of Courts. It is common knowledge that this Court has been making a justifiably liberal approach in matters instituted in this Court. But the message does not appear to have percolated down to all the other Courts in the hierarchy.

Further, the Court provided six guidelines to be kept in mind by adjudicatory authorities while liberally construing a prescribed limitation period:

1. Ordinarily a litigant does not stand to benefit by lodging an appeal late.
2. Refusing to condone delay can result in a meritorious matter being thrown out at the very threshold and cause of justice being defeated. As against this, when delay is condoned, the highest that can happen is that a cause would be decided on merits after hearing the parties.
3. "Every day's delay must be explained" does not mean that a pedantic approach should be made. Why not every hour's delay, every second's delay? The doctrine must be applied in a rational common-sense pragmatic manner.
4. When substantial justice and technical considerations are pitted against each other, the cause of substantial justice deserves to be preferred, for the other side cannot claim to have a vested right in injustice being done because of a non-deliberate delay.
5. There is no presumption that delay is occasioned deliberately, or on account of culpable negligence, or on account of mala fides. A litigant does not stand to benefit by resorting to delay. In fact, he runs a serious risk.
6. It must be grasped that the judiciary is respected not on account of its power to legalize injustice on technical grounds but because it is capable of removing injustice and is expected to do so.

Thus, the Supreme Court's preference for a "justice oriented" approach over a technical approach is evident. While these guidelines were given by the Court in relation to Order XXI of the Code of Civil Procedure, 1908, the NGT has relied on them while overlooking a delay beyond the statutory limitation period prescribed under Section 16 of the NGT Act, 2010.[143]

In *Paryavana Sanrakshan Sangarsh Samiti Lippa v. Union of India & Ors*,[144] an order of the MoEF granting approval for the diversion of 17.68 hectares of forest land for the construction of a hydroelectric power plant was challenged before the NGT. While the appeal in this case was filed after the thirty-day deadline, it was within the sixty-day extension period provided in the proviso to Section 16 of the NGT Act, 2010. In fact, the appeal was filed on the ninetieth day from the date on which the MoEF's order was communicated to the appellant. Accordingly, the moot question before the Tribunal was whether it could entertain the appeal on the basis of the existence of a sufficient cause for delay.

The memorandum accompanying the appeal provided insight into the reasons for the delay. It stated that the appellant is an organization based in the village Lippa, which is located in the interiors of Himachal Pradesh. Due to the remote location of the village, it is difficult for residents to access other parts of the country. In addition to the high cost of travelling, it takes almost two days to reach Delhi from Lippi. Further, these difficulties had been aggravated due to the monsoon season and frequent landslides. The cumulative effect of these conditions resulted in the delay in filing the appeal by the appellants.

The NGT relied on the six guidelines of the Supreme Court in *Collector, Land Acquisition, Anantnag*, and held that mere technicalities should not come in the way of justice.[145] Given that there was no negligence attributable to the appellant and it did not stand to gain due to the delay, the Tribunal condoned the delay due to the demonstration of sufficient cause.

The Tribunal's interpretation of what constitutes a sufficient cause is in accordance with the overarching nature of environmental litigation. Even though, generally, litigants approach the Tribunal with an environmental matter, the impact of any environmental degradation is well beyond the parties to the case. Thus, the Tribunal has to look at the larger public interest and, to this extent, view the case in a non-adversarial manner.

Complementing the six guidelines of the Supreme Court in this regard, the NGT has endorsed the following principles in relation to the interpretation of sufficient cause:[146]

1. The term "sufficient cause" has to be understood and applied in a reasonable, pragmatic, practical, and liberal manner depending on the facts and circumstances of each case. The interpretation has to advance substantial justice, when delay is not due to dilatory tactics, want of bona fides, deliberate inaction, or negligence attributable to the appellant.

2. While considering reasons for condonation of delay, the Tribunal will be more liberal with reference to applications for setting aside abatement. While the Tribunal will keep in mind that a valuable right accrues to the legal representatives of the deceased respondent when an appeal abates, it will not punish an appellant with foreclosure of the appeal due to unintended lapses.

3. The decisive factor in condoning delay is the sufficiency of a satisfactory explanation, rather than the length of delay.

4. The degree of leniency shown by the Tribunal depends on the nature of the application and the facts and circumstances of each case. For instance, the Tribunal would view a delay in making an application in a pending appeal more leniently than a delay in the institution of an appeal. Further, the Tribunal is likely to view applications involving delays on account of a lawyer more leniently than applications involving delays due to lapses by a litigant.

The NGT has further held that the law of limitation was founded on public policy and is enshrined in the maxim "interest reipublicae ut sit finis litium", which means that it is in the general interest of the society that litigation must come to an end.[147] It has stated:

> [The] law of limitation is relatable to the principle of public policy. Legislative intent behind prescribing limitation is to further the cause of public policy, on the one hand and to aid the doctrine of finality, on the other. This would impliedly help in expeditious disposal of cases. In our considered view, it is always better to adopt a balanced approach with reference to the facts and circumstances of a given case. A strict interpretational approach may subserve the cause of justice while too liberal an approach may defeat the ends of justice. The law of limitation, therefore, must receive a reasonable construction with the aid of the principle of plain reading. Wherever the Court/Tribunal finds sufficient cause being shown and conduct of the applicant being bonafide, that is to say his approach and attitude is not that of negligence and inaction, he has approached the Court with clean hands and true facts and that there would be no grave and irretrievable injustice done to the other parties, the judicial discretion of the Court may be tilted more towards condoning the delay rather than shutting the doors to justice right at the threshold.

Thus, from the NGT's holding, it is clear that "sufficient cause" has to be construed liberally, and the Tribunal should be inclined to determine the cause on merits rather than dismissing the petition on grounds of delay. It is noteworthy that even after sufficient cause has been demonstrated by a party, the party is not entitled to condonation of delay as a matter of right.[148] The NGT condones the delay in exercise of discretionary jurisdiction vested upon it. Accordingly, in addition to proof of sufficient cause, other factors such as the bona fides and negligence attributable to the appellant play a decisive role.

While the discretionary power of the NGT enables it to condone delay due to the presence of sufficient cause for the delay, such an equitable power does not enable it to extend the limitation period beyond the statutorily prescribed period.[149] In other words, the provisions stipulating the limitation period cannot be liberally construed to frustrate the purpose with which they were enacted. Thus, the sixty-day extension period provided under the provisos to Sections 14 and 16 of the NGT Act, 2010, has to be strictly construed without further extension.

This view has been upheld by the NGT in *Nikunj Developers & Ors. v. the State of Maharashtra & Ors.*[150] The NGT has held that the language of the provisos to Sections 14 and 16 is unambiguous, and it is amply clear that the Tribunal loses jurisdiction to condone delay after the limitation period of ninety days.[151] Relying on the Supreme Court's holding in *Hiralal Ratanlal v. STO* – wherein the Supreme Court gave precedence to the literal interpretation of a statute – the NGT has held that the legislative intent is clear from the literal reading of the provisions. [152]

In another case, the NGT has unequivocally held that the outer limit of ninety days for the institution of a petition or appeal provided under Sections 14 and 16 is "unexceptionally mandatory".[153] Accordingly, in the same case, the NGT barred the institution of an appeal due to a delay of 104 days.[154] Therefore, even on equitable grounds, the NGT lacks the jurisdiction to condone delay beyond the statutorily prescribed limitation period.

2.3.5.2   Interpretation of Cause of Action under Section 14

Since the limitation periods provided under Sections 14 and 16 of the NGT Act, 2010, are mandatory, there can be cases wherein despite the existence of sufficient cause a worthy appeal of petition can be dismissed due to the technical bar of limitation. To address this concern, the NGT has liberally interpreted when a "cause of action" first arises under Section 14, as the limitation period commences from this date.

A "cause of action" refers to the entire set of facts that give rise to an enforceable claim.[155] The term is broad enough to cover each fact that a litigant must prove to obtain a judgment. In other words, it refers to the set of facts that, in consonance with the law, accord a right to a petitioner to obtain relief against a defendant.[156] In addition, the cause of action has to be construed from the pleadings as a whole. It is not permissible to cull out a sentence or passage, without context, to establish a separate cause of action.[157]

The cause of action, as understood under civil jurisprudence, has to be examined differently in the context of the NGT Act, 2010. Invariably, it must bear a nexus with matters relating to the environment. To commence the limitation period, the cause of action should satisfy all the conditions under Section 14(1). Accordingly, it should, necessarily, involve a substantial question relating to the environment and should relate to the implementation of the statutes specified under Schedule I of the NGT Act, 2010.[158]

For instance, the Tribunal has held that the limitation period under Section 14 would not be triggered simply due to the fact of acquisition of land for a project or due to the issuance of notifications under the relevant land acquisition laws.[159] The facts, ipso facto, are incapable of triggering the limitation period. It is necessary that the facts giving rise to a cause of action must involve a substantial question relating to the environment.

The NGT has liberally interpreted the requirement of cause of action in cases involving continuing pollution by elaborating on the concept of continuing cause of action. This is a concept found in civil jurisprudence on limitation, and the Tribunal has co-opted it to further environmental justice. In *Forward Foundation & Ors. v. State of Karnataka & Ors.*, the NGT was faced with continuing pollution of the entire ecosystem surrounding the Bellundur Lake on account of a commercial activity.[160] In arriving at its decision, the

Tribunal made a distinction between the first cause of action and recurring or continuing cause of action.[161]

The former refers to a definite point in time when the requisite ingredients constituting a cause of action are satisfied for the first time. In other words, it is the first time that the petitioner or appellant has a right to obtain relief from the Tribunal. In contrast, the latter refers to each successive set of facts which, when independently considered, accord a similar right to the petitioner or appellant to invoke the jurisdiction of the Tribunal.

The NGT relied on the Supreme Court's decision in *State of Bihar v. Deokaran Nenshi & Anr.*[162] to make this distinction. In that case, the Supreme Court dealt with Sections 66 and 79 of the Mines Act, 1952, which, akin to Section 14 of the NGT Act, 2010, contained a limitation period of six months post the first cause of action. The Supreme Court held:[163]

> A continuing offence is one which is susceptible of continuance and is distinguishable from the one which is committed once and for all. It is one of those offences which arises out of a failure to obey or comply with a rule or its requirement and which involves a penalty, the liability for which continues until the rule or its requirement is obeyed or complied with. On every occasion that such disobedience or non-compliance occurs and recurs, there is the offence committed. The distinction between the two kinds of offences is between an act or omission which constitutes an offence once and for all and an act or omission which continues and therefore, constitutes a fresh offence every time of occasion on which it continues. In the case of a continuing offence, there is thus the ingredient of continuance of the offence which is absent in the case of an offence which takes place when an act or omission is committed once and for all.

Unlike Section 14 of the NGT Act, 2010, the Mines Act, 1952, contains a provision stating that in the event of a continuing offence, the period of limitation would be computed from each point of time during which the offence continues. Nevertheless, the NGT liberally construed cause of action under Section 14 to extend to encompass continuing cause of action. Accordingly, the Tribunal held that the grant of an environmental clearance was a separate cause of action from the environmental damage done to the ecosystem of the lake. Thus, it held that the limitation period would commence from the date of the subsequent cause of action.

Further, the NGT has clarified that the law of limitation is concerned with only the legal injury and not the consequences of the injury.[164] If a wrongful act causes a legal injury which is complete, there is no continuing wrong even though the ensuing damage may continue. In other words, there is a distinction between the continuance of a legal injury and the continuance of its injurious effects.[165]

An applicant has the right to invoke the jurisdiction of the NGT upon a single cause of action while claiming multiple reliefs therein. This is in consonance with Rule 14 of the National Green Tribunal (Practice and Procedure) Rules, 2011, which provides that several reliefs can be claimed by an applicant provided these reliefs are consequential to one another and are based on a single cause of action. Accordingly, different causes of action may result in the institution of different applications. Thus, there is an exclusion of joinder of causes of action under the 2011 Rules.[166]

Multiple causes of action can be of two types. First, causes of action that arise simultaneously and, second, causes of action that arise at different or successive points in time. In the former, the cause of action accrues at the time of completion of the wrong or injury. In the latter, however, if each subsequent cause of action is distinct and complete, it will give rise to a fresh cause of action at each subsequent time of occurrence.[167]

To this effect, the NGT has provided an illustrative example.[168] When an order granting or refusing an environmental clearance is passed, a right to approach the Tribunal accrues to an aggrieved person. Subsequently, if any of the terms of the environmental clearance are not fulfilled by the project proponent, a distinct cause of action arises, and a separate right accrues to an aggrieved person to approach the Tribunal. Thus, an aggrieved person who did not approach the NGT within the limitation period in the first instance can still separately approach the Tribunal by challenging the non-compliance of terms of the environmental clearance. In this case, the limitation period will commence from the date of non-compliance with the conditions of the environmental clearance.

Thus, a recurring or continuous cause of action may give rise to a fresh cause of action resulting in a fresh accrual of the right to sue. In such cases, the subsequent legal injury would be independent of the first legal injury and would accord an independent right to sue.[169] In addition, the NGT has clarified that the independent character of the recurring or continuing cause of action would not be materially altered simply due to the fact that it has a reference to an event which, although independent and complete, had occurred earlier.[170]

Accordingly, the NGT has interpreted the words "cause of action for such dispute *first arose*" (emphasis supplied) in Section 14 as not impacting the computation of limitation period in the event of an independent, composite, and recurring cause of action.[171] The concept of "cause of action first arose" is limited to the same event or series of events that have a direct linkage and the same source. In other words, while separate and independent causes of action give rise to a separate limitation period, acts which stem from the same event and are merely different stages of the same event do not invite a separate limitation period.

For instance, an appellant cannot challenge the legality of an environmental clearance at one stage and its impacts at a later stage. This is because both events have a common cause of action – that is, the grant of an environmental clearance. On the other hand, if the terms of the environmental clearance are amended subsequently, a new limitation period ensues as this gives rise to a separate cause of action.[172] Likewise, the non-compliance with the terms of the environmental clearance gives rise to a distinct cause of action.

Based on this reasoning, the NGT, in *Doaba Paryavaran Samiti v. Union of India*, has further elucidated on recurring or continuing cause of action.[173] The case dealt with harm caused to the wildlife and ecosystem of the Kedarnath Wildlife Sanctuary in Uttrakhand on account of a helicopter service. The helicopter service was started in 2006, and the petitioner had approached the Tribunal in 2015 – that is, nine years after the first cause of action arose.

The respondents argued that the petition was time barred as the phrase "cause of action ... when arose" under Section 14(3) ought to be literally interpreted. However, the Tribunal elaborated upon the distinction between the first cause of action and a continuing or recurring cause of action. It held that when an offence is committed and repeated, it is a case of a continuing offence. For instance, a project proponent commits a new offence each day that she operates her factory without a license.[174] The Tribunal relied on the Supreme Court's holding in *Maya Rani Punj v. Commissioner of Income Tax, Delhi*,[175] wherein the Court held that the non-filing of tax returns by a person gave rise to a fresh offence on each day of non-compliance. Therefore, the Tribunal held:[176]

> If the helicopters are flying at a height which is not permissible or without permission from the Board in accordance with law and are causing adverse impacts upon the above, each flight would be an independent cause of action which will be a recurring cause of action where the expression cause of action first arose appearing under Section 14(3) of the Act would not be attracted....

From the above discussion, we see that the NGT has furthered substantial justice by liberally construing when a cause of action first arises under Section 14(3). The NGT has been able to circumvent the practical challenges posed by a strict limitation period by reading the concept of continuing or recurring cause of action into the NGT Act 2010. Thus, the Tribunal has ensured that procedural hurdles do not come in the way of addressing environmental issues that have far-reaching consequences.

2.3.5.3   Threshold of Communication Required under Section 16

The limitation period of thirty days under Section 16 of the NGT Act, 2010, starts from the date when the order or decision is "communicated" to the appellant. In accordance with the justice-oriented approach of the Tribunal, the NGT has liberally interpreted communication to the appellant.

In *Sajal Kumar v. Union of India*,[177] an order granting environmental clearance for a coal mine was passed by the MoEF on 24 May 2012. An appeal challenging the environmental clearance should have been filed within thirty days of this order – that is, on 13 July 2012. However, admittedly, the appeal was filed on 30 August 2012.

The appellant claimed that he had not received any intimation of the order passed by the MoEF. He argued that the order was not displayed on the website or in any newspaper and, thus, he did not have sufficient information to file an effective appeal within the thirty-day time period under Section 16. Further, he argued that a copy of the order was not made publicly available before 27 July 2012 by the Public Information Officer at the Chhattisgarh Environment Conservation Board. The respondents countered by producing newspaper articles published shortly after the granting of the environmental clearance. These articles stated that such an order had been passed by the MoEF and gave technical details regarding the address and capacity of the coal mine.

The NGT, in arriving at its decision, relied on the six guidelines of the Supreme Court in *Collector, Land Acquisition, Anantnag*.[178] It held that there was no negligence on the part of the appellants as the order granting the environmental clearance was not uploaded on MoEF's website until after the thirty-day period had elapsed.

Further, the Tribunal held that the communication needed to be effective. Accordingly, publishing information in newspapers that an order granting environmental clearance had been passed amounted to a "cryptic notice" and was not enough to meet the threshold of communication required under Section 16 of the NGT Act, 2010. It held that communication of the order was necessary to equip the appellant with adequate information to file an effective appeal. Accordingly, the MoEF ought to have published the entire order and not just information related to its passing.

In *Save Mon Region Federation & Anr. v. Union of India*, an environmental clearance was granted by the MoEF for the construction of a 780 MW hydroelectric project in Arunachal Pradesh.[179] Several environmentally sensitive citizens of the Monpa indigenous community challenged the environmental clearance due to environmental concerns. Admittedly, the appeal was filed after the thirty-day period under Section 16. However, it was within the sixty-day extension period provided in the proviso to the section. One of the main preliminary issues before the NGT related to which date the limitation period would begin. In other words, the Tribunal had to determine the date from which the order granting the environmental clearance was deemed to be "communicated" to the appellant.

In arriving at the answer, the NGT discussed the threshold for communication required under Section 16. Let us look at the relevant excerpts from the judgment to understand the Tribunal's reasoning in more detail:

National Green Tribunal

(Principal Bench, New Delhi)

SAVE MON REGION FEDERATION & ANR. v. UNION OF INDIA

[Appeal No. 39 of 2012, Order Dated 14 March 2013]

Swatanter Kumar, J. (Chairperson);

P. Jyothimani, J. (Judicial Member);

Dr. D.K. Agrawal (Expert Member);

Dr. G.K. Pandey (Expert Member);

A.R. Yousuf (Expert Member)

*　　*　　*

Relevant Extracts:

1.   The Ministry of Environment and Forests (for short 'MoEF') accorded clearance for construction of 780 Mega Watts Naymjang Chhu Hydroelectric Project in Tawang district of Arunachal Pradesh. The applicant is an organization based in Tawang, consisting of citizens of Monpa indigenous community who advocate environmentally and culturally sensitive development in the ecologically and geologically fragile, seismically active and culturally sensitive Mon-Tawang region of the State. The applicant being aggrieved from the order dated 19th April, 2012 has preferred an appeal questioning the legality and correctness of the said order.

2.   The appeal apparently and admittedly has been filed beyond 30 days from the date of communication of the order to the appellant. The appeal being barred by time, is accompanied by an application (MA No. 104 of 2012) praying for condonation of delay in filing the appeal. In view of the objections raised with regard to the maintainability of the appeal in as much as it is barred by time, we have to deal with the question of limitation at the first instance and before we dwell upon the merits of the case. Thus, in view of the limited controversy, we shall refer only to the necessary facts relating to the application for condonation of delay.

3.   The MoEF granted Environmental Clearance to the project vide its order dated 19th April, 2012. According to the applicant he received no information of passing of the order till 17th May, 2012, when the applicant visited Delhi and came to know that a news item had appeared, mentioning about the environmental clearance. On 15th May, 2012, one Himanshu Thakker informed the MoEF that its website had no information of the

said Environmental Clearance. He also mentioned of the non-availability of the compliance reports on the website. Even the Central Information Commissioner had passed an order on 18th January, 2012 stating that the Environmental Clearance should be uploaded on the website at the earliest and should be available to the public. Immediate non-placing of the order dated 19th April, 2012 on the website, thus, was in violation of the order of the Central Information Commissioner dated 18th January, 2012. The MoEF uploaded the order on its website on 22nd May, 2012. However, still as per the email of the Director of MoEF dated 5th June, 2012, (Annexure R1/2) the Environmental Clearance could not be made available as on that date. In this email to Himanshu Thakker the Director (MoEF) stated that she had tried her level best to upload the Environmental Clearance but there were glitches in the synchronization of their new website with the old one. The said order could only be downloaded by the applicant from the website of MoEF on 8th June, 2012, the date on which applicant claims the completion of communication of the order. The applicant could download the copy of the Scoping (ToR) Clearance granted to the Project Proponent only on 24th June, 2012. The applicant came to Delhi on 4th July, 2012 for obtaining Form-I, which was received by him on 12th July, 2012. He filed the appeal on 17th/18th July, 2012, i.e. on the 90th day from the date of clearance, i.e. 19th April, 2012. It is further the contention of the applicant that he got copy of the Environmental Clearance only on 8th June, 2012 and could prepare the appeal on 17th July, 2012 which was received in the Registry of the NGT on 18th July, 2012. Therefore, according to the applicant, the appeal has been filed within the extended period of 60 days but beyond the prescribed limitation of 30 days and there being sufficient cause for non-filing of the appeal within 30 days, the delay in filing the appeal may be condoned and the appeal be heard on merits.

4. The MoEF, in its reply, has taken up the stand that the minutes of the Expert Appraisal Committee (EAC) for the River Valley and the Hydro Electric Power (HEP) Projects are displayed on the Ministry's website in a timely manner. It is admitted that the Environmental Clearance was granted to the applicant on 19th April, 2012 and was displayed on the website on 22nd May, 2012. In terms of EIA Notification 2006, the Project Proponent was required to submit the EIA and EMP reports along with the proceedings of public hearing as prayed.... According to the MoEF, even after getting the copy of the Environmental Clearance on 8th June, 2012, the appeal has not been filed within 30 days and as such, the applicant cannot shift the burden onto the Ministry on the ground of negligence, omission and carelessness.

9. In the rejoinder filed on behalf of the applicant, besides reiterating the facts already noted, it has also been averred that the Project Proponent, Respondent No.3, to whom the Environmental Clearance was granted, has no website in existence even till date. Also, the website of the MoEF does not reflect the complete information. It is contended that the expression 'date on which the order is communicated to him' appearing in the relevant provisions of the NGT Act signifies not merely constructive communication but the actual communication, satisfying all mandatory requirements. The Environmental Clearance was not available on the website of the MoEF till 8th June, 2012....

10. Undisputedly and admittedly, this is not a case where the appeal has been filed beyond the period of 90 days (i.e. within 30 days from the date of which the order or decision is communicated to him plus further period of 60 days, as permissible under the NGT Act). Thus, we are called upon to decide if there exists sufficient cause for filing the appeal beyond 30 days but within 90 days from the date of communication of the order.

11. The framers of law have worded the limitation provision somewhat differently. It has been worded in the negative language by stating that the Tribunal could condone the delay where the appeal is filed beyond 30 days but not exceeding the further period of 60 days. The legislative intent of applying the period of limitation with its rigors to the appeals under the NGT Act, is clear and unambiguous from the language of the Section itself. The bare reading of the above provision shows that legislature has used the following significant expressions which require clear interpretation by the Tribunal:

    a. Within a period of 30 days from the date on which the order or decision or direction or determination is communicated to him.

    b. If the Tribunal is satisfied that the appellant was prevented by sufficient cause from filing the appeal within the said period.

    c. Allow it to file an appeal within a further period not exceeding 60 days.

    ... Thus, we are required to examine the interpretation and application of these expressions to enable us to appropriately address and answer the controversy in issue in the present case.

13. The legislature, in its wisdom, has used the expression 'communicated to him' under Section 16 of the NGT Act in contradistinction to 'serving', 'receiving', 'delivery' or 'passing' of the order. Normally, these are the expressions which are used in the provisions relating to limitation. Generally, limitation is to be reckoned from the date which is relatable to these expressions. For instance,

the period of limitation may commence from the date the order is received by or served upon an individual, as presented in the relevant provisions. The expression 'communication' is neither synonymous nor even equivalent in law to the above mentioned expressions. The above-mentioned expressions require merely a unilateral act, that is, dispatch of the order, receipt of the order or service of the order upon an individual. But the act of communication cannot be completed unilaterally. It does require the element of participation by two persons, one who initiates communication and the other to whom the communication is addressed and who receives the same, i.e. the intended receiver.

At this stage, we may examine what is the legal meaning and connotation of the expression 'communication'. "Communication" is initiated by transforming a thought into words, act and expression. It is then converted into a message which is transmitted to the receiver. The receiver understands the message. It may or may not evoke a response. There may be cases where only the sender and the receiver alone are not of significance but even the channel of communication may have some importance. The Black's Law Dictionary, 9th Edition, explains 'communication' as:

> "1. The expression or exchange of information by speech, writing, gestures, or conduct; the process of bringing an idea to another's perception.
>
> 2. The information so expressed or exchanged."

16. ... [It] is clear that 'communication' is made by one and received by another. It requires sufficient knowledge of the basic facts constituting the communication. The action of communicating is precisely sharing of knowledge by one with another of the thing communicated. Communication, particularly to the public, has to be by methods of mass communication, like satellite, website, newspapers etc. 'Communicated' is a strong word. It requires that sufficient knowledge of basic facts constituting the grounds of the order should be imparted fully and effectively to the person.

17. The expression 'is communicated to him', thus, would invite strict construction. It is expected that the order which a person intends to challenge is communicated to him, if not in *personam* than in *rem* by placing it in the public domain. 'Communication' would, thus, contemplate complete knowledge of the ingredients and grounds required under law for enabling that person to challenge the order. 'Intimation' must not be understood to be communication. 'Communication' is an expression of definite connotation and meaning and it requires the authority passing the order to put the same in the public domain by using proper means of communication. Such

Communication will be complete when the order is received by him in one form or the other to enable him to appropriately challenge the correctness of the order passed.

18. Law gives a right to 'any person' who is 'aggrieved' by an order to prefer an appeal. The term 'any person' has to be widely construed. It is to include all legal entities so as to enable them to prefer an appeal, even if such an entity does not have any direct or indirect interest in a given project. The expression 'aggrieved', again, has to be construed liberally. The framers of law intended to give the right to any person aggrieved, to prefer an appeal without any limitation as regards his locus or interest. The grievance of a person against the Environmental Clearance may be general and not necessarily person specific. This provision of Section 16 requires communication of the order to such person(s). The expression 'him' takes within its ambit 'any person' who is aggrieved by an order. Therefore, the expression 'communication' accordingly has to receive a more generic and at the same time, definite meaning. The nature of the communication has to be such that it reaches the public at large, as that appears to be the legislative intent. A person is expected to, and can, only act when the order is put in public domain. He is expected to download the same from the website of the concerned Ministry/Department, and if he so requires thereafter, make an application for receiving specific information. However, the content of the order is required to be communicated by the MoEF as well as by the Project Proponent.

19. The limitation as prescribed under Section 16 of the NGT Act, shall commence from the date the order is communicated. As already noticed, communication of the order has to be by putting it in the public domain for the benefit of the public at large. The day the MoEF shall put the complete order of Environmental Clearance on its website and when the same can be downloaded without any hindrance or impediments and also put the order on its public notice board, the limitation be reckoned from that date. The limitation may also trigger from the date when the Project Proponent uploads the Environmental Clearance order with its environmental conditions and safeguards upon its website as well as publishes the same in the newspapers as prescribed under Regulation 10 of the Environmental Clearance Regulations, 2006. It is made clear that such obligation of uploading the order on the website by the Project Proponent shall be complete only when it can simultaneously be downloaded without delay and impediments. The limitation could also commence when the Environmental Clearance order is displayed by the local bodies, Panchayats and Municipal Bodies along with the concerned departments of the State Government displaying the same in the manner afore-indicated. Out of the three points, from which the limitation

could commence and be computed, the earliest in point of time shall be the relevant date and it will have to be determined with reference to the facts of each case. The applicant must be able to download or know from the public notice the factum of the order as well as its content in regard to environmental conditions and safeguards imposed in the order of Environmental Clearance. Mere knowledge or deemed knowledge of order cannot form the basis for reckoning the period of limitation.

*   *   *

Thus, communication of the order or decision in question needs to be effective to qualify as communication under Section 16 of the NGT Act, 2010. To be effective, the communication needs to equip any aggrieved person from the public with sufficient knowledge of the basic facts and contents of the order in question. It needs to equip such an aggrieved person with sufficient knowledge to file an effective appeal. Merely publicizing the fact that an order has been passed is not enough. All the relevant contents of the order need to be publicized as well.

Further, given that the publication needs to be made to the public, it needs to be made through means of mass communication such as newspapers and the website of the authority concerned. Accordingly, such dissemination of necessary information will only be complete when the same is readily accessible to the public. In other words, the order or decision would be deemed to be communicated to the public when it is readily downloadable or accessible from the concerned website without delay or impediments. Therefore, the limitation period of thirty days provided under Section 16 commences from the date on which the order under challenge is fully accessible by the public at large.

2.4   DETERMINATION OF ENVIRONMENTAL COMPENSATION

Environmental compensation is the bedrock of environmental adjudication.[180] In addition to ensuring substantive and distributive environmental justice, a strong environmental compensation regime reflects the ability of the adjudicatory body to address complex issues affecting the environment. In other words, in addition to compensating the affected stakeholders, the determination of compensation reflects the quality of scientific analysis undertaken by the Tribunal. It demonstrates both the accuracy of the Tribunal's assessment of environmental damage in a case and how effectively it dealt with scientific uncertainty.

As noted in Chapter 1, one of the foremost reasons for the creation of the NGT was that the higher judiciary found itself to be ill-equipped to scientifically determine the quantum of environmental damage. Since the environmental damage was not usually scientifically assessed, the ensuing environmental compensation also bore less semblance to the actual damage.

This was starkly exemplified in the aftermath of the infamous Bhopal Gas Tragedy in December 1984. Officially, the leakage of methyl isocyanate from the premises of Union Carbide India Limited caused the death of approximately 3,000 people and exposed over 500,000 people to the toxic fumes.[181] The unofficial number is significantly higher. Estimates state that at least 15,000 to 20,000 people have died prematurely in the subsequent two decades after the disaster.[182] In fact, children continue to be born with mental and bodily impairments even today.[183] The tragedy has been termed as one of the worst human-induced disasters in history.

In addition to the catastrophic impact on human lives, the ensuing environmental damage has been devastating. Several thousands of animals were killed, and the poisonous gas was absorbed into local rivers and water bodies, making them hazardous for fish and local consumption. Further, the gas was absorbed by the soil in neighbouring fields, making the vegetation and crops unfit for human or animal consumption.[184]

Despite such disastrous consequences to human health and environment, the Supreme Court failed to hold Union Carbide proportionately liable. In total, the Court levied an environmental compensation on the company amounting to a mere USD 470 million (approximately INR 715 crore then). The compensation amount was based on a disputed estimate that only 3,000 people had died and 102,000 people suffered permanent disabilities on account of the gas leak. While the decades following the gas leak have demonstrated conclusively that these estimates were flawed, the amount was not even enough to adequately compensate the persons included.[185]

Further, the compensation ordered by the Court was negligible in comparison to the corresponding multi-billion dollar lawsuit filed by a lawyer in the United States (US).[186] Upon the announcement of the court settlement and the compensation amount, the shares of Union Carbide rose 7 per cent in value.[187] Had the compensation awarded by the Supreme Court been paid at the same rate as that awarded by US courts to asbestosis victims (Union Carbide had mined asbestosis between 1963 and 1985), the liability of the company would have been more than USD 10 billion – that is, twenty times the compensation levied.[188] In fact, subsequently, the Central government moved the Supreme Court in December 2010 and demanded additional compensation on account of the disaster to the tune of INR 7,844 crore (more than USD 1 billion).[189]

It is a matter of public record that Union Carbide did not cooperate with the Indian government and the Supreme Court.[190] It tried to manipulate and suppress scientific data relating to the gas leak. Even to date, the company has not conclusively revealed details relating to the chemical composition of the gas cloud that killed thousands of people to enable effective treatment. Adding insult to injury, Union Carbide did not even clean up its industrial site properly after discontinuing operations in India. For more than two decades after the closure, the plant kept spewing toxic and poisonous chemicals that percolated into local water bodies and groundwater.[191]

In addition to highlighting the lack of environmental regulations and laws, the entire incident revealed the judiciary's inability to scientifically assess environmental damage and compensation. In the aftermath of the disaster, with the aim of strengthening environmental protection, the legislature enacted several environmental regulations, inter alia, such as the Environment Protection Act, 1986, Hazardous Waste (Management and Handling) Rules, 1989, and the Environmental Impact Assessment Notification, 1994. Though the Water Act, 1974, and Air Act, 1981, existed prior to the gas leak, the new laws enacted (especially the Environmental Protection Act, 1986) ensured effective coordination between existing state and central authorities.

In addition, the Supreme Court subsequently developed environmental jurisprudence in a manner that held polluters accountable. In addition to using doctrines such as polluter pays, precautionary principle, and sustainable development, the Court modified and adapted the application of tortious principles such as strict liability and absolute liability in environmental cases.[192]

Despite the enactment of these new laws and the Supreme Court's stringent approach, it was felt that the judiciary was not equipped to quantify environmental damage and award proportionate compensation. For instance, while courts applied the principle of sustainable development, both parties produced differing scientific expert views about how much environmental compensation was necessary to achieve sustainable development. Adding to this, as noted in Chapter 1, the inherent scientific uncertainty contained in most estimates made it more difficult for the judiciary to award proportionate environmental compensation.

Thus, the NGT was created with a view to furthering environmental justice through scientific calculation of environmental damage and compensation. This is necessary to ensure adequate rehabilitation of humans and the environment. Accordingly, Section 15 of the NGT Act, 2010, states that the Tribunal may provide:

a) Relief and compensation to victims of pollution and other environmental damage arising under the enactments specified in Schedule I (including accidents arising out of handling of hazardous wastes)
b) Restitution of damaged property
c) Restitution of environment

This restitution and compensation levied by the NGT is in addition to the relief payable under the Public Liability Insurance Act, 1991.[193] Further, the Tribunal can choose to divide the compensation or relief payable under separate heads specified under Schedule II, which include[194]

a) Death
b) Permanent, temporary, total or partial disability or other injury or sickness
c) Loss of wages due to total or partial disability or permanent or temporary disability

d) Medical expenses incurred for treatment of injuries or sickness
e) Damages to private property
f) Expenses incurred by the government or any local authority in providing relief, aid, and rehabilitation to the affected persons
g) Expenses incurred by the government for any administrative or legal action or to cope with any harm or damage, including compensation for environmental degradation and restoration of the quality of environment
h) Loss to the government or local authority arising out of, or connected with, the activity causing any damage
i) Claims on account of any harm, damage, or destruction to the fauna including milch and draught animals and aquatic fauna
j) Claims on account of any harm, damage, or destruction to flora including aquatic flora, crops, vegetables, trees, and orchards
k) Claims including cost of restoration on account of any harm or damage to environment including pollution of soil, air, water, land, and eco-systems
l) Loss and destruction of any property other than private property
m) Loss of business or employment or both
n) Any other claim arising out of, or connected with, any activity of handling of hazardous substance

Section 17 further states that where the death or injury is caused to any person (excluding a workman or workwoman) or property on account of an accident or an activity governed by any enactment specified under Schedule I, the person responsible for the pollution should be liable to pay compensation or relief under all or any of the heads specified above. In addition, if such death or injury cannot be attributed to any single activity and is a combined or resultant effect of several such activities, then the NGT may apportion liability and compensation amongst those responsible on an equitable basis.[195]

While the NGT Act, 2010, provides suggestive heads under which compensation can be awarded, depending on the circumstances of each case, the NGT wields significant discretion in relation to the assessment and quantum of compensation. The only guidance with respect to the calculation of such compensation is under Section 20, which simply states that the Tribunal should apply the principle of sustainable development, precautionary principle, and the polluter pays principle while passing an order or award. Thus, the Tribunal has complete discretion in relation to determining the manner of rehabilitation, restitution, relief, and compensation to be awarded.

This discretion is necessary to allow the Tribunal's technical and scientific expertise to come into play. Let us now explore the dominant trends in the Tribunal's awarding of compensation and analyse whether it has been able to utilize its scientific expertise to fill the void left by the higher judiciary. Subsequently, we will exemplify these trends through a case study on *Manoj Mishra v. Union of India.*[196] Thereafter, through a comparative analysis, we will highlight what the NGT can learn about compensation determination from courts in the US and United Kingdom (UK). This will entail a discussion of the Resource Equivalence Analysis approach.

2.4.1 DOMINANT TRENDS IN THE NGT'S DETERMINATION OF COMPENSATION

As noted, the legislative intent to confer wide discretion on the NGT in determining and awarding compensation is apparent from the scheme of the NGT Act. The NGT Act, 2010, does not prescribe any minimum or maximum amount of compensation that needs to be given. Due to this wide discretion, the NGT has been able to award unprecedented sums of environmental compensation. For instance, in February 2016, the NGT ordered companies involved in illegal mining along the river Yamuna to pay INR 252.5 crore as environmental compensation.[197] More recently, in February 2018, the NGT awarded INR 195 crore as compensation payable to compensate for the environmental damage caused by M/s Goel Ganga Developers India Pvt. Ltd. due to illegal construction activities.[198] While these high compensation amounts are a much-needed change, further scrutiny through analysis of case law reveals that they are an exception and not the norm.

The recent trend of the NGT with respect to determining environmental compensation in cases involving a lack of consent to operate seems to be to make the project proponent pay between 5 per cent and 10 per cent of the project cost.[199] This trend started in 2014 when the NGT arbitrarily adopted[200] the Supreme Court's approach to determining compensation in *Goa Foundation v. Union of India & Ors.*[201]

In *Goa Foundation*, the Supreme Court was faced with the issue of determining the environmental damage caused due to certain illegal mining in Goa. In arriving at the compensation amount, the Court held that the project proponents would have to pay 10 per cent of the "sale proceeds" to a public fund – Goan Iron Ore Permanent Fund – as compensation.[202] The Court felt that this was an appropriate compensation, given that mining could not be completely stopped due to its contribution towards employment and revenue generation for the state.[203] Accordingly, it held that if mining had to continue, determining compensation on the basis of sale proceeds would be apt as it would directly impact the profitability of the project.[204]

This approach adopted by the Supreme Court, however, was not intended to be a precedent for determining environmental compensation in all cases. This is evident from the fact that the Court had specifically based its decision on the special considerations prevalent in the case due to the economic significance of mining in Goa. In fact, to arrive at the compensation amount as 10 per cent of the sale proceeds, the Court had relied on its earlier decision in *Samaj Parivartana Samudaya v. State of Karnataka*,[205] wherein it had held that 10 per cent of the sale proceeds from the sale of iron ore should be used as compensation.

Thus, the approach, at best, can be a precedent for cases involving illegal mining in regions such as Goa. Clearly, considerations of the state's dependency on mining for revenue and employment generation had gone into arriving at the compensation. Thus, had the considerations been different – in that the Supreme Court was concerned with an activity which did not contribute largely to the State's overall economic development – and had the Supreme Court banned mining altogether, it is very likely that the approach to determining compensation would have been significantly different.

However, the NGT has, without paying heed to this context in *Goa Foundation*, co-opted this approach in several cases that have had very different considerations.[206] This was first exemplified in *Forward Foundation v. State of Karnataka*.[207] The case dealt with unauthorized construction in a Special Economic Zone by two companies without receiving the requisite environmental clearance.[208] Even after receiving the environmental clearance, the companies continued to flout the conditions stipulated therein.[209] The NGT, in its judgment, observed that the project fell under the ecologically sensitive area between the Agara and Bellandur lakes and was a threat to the entire ecosystem. Additionally, the project activities affected the wetlands and stormwater drains.[210] Despite the serious environmental damage involved, the NGT unduly co-opted the Supreme Court's approach in *Goa Foundation* and imposed an environmental penalty amounting to a mere 5 per cent of the project cost.[211] Let us analyse the relevant portions of the judgment below.

National Green Tribunal

(Principal Bench, New Delhi)

THE FORWARD FOUNDATION: A CHARITABLE TRUST & ORS. v. STATE OF KARNATAKA & ORS.

[Original Application No. 222 of 2014, Order Dated 7 May 2015]

Swatanter Kumar, J. (Chairperson);
U.D. Slavi, J. (Judicial Member);
Dr. D.K. Agrawal (Expert Member);
A.R. Yousuf (Expert Member)

*   *   *

Relevant Extracts:

1.   … The three applicants are either a registered charitable trust and/ or a Society, registered under the relevant laws in force. They claim to be keenly interested in protecting the environment and ecology, particularly, in the State of Karnataka. Their principal grievance is in relation to certain commercial projects that are being developed by respondent nos. 9 & 10 in a large-sized, mixed use development project/building complex, including setting up of a SEZ park, Hotels, Residential Apartments and a Mall,

covering approximately 80 acres on the valley land immediately abutting the Agara Lake and more particularly identified as lying between Agara and Bellandur Lakes, exposing the entire eco system to severe threat of environmental degradation and consequential damage. According to them, it is of alarming significance that the Project has encroached an Ecologically Sensitive Area, namely, the valley and the catchment area and Rajakaluves (Storm Water Drains) which drains rain water into the Bellandur Lake. Thus, in the interest of environment and ecology, they have approached the Tribunal with the above prayers.

2. Shorn of any unnecessary details, the precise facts leading to the filing of this application are that, according to these applicants, the ecologically sensitive land was allotted by the Karnataka Industrial Area Development Board (for short the 'KIADB'), respondent no. 7 herein, to respondent nos. 9 & 10 vide Notifications dated 23rd April, 2004 and 7th May, 2004, respectively. This land was allotted for setting up of Software Technology Park, Commercial and Residential complex, hotel and Multi Level Car Parks. The Master Plan formulated by the Bangalore Development Authority (for short the 'BDA'), respondent no. 8, identifies the allotted land as 'Residential Sensitive', though the same land was identified in the draft Master Plan as 'Protected Zone'. It is stated by the applicant that the Revenue Map in respect of properties as referred in the land lease Agreements has multiple Rajakaluves. The development projects in question sit right on the catchment and wetland areas which feeds the Rajakaluves, which in turn drain rain water into Bellandur Lake. The project will thus encroach two Rajakaluves of 1.38 acres and 1.23 acres each. The satellite digital images of the area from year 2000 to 2012 clearly show encroachment upon these Rajakaluves, as well as, the manner in which they are covered by this construction. The State Level Expert Appraisal Committee (for short the 'SEAC'), which was to assist State Level Environment Impact Assessment Authority (for short the 'SEIAA'), held its meetings on various dates to examine the project. It had required respondent no. 9 to submit a revised NOC from the Bangalore Water Supply and Sewerage Board (for short the 'BWSSB'), respondent no. 5 herein, for the project in question. It was also observed that the project lies between the above stated two lakes. Respondent no. 9 was also directed to take protective measures to spare the buffer zone around Rajakaluves and also to commit that no construction would be carried out in the buffer zone. In the meeting of 11th November, 2011, it was recorded that the project proposes car parking facility for 14,438 cars in that environmentally sensitive area.

3. It is the case of respondent no. 5 that such NOC was issued but it covers only an area of 17,404 sq mtr, whereas the total built up area as noted by the SEAC

is 13,50,454.98 sq mtr. It is alleged by the applicants that respondent no. 9 obtained NOC from respondent no. 5 by concealing material facts and by misrepresenting that NOC is required only for residential units, which forms a very minuscule part of the total project.... The applicant contends that the grant of consent by the KSPCB to respondent no. 9 also contained a condition with regard to obtaining Environmental Clearance from the Competent Authority and no construction was to commence until such clearance was granted.

4.   According to the applicants, respondent no. 9 violated the conditions and commenced construction of the project. There was also violation of the stipulations stated in the approval of the SEAC, in relation to buffer zone and construction over Rajakaluves. The construction has been commenced over the ecologically sensitive area of the Lake Catchment area and valley, with utter disregard to the statutory compliances. Referring to these blatant irregularities the applicant submits that the conversion of land from 'Protected Zone' to 'Residential Sensitive' area is violative of the law. The Project is right in the midst of a fragile wetland area which ought not to have been disturbed by the development activity. The fragile environment of the catchment area has been exposed to grave and irreparable damage. It has severely disturbed and damaged the Rajakaluves. It is also alleged that respondent nos. 9 & 10 have started to level the land by filling it with debris, thus causing damage to the drains. It is further stated that the conditions with regard to no-disturbance to the Storm Water Drains, natural valleys and buffer area in and around the Rajakaluves have been violated. This has in turn, affected the ground water table and bore wells which are the only source of water for thousands of households. Fishing and agriculture which depends on Bellandur Lake are also severely affected.... It is submitted that SEIAA in its meeting dated 29th September, 2012, decided to close the file pertaining to respondent nos. 10 due to non-submission of requisite information and the application therefore was rejected in November, 2012. Despite the rejection, respondent no. 10 commenced construction on the project in full swing.

79.   The cumulative effect of the above discussion would be that there is a definite possibility of environment, ecology, lakes and the wetlands being adversely affected by these projects. There are multiple public authorities including SEIAA involved in regulating such projects and they are also responsible for protecting interest of environment and ecology while keeping in mind the settled canon of sustainable development. It is the contention of the respondent nos. 9 and 10 that there are large numbers of other projects located around these lakes. If that be so, then we have no hesitation in observing that various regulatory authorities including SEIAA ought to have examined the

cumulative Environmental Impact Assessment in these cases on the water bodies as the protection of the water bodies, the wetland and the catchment areas of the lakes is the obligation of these authorities.

80. It was vehemently contended before us that the construction of the projects is nearing completion and huge money of respondent nos. 9 and 10 including investments made by various land and other area purchasers is at stake. Thus, according to these respondents, the application should be declined by the Tribunal only on that fact. We are not impressed with this contention at all. The respondents have started the construction even prior to the grant of Environmental Clearance and instigated the public to invest money. They cannot be permitted to take advantage of their own wrong. However, it may also not be in the interest of justice and particularly, while applying the Principle of Sustainable Development in terms of Section 20 of the NGT Act, that these properties be demolished but that does not mean that they should not be directed to take all measures and precautions, even if it results in necessary demolition of some parts of the projects in the interest of environment, ecology and protection of lakes and wetlands. It cannot be disputed that there is serious scarcity of water in the city of Bangalore. Impact of these projects on water bodies ought to have been of fundamental consideration before the authorities concerned. In our considered view, they have failed to take complete notice of this fact and act objectively in light of the laws in force.

81. The project proponents, i.e. respondent nos. 9 and 10 submitted their respective applications for grant of Environmental Clearance to the concerned authorities in the year 2011 and 2012 respectively. The Environmental Clearance was granted to the Project proponents on 17th February, 2012 and 30th September, 2013 respectively. However, construction activities had been carried out by the project proponents much prior to the grant of Environmental Clearance. There is not even an iota, much less valid, reason placed by the project proponents before the Tribunal as to why the applications for Environmental Clearance were moved at such belated stage and why construction was started prior to grant of Environmental Clearance. The provisions of the EIA Notification, 2006 which was in force at all relevant times does not permit carrying on of any construction or any other activity in relation to the project prior to the grant of Environmental Clearance…. The project proponents are clear defaulters of compliance of the statutory provisions. They cannot take advantage of their own wrong of raising construction prior to submission of the application for Environmental Clearance and even grant of Environmental Clearance. The respondent nos. 9 & 10 are intentional defaulters. They violated the law being fully conscious of their obligations under different laws

in force. The authorities concerned had sanctioned the building plans of these respondents subject to a specific stipulation that such sanction was subject to grant of other clearances including Environmental Clearance under different laws. Since the construction and allied activities were being carried on contrary to law, they even would be deemed to have caused pollution not only of the environment but more particularly of the lakes and caused obstructions of the Rajakaluves in the area. Applying the Principle of 'Polluter Pays' as contemplated under Section 20 of the NGT Act, the project proponents must be held liable to pay compensation for restoration and restitution of the environmental pollution and degradation. There is sufficient material on record to show that there has been environmental degradation. From the date of grant of Environmental Clearance, the construction is supposed to be carried on in accordance the conditions of the Environmental Clearance and with due protection of the environment, which the respondents have failed to comply with. The project proponents are liable to pay compensation under the 'Polluter Pays' Principle, for the illegal and unauthorised construction carried on in violation of the environmental laws and prior to grant of Environmental Clearance. One who violates law renders itself liable for consequences of such violations. The mining, excavation and construction work adversely affected the Lakes and the Rajakaluves. The possible risk and degradation, due to construction and operation of the project include actual damage and even threats to environment and ecology pertaining to pollution, encroachment, eutrophication, illegal mining of soil, loss of Biodiversity, ungoverned human activities and cultural misuse. The consequential damage and degradation of environment and ecology from the activities of these projects can broadly be placed under two distinct heads, while invoking the Polluter Pays Principle.

82.   It may not be possible to determine the above compensation with exactitude but that does not mean that the project proponents can avoid liability in that regard…. The afore-noticed project activities and construction started much prior to moving of application and grant of Environmental Clearance. The principle which has often been adopted by the Courts, including the Hon'ble Supreme Court in the case of *Goa Foundation v. Union of India and Ors.*, (2014) 6 SCC 590, is to direct deposit of certain percentage of the cost of the project at the first instance. In the case of Goa Foundation, the Supreme Court had directed deposit of 10 per cent of the value of the mineral extracted. In the case of Krishankant Singh v. National Ganga River Basin Authority 2014 ALL (I) NGT REPORTER 3 DELHI 1, this Tribunal directed Simbhaoli Sugar Mills which had operated without consent of the concerned Board for a long period and had polluted the environment, Phuldera drain as well as the underground water, to pay a compensation of Rs. Five Crores.

The said sugar factory had operated with the consent of the Board prior and subsequent to this period. The compensation was imposed for flouting the law and for causing the pollution. It may be noticed that the appeal against the said judgment of the Tribunal was dismissed by the Supreme Court in Civil Appeal No. Civil Appeal No. 10434 OF 2014 vide its order dated 21st January, 2015. This liability primarily accrues on account of the illegal and unauthorised activities carried on by the Project Proponents. These are purely commercial ventures of respondent nos. 9 & 10 to make high profits, while causing environmental and ecological degradation and also by carrying on illegal and unauthorised activities, particularly, for the period prior to grant of Environmental Clearance.

83. ... We have already indicated that at this stage the entire amount of compensation payable on various counts by the Project Proponent cannot be determined with exactitude, however, liability to pay for violation of law, raising construction unauthorizedly and illegally, renders the Project Proponent liable to pay the environmental compensation forthwith. The final amounts for restoration of environment and ecology would be determined by the Committee constituted in this judgment. We are of the considered view that 10 per cent of the project cost may be somewhat on the higher side and to maintain the equitable balance between the default and the consequential liability of the applicant, we direct the Project Proponents to pay at the first instance compensation for their default at the rate of 5 per cent of the cost of the project. In light of this, Respondent No. 10 would be liable to pay a sum of Rs 22.5 crores and Respondent No. 9 would be liable to pay a sum of 117.35 crores.

* * *

NOTES AND QUESTIONS

1. The NGT highlights the serious environmental damage that has taken place due to the illegal construction activities of the project proponent. In particular, the illegal mining, excavation, and construction work adversely affected the lakes and the *rajakaluves* (canals that were responsible for the water flow into the lakes). There was a substantial loss of soil cover, biodiversity, and the entire ecosystem near the lakes. Do you think that the NGT's methodology for determining compensation sufficiently addresses the ecological damage caused?
2. The NGT holds that the precise amount of environmental compensation cannot be ascertained with exactitude. However, it relies on the Supreme Court's approach

to compensation in *Goa Foundation* and imposes an environmental compensation amounting to approximately INR 140 crore (INR 22.5 crore + INR 117.35 crore). Based on our prior discussion on *Goa Foundation*, wherein we highlighted the case-specific considerations on which the Supreme Court based its assessment of compensation, do you think that the NGT's co-option of the same approach was appropriate in the present case?

Further, the Court had held that 10 per cent of the "sale proceeds" would be the appropriate compensation as this would directly impact the profitability of the project. In contrast, the NGT awarded 5 per cent of the "project cost" as compensation. Do you think this is appropriate? Although the Tribunal relied on *Goa Foundation* for determining compensation, do you think the approach adopted by the NGT differs significantly from the approach adopted by the Court? Practically, what would be the difference between basing compensation as a percentage of the sale proceeds and the project cost?

3. What do you think is the consequence of pegging environmental compensation to a variable relating to the project's balance sheet or income statement? Should this be made a blanket practice for all cases involving a lack of consent to operate? Further, do you think such an approach incentivizes potential polluters to pollute if the project is still profitable after taking into account the eventual environmental compensation?

4. The Tribunal states that the project proponents must be held liable to "pay compensation for restoration and restitution of the environmental pollution and degradation". However, it does not engage in a detailed analysis of the extent of environmental degradation caused. In fact, the reason that the Tribunal holds that the environmental compensation cannot be determined with exactitude is that the Tribunal does not adequately determine the extent of environmental damage caused. While INR 140 crore (approximately) seems to be a large sum of money when seen in isolation, it might be inadequate if the actual amount required for restoration and restitution of the environment is more. Thus, do you think that pegging environmental compensation at 5 per cent of the project cost, irrespective of the actual environmental damage, is appropriate? If no, what would an alternative method be for determining compensation?

*   *   *

As seen from the relevant excerpts of the judgment, the NGT arbitrarily co-opts the Supreme Court's approach to compensation without paying heed to the specific factual context present in *Goa Foundation*. The Court had held that it could not ban mining altogether in the state of Goa due to its significant employment and revenue generation. The present case, on the other hand, dealt with the illegal construction of hotels, shopping complexes, and residential areas. There was no economic significance of the construction activity – which could easily be banned – akin to the significance of mining in *Goa Foundation*.

Further, while the NGT overtly based its assessment of compensation on the Court's approach in *Goa Foundation*, it significantly different in two aspects. First, the NGT reduced the compensation amount from 10 per cent to 5 per cent without providing any reasoning for the reduction. It simply stated that "10 per cent of the project cost may be somewhat on the higher side" and that it was necessary to lower the compensation percentage to 5 per cent so as to "maintain the equitable balance between the default and the consequential liability".[212] However, an equitable balance between the default and consequential liability can only be maintained when the extent of environmental damage can be reasonably estimated. Since the NGT did not engage in such an endeavour, it is not clear how the compensation levied would strike such a balance.

Second, instead of basing compensation on a percentage of the sale proceeds like the Court, the NGT based its compensation on a percentage of the project cost. The Court had used sale proceeds as it thought that this would be the most effective way of impacting the profitability of the project proponent. This is because in most mining operations, the mining site is leased from the government and the total project cost is significantly less than the sale generated. Likewise, in infrastructural projects such as the construction project in *Forward Foundation*, it is common practice – especially in Special Economic Zones – that the cost of the project is substantially lower than the eventual price at which the projects are sold. This is because of tax exemptions and the low cost of land allotted by the government to develop the area. For instance, if a developer constructs a shopping complex for INR 100 crore, he or she is likely to sell it further for five or six times the cost to prospective buyers. Thus, the NGT's decision to determine compensation as a percentage of the project cost does not affect the profitability of the project proponent as much as basing it on a percentage of sale proceeds.

What emerges from this discussion is a trend of the NGT to award compensation without paying heed to the actual amount of environmental damage. The compensation is not based on any scientific methodology or quantitative assessment. Rather, it is pegged arbitrarily on an economic variable which has no conspicuous nexus with the underlying environmental damage. In fact, even the high amount of compensation – totalling to INR 195 crore – mentioned at the beginning of this section was a result of this trend. While awarding the compensation, the NGT stated:[213]

Goel Ganga Developers India Private Limited shall pay environmental compensation cost of ₹190 crore or 5% (five per cent) of the total cost of project to be assessed by State Expert Appraisal Committee (SEAC), whichever is more, for restoration and restitution of environment damage and degradation caused by the project proponent by carrying out the construction activities without the necessary prior environmental clearance within a period of one month. In addition to this, it shall also pay a sum of ₹5 crore for contravening mandatory provision of several environment laws in carrying out the construction activities in addition to and exceeding limit of the available environment clearance and for not obtaining the consent from the Board.

The case involved grave environmental damage on account of the illegal construction of 12 buildings including 552 residential flats, 50 shops, and 34 offices. M/s Goel Ganga Developers India Pvt. Ltd. had flouted several conditions stipulated in the environmental clearance and had intentionally violated several municipal laws. Further, there was intentional suppression of material facts by the company and several governmental officers of the Pune Municipal Corporation.[214]

Despite noting the disastrous effects on the local environment due to the construction activities, the NGT did not conduct a scientific analysis of the extent of environmental damage. Rather, it based its compensation on the trend we have highlighted and pegged the compensation at 5 per cent of the project cost or INR 190 crore, whichever is higher. Thus, while the total compensation of INR 195 crore seems significant when viewed in isolation, it is possible that it could be inadequate for the restitution of the environment given that the actual amount of environmental damage was not determined.

In fact, on appeal to the Supreme Court, one of the main contentions of M/s Goel Ganga Developers India Pvt. Ltd. was that the NGT had not based its assessment on any scientific methodology.[215] Let us analyse the Supreme Court's response to this contention in its judgment:[216]

Supreme Court of India

(Principal Bench, New Delhi)

M/S GOEL GANGA DEVELOPERS INDIA PVT. LTD. v. UNION OF INDIA

[Civil Appeal No. 10854 of 2016, Order Dated 10 August 2018]

Deepak Gupta, J.

* * *

Relevant Extracts:

52. The main case of the original applicant is that the damages should be assessed on a scientific basis by calculating the damage caused to the environment by the project proponent on the basis of 'Carbon Footprint'. In the absence of detailed submissions, we find ourselves *totally unequipped* to go into this aspect of the matter. (Emphasis supplied)

53. In the original application filed by the original applicant before the NGT, there is no reference to Carbon Footprint. Even when evidence was initially led, no reference was made to the same. The concept of Carbon Footprint was introduced by the original applicant only in his affidavit dated 18.05.2016. In fact, according to the project proponent this affidavit was not even filed on 18.05.2016. It appears to us that there is no order of the NGT specifically permitting the original applicant to file such an affidavit. The submission of original applicant is that he was orally permitted to file the same. These disputed questions would have been only decided by the Original Bench and, therefore, we have already set aside the order passed in the review application dated 08.01.2018.

54. Courts cannot introduce a new concept of assessing and levying damages unless expert evidence in this behalf is led or there are some well established principles. We find that no such principles have been accepted or established in the present case. When there are no pleadings in this regard we fail to understand how the concept of Carbon Footprint can be introduced after evidence has been closed, at the stage of arguments. *We cannot assess the impact in actual terms and, therefore, we can only impose damages or costs on principles which have been well settled by law.* (Emphasis supplied)

55. We may also note that the method to which the original applicant referred to is not part of any law, rule or executive instructions. This method is no doubt used to compensate and impose damages on nations but we cannot apply this method while imposing damages on a person who violates the EC. We may also add that the calculation made by the original applicant in his affidavit dated 18.05.2016 filed before the NGT are based on assumptions some of which we have not found to be correct namely – (1) use of ground water; (2) reduction of Cultural Centre space; (3) construction of basements etc.

56. We may make it clear that we are not laying down the law that damages cannot be assessed on the basis of Carbon Footprint. In a case where expert evidence in this behalf is led or on the basis of empirical data it is established that by applying the principles of Carbon Footprint damages can be assessed, the Court may, in the facts and circumstances of the case, rely upon such data but, in the present case, there is no such reliable material.

57. Having held so we are definitely of the view that the project proponent who has violated law with impunity cannot be allowed to go scot-free. This Court has in a number of cases awarded 5% of the project cost as damages. This is the general law. However, in the present case we feel that damages should be higher keeping in view the totally intransigent and unapologetic

behaviour of the project proponent. He has maneuvered and manipulated officials and authorities. Instead of 12 buildings, he has constructed 18; from 552 flats the number of flats has gone up to 807 and now two more buildings having 454 flats are proposed. The project proponent contends that he has made smaller flats and, therefore, the number of flats has increased. He could not have done this without getting fresh EC. With the increase in the number of flats the number of persons, residing therein is bound to increase. This will impact the amount of water requirement, the amount of parking space, the amount of open area etc. Therefore, in the present case, we are clearly of the view that the project proponent should be and is directed to pay damages of Rs.100 crores or 10% of the project cost whichever is more. We also make it clear that while calculating the project cost the entire cost of the land based on the circle rate of the area in the year 2014 shall be added. The cost of construction shall be calculated on the basis of the schedule of rates approved by the Public Works Department (PWD) of the State of Maharashtra for the year 2014. In case the PWD of Maharashtra has not approved any such rates then the Central Public Works Department rates for similar construction shall be applicable. We have fixed the base year as 2014 since the original EC expired in 2014 and most of the illegal construction took place after 2014. In addition thereto, if the project proponent has taken advantage of Transfer of Development Rights (for short 'TDR') with reference to this project or is entitled to any TDR, the benefit of the same shall be forfeited and if he has already taken the benefit then the same shall either be recovered from him or be adjusted against its future projects. The project proponent shall also pay a sum of Rs. 5 crores as damages, in addition to the above for contravening mandatory provisions of environmental laws.

∗   ∗   ∗

The project proponent, on appeal, contended that the NGT ought to have determined the compensation on a "scientific basis" according to the actual "damage caused to the environment". It submitted that the calculation of the amount should have been based on the project's "carbon footprints" rather than being pegged at a percentage of the project cost. In response, the Supreme Court unequivocally stated that it was "totally unequipped" to deal with the matter due to the absence of details in the submission.[217]

Further, the Court opined that determining environmental compensation on the basis of carbon footprints was not appropriate as no expert evidence was led in this regard, and the concept was not based on well-established principles of law. However, it clarified that this did not bar determining compensation on carbon footprints in successive cases.

In relation to the calculation of the compensation by the NGT, the Court held that the trend of awarding 5 per cent of the project cost as environmental compensation amounted to "general law", as the Court had used this in several cases. However, given that the project proponent had intentionally suppressed material facts and had manipulated official authorities, the Court held that the correct assessment of compensation would be 10 per cent of the project cost.

Ironically, however, the Court reduced the compensation from INR 190 crore (awarded by the NGT) to INR 100 crore or 10 per cent of the project costs, whichever would be higher. No reasons were presented for the reduction in the amount. As noted previously, the issue with this approach of the Court and the Tribunal is that it disregards actual environmental damage. In other words, there is no nexus between the compensation levied and the actual amount needed to restore the environment to its original condition. This was acknowledged by the Court when it held:[218]

> We cannot assess the impact in actual terms and, therefore, we can only impose damages or costs on principles which have been well settled by law.

While the Court acknowledged this, it equally emphasized how the current trend was appropriate and was a part of the general law. However, it remains unclear why the Court would not order a scientific assessment of the environmental impact and why the current trend is preferable.

This trend is problematic as it allows a potential polluter to do a cost–benefit analysis before undertaking a project. Given that the environmental compensation, irrespective of the level of pollution, is expected to be pegged at between 5 and 10 per cent of the project cost, it is likely to incentivize a potential polluter to proceed with the project if the project can still be reasonably profitable. In other words, instead of acting as a deterrent, the environmental compensation, in its current form, is likely to be viewed as an environmental fee or cess by a potential polluter which becomes a part of the calculation of the cost of the project. Therefore, this trend has effectively converted the polluter pays principle into "pay and pollute" (the polluter pays principle is discussed in detail in the next chapter).

We believe that this trend should be discouraged and the NGT should, instead of having a blanket practice of awarding a certain percentage of the project cost, determine compensation on a case-by-case basis as per the actual amount of environmental damage. This will not only disincentivize a potential polluter from polluting but also allow the Tribunal to award stringent and appropriate compensation in cases where the pollution is more significant.

Additionally, this reflects the NGT's inability to use its technical expertise to scientifically quantify environmental damage. In fact, despite holding that there is significant environmental damage in some cases, the NGT has unequivocally relied on "guesswork" to compute environmental compensation.[219] Let us analyse one such case in detail below.

KRISHAN K. SINGH v. M/s TRIVENI ENGINEERING INDUSTRIES LTD.

[Original Application No. 317 of 2014, Order Dated 10 December 2015]

Swatanter Kumar, J. (Chairperson);
M.S. Nambiar, J. (Judicial Member);
Dr. D.K. Agrawal (Expert Member);
A.R. Yousuf (Expert Member)
Ranjan Chatterjee (Expert Member)

*　*　*

Relevant Extracts:

1. The applicant, Krishan Kant Singh had instituted an Original Application No. 299 of 2013 before the Tribunal with an allegation that respondent Simbhaoli Sugar Mills and Distillery and Gopalji Dairy were discharging their untreated trade effluents in the Simbhaoli Drain and were causing pollution in the River Ganga. Thus, he prayed that the Central Pollution Control Board (for short 'CPCB') be directed to assess the pollution caused, both to the ground water as well as the River and that appropriate orders, including imposition of fine and penalty, be passed against these units...

2. During the pendency of this application (O.A. 299 of 2013), the CPCB filed a report dated 7th February, 2014 mentioning the names of industries, which were polluting and/or highly polluting industries and were discharging their effluents directly or indirectly into the River Ganga or its tributaries. Vide order dated 22nd April, 2014, Tribunal directed the Uttar Pradesh Pollution Control Board (for short 'UPPCB') to issue notice to such industries and directed them to appear before the Tribunal. In furtherance to the said order the UPPCB on 6th May, 2014, issued notices to nearly 956 industries which were polluting River Ganga or its tributaries by discharging their untreated effluents in it.... M/s. Triveni Engineering Industries Ltd. (for short 'industry') was one of such industries to whom notice had been issued vide order dated 22nd April, 2014.

4. The industry was directed to submit a time-bound Action Plan within 20 days to achieve Zero Liquid Discharge. The industry was to reduce spent wash storage capacity up to 30 days of spent wash generation and demolish the extra storage capacity. The industry was also directed to initiate immediate action for utilization of the spent wash stored. These were the directions issued in accordance with provisions of the Environment (Protection) Act, 1986 (for short 'the Act of 1986').

5. The industry was further required to furnish a Bank Guarantee of Rs. 10 Lakhs to ensure that the conditions stated in the order dated 9th October, 2012, were complied with. The industry respondent on 10th December, 2012, informed the CPCB that it was a Zero Liquid Discharge Industry as far as distillery section is concerned and that it has also complied with other conditions of the consent order.…

6. A joint inspection was conducted by a team of officers from the CPCB and the UPPCB on 1st September, 2014. Prior thereto, in furtherance to the order of the Tribunal dated 6th May, 2014, the UPPCB had filed a status report dated 17th June, 2014, stating that the industry had taken anti-pollution measures and proper mechanism for treating the effluents. In the joint inspection report of 1st September, 2014 also, it was recorded that the industry is a Zero Liquid Discharge distillery; that treated effluent is disposed of by Bio Composting leading to Zero Liquid Discharge and that there is no disposal of treated effluent either on land and/or on surface. All concerned permissions, consents and approvals as required were also reported to be in place.… However, still the question that remains to be examined and answered in the present application is whether for the past pollution caused by the industry, it should be directed to pay environmental compensation in terms of the Sections 15 and 17 of the National Green Tribunal Act, 2010 (for short the 'Act of 2010') and on the Polluter Pays Principle. There is no doubt that all the reports are consistent and clearly indicate that prior to the issuance of directions under Section 5 of the Act of 1986 by the CPCB on 9th October, 2012, this industry was a seriously polluting industry. It had polluted the ground water and had indiscriminately discharged its effluents on the land within and outside its premises. It is only when the direction under Section 5 of the Act of 1986 were issued and the industry in default was threatened with closure, that it took effective steps to prevent and control pollution resulting from its activities, of both water and air. It is only after complying with the conditions imposed, submission of the Action Plan and taking steps like installation of anti-pollution devices, that this industry has become compliant. This obviously means that prior thereto, the industry was a non-compliant and polluting industry. Another aspect of this case is that this industry has committed even other defaults. It operated for some period without obtaining the consent of the Board, which is illegal and violative of the specific provisions of the Water Act and the Air Act. Secondly, there are periods when the industry had violated the conditions of the consent order and even continued to operate in violation thereof.

20. As we have already noticed, that the statutory provisions/environmental laws in India place an unequivocal obligation upon the person or industry not to

carry out any activity which is hazardous or otherwise polluting, except with the consent of the Board. Therefore, the onus to show that the activity is being carried on with the consent of the Board or the competent authority and that such activity is being continued strictly in terms of the consent order within the prescribed parameters of emissions or discharge, is upon the industry/unit. In such cases, the primary burden of proof, as distinguished from the substantive burden of proof, would lie upon the applicant who approaches the Tribunal. The primary burden would be with reference to preponderance of probabilities, while the substantive burden to prove to the contrary would shift and lie upon the industry. The industry would have to discharge its burden on both these aspects afore-stated.

21. Undisputedly, the industry has polluted the ground water and air, has operated without consent of the Board, has breached the conditions of the consent order and has failed to discharge its legal obligations. For this reason, the industry would be liable to pay Environmental Compensation. At this stage it is not possible to determine with certainty the extent of pollution caused and consequences of the violations committed by the industry and therefore some kind of *guesswork* has to be applied by the Tribunal to direct payment of Environmental Compensation in terms of Sections 15 and 17 of the Act of 2010. In this regard we may refer to the judgment of the Tribunal in *Krishan Kant Singh v. National Ganga River Basin Authority*, MANU/GT/0130/2014 : 2014 ALL (I) NGT REPORTER (3) (DELHI) 1:

> "51. It is not possible to assess exact environmental damage and the cost of restoration thereof in view of the long period involved in the present case and the fact that the statutory Boards empowered to prevent and control pollution have not performed their statutory duties in accordance with the spirit and object of the environmental Acts and jurisprudence. This unit is responsible for causing great environmental pollution of different water bodies including Phuldera drain, the Syana Escape canal, the River Ganga and even the groundwater in and around the area of this industrial unit. Besides scientific data of inspection by the Expert teams, officers of the Pollution Control Board, analysis report and the fact that the water in the Phuldera drain had turned brown, even to the naked eye, demonstrates the extent of pollution caused by this unit. Considering the magnitude of the pollution caused by the unit, its capacity and prosperity, responsibility of the unit to pay compensation cannot be disputed on any plausible cause or ground. The Supreme Court in ... *M.C. Mehta v. Union of India* MANU/SC/0092/1986 : (1987) 1 SCC 395, the Court further stated that the plea of reasonable care and that the damage to environment occurred without specific negligence on

the part of the unit is not a sustainable defence to a direction of payment of compensation for causing environmental damage. The court further held that magnitude, capacity and prosperity of the unit are the relevant considerations for determining the extent of the liability in such case. Applying these principles to the facts of the present case, there can hardly be any dispute that it is a polluting unit. It is also beyond controversy that this unit has operated without consent of the Boards from 1974 till the year 1991, thereafter, it committed default in compliance of the conditions of the consent right up to the year 2000. Even thereafter, it did not strictly comply with the conditions and directions issued by the respective Boards. This unit is a direct source of polluting River Ganga.

The unit is a profit making unit. No record has been produced before the Tribunal to establish anything to the contrary. Though, it may not be possible to determine with exactitude the exact amount of compensation payable on account of damage to environment because of the long period involved and also for the reason that even scientifically the extent of damage and amounts required for restoration and restitution thereof cannot be determined at this stage now. Cleaning and removal of sludge from Phuldera drain, treatment of other pollutants flowing in the said drain, preventing any discharge into the Syana Escape Canal and making River Ganga pollution free are the basic needs which require attention of the Expert bodies particularly, in the facts and circumstances of this case. We fix a compensation of Rs. 5 crores which shall be deposited with the UPPCB and shall be spent for that purpose alone by and joint team of CPCB and UPPCB, including for removal of sludge and all pollutants in the Syana Escape Canal till it joins river Ganga. This amount shall also be used for preventing ground water pollution."

22. In view of the Principles of Law afore-stated and the circumstances of the present case, it is a clear case of intended violations. The Industry has not acted appropriately, has operated without consent intermittently violated the conditions of the consent order and has also polluted the environment. The onus to show that it had strictly applied with the specified standards lay on the industry. The industry certainly has not completely discharged its onus. Even, if we were to assume for the sake of arguments that it was not a case covered under the principle of strict liability, still the applicant had discharged its primary onus shifting heavy burden to prove to the contrary upon the industry. As a result of cumulative discussion above, we are of the considered view that the industry is liable to pay environmental compensation besides the directions that the Tribunal has issued in the present case.

27. Having rejected the various contentions raised on behalf of the industry, we partly allow the application while passing the following directions:

   1. In view of the above directions, this industry shall be liable to pay a sum of Rs. 25 Lakhs as an environmental compensation. The amount shall be paid in equal share to the Central Pollution Control Board and UP Pollution Control Board which will also include the expenses incurred by the Board in conducting different inspections of the industry under the orders of the Tribunal or otherwise.

   2. The amount shall be used for preventing and controlling pollution as well as for restoration of the environment, ecology and ground water around the industry….

*   *   *

NOTES AND QUESTIONS

1. The NGT, unequivocally, acknowledges its reliance on "some kind of guesswork" while determining the extent of pollution caused by the project proponent, as well as the ensuing environmental compensation necessary for restoring the environment to its original position. Thus, the inability of the Tribunal to scientifically assess environmental damage coupled with the lack of quantitative assessment while determining environmental compensation is evident. While the NGT holds that M/s Triveni Engineering Industries Ltd. has undisputedly operated without consent and had seriously polluted groundwater and air, it does not explain how an environmental compensation of INR 25 lakh would be sufficient for the restitution of the environment.

   Further, the NGT does not specify any methodology or calculation in relation to how it arrived at the compensation amount. It simply states the compensation amount without any explanation. Due to this, the NGT's holding seems arbitrary and illogical as it bears no semblance to the factual reality of the case.

2. In arriving at the environmental compensation, the NGT targets the profitability of the project proponent. It relies on its earlier decision in *Krishan Kant Singh v. National Ganga River Basin Authority*,[220] wherein it had held: "The unit is a profit-making unit. No record has been produced before the Tribunal to establish anything to the contrary." Do you think the profitability of a project proponent (irrespective of whether it is incorporated or not) should determine the environmental compensation to be paid? In other words, if the same amount of environmental damage has occurred, should two persons be treated differently based on their individual profitability? Should the person earning more be liable to compensate more towards environmental restitution

due to his or her increased capacity to pay? Or should the compensation levied be proportionate to the environmental damage caused by the person concerned?

3. Though the NGT seems to be concerned with impacting the profitability of the project proponent while determining environmental compensation, its actions say otherwise. A levy of a mere INR 25 lakh is unlikely to act as a deterrent to future pollution. Particularly, this amount is abysmally low when seen in the context of the annual turnover and net profit of M/s Triveni Engineering Industries Ltd. As per the annual report of the company filed for the financial year 2014–2015, the net turnover was INR 2,061 crore and the net profit was INR 153 crore after the production of approximately half a million tonnes of sugar.[221] Thus, the environmental compensation levied was 0.0121 per cent of the annual turnover and 1.63 per cent of the net profit of the company for the year immediately preceding the judgment. Moreover, given that the pollution had happened over several years, the compensation amount is appallingly low when compared to the cumulative earnings of the company during that period.

4. Like in other cases discussed previously, the Tribunal simply holds that a scientific determination of environmental damage is not possible with certainty. However, the NGT does not provide reasons regarding why such a determination is not possible or why it cannot be done at a later date. The lack of explanation regarding why a scientific determination of environmental damage should not be conducted to ascertain the actual extent of damage goes against the very reason for the creation of the NGT. What kind of problems do you think will result from this trend in the long run?

*　　*　　*

As noted above, in *Krishan Kant Singh v. National Ganga River Basin Authority*,[222] the Tribunal was concerned with impacting the profitability of the project proponent. In that case, some of the major factors that played a role in determining environmental compensation were the "magnitude, capacity, and prosperity of the unit".[223] However, as analysed above, the actual compensation levied by the Tribunal was not based on any scientific analysis and was not commensurate with the profitability of the polluting project.

Referring to the above case, the NGT in *M/s. DSM Sugar Distillery Division v. Shailesh Singh & Ors.*, once again, overtly relied on "guesswork" to compute environmental compensation.[224] Similar to M/s Triveni Engineering Industries Ltd., M/s DSM Sugar Distillery Division had been operating a sugar factory without fulfilling the conditions stipulated in the consent order of the State Pollution Control Board (SPCB) of Uttar Pradesh, for several years. The pollution from the factory had severely contaminated the underground water and soil in the vicinity of the factory.

The NGT, while relying on guesswork, levied an environmental compensation of a mere INR 1 crore on the company. This amount is negligible when compared to the annual turnover of M/s DSM Sugar Distillery Division. For the financial year 2014–2015, immediately before the Tribunal's decision, the annual turnover for the company was INR

1,863 crore. Accordingly, despite the serious environmental damage involved over several years, the compensation levied was a mere 0.0485 per cent of the annual turnover for the company.[225] Since the pollution occurred over several years, the compensation is even oven lower when compared to the cumulative turnover of the company during the years of pollution.

As usual, the NGT did not provide any details regarding how it arrived at this amount or how this amount was commensurate with the actual environmental damage. Decisions like these make the workings of the Tribunal less transparent and arbitrary. The Centre for Science and Environment (CSE) has conducted a detailed analysis of this trend by comparing the compensation awarded in similar cases involving pollution by sugar factories to the respective annual turnover and profit of the polluting companies. A tabular excerpt of this analysis is produced in Table 2.2.

From the above analysis, it is evident that though the NGT intends to affect the profitability of polluters, in practice it is unable to do so. The environmental compensations levied by the Tribunal are a miniscule fraction of the annual turnovers of the polluters. Due to the lack of rationale behind the calculation of compensation, the polluter only pays a token amount for the pollution and only a fraction of the large clean-up costs. Thus, the costs of pollution are not internalized by the polluter.

The 956 sugar and distillery factory units in question were classified by the Uttar Pradesh Pollution Control Board as grossly polluting industries (GPIs). A glance at the company profiles of these sugar plants highlights that they are some of the biggest and most profitable in India.[226] Admittedly, these GPIs were responsible for a large amount of pollution in River Ganga. However, the NGT's practice of awarding such low environmental compensation in these cases is likely to not act as a deterrent for future pollution.

Even if the NGT did not intend to scientifically calculate environmental compensation, it could have at the very least imposed a higher amount in relation to the turnover of the polluters. According to a report prepared by the Central Pollution Control Board, an environmental compensation of 3 per cent of the turnover of the polluting companies was deemed reasonable and would not subject the polluters to undue economic hardships.[227] Thus, had the NGT relied on this suggestion, the environmental compensation levied on M/s Triveni Engineering Industries Ltd. would have increased from INR 25 lakh to INR 61.83 crore.

The research conducted by the CSE also highlights that most penalties levied by the NGT are provisional in nature.[228] Frequently, the NGT imposes an "initial" penalty or fine and then constitutes an investigative committee to assess the situation further. This initial amount is usually not based on any scientific assessment of the environmental damage, and in almost all cases, the project proponent does not make any payments until the submission of the expert committee report.[229]

Since the NGT's determination of compensation is not based on any quantitative assessment, the trend of pegging environmental compensation to a percentage of the

Table 2.2   Analysis of compensation awarded and turnover of the sugar distillery industry in Uttar Pradesh

Case and Company	Compensation	Annual Turnover of Project Proponent	Relation between Compensation and Annual Turnover
Case: *Krishan Kant Singh v. National Ganga River Basin Authority and Ors.* (OA No. 299/2013, Judgment dated October 2014) **Company:** Simbhaoli Sugar Mills	INR 5 crore	INR 864 crore (As per the Annual Report of the company 2013–2014)	The penalty levied is negligible and amounts to a mere 0.57 per cent of the annual turnover of the company.
Case: *Krishan Kant Singh & Ors v. Daurala Sugar Works Distillery Unit* (OA No. 328/2014, Judgment dated November 2015) **Company:** Daurala Sugar Works Distillery Unit (a wing of DCM Shriram Industries Ltd.)	INR 1 crore	INR 1,329 crore (As per the Annual Report of the company 2014–15)	The penalty levied is negligible and amounts to a mere 0.07 per cent of the annual turnover of the company.
Case: *DSM Sugar Distillery Division v. Shailesh Singh & Ors.* (Review Application No. 13/2015 in OA No. 35/2015, Judgment dated December 2015) **Company:** DSM Sugar Distillery Division	INR 1 crore	INR 1,864 crore (As per the Annual Report of the company 2014–2015)	The penalty levied is negligible and amounts to a mere 0.05 per cent of the annual turnover of the company.
Case: *Krishan Kant Singh v. Triveni Engineering Industries Ltd.* (OA no. 317/2014 Judgment dated December 2015) **Company:** Triveni Engineering Industries Ltd.	INR 25 lakh	INR 2,061 crore (As per the Annual Report of the company 2014–15)	The penalty levied is negligible and amounts to a mere 0.012 per cent of the annual turnover of the company.

Source: Centre for Science and Environment; Bhushan, Banerjee, and Bezbaroa, *Green Tribunal, Green Approach*, 39.

project cost has led to a situation wherein the compensation either grossly underestimates or overestimates the environmental damage involved. While the cases discussed previously – *Krishan K. Singh v. M/s Triveni Engineering Industries Ltd.* and *M/s. DSM Sugar Distillery Division v. Shailesh Singh & Ors.* – exemplify instances wherein the compensation was not adequate in relation to the environmental damage involved, the overestimation of compensation is aptly demonstrated in *Ajay Kumar Negi v. Union of India*.[230]

Ajay Kumar Negi involved damage to the forest cover in the Tidong basin in Himachal Pradesh due to the construction of a hydroelectric project.[231] The project proponent had violated several conditions of the environmental clearance with respect to forests.[232] As a result, in line with the trend discussed, the Tribunal awarded an environmental penalty to the project proponent amounting to INR 5 crore.[233]

However, this amount bore very little semblance with the ground realities of the case as the project proponent had already paid all costs required under forest laws. Additionally, prior to the case being filed with the NGT, the project proponent had compensated the *gram panchayat* (village council) and the Forest Department and had paid all amounts asked by several governmental authorities before the matter came up to the NGT.[234]

Realizing its mistake, the NGT, in a later order dated 4 April 2016, completely changed its stance with respect to the compensation levied and held that the "stage is not yet matured for relief as solicited, particularly, damage to environment, if any, arising out of the project activity is yet to be completely assessed".[235] The reason for this sudden change was that the same expert committee, which was instrumental in the levy of the initial compensation, subsequently held that the livelihood of the people was "least likely to be affected by the project operation" and that there was no apparent threat of irreversible damage to the forest cover.[236]

Accordingly, the Tribunal went from holding that there was serious environmental damage and levying an environmental compensation of INR 5 crore to holding that the stage for damages had not arisen. In doing so, the NGT ought to have explained why the initial compensation was levied in the first place. Rather than levying an arbitrary amount and later revoking it, the NGT should have admitted that it did not have adequate data to arrive at a compensation amount.

If this trend continues, and compensation is largely based on considerations extraneous to the actual environmental damage in a case, it is likely to erode public confidence in the Tribunal's ability to effectively adjudicate environmental matters and provide the necessary rehabilitation. To further explore the ill effects of this trend, let us discuss the case of *Manoj Mishra v. Delhi Development Authority & Ors.* We intend to highlight the issues with the approach adopted by the NGT to determine initial compensation and discuss how the result might have been different had the Tribunal undertaken an actual scientific analysis.

2.4.2   CASE STUDY: LACK OF SCIENTIFIC DETERMINATION OF ENVIRONMENTAL COMPENSATION – THE ART OF LIVING CASE

Manoj Misra v. Delhi Development Authority & Ors. (hereinafter, the *Art of Living Case*) is arguably one of the most controversial cases in the history of the NGT. The case became highly publicized, and several news channels covered it due to the alleged penalty amount involved as well as its substantial reduction subsequently by the Tribunal.[237] The case involved a cultural event organized by the Art of Living Foundation, a non-governmental and not-for-profit organization, called the World Cultural Festival (WCF) on the banks of River Yamuna from 11 to 13 March 2016.[238]

As a background on the project proponent, the Art of Living Foundation is an educational, humanitarian, and spiritual organization founded in 1981 by Sri Sri Ravishankar. Through its 10,000+ centres, it has a presence in over 156 countries, and its breathing and meditation techniques have reached over 450 million people worldwide. In addition to its meditation and stress relief workshops, the Art of Living Foundation has engaged in various humanitarian and environmental initiatives.

Accordingly, in recognition of the impact of such initiatives, Sri Sri Ravishankar has received some of the highest civilian awards of several countries such as Canada, Russia, Mongolia, Colombia, Peru, and Paraguay. In fact, he was awarded the Padma Vibhushan – the highest annual civilian award of India – just a few days after the WCF in March 2016.

While the preparation of the WCF began several months prior to the event, an application was filed in the NGT in February 2016 raising concerns regarding the environmental impact of the WCF on the riverbank and floodplain.[239] The initial estimate of the environmental compensation based on a simple "visual assessment" conducted by the expert committee was approximately INR 120 crore.[240] This estimate was later reduced to INR 28.73 crore.[241] Finally, the Tribunal asked the Art of Living to deposit INR 5 crore and specified that this was not a penalty.[242] Out of this amount, only INR 25 lakhs was required to be deposited as a condition precedent for going ahead with the event.

This drastic reduction from the initially estimated compensation of INR 120 crore to INR 5 crore garnered a lot of media attention and coverage. This led some academics to argue that the reduction in the penalty amount was a consequence of the fact that several politically influential people, including the prime minister of India, had attended the WCF.[243] For instance, Gitanjali Nain Gill has argued:[244]

> The AOL [Art of Living] episode exposes a weakness in India's environmental regulatory system, demonstrating the willingness of authorities to bend rules at the dictate of the affluent and influential.

This is an overly simplistic conclusion. It is not based on an understanding of the NGT's approach to compensation determination and ignores the NGT's own admission to not conducting a scientific analysis of the extent of environmental damage in the judgment.[245] When the eventual compensation amount of INR 5 crore is seen in the light of the trends discussed in the previous section, it does not stand out.

As discussed previously, the NGT has levied an initial penalty of INR 5 crore in cases involving allegations of much more serious environmental damage, as well as in cases involving no material environmental damage (requiring the NGT to revoke its initial penalty amount).[246] Thus, at best, the INR 5 crore penalty is a plug that the NGT is habituated to using in cases wherein it does not scientifically assess environmental damage.

Accordingly, arguing that the reduction in penalty was due to political influence ignores these issues at the heart of the Tribunal's adjudication mechanism. Now, through an in-depth analysis, we will endeavour to highlight that the reduction in the estimated compensation was a natural result of the lack of scientific analysis undertaken by the NGT. In doing so, we will analyse the preliminary and final reports submitted by the Expert Committee set up by the NGT and the general approach of the Tribunal in relation to quantifying environmental damage.

2.4.2.1 According to the Chairperson of the Expert Committee, the estimated compensation amount was an "inadvertent mistake" and was "not based on any scientific assessment".

In both reports (preliminary and final) the Expert Committee stated that the entire floodplain had been "completely destroyed" and that "the natural vegetation consisting of reeds and trees has been completely removed".[247] The reports further claimed that the ground was "totally devoid" of water bodies and that "no plant cover was visible anywhere" following the WCF.[248] However, it was a matter on record that illegal agriculture was being practised on the event site several years prior to the event and that all the vegetation had already been cleared to make room for growing crops.

In fact, the Tribunal, in its judgment, unequivocally notes that the petitioner first learnt about the event from the local farmers practising agriculture on the event site.[249] This illegal farming was being carried out with the acquiescence of the Delhi Development Authority (DDA), which is the governmental agency responsible for overseeing the event site.[250] Further, after receiving permission from the DDA to hold the event, the Art of Living Foundation compensated the farmers of village Kilkori – to whom the land belonged – by paying a fee in lieu of their harvest.[251] This is also evidenced by the fact that the farmers who wished to retain their agricultural land filed a petition in the Delhi High Court, which was subsequently dismissed, as the High Court held that the occupation of land by the farmers was illegal.[252]

The same members of the Expert Committee, namely Professor Brij Gopal, Professor C.R. Babu, and Professor A.K. Gosain – who had conducted the initial site visit wherein an estimated compensation amount of INR 120 crore was proposed based on a mere "visual assessment" – had conducted extensive research on the same floodplain area in 2013. Ironically, as a result of this research, they had concluded that the area of the event was already devoid of natural vegetation and biodiversity.

Based on these conclusions, these members had submitted a report in 2013 to the NGT titled "Restoration and Conservation of River Yamuna", wherein they unequivocally stated that the life-supporting potential of the river had already been lost and that "the flowing water, the river bed, the floodplain forest and grassland ecosystems are *locally extinct*" (emphasis supplied).[253] Additionally, the report stated that "the floodplain biodiversity has been significantly altered and reduced such that the natural functions of the floodplains are lost".[254] Furthermore, it stated:

Delhi urban stretch of 22 KM in the downstream of Wazirabad barrage up to Okhla barrage [this is the site of the WCF] is *critically polluted* and dry weather flow is almost the treated and untreated sewage from 22 drains and the fresh water flow from upstream or lateral connection and it is perhaps *the most polluted river stretches in the country with zero DO* [dissolvable oxygen] and over 30 mg/1 BOD levels. (Emphasis supplied)

Accordingly, on the one hand, the Expert Committee members in the 2013 report stated that there is zero dissolvable oxygen in the stretch of the River Yamuna adjacent to the event site and, therefore, no fish or marine life can survive in that portion of the floodplain. On the other hand, the same Expert Committee members in the report submitted to the NGT in the impugned case stated that Art of Living will be responsible for the "restoration of the fauna such as fish".[255]

Further, while the same members had previously concluded in 2013 that the floodplain biodiversity had already been significantly reduced and that the floodplain ecosystems were "locally extinct",[256] in 2016, they concluded that "*all* the vegetation has to be restored" (emphasis supplied)[257] by the Art of Living Foundation through the WCF.

This begs the question that if according to the same Expert Committee members, the area of the floodplain where the WCF was held was already so polluted three years prior to the event, why would they inflate the compensation estimates and hold the Art of Living responsible for the "complete destruction of all vegetation"? Moreover, why would they not hold other governmental authorities such as the DDA accountable for the environmental degradation that had already happened prior to the WCF?

This becomes more problematic given that the Expert Committee, while explaining the loss of vegetation and biodiversity in the floodplain, held that the total loss "cannot be readily visualised and documented" and that "this is an '*invisible loss*' of biodiversity, which cannot be easily assessed" (emphasis supplied).[258] In fact, the Art of Living Foundation presented evidence by way of satellite images demonstrating that the total number of trees before and after the WCF were exactly the same.[259] However, this was not addressed by the Tribunal.

The NGT does not explain what an "invisible loss" entails. Further, it remains silent with respect to why this loss seems invisible and not capable of being documented given that just three years prior to the WCF, the same members of the Expert Committee were able to succinctly quantify the damage done to the event site.

Significantly, it did not address how a compensation estimate of INR 120 crore can be based on an invisible loss that cannot be visualized or documented. Clearly, this estimate was not based on any scientific quantification of environmental damage. This is further evident from the fact that the chairperson of the Expert Committee, Shashi Shekhar (then the secretary to the Ministry of Water Resources, River Development, and Ganga Rejuvenation), in a letter dated 3 March 2016, addressed to the NGT, unequivocally rejected the conclusions drawn by the Expert Committee and stated: [260]

One of the suggestions by the Committee that inadvertently got recommended was regarding penalty of Rs. 120 crores on AOL for restoring the Yamuna floodplain destroyed for their function. This *inadvertent mistake* was largely due to the fact that I was running high fever and I could not see the entire report prepared by the experts.... Rs. 120 crore as assessed by the experts was tentative and the figure emerged as spontaneous suggestion. It was *not based on any scientific assessment.* (Emphasis supplied)

The chairperson of the Expert Committee unequivocally denounced the report, along with the estimated compensation put forth by his own committee, as it was unscientific. As noted, in addition to the estimated environmental compensation of INR 120 crore, all conclusions drawn by the Expert Committee in relation to the extent of environmental damage caused by the WCF were based on this single visual assessment. Clearly, this approach was not based on any scientific quantification of environmental damage. However, unlike other cases where the NGT has admitted to resorting to "some kind of guesswork",[261] the NGT, in this case, made no such admission and proceeded to base the environmental compensation on a non-attributable loss.

While this trend of the NGT to not quantify environmental compensation on the basis of actual environmental damage is not new (as discussed in the previous section), it often results in situations in which the Tribunal has to modify the initial compensation as it lacks any scientific basis. As discussed previously in the case of *Ajay Kumar Negi v. Union of India*, wherein the NGT imposed an initial environmental penalty and later revoked it on account of lack of scientific evidence, such frequent modifications are likely to result in an erosion of public confidence in the NGT's adjudication.

The *Art of Living Case* aptly demonstrates this erosion. While the subsequent reduction in the compensation amount was a direct result of the unscientific nature of the initial assessment, it led several media houses and academics to naively state that the reduction was due to political pressure.

2.4.2.2   Alleging compaction and levelling without scientific analysis

After realizing that the initial estimate of INR 120 crore was baseless, the Expert Committee recommended a lower compensation of INR 28.73 crore.[262] When this 76 per cent reduction in the compensation amount is seen in isolation, it seems arbitrary and based on political factors. However, when the reduction is seen in light of the fact that the initial estimate of INR 120 crore was based on an invisible loss without any quantification of actual environmental damage, the reduction seems only natural.

The new estimated compensation of INR 28.73 crore by the Expert Committee was for undoing the compaction and levelling of the floodplain on the event site. However, this assessment too was not based on any scientific inquiry.

For a scientific analysis to be done, the NGT ought to have determined the baseline condition of the event site prior to the WCF to quantify any deviation from it. This is both logical and internationally recognized as the most appropriate method for determining compensation as the amount of compensation is based on the extent of alteration in the baseline condition that existed prior to the project.[263] (This is discussed in further detail in the next section where we discuss the most appropriate method of determining environmental compensation.)

The NGT, however, did not determine the baseline condition of the event site that existed prior to the WCF and did not conduct any scientific analysis of the damage apart from the visual assessment. The most widely acknowledged and used test for determining soil compaction is the California Bearing Ratio (CBR) Test.[264] It involves taking soil samples before and after a specified date and then carrying out the test to determine the compaction, if any.[265] Since the Expert Committee did not collect any soil samples to arrive at a factual conclusion for the level of compaction, the Art of Living Foundation requested the NGT to allow it to voluntarily conduct the CBR Test before the WCF. However, the NGT denied permission for conducting the test and disposed of the application without providing any reasons.[266]

This is similar to a situation discussed earlier in *M/s Goel Ganga Developers India Pvt. Ltd. v. Union of India*, wherein on appeal, the project proponent argued that the compensation determined by the NGT lacked a scientific basis. This argument was based on the reasoning that the NGT had not determined the actual extent of the environmental damage and had arbitrarily awarded 5 per cent of the project cost as compensation. Accordingly, on appeal, M/s Goel Ganga Developers India Pvt. Ltd. had requested the Supreme Court to reassess the compensation based on its "carbon footprints".[267] The Court, however, declined to interfere by stating that it was "totally unequipped" to review the matter.[268]

While there are other scientific methods to calculate the compensation in addition to the carbon footprints of the project proponent, the main point of the argument is that the Tribunal should base its estimate of compensation on at least one such scientific method rather than basing it on extraneous considerations. Likewise, in the *Art of Living Case*, although there are several other scientific methods to assess the level of soil compaction in addition to the CBR Test, at the very least a sample of soil prior to the event should have been compared to a sample of soil after the event to determine the level of compaction, if any. However, no such analysis was done, and the claim of levelling was made simply on the basis of a visual assessment.

Alleging compaction of soil without actually taking samples and testing is problematic. The soil type of the northern floodplains, including the event site, is predominantly sandy. This has been admitted by the members of the Expert Committee in their 2013 report, which characterizes the soil in the area as being primarily made up of sand and gravel.[269] Scientifically speaking, the pressure–void ratio curves for sandy soil show that over 90 per cent of the compaction of loose sand takes place within two minutes of it being deposited.[270] In other words, due to the nature of sandy soil, most of the compaction takes place very soon after it is deposited.

Invariably, further compaction of the sand in the event site, if any, took place years ago due to the construction of roads and illegal agriculture forming dense sand which was present at the event site prior to the WCF. In fact, even when high pressure is applied to such dense sand, usually negligible compaction is witnessed.[271] Nevertheless, the Art of Living Foundation, to address concerns regarding soil compaction, built what it called the world's first "floating stage" made from scaffoldings and rods rather than a concrete foundation (see Images 2.1–2.3).

The construction of the stage in such a lattice-like manner with thousands of scaffoldings, according to the Art of Living Foundation, ensured that there would be no compaction of soil beneath the stage due to the reduction of weight per unit area. The extent to which this was able to ensure the non-compaction of soil would have been answered only if the NGT and the Expert Committee had agreed to undertake a scientific analysis of the actual level of compaction at the request of the Art of Living Foundation.

Therefore, even if there appeared to be compaction caused to the sandy soil in the event area during the visual assessment, it ought to have been evidenced by taking soil samples before and after the event to demonstrate the extent of deviation from the baseline condition.

Image 2.1   Construction of the floating stage prior to the World Cultural Festival

Source: Written submissions filed in the *Art of Living Case*. Photograph submitted by respondents in *Manoj Mishra v. Delhi Development Authority*, Original Application No.65 of 2016 (Principal Bench, NGT, India).

Image 2.2   One-foot-by-one-foot graft footing of each scaffolding

Source: Written submissions filed in the *Art of Living Case*. Photograph submitted by respondents in *Manoj Mishra v. Delhi Development Authority*, Original Application No.65 of 2016 (Principal Bench, NGT, India).

Image 2.3   Scaffolding structure beneath stage

Source: Written submissions filed in the *Art of Living Case*. Photograph submitted by respondents in *Manoj Mishra v. Delhi Development Authority*, Original Application No.65 of 2016 (Principal Bench, NGT, India).

2.4.2.3   Selection bias in collecting evidence

Selection bias refers to the selection of individuals, groups, or data in a manner that adequate randomization is not achieved. In this section, we endeavour to demonstrate how the Expert Committee, by drawing conclusions from certain images without their seasonal context and not relying on other available images, committed this error.

As noted, the NGT ought to have determined the baseline condition of the event site prior to the WCF. Instead, the Expert Committee conducted a simple visual assessment and concluded that there was an "invisible loss" of biodiversity that could not be readily assessed or documented. While it was evident that this was inadequate to determine the actual quantum of the environmental damage, if any, the Expert Committee supplemented its visual assessment with only a single satellite image dated 5 September 2015 (despite the availability of several images) for determining the condition of the event site prior to the event.

This pre-event image (refer to Image 2.4) was taken during the peak monsoon season and was compared to a post-event image (refer to Image 2.5) taken during the dry season of March 2016, from Google Earth. When these pictures are seen in isolation, it seems that there has been a significant loss of green cover. However, when the seasonal context is considered, it shows an entirely different picture (refer to Images 2.6 and 2.7).

Image 2.4   A satellite image of the event site taken during peak monsoon season on 5 September 2015, prior to the event

Source: Written submissions filed in the *Art of Living Case*. Photograph submitted in the *Art of Living Case* (accessed 25 December 2021). Map Data: ©2015 Google.

Image 2.5 A satellite image of the event site taken during the dry season on 28 March 2016, after the event

Source: Written submissions filed in the *Art of Living Case*. Photograph submitted in the *Art of Living Case* (accessed 25 December 2021). Map Data: ©2015 Google.

Image 2.6 A satellite image of the event site taken during the dry season in June 2012, showing farming prior to the event

Source: Written submissions filed in the *Art of Living Case*. Photograph submitted in the *Art of Living Case* (accessed 25 December 2021). Map Data: ©2015 Google.

Image 2.7   A satellite image of the event site taken during the monsoon season in September 2016, after the event

Source: Written submissions filed in the *Art of Living Case*. Photograph submitted in the *Art of Living Case* (accessed 25 December 2021). Map Data: ©2016 Google.

If we were to compare Image 2.6 (pre-event, dry season) and Image 2.7 (post-event, monsoon season) without the seasonal context, the likely conclusion would be that the WCF improved the green cover and helped revive the natural vegetation. This is because Image 2.6 is a pre-event satellite image taken during the dry season, while Image 2.7 is a post-event picture taken during the monsoon season (this is like comparing apples and oranges!).

In fact, if Image 2.4 (pre-event, monsoon season) is compared with Image 2.7 (post-event, monsoon season), it shows a negligible change in the green cover of the area. This is because both pictures are taken during the monsoon season, and an equitable comparison is possible. Likewise, if Image 2.5 (post-event, dry season) is compared with Image 2.6 (pre-event, dry season), it shows similar dryness of the area. Accordingly, the appropriate comparison that the Tribunal ought to have undertaken was of the same season across the years.

This demonstrates the issue with relying on just two satellite images, when several other similar satellite images are readily available, to conclude that there has been a loss of natural vegetation and green cover. In other words, even if the Expert Committee and the NGT deemed it necessary to rely on satellite images, they ought to have examined several images to fully appreciate the seasonal context. Ideally, the satellite image taken in September 2015 (Image 2.4) should have been compared with the satellite image taken in September 2016 (Image 2.7).

Given that all estimates of compensation put forth by the Expert Committee were based on an unscientific visual assessment augmented by a comparison between Image 2.4 and Image 2.5, without the necessary seasonal context, further reduction in the compensation amount was only natural.

2.4.2.4   The Expert Committee admits to not conducting a scientific analysis due to a paucity of time and resources

As noted previously, the NGT stated that there was illegal agriculture happening on the event site for several years prior to the WCF. In this regard, the main contention of the Art of Living Foundation before the Tribunal was that the damage being attributed to it was already done by illegal farmers and municipal activity, much before the idea of organizing the WCF was conceived. Thus, it prayed before the NGT to instruct the Expert Committee to delineate the damage done before and after the event.

While this seems logical, the Expert Committee, in its final report, stated that it was unable to differentiate between the compensation required to restore the floodplain as a whole and the compensation required to undo the damage caused by the event.[272] In other words, it held that it could not distinguish between the damage done to the event site prior to the event and the damage attributable to the Art of Living Foundation. This is acknowledged by the NGT in its judgment.[273]

Further, the Expert Committee substituted the term "ecological restoration" in its preliminary report for "ecological rehabilitation" in the final report. This was done as the Expert Committee was unable to clearly attribute costs required for restoration due to the WCF. In the final report, the Expert Committee stated that ecological "restoration" was not possible as the ecological damage attributable to Art of Living Foundation due to the WCF could not be ascertained.[274]

This is ironic as not only could the baseline condition of the event site have been determined prior to the event, but it could have also been determined after the event. This is because the entire area of the concerned floodplain was 9,300 hectares, while only 25 hectares were used for the WCF. Thus, had the NGT and the Expert Committee desired, it would have been possible to determine the baseline condition of the event site by comparing samples from the event site to samples of the adjacent floodplain area after the event.

In fact, the primary reason that the Expert Committee provided for not being able to quantify the damage and determine the baseline condition was:[275]

Estimate of the costs of restoration requires the preparation of a Detailed Project Report that may take *several months to a year besides financial resources*. (Emphasis supplied)

Therefore, the Expert Committee admitted that while it was possible to do a scientific analysis and calculate the environmental damage attributable to the Art of Living Foundation, if any, it did not do so due to a lack of financial resources and time. Moreover, irrespective of the fact that it did not quantify the environmental damage attributable to the Art of Living Foundation, the Expert Committee still recommended making the Art of Living Foundation bear the costs of rehabilitating the entire floodplain area, which included damage done prior to the event.

Thus, it is clear that the NGT did not lack the expertise to scientifically quantify the environmental damage done by the WCF. Rather, it chose to not conduct a detailed and scientific analysis. While not conducting a scientific analysis is certainly more convenient, this approach has the potential to shake public confidence, as is evident from several news and media reports at the time.[276]

The common person is unlikely to go into the specifics of a case and is likely to rely on the headlines. Accordingly, when such a person sees a drastic reduction in environmental compensation from INR 120 crore to INR 5 crore, without realizing that the initial estimate of INR 120 crore was admittedly based on an unscientific analysis, he or she is likely to lose trust in the effective functioning of the Tribunal.

Given that there was no scientific quantification of environmental damage and the resulting compensation, even the final amount of INR 5 crore was arbitrarily given by the NGT. Similar to the case in *Ajay Kumar Negi v. Union of India*, wherein the NGT, without any reasoning, levied an environmental compensation of INR 5 crore (which it later revoked due to lack of scientific evidence), the NGT in the *Art of Living Case* specified that the amount was not a "penalty".[277] Rather, it held that this was an "initial" amount that the Art of Living Foundation must pay for the rehabilitation of the area. Interestingly, the NGT made no attempt to specify the exact damage that the Art of Living Foundation had done in lieu of which the compensation was levied.

2.4.2.5   The NGT did not adequately hold governmental bodies accountable

While the final compensation amount imposed on the Art of Living Foundation, albeit not a penalty, was INR 5 crore, the amount levied on governmental authorities that had been grossly negligent was significantly less. Despite holding that the DDA – the main authority having jurisdiction over the event site – grossly erred in granting permission to the Art of Living Foundation for holding the WCF, the NGT did not impose any compensation on it. Further, despite holding that the Delhi Pollution Control Committee (DPCC) erred in performing its duty to ensure that there was no environmental damage, the Tribunal levied a paltry penalty of INR 1 lakh on it.[278]

Additionally, prior to the event, the Art of Living Foundation had also taken permissions from, inter alia, the MoEF, the Uttar Pradesh Irrigation Committee (UPIC), the Delhi Disaster Management Authority (DDMA), and the Irrigation and Flood Control Department of Delhi (IFCD). However, despite holding that these departments had wrongly granted the permission, the NGT did not impose any penalty on them and did not hold them accountable in any manner.

This special treatment for governmental authorities finds another parallel with the case of *Ajay Kumar Negi*. In that case, despite holding that the Forest Department did not perform its duties and could not explain the discrepancy between the number of trees allegedly damaged by the project proponent (398 trees) and its estimate (4,815 trees), the NGT did not impose any costs on it.[279] In fact, while the project proponent in the case had been depositing the necessary sums of money over several years to the Forest Department, the Forest Department had not used the deposit for any environmental restoration.[280] Accordingly, even though the NGT took note of the laxity and the gross negligence of the Forest Department, it did not hold it accountable in any way.

Similar to *Ajay Kumar Negi*, the INR 5 crore deposited by the Art of Living Foundation in 2016 has not been used by the relevant authorities for ecological rehabilitation to date. This trend of not holding governmental authorities accountable is problematic in two ways. First, it undermines the role of these agencies in curbing environmental pollution by normalizing their negligence and disregard. Second, it does not provide adequate deterrence against such dereliction.

Further, it creates a sense of uncertainty for any project proponent. For instance, as discussed, the Art of Living Foundation had taken permission from several governmental authorities before commencing the preparations of the WCF. However, the NGT did not hold these governmental authorities proportionately liable for granting permission for the event. Instead, all the burden was shifted onto the project proponent who seemingly thought that it was operating within the legally permissible limits having taken the governmental approvals.

Therefore, this trend of the NGT of not holding governmental authorities responsible by levying adequate compensation on them should be discouraged.

* * *

Through the above case study, we have sought to highlight the issues with the present adjudication mechanism of the NGT. In particular, we have endeavoured to demonstrate how these issues led to the substantial reduction in the compensation amount from INR 120 crore to INR 5 crore in the *Art of Living Case*. In doing so, we have emphasized that this reduction in the compensation amount was a natural consequence of the unscientific analysis undertaken by the NGT and the lack of will displayed by the Tribunal to quantify the actual environmental damage. The main points of the discussion are summarized below:

1. The initial estimate of INR 120 crore was based on a mere visual assessment conducted by the Expert Committee which did not involve a scientific

analysis. The chairperson of the Expert Committee, Mr Shashi Shekhar, denounced the compensation estimate put forth by his own committee and stated that it was "an inadvertent mistake" that was "not based on any scientific assessment".

In addition to being unscientific, the estimated compensation was based on a misplaced allegation that the natural vegetation and water bodies in the floodplain had been completely destroyed. The reason this was misplaced is due to the fact that the same Expert Committee members who made this allegation had submitted a report, after extensive research on the same floodplain area, to the NGT in 2013 titled "Restoration ad Conservation of River Yamuna", wherein they had concluded that the area was already devoid of natural vegetation, plant cover, and water bodies. In the report, the members had unequivocally held that the riverbed, floodplain forest, and grassland ecosystems were "locally extinct".

Further, it was a matter on record that there was illegal agriculture taking place on the event site for several years prior to the WCF. Thus, the Tribunal ought to have considered the state of the floodplain prior to the event and then compared it to the state of the floodplain after the event.

Finally, given the unscientific nature of the assessment, the Expert Committee based the initial estimate of the compensation on an "invisible loss" that was not capable of being readily visualized or documented.

2. Accordingly, the estimated compensation was reduced from INR 120 crore to INR 28.73 crore by the Expert Committee. This revised amount was primarily based on the alleged compaction of the event site by the Art of Living Foundation. However, this estimate too was based on the single visual assessment conducted by the Expert Committee, which was admittedly unscientific.

The Art of Living Foundation claimed that its use of the world's first "floating stage" significantly reduced soil compaction. Nevertheless, to determine the actual extent of compaction, if any, pre-event samples ought to have been compared with post-event samples of the soil from the event site.

In fact, during the hearings before the Tribunal, the Art of Living Foundation filed a separate application praying that the NGT should direct the Expert Committee to conduct the CBR Test – one of the most widely acknowledged tests for determining soil compaction – to quantify the actual extent of compaction of the soil. However, this application was denied by the Tribunal without providing any reasons.

The main point here is not whether the CBR Test is the most appropriate method of determining soil compaction. Rather, it is that the NGT ought to have supplemented its visual assessment with some scientific estimate of actual compaction. Such a scientific analysis would invariably involve the determination of the baseline condition of the event site prior to the event and the subsequent deviation from this condition.

3.   The unscientific visual assessment was only supplemented by two satellite images. These images (refer to Images 2.4 and 2.5), however, were taken without their seasonal context and were compared to make it seem like there is a loss of green cover in the event site due to the WCF. Since a pre-event image taken during the monsoon season was compared with a post-event image taken during the dry season, it made it seem that the loss of green cover was only due to the event.

     We have provided similar satellite images taken directly from the respondent's pleadings in the case to highlight the seasonal context. When Image 2.6, a pre-event image taken during the dry season, is compared with Image 2.7, a post-event image taken during the monsoon season, it seems that the WCF has actually helped grow the green cover in the event site.

     Thus, given that the Expert Committee relied on only two satellite images, despite the presence of several other images, to arrive at its conclusion of loss of green cover on account of the event, it led to selection bias.

4.   The Expert Committee, in its final report, admitted that it could not differentiate between the damage done to the event site prior to the event and the damage done on account of the event. Accordingly, the Committee substituted the term "ecological restoration" used in its preliminary report for "ecological rehabilitation" in the final report. It stated that ecological restoration was not possible as the damage done by the Art of Living Foundation due to the WCF could not be ascertained.

     This is ironic given that the same Expert Committee members, in their 2013 report submitted to the NGT, were able to scientifically ascertain the condition of the floodplain and the extent of environmental damage done. Moreover, determining the pre-event baseline condition would not have been very arduous given that the floodplain area was 9,300 hectares while only 25 hectares were used for the WCF.

     The primary reason that the Expert Committee provided for not conducting such a scientific analysis to determine compensation was that it would take "several months to a year besides financial resources". In other words, the Committee stated that while it was possible to determine the actual environmental damage caused by the Art of Living Foundation, it chose to not do so. Thus, the lack of will to correctly estimate environmental compensation is evident.

5.   Due to the unscientific assessment of compensation, the NGT had to drastically reduce the compensation amount. Finally, it levied an initial amount of INR 5 crore on the Art of Living Foundation while stating that this amount was not a penalty. The governmental authorities responsible for

granting permission to the Art of Living Foundation, however, were not held adequately accountable.

Despite holding that the DDA and the DPCC had been grossly negligent and had erred in granting permission for the WCF, the NGT did not hold them proportionately liable. It did not impose any costs on the former and imposed a paltry sum of INR 1 lakh on the latter.

Further, prior to the event, the Art of Living Foundation had taken permission from multiple governmental authorities such as the MoEF, the UPIC, the DDMA, and the IFCD. However, despite holding that these departments had wrongly granted the permission, the NGT did not impose any penalty on them and did not hold them accountable in any manner.

As we have discussed in previous sections, this trend of the NGT to unscientifically determine environmental compensation goes against its raison d'être. One of the most important reasons for the creation of the NGT was that the higher judiciary in India was unequipped to scientifically quantify environmental damage and the resulting compensation. However, despite having expert members, the NGT is unable to scientifically quantify environmental damage. As discussed, the compensation amount is frequently based on an arbitrary percentage of the project cost which does not have any semblance to the actual compensation required to undo the environmental damage.

Moreover, in cases such as the *Art of Living Case* and *Ajay Kumar Negi v. Union of India*, wherein the NGT makes no attempt to determine the baseline condition that existed prior to the damage, the Tribunal arbitrarily awards an initial compensation of INR 5 crore. Thus, this amount of INR 5 crore is used by the Tribunal as a placeholder which can later be revoked if there is no actual damage found later. Since this amount is not based on the actual environmental damage, it is usually revoked or significantly modified.

Thus, the NGT based its conclusions on an unscientific visual assessment, did not determine the baseline condition of the event site prior to the event, erred by committing selection bias in relying on supplementary evidence, and admitted that the damage done to the floodplain area could not be specifically attributed to Art of Living Foundation. In the light of this, it is not difficult to see why the environmental compensation was eventually reduced from INR 120 crore to INR 5 crore. In fact, due to the complete lack of methodology in quantifying environmental damage coupled with the unscientific determination of compensation, any amount levied as compensation seems arbitrary.

Furthermore, at the very least, conducting a scientific analysis would have yielded better results than the simple visual assessment upon which all compensation estimates were based. In addition to being backed by scientific data, such a comparison with the baseline condition would allow the Tribunal to make an informed estimate of the compensation in the first instance.

2.4.3   INTERNATIONAL BEST PRACTICES FOR DETERMINING ENVIRONMENTAL COMPENSATION: THE RESOURCE EQUIVALENCY ANALYSIS

In the previous section, we have discussed how there exists no particular methodology that the NGT follows for determining the quantum of environmental compensation. As noted, such determinations are often based on considerations that are not in line with the ground realities of a case. In this section, however, we seek to highlight some of the international best practices that are used in the US and the European Union (EU) in relation to quantifying environmental damage. In doing so, we endeavour to highlight how these can be applied by the NGT to yield a more scientific and stable estimate of environmental compensation on a regular basis.

While one of the key objectives of the polluter pays principle is to ensure that the polluter internalizes the cost of pollution, the quantification of such damage has been challenging. Historically, the focus of environmental liability in the developing parts of Europe and Asia – particularly Eastern Europe, the Caucasus, and Central Asia – has been on the fact of harm to the environment and the resulting monetary compensation to the state even in cases where the damaged environment cannot be restored.[281] This primarily finds expression in the form of an imposition of a penalty when environmental damage has crossed a certain threshold.[282] In other words, the focus in these countries has been on the legal harm whereby the pollution exceeds permissible standards rather than the environmental harm and subsequent environmental restoration.

For instance, according to Articles 9 and 10 of Moldova's Methodology for Assessing Environmental Damage Caused by Violation of Water Legislation, a polluter is liable to pay environmental compensation if the pollution has crossed certain thresholds even if such pollution has not resulted in any actual environmental damage.[283] Similar provisions can be found in Indian environmental legislation as well.[284]

In contrast, the EU's Environmental Liability Directive (ELD) defines environmental damage in terms of the harm caused to protected species, natural habitats, water, and land if its contamination threatens human health.[285] Similarly, albeit broader in scope, the US definition encompasses loss, injury, or destruction of natural resources including reasonable costs of its assessment.[286] Both the EU and the US definitions focus on the remediation and restoration of the environment rather than just the fact of environmental harm.

Accordingly, there exist primarily two ways of quantifying environmental damage.[287] The first method involves determining the monetary value of the damage by determining the economic value of natural resources through methods such as hedonic pricing, travel cost method, and stated preference techniques.[288] Broadly, these methods can be seen as monetary in nature as they involve ascribing an economic value to a natural resource, by determining how much people are willing to pay for using it or willing to be compensated for its non-availability.

There are two problems with this approach. First, it involves a great deal of subjectivity. Irrespective of the method used, it is very difficult to determine a reasonable amount that people would be willing to pay for a certain resource. Additionally, this method is not well suited for valuing natural resources such as biodiversity as determining their non-use value through this method becomes difficult and subjective.[289]

For example, let us consider two lakes that are similar in all ecological respects but are situated at different distances from a human settlement. Also, let us assume that there are two similar factories located adjacent to each of these lakes which are polluting equally. If we were to follow this approach to determining environmental compensation, invariably the lake that is closer to the human settlement and is more useful for recreational purposes will be valued more.

This also highlights the second issue with this approach, which is the inherent anthropocentrism. The *Cambridge Dictionary* defines anthropocentrism as considering humans and their existence as the most important and central fact in the universe.[290] It refers to the paradigm that interprets and values everything around us in terms of human values and experiences. Accordingly, this method is anthropocentric as it values the environment in terms of human wants and desires rather than valuing it due to its inherent worth. Thus, even though both lakes perform similar ecological functions in our hypothetical example, they are likely to be valued differently based on their fulfilment of human needs.

Due to the shortcomings of this method, "resource equivalency methods" were developed in the 1990s as the Organisation for Economic Co-operation and Development (OECD) countries felt the need to base environmental compensation on the assessed need to restore affected natural resources and their services.[291] These methods focus on the remediation of natural resources rather than the market value that can be ascribed to them. Unlike the monetary approach which is anthropocentric, this approach is ecocentric.

Ecocentrism refers to the paradigm that places importance on all life and the environment as a whole, rather than on parts of the environment which are more useful to humans. This approach is ecocentric as it values environmental compensation on the basis of the actual costs required to remediate the natural resources and their services in the ecosystem, rather than valuing the compensation on the basis of how useful these resources are to humans. In fact, the preference for ecocentrism over anthropocentrism is evident from the fact that Annexure II of the ELD unequivocally states a preference for resource equivalency methods over monetary methods.

The determination of environmental compensation in India lies somewhere in the middle of these two approaches. Schedule II of the NGT Act provides heads under which compensation or relief for damage can be claimed. These heads include inter alia, loss of employment, damage to property, expenses or loss incurred by the government for providing relief or restoration of the environment, and damage or harm caused to flora and fauna.[292] These heads encompass features of both methods as they strive to take into account both the monetary value of the environmental damage caused by paying the required amount to the state and the harm caused to natural resources.

In practice, however, the NGT tends to impose environmental compensation for restoration of the environment and directs governmental authorities to take the necessary restitutive actions. While this seems in line with the approach taken by the OECD countries and the ELD, as noted previously, the final determination of compensation bears little semblance to the approach taken. In other words, while the NGT claims to assess environmental compensation on the amount needed for remediating the environment, the trends discussed previously demonstrate that the final compensation is usually not based on the actual environmental damage.

As seen in the *Art of Living Case*, the three estimates of compensation – INR 120 crore, INR 28.73 crore, and INR 5 crore – were not based on any scientific assessment and were not calculated by taking into account the actual remediation costs. Further, as discussed, the general trend of the NGT is to peg environmental compensation at 5 per cent of the project cost, irrespective of the damage caused by the pollution. Thus, while the NGT is seemingly in line with the resource equivalency methods, in practice it lacks a scientific methodology for calculating environmental compensation.

Further, as will be discussed in subsequent sections, the compensation awarded by the NGT is rarely deposited by the project proponent. Even in cases where the amount is deposited, it is rarely employed by governmental authorities for environmental remediation and restoration. For instance, the INR 5 crore deposited by the Art of Living Foundation as environmental compensation remains unutilized to date. Given these issues, let us explore what the resource equivalency analysis (REA) entails and how its adoption by the NGT can yield more accurate compensation estimates.

2.4.3.1   The Resource Equivalency Analysis

The REA focuses on the remediation of the environment. Before determining the appropriate remediation methods, it is important to determine the actual extent of environmental damage. The quantum of damage is best measured in relation to a "baseline condition" of the natural resource or environment. The ELD defines baseline condition as follows: [293]

> [T]he condition at the time of the damage of the natural resources and services that would have existed had the environmental damage not occurred.

This estimation is done on the basis of the best information available. After the baseline condition has been determined, the ELD provides for remedying of the environmental damage by way of primary, complementary, and compensatory remediation:[294]

a)   "Primary" remediation is any remedial measure which returns the damaged natural resources or impaired services to the baseline condition.

b) "Complementary" remediation is any remedial measure that is undertaken in relation to the damaged natural resources or impaired services which accounts for the fact that primary remediation does not fully result in the restoration of the damaged resources or services.

c) "Compensatory" remediation refers to any action that is taken to account for any interim losses of natural resources or services that occur from the date of the damage until primary remediation has achieved its full effect.

These methods of remediation are undertaken in a stepwise manner. Complementary remediation is only undertaken when primary remediation does not result in the restoration of the environment to its baseline condition. Likewise, compensatory remediation will only be undertaken when there are significant interim losses.

To determine the quantum of remediation that is required to adequately compensate for past, present, and future losses, both the ELD and the US's Natural Resource Damage Assessment regulations use the REA.[295] In simple terms, the REA tries to equate the value of the environmental damage to the value of environmental gains from remediation work. It includes the following three methods of assessing the type of remediation required:[296]

a) Resource-to-resource method: This method involves remediation that matches the actual lost natural resources with the remediated ones. It involves assessing the extent to which the organisms and biodiversity, that had been damaged, have been remediated. The US National Oceanic and Atmospheric Administration uses a similar approach called the habitat equivalency analysis wherein the damage to the habitat is compared with the gains from remediation.

b) Service-to-service method: This method involves remediation that matches the loss of services or functions of the natural resources to the gains made to these natural services through remediation. For instance, the loss of a lake affects both the natural functions that the lake would perform in the ecosystem and the loss of public services such as fishing and recreation.

c) Value-to-value method: This method is usually applied when both the resource-to-resource method and the service-to-service method do not satisfactorily remediate the losses. For instance, in cases where the natural resource is completely destroyed and its restoration is not possible, then the appropriate method of remediation is to provide an alternative natural resource which is equivalent in value. Accordingly, this method involves estimating the value of the lost resource or services and then selecting remediating alternatives that have an equivalent monetary value. However, unlike monetary methods discussed earlier, the value referred to under this method is based on the value added to the ecosystem as well as the fulfilment of human needs.

Accordingly, the REA involves three main steps:[297]

a) The first step in the REA is to quantify the environmental damage in terms of the extent and degree of lost natural resources or services.
b) The second step involves identifying and evaluating different remediation options in terms of the quantity and quality of replaced natural resources and services that are likely to be provided.
c) Finally, the REA requires the adjustment of the remediation timeline and degree to compensate for lost resources and services over time.

An example of the REA in action is seen in the trout remediation in Coeur d'Alene River Basin in Idaho, US. For more than a century, hazardous heavy metals such as lead, zinc, and cadmium had been released into the river basin due to mining and mineral processing. This resulted in a drastic loss of aquatic habitat and resources.

The damage to the aquatic habitat, including surface water, fish, and other aquatic organisms, was calculated on the basis of replacing the ecosystem functions of the lost habitat. Costs were estimated for regaining the lost natural services by using the trout population density as a metric. In particular, the response of the trout population to the improvement in water quality was assessed and empirical data from different water streams was used to estimate the total cost of remediating the impacted area.

Further, remediation alternatives were included in the compensation estimates in lieu of areas that could not be fully revived. These alternatives included enhancing the physical habitat of nearby streams to enable fish spawning and revival. Thus, losses to the habitat on account of the contamination were compared to the gains from remediation methods. The final compensation accounted for costs required to return to the baseline condition as well as costs required to compensate for losses in the interim. Accordingly, the compensation estimate based on the REA ranged from USD 64.4 million to USD 177.9 million.

There are, however, some challenges with the REA. The most significant challenge involves the estimation of the loss of natural resources and services. Estimating environmental loss is often based on a unit of measure of damage that adequately matches the gains from remediation.[298] This unit of measure varies on a case-to-case basis. For instance, in the aforementioned example of the Coeur d'Alene River Basin, one of the major units of measurement was the trout population in the basin.

Likewise, other units of measurement depending on the facts of a case can include measures of vegetation density, microorganism concentration, biomass, and the number of trees and animals lost.[299] Once the unit of measurement is chosen for determining the environmental loss, the same unit should be used while gauging the impact of remediation.

The selection of such a unit of measurement involves subjectivity and there is no objective standard for determining which unit should be used. Nevertheless, arriving at an estimated compensation through this method is significantly more scientific and accurate than the method used by the NGT. The REA, at the least, attempts to base compensation on the actual costs required to undo the environmental damage and return the environment to the baseline condition.

If we apply the REA to the *Art of Living Case*, it is likely to yield a very different result. As noted, the NGT did not determine the baseline condition of the event site before estimating compensation. It did not collect soil samples prior to the event. Further, it restrained the Art of Living Foundation from voluntarily conducting the CBR Test to determine the pre-event and post-event compaction of the soil.

If the NGT were to apply the REA in this case, however, the first step would be to determine the baseline condition which would enable the tribunal to quantify any deviation. In doing so, not only would it have to collect data on the soil compaction levels prior to the event, it would have to also prepare an estimation of the resource value of the event site by deciphering the value of natural resources present and natural services rendered by the microorganisms, vegetation, and the floodplain as a whole.

After the baseline condition has been determined, in line with the REA the Tribunal would then quantify the environmental damage in terms of the extent of lost resources and services and compare this with the baseline condition. Once the deviation from the baseline condition has been determined, the Tribunal would then evaluate and select the appropriate remediation methods. Given that the NGT Act gives the Tribunal ample discretion in adopting the course for determining compensation and the type of remediation, the Tribunal can take into account some of the following criteria, inter alia, provided in Annex II of the ELD:

a) Effect of each remediation option on public health and safety
b) Cost of implementing each option
c) Likelihood of success of each option
d) Extent to which each option will prevent future damage on account of the implementation of such option
e) The amount of time that will be required for the remediation options to be effective in restoring the environmental damage
f) Extent to which option takes account of relevant social, economic, cultural, and other locally specific concerns and factors

Thus, after evaluating each of the remediation options based on these criteria, the Tribunal would select the appropriate remediation option and proceed with the remediation.

Accordingly, it would determine the degree to which primary remediation would be effective in reversing the environmental damage towards the baseline condition. Based on this evaluation, the Tribunal would gauge the need for complementary and compensatory remediation in accordance with the gaps left by the primary remediation and interim losses, respectively.

Perhaps the most significant result yielded by the application of this methodology would be that the NGT would not have to substantially lower its compensation estimate by more than 95 per cent (from INR 120 crore to INR 5 crore). Thus, even if the baseline condition is difficult to determine – which is unlikely to be the case as it can be determined from the adjacent parts of the floodplain – following the REA would, at the very least, allow the NGT to give cogent reasons as to why it is difficult to estimate the deviation from the baseline condition caused by the environmental damage. Additionally, in such a case the NGT would be able to justify why a value-to-value remediation would be preferred over a resource-to-resource remediation given that restitution of the natural resource is not entirely possible.

Overall, following the REA will allow the NGT to determine more appropriate environmental compensation on a case-by-case basis, which bears a rational nexus with actual damage. In cases where the extent of environmental damage is hard to determine, it will allow the Tribunal to provide cogent reasons for arriving at the compensation amounts. This will ensure that compensation estimates are stable and do not vary drastically. Finally, the REA will enable the NGT to deal with scientific uncertainty more effectively and live up to the intention behind its creation.

2.4.4   THE FORMULA-BASED APPROACH: A NEW TREND IN ENVIRONMENTAL COMPENSATION?

In the previous section, we have argued that the environmental compensation should be based on, inter alia, the actual remediation cost of restoring the lost natural habitat, rather than the present practice of the Tribunal to peg the compensation to an economic variable of the project or the project proponent in most cases. Recently, for the first time in India, such an attempt has been made by the CPCB's in-house Committee on Methodology for Assessing Environmental Compensation and Action Plan to Utilize the Fund. In its report dated 15 July 2019, the Committee, based on a request from the NGT[300] to give effect to the polluter pays principle, has sought to provide guidelines with respect to the assessment and calculation of environmental compensation.[301] In this section, we will examine whether the approach adopted by the Committee meets its objective to base the environmental compensation on actual remediation costs and whether the NGT should adopt the same.

In the report, the Committee listed the following six instances that it deemed to be appropriate for levying environmental compensation:

a) Discharges in violation of consent conditions, mainly prescribed standards/consent limits.

b) Not complying with the directions issued, such as direction for closure due to non-installation of online continuous emission/effluent monitoring systems (OCEMS), non-adherence to the action plans submitted, and so on.

c) Intentional avoidance of data submission or data manipulation by tampering with the Online Continuous Emission/Effluent Monitoring systems.

d) Accidental discharges lasting for short durations resulting in damage to the environment.

e) Intentional discharges to the environment – land, water, and air – resulting in acute injury or damage to the environment.

f) Injection of treated/partially treated/untreated effluents to ground water.

The Committee has suggested that environmental compensation in the first three cases, that is, (a), (b), and (c), should be based on the following formula:

$$\text{Environmental Compensation} = PI \times N \times R \times S \times LF$$

Where PI = pollution index, N = number of days for which violation has taken place, R = factor in rupees, S = scale of operation, and LF = location factor.

(While the report provides certain other formulae for calculation of compensation in certain other situations, they fall prey to the issues highlighted later, and are hence not discussed.)

The first factor is the PI, which is a number between 0 and 100. An increasing value of PI denotes the increasing degree of pollution hazard from the particular industrial sector. It is calculated after considering the quality and quantity of emissions or effluents generated, types of hazardous wastes generated, and the consumption of resources by a particular industry.[302] The CPCB has directed that industrial sectors should be categorized into Red (60–100), Orange (41–59), and Green (21–40), and that the average pollution index of 80, 50, and 30, respectively, may be taken for calculating the environmental compensation.

The second factor is the number of days (N) for which the violation takes place. It is the difference between the date of observation of the violation and the date of compliance. The third factor is a factor in rupees (R) and may be a minimum of 100 and a maximum of 500. The CPCB has suggested considering R as 250 for the purpose of the calculation of compensation. This variable seems to be inserted as a multiplier and to provide leeway in cases where the compensation seems inadequate. The fourth factor relates to the categorization of the size (S) of the industry. The value is 0.5 for micro or small, 1 for medium, and 1.5 for large industries or units. The last factor is a location factor (LF) of the industrial unit and the population of the city or town that it is located nearby. For industrial units located within a municipal boundary or up to 10-kilometre distance from such boundary, the following factors may be used:

Population (in millions)	Location Factor (*LF*)
1 to <5	1.25
5 to <10	1.5
10 and above	2.0

The CPCB has suggested that in the event that the industrial unit is outside the 10-kilometre radius of a municipal boundary, or is near a town or city that has a population of less than 1 million, the value of *LF* is presumed to be 1. For notified Ecologically Sensitive Areas, the value of *LF* is suggested to be 2.

Further, the report suggests that in any case, the minimum compensation should be INR 5,000 per day, and to include a deterrent effect for repeated violations the compensation can be increased on an exponential basis, that is, by two times on the first repetition, four times on the second violation, and eight times on further repetitions. Accordingly, the report provides the following sample calculation of environmental compensation across different industrial categories:

Industrial Category	Red	Orange	Green
Pollution Index (PI)	60–100	41–59	21–40
Average PI	80	50	30
R		250	
S		0.5–1.5	
LF		1.0–2.0	
Environmental Compensation (per day)	**10,000–60,000**	**6,250–37,500**	**5,000–22,500**

In relation to the next three cases identified by the report, that is, (d), (e), and (f), the report suggests that the compensation may contain two parts – immediate relief and long-term measures (such as remediation). Further, the report suggests that in all such cases "detailed investigations are required from expert institutions/organisations", and a comprehensive plan for remediation should be prepared and executed under the supervision of a committee consisting of representatives of the relevant SPCB, CPCB, and the expert organization.

The stated purpose of this formula, according to the report, is to strengthen the application of the polluter pays principle by basing environmental compensation on the "quantity and quality" of environmental harm and enabling remediation of lost or damaged natural resources.[303] Let us examine the components of the formula to analyse whether its application has the potential to meet this objective.

The formula, at the outset, is based on factors that can be reasonably determined. This is because the value attached to each factor such as the pollution index of an industry, size, proximity to a municipality, and the number of days of pollution can be calculated with ease. Thus, it is convenient in its application and is likely to save judicial time and resources. However, by basing the compensation on these variables rather than actual remediation costs, it is placing convenience over the stated aim of the formula. This is because each of the factors is applicable only at a generic level, if at all, to the reality of a particular industry and is unlikely to have any significant correlation to the actual environmental damage in a particular case.

For instance, the value of the first factor – PI – of a particular industry is calculated by SPCBs based on the guidelines provided by the CPCB, which takes into account the average quantity and quality of emissions in a particular sector. Thus, this does not take into account the outliers in any industry, which can pollute substantially in excess of the sectoral average. Moreover, there are many companies and plants that produce multiple chemicals and products that do not neatly fit into a single industry, and hence assigning a particular industry's value might not be appropriate. Perhaps more significantly, the pollution index looks at the average pollution of an industry during its normal period of operation. When there is a violation of consent limits, directions issued, or intentional data manipulation (refer to cases (a), (b), and (c) above to which this formula applies), it is likely to be very different and might not always be reflected by a generic pollution index of an industry. This problem is only exacerbated by the CPCB's suggestion to use "average PI" for each of the three zones – Red (80), Orange (50), and Green (30) – thereby divorcing the actual extent of pollution from the factual reality and specifics of a particular case.

Similarly, the factor relating to the size of operation (S) seems to be detached from the actual facts of a case. The according of a blanket value of 0.5 for micro or small, 1 for medium, and 1.5 for large industries or units seems arbitrary. It does not take into account that small industrial units can cause massive pollution and discharge, while large units might not be polluting as much. Accordingly, this is similar to the present trend of the NGT wherein it considers the profitability, size, and turnover of the project proponent while awarding compensation, rather than basing it on the actual extent of pollution.[304] Thus, this punishes an enterprise merely due to its size or scale, without regard to actual damage, and is likely to result in under-compensation or over-compensation in cases.

The factor relating to the location (LF) of an industrial unit is equally problematic. By basing the degree of compensation on the proximity of a project to a municipality and the human population therein, it is not only very anthropocentric but also loses sight of the fact that most large-scale projects (such as those related to mining or excavation) are in rural areas, with low population and significant ecology. This directly goes against the idea of remediation of natural resources and habitat as there is no necessary correlation between the proximity to a municipality or the population of a city or town and the environmental damage. Moreover, any damage done by an industrial unit operating outside the 10-kilometre radius of a municipality or near a town with a population under 1 million is accorded the *LF* value of 1, which in terms of the formula adds nothing (given that 1 when multiplied by another number remains the number). In other words, the location factor in the formula treats any damage done to the environment outside the prescribed municipal and population limits as redundant.

The factor taking into account the number of days of pollution (*N*) is suggested to commence from the day of observation of the pollution. Accordingly, this does not take into account the actual date of the start of the pollution. Finally, the only factor that seems to be not based on generic or arbitrary considerations is the rupees factor (*R*). However, this does not appear to be based on any consideration at all and seems to have been inserted to allow the Tribunal some leeway in situations that warrant more or less compensation.

The issues highlighted above with each individual factor in the formula can be understood with the help of a hypothetical example. If we have a small (*S*) industrial plant, belonging to a green industry (*PI*), outside the 10-kilometre radius of the nearest municipality (*LF*), and there has been an excess discharge for a few hours of a chemical that has seriously damaged the nearby environment, applying the formula the compensation is extremely inadequate. The environmental compensation, in this example, would be in a range between: Environmental Compensation (INR 1,050 to INR 10,000) = *PI* (21 to 40) × *N* (1) × *R* (100 to 500) × *S* (0.5) × *LF* (1).

Thus, the compensation would range between INR 1,050 and INR 10,000. Perhaps realizing how low the compensation could be based on the formula, the report suggests that the minimum compensation per day should be INR 5,000. However, even if the upper limit of INR 10,000 in the aforementioned example is taken, it is completely detached from the actual environmental damage in a particular case. Therefore, the objective of the formula to give effect to the polluter pays principle by enabling effective remediation of the environment to its original condition is not met.

Similar to the present trend of the NGT (discussed earlier in the chapter), a potential polluter is likely to continue with a polluting project if the project is reasonably profitable after considering the maximum environmental compensation that might be levied under the formula, given the industry of its operation. Thus, in many ways, this exacerbates the present challenges with the determination of environmental compensation, and is likely to continue the present trend of turning the polluter pays principle into "pay and pollute". Nevertheless, the report seems to make some progress by suggesting a full-scale scientific inquiry to ascertain the actual cost of remediation efforts in relation to cases (d), (e), and (f). As noted, the report suggests that the compensation may contain two parts – immediate relief and long-term measures – and does not provide a formula for this calculation. This is helpful in shifting the focus towards remediation and basing the compensation on the actual facts of a case. However, as noted previously in the case study on the *Art of Living Case*, the NGT is already aware that the compensation needs to be based on the actual environmental damage, which is determined after a scientific investigation. Given the lack of guidance with respect to how the remediation calculation should be done, it is unclear how impactful the report is likely to be in changing the NGT's present methodology.

Given the recentness of the report, the application of the formula by the NGT has been limited. In *Anwar Hussain Ansari, Jhamumo Alpsankhyak Morcha v. State of Jharkhand*,[305] the NGT received a letter alleging the discharge of pollutants such as hypochlorite and other toxic effluents into the groundwater by M/s Aditya Birla Chemicals, without any safeguards. The letter prayed for remedial action. The joint inspection conducted by the SPCB reported increased values of sodium, chloride, total dissolved solids (TDS), potassium, and a highly acidic pH value of 3.0 in the surrounding drainage system. After confirming that the industrial unit had discharged these effluents into the river, the NGT calculated the compensation to be levied based on the aforementioned formula proposed by the report, as the case fell squarely under case (a), identified by the report (discharges beyond the prescribed limit). Employing the formula, the NGT observed:

Environmental Compensation (EC) = PI × N × R × S × LF

Where, PI = Pollution index of industrial sector (here-80 for red category industrial sector),

N = Number of days of violation took place (here – 545 days has been considered, from date of complaint submitted to Hon'ble NGT vide letter dated 22.07.2018 to continuous violation observed during 5 inspections carried out in between and also same violation observed during inspection of joint team dated 17.01.2020)

R = A factor in Rupees for EC which may be a minimum of 100 to maximum of 500 (R to be taken as 250 in case of violation)

S – Factor for scale of Operation of the facility (here 1.5, for large scale industry)

LF = Location factor (Here 1.25, for 1 million to <5 million population)

As per the EC formula, EC has been calculated as follows:

Environmental Compensation (EC) = PI × N × R × S × LF

$$= 80 * 545 * 250 * 1.5 * 1.25 = 2,04,37,500/-$$

The unit is liable to pay total environmental compensation amount of Rs. 2,04,37,500/- for affecting the quality of North Koel river by discharging effluent through Chhaliya drain for the period of 22.07.2018 to 17.01.2020.

It remains largely unclear as to how the amount of INR 20,437,500 would be adequate for the remediation process. Even though the applicant in the impugned case specifically prayed for remediation, there is no discussion in the judgment on what was the actual extent of damage to the environment and how this amount levied was proportionate. Moreover, the issues with the formula's application highlighted above become clear if some facts are tweaked. For instance, the value accorded to the location factor (*LF*) in the case was 1.25, as the population of the nearest municipality was between 1 and 5 million. Had the incident happened near a city with a population of more than 10 million, the resulting compensation would have increased to INR 32,700,000, that is, a 60 per cent increase, even though the environmental damage and the remediation costs in both cases were exactly the same. Thus, in addition to the inherent anthropocentrism, the calculation of the compensation has no nexus with the actual remediation costs prayed due to the design of the formula.

Similar issues are observed in *Adil Ansari v. C.I. Gupta Exports Pvt. Ltd. and Ors.*,[306] wherein the NGT adjudicated on the allegations of discharge of effluents and illegal extraction of groundwater by the defendant. The case is presently sub judice (as of March 2022), and the investigation has revealed the intentional illegal extraction of groundwater by the defendant, coupled with the discharge of highly acidic effluents and hazardous wastes into the neighbouring water supply system. Additionally, there has been a leakage in the sewage treatment plant into a pond adjacent to the industrial unit, leading to a mixing of industrial and domestic effluents. In the latest order, the NGT has calculated the environmental compensation as follows:

Environmental Compensation (EC) = PI × N × R × S × LF

PI = Pollution index of industrial sector (here-80, for red category industrial sector),

N = Number of days of violation took place (here-203 days, from date of inspection carried out by the joint team and found violation of ZLD norms dated 28.03.2019 to date of inspection of 2nd inspection of the joint team dated 16.10.2019)

R = A factor in Rupees for Penalty (R to be taken as 250)

S = Factor for scale of Operation of the facility (here-1.5, for large scale industry)

LF = Location factor (Here-1, for less than 1 million population)

A). 28.03.2019 – 25.06.2019

　　(EC = PI*N*R*S*LF)

　　　　= 80* 90*250*1.5*1

　　　　= 27,00,000/-

B). 26.06,2019 – 23.09.2019

　　(EC = PI*N*R*S*LF)*2

　　　　= 80*90*250*1.5*1*2

　　　　= 54,00,000/-

C). 23.09.2019 – 16.10.2019

(EC = PI *N*R*S* LF)*4

= 80*23*250*1.5*1*4

= 27,60,000/-

Total EC (A+B+C) = Rs. 1,08,60,000/-

Similar to *Anwar Hussain*, there is no discussion by the Tribunal of the actual environmental damage that has taken place in terms of costs, which would only be determined after a detailed scientific investigation. Accordingly, there is no discussion of how the final environmental compensation is adequate to remediate the contaminated groundwater and pond to their original condition. Moreover, tweaking any of the factors in the formula such as the proximity to a municipality, population of a neighbouring town, or size of the unit would yield a very different compensation amount, even though the actual environmental damage would be the same.

Therefore, in conclusion, in the light of all the reasons highlighted in our discussion above, the NGT should nip the trend of adopting the CPCB's formula for determining environmental compensation in the bud. Instead, as suggested in the section on the resource equivalence analysis, the compensation should be based on the actual costs of remediating the environment after conducting a scientific assessment of the same.

2.5　PROCEDURE AND PRACTICE

As we have observed from Chapter 1, environmental adjudication is inherently more technical and complex than ordinary adjudication. It invariably involves scientific assessment of environmental damage and compensation. As we will discuss later in Chapter 3, many times the environmental or health-related impact of an industrial activity is not apparent and scientific studies are undertaken to reasonably estimate this. Due to these reasons, standard civil procedural requirements are not always suited to the needs of environmental adjudication. This has been recognized right from the early years of environmental adjudication.[307] For instance, in response to the infamous 1969 oil spill in the Santa Barbara Channel in the US, a senator stated:[308]

> A statement of national policy for the environment like other major policy declarations is in large measure concerned with principle rather than detail; with an expression of broad national goals rather than narrow specific procedures for implementation. But if goals and principles are to be effective, they must be capable of being applied in action.

This recognition was also seen by the Supreme Court in the *Oleum Gas Leaks Case*,[309] wherein standard civil procedures of evidence and burden of proof would not have adequately held the polluters accountable. Accordingly, the Court had to devise a new procedural standard of absolute liability that did not accord any standard alibis to the project proponent, to ensure that the costs of pollution are internalized. The need for procedural flexibility in environmental cases also comes from the recognition that the application of standard procedural laws can lead to a delay in justice. Environmental matters, inherently, require speedier resolution given the potential risk of irreversible environmental damage if a pollutive activity is allowed to continue.

Due to these, by the time the judiciary-led call for environmental courts culminated in action by the legislature, there was consensus on allowing procedural flexibility to environmental courts to ensure expedient adjudication.

India's first legislation aimed at establishing an environmental court – the National Environment Tribunal Act, 1995 – echoed this consensus. Under Section 5(3), it clearly prescribed the non-application of the Code of Civil Procedure[310] to the environmental courts established under the legislation:

> The Tribunal shall not be bound by the procedure laid down by the Code of Civil Procedure, 1908, but shall be guided by the principles of natural justice and, subject to the other provisions of this Act and of any rules, the Tribunal shall have power to regulate its own procedure including the fixing of places and times of its inquiry.

Thus, it was recognized that environmental courts ought to have the power to regulate their own procedure to ensure efficient disposal of environmental matters. To this effect, it was held that the NET would not be bound by the standard civil procedure. Nevertheless, the NET Act, 1995, was never notified by the legislature and, as a result, the NET was never established. It remained on paper. The procedural flexibility, however, was retained during the second attempt to establish an environmental court in India. Accordingly, the National Environmental Appellate Authority Act, 1997, incorporated the procedural autonomy of the NEAA as a distinct feature under Section 12 of the legislation. As we have discussed in Chapter 1, the NEAA was mostly staffed with bureaucrats and was largely seen as dysfunctional. It remained without a chairperson for almost a decade.

Nevertheless, despite the failures of the two predecessors of the NGT, procedural flexibility remained a constant theme. The 186th Report of the Law Commission of India also noted, in its final recommendations, that the proposed environmental courts must be freed from the application of the Code of Civil Procedure, 1908, as well as the Indian Evidence Act, 1872. These suggestions were duly noted and incorporated in Section 19 of the NGT Act, which states:

> (1) The Tribunal shall not be bound by the procedure laid down by the Code of Civil Procedure, 1908, but shall be guided by the principles of natural justice.

(2) Subject to the provisions of this Act, the Tribunal shall have power to regulate its own procedure.

(3) The Tribunal shall also not be bound by the rules of evidence contained in the Indian Evidence Act, 1872.

Furthermore, the NGT has been granted all the powers of a civil court under Section 19(4) of the NGT Act. These powers include

a) summoning and enforcing the attendance of any person and examining him on oath;
b) requiring the discovery and production of documents;
c) receiving evidence on affidavits;
d) subject to the provisions of Sections 123 and 124 of the Indian Evidence Act, 1872 (1 of 1872), requisitioning any public record or document or copy of such record or document from any office;
e) issuing commissions for the examination of witnesses or documents;
f) reviewing the Tribunal's own decision;
g) dismissing an application for default or deciding its *ex parte*;
h) setting aside any order of dismissal of any application for default or any order passed by it *ex parte*;
i) passing an interim order (including granting an injunction or stay) after providing the parties concerned an opportunity to be heard, on any application made or appeal filed under the NGT Act; and
j) passing an order requiring any person to cease and desist from committing or causing any violation of any enactment specified in Schedule I to the NGT Act.

The NGT is deemed as a civil court for the purposes of Section 195 and Chapter XXVI of the Code of Criminal Procedure, 1973, and proceedings before the Tribunal are considered as judicial proceedings for the purposes of the Indian Penal Code, 1860.[311] Accordingly, Section 25 prescribes that an award, decision, or order of the Tribunal is executable as a decree of a civil court and that the Tribunal has the powers of a civil court for this purpose.

Further, Section 35 empowers the Central government to frame rules on various aspects of the NGT's functioning, such as who can appear before the Tribunal, the procedure for hearing, the transfer of cases by the chairperson, salaries and allowances, and the constitution of the Selection Committee and manner of appointment of members. Although, any rules made under this section become operative on the date of notification, they need parliamentary assent to stay valid. Invoking the powers conferred under this section, the National Green Tribunal (Practice and Procedure) Rules, 2011, were notified.

These rules specify the detailed requirements for, inter alia, filing applications and appeals in the NGT.

The objective behind the procedural autonomy and flexibility provided under Section 19 has been recognized and affirmed by the NGT in *Vitthal Gopichand Bhungase v. Gangakhed Sugar and Energy Ltd.*[312] The case involved environmental damage that was increasing quickly with the passage of time. Disregarding conventional procedural requirements, the NGT proceeded to hear the case urgently without even framing the preliminary issues. In this regard, the Tribunal held:[313]

> Section 19, gives sufficient flexibility to the working of the Tribunal in conducting trial of the Applications…. We are much concerned with Sub-section (2) of Section 19, which categorically states that the Tribunal shall have power to regulate its own procedure. Needless to say, there is no inherent right available to Gangakhed Sugar Factory, to urge this Tribunal to frame the preliminary issues as sought. In other words, Applicant-Gangakhed Sugar Factory, cannot insist that without framing such preliminary issues, the main Application shall not be proceeded with. It is the discretion of this Tribunal to either frame preliminary issues or to call upon the parties to go ahead with the trial of the matter for final adjudication. For, the Law itself has set out limitation of six (6) months as expected duration for disposal of such Application. The intention of Legislature, therefore, clearly is to avoid procedural impediments and to ensure expeditious final decision in such matters.

This case demonstrates the need for procedural flexibility in routine environmental cases. Ordinarily, the non-framing of issues is an offence that can later annul the entire proceedings in a civil court.[314] However, given that time is of the essence in many environmental cases, the NGT has the procedural autonomy and flexibility to prioritize the expeditious disposal of cases rather than fulfilling procedural requirements. The NGT, in the aforementioned case, demonstrates this by foregoing the standard procedural requirement of framing issues in the overall interest of justice.

Similarly, in *Janardan Kundalikrao Pharande v. Ministry of Environment & Forest*,[315] the Tribunal had allowed the applicants to amend their pleadings without issuing notice to the respondents of such amendment. Moreover, the applicants did not file a composite copy of the original pleadings along with the amendment in the format as per Rule 10 of the National Green Tribunal (Practice and Procedure) Act, 2011. The amendment, however, mostly pertained to information about intervening events and did not materially alter the substance of the submissions. The respondents objected to this concession accorded by the NGT as they had not been notified of the changes to the pleadings. In rejecting the respondents' objection, the NGT held:[316]

> All said and done, the amendment is not of substantial nature, nor it causes any prejudice to the rights of Respondent No. 2 Jubilant Industry. The amendment only

highlights the intervening developments. So far as the procedural part is concerned, it may be stated that Section 19 of the National Green Tribunal Act, 2010 gives flexibility to the Tribunal in such matters. The procedural Rules of the Code of Civil Procedure are not applicable to the proceedings before the National Green Tribunal. *Unless certain adverse order is to be passed which will cause serious impact on the rights of party, it may not be essential to hear the party.* The provision of Section 19 of the National Green Tribunal Act shows that only principles of natural justice need to be followed. (Emphasis supplied)

This case demonstrates the significant discretion accorded to the NGT with respect to governing its own procedure. Ordinarily, notifying the other party of changes in the initial pleadings is essential in civil disputes. This is the case even if there is no material bearing on the substance of the original pleadings in the opinion of the court. The Tribunal, however, dispenses with this requirement in the interest of minimizing environmental damage and ensuring expeditious disposal of cases. Significantly, while Section 19(1) states that the NGT should be guided by the principles of natural justice, the NGT held that it is not essential to hear a party unless an adverse order is passed that prejudicially impacts the rights of that party.

Being vested with all the powers of a civil court, the Tribunal has made use of such powers effectively. For instance, the NGT has consistently used bailable warrants against recalcitrant parties for the purpose of compelling appearance. In *Ramubhai Kriyabhai Patel v. Union of India*[317] the Tribunal issued bailable warrants to parties that refused to appear before it. This was done in exercise of the powers under Section 19(4)(a) of the National Green Tribunal Act, 2010, read with Order XV I Rule 10(3) and Section 151 of the Code of Civil Procedure, 1908. Exercise of such power to ensure the appearance of parties has been effectively used by the NGT in several cases.[318]

Another important aspect of the NGT's procedural autonomy is its power to review its own decision. Since the NGT's powers are analogous to that of a civil court in the matter of exercising review, its exercise of this power must adhere to Order XLVII, Rule 1 of the Civil Procedure Code, 1908. Accordingly, the NGT has been insistent on not allowing review petitions to be filed in cases where they are not warranted. As such, the Tribunal has been particular about ensuring that the grounds mentioned under Rule 1 are fulfilled.

The case of *Goel Ganga Developers India (P) Ltd. v. Union of India*[319] contains a detailed discussion of the review powers of the NGT. In this case, the appellants assailed the validity of an order passed by the NGT in review of its earlier decision before the Supreme Court. The case involved the construction of residential areas in violation of the conditions attached to the environmental clearance. Initially, the NGT ordered payment of environmental compensation by the project proponent. However, the applicant filed for review praying that the constructions should be demolished. The applicant contended that the Tribunal had committed an error apparent on the face of the record in passing the impugned order. The Tribunal admitted the review petition, and greatly enhanced the compensation. However, the review petition was adjudicated by a different bench than the one that had delivered the earlier decision.

Meanwhile, the respondents had already filed an appeal against the first decision in the Supreme Court. One of the key questions raised before the Supreme Court was regarding the validity of the review decision rendered by the NGT. The Supreme Court discussed the scope of the NGT's power vis-à-vis review of its own decisions in detail and stated:[320]

> Section 19(4)(*f*) of the National Green Tribunal Act, 2010, provides that the Tribunal shall have the same powers as are vested in civil courts while trying a suit in respect of matters relating to review of its decisions. Therefore, the power of review vested with NGT is akin to the power vested with the civil court. As such, the principles which govern the exercise of review jurisdiction before a civil court will apply with equal force to NGT.... Rule 22(2) of the National Green Tribunal (Practices and Procedure) Rules, 2011 provides that a review application shall ordinarily be heard by the Tribunal at the same place of sitting which has passed the order unless the Chairperson may, for reasons to be recorded in writing, direct it to be heard by the Tribunal sitting at any other place.... The normal rule that the same Bench should hear the review application should not be disturbed unless it is virtually impossible for the original Bench to hear the matter or the members of the Bench themselves opt not to hear the matter.

Further, the Court continued:[321]

> "In this behalf, we must remind ourselves that the power of review is a power to be sparingly used." As pithily put by V.R. Krishna Iyer, J., "A plea for review, unless the first judicial view is manifestly distorted, is like asking for the moon". The power of review is not like appellate power. It is to be exercised only when there is an error apparent on the face of the record. Therefore, judicial discipline requires that a review application should be heard by the same Bench. Otherwise, it will become an intra-court appeal to another Bench before the same court or tribunal. This would totally undermine judicial discipline and judicial consistency.

Accordingly, the Court set aside the increased compensation rendered in the review decision as the proper procedure was not followed by the Tribunal. Additionally, the Court also added that the NGT should not have entertained the review application, given that an appeal had already been filed at the Supreme Court. Through this decision, the Court has clarified the scope of review jurisdiction that can be exercised by the NGT. Unlike appellate jurisdiction, the power of review, as per the Court, has to be exercised very sparingly and only in extraordinary situations. It must only be exercised when there is an error apparent on the face of the record. Moreover, a review application must only be heard by the same bench that had pronounced the original decision as otherwise, it will amount to an intra-tribunal appeal. The only situations in which a review application can be heard by a different bench is when it is "virtually impossible".

The general power of judicial review of the NGT has also come under the scrutiny of the Court. While the NGT, in *Wilfred J. v. Ministry of Environment & Forests*,[322] has held that the scheme of the NGT vests the inherent power of judicial review with the Tribunal, the Supreme Court has held otherwise:[323]

> ... the NGT has no general power of judicial review akin to that vested under Article 226 of the Constitution of India possessed by the High Courts of this country.

We have discussed earlier in this chapter the debate around the NGT's power of judicial review in detail. Refer to the section on NGT's jurisdiction titled "NGT's Scope of Judicial Review" (section 2.3.4) for a more detailed analysis of the Tribunal's power of judicial review.

Overall, the NGT Act accords significant procedural autonomy and flexibility to the Tribunal. This is in line with the broad consensus that environmental matters require procedural flexibility to avoid delays and to dispose of cases expeditiously. As we have discussed, usually time is of the essence in environmental cases as the environmental damage is usually ongoing. The NGT has used this procedural flexibility judiciously to ensure that procedural impediments do not come in the way of environmental justice.

2.6   APPEAL AND BAR TO JURISDICTION

The NGT Act, under Section 22, provides that any person aggrieved by an order or award of the Tribunal "may" file an appeal to the Supreme Court within ninety days of the communication of the decision to such a person. This appeal can be filed on any grounds specified in Section 100 of the Code of Civil Procedure, 1908. The grounds are, inter alia, where there is a substantial question of law involved or where the order was delivered *ex parte*. In addition, the Supreme Court can entertain such an appeal after the expiry of ninety days if it is satisfied that there was a sufficient cause for the delay.

The preamble of the NGT Act clearly notes that the expeditious disposal of environmental cases is one of the main objectives behind the establishment of the NGT. In line with this objective, the Act does not provide for an appeal to the High Courts and only mentions that an appeal may lie to the Supreme Court. This is because incorporating an appeal to the High Courts would invariably lead to further delays, thereby running counter to the objective of dispensing timely environmental justice.

In furtherance of the same objective, Section 29 of the NGT Act bars the jurisdiction of civil courts from entertaining any appeals in respect of any matter that the NGT is empowered to determine. Further, it provides that no civil court has jurisdiction to settle any dispute or entertain any question relating to any matter which may be adjudicated upon by the NGT. This bar of jurisdiction extends to issuing injunctions in relation to such matters by civil courts.

Within a few months of the enactment of the NGT Act, a writ petition was filed in the Madras High Court challenging the constitutionality of this provision and the entire Act.[324] It was contended that the bar of jurisdiction applicable to all civil courts and vesting all environmental matters exclusively with the NGT would severely curtail access to justice for the underprivileged living in remote areas. Accordingly, an interim direction was sought to restrain the Central government from appointing any further members to the NGT. In response, the High Court ordered an injunction restraining further appointments. Subsequently, however, the Supreme Court reversed this decision.[325]

The meaning and object of Section 29 have been appreciated by the Supreme Court in *Bhopal Gas Peedith Mahila Udyog Sangathan v. Union of India*,[326] wherein the Court opined:[327]

> Keeping in view the provisions and scheme of the National Green Tribunal act, 2010, particularly Sections 14, 29, 30 and 38(5), it can safely be concluded that the environmental issues and matters covered under the NGT Act, Schedule I should be instituted and litigated before the National Green Tribunal. Such approach may be necessary to avoid likelihood of conflict of orders between the High Courts and NGT. Thus, in unambiguous terms, we direct that all the matters instituted after coming into force of the NGT Act and which are covered under the provisions of the NGT Act and/or in Schedule I to the NGT act shall stand transferred and can be instituted only before NGT. *This will help in rendering expeditious and specialized justice in the field of environment to all concerned.* (Emphasis supplied)

Through this order, the Supreme Court transferred all cases involving environmental matter covered by the NGT Act from High Courts and civil courts to the Tribunal. This was done in furtherance of rendering expeditious and specialized environmental justice. In *Ratnagiri Nagar Parishad v. Gangaram Narayan Ambekar*,[328] despite the aforementioned holding of the Supreme Court, the Bombay High Court proceeded to hear an appeal from a civil court in a matter that clearly fell within the ambit of the NGT Act. Taking note of this discrepancy, the Supreme Court held:[329]

> We find it imperative to place on record a caution for consideration of the courts of competent jurisdiction that the cases filed and pending prior to coming into force of the NGT Act, involving questions of environmental laws and/or relating to any of the seven statutes specified in Schedule I of the NGT Act, should also be dealt with by the specialized tribunal, that is, NGT, created under the provisions of the NGT Act. The courts may be well advised to direct transfer of such cases to NGT in its discretion, *as it will be in the fitness of administration of justice.* (Emphasis supplied)

Consequently, the Supreme Court quashed the decisions rendered by the civil court as well as the High Court. Nevertheless, the concerns with respect to a lack of justice remain. As discussed in Chapter 1, the Standing Committee on Science and Technology, Environment and Forests, which had submitted its 203rd Report on The National Green Tribunal Bill, 2009, had expressed serious concerns with respect to a lack of access to justice:[330]

> The Committee feels that the National Green Tribunal which claims itself to be a mechanism aimed at effective and expeditious disposal of civil cases relating to environmental protection and conservation of forests does not exude much confidence given its infrastructural framework, particularly in view of the geographical vastness of our country.... Thus, the poor and the tribal people living in remote areas will be deprived of the opportunity to approach civil courts for redressal of their grievances on substantial question relating to environment.

As will be discussed in Chapter 4, the ouster of jurisdiction from 13,000 civil courts in the country has seriously impacted the access to justice in remote rural areas which are the most vulnerable to environmental degradation. Adding to this, all zonal benches of the NGT have been shut down due to a lack of appointments in the past two years.[331] Moreover, even the Principal Bench in New Delhi is operating below the minimum required quorum. Thus, we are presently in a situation wherein all environmental cases in India are being heard by seven members (including the chairperson) of the NGT in New Delhi.[332]

While the issue of bar of jurisdiction with respect to appeals to civil courts under Section 29 is settled, there remain diverging views with respect to the ouster of the appellate jurisdiction of the High Courts under Section 22. This is because while Section 22 provides that an appeal may lie to the Supreme Court, it does not expressly bar the jurisdiction of the High Courts. Consequently, there has been immense ambiguity in relation to whether High Courts can entertain appeals from the orders and awards of the NGT.

As discussed, an appeal to only the Supreme Court is in line with the overall objective of the NGT Act to promote expeditious disposal of environmental cases. However, disregarding this legislative intention, the Madras High Court, in *Kollidam Aaru Pathukappu Nala Sangam v. Union of India*,[333] held that the jurisdiction of the High Courts under Article 226 to entertain a writ petition against the order of the NGT is not barred by the provisions of the NGT Act. It has opined that the bar on jurisdiction envisaged by the Act, if any, is applicable only to lower courts.

In arriving at this conclusion, the Madras High Court placed reliance on the ratio of *L. Chandra Kumar v. Union of India*,[334] where the Supreme Court had held that "the jurisdiction conferred upon the High Courts under Articles 226 & 227 and upon the Supreme Court under Article 32 is a part of the inviolable basic structure of the Constitution".[335] Thus, the High Court held that Section 22 of the NGT Act could not take away the jurisdiction of the High Courts under Article 226 as this was a part of the basic structure of the Constitution.

The High Court reasoned that Section 29 of the NGT Act, which bars the jurisdiction of the civil courts, could be compared with Section 28 of the Administrative Tribunals Act, 1985. In *L. Chandra Kumar*, the Supreme Court had struck down Section 28 of the Administrative Tribunals Act, to the extent that it excluded the jurisdiction of High Courts under Articles 226 and 227 of the Constitution. Furthermore, the Supreme Court had declared all similar "exclusion of jurisdiction" clauses as unconstitutional.

However, unlike the NGT Act, which expressly provides that the appeal from the Tribunal should lie with the Supreme Court, the Administrative Tribunal Act, 1985, in question before the Supreme Court in *L. Chandra Kumar* expressly excluded the jurisdiction of all courts apart from labour courts and the Supreme Court.[336] Thus, there was a fundamental distinction between Section 29 of the NGT Act and Section 28 of the Administrative Tribunals Act, 1985. This was, however, not considered by the Madras High Court while arriving at its decision to hear appeals from the NGT under Articles 226 and 227 of the Constitution.

In contrast to the Madras High Court, the Bombay High Court, in view of the legislative intent of the NGT Act, has declined to hear appeals from the NGT and has directed appellants to approach the Supreme Court under Section 22 of the Act.[337] While the Bombay High Court agreed with *L. Chandra Kumar* to the extent that the jurisdiction of the High Courts could not be excluded, it held that the writ jurisdiction of the High Courts under Articles 226 and 227 of the Constitution has to be sparingly used, such as in situations of gross breach of principles of natural justice or issues of jurisdiction.[338] An appeal from the NGT was not one of those rare occasions, because the NGT Act provided for an "effective alternate remedy".[339] To this effect, the Bombay High Court relied on the Supreme Court's reasoning in *United Bank of India v. Satyawati Tondon*, wherein it was held:[340]

> Unfortunately, the High Court overlooked the settled law that the High Court will ordinarily not entertain a petition under Article 226 of the Constitution if an effective remedy is available to the aggrieved person…. (Emphasis supplied)

Thus, the High Court rightly held that Section 22 of the NGT Act provides an effective alternate remedy, and in line with the legislative intent behind the Act, the appeals from decisions of the Tribunal should ideally be directed to the Supreme Court.[341]

In furtherance of this line of reasoning, the Telangana High Court initially refused to hear an appeal from an order of the NGT on the pretext that the statutory appeals from the NGT lie with the Supreme Court.[342] However, it subsequently agreed to hear the appeal as one of the primary contentions was with respect to the breach of principles of natural justice.[343] This is the correct approach and is in line with the reasoning of the Supreme Court. Moreover, it is in consonance with the underlying legislative intent to enable expeditious disposal of cases by the Tribunal. It is recommended that all High Courts adopt the Bombay High Court's reasoning and not entertain appeals under Articles 226 and 227 of the Constitution unless grave issues of jurisdiction or violation of the principles of natural justice are involved. This will ensure that environmental adjudication of the NGT is both effective and expeditious.

2.7   ENVIRONMENT RELIEF FUND

Section 24 of the NGT Act states that where any amount is ordered to be paid by the Tribunal, by way of compensation or relief, on the ground of environmental damage, the amount shall be credited to the Environmental Relief Fund (ERF). Notwithstanding anything contained in the Public Liability Insurance Act, 1991, this compensation or relief amount credited to the ERF can be utilized for environmental purposes by any person or authority that the Tribunal prescribes.

The provenance of the ERF can be traced back to the Public Liability Insurance Act, 1991. In turn, the provenance of the Public Liability Insurance Act, 1991, can be traced back to the inability of the government to effectively meet the requirements of immediately dispersing environmental compensation to victims of hazardous accidents such as the Bhopal Gas Tragedy (1984). The judicial experience with adjudicating cases connected to the Bhopal Gas Tragedy had proved daunting, and it was largely felt that polluters dealing with hazardous substances ought to be held absolutely liable.

Accordingly, the impetus for the Public Liability Insurance Act and the ERF came from the Supreme Court's pronouncements, after the 1984 disaster, in cases such as the *Oleum Gas Leak Case*[344] and *Union Carbide Corporation v. Union of India*[345] that established the absolute liability doctrine. Accordingly, there emerged a widespread consensus on the need for the establishment of a fund that could provide immediate relief in case of an environmental accident. This consensus led to the creation of the ERF.[346]

Rule 35 (1) of the National Green Tribunal (Practices and Procedure) Rules, 2011, prescribes that the payment ordered by the NGT must be submitted to the ERF within thirty days from the date of the order, or as otherwise ordered by the Tribunal. When Section 24 of the NGT Act is read with Rule 35(1), it is amply clear that the requirement to deposit money into the ERF is a mandatory provision. However, the NGT does not order the amount to be remitted to the ERF in all cases.[347] In fact, reports indicate that the NGT rarely directs awards to be deposited into the ERF.[348]

A recent report titled *The Management of Environment Relief Fund* by the Vidhi Centre for Legal Policy has highlighted critical findings in relation to the application and utilization of the ERF by the NGT.[349] The report studied a total of 116 significant decisions by the NGT, between 2014 and 2019, where the total environmental compensation awarded by the NGT was INR 645 crore. However, out of these 116 cases, the Tribunal directed the amount to be paid to the ERF only in 13 cases.[350] The total amount of compensation directed to be deposited in the ERF under these 13 cases was INR 90 lakh.

Further, in 99 out of the 116 cases studied, the NGT ordered the amount to be paid to the victims of pollution or government authorities like the SPCBs and the Forest Officer. The total amount of compensation directed to be paid directly to the victims or the governmental authorities in these cases was INR 343.75 crore. Moreover, in 4 out of the 116 cases studied, the Tribunal did not specify where the amount awarded should be deposited. Surprisingly, the total amount of compensation involved in these cases amounted to INR 300.35 crore! The Report concluded:[351]

> Irrespective of whether or not any NGT direction specifically stated that the amount awarded as compensation or relief should be deposited with the ERF, it is clear, from a reading of section 24 of the NGT Act and section 35 of the NGT (Practice and Procedure) rules that the award must be deposited to ERF. While the amount awarded by the NGT as of December 2019 is approximately 645 crores, only Rs 2 crores appears to have been deposited with the ERF.

> Even if it is assumed that orders of the NGT awarding compensation have been appealed to the SC under section 22 of the NGT Act, there is a glaring disparity between the total amount awarded by the NGT and the amount credited with the ERF.

The Vidhi report highlights that despite the mandatory nature of Section 24 of the NGT Act, in practice the NGT does not order the compensation amount to be deposited in the ERF in a majority of cases. The report further postulates that these trends are indicative of the following possibilities:[352]

- Amounts awarded by the NGT are not first credited to the ERF before disbursal as required by the NGT Act and its rules and are instead directly disbursed to victims or government authorities.
- An overwhelming proportion of orders awarding compensation have been appealed to SC and have not yet been disposed of.
- There is simply no compliance with orders of the NGT awarding compensation or relief, that is, money is neither being credited to the ERF nor is it being directly disbursed.

Another groundbreaking report by the CSE[353] reveals that even out of the limited number of cases in which the NGT has specifically ordered that the compensation should be deposited with the ERF, the amount has actually been deposited in the ERF in only two cases.[354] Further, akin to the Vidhi report, the CSE report concluded that every time the NGT ordered an amount to be paid to an entity other than the ERF, it was going against the mandate of Section 24 and was, thereby, exceeding its jurisdiction.[355]

Further, the management of the ERF, in respect of the NGT's awards, has been less than optimal. While the United India Insurance Company Limited has been the Fund Manager of the ERF ever since it was first appointed in 2008, the Vidhi report highlights:[356]

> As per verified documents, the Fund Manager has not kept any separate account for contributions to the ERF as a result of awards or orders made by the NGT for compensation or relief for environmental damage. Instead, they appear to have been included as 'Others' for audit purposes. The first contribution to the 'Others' category came in the year 2012–13, and the total contribution stands at Rs 2.24 Crores as on March 2019. The Fund Manager informed Vidhi that a new account for compensation or relief awarded by the NGT has been opened recently, but we were unable to access any official documentation to this effect.

These instances clearly indicate deficiencies in the management of the ERF. This highlights one of the main challenges that the NGT is presently facing. The Tribunal is unable to ensure that its orders and awards are implemented, and the amounts deposited are actually utilized towards remediation of the environment or disbursed to victims of environmental damage. This is because there is virtually no oversight mechanism to ensure that the payment to the ERF is complied with.[357]

Moreover, this problem is further compounded by the fact that there are several layers of red tape and bureaucratic jargon to traverse to obtain vital information with regard to a particular project and the payment to the ERF. The CSE report highlights the opacity that persists within the United India Insurance Company Limited with respect to information about the management of the fund. It states:[358]

> Efforts were then made to contact the Ministry of Environment and Forests and the United India Insurance Company Ltd (UIICL) to inquire into the status of payments made into the fund. However, the contacted persons at the UIICL expressed reluctance to share information without official sanction. After that, a PIL was filed with the relevant authority requesting information about whether payments were made into the fund as directed, and also whether any of the deposited money had been disbursed. There has so far been no response to the filed PIL.

> Evidently, there is no clear oversight mechanism to evaluate whether payments have been made or not. The process of gaining information is bureaucratic and ambiguous. In the absence of any clear centralized mechanism, tracking and reviewing ground implementation of NGT directions becomes a case-to-case pursuit by individuals.

Thus, the need of the hour is a transparent and efficient monitoring mechanism for ensuring that the ERF is utilized for the intended purposes. Given the opacity in the management of the fund, it becomes difficult to assess whether the NGT's orders and awards are being complied with on the ground. In addition, given the fact that the NGT does not have contempt powers, there are serious concerns with respect to the effectiveness of the NGT's adjudication in general.

Another factor which leads to poor compliance with the NGT's orders is the high number of appeals filed against the Tribunal's decisions in the Supreme Court.[359] It is observed that even though Section 22 of the NGT Act prescribes that appeals will lie only where a substantial question of law is involved, most cases where the compensation levied is high are appealed.[360] Furthermore, Section 35(1) of the NGT Act grants power to the Central government to frame rules regarding the manner and purposes for which amounts credited to the ERF shall be utilized. However, no such rules have been formulated to date. Consequently, the ERF has, for the most part, remained unutilized for the majority of its existence.[361]

The ERF holds great potential to expedite environmental adjudication. It can act as a means of providing monetary relief in an expedited manner. This would positively impact the overall state of access to environmental justice in India. It would also ensure that protracted litigation does not deter victims of environmental damage from asserting their rights. Given the ERF's important position within the overall framework of the NGT, there is a need for a systemic overhaul of the management of the ERF. This would require reforms not only in the way the NGT adjudicates but also on the part of regulatory authorities charged with overseeing the operation of the fund. Increasing transparency and access to information could also ensure better compliance levels, due to the additional oversight of private parties, activists, researchers, and so on.

2.8   COSTS AND PENALTIES

2.8.1   COSTS

The power to impose costs on litigating parties for frivolous and vexatious litigation is a necessary power to ensure that precious judicial resources and time are not wasted. This becomes particularly important in matters of environmental law as time is of the essence in most cases and the requirement of *locus standi* is considerably relaxed. The NGT Act confers such a power on the Tribunal. Section 23 of the Act states that the Tribunal has the power to impose costs while disposing of an application if it holds that the claims made are vexatious, frivolous, or not maintainable. The reasons for such a holding have to be expressly recorded in writing, and the Tribunal, in addition to imposing costs, can also take away benefits accorded to a party by way of an injunction.

The express provision of such a power was a noteworthy addition in the Act, especially when compared to the NGT's predecessors. The first legislation establishing an environmental tribunal – the NEAA Act, 1995 – did not contain any provisions expressly granting such a power to the NEAA. Similarly, the second such legislation – the NEEA Act, 1997 – followed the same scheme and lacked any such provision to award costs.

The 186th Report of the Law Commission of India,[362] through a comparative analysis, delved into the structure of environmental courts in New Zealand that have the power to impose costs on litigants. The Report noted:[363]

> [T]here is some criticism of the Court's power to impose costs against unsuccessful parties but imposition of *costs* is a normal feature of litigation *except where plans or policy statements or public interest is involved*. It is however pointed out by critics as to why costs could go as high as $8,500 upto $20,000, and that for that reason threats by developers about costs could discourage genuine objections.

It is likely that these observations were in the mind of the legislature while enacting Section 23 and according the power to award costs to the Tribunal. The power to award costs bears considerable significance in the context of the PIL regime that had been at the forefront of Indian environmental litigation, prior to the establishment of the NGT. As discussed in Chapter 1, one of the vital characteristics of PIL was the expansion of *locus standi*. However, with the ease of approaching the Court also came the increased possibility of misusing the judicial process. Accordingly, while recognizing the significance of the expansion of *locus standi*, the Supreme Court has taken note of how PIL has been subjected to blatant abuse by unscrupulous litigants.[364]

In *Balco Employees' Union* v. *Union of India*,[365] the Court took note of the trend of misusing the PIL process and proposed two measures to discourage such misuse. First, it held that the *locus standi* should be restricted to individuals who are "acting *bona fide*". Second, it held that the imposition of "exemplary costs" would act as a deterrent against frivolously filed PILs. In furtherance of this logic, the NGT, in *Baijnath Prajapati v. Ministry of Environment and Forests*,[366] stated:[367]

> This Tribunal is expected to ensure effective environmental management and conservation, give relief and compensation for damages to persons and property and connected matters and at the same time ensure sustainable development. In this regard, the jurisdiction of this Tribunal should not be invoked for frivolous litigation that unnecessarily consumes the time of the Tribunal without serving the purpose for which the Tribunal was constituted.

In this case, the Tribunal found that the appellant had dragged numerous parties into litigation "in a flippant manner", which amounted to an abuse of the Tribunal's due process. Accordingly, the Tribunal imposed costs of INR 50,000 on the appellant. Similarly, in *Rana Sen Gupta v. Union of India*,[368] the applicant was a self-proclaimed activist and had challenged the environmental clearance granted to a project. The Tribunal, after examining the record, noted:[369]

We do not find any tangible material which would plausibly show that the Appellant has credentials as expert in the field of steel and iron industries and we are at a loss to know in what manner he is working for the welfare of unrepresented members of the public. It is not his case that he represents any NGO. His self-proclaimed status as 'public spirited citizen' is of no much avail. There is absolutely no record to show that he participated in the public consultation process and raised any issue regarding the environment or socio-economic adverse impact on account of establishment of the proposed project.

Consequently, the appeal was dismissed, and costs of INR 50,000 were imposed on the appellant by the NGT. Further, the Tribunal has shown a consistent distaste for applications filed out of personal acrimony under the guise of PIL, and has imposed costs on the erring party in such cases.[370]

2.8.2   PENALTIES

As we have discussed in the preceding section on the ERF, the lack of implementation of the NGT's decisions remains a concern. As a result, a provision vesting the NGT with the power of punishing persons in its contempt becomes a necessity. The NGT's predecessors lacked such powers. The NET Act, 1995, under Section 25, prescribed that any party not complying with the directions of the NEAA could be punished with imprisonment up to three years, or with a fine up to INR 10 lakh, or with both. Similarly, the NEAA Act, 1997, incorporated a similar provision under Section 19, which prescribed that non-compliance with the NEAA's directions would be punishable with imprisonment for up to seven years, or with a fine up to INR 1 lakh, or both.

However, while the aforementioned sections stated that there would be imprisonment for the violation of the orders of the NET and the NEAA, these offences were triable only under the ordinary criminal courts. In effect, the NET and the NEAA did not have powers to hold persons guilty of their contempt. This problem was recognized in the 186th Report of the Law Commission of India:[371]

> The Commission is of the view that having regard to the fact that big industries which pollute the environment (or our streams, lakes and rivers or air) come before the Court, there is need to invest the Court with contempt powers so that the Court can, by way of summary proceedings, see that its orders are *effectively implemented instead of taking out lengthy proceedings by way of execution or proceedings under the criminal law.* (Emphasis supplied)

Thus, the Law Commission rightly identified the issues with respect to the implementation of orders on the ground and held that it is necessary to vest an environmental court with contempt powers to ensure expeditious compliance. This was necessary as otherwise, the lengthy proceedings in a criminal court would defeat the purpose of expeditious disposal of environmental matters.

However, this recommendation was disregarded while drafting the NGT Act. Section 26 of the Act is similar to the sections of the NET Act, 1995, and the NEAA Act, 1997, that we have discussed. It provides that any person who fails to comply with any direction of the Tribunal shall be punishable with imprisonment for a term which may extend to three years, or with a fine which may extend to INR 10 crore, or with both. In case the non-compliance continues, the person would be punishable with an additional fine of up to INR 25,000 for every day during which such non-compliance continues after conviction for the first such instance of non-compliance.

The section further prescribes that in case a company fails to comply with any direction of the Tribunal under this Act, such company shall be punishable with fine which may extend to INR 25 crore. In case non-compliance continues, there can be an additional fine which may extend to INR 1 lakh for every day during which such non-compliance continues after conviction for the first instance of non-compliance. As in the case of the NET and the NEAA, these offences are only triable by criminal courts as the NGT lacks criminal jurisdiction.

Further, these offences have been declared to be non-cognizable.[372] According to Section 30(2) of the NGT Act, the offences under the Act cannot be tried by a court inferior to that of a Metropolitan Magistrate, or a Judicial Magistrate of the first class. Therefore, the Tribunal, by deliberate legislative design, has not been granted contempt powers. As we will discuss in the next chapter, this has proven detrimental to the implantation of the NGT's decisions. Further, Justice Swatanter Kumar – the longest serving chairperson of the NGT – has stated in an interview (featured in Chapter 4) that the NGT ought to be accorded contempt powers by the legislature.

Therefore, in line with the Law Commission's recommendations, and following the model of New Zealand's environmental courts, the NGT should be granted contempt powers through summary proceedings. This would enable the NGT to tackle the problem of non-compliance and non-enforcement of its orders and would act as a strong deterrent.

NOTES

1. National Green Tribunal Act, 2010 (Act 19 of 2010) (India).
2. The National Environmental Tribunal, 1995 (Act 27 of 1995) (India).
3. The National Environmental Appellate Authority, 1997 (Act 22 of 1997) (India).
4. *A.P. Pollution Control Board v. M.V. Naidu (I)*, (1999) 2 SCC 718 (Supreme Court of India); *A.P. Pollution Control Board v. M.V. Naidu (II)*, (2001) 2 SCC 62 (Supreme Court of India).
5. Law Commission of India, "Proposal to constitute Environmental Courts" (17th Law Commission, 186th Report, 2003).
6. National Green Tribunal Act, 2010 (Act 19 of 2010) (India).

7. Ibid.

8. United Nations Conference on the Human Environment, UNGA Res 2994 (XXVII) (15 December 1972) (A/RES/2994).

9. "Report of the United Nations Conference on Environment and Development", United Nations Conference on Environment and Development (Rio De Janeiro 3–14 June 1992) (12 August 1992) UN Doc A/CONF.151/26 Rev.1 (Vol. 1).

10. Ibid.

11. Ibid.

12. The Constitution of India.

13. National Green Tribunal Act, 2010 (Act 19 of 2010) (India).

14. Maya Ramesh, "Nearly a Decade Old, Is the National Green Tribunal Losing Its Bite?" *The Wire* (11 May 2019), https://thewire.in/environment/nearly-a-decade-old-is-the-national-green-tribunal-losing-its-bite (accessed 18 December 2019).

15. Ibid.

16. Kumar Sambhav Shrivastava, "Green Tribunal Gets Short Shrift" *Down to Earth* (4 July 2015), https://www.downtoearth.org.in/news/green-tribunal-gets-short-shrift-38426 (accessed 18 December 2021).

17. Geetanjoy Sahu, "Ecocide by Design? Under Modi, Vacancies at National Green Tribunal Reach 70%", *The Wire* (15 February 2018) , https://thewire.in/politics/ngt-political-apathy-vacancies (accessed 18 December 2021).

18. Debayan Roy, "NGT Working with Just Six Members Instead of at Least 21, Zonal Benches Vacant for Two Years Now" (New Delhi, 1 November 2019), https://theprint.in/environment/ngt-working-with-6-members-instead-of-at-least-21-zonal-benches-vacant-for-2-yrs-now/314616/ (accessed 18 December 2021).

19. Ibid.

20. Ibid.

21. Dhananjay Mahapatra, "Kolkata May Lose Green Tribunal Bench to Guwahati or Ranchi", *Times of India* (New Delhi, 10 July 2013), https://timesofindia.indiatimes.com/city/kolkata/Kolkata-may-lose-green-tribunal-bench-to-Guwahati-or-Ranchi/articleshow/20996616.cms (accessed 18 December 2021).

22. *Union of India v. Vimal Bhai*, Order dated 13 July 2012 in Special Leave to Appeal (Civil) No. 12065 of 2009 (Supreme Court of India).

23. Raghuveer Nath and Armin Rosencranz, "Evaluating the National Green Tribunal after Nearly a Decade: Ten Challenges to Overcome", *NLIU L. Rev.* 9, no. 1 (2019): 1–39,23–27; see also *Union of India v. Vimal Bhai*: Orders dated 12 May 2011, 11 July 2011, 19 September 2011, 14 October 2011, 28 November 2011, 14 December 2011, 16 March 2012, 19 March 2012, 9 April 2012, 3 May 2012, 13 July 2012, 26 September 2012, 10 October 2012, 6 December 2012, 4 April 2013, 2 August 2013, 27 August 2013, 12 September 2013 in Special Leave to Appeal (Civil) No. 12065 of 2009.

24. Ibid.

25. *Union of India v. Vimal Bhai*, (2014) 13 SCC 766 (Supreme Court of India).

26. NGT Website, "National Green Tribunal FAQs", https://greentribunal.gov.in/faqs (accessed 18 December 2021).

27. Section 4(1)(a), The National Green Tribunal Act, 2010 (Act 19 of 2010) (India).

28. Section 4(2), The National Green Tribunal Act, 2010 (Act 19 of 2010) (India).

29. Section 6(1), The National Green Tribunal Act, 2010 (Act 19 of 2010) (India).

30. Section 6(2), The National Green Tribunal Act, 2010 (Act 19 of 2010) (India).

31. Section 6(3), The National Green Tribunal Act, 2010 (Act 19 of 2010) (India).

32. NGT Website, "Methodology of the NGT", https://greentribunal.gov.in/methodology-ngt (accessed 18 December 2021).

33. Section 5(1), The National Green Tribunal Act, 2010 (Act 19 of 2010) (India).

34. Section 5(1), The National Green Tribunal Act, 2010 (Act 19 of 2010) (India).

35. Section 5(2)(a), The National Green Tribunal Act, 2010 (Act 19 of 2010) (India).

36. Section 5(2)(a), The National Green Tribunal Act, 2010 (Act 19 of 2010) (India).

37. Section 5(2)(b), The National Green Tribunal Act, 2010 (Act 19 of 2010) (India).

38. Section 5(4), The National Green Tribunal Act, 2010 (Act 19 of 2010) (India).

39. Section 5(4), The National Green Tribunal Act, 2010 (Act 19 of 2010) (India).

40. Rule 7(1)(a), The National Green Tribunal (Manner of Appointment of Judicial and Expert Members, Salaries, Allowances and other Terms and Conditions of Service of Chairperson and other Members and Procedure for Inquiry) Rules, 2010 (India).

41. Rule 7(1)(b), The National Green Tribunal (Manner of Appointment of Judicial and Expert Members, Salaries, Allowances and other Terms and Conditions of Service of Chairperson and other Members and Procedure for Inquiry) Rules, 2010, National Green Tribunal Act, 2010 (Act 19 of 2010).

42. Rule 7(1)(c), The National Green Tribunal (Manner of Appointment of Judicial and Expert Members, Salaries, Allowances and other Terms and Conditions of Service of Chairperson and other Members and Procedure for Inquiry) Rules, 2010, National Green Tribunal Act, 2010 (Act 19 of 2010).

43. Section 7, The National Green Tribunal Act, 2010 (Act 19 of 2010) (India).

44. Section 7, The National Green Tribunal Act, 2010 (Act 19 of 2010) (India).

45. Section 7, The National Green Tribunal Act, 2010 (Act 19 of 2010) (India).

46. Section 7, The National Green Tribunal Act, 2010 (Act 19 of 2010) (India).

47. Section 10, The National Green Tribunal Act, 2010 (Act 19 of 2010) (India).

48. Section 10 (2), The National Green Tribunal Act, 2010 (Act 19 of 2010) (India).

49. Section 10 (3), The National Green Tribunal Act, 2010 (Act 19 of 2010) (India).

50. Government of India, Ministry of Environment and Forests, Environmental Impact Assessment S.O. 1533(E) (14 September 2006).

51. *Madras Bar Association v. Union of India*, 2021 SCC OnLine SC 463 (Supreme Court of India).

52. *Madras Bar Association v. Union of India*, 2020 SCC OnLine SC 962 (Supreme Court of India).

53. *Rojer Mathew v, South India Bank Limited*, (2020) 6 SCC 1 (Supreme Court of India).

54. Srishti Ojha, "Tribunal Reforms: "Government Hasn't Honoured Our Judgement", Says CJI Ramana", *LiveLaw* (24 February 2022), https://www.livelaw.in/top-stories/tribunal-reforms-governmeIsnt-honoured-our-judgement-says-cji-ramana-192718?s=08 (accessed 3 March 2022).

55. *T.N. Godavarman Thirumulpad v. Union of India*, (1997) 2 SCC 26 (Supreme Court of India).

56. *Tribunal on Its Own Motion v. MoEF & Ors.*, Judgment Dated 4 April 2014 in Appeal No. 16 of 2013, para 21 (National Green Tribunal, India).

57. Section 14(3), The National Green Tribunal Act, 2010 (Act 19 of 2010) (India).

58. Section 15(5), The National Green Tribunal Act, 2010 (Act 19 of 2010) (India).

59. Section 15(3), The National Green Tribunal Act, 2010 (Act 19 of 2010) (India).

60. Section 17(1), The National Green Tribunal Act, 2010 (Act 19 of 2010) (India).

61. Section 17(3), The National Green Tribunal Act, 2010 (Act 19 of 2010) (India).

62. *M.C. Mehta v. Union of India*, 1987 SCR (1) 819 (*Oleum Leak Case*) (Supreme Court of India).

63. Section 18(2), The National Green Tribunal Act, 2010 (Act 19 of 2010) (India).

64. Roy, "NGT Working with Just Six Members Instead of at Least 21, Zonal Benches Vacant for 2 Years Now".

65. Ibid.

66. Section 38(1), The National Green Tribunal, 2010 (Act 19 of 2010) (India).

67. Meaning of the right to bring an action. In Bryan Garner (ed), *Black's Law Dictionary* (7th edn., West Publishing Co.1999), 952.

68. *T.N. Godavarman Thirumulpad v. Union India*, (1997) 3 SCC 312 (Supreme Court of India).

69. Ibid.

70. *Visitor, Amu and Ors. v. K.S. Mishra*, Judgment dated 6 September 2007 in Appeal (Civil) 4102 of 2007 (Supreme Court of India).

71. Shibani Ghosh, "Case Note: Access to Information as Ruled by the Indian Environmental Tribunal: *Save Mon Region Federation v. Union of India*", *Review of European Comparative and International Environmental Law* 22, no. 2 (2013): 202–206.

72. Shrivastava, "Green Tribunal Gets Short Shrift".

73. Maitri Porecha, "National Green Tribunal Reeling under Vacancies", *Hindu Business Line* (New Delhi, 29 October 2019), https://www.thehindubusinessline.com/news/national-green-tribunal-reeling-under-vacancies/article29821953.ece (accessed 18 December 2021).

74. Gitanjali Nain Gill, *Environmental Justice in India: The National Green Tribunal* (London: Routledge, 2016), 79.

75. *Gulam Qadir v. Special Tribunal and Another*, (2002) 1 SCC 33 (Supreme Court of India).

76. *Betty C Alvares v. State of Goa*, Judgement Dated 14th February 2014 in Application No.63 of 2012 (Western Zone, National Green Tribunal, India).

77. Ibid.

78. *Court on Its Own Motion v. State of Himachal Pradesh & Ors.*, Original Application No. 446 of 2018 (National Green Tribunal, India).

79. *Baijnath Prajapati v. MoEF*, NGT Appeal No. 18 of 2011 (National Green Tribunal, India).

80. Nitin Sethi, "NGT Does Not Have Power to Act Suo Motu: Government", *The Hindu* (11 September 2013), https://www.thehindu.com/todays-paper/tp-national/ngt-does-not-have-powers-to-act-suo-motu-government/article5114766.ece (accessed 19 December 2021).

81. Anubhuti Vishnoi, "Ministry of Environment and Forests States That NGT Has No Power to Initiate Suo Moto Proceedings", *Indian Express* (New Delhi, 26 August 2013), http://archive.indianexpress.com/news/no-suo-motu-powers-provided-for-you-moef-tells-green-tribunal/1160046/ (accessed 19 December 2021).

82. Utkarsh Anand, "NGT Gives itself Powers of a Court", *Indian Express* (New Delhi, 18 July 2014), https://indianexpress.com/article/india/india-others/ngt-gives-itself-powers-of-a-court/ (accessed 19 December 2021).

83. PTI, "NGT Says It Has Power to Institute Suo Motu Proceedings Cannot Keep Hands Tied", *The Week* (New Delhi, 3 June 2020), https://www.theweek.in/wire-updates/national/2020/06/03/lgd5-green-gas-leak-suo-motu.html#:~:text=New%20Delhi%2C%20Jun%20 3%20(PTI,at%20least%2011%20people%20had (accessed 19 December 2021).

84. Nitin Sethi, "Green Tribunal Does Not Have Power to Act Suo Motu Says Government", *The Hindu* (New Delhi, 12 September 2013), https://www.thehindu.com/news/national/green-tribunal-does-not-have-powers-to-act-suo-motu-says-govt/article5118106.ece (accessed 19 December 2021).

85. Ibid.

86. *Court on Its Own Motion v. State of Himachal Pradesh*, 2014(1) All India NGT Reporter Part 3, 66.

87. *Tribunal on Its Own Motion v. Ministry of Environment & Forests*, Original Application No. 16 of 2013 (NGT Central Zonal Bench, India).

88. Ibid.

89. *Tribunal on Its Own Motion v. Govt. of NCT of Delhi & Ors.*, Original Application No. 496 of 2016 (National Green Tribunal, India).

90. Ibid.

91. *P. Sundararajan v. The Deputy Registrar*, National Green Tribunal, Sothern Zone, 2015 SCC OnLine Mad 10338 (High Court of Madras, India).

92. J. Stalin, "Madras High Court Restrains NGT from Initiating Suo Moto Proceedings", *Deccan Chronicle* (Chennai, 19 March 2019) https://www.deccanchronicle.com/140104/news-current-affairs/article/madras-hc-restrains-green-tribunal-initiating-suo-moto (accessed 20 December 2021).

93. *Down To Earth*, "NGT Must Have Suo Moto Powers" (30 November 2014), https://www.downtoearth.org.in/interviews/ngt-must-have-suo-moto-powers-47542 (accessed 20 December 2021).

94. *Union of India v. Major General Shri Kant Sharma*, (2015) 6 SCC 773 (Supreme Court of India).

95. *P. Sundararajan v. The Deputy Registrar*.

96. *Municipal Corporation of Greater Mumbai v. Ankita Sinha & Ors.*, 2021 SCC OnLine SC 897.

97. *Goa Foundation v. Union of India*, (2014) 6 SCC 590 (Supreme Court of India).

98. Arati Menon, "Tiger Is Not the Only Animal That Needs Saving", *DailyO* (28 April 2016), https://www.dailyo.in/politics/project-tiger-incredible-india-wildlife-amitabh-bachchan-panama-papers-corbett-animals/story/1/10324.html (accessed 20 December 2021).

99. Jeremy Hance, "Tigers Gobble Up 49 Percent of India's Wildlife Conservation Funds, More Imperiled Species Get Nothing", *Mongabay* (12 February 2013), https://news.mongabay.com/2013/02/tigers-gobble-up-49-percent-of-indias-wildlife-conservation-funds-more-imperiled-species-get-nothing/ (accessed 20 December 2021).

100. *Rajkumar Shivhare vs. Assistant Director, Directorate of Enforcement*, (2010) 4 SCC 772, para 34 (Supreme Court of India).

101. *State of Uttar Pradesh v. Mohammad Nooh*, AIR 1958 SC 86, para 11.

102. Ibid.

103. Prakhar Chauhan and Raghuveer Nath, "The Dilution of Article 32: Convenience over Right", *GNLU L.Rev.* 7 (2020): 1.

104. *Kharak Singh v. State of Uttar Pradesh*, AIR 1963 SC 1295.

105. *State of Uttar Pradesh v. Mohammad Nooh.*

106. *Nivedita Sharma v. Cellular Operators Association of India & Ors.*, (2011) 14 SCC 337 (Supreme Court of India).

107. *Thansingh Nathmal v. Superintendent of Taxes*, 1964 AIR SC 1419.

108. *Cicily Kallarackal v. Vehicle Factory*, (2012) 8 SCC 524 (Supreme Court of India).

109. Ibid.

110. *Union of India v. Major General Shri Kant Sharma.*

111. *P. Sundararajan v. The Deputy Registrar.*

112. *State of Uttar Pradesh v. Mohammad Nooh.*

113. Ibid., para 15.

114. Ibid., para 15.

115. *Bal Krishna Agarwal (Dr.) v. State of Uttar Pradesh*, (1995) 1 SCC 614 (Supreme Court of India).

116. *State of Uttar Pradesh v. Mohammad Nooh*, para 11.

117. Nupur Chowdhury and Nidhi Shrivastava, "The National Green Tribunal in India: Examining the Question of Jurisdiction", *Asia Pacific Journal of Environmental Law* 21, no. 2 (2018): 190–216, https://www.teachenvirolaw.asia/sites/default/files/jurisdiction-ngt-nupur-nidhi-2018.pdf (accessed 20 December 2021).

118. *Mahavir Singh v. Union of India & Ors.*, 2013 SCC OnLine Del 690 (Delhi High Court, India).

119. *Salaya Machhimar Boat Association through Vice-President v. Union of India & Others*, AIR 2015 Guj 70 (Gujarat High Court, India).

120. *Somasekharan Nair v. District Collector*, (2016) SCC OnLine Mad 25089 (Madras High Court, India).

121. *Adarsh Coop. Housing Society Ltd. v. Union of India*, MANU/SC/0375/2014 (SLP (C) Nos. 27327 and 28512 –13 / 2013) (Supreme Court of India).

122. *Aman Sethi v. State of Rajasthan*, 2015 SCC OnLine NGT 164, para 15 (National Green Tribunal, India).

123. *Minerva Mills Ltd. & Others v. Union of India and Ors.*, AIR 1980 SC 1789.

124. *S.P. Sampath Kumar v. Union of India & Ors.*, AIR 1987 SC 386.

125. *L. Chandra Kumar v. Union of India*, (1997) 3 SCC 261 (Supreme Court of India).

126. Ibid.

127. Ibid.

128. Ibid., 274.

129. Ibid., 274.

130. *Kollidam Aaru Pathukappu Nala Sangam v. Union of India*, 2014 SCC OnLine Mad 4928 (Madras High Court, India).

131. Ibid.

132. *Wilfred J. & Anr. v. MoEF*, 2014 SCC OnLine NGT 6860 (Principal Bench, NGT, India).

133. *Central India Ayush Drugs Manufacturers Association v. State of Maharashtra*, 2016 SCC OnLine Bom 8813.

134. Ibid., para 27.

135. *Tamil Nadu Pollution Control Board v. Sterlite Industries & Ors.*, 2019 SCC Online SC 221 (Supreme Court of India).

136. Ibid., para 53.

137. *Wilfred J. & Anr. v. MoEF*.

138. Ibid.

139. *Vimal Bhai v. Union of India*, Order dated 29 September 2005 in Writ Petition (Civil) No. 17682/2005, W.P.(C) No. 17683/2005 and W.P.(C) No. 17684/2005 (High Court of Delhi, India).

140. Ibid.

141. *Ram Nath Sao v. Gobardhan Sao & Ors.*, (2002) 3 SCC 195 (Supreme Court of India).

142. *Collector, Land Acquisition, Anantnag & Anr. v. Mst. Katiji & Ors.*, (1987) 2 SCC 107 (Supreme Court of India).

143. Ibid.

144. *Paryavana Sanrakshan Sangarsh Samiti Lippa v. Union of India*, 2011 SCC OnLine NGT 5 (Principal Bench, National Green Tribunal, India).

145. *Collector, Land Acquisition, Anantnag & Anr. v. Mst. Katiji & Ors.*

146. *Save Mon Region Federation & Anr. v. Union of India*, Judgment dated 7 April 2016 in Appeal No. 39 of 2012 (Principal Bench, NGT, India).

147. Ibid., para 29.

148. *Save Mon Region Federation & Anr. v. Union of India*, para 34; *P.K. Ramachandran v. State of Kerala*, (1997) 7 SCC 556 (Supreme Court of India).

149. *Save Mon Region Federation & Anr. v. Union of India*, para 34.

150. *Nikunj Developers & Ors. v. the State of Maharashtra & Ors.*, Order dated 14 March 2013 in Appeal No. 76 of 2012 (Principal Bench, NGT, India).

151. Ibid., para 19.

152. *Hiralal Ratanlal v. STO*, (1973) 2 SCR 502 (Supreme Court of India).

153. *Sunil Kumar Samanta v. West Bengal Pollution Control Board*, Judgment dated 24th July 2014 in M.A. No. 573 of 2013 in Appeal No. 67 OF 2013 (Principal Bench, NGT, India).

154. Ibid., para 55.

155. *Forward Foundation v. State of Karnataka & Ors.*, 2015 SCC OnLine NGT 5, para 23 (Principal Bench, NGT, India).

156. Ibid.

157. *Uddhav Singh v. Madhav Rao Scindia*, (1977) 1 SCC 511 (Supreme Court of India); *A.B.C. Laminart Pvt. Ltd. v. A.P. Agencies,* AIR 1989 SC 1239.

158. Section 14, The National Green Tribunal Act, 2010 (Act 19 of 2010).

159. *Kehar Singh v. State of Haryana*, Judgment dated 12th September 2013 in Application No. 124 of 2013, para 24 (Principal Bench, NGT, India); *J. Mehta v. Union of India and Ors.*, Judgment/Order dated 24th October 2013 in Application No. 88 of 2013 (Principal Bench, NGT, India).

160. *Forward Foundation v. State of Karnataka & Ors.*

161. Ibid., para 25.

162. *State of Bihar v. Deokaran Nenshi & Anr.*, (1972) 2 SCC 890 (Supreme Court of India).

163. Ibid.

164. *Forward Foundation v. State of Karnataka & Ors*, para 28.

165. The NGT has cited the Supreme Court in *Khatri Hotels Pvt. Ltd. & Anr. v. Union of India*, (2011) 9 SCC 126 (Supreme Court of India) and *Bal Krishna Savalram Pujari & Ors. v. Dayaneshwar Maharaj Sansthan & Ors.*, AIR 1959 SC 798.

166. *Forward Foundation v. State of Karnataka & Ors*, para 29.

167. Ibid., para 28.

168. Ibid.

169. Ibid., para 32.

170. Ibid., para 25.

171. Ibid., para 32.

172. Ibid., para 32.

173. *Doaba Paryavaran Samiti v. Union of India*, Judgment dated 10th December 2015 in Original Application No. 327 of 2015 (Principal Bench, NGT, India).

174. Ibid., para 27.

175. *Maya Rani Punj v. Commissioner of Income Tax, Delhi*, (1986) 1 SCC 445 (Supreme Court of India).

176. *Doaba Paryavaran Samiti v. Union of India*, para 23.

177. *Sajal Kumar v. Union of India*, Judgment dated 18th December 2012 in Miscellaneous Application No. 131 of 2012 (Arising out of Appeal No. 46 of 2012) (Principal Bench, NGT, India).

178. *Collector, Land Acquisition, Anantnag & Anr. v. Mst. Katiji & Ors.*

179. *Save Mon Region Federation & Anr. v. Union of India.*

180. Raghuveer Nath and Armin Rosencranz, "Determination of Environmental Compensation: The Art of Living Case", *National University of Juridical Sciences L. REV.* 12, no. 1 (2019): 1–20.

181. Edward Broughton, "The Bhopal Disaster and Its Aftermath: A Review" *Environ Health* 4 (10 May 2005): 1–19, 6, https://ehjournal.biomedcentral.com/articles/10.1186/1476-069X-4-6 (accessed 20 December 2021).

182. Ibid.

183. Ibid.

184. Ibid.

185. Press Trust of India, "Bhopal Gas Tragedy: 33 Years On, Survivors Still Wait for Adequate Compensation", *Deccan Chronicle* (Bhopal, 3 December 2017), https://www.deccanchronicle.com/nation/current-affairs/031217/bhopal-gas-tragedy-33-yrs-on-survivors-still-await-adequate-compensation.html#:~:text=for%20more%20compensation.-,The%20US%20company%2C%20which%20then%20owned%20the%20chemical%20plant%20in,a%20Madhya%20Pradesh%20minister%20said.&text=The%20Rs%20715%20crore%2Dcompensation,by%20the%20leak%2C%20he%20said (accessed 20 December 2021).

186. Ibid.

187. Kim Fortun, *Advocacy after Bhopal: Environmentalism, Disaster, New Global Orders* (Chicago: University of Chicago Press, 2001), 259.

188. Ibid.

189. Japnam Bindra, Bhopal Gas Tragedy: New SC Bench to Hear Compensation Case", *Mint* (29 January 2020), https://www.livemint.com/news/india/bhopal-gas-tragedy-new-sc-bench-to-hear-compensation-case-11580279138703.html (accessed 20 December 2021).

190. Ibid.

191. Ibid.

192. See *M.C. Mehta v. Union of India,* (1987) 1 SCC 395 (Supreme Court of India):

> An enterprise which is engaged in a hazardous or inherently dangerous industry which poses a potential threat to the health and safety of the persons working in the factory and residing in the surrounding areas owes an absolute and non-delegable duty to the community to ensure that no harm results to anyone on account of hazardous or inherently dangerous nature of the activity which it has undertaken … if *any harm* results on account of such activity, the enterprise must be *absolutely liable to compensate for such harm* and it should be no answer to the enterprise to say that it had taken all reasonable care and that the harm occurred without any negligence on its part.

193. Section 15(2), The National Green Tribunal Act, 2010 (Act 19 of 2010).

194. Section 15(3), The National Green Tribunal Act, 2010 (Act 19 of 2010).

195. Section 17(2), The National Green Tribunal Act, 2010 (Act 19 of 2010).

196. *Manoj Mishra v. Union of India*, M.A. No. 65 of 2016 (Principal Bench, NGT, India).

197. Aniruddha Ghosal and Sowmiya Ashok, "Inside the NGT as It Turns Seven", *Indian Express* (New Delhi 26 June 2018), https://indianexpress.com/article/india/ngt-national-green-tribunal -delhi-smog-pollution-swatanter-kumar-inside-the-ngt-as-it-turns-seven-4943859/ (accessed 21 December 2021).

198. HT Correspondent, "NGT Slaps ₹195 Cr. Fine on Pune's Goel Ganga Developers for Environmental Damage", *Hindustan Times* (Pune, 9 January 2018), https://www.hindustantimes. com/pune-news/ngt-slaps-195-cr-fine-onpune-s-goel-ganga-developers-for-environmental- damage/story-eHVl8micvPT7X3Bp58ZEcO.html (accessed 20 December 2021).

199. *Goa Foundation v. Union of India*.

200. Ibid.

201. Ibid.

202. Ibid., 632.

203. Ibid., 632–633.

204. Ibid., 633.

205. *Samaj Parivartana Samudaya v. State of Karnataka,* (2013) 8 SCC 154,173 (Supreme Court of India).

206. See generally *S.P. Muthuraman v. Union of India*, 2015 SCC OnLine NGT 169, para 163 (National Green Tribunal, India); *Manoj Misra v. Union of India*, 2015 SCC OnLine NGT 840, para 94 (National Green Tribunal, India); *Krishan Lal Gera v. State of Haryana*, Appeal No. 22 of 2015 (National Green Tribunal, India); *Sunil Kumar Chugh v. Secretary Environment Department*, Appeal No. 66 of 2014 (National Green Tribunal, India); Chandra Bhushan, Srestha Banerjee, and Ikshaku Bezbaroa, *Green Tribunal, Green Approach: The Need for Better Implementation of the Polluter Pays Principle* (New Delhi: Centre for Science and Environment, 2018), 8.

207. *Forward Foundation v. State of Karnataka & Ors.*

208. Ibid., para 2.

209. Ibid., para 43.

210. Ibid., para 4.

211. Ibid., para 84.

212. Ibid., para 84.

213. *Mr. Tanaji Balasaheb Gambhire v. The Union of India*, 2018 SCC OnLine NGT 302 (Western Zone Bench, NGT, India); see also HT Correspondent, "NGT Slaps ₹195 Cr Fine on Pune's Goel Ganga Developers for Environmental Damage".

214. *Mr. Tanaji Balasaheb Gambhire v. The Union of India*.

215. *Goel Ganga Developers v. Union of India*, (2018) 8 SCC 257 (Supreme Court of India).

216. Ibid.

217. Ibid., 286.

218. Ibid., 286.

219. *Krishan Kant Singh vs Triveni Engineering Industries Ltd.*, Judgment dated 10th December 2015 in Original Application No. 317 of 2014 (Principal Bench, NGT, India).

220. *Krishan Kant Singh v. National Ganga River Basin Authority*, 2014 SCC OnLine NGT 5640, para 51 (Principal Bench, NGT, India).

221. Bhushan, Banerjee, and Bezbaroa, *Green Tribunal, Green Approach,* 39.

222. *Krishan Kant Singh v. National Ganga River Basin Authority*, para 51.

223. Ibid., para 51.

224. *M/s. DSM Sugar Distillery Division v. Shailesh Singh & Ors.*, Judgment/Order dated 10th December 2015 in Review application No. 13 of 2015 in Original Application No. 35 of 2015 (Principal Bench, NGT, India).

225. Bhushan, Banerjee, and Bezbaroa, *Green Tribunal, Green Approach*, 39.

226. *M/s. DSM Sugar Distillery Division v. Shailesh Singh & Ors.*.

227. Central Pollution Control Board, Ministry of Environment and Forests, "National Ambient Air Quality Status 2009" (January 2011), 12, https://cpcb.nic.in/openpdffile.php?id=UHVib GljYXRpb25GaWxlLzYzMF8xNDU3NTA2Mjk1X1B1YmxpY-2F0aW9uXzUxNF9haXJxd WFsaXR5c3RhdHVzMjAwOS5wZGY (accessed 21 December 2021).

228. Bhushan, Banerjee, and Bezbaroa, *Green Tribunal, Green Approach*, 30.

229. Ibid., 30.

230. *Ajay Kumar Negi v. Union of India*, 2015 SCC OnLine NGT 666 (Principal Bench, NGT, India).

231. Ibid.

232. Ibid., para 3.

233. Ibid., para 22.

234. Ibid., para 7.

235. *Ajay Kumar Negi v. Union of India*, 2016 SCC OnLine NGT 457, para 16 (Principal Bench, NGT, India).

236. Ibid., para 12.

237. See generally *Indian Express*, "Full Text of NGT Judgment on Sri Sri Ravi Shankar's World Culture Festival" (New Delhi, 10 March 2016), https://indianexpress.com/article/india/ india-news-india/ngt-sri-sri-ravi-shankar-world-culture-festival/ (accessed 21 December 2021).

238. *Manoj Misra v. Delhi Development Authority*, 2017 SCC OnLine NGT 966 (Principal Bench, NGT, India).

239. Ibid.

240. Ibid., para 42.

241. Ibid., para 42.

242. *Manoj Mishra v. Delhi Development Authority*, 2016 SCC OnLine NGT 1556, para 7 (Principal Bench, NGT, India).

243. See generally Debobrat Ghose, "NGT v AOL: How the Green Tribunal Flouted Its Own Order against Sri Sri's Organisation", *FirstPost India* (New Delhi, 11 March 2016), https:// www.firstpost.com/india/ngt-vs-aol-how-the-green-tribunal-flouted-its-own-order-against- sri-sris-organisation-2670494.html (accessed 21 December 2021); SCOI Report, "How Art

of Living Managed to Circumvent the NGT Ruling", *Legally India* (12 March 2016), https://www.legallyindia.com/the-bench-and-the-bar/how-art-of-living-managed-to-circumvent-the-ngt-ruling-and-get-away-paying-only-rs-2-5-cr-despite-its-open-defiance-20160312-7312 (accessed 21 December 2021).

244. Gitanjali Nain Gill, *Environmental Justice in India: The National Green Tribunal* (London: Routledge 2016).

245. Ibid.

246. Ibid.

247. See Nath and Rosencranz, "Determination of Environmental Compensation"; *Manoj Mishra v. Delhi Development Authority*, 2016 SCC OnLine NGT 1556, para 5.

248. *Manoj Mishra v. Delhi Development Authority*, 2016 SCC OnLine NGT 1556, para 5.

249. *Manoj Mishra v. Delhi Development Authority*, Order dated 31 March 2016 in O.A. No. 65 of 2016 (Principal Bench, NGT, India).

250. Ibid.

251. Ibid.

252. *Ram Singh v. Government of NCT of Delhi*, Civil Misc. Petition No. 1988 of 2016 and Writ Petition (Civil) No. 483 of 2016 (Delhi High Court, India).

253. Brij Gopal, C.R. Babu, and A.K. Gosain (Expert Committee constituted by MoEF), "Restoration and Conservation of River Yamuna – Final Report" (MoEF, submitted to the National Green Tribunal with reference to Main Application No. 06 of 2012 based on Order dated 24th September 2013).

254. Ibid.

255. Ibid.

256. Ibid.

257. Ibid.

258. Ibid.

259. Ibid.

260. Letter from Mr Shashi Shekhar to the National Green Tribunal, D.O. No. 5 (UIR, RD 1 GR)/Misc./2016 (3 March 2016).

261. *Krishan Kant Singh v. National Ganga River Basin Authority*; see also Bhushan, Banerjee, and Bezbaroa, *Green Tribunal, Green Approach*.

262. *Manoj Misra v. Delhi Development Authority*, 2017para 42.

263. See Council Directive (EC) 2004/35 on environmental liability with regard to the prevention and remedying of environmental damage [2004] OJ L143/56, https://eur-lex.europa.eu/legal-content/EN/TXT/PDF/?uri=CELEX:32004L0035&from=EN (accessed 21 December 2021).

This section of the paper contains paraphrases from authors' previous work titled "Determining Environmental Compensation in India: Lessons from a Comparative Perspective" submitted to Environmental Policy and Law.

264. Muralidhara H.R., Yashas S.R., and Harish S.N., "Effect of California Bearing Ratio on the Properties of Soil", *American Journal of Engineering Research* 5, no. 4 (2016): 28–37.

265. Ibid.

266. *Manoj Mishra v. Delhi Development Authority*, Order/Judgment in Miscellaneous Application No. 311 of 2016 in Original Application No. 65 of 2016 (Principal Bench, NGT, India).

267. *Goel Ganga Developers v. Union of India.*

268. Ibid.

269. Letter dated 3 March 2016 from Mr Shashi Shekhar to the National Green Tribunal, D.O. No. 5 (UIR, RD 1 GR)/ Misc./2016.

270. V.N.S. Murthy, *Textbook of Soil Mechanics and Foundation Engineering* (Geotechnical Engineering Series, 4th edn) (New Delhi: CBS Publishers & Distributors/Alkem Company (S), 2015).

271. Ibid.

272. *Manoj Misra v. Delhi Development Authority*, 2017, para 41.

273. Ibid., para 41.

274. Ibid., para 41.

275. Ibid., para 41.

276. Ibid., para 41.

277. Ibid., para 24.

278. *Manoj Mishra v. Delhi Development Authority*, 2016 SCC OnLine NGT 114, para 4 (Principal Bench, NGT, India).

279. *Ajay Kumar Negi v. Union of India*, 2015 SCC OnLine NGT 666 (Principal Bench, NGT, India).

280. Ibid., para 4.

281. Organisation for Economic Co-operation and Development, *Liability for Environmental Damage in Eastern Europe, Caucasus and Central Asia (EECCA): Implementation of Good International Practices* (Paris: OECD, 2012), http://www.oecd.org/env/outreach/50244626.pdf (accessed 21 December 2021).

282. Ibid., 11.

283. Organisation for Economic Co-operation and Development, *Liability for Environmental Damage in Eastern Europe, Caucasus and Central Asia (EECCA).*

284. The National Green Tribunal Act, 2010 (Act 19 of 2010).

285. Environment Liability Directive 2004/35, www.ec.europa.eu/environment/legal/liability/index.htm (accessed 22 December 2021).

286. Comprehensive Environmental Response, Compensation, and Liability Act of 1980 § 107(a)(4)(c), 42 U.S.C. § 9601 (1980); see also Raghuveer Nath and Armin Rosencranz, "Determining Environmental Compensation in India: Lessons from a Comparative Perspective", *Environmental Policy and Law* 49, nos. 4–5 (2019): 246–252.

287. *Samaj Parivartana Samudaya & Ors. v. State of Karnataka & Ors.*, Writ Petition No. (C) 562 Of 2009.

288. Ibid.

289. Ray Adams and Margaret Wu (eds.), *Programme for International Student Assessment – Manual for the PISA 2000 Database* (Organisation for Economic Co-operation and Development, Paris 2000); see also Ibid.

290. *Cambridge Advan'ed Learner's Dictionary & Thesaurus*, "anthropocentric", https://dictionary.cambridge.org/dictionary/english/anthropocentric (accessed 21 December 2021).

291. *Samaj Parivartana Samudaya & Ors. v. State of Karnataka & Ors.*, Writ PeIion No. (C) 562 of 2009.

292. Schedule II, National Green Tribunal Act, 2010 (Act 19 of 2010) (India).

293. Environment Liability Directive 2004/35, www.ec.europa.eu/environment/legal/liability/index.htm (accessed 22 December 2021).

294. Ibid., Annexure II.

295. Nath and Rosencranz, "Determining Environmental Compensation in India".

296. US Environmental Protection Agency Website, "Natural Resource Damages: A Primer" (undated, but confirmed on 5 October 2019), https:// www.epa.gov/superfund/natural-resource-damages (accessed 22 December 2021), and the documents and other pages referred to therein; see also Nath and Rosencranz, "Determining Environmental Compensation in India".

297. Environment Liability Directive 2004/35, www.ec.europa.eu/environment/legal/liability/index.htm (accessed 22 December 2021). See also United States Environmental Protection Agency, "Natural Resource Damages: A Primer"; Nath and Rosencranz, "Determining Environmental Compensation in India".

298. Ibid.

299. Ibid.

300. *Paryavaran Suraksha Samiti & Anr. v. Union of India & Ors.*, Original Application No. 593 of 2017, W.P. (CIVIL) No. 375 of 2012.

301. Central Pollution Control Board, *Report of the CPCB In-House Committee on Methodology for Assessing Environmental Compensation and Action Plan to Utilize the Fund* (New Delhi: Central Pollution Control Board, 2019).

302. Ibid., 4.

303. Ibid., 4.

304. *Manoj Mishra v. Delhi Development Authority*, Original Application No. 65 of 2016 (National Green Tribunal, India); *M/s. DSM Sugar Distillery Division v. Shailesh Singh & Ors.*, Judgment/Order dated 10th December 2015 in Review application No. 13 of 2015 in Original Application No. 35 of 2015 (Principal Bench, NGT, India).; *Krishan Kant Singh v. National Ganga River Basin Authority*, 2014 SCC OnLine NGT 5640, para 51 (Principal Bench, NGT, India); *Tanaji Balasaheb Gambhire v. The Union of India*.

305. *Anwar Hussain Ansari, Jhamumo Alpsankhyak Morcha v. State of Jharkhand*, 2020 SCC OnLine NGT 1980 (National Green Tribunal, India).

306. *Adil Ansari v. C.L. Gupta Exports Pvt. Ltd. and Ors*, Order dated 3 December 2020 in I.A. No. 273/2020 in Original Application No. 220/2019 (National Green Tribunal, India).

307. Scott C. Whitney, "The Case for Creating a Special Environmental Court System", *William and Mary Law Review* 14, no. 3 (1972–73), article 2, https://scholarship.law.wm.edu/cgi/viewcontent.cgi?article=2625&context=wmlr (accessed 22 December 2021).

308. S. Rep. No. 91-296 (1969); see also Council on Environmental Quality, *Third Annual Report of the Council on Environmental Quality* (Washington D.C.: CEQ, 1972), 222.

309. *Oleum Leak Case.*

310. The Code of Civil Procedure, 1908 (Act 5 of 1908) (India).

311. Section 19(5), National Green Tribunal Act, 2010 (Act 19 of 2010) (India).

312. *Vitthal Gopichand Bhungase v. Gangakhed Sugar and Energy Ltd.*, 2016 SCC OnLine NGT 3893 (National Green Tribunal, India).

313. Ibid., para 10.

314. *Seela Venkata Subbaiah v. Jinka Muni Swamy*, 1997 (6) ALT 654 (Andhra Pradesh High Court, India).

315. *Janardan Kundalikrao Pharande v. Ministry of Environment & Forest*, 2014 SCC OnLine NGT 1651 (National Green Tribunal, India).

316. Ibid., para 19.

317. *Ramubhai Kriyabhai Patel v. Union of India*, 2013 SCC OnLine NGT 3199 (National Green Tribunal, India).

318. See generally *Shamsunder Shridhar Dalvi v. Govt. of India*, 2014 SCC OnLine NGT 2122 (National Green Tribunal, India); *Suo Motu Uttarakhand Human Rights Commission v. Chief Secretary*, Govt. of Uttarakhand 2016 SCC OnLine NGT 1436 (National Green Tribunal, India).

319. *Goel Ganga Developers v. Union of India.*

320. Ibid., para 34.

321. Ibid., para 41.

322. *Wilfred J. & Anr. v. MoEF.*

323. *Tamil Nadu Pollution Control Board v. Sterlite Industries & Ors.*

324. *M. Naveen Kumar v. Union of India & Anr.*, Writ Petition No. 128644 of 2010 (Madras High Court, India); *Outlook*, "National Green Tribunal Act 2010 Challenged" (Chennai 25 December 2010), https://www.outlookindia.com/newswire/story/national-green-tribunal-act-2010-challenged/706348 (accessed 22 December 2021).

325. *Union of India v. Vimal Bhai*, Order dated 21st April 2011 in Special Leave to Petition (Civil) No.12065 of 2009 (Supreme Court of India).

326. *Bhopal Gas Peedith Mahila Udyog Sangathan v. Union of India*, (2012) 8 Supreme Court Cases 326 (Supreme Court of India).

327. Ibid., para 40.

328. *Ratnagiri Nagar Parishad v. Gangaram Narayan Ambekar*, (2020) 7 SCC 275 (Supreme Court of India).

329. Ibid., para 14.

330. Department-Related Parliamentary Standing Committee on Science & Technology, Environment & Forests, "Report on the National Green Tribunal Bill, 2009, Presented in Parliament of India – Rajya Sabha" (203rd Report, November 2009), http://164.100.47.5/newcommittee/reports/EnglishCommittees/Committee%20on%20S%20and%20T,%20Env.%20and%20Forests/For%20Net.htm (accessed 2 December 2021).

331. Roy, "NGT Working with Just Six Members Instead of at Least 21, Zonal Benches Vacant for Two Years Now".

332. Ibid.

333. *Kollidam Aaru Pathukappu Nala Sangam v. Union of India.*

334. *L. Chandra Kumar v. Union of India.*

335. Ibid., para 100.

336. Ibid.

337. *Shri Anil Hoble v. Kashinath Jairam Shetye*, 2015 SCC OnLine Bom 3699 (Bombay High Court, India).

338. Ibid., para 16.

339. *Shri Anil Hoble v. Kashinath Jairam Shetye.*

340. *United Bank of India v. Satyawati Tandon* (2010) 8 SCC 110, para 43 (Supreme Court of India).

341. *Goa Foundation v. Union of India*, Order in Writ Petition (Civil) No. 435 of 2012, para 22.

342. Special Correspondent, "High Court to Hear Appeal against NGT Order", *The Hindu* (Hyderabad, India 1 March 2019), https://www.thehindu.com/news/cities/Hyderabad/high-court-to-hear-appeal-against-ngt order/article26401062.ece (accessed 22 December 2021).

343. Ibid.

344. *Oleum Leak Case.*

345. *Union Carbide Corporation v. Union of India*, AIR 1992 SC 248 (Supreme Court of India).

346. Bhushan, Banerjee, and Bezbaroa, *Green Tribunal, Green Approach.*

347. Ibid.

348. Ibid., 18.

349. Debadityo Sinha, *The Management of Environment Relief Fund* (New Delhi: Vidhi Centre for Legal Policy, 2020), https://vidhilegalpolicy.in/wp-content/uploads/2020/03/Management_of_ERF_Debadityo_Sinha_VCLP_2020.pdf (accessed 22 December 2021).

350. Ibid.

351. Ibid.

352. Ibid.

353. Environment Liability Directive 2004/35, https://eur-lex.europa.eu/legal-content/EN/TXT/PDF/?uri=CELEX:32004L0035&from=EN (accessed 22 December 2021).

354. Bhushan, Banerjee, and Bezbaroa, *Green Tribunal, Green Approach,* 19.

355. Ibid., 19.

356. Sinha, *The Management of Environment Relief Fund.*

357. Environment Liability Directive 2004/35, https://eur-lex.europa.eu/legal-content/EN/TXT/PDF/?uri=CELEX:32004L0035&from=EN (accessed 22 December 2021).

358. Bhushan, Banerjee, and Bezbaroa, *Green Tribunal, Green Approach*, 20.

359. Ibid.

360. Ibid.

361. Gopal, Babu, Gosain, "Restoration and Conservation of River Yamuna".

362. Law Commission of India, "Proposal to constitute Environmental Courts".

363. Ibid., 67.

364. See generally *State of Uttaranchal v. Balwant Singh Chaufal*, Civil Appeal Nos.1134–1135 of 2002 (Supreme Court of India); *S.P Gupta v. Union of India*, AIR 1982 SC 149; *Dattaraj Nathuji Thaware v. State of Maharashtra* Special Leave Petition (Civil) 26269 of 2004 (Supreme Court of India); *Holicow Pictures (P) Ltd. v. Prem Chandra Mishra* Appeal (Civil) 5671 of 2007 (Supreme Court of India); *Chhetriya Pardushan Mukti Sangharsh Samiti v. State of U.P.*, AIR 1990 SC 2060 (Supreme Court of India).

365. *B'lco Employees' Union v. Union of India* (Transfer Case) (Civil) 8 of 2001 (Supreme Court of India).

366. *Baijnath Prajapati v. Ministry of Environment and Forests* 2012 SCC OnLine NGT 21 (National Green Tribunal, India).

367. Ibid., para 7.

368. *Rana Sen Gupta v. Union of India Judgment* Dated 22nd March 2013 in Appeal No. 54 of 2012 (Supreme Court of India).

369. Ibid., para 14.

370. *Vijay Singh v. Balaji Grit Udyog*, Appeal No. 2 of 2014 (Principal Bench, National Green Tribunal, India)

371. Law Commission of India, "Proposal to constitute Environmental Courts", 151.

372. Section 30(1), The National Green Tribunal Act, 2010 (Act 19 of 2010) (India).

3

INTERPRETATION AND APPLICATION
OF ENVIRONMENTAL PRINCIPLES

Article 51 of the Indian Constitution states that the state shall foster respect for international law and treaty obligations. To give effect to this provision, Article 253 of the Constitution empowers the parliament to make any law for implementing obligations under international treaties, conferences, or agreements. In particular, the preamble to the NGT Act states that the creation of the NGT symbolizes the fulfilment of India's obligations under the United Nations Conferences on the Human Environment (Stockholm, 1972) and Environment and Development (Rio de Janeiro, 1992). These conferences call upon member states to, inter alia, provide effective access to judicial and administrative proceedings and to develop national laws regarding liability and compensation for victims of environmental pollution and damage.[1]

While there are several internationally recognized norms and principles,[2] three main principles form the bedrock of environmental jurisprudence in the Indian context. These three principles are sustainable development, the precautionary principle, and the polluter pays principle. While these have been extensively used by the Supreme Court in several important environmental cases,[3] the NGT Act is the first legislation that codifies these principles. Section 20 of the NGT Act states:

> The Tribunal shall, while passing any order or decision or award, apply the principles of sustainable development, the precautionary principle and the polluter pays principle.

Overall, the NGT Act accords significant discretion to the Tribunal in relation to how it should adjudicate and award compensation. Given this context, Section 20 assumes greater significance as it is the only guiding provision contained in the NGT Act, which provides directions with respect to how the Tribunal should pass an order or award. The use of the word "shall" indicates that it is a mandatory provision and that the NGT is obligated to base its decision on these three principles, if they are applicable.

Accordingly, these principles have formed an integral part of most decisions of the NGT and are intricately linked with its jurisprudence. As we will discuss, most landmark cases of the NGT have relied on these principles to provide environmental justice. Through this chapter, we explore the significance of these three principles. In doing so, we highlight their origin and evolution in the international context, their interpretation and application by the Supreme Court of India, and their use by the NGT.

3.1   PRINCIPLE OF SUSTAINABLE DEVELOPMENT

3.1.1   INTRODUCTION TO SUSTAINABLE DEVELOPMENT

"Sustainability" has probably become a buzzword today. We prefer to buy clothes that are made through a sustainable process. We like to consume food that has been grown sustainably. Governments and municipalities seek to make sustainable cities for people to live in. Also, since the 1980s we have been hearing and talking about sustainable development, especially after evidence of climate change, human-induced natural disasters, and loss of ecosystems due to infrastructural activities have come to light.[4]

The concept of sustainability, however, can be traced back to at least the early 1700s during the European Enlightenment.[5] Nevertheless, this does not imply that sustainability is a European concept. For several hundreds and thousands of years, indigenous communities in various parts of the world, including Europe, the Americas, China, and India, have been living in a sustainable manner.[6] It is the unsustainable use of natural resources and the ensuing social and economic repercussions that ignited the modern interest in sustainability. Thus, it is not a coincidence that the sustainability movement can trace its roots back to Europe in the early phases of the Industrial Revolution.[7] After all, it is an unsustainable society that needs to think in terms of sustainability.

In 1798, Thomas Malthus, an English country parson, argued that the poor would remain poor due to their likelihood of having several children.[8] During his time, the poor were likely to have more children as some children were expected to die in their infancy due to high infant mortality in the eighteenth century. His solution was to encourage the poor masses to marry later and have fewer children. At its core, Malthus' argument is not about growth or economic development. Rather, according to his understanding, it is about the unsustainability of overpopulation and the impossibility of equality.

The eighteenth century saw rapid economic expansion due to technological innovations brought forth by the Industrial Revolution. Largely, however, this development came at the expense of the environment, which was seen as an inexhaustible resource that existed for the fulfilment of human needs and desires.[9] It is not surprising that the environment or natural resources do not feature in Malthus' theory on poverty.[10]

During the Industrial Revolution, Adam Smith formulated the classical theory of capitalism, which assumed the need for a deregulated economy based on the growth of material consumption, population, and private wealth.[11] Goods that were earlier painstakingly crafted by hand began to be mass produced with the invention of machines such as the spinning jenny, the power loom, and the steam engine. Coal was the main fuel used by factories, and major European cities were covered in dark clouds of smoke. A conservative estimate puts the pollution levels during this time as being fifty times higher than before the Revolution. In fact, even as late as 1952, smog covered the entire city of London and killed more than 4,000 people.[12]

While the European Enlightenment period is widely regarded as the beginning of modern-day capitalism, it is also the source of the modern-day concept of sustainability. Saxon mining administrator and forestry expert Hans Carl von Carlowitz coined the term *Nachhaltigkeit* – meaning "sustainability" in German – in 1713.[13] He used this term in the context of a timber crisis that had gripped Saxony and several parts of Europe in the early eighteenth century.

Carlowitz ran a profitable silver mining operation which needed a steady supply of wood to keep the mining shafts warm. During this time, fuelwood was the main source of energy as coal displaced it only towards the end of the eighteenth century. Given the shortage of timber for fuel, Carlowitz called for the suitable use of forests, which would ensure a steady supply. His treatise on sustainable forestry drew on the works by John Evelyn in England and Jean-Baptiste Colbert in France in the seventeenth century.[14]

In fact, John Evelyn's book titled *Sylva* is relevant even today in terms of its recognition of problems posed by rapid industrialization, rapid conversion of forests into farmland, and the risk of people being blinded by the greed of profits.[15] Evelyn called for altering our approach towards industrialization, placing a duty on citizens to take part in efforts to safeguard the environment, and celebrating the intrinsic value of the environment.[16]

The basic idea that underpinned the works of Carlowitz, Evelyn, and Colbert was that human beings must learn to live and thrive within limits. This was reiterated by John Stuart Mill in the mid-nineteenth century when he spoke of the idea of a stationary state of capitalism.[17] This was based on the notion that economic growth must not continue endlessly, and that economic growth should eventually culminate to a point where everyone is prosperous.[18] This idea found ground with other early environmentalists who understood that economics and social well-being are intrinsically connected to the environment.[19]

The origin of the contemporary notion of the "Three E's" of sustainability – environment, economics, and equity – can be traced to this belief system.[20] This idea of placing sustainable limits on economic growth led the Club of Rome to publish its famous report titled *The Limits to Growth* in 1972, which drew upon the works of Malthus and highlighted the environmental unsustainability of overpopulation.[21] This report advocated for a form of development wherein human needs are met by not risking a collapse of the global economic system. Similar to Mill's notion of a stationary state of capitalism, the report propounded a "state of global equilibrium".[22]

These ideas of sustainability later found tacit recognition at an international level during the United Nations Conference on the Human Environment in Stockholm (1972).[23] The central theme of the 1972 conference was to defend and improve the "human environment" for present and future generations.[24] Principle 2 of the declaration states:

> The natural resources of the earth, including the air, water, land, flora and fauna and especially representative samples of natural ecosystems, must be safeguarded for the benefit of present and future generations through careful planning or management, as appropriate.

The anthropocentrism is evident in the declaration. In fact, under Principle 5 the declaration unequivocally states, "Of all things in the world, people are the most precious." Nevertheless, this conference marked the first international enunciation of principles calling for limitations on the unrestrained exploitation of the global environment and implied the sustainable use of natural resources. Since the Stockholm Declaration, similar global conferences have been held every decade.[25]

The first explicit use of the term "sustainable development", however, was made more than a decade later by the World Commission on Environment and Development in its report titled *Our Common Future*.[26] This report has been referred to popularly as the Brundtland Report, and its definition of the term is still widely used. The report defines sustainable development as: [27]

> Development that meets the needs of the present without compromising the ability of future generations to meet their own needs.

This definition stresses the survival and existence of human beings. To this effect, it underpins the need to utilize natural resources in a manner that not only meets the present needs but also ensures that the needs of future generations are not impacted. Thus, it calls for the sustainable use of natural resources in a manner that does not irreversibly damage the environment and allows the future generations same access to these resources.

This definition of sustainable development contains elements of a related concept called "intergenerational equity", which was coined by economist James Tobin in 1974.[28] According to Tobin, trustees of endowed institutions were "guardians of the future against the claims of the present", and they were responsible for ensuring equity among generations.[29] At its core, the principle states that every generation holds the Earth in common with members of past, present, and future generations.[30] As seen in the Brundtland Report's definition, this idea forms the basis of the modern implications of sustainable development.

Shortly after the Brundtland Report, the first enunciation of sustainable development at a global level took place during the United Nations Conference on Environment and Development in Rio de Janeiro in 1992.[31] The Rio Declaration reaffirmed the Stockholm Declaration of 1972 and added some salient points to it. It held, under Principle 4, that to achieve sustainable development, environmental protection shall constitute an integral part of the development process of states. In line with the concept of intergenerational equity, it held that the right to development must be fulfilled so as to equitably meet the developmental and environmental needs of the present and future generations.[32]

Further, the Rio Declaration held that states shall conserve, protect, and restore the health and integrity of the Earth's ecosystem. In doing so, it held that there were "common but differentiated responsibilities" between developed and developing countries.[33] Additionally, it underpinned the need for inclusive development,[34] eradication of poverty,[35] and transnational cooperation through sharing of new technologies and the abandonment of the use of hazardous substances to ensure sustainable development.[36]

Nevertheless, sustainable development, similar to the Stockholm Declaration of 1972, continued to be defined in anthropocentric terms. Principle 1 of the Rio Declaration states:

> Human beings are at the centre of concerns for sustainable development. They are entitled to a healthy and productive life in harmony with nature.

In fact, this anthropocentric trend is clearly visible in the Johannesburg Declaration on Sustainable Development of 2002 and the United Nations Conference on Sustainable Development of 2012, Rio de Janeiro. In both declarations, human beings are the central focus and the use of natural resources is deemed sustainable only if they are utilized in a way that does not cause harm to present and future generations of human beings.[37] In fact, flora and fauna need to be sustainably maintained as they are necessary for the survival of mankind.[38] This is clearly visible from the Rio Declaration on Environment and Sustainable Development of 2012, which states:[39]

> We recognize that people are at the centre of sustainable development and in this regard we strive for a world that is just, equitable and inclusive, and we commit to work together to promote sustained and inclusive economic growth, social development and environmental protection and thereby to benefit all.

The aforementioned conferences and declarations have helped put the principle of sustainable development on the global stage. Over the years, the principle of sustainable development has become an integral part of a host of international legal instruments such as the United Nations Framework Convention on Climate Change,[40] the United Nations Convention to Combat Desertification and Drought,[41] and the International Treaty on Plant Genetic Resources.[42] Nevertheless, while there is wide acceptance of the principle globally, the anthropocentrism implied within the declarations belittles the intrinsic value of the environment. The environment is deemed valuable only to the extent that it is useful for the survival and prosperity of human beings.

In addition to the anthropocentrism, some scholars have criticized the principle for its vagueness and its inability to produce tangible results.[43] This inability has been attributed to the failure to strike a balance between the principle and policy considerations in actual situations.[44] Further, the principle is viewed as being unable to create a defined legal standard of behaviour due to the difficulty in defining the parameters of such behaviour.[45] As previously noted, sustainable development is a balance of economic, environmental, and sustainable considerations. However, there exists no scientific formula or a standardized equation that helps achieve a balance between these competing variables, and often political considerations decide which variable to favour.[46]

Accordingly, the principle's inherent anthropocentrism, vagueness, and inability to provide effective standards for behaviour have led some scholars to question its relevance in resolving international disputes.[47] For instance, John Gillroy has argued that, unlike general legal principles, sustainable development is incapable of generating legal rules as it is comprised of competing sub-principles.[48] Gillroy states that the principle of sustainable development should be seen as an overarching "meta-principle" of law, which is comprised of four substantive and four procedural principles that are constantly competing with each other.

According to Gillroy, the four substantive sub-principles contained in sustainable development are: (1) prevention; (2) precaution; (3) the right to equitable development; and (4) the right to use internal resources so as not to harm other states. The four corresponding procedural sub-principles of sustainable development are: (1) integration of environment and development; (2) concern for future generations and their welfare; (3) common but differentiated responsibility; and (4) the principle of polluter pays.[49]

Thus, the principle of sustainable development can be seen as a parent principle that encompasses the precautionary principles and the polluter pays principle (we will be discussing these principles in subsequent sections). According to Gillroy, continuous conflict between the four substantive principles and the four procedural principles prevents sustainable development from producing legal rules that may be useful in resolving legal disputes. This is because the scope of each of these sub-principles is inherently unclear and the weightage accorded to each of them differs based on the facts of a case and various policy considerations.[50] For instance, if a polluter pollutes a certain portion of an area but still leaves adequate natural resources for future generations, it is unclear what the standard application should be of the sustainable development principle.

Nevertheless, despite these criticisms of the principle, sustainable development has to some extent been recognized and used as a legal principle in international disputes. For instance, in arriving at a decision the the Appellate Body of the World Trade Organization (WTO) employed the principle of sustainable development as an aid in the *Shrimp Turtle Case* dispute and drew specific legal consequences from the principle.[51] The case involved a complaint filed by India, Malaysia, and Pakistan in 1997 against the United States (US) claiming that the latter's ban on the import of certain shrimp products was unreasonable and illegal. The ban was imposed for the protection of endangered sea turtles that were either directly or indirectly adversely affected by shrimp cultivation. One of the arguments put forth by the complainant countries was that the expression "exhaustible natural resources" applied only to resources that were incapable of biological reproduction such as coal and petroleum reserves.[52] Thus, they contended that the US could not treat shrimp as an exhaustible resource.

Interestingly, the WTO Agreement between the countries referred to sustainable development as an objective of the WTO system. The Appellate Body, in its decision, held that there was ample evidence to suggest that endangered species could be considered as "exhaustible" even though individual members had reproductive capabilities.[53] Further, it held that states had an inherent right to take trade actions to protect the environment and endangered species.[54] Thus, while the US lost the case, it was due to its discriminatory trade practices within the group of countries banned and not due to the ban itself.

The International Court of Justice (ICJ), in comparison to the WTO, has employed the principle of sustainable development as a distinct legal principle rather than as a part of an agreement. Although the ICJ had included the principle in an Advisory Opinion in 1996,[55] the *Gabcikovo-Nagymaros*[56] *Case* in 1997 was the first time that the principle was used as a part of the ICJ's jurisprudence. The case involved a dispute regarding the development of a system of locks on the Danube River pursuant to a 1977 treaty between Hungary and Czechoslovakia.

While the aim of the project was to generate hydroelectricity and protect against flooding, Hungary decided to abandon the project in 1989 due to serious environmental (threats to groundwater and wetlands) concerns raised by scientists and environmentalists. In response, Slovakia attempted to unilaterally continue the project and diverted the river towards its territory. While the parties before the ICJ prayed for the Court to look at the 1977 treaty, in determining the case the ICJ looked beyond the treaty and referred to customary international law and international conventions.[57] In relation to sustainable development, it held:[58]

> Throughout the ages, mankind has, for economic and other reasons, constantly interfered with nature. In the past, this was often done without consideration of the effects upon the environment. Owing to new scientific insights and to a growing awareness of the risks for mankind ... new norms and standards have been developed, set forth in a great number of instruments during the last two decades. Such new norms have to be taken into consideration, and such new standards given proper weight, not only when states contemplate new activities but also when continuing with activities begun in the past. This need to reconcile economic development with protection of the environment is aptly expressed in the concept of sustainable development. For the purposes of the present case, this means that the Parties together should look afresh at the effects on the environment of the operation of the [Slovakian] power plant.

While the ICJ implored the parties to use sustainable development in sovereign decision-making, it stopped short of declaring the principle as a part of customary international law.[59] Nevertheless, later, the ICJ recalled these observations in the *Pulp Mills Case*, and while it still did not recognize the principle as a part of customary international law, there was a recognition of it as a reasonable state practice.[60] Given these international developments and the increasingly wide incorporation of sustainable development in international agreements and state practice, it is only a matter of time before the principle will acquire the formal status of being a part of customary international law.

At its core, given the present challenges highlighted earlier, the principle of sustainable development can be seen as a modifying norm that primarily exerts normative influence as an interpretative tool when used by judges.[61] This interpretative function is important as judges have been able to use the principle to legitimize the use of evolutive treaty interpretation, resolve conflicts, and reinterpret conventional obligations.[62] Beyond this interpretative function, the principle mainly regulates state conduct.[63] While the exact standard of the obligation imposed by the principle may be unclear, it nevertheless exerts some degree of influence in state practice. It has been argued that such obligations as those imposed by the principle are known as obligations of means or of best efforts.[64] Thus, states are ultimately obligated to promote sustainable development.

Sustainable development, from the seventeenth century to date, has evolved and matured from a concept to a legal principle, although with limited influence, which is internationally recognized and widely acknowledged by countries. Overall, the principle is a parent principle from which several other environmental principles emerge, such as the precautionary principle and polluter pays principle. The principle purports to protect the environment from the excesses of unrestrained capitalistic development and seeks to ensure adequate natural resources for future generations. It is a synergic principle that seeks to meet human needs while safeguarding the environment. To further understand the operation and practical contours of the principle of sustainable development, let us now examine its application by the Supreme Court and the NGT.

3.1.2   THE INDIAN SUPREME COURT AND THE PRINCIPLE OF SUSTAINABLE DEVELOPMENT

From the previous discussion, we have seen how the principle of sustainable development has now been recognized as an international environmental principle due to its wide recognition in international treaties and conventions. Around the time when the Brundtland Report published the most widely recognized definition of sustainable development in 1987, India was struggling to comprehensively deal with environmental issues.

In 1984, the Bhopal Gas Tragedy had shaken the entire country. At least 30 tonnes of methyl isocyanate gas had leaked into the city of Bhopal from Union Carbide's factory, killing more than 15,000 people and permanently affecting more than 600,000 people (Image 3.1).[65] The rate of stillbirths and the infant mortality rate grew by 300 per cent

Image 3.1 Dead bodies being rounded up after the tragedy in December 1984, Bhopal

Source: Sunita Narain and Chandra Bhushan, "30 Years of Bhopal Gas Tragedy: A Continuing Disaster", *Down To Earth* (15 December 2014), https://www.downtoearth.org.in/coverage/environment/30-years-of-bhopal-gas-tragedy-a-continuing-disaster-47634 (accessed 24 December 2021).

and 200 per cent, respectively, in the affected area.[66] Within a few days of the disaster, people wobbled on streets vomiting and dying, trees became barren, and the city ran out of cremation grounds. It was one of the worst man-made natural disasters in history.[67]

There had been warning signs of the impending disaster before the calamity. As early as in 1976, trade unions complained about the pollution within the Union Carbide factory. Shortly thereafter, a worker died on account of accidently inhaling a large amount of toxic phosgene gas. In fact, local newspapers reported news of a coming disaster months before the 1984 disaster, with a headline reading, "Wake Up People of Bhopal, You Are on the Edge of a Volcano".[68] Despite these warnings, precaution was not taken. The Indian environmental jurisprudence back then had not evolved to apply the principle of sustainable development in the form of the precautionary principle.

The Government of India began legal proceedings against Union Carbide right after the gas leak and passed the Bhopal Gas Leak Act, 1985, which allowed the government to act as a legal representative for all victims of the tragedy. In response, Union Carbide offered a meagre amount of USD 5 million as a relief fund to India. The government turned down this offer and asked for USD 3.3 billion. Eventually, an out-of-court settlement was reached, and Union Carbide was required to pay only USD 470 million in settlement of all possible claims.[69] The approval of this paltry settlement between the government and Union Carbide is widely regarded as one of the greatest failures of the Supreme Court.[70] Not only did the Court fail to uphold basic human rights and dignity, it also shred the victims and their families of their dignity.

As noted in Chapter 2, the compensation ordered by the Court was negligible relative to the corresponding multi-billion dollar lawsuit filed by a lawyer in the US.[71] Upon the announcement of the court settlement and the compensation amount, the shares of Union Carbide rose 7 per cent in value.[72] Had the compensation awarded by the Supreme Court been paid at the same rate as that awarded by US courts to asbestosis victims (Union Carbide had mined asbestosis between 1963 and 1985), the liability of the company would have been more than USD 10 billion, that is, twenty times the compensation levied.[73] In fact, subsequently, the Central government moved the Supreme Court in December 2010 and demanded additional compensation on account of the disaster to the tune of INR 7,844 crore (more than USD 1 billion).[74]

It is a matter of public record that Union Carbide did not cooperate with the Indian government and the Supreme Court.[75] It tried to manipulate and suppress scientific data relating to the gas leak. Even to date, the company has not conclusively revealed details relating to the chemical composition of the gas cloud that killed thousands of people to enable effective treatment. Adding insult to injury, Union Carbide did not even clean up its industrial site properly after discontinuing operations in India. For more than two decades after the closure, the plant kept spewing out toxic and poisonous chemicals which percolated into local water bodies and ground water.[76] The effects of this are visible in Image 3.2.

After more than thirty-five years, the battle for justice and adequate compensation still wages on. Children continue to be born with deformities and diseases primarily because chemical wastes continue to remain dumped around Union Carbide's factory, contaminating the ground water that people drink. This could have been managed had the government been provided with information about the chemical used by Union Carbide and the treatment for it.[77] In fact, even as recently as 2014, the Indian Council of Medical Research (ICMR) stated that "the exact causative agent of the Bhopal Gas Disease is unknown".[78] The main reason for this is that Union Carbide used trade secrecy as an excuse to withhold crucial information regarding the exact composition of the chemical that killed thousands.[79]

In fact, even today, there is another impending disaster in the same area which has the propensity to negatively impact even more people. Approximately, 350 tonnes of chemical waste continues to be kept in a leaking shed at the same disaster site.[80] Given that these chemicals remain in the environment for hundreds of years, if the government does not prepare a proper plan to dispose of this waste, it is likely to seriously endanger people and the environment in the vicinity.

Image 3.2   This is a picture of Vineeta Kumar and her disabled son Abhay, taken in Dwarker Nagar, Bhopal. Abhay's congenital disability was caused due to the consumption of carcinogenic and mutagenic water from the area surrounding the Union Carbide factory, which was abandoned nearly four decades ago.

Source: *The Logical Indian*, "Heart-Wrenching Images Showing the Devastating Effects of the Bhopal Gas Tragedy Even After 32 Years" (Photo published on The Logical Indian on 3 December 2015), https://thelogicalindian.com/news/the-bhopal-gas-tragedy/ (accessed 24 December 2021).

While several reasons contributed towards the appalling approach of the Supreme Court, such as India's dependency on foreign capital and the lack of governmental will, one of the primary reasons that Union Carbide could escape proportional liability was due to the inadequacy of environmental jurisprudence with the Supreme Court.[81] Even though laws such as the Water (Prevention and Control of Pollution) Act, 1974, the Wildlife (Protection) Act, 1972, and the Forest (Conservation) Act, 1980, were in place, these were not designed to handle a disaster of the magnitude of the Bhopal Gas Tragedy. Additionally, the Supreme Court did not have the benefit of general international environmental principles to impose strict liability on the polluter.

Given this context, it is not surprising that in subsequent years, the Supreme Court welcomed the enunciation of international principles such as sustainable development and applied them in the domestic context. To date, the Supreme Court has employed the concept of sustainable development as a legal principle in several cases, elevating the principle from an international environmental norm to a perennial independent legal principle applicable in India.[82]

The first use of the principle of sustainable development by the Court was in *State of Himachal Pradesh v. Ganesh Wood Products,*[83] where the Court took up the issue of uncontrolled felling of *khair*[84] trees by *kattha*[85] industries in the state of Himachal Pradesh. The petition was filed in order to prohibit more *kattha* industries from setting up. The Court for the first time drew upon the growing recognition of the principle of sustainable development by examining the Brundtland Report[86] and then held: [87]

> The obligation of sustainable development requires that a proper assessment should be made of the forest wealth and the establishment of industries based on forest produce should not only be restricted accordingly but their working should also be monitored closely to ensure that the required balance is not disturbed.

The Court prohibited any new factories from being set up and directed that an expert panel under the relevant High Court should be set up to report on the sustainability of the new industries. In many ways, this reporting and assessment mechanism used by the Court can be seen as a precursor to the Environmental Impact Assessment (EIA) that we have today to ascertain the sustainability of projects. (EIA is discussed in greater detail in the next chapter.)

Shortly thereafter, the Court developed the principle further in *Vellore Citizens Welfare Forum v. Union of India.*[88] The court declared: [89]

> The traditional concept that development and ecology are opposed to each other is no longer acceptable. Sustainable Development" is the answer.

The Court drew upon the international dialogue of the principle. After citing the Stockholm Declaration of 1972, the Brundtland Report of 1987, and the Rio Declaration of 1992, it endorsed the concept as a balance between ecology and development. Notably, the Court went a step further than the ICJ in the *Gabcikovo-Nagymaros Case*[90] and held that the principle of sustainable development was, in its interpretation, a part of international law.

Further, in line with Gillroy,[91] the Court interpreted sustainable development as an overarching principle that contains other environmental principles such as intergenerational equity, use and conservation of natural resources, environmental protection, obligation to assist and cooperate, eradication of poverty, and financial assistance to developing countries. Moreover, it held that the precautionary principle and the polluter pays principle are two integral components of sustainable development. However, unlike Gillroy, the Court did not interpret these components of sustainable development as being in competition with each other and affirmed the use of the principle as a legal norm.

This interpretation of the Supreme Court was critical in developing a legal mechanism to hold a polluter liable and to protect against potential pollution. Such an interpretation gave legal sanctity to the polluter pays principle and the precautionary principle as individual legal norms that could be applied within the larger context of sustainable development. Accordingly, by applying these two sub-principles with sustainable development in mind, the Court ordered polluting industries to pay compensation and shut down factories that failed to meet environmental standards.

The Court's interpretation and application of sustainable development in the *Vellore Case* was robustly echoed in later cases such as *M.C. Mehta v. Union of India*[92] (popularly known as the *Lakes Case*) and *In. Re. Delhi Transport Department.*[93] In both of these cases, the Court recognized following sustainable development as a constitutional duty of the government when undertaking developmental activities. Further, in *S. Jagannath v. Union of India*,[94] the Court held that the principle imposed a positive obligation on the government to ensure that industries conform to sustainable development. It took cognizance of rapidly depleting shrimp stocks and directed the government to set up a dedicated authority to regulate the shrimp industry and ensure its conformance to sustainable development.

Similarly, in the *Taj Trapezium Case*,[95] the Court reiterated the positive obligation imposed on the government under the principle and held that the government must endeavour to strike a balance between development and ecology, and that there should not be a trade-off between the two. The case involved, inter alia, the discolouration of the Taj Mahal due to pollution and acid rain. In response, the Court further developed the principle and proposed a method of assessing the sustainability of a certain developmental activity. According to the Court, the sustainability of a project could be ascertained by examining whether the activity intended exceeds the "carrying capacity"[96] of the ecosystem in which it was located.[97] This involves studying the fragility of an ecosystem and its likely response to a potential pollutive activity.

If a potential industry is located near a fragile ecosystem, then that industry should refrain from environmentally risky behaviour and should ideally relocate elsewhere if there is tangible harm likely to be caused to the surrounding environment. Accordingly, this involves an assessment of foreseeable environmental damage and the extent of mitigation possible through preventive measures. This is in line with the precautionary principle which is a component of sustainable development. In fact, the requirement of assessing the carrying capacity of the ecosystem was reemphasized by the Supreme Court in several cases,[98] and eventually found recognition in the EIA Notification, 2006.[99]

These judgments of the Court, in the aftermath of the Bhopal Gas Tragedy, reflect a strong intent to understand and apply international environmental principles in the domestic context. While the ICJ fell short of holding that the principle forms a part of customary international law, the Supreme Court did not. In addition to holding that the principle is a part of customary international law, it interpreted the principle as imposing a positive legal obligation on the government and any person undertaking an activity that is likely to interfere with the environment. Accordingly, such an interpretation enabled the Court to deploy the principle in a manner which held governmental actions to a high standard and enforced stricter regulations on industrial activities.

However, the Supreme Court gradually began to dilute its stringent approach and adopt a softer iteration of sustainable development.[100] On the other hand, some viewed this shift as being counterproductive.[101]

This shift to a softer approach is apparent in the case of *Consumer Education & Research Society v. Union of India*.[102] In this case, the Chinkara Wildlife Sanctuary – a state protected wildlife sanctuary – lost its protected status because of a decision made by state government. The decision was challenged on the ground that this de-notification was not made with due regard to the possible environmental impacts on the wildlife and biodiversity in the sanctuary and was made to appease the government's pro-development agenda. Despite stating that the state authorities ought to have examined relevant material and should have considered the environmental impact of their decision in greater depth, the Court held that this was not reason enough to set aside their decision.

According to the Court, as long as some deliberation and examination had gone into the decision-making process of the state authorities, it could not interfere and stipulate exactly which information ought to have been considered. This is problematic as it significantly lowers the burden on the government, imposed by earlier decisions such as in *S. Jagannath v. Union of India*[103] and the *Taj Trapezium Case*,[104] in terms of the number and degree of environmental aspects that should be considered to uphold sustainable development. The following paragraph demonstrates this aptly:[105]

> This forest in the notified and de-notified areas in an edaphic thorn forest. It is a desert forest but with *large number of trees*. It has been identified as a *potential site for designation as a bio-sphere reserve* by an Expert Committee constituted by the Ministry of Environment and Forest. It has been put in a *"Rich Area Category"*, from bio-diversity point of view, by the Gujarat Ecology Commission. Even the Union of India in its affidavit has stated the de-notified area of the sanctuary includes many areas of high and *very high flora and fauna value* and these areas form an integral part of the Narayan Sarovar Sanctuary. The Rapid Impact Assessment Report by the Wildlife Institute of India has pointed out that any reduction in the area of that sanctuary will reduce the number of species of trees. It is also at the same time true, as pointed out by the government, that this part of the Kutchh district is a *backward area*. There is no other possibility of industrial development in that area, though it contains rich mineral deposits. *Therefore, if an attempt is made by the state legislature and the state government to balance the need of the environment and the need of economic development it would not be proper to apply the principle of prohibition in such a case.* The reports of the three committees only point out the ecological importance of the area and express an apprehension, that any major mining operation within the notified area and large scale industrialization near about the sanctuary as originally notified, may adversely affect the ecological balance and bio-diversity of that area. It would, therefore, be proper and safer to apply the 'principle of protection' and the 'principle of polluter pays' keeping

in mind the principle of sustainable development and the 'principle of inter-generation equity'. (Emphasis supplied)

The irony in the Court's decision is clearly reflected in the aforementioned excerpt. On one hand, the Court recognizes the ecological significance of the de-notified sanctuary and the likely environmental impact by highlighting the following points:

1. The sanctuary has a large number of trees, and the biodiversity is so significant that the expert committee appointed by the MoEF held that it has the potential to be classified as a biosphere reserve.
2. The concerned area has a very high flora and fauna value and, according to the Wildlife Institute of India, any reduction in the area of the sanctuary will inevitably lead to a reduction in the species of trees.
3. Any major mining activity or large-scale industrialization could adversely affect the ecological balance and biodiversity in the sanctuary.

On the other hand, the Court holds that its intervention is not warranted if the state government has made an attempt to "balance the need of the environment and the need of economic development". The Court does not shed any light on how such a balance is being maintained. While it states that the area is backward and that there are no other possibilities of industrial development in the area apart from the proposed mineral mining, it does not explain how a balance is "being" maintained. Clearly, developmental needs are being preferred at the cost of the environment.

Further, this sets a dangerous precedent in that any activity for economic development, carried out in an area which has no other alternatives for similar development, should be allowed irrespective of the environmental damage as this is viewed as balancing economic and environmental needs. Further, by holding that the precautionary principle and the polluter pays principle are not applicable in such a scenario, the Court effectively held that the principle of sustainable development is not applicable. Such a holding runs counter to the earlier cases discussed wherein the Court unequivocally interpreted the principle of sustainable development as imposing a positive obligation on the government.[106]

Further, such deference to the executive, if the executive can demonstrate some deliberation on an environmental issue even if all relevant materials are not considered, is unwarranted and is opposed to sustainable development which holds the legislature accountable to a higher threshold. Lowering the threshold to such an extent also grants considerable leeway to industries and governmental agencies which might collude for the grant of a particular project, irrespective of the environmental damage.

This diluted reinterpretation of sustainable development was carried forward by the Supreme Court in *Narmada Bachao Andolan v. Union of India*,[107] wherein the Court was concerned with the construction of the Sardar Sarovar Dam – the world's second-largest hydroelectric dam.[108] The Sardar Sarovar Dam was proposed to be constructed on the

Narmada River and was capable of generating large amounts of hydroelectric power and ensuring a reservoir of water during the drought season. Thus, it was viewed as being important from an industrial standpoint.

From the outset, the governmental agencies had only highlighted the developmental aspect of the dam and its commercial use for irrigation and drinking water. Due to this propaganda, the World Bank had agreed to support the project in 1985. However, several social and environmental groups came out in fierce protest of this project as many scientific reports indicated that there would be considerable damage to the environment.[109] Notably, the Narmada Bacha Andolan, led by Medha Patkar, raised several issues with the construction of the dam, such as the displacement of more than 40,000 families.[110] This led the World Bank to form an independent commission in 1991 to reassess its position. The commission published the Morse Report, which firmly condemned the lack of a plan for resettlement and rehabilitation.[111] Shortly thereafter, the World Bank withdrew its support from the project.

The construction of the dam entailed massive flooding of villages and productive land.[112] It had a negative impact on downstream aquatic life, led to waterlogging and salination of water, massive deforestation, silting of the river bed, and destruction of natural wildlife habitat.[113] Adding insult to injury, the displacement of marginalized groups and tribal communities without adequate financial compensation has been at the heart of the issue, and the Maharashtra and Gujarat state governments were responsible for serious violations to the right to life, livelihood, and rehabilitation.[114]

Despite these serious concerns raised against the construction of the dam, the Supreme Court held that the threshold for sustainable development had been met since the government had ascertained the possible adverse environmental and social impacts in a report prepared by it.[115] It reasoned that since the adverse impacts were already known, the precautionary principle was not applicable.[116] In this regard, the Court held:[117]

> It appears to us that the precautionary principle and the corresponding burden of proof on the person who wants to change the status quo will ordinarily apply in a case of polluting or other project or industry where the extent of damage likely to be inflicted is not known. When there is a state of uncertainty due to lack of data or material about the extent of damage or pollution likely to be caused then, in order to maintain the ecology balance, the burden of proof that the said balance will be maintained must necessarily be on the industry or the unit which is likely to cause pollution. On the other hand where the effect on ecology or environment of setting up of an industry is known, what has to be seen is that if the environment is likely to suffer, then what mitigative steps can be taken to offset the same. Merely because there will be a change is no reason to presume that there will be ecological disaster. It is when the effect of the project is known then the principle of sustainable development would come into play which will ensure that mitigative steps are and can be taken to preserve the ecological balance. Sustainable development means

what type or extent of development can take place which can be sustained by nature/ecology with or without mitigation.

This is extremely problematic on three accounts. First, the Supreme Court severely dilutes the burden of proof of any person changing the environmental *status quo* by holding that the burden of proof is on such a person only in instances where there is uncertainty with respect to the quantum of environmental damage (this will be discussed in further detail in the next section on the precautionary principle). If this is followed, any industry or activity causing pollution which can be readily estimated does not have to discharge the burden of proof levied by the precautionary principle even though it is changing the environmental *status quo*.

Second, the Court clearly displays a preference for mitigation rather than prevention, despite the serious environmental concerns evident from all scientific reports presented to the Court. It holds that as long as the environmental impact of an activity is known, prevention should not be exercised and rather the focus should shift towards mitigation. If such reasoning is taken to its logical conclusion, any developmental activity proposed by the government, whose environmental impact can be estimated, will always be allowed subject to certain mitigation irrespective of the quantum of environmental damage involved.

Third, the Court's preference for development over environmental protection is implied though its definition of sustainable development. It defines sustainable development as development that can be "sustained by nature/ecology with or without mitigation". This definition presupposes that development with take place as long as the environment can sustain itself after it. Given the extremely low threshold for what is deemed as sustenance of the environment seen from the massive environmental damage done by the Sardar Sarovar Dam, this definition ought to be changed. Further, the question of the carrying capacity of the ecosystem in the concerned area did not come up as several ecosystems were entirely annihilated by the construction. Accordingly, the fact that no regulatory framework was put in place by the Court suggests that there was nothing left to initiate mitigation.

The Court, through this judgment, betrayed its own interpretation of sustainable development discussed earlier[118] and seriously diluted the application of the principle of sustainable development. Not surprisingly, this decision became a precedent through which the Court justified the construction of large-scale projects that seriously damaged the environment on the reasoning that the degree of harm was known to some extent and mitigation could be done.[119]

In a similar manner, the Supreme Court dealt with environmental concerns involving the Tehri Dam in *N.D. Jayal v. Union of India*.[120] However, in contrast to its treatment of sustainable development in the aforementioned *Sardar Sarovar Dam Case*, the Court first unequivocally held that sustainable development is "necessary to guarantee 'right to life' under Article 21" of the Constitution. Further, it held that weighty concepts such as interpretational equity,[121] public trust doctrine,[122] and the precautionary principle,[123] which had been declared as inseparable ingredients of our environmental jurisprudence, could only be nurtured by ensuring sustainable development.

While the Court, through these statements, tried to reinstate sustainable development's significance, it went on to allow the construction of the dam despite serious environmental concerns by employing the same reasoning as the *Sardar Sarovar Dam Case*.[124] In the judgment, the Court noted that there would be complete underwater submersion of thirty-seven villages and partial submersion of eighty-eight villages. While there had been several environmental violations during the construction, the Court directed the government to continue the construction without violating the relevant norms in future. This, again, demonstrates the Court's reluctance to significantly intervene in large-scale infrastructural and developmental government projects.

At this juncture, it is important to examine *Karnataka Industrial Areas Development Board v. C. Kenchappa*,[125] which contains one of the most elaborate discussions on the principle of sustainable development by the Supreme Court. The case involved a writ petition filed by agriculturalists who were aggrieved by the acquisition of large swathes of agricultural land by the Karnataka Industrial Areas Developmental Board for industrial purposes. The agriculturalists prayed that the Court ought to stop the procurement of agricultural land as the land was essential for cattle grazing and related agricultural activities.

The Court engaged in a long discussion wherein it traced the significance and historical development of sustainable development and highlighted how it imposes a positive obligation on the government to balance ecology and development.[126] Further, like the aforementioned *Tehri Dam Case*, the Court held that the principle forms an integral part of the Indian constitutional scheme.[127]

While these reiterations and assertions made it seem that the Court was reverting to its initial stringent application of the principle, the conclusion in the case was very different. The Court did not penalize the Board in any manner and placed two rather toothless preconditions on the state government. First, it held that the government must ensure that in future the ecology is not gravely harmed. Second, it held that the State Pollution Control Board must be consulted in future before undertaking such activities.

It is difficult to tally these conditions imposed with the preceding interpretation of the principle expounded by the Court. Invariably, the Court disregarded the precautionary aspect of sustainable development and leaned in favour of developmental activities. Further, akin to the dam cases discussed above, it set a very low standard that the government needs to meet to discharge its duty under the principle. Accordingly, the government is not held accountable in any way for the environmental damage done.

In 2011, the Court, in *Lafarge Umiam Mining (P) Ltd. v. Union of India*,[128] clearly acknowledged and justified the restraints it had been placing on the application of sustainable development. The Court drew upon the constitutional doctrine of proportionality and stated that it must be the guiding doctrine in matters concerning the environment as it forms a part of judicial review.[129]

In effect, the Court held that its review of a governmental decision regarding the use of natural resources or impacting the environment could not be based on the merits of the decision. Rather, such a review was limited to a judicial review wherein the Court would only review the decision-making process.[130] The Court held that as per the doctrine of proportionality, its review of the governmental decision would be limited to the following questions:[131]

1. Have all relevant factors been taken into account?
2. Have extraneous factors influenced the decision?
3. Is the decision strictly in accordance with legislative policy underlying the law (if any) that governs the field?
4. Is the decision-making authority fully informed and has taken its decision based on correct principles (such as natural justice) and is such a decision free from bias or restraint?

Thus, according to the Court, once the government could show that it had considered all relevant aspects relating to environmental and social consequences and that the decision was free from bias, the Court could not intervene with the correctness of the decision. This is a drastic reduction in the interpretation of the principle of sustainable development from a positive legal obligation[132] to a policy decision which cannot be questioned by the Court. In fact, the following statement of the Court runs counter to all previous interpretations of the principle of sustainable development that we have highlighted:[133]

> It cannot be gainsaid that utilization of the environment and its natural resources has to be in a way that is consistent with principles of sustainable development and intergenerational equity, but balancing of these equities may entail policy choices. In the circumstances, barring exceptions, decisions relating to utilization of natural resources have to be tested on the anvil of the well-recognized principles of judicial review.

This interpretation of the application of the principle completely dilutes the obligation that it previously imposed on the government or any person changing the *status quo* of the environment and, effectively, pays only lip service to the international obligations which have been duly recognized and previously enforced. The Court seems to view sustainable development as one of many policy considerations that the executive needs to balance rather than a positive legal obligation that ought to be enforced.

Accordingly, the Court holds that once the decision has met the aforementioned procedural requirements, the doctrine of "margin of appreciation" in favour of the decision-maker would come into play. While this implied trust in the executive's developmental agenda, which was also seen before in the *Sardar Sarovar Dam Case*[134] and the *Tehri Dam Case*,[135] the principle of sustainable development was reduced to a mere policy decision whose correctness could not be tested by the Court on merit.

This extremely low threshold for fulfilling the obligation of sustainable development by merely stating that it was "considered" during the decision-making process allows the government to shrug off any environmental concerns by simply stating that they were taken into account. By limiting itself to the procedural correctness of a decision, the Supreme Court has done a great disservice to the principle of sustainable development and environmental justice.

Compounding this problem further is the fact that the doctrine of margin of appreciation runs with the assumption that the policymaker is acting on sound knowledge and for the benefit of the larger public.[136] This doctrine's application in the context of environmental damage is unwarranted as it assumes that governmental agencies always act honestly and free of external forces that may nudge them in a certain direction. Additionally, the doctrine of proportionality shields non-compliance to environmental norms by the government from being dealt with in a punitive manner by limiting the scope of the Court's interference to procedural correctness.

This unwarranted logic was continued in *Sterlite Industries (India) Ltd. v. Union of India*,[137] wherein the Supreme Court set aside a High Court decision that quashed an environmental clearance. The High Court had set aside the clearance on the ground that the public hearing requirement under the Environment (Protection) Act, 1986, had not been fulfilled. The Supreme Court, however, held that this provision was non-mandatory and set aside the High Court's decision. In doing so, it stated that judicial review of an environmental decision-making process can be exercised only on the grounds of illegality, irrationality, and procedural impropriety by the decision-making body.[138]

As noted previously, this hyper-technical approach by the Supreme Court does injustice to the principle of sustainable development and reduces its application to mere procedural correctness. As long as the government claims that it took into account sustainable development factors and it can provide some relevant material that it considered, the Court cannot question the decision on merits. It is surprising that the Court has read the principle of sustainable development as a part of judicial review and has abandoned its earlier stance of viewing the principle as an independent obligation. This is because usually the Court has been criticized for often overstepping its judicial boundaries and deciding cases on the basis of policy considerations.[139] In issues other than the environment, the Court has often questioned policy considerations on merit.[140]

From this long discussion of several cases, we see that the Supreme Court has, over time, diluted its own interpretation and application of sustainable development. From the expansive interpretation of the principle in the aftermath of the Bhopal Gas Tragedy, wherein the Court held that the principle formed a part of customary international law and imposed a positive legal obligation on the executive, the Court has diluted the principle to be applicable only in relation to ensuring the procedural correctness of a governmental decision. Interestingly, even while the Court upholds the latter diluted interpretation in a case, it usually does so after glorifying the significance of the principle and how it forms a part of the fundamental right to life under Article 21.

Clearly, the recent decisions of the Supreme Court discussed demonstrate that the Court only does lip service to its earlier robust and stringent interpretation of sustainable development. This still leaves the question open with respect to which interpretation of the Court is still valid. Is the initial strong application of the principle wherein it was seen as imposing a positive legal obligation on the executive still valid despite the subsequent dilution by the Court? This is yet to be conclusively decided by the Court. From the cases that we have discussed, it seems that the answer lies in the factual matrix of each case and the importance of a certain project towards the infrastructural development of a certain area.

Given the diluted application of the principle of sustainable development by the Supreme Court, let us now examine whether such a shift percolated into the NGT's jurisprudence.

3.1.3   THE NGT AND THE PRINCIPLE OF SUSTAINABLE DEVELOPMENT: INTERPRETATION AND APPLICATION

At the outset, it is important to note that, unlike the Supreme Court, the NGT is statutorily bound to employ the principle of sustainable development while delivering an award or decision under Section 20 of the NGT Act. This statutory obligation ensures that the principle is examined by the Tribunal in each case, if applicable. However, since the NGT Act does not define what the principle entails, the NGT broadly applies the principle by paying heed to international interpretations as well as domestic precedents.

Hence, due to these reasons, the principle of sustainable development has become an integral part of the NGT's jurisprudence. Additionally, many cases before the NGT involve issues relating to environmental clearance, wherein either the clearance has not been granted or the conditions stipulated therein have not been fulfilled.[141] These cases necessarily involve issues relating to sustainable development as the NGT has a choice with respect to quashing the clearance or allowing the project to continue despite violations.

We find that in most judgments rendered by the NGT dealing with environmental clearances, the Tribunal consistently takes a moderate approach whereby it does not interfere with the clearance if most relevant concerns highlighted have been substantially fulfilled.[142] Where there are serious deficiencies, including cases where a project has begun despite not receiving the mandatory environmental clearance, the Tribunal usually allows the project to continue after attaching additional conditions that need to be fulfilled along with a nominal environmental compensation. This trend, in effect, is similar to the Supreme Court's diluted approach with certain added safeguards.

The indispensable nature of EIA, and the environmental clearances granted therein, with respect to ensuring sustainable development has been acknowledged by the NGT on several occasions.[143] The Environmental Impact Assessment Notification, 2006 (discussed in greater depth in the next chapter), requires a comprehensive assessment of the environmental and social impacts of a proposed project prior to its commencement. The process involves screening, scoping, collecting baseline data, impact prediction, undertaking a public hearing, and exploring mitigation measures.[144] Significantly, the risk assessment involves taking into account potential environmental impacts, socio-economic impacts, cultural impacts, and human health impacts of a proposed project.[145]

In many ways, the EIA process is a refined version of the reporting mechanisms that the Supreme Court used to set up under the aegis of sustainable development during its initial robust interpretation of the principle.[146] Thus, it is not surprising that the EIA process is intricately linked to the Tribunal's application of sustainable development as it highlights the costs and benefits of a proposed project. Accordingly, the NGT, in *K.G. Mathew v. State of Kerala*[147] has held:[148]

> Environmental Impact Assessment (EIA) is an important management tool for ensuring optimal use of natural resources for sustainable development and was introduced in the year 1978–1979 in India, to facilitate project proponents in collection of environmental data and formulation of environmental management plans.

The Tribunal has therefore underpinned the need for strengthening of the EIA process to ensure that the principle of sustainable development is upheld when developmental activities are undertaken. However, as will be discussed in the next chapter, the potential dilution of the EIA process proposed by the present government is likely to fundamentally shake the NGT's adjudication process and the application of the principle of sustainable development. Let us now discuss the NGT's interpretation and application of the principle through cases to understand the contours of its impact.

In *Rohit Choudhury v. Union of India*,[149] the Tribunal did not shy away from taking stringent action against the polluter when the gross environmental violations came to light. The case was concerned with numerous mining projects that had been constructed in an area that was conspicuously within the "No Development Zone" around the Kaziranga Wildlife Sanctuary. Noticing the patent illegality of these projects, the Tribunal ordered the closure of these units. Additionally, the authorities involved, namely the state of Assam and the MoEF, were reprimanded for the dereliction of their duties and were directed to pay costs for the restoration of the area impacted by the polluting units. This was a welcome decision given the ecological fragility of the area and the endangered wildlife that were present in the wildlife sanctuary. Moreover, such a decision served as a deterrent to other governmental agencies from acting in a callous and negligent manner.

The application of sustainable development, along with its two sub-principles, namely the precautionary principle and the polluter pays principle, in the aforementioned case was straightforward as the environmental violation and damage were conspicuous. However, in cases where the environmental impact is not as apparent, the NGT does not apply the principle of sustainable development in a similar manner.

For instance, in *Sterlite Industries (India) Ltd. v. Tamil Nadu Pollution Control Board*,[150] the Tribunal dealt with an appeal from an order of the Tamil Nadu Pollution Control Board that had ordered the closure of Vedanta's copper smelting plant after workers complained of environmental damage and various health problems. While arriving at its decision, the NGT relied on sustainable development and held:[151]

> The right to development itself cannot be treated as a mere right to economic betterment or cannot be limited as a misnomer to simple construction activities. It encompasses much more than economic well-being and includes within its definition the guarantee of fundamental human rights. It includes the whole spectrum of civil, cultural, economic, political and social process, for the improvement of people's well-being and realisation of their full potential. It is an integral part of human rights. Of course, development is the essence of any pragmatic and progressive society. But essentially, development besides being inter-generational, must be balanced to its ecology and environment. Sustainable development means that the richness of the earth's bio-diversity would be conserved for future generations by greatly slowing or if possible halting extinctions, habitat and ecosystem destruction, and also by not risking significant alterations of the global environment that might – by an increase in sea level or changing rainfall and vegetation patterns or increasing ultraviolet radiation – alter the opportunities available for future generations.

Right after stating this, the NGT quoted the principle's interpretation under the Brundtland Report. Up to this point, it seems that the NGT's interpretation of the principle was in line with the Supreme Court's initial robust interpretation in the aftermath of the Bhopal Gas Tragedy. However, the Tribunal subsequently held that the principle of proportionality was applicable when applying the principle of sustainable development:[152]

> While applying the concept of sustainable development, one has to keep in mind the "principle of proportionality" based on the concept of balance. It is an exercise in which courts or tribunals have to balance the priorities of development on the one hand and environmental protection on the other. So sustainable development should also mean the type or extent of development that can take place and which can be sustained by nature/ecology with or without mitigation. In these matters, the required standard now is that the risk of harm to the environment or to human health is to be decided in public interest, according to a 'reasonable person's test'.

This reasoning is in line with the subsequent diluted approach taken by the Supreme Court (discussed in the previous section). However, it is noteworthy that, unlike the Supreme Court, the Tribunal holds that the principle of proportionality entails that it has to balance the needs of development with environmental protection. Where the Supreme Court had deferred to the judgment of the executive and had held that its scope of review is limited to procedural correctness,[153] the aforementioned statement of the Tribunal shows that it is responsible for ensuring this balance is maintained. This interpretation demonstrates that the Tribunal's application of the principle is not similar to the Supreme Court's application of the principle as a part of judicial review.

Having stated this, however, the NGT went on to reverse the decision of the Tamil Nadu State Pollution Control Board which had ordered the closure of the plant. The Tribunal held that the closure of the plant had been directed on entirely vague presumptions, devoid of any scientific backing. In arriving at this decision, the Tribunal, nevertheless, tried to apply the precautionary principle. However, it held that since no scientific evidence whatsoever had been supplied by the pollution control board in relation to the allegations, the precautionary principle was not applicable. In this regard, the NGT held:[154]

> The cumulative view of the facts and circumstances of the present case shows that the case at hand is not a case of promoting development at the cost of the environment. It has not been established that the industrial activity carried on by the appellant-company prejudicially and in any way compromises either the environment or the interests of the future generations…. There is no cogent or reliable evidence or reasonable scientific data, even by necessary implication, to contribute the leakage of SO2 in excess of the prescribed parameters to the plant of the appellant-company. Nothing on record justifies the invocation of precautionary principle. In fact, it is a punitive action in the garb of a preventive measure.

This demonstrates the fundamental difference between the Supreme Court and the NGT. While the approach adopted by the Tribunal and the Supreme Court is similar, due to the statutory obligation under Section 20 of the NGT Act, the Tribunal is bound by considerations of sustainable development and its sub-principles. Thus, unlike the Supreme Court – which preferred mitigation to precaution in several cases discussed earlier[155] – the NGT had to justify why the precautionary principle was not applicable rather than merely relying on mitigation. This decision was subsequently overturned by the Supreme Court on technical grounds that the NGT did not have the ordinary powers of judicial review akin to the Supreme Court under Article 32 and akin to the High Courts under Article 226 of the Constitution.[156] (The Supreme Court's holding is discussed in greater detail in the previous chapter.)

Similarly, in *Gaur Green City Residents Welfare Association v. State of Uttar Pradesh*,[157] the applicant challenged the installation of a Gas Insulated Power Sub-station (GIS) within a Green Belt adjoining a highway. The rules and regulations involved clearly allowed such an installation. Nevertheless, the applicant alleged that the installation of the GIS had caused the illegal felling of many trees in the Green Belt, and that the electro-magnetic field released from the GIS was likely to result in leukaemia in children and old persons. Further, the applicants alleged that the Green Belt had been reduced from 300 metres to 100 metres due to the construction of the GIS.

The NGT held that the designation of an area as a "Green Belt" was a matter of policy and not a matter of right for residents of any locality.[158] Further, while the applicant demonstrated several scientific articles and studies in support of its contention that the GIS would increase the risk of leukaemia, the NGT held that the World Health Organization had provided guidelines stating that extremely low-frequency electromagnetic fields were not hazardous to human health.[159] The Tribunal scientifically assessed the frequencies emitted by different components of the GIS and looked at similar installations in the United Kingdom (UK). Additionally, the Tribunal cross-examined the expert witness presented by the applicant and held that he did not possess any experience in the relevant subject. Accordingly, in relation to the principle of sustainable development, the NGT held:[160]

> The need to have electricity connection for residents is more important as compared to illusory apprehension projected by the Applicant (RWA). In our considered view, installation of the GIS Power Substation on the small part of the Green Belt is in keeping with principle of sustainable development. There cannot be duality of opinion that any development should be compatible with the Environment. Still, however, the Applicant must prove real possibility of threat to the environment or dangerous impact of such development on human beings.

Thus, the NGT dismissed the petition and viewed the activity to be in line with the principle of sustainable development.

In *Sarang Yadwadkar v. Commissioner, Pune Municipal Corporation*,[161] the Tribunal was faced with the construction of a road that had encroached into the "No Development Zone" of the Mutha River. Several other civil constructions had also been erected by various parties within the zone. In addition to the apparent infraction, the road construction also suffered from a seriously flawed environmental clearance process and a clear disregard for environmental norms on part of the developmental authorities.

The Tribunal's response to these serious concerns, however, was moderate. Although it attached various conditions to the environmental clearance, it allowed the authorities to proceed with the illegal construction even though the need for the specific road had already been met by the construction of an alternate road. In relation to other buildings constructed in the No Development Zone, the Tribunal merely directed the authorities to take action against unauthorized constructions. While the Tribunal generally cited the conventional precedents of sustainable developments we have been discussing, its decision, in our opinion, was based on the following statement in the judgment:[162]

> As already indicated, we are a developing country, and therefore, have to take *somewhat liberal approach towards development* but certainly not by compromising the environmental interest. (Emphasis supplied)

Apparent in the case is the Tribunal's inability to incorporate an element of deterrence in its action against statutory authorities that blatantly violate environmental norms. In the absence of any punitive mechanism, the governmental authorities generally pay little heed to proper legal procedures in environmental matters.[163] This perpetuates a system of faulty compliances that not only create grounds for litigation but also defeat the purpose of many environmental laws. As seen in the compensation section of the previous chapter, the NGT frequently does not hold governmental authorities accountable despite gross negligence on their part. Further, even though the principle of sustainable development is necessarily invoked by the Tribunal due to a statutory obligation, in practice the NGT seems to take a "somewhat liberal approach towards development". This is done by not holding governmental authorities proportionally liable and by allowing projects to continue even though they have flouted several environmental norms and have caused serious environmental damage.

In a similar manner, in *Laxmi Suiting v. State of Rajasthan*[164] the Tribunal was concerned with the pollution caused by effluents discharged by fabric industries into water bodies in Rajasthan. The Tribunal, just as in the *Goa Foundation Case*[165] discussed in the previous chapter, took note of the particular importance of the fabric industry to the economy and tradition of Rajasthan. Therefore, to strike a balance, the Tribunal held:[166]

> Keeping in view the principle of sustainable development, the peculiar facts and circumstances of the case and the time for which these industries have been in operation, we do not propose to direct their closure forthwith but would issue appropriate directions to enable them to operate while ensuring that there is no pollution…. A concerted effort by all the stakeholders has to be taken in order to ensure effective control and prevention of pollution while permitting development without irretrievably damaging the environment.

Even the Supreme Court, in the *Vellore Case,*[167] directed the closure of tanneries that had been repeatedly flouting environmental norms despite the importance of tanneries in terms of revenue generation for the state. The NGT, however, took a different stance in this case. While the additional directions are welcome, the blatant disregard that the industries had been demonstrating towards environmental norms for several years deserved a more serious punitive measure. As noted, decisions such as these, wherein the environmental compensation levied by the Tribunal is insignificant (refer to the previous chapter for the inadequacy of compensation) and the polluting industry is allowed to continue operations, are unlikely to deter future pollution.

While this has been the general trend, the NGT has, nevertheless, upheld the stringent application of sustainable development in certain exceptional cases. In *State Pollution Control Board v. Swastik Ispat Pvt. Ltd.,*[168] the Tribunal was concerned with the legality of a "Bank Guarantee System" started by the Odisha Pollution Control Board. Under this system, an industry assessed to be violating environmental norms was required to furnish a bank guarantee that would be forfeited if the industry failed to comply with the conditions laid down by the Board in the event of a default.

One of the main arguments behind the Board's adoption of the system was that such a system helped promote sustainable development. This was because industrial activity was not automatically prohibited but was permitted to carry on subject to compliance with the conditions imposed.[169] Thus, the Board's invocation of the principle to justify the bank guarantee system provided a novel interpretation of the concept of sustainable development. The Tribunal agreed with such an invocation of the principle and held:[170]

> Striking a balance between environmental interest and sustainable development would require the expert bodies like the Boards to follow a path which would permit industrial growth and still protect the environment without allowing any irretrievable injury to the environment. In view of that, it will certainly be permissible in law for an expert body to provide an opportunity to a unit to attain the prescribed standards of emission or effluent discharge before it is directed to be closed in exercise of the powers vested in the Board. Such approach would be in consonance with the scheme of the Air Act. More so, it will make a provision also to ensure restoration or rectification of the environmental damage done by the unit at its cost in the case of default.

Accordingly, potential polluters were asked to furnish an amount of money in advance which could be realized if they defaulted on their environmental obligations. Thus, the Tribunal upheld the imposition of an unprecedented bank guarantee by the Board as it was deemed to be in line with sustainable development.

In *Save Mon Region Federation v. Union of India,*[171] the appellants challenged the environmental clearance granted for the construction of a hydroelectric dam on the Naymjang Chhu River. The bone of contention was that the scoping process under the EIA and the Expert Appraisal Committee had not considered the fact that the dam was located in the habitat of the endangered black-necked crane, which also had material religious significance for the indigenous population. The EIA was further marred by various deficiencies in its consideration of the potential effects of the dam on the river basin.

Due to these apparent and serious violations of the EIA process, the Tribunal suspended the environmental clearance granted to the dam and held:[172]

> It is true that hydel power project provides ecofriendly renewable source of energy and its development is necessary, however, we are of the considered view that such development should be 'sustainable development' without there being any irretrievable loss to environment. We are also of the view that studies done should be open for public consultation in order to offer an opportunity to affected persons having plausible stake in environment to express their concerns following such studies. This would facilitate objective decision by the EAC on all environmental issues and open a way for sustainable development of the region.

Further, the MoEF was directed to undertake an environmental flow study to determine and implement measures to protect the black-necked crane and its habitat. The Expert Appraisal Committee was also directed to prepare a new appraisal of the report. The response of the Tribunal is commendable as its strong application of sustainable development stopped a clearance that would have destroyed the habitat of an endangered crane. Unlike other cases wherein despite serious flaws in the EIA process projects were allowed to continue with safeguards, the suspension of the clearance in this case is likely to act as a deterrent.

In addition to the suspension of the clearance, the strong deployment of the principle allowed the Tribunal to set up strong preconditions for the project and ensured adequate regulatory oversight. This is a much better balancing act of environmental and developmental concerns.

Akin to the public interest regime that preceded the creation of the NGT, the NGT has, in several cases,[173] taken *suo motu* jurisdiction of cases involving environmental damage. For instance, in *In Re Court on Its Own Motion v. State of Himachal Pradesh*,[174] the NGT was concerned with the environmental degradation in environmentally sensitive areas around the Rohtang Pass in Ladakh on account of tourist hotspots. Citing a scientific study, the NGT held that black carbon released from vehicle use around the sensitive area was a major contributor to the melting of Himalayan glaciers.

The Tribunal reiterated that Indian citizens had a fundamental right to a clean and safe environment under Article 21 of the Constitution, as well as a corresponding fundamental duty to protect and improve the natural environment under Article 51A(g) of the Constitution. Further, in the light of the directive to the state to protect and improve the environment under Article 48A of the Constitution, the NGT directed the state of Himachal Pradesh to undertake sweeping measures such as conducting random pollution checks, restricting transport in certain areas to only vehicles driven by natural gas and electricity, and implementing a reforestation programme. Additionally, the Tribunal set up a monitoring committee that would report on the progress every quarter.

Interestingly, the NGT has interpreted the principle of sustainable development to be integral to the discharge of corporate social responsibility (CSR) on the part of corporations. In *Ramdas Janardan Koli v. Secretary, Ministry of Environment and Forests*,[175] the Tribunal was concerned with certain construction activities undertaken by the Jawaharlal Nehru Port Trust, Mumbai. The construction had allegedly destroyed mangroves, which were the main breeding grounds for fish populations in the area, thereby leading to a loss of livelihood for the local fishermen. In this regard, the Court rendered an important decision highlighting the role of corporations as stakeholders in ensuring sustainable development. It held:[176]

The Respondents also cannot thwart legal responsibility which emanates from Corporate Social Responsibility to promote 'sustainable development'. The positive impact of the CSR initiative with respect to local communities and environment can be observed. The environment represents the accumulation of the material resources to be shared by all actors in a country. The Corporations in their creation of economic goods exploit these precious resources. However, these rewards are accompanied with evils in the form of pollution, congestions, stripped resources, and overall environmental degradation. Corporate Social Responsibility is a management concept whereby companies integrate social and environmental concerns in their business operations and interactions with their stakeholders.... The concept of 'sustainable development' has co-relation with eradication of poverty, which is offshoot of the project and project activity must be balanced against conservation of environment.

The United Nations Industrial Development Organization defines CSR as a management concept that requires a company to achieve a balance between economic, environmental, and social imperatives, while at the same time addressing the expectations of shareholders and stakeholders.[177] India, on 1 April 2014, became the first country in the world to legally impose CSR as an obligation on companies. Section 135 of the Companies Act requires companies meeting a certain threshold to ensure that at least 2 per cent of the average net profits of the company made in the preceding three financial years are used in pursuance of CSR. Given this context, reading sustainable development as a part of CSR strengthens the application of the principle by grounding it in corporate law as well.

Thus, the positive obligation imposed by the principle on corporations is in line with the Supreme Court's initial robust interpretation of the principle. Based on such an interpretation, the Court directed the corporations involved to adequately compensate the fisherman who had suffered as a result of their actions in addition to paying compensation for the restoration of environmentally impacted areas.

The NGT, in some cases,[178] has also shown contempt for projects that are undertaken with a wilful and blatant disregard for the law and established procedure. In cases where the error is totally apparent and appears to be intentional, the Tribunal has refused to engage in balancing the pros and cons of the projects and has proceeded to deal with such projects stringently. Accordingly, it has held:[179]

> This Doctrine of Balancing comes into play only when the acts are done in accordance with law and in obedience to law. Unauthorized and illegal activities contrary to law cannot squarely fall within the framework of Sustainable Development. It is a settled principle of law that nobody can be permitted to take advantage of his intentional wrongs or intentional flouting of law.... There is a clear line of distinction between the case of willful disobedience and acts done in excess but in accordance with law.

This is an important clarification with respect to the defence of balancing environmental and developmental needs that is often deployed by governmental agencies and corporations. As discussed previously, the Supreme Court and the NGT have generally deferred to governmental activities despite the grave environmental concerns involved.[180] Further, the NGT has usually allowed projects to continue despite violations of environmental norms such as beginning operations without an environmental clearance. Given this context, such a holding is welcome. However, in our view, such an application of the principle of sustainable development should not be limited to cases of blatant disregard for the law. The positive obligation contained within the principle should be applied by the NGT in other cases as well to hold governmental and corporate activities to a high standard.

Following the Supreme Court's directions,[181] the NGT has also paid heed to the concept of carrying capacity in relation to sustainable development. In relation to urban sustainability, the Tribunal has held that urban carrying capacity is an important conceptual tool that must guide a welfare state in promoting sustainable development.[182] In this context, the Tribunal has applied this concept to assess how many people can be permitted into an area without risking the environmental degradation of the area. This assessment allows the Tribunal to balance the demand for natural resources with the sustainable capacity of such resources and is essential to improve the living quality for residents.

The Tribunal has warned that measures such as the odd–even vehicular scheme in Delhi, limiting the flow of tourist vehicles, and restraining the timing of firecrackers during festivals are emergency measures that may help only temporarily.[183] Accordingly, it has held that a long-term assessment of the carrying capacity of the ecosystem coupled with devising measures to restrict overuse is critical to ensure sustainable development.

While the NGT has admitted that several developmental projects that disregard the concept of carrying capacity have caused irreversible environmental and ecological damage,[184] its compensation mechanism needs to improve to facilitate a stronger change. As discussed in Chapter 2, the present trend of the NGT is to peg environmental compensation at a certain percentage of the project cost or other economic variable, irrespective of the actual environmental damage. In several cases, this has resulted in situations wherein the environmental compensation either grossly underestimates or overestimates the environmental damage (see the case study on the *Art of Living Case* in Chapter 2).

The main reason for the lack of nexus between the actual environmental damage and the compensation is that the NGT, frequently, does not scientifically assess the extent of environmental damage. It does not determine the environmental baseline condition that existed prior to the damage so as to calculate the extent of deviation from this condition. As suggested in the previous chapter, an overhaul of the NGT's compensation methodology is necessary to ensure that polluters pay adequate compensation to rehabilitate the lost habitat or natural resources. This will ensure that the positive obligation inherent in sustainable development is carried out.

In conclusion, the Supreme Court had left a difficult interpretative task before the NGT with respect to sustainable development. As discussed, the initial robust interpretation of the Court did not tally with the subsequent dilution in the application of the principle. Thus, the NGT was left with the difficult task of reconciling the two extreme positions of the Supreme Court and developing its own jurisprudence. The Tribunal has certainly risen to this challenge and has interpreted the principle in line with robust international and domestic precedents.

Significantly, the NGT has upheld the positive legal obligation imposed by the principle to hold developmental activities accountable to a high standard. It has expanded the principle to hold corporations responsible by reading the principle into CSR activities. The use of the principle by the Tribunal has been particularly useful in cases where there is a blatant violation of the law. However, where such disregard is not blatant, the NGT has taken a moderate approach by allowing polluting projects to continue by adding more environmental conditions.

This trend has demonstrated the Tribunal's inability to provide an effective deterrent as potential polluters are likely to violate environmental norms with the knowledge that even if they are caught the project will not be stopped. Additionally, while the NGT has not deferred to governmental projects in the same manner as the Supreme Court in the past, it still does not adequately hold governmental authorities accountable. Thus, while the NGT has favoured the stringent application of the principle of sustainable development – which is definitely preferred over the diluted application of the principle by the Supreme Court – there is more room for improvement. Let us now discuss some important judgments of the NGT, which reflect the trends highlighted in this section, in greater detail.

3.1.4   SUSTAINABLE DEVELOPMENT – CASE EXCERPTS AND ANALYSIS

National Green Tribunal

(Principal Bench, New Delhi)

SARANG YADWADKAR V. COMMISSIONER, PUNE MUNICIPAL CORPORATION

[Original Application No. 2 of 2013, Judgment Dated 11 July 2013]

Swatanter Kumar J. (Chairperson);
U.D. Salvi J. (Judicial Member);
Dr. D.K. Agrawal (Expert Member);
Prof. A.R. Yousuf (Expert Member);
Dr. R.C.Trivedi (Expert Member)

*   *   *

Relevant Extracts:

1.   The applicant and others, social activists, challenge the construction of the road from Vitthalwadi to National Highway-4 bypass, which is being constructed under the Draft Development Plan on the ground that the Draft Development Plan has not been approved by the State Government, no

permission from Irrigation Department has been taken and the road touches the Vitthalwadi Temple and its surrounding areas which are Grade I Heritage Buildings and even permission from Archaeological Department has not been taken. This construction, according to the applicants, is bound to cause massive environmental, ecological and social damage. The construction of the road is being carried out in the river bed i.e. within the "blue line". Thus, the applicants pray that the on-going construction work should be stopped immediately and the respondents; any other person or agencies should be restrained from dumping any debris or construction material; the entire debris and soil dumping should be directed to be removed and finally the boundaries of the river should be expressly defined and marked by the local government in conjunction with Irrigation Department and the Archaeological Department.

2.   ... The respondents, according to the applicants, are constructing the road within the Mutha river bed itself and have elevated the level of the road by 20 ft. to 30 ft. by way of illegal dumping rubble and earth and tens of thousands of truckloads of debris and soil are dumped right in the river bed for elevating the road. As a result, there has been reduction of the width of the river Mutha by about 55% and it is bound to result in increased floods in the surrounding densely populated residential areas during rainy season...

13.   ... It is the case of Respondent No.1 with some emphasis that construction of an elevated road on pillars and beyond the river bed would involve unnecessary and extraordinary high expenditure to Respondent No.1, which would ultimately be a liability on public exchequer. Construction of the road would help in overcoming problem of the suburban area beyond the proposed road. Construction of the road does not give rise to the issues raised by the applicant, like environmental, ecological and that of social damage. According to Respondent No.1, the road would also significantly help in reducing traffic load on Sinhagad Road and would save time and fuel of the population located between the river and Sinhagad Road. It is expected that BRT Bridge, once implemented on Sinhagad Road shall raise public transport commuting from 8–9% to 32–35% bringing change in life style and commuting pattern of the citizens.

14.   This Respondent thus has prayed that the project may be continued as delay in completion of the project will have serious financial repercussions.

20.   Now we shall deal with the next contention raised on behalf of the applicant that Irrigation Department has not granted any permission to Respondent

No.1 to carry out the road project at all and in any case on the river bed or the blue line area. Further, the contention is that even if such permission has been granted at any subsequent stage to the filing of the present application, even then it has not been granted by the competent authority, as in terms of the circular dated 21st September, 1989, issued by the State of Maharashtra, the construction below red line in the river bed is prohibited.

21. This contention of the applicant can safely be dissected into two parts. First relates to the factum of granting or otherwise of the permission by Irrigation Department of the State of Maharashtra, while the other relates to competence and correctness of such permission, if issued. As far as the first part-point of fact is concerned, there is no dispute that at the time of institution of the present application, no permission whatsoever had been granted by the Department of Irrigation to Respondent No.1. There also cannot be any dispute to the fact that the work of the project had been commenced by Respondent No.1 without having been granted any such permission. It is only when the counsel appearing before the Tribunal had stated that no such permission had been granted.... Finally, permission was granted by the Executive Engineer, Khadakwasla Irrigation Division, Pune, to Respondent No.1.... It is not understandable as to how Respondent No.1 started the work of the project without seeking such permission when admittedly, it was mandatory for Respondent No.1 to do so.

22. Be that as it may, the fact of the matter is that as of now, Irrigation Department has granted NOC to Respondent No.1. Thus the matter has to proceed further from that stage. The latter part of the submission of the counsel for the applicant relates to non-construction in the prohibited zone and who was competent to vary the said restriction and if so, to what extent? The circular dated 21st September, 1989 was issued by the Assistant Secretary, Irrigation Department, Government of Maharashtra. This circular related to issuance of necessary instructions in connection with demarcation of flood lines, the guidelines in respect of flood zone and respective flood lines and use of land in the flood zone in Chapter 8 of the Dam Safety Manual, 1984. This circular importantly noticed that the flood lines are of two types – blue line which prohibits the construction in an area due to probability of flood during any year; and red line shows water level upto which flood can occur during any year depending upon rainfall, but generally 1 in 100 years. The contour line deciding the boundary of prohibitive zone on both banks of the river is called blue line...

23. According to the applicants, on the co-joint reading of the provisions of the Manual and the circular issued by the Government, the Chief Engineer and

any other officer of Irrigation Department is not vested with the powers to vary the terms of the said circular. To counter this, Respondent No.1 and the State have relied upon Appendix 42 of Maharashtra Public Works Manual, showing administrative and financial powers in terms of which the Chief Engineer possesses full powers in regard to technical sanction of original works classified under all major heads...

24. From the bare reading of the above circular dated 21st September, 1989, it is clear that the main river bed and the area on both the banks of the river required to carry the controlled discharge from the Dam and the catchment area below the Dam, which is the prohibited zone. The line deciding the boundary of this prohibited zone on both banks of the river is called the blue line. The prohibited zone requires that no construction can be raised in that area.... Two aspects are very clear – one that the circular has been issued by the Assistant Secretary concerned on behalf of the Government without any power of delegation and secondly, the circular does not admit of any exceptions. In these circumstances, the only way to get over the restriction of the circular is that the competent authority in the Government had to withdraw or modify the circular. The Chief Engineer of Irrigation Department admits the above position. However, he claims to have the authority to issue the NOC for construction of the road including the blue line on the strength of the Maharashtra Public Works Manual (Appendix 42). Vesting of financial and administrative powers for the works stated under the Maharashtra Public Works Manual is one thing and cannot be stretched to the extent of empowering the said Chief Engineer to overrule or render ineffective a circular issued by the competent authority in the State in exercise of his executive powers. The Chief Engineer is not vested with the power to vary the terms of the circular, and that too to the extent of violation.....

25. Another facet of this aspect is that the circular had been issued by way of guidelines in respect of flood zone, respective flood line and use of land in the flood zone. It was read in conjunction with the Dam Safety Manual. It was issued with the intention to prevent heavy damage that may occur along the river due to heavy rain and flood water during monsoon. It was also to prevent undue interference with the flow of the river and the ecology of the area in question. The floods result from heavy rains or from release of water from the Dam; it is stated to be so close to the site where the road was being constructed. It is to prevent damage to persons and property on the one hand and protect environment on the other. Both these purposes are being interfered with by issuance of NOC by the Chief Engineer, which apparently

was not within his competence…. The cumulative effect of the above circular and the correspondence referred to above is that until 15th April, 2013, no permission had been granted by the authorities of Irrigation Department for commencement of the work of the project and the construction work being carried out by Respondent No.1 of the project in question was not in accordance with law.

26. Despite the fact that the Chief Engineer of the Irrigation Department was not competent to negate the circular dated 21st September, 1989 issued by the State Government of Maharashtra, and had any competence to issue NOC permitting construction even on the blue line and also keeping in mind that more than 40% of the work of the project had been completed without even any permission from the Department of Irrigation and other competent authorities, still we have to examine as to whether this development (i.e. the completion of the project) should be permitted in the larger interest of development or not. If the answer to the above be in affirmative, then subject to what conditions further work of the project should be permitted. From the above facts and the records before us, it is clear that Respondent No.1 had not obtained either the SEIAA clearance or clearance from Archaeological Department. It had also not obtained NOC from Irrigation Department before it commenced the work of the project. Clearance by Archaeological Department was granted on 15th April, 2011 and NOC by Irrigation Department was given on 15th April, 2013. It is not in dispute before us that more than 40% work of the project has been completed on which large public funds have been spent. The Tribunal has either to direct demolition of the road already constructed with a further direction that the project be abandoned and no further construction be carried out or to permit completion of the project subject to certain specific conditions while protecting the environmental interest to the extent possible with reference to the facts and circumstance of the present case. This is where the judicial discretion of the Tribunal is to be exercised while striking a balance between development on the one hand and environmental protection on the other. Developmental and environmental needs have to be seen in complement to each other and not in antagonistic terms….

30. The above stated principles illustratively demonstrate that judicial balance of both these concepts would not permit undue significance being attached to either of them at the cost of the other. The concept of sustainable development in essence admits to balance the scale between the quantity of development and the quality of environment…. The principle of sustainable development takes within its ambit the application of the 'principle of

proportionality' and the 'precautionary principle'. In other words, one must, while permitting development, not only ensure that no substantial damage is caused to the environment but also take such preventive measures which would ensure no irretrievable damage to the environment even in future on the premise on intergenerational equity. All these principles have to be examined and applied on the touch stone of "reasonable person's test".… The precautionary principle can be explained to say that it contemplates that an activity which poses danger and threat to environment is to be prevented. Prevention is better than cure. It means that the State Governments and the local authorities are supposed to anticipate and then prevent the causes of environmental degradation.…

34. Now let us revert to the facts of the present case. 2.35 km long road is sought to be constructed with the width of 24 metres, connecting Vitthalwadi to NH-4 bypass. This road is being constructed certainly at some portion in the river bed i.e. the prohibited zone (blue line)… Between the blue line and the red line, there are structures in existence like Atharva Terace Apartments, River View Residency Apartments on the one hand while Puja Park, Nimraj Nagar, Gayatri, Radhakrishna, Kudale Patil, Anand Park, Jal Tarang, Shrm Saffale, Jal Vihar, Jal Pugan, Sham Sundar Apartments on the other, which are structures on or even inside the blue line. Major part of the high rise road is being constructed inside the blue line and to a large extent in the river bed. During the course of hearing, we were informed that the Sham Sundar Apartments/structure has been issued notice by Respondent No.1 for demolition on certain grounds.

36. [I]t is very important to avoid environmental damage and in the interest of ecology, flood plains are maintained properly. As the flood plains provide important ecological services…. These services or benefits would be adversely affected by any encroachment of the flood plains. In the present case, the total flood plain proposed to be encroached is 2.35 km.

37. These, amongst others, are a few disadvantages of the project in question besides there being logistic deficiencies like lack of permission or grant of improper permission. The need for the project is sought to be justified on the ground of larger public interest i.e. providing an alternative route to the commuters as well as to reduce vehicular pollution. It is expected to solve public transportation problem of about 5 lakh citizens who rely on the Sinhagad Road, as their main connectivity by the arterial road to the city. It is likely to reduce travel time as well as pollution level. On the contrary, the applicant's main contention is that besides causing degradation of the

environment, the intention of Respondent No.1 is to help the property grabbers unauthorisedly by reclaiming the land, falling even within the red/blue line and to give them undue advantage…. Of course, this allegation has been refuted by Respondent No.1. It is also argued on behalf of Respondent No.1 that raising construction on elevated pillars would prove much more expensive than its construction by compacting and earth filling. This argument does not impress us. If the Corporation-authorities have taken a decision to take up the project in public interest, then it must also bear its cost and higher cost, if necessary and also unavoidable in the larger environmental interest. The authorities cannot be permitted to cause irreversible damage to the environment and ecology of the area and even expose the inhabitants of the vicinity to undue flood risks on the ground that the project is being taken up in public interest merely for providing an alternative road and for reducing the vehicular pollution. Firstly, Respondent No.1 has not placed any scientific data or analysis on record before us in support of its contention, even for the sake of arguments, that there would be reduction in environmental pollution and great convenience will accrue to the public by reduction in the travel time. Applying the principle of proportionality, even if an alternative route is provided, still the balance would tilt in favour of environment and we would still require Respondent No.1 to carry out the project subject to such conditions which would strive equitable balance between the development on the one hand and the environment on the other. If Respondent No.1 is of the firm view, and particularly in view of the NOC dated 15th April, 2013 having been issued by Irrigation Department, to carry out the project, then it has to be subject to such stringent conditions as would protect the environment and ecology as well as greater public interest by preventing floods etc. Keeping in view the above rival contentions and the facts of the present case, normally, we would have accepted the petition and prohibited carrying out the project any further with the specific demolition of the part of the road. The road can be raised by elevated pillars in the area that will fall within the blue line or inside the blue line. The construction of elevated pillars at that stage would neither obstruct the flow of the river nor narrow the flood plain. Furthermore, it will also help the storm or drain water to freely join the river during larger part of the area.

38. However, keeping in mind the public interest, that by imposition of certain conditions, environmental and ecological interests can be safeguarded, we would permit Respondent No.1 to complete the project. Accordingly, we impose the following conditions subject to which the project could continue:

(a) The interim order dated 4th January, 2013 and subsequent interim orders shall stand vacated and Respondent No.1 would be permitted to carry out and complete the project of building only 24 metre wide road from Vitthalwadi to NH-4 bypass as shown in Annexure R-2/1 strictly and subject to the conditions stated hereinafter.

(b) Respondent No.1 shall make every effort to realign the road to bring it as far as possible closer to and beyond the blue line, right from chainage of 0+400 to 1+750 of Exh. Annexure 2/1. It shall ensure to extend the least part of the project in the river bed/blue line.

(c) The road/project shall be constructed on elevated pillars alone in the area that falls within the blue line.

(d) We direct Respondent No.1 to remove the debris dumped at the present site and shift the same to the red line by following 1 in 25 years rule.

(e) A massive plantation should be undertaken on both sides of the river, also in the no-development zone by Respondent No.1 as well as the State Government of Maharashtra. Adequate protective measures should be undertaken to prevent flooding and submerging of the residential area along the proposed road.

(f) The conditions imposed by the Chief Engineer, Irrigation Department, vide his NOC dated 15th April, 2013 shall mutatis mutandis be part of the present directions. The same shall be read in aid and not in derogation to the conditions stated in this order.

(g) As already noticed and highlighted during the course of the hearing, a large number of structures have come up at and even inside the blue line of the river Mutha. Respondent No.1 itself has issued notice to some of such structures for demolition. Thus, in the peculiar facts and circumstances of the case, we further direct that Respondents No.1, 3 and 4 shall take appropriate steps against unauthorised constructions, if any, raised on and inside the blue line and pass order of demolition or such other order as is permissible in accordance with law. We also direct the said authorities to ensure that no encroachment is permitted and no construction in future is permitted on and inside the blue line of the river Mutha.

39. ... If the conditions imposed under this order are found to be onerous by the State, particularly Respondent No.1, then they can even give up the project on river Mutha as an alternative road on the other side of the river has already been constructed to provide the connectivity. In the event the

Department decides to give up the road project, it shall be incumbent on it to remove all debris from within the blueline that has been used to create the high rise road segment. It is stated to be a 100 ft. wide road on the left bank of the river Mutha giving connectivity with the same bypass. Thus, in the present case, Respondent No.1 has options and alternatives available to it while ensuring that both the public interest and the environment do not suffer.

* * *

NOTES AND QUESTIONS

1. The case highlights the technical and apathetic approach taken by public authorities with respect to environmental norms and concepts such as sustainable development. The project in the above case was initiated without undergoing any scrutiny of its environmental impacts. It was only when litigation was initiated that the Irrigation Department's clearance was obtained. To add to the long list of violations, the Irrigation Department's clearance had been given without any regard for the environmental norms governing the subject. The project had virtually circumvented any sort of environmental assessment, had it not been for the applicants and the Tribunal.

2. The deficiencies of the NGT's moderate approach towards errant authorities came to the fore a few years later when Pune saw flooding attributable to the encroachments on the riverbed which had lessened the carrying capacity of the river. These encroachments were as much a result of executive complacency as of private misadventures. This came despite the Tribunal directing authorities to demolish and remove all encroachments. As such, the effectiveness and on-ground compliance of the NGT's directions become highly debatable. Does the Tribunal need to improve follow-up processes and do more to improve the implementation of its orders?

3. Despite having shown a conspicuous and blithe disregard for environmental norms, the authorities involved in the instant case were not reprimanded or held accountable in any way. The Tribunal, too, did not take any action against the complacency of the authorities. Should the Tribunal consider adopting stricter measures to hold errant authorities to account so as to sufficiently deter authorities from ignoring environmental norms? How far can concepts such as sustainable development be affected without creating a system of stringent accountability for public authorities?

* * *

National Green Tribunal

(Principal Bench, New Delhi)

STATE POLLUTION CONTROL BOARD, ODISHA V. M/S SWASTIK ISPAT PVT. LTD. AND OTHERS

[Appeal No. 68 of 2012, Judgment Dated 9 January 2014]

Swatanter Kumar J. (Chairperson);
U.D. Salvi J. (Judicial Member);
Dr. D.K. Agrawal (Expert Member);
Prof. A.R. Yousuf (Expert Member);
Dr. R.C.Trivedi (Expert Member)

* * *

Relevant Extracts:

2. We may, at the outset, refer to the facts of both the cases giving rise to the present appeals. The State Pollution Control Board, Odisha, (for short the 'Board'), is a statutory body, constituted under the provisions of the Water (Prevention and Control of Pollution) Act, 1974 (for short the 'Water Act') and the Air (Prevention and Control of Pollution) Act, 1981 (for short the 'Air Act'). The Board, in exercise of its powers, introduced bank guarantee system vide its Resolution No.17617 dated 18th August, 2003. The said resolution reads as under:

> "A number of Acts & Rules have been enacted for the purpose of preventing pollution from different sources & for protection of the environment. Basing on these Acts, the Central Pollution Control Board, State Govt. & the State Pollution Control Boards are empowered to file complaint cases resulting in the closing down of defaulting industries through disconnection of electricity & water supply. There is hardly any other provision to pressurise defaulting industries to install required pollution control system or to impress upon them to upgrade their existing pollution control systems so as to comply with the prescribed norms... It has been experienced that the orders of closure and disconnection of electricity etc. served on the industries at times create social problems like non-payment of wages to its workers due to lack of adequate provisions in the Act. Under such prevailing circumstances, a new instrument namely Bank guarantee system has been introduced by the West Bengal Pollution Control Board. Such an imposing of Bank guarantee has already come

up before the judicial scrutiny in the Hon'ble High Court of Calcutta in the matter of WP5938(W) of 2000 wherein the letter has notionally endorsed the State Board to monitor the policy of Bank Guarantee towards effective pollution control.... After going through the concept paper prepared by the C.P.C.B., the Board unanimously resolved to introduce the Bank guarantee system for the defaulting industries in the following manner.

a)   Industry that fails to install necessary pollution control equipment so as to meet the prescribed standard.

b)   Industry whose pollution control equipment are inadequate to meet the prescribed standard.

At the first instance, show cause notice will be issued to the defaulting industry indicating the intention of issuing direction for closure. Then the industry will be asked to furnish a time bound action plan for installation of pollution control equipment or up gradation of the existing pollution control system. Simultaneously the industry will be asked to furnish Bank Guarantee of a stipulated amount for implementing the action plan. If the industry fails to comply within the timeframe, the amount of Bank Guarantee will be forfeited...."

10   ... On 8th November, 2011, the industry of Respondent No.1 was again inspected and an inspection report dated 11th November, 2011 was prepared. Respondent No.1, after inspection, submitted the bank guarantee on 3rd April, 2012 for a sum of five lakh rupees, valid till 30th June, 2012. Thereafter, no action was taken by the Board. In fact, vide order dated 4th April, 2012, the Board granted consent to Respondent No.1 to operate till 31st March, 2013. The Assistant Environmental Scientist, the Environmental Engineer and the Sr. Environmental Engineer of the Board made a recommendation on 24th April, 2012 that the bank guarantee be forfeited in view of non-satisfactory performance and non-compliance with the environmental clearance conditions, and as a result thereof, the Board, vide its letter dated 26th May, 2012 requested the Indian Overseas Bank to forfeit the bank guarantee amount of five lakh rupees. The Bank, vide its letter dated 5th July, 2012 intimated the Board that the bank guarantee amount of five lakh rupees stood forfeited and submitted a bank draft of five lakh rupees in that behalf. The action of the Board was challenged by Respondent No.1 by filing an appeal before the appellate authority under the Air Act.... [T]he Board has preferred the present appeal contending that the resolution of the Board requiring an industry to furnish a bank guarantee is in accordance

with law. The Board has been vested with the power of issuing direction of closing an industry, and therefore, is requiring the industry to furnish a bank guarantee as a condition for grant and continuation of the consent, and it being less rigorous, would be permissible in law. It is a financial tool to achieve sustained compliance with the prescribed environmental parameters. The decision of the Board is not penal but is regulatory and compensatory in nature. Both these aspects are essential requirements for a clean and decent environment and are in consonance with the preambles of the Air Act and the Water Act. The industry has committed persistent violation of the terms and conditions of the consent order and the prescribed parameters....

10. As opposed to this, the contention on behalf of the private respondent-industry is that the Board is not vested with any power to ask for a bank guarantee. Such exercise of power is not backed by any statutory provision. The imposition of such condition is punitive in nature, and is therefore, beyond the scope of Section 31A of the Air Act. However, if any penalty is to be imposed, it has to be in accordance with the provisions of Chapter VI of the Air Act. Recourse to any other provision by implication or otherwise would be impermissible. Asking for furnishing of the bank guarantee itself is a penalty and so is its invocation. The only power vested with the Board is to prosecute the industry or direct its closure in accordance with law....

32. Keeping in view the legislative scheme and the object of the Air Act, it is evident that the Board is not incapacitated to issue a direction which may not be prohibitory or of closure in substance and application, but may be regulatory with an object to ensure that anti-pollution devices and anti-pollution measures are adopted to prevent and control pollution. For this purpose, the Board may require an industry to furnish a bank guarantee which would serve dual purposes. On the one hand, it would provide incentive to an industry to install anti-pollution devices so as to ensure non-encashment of the bank guarantee, while on the other, in the event of default, resulting in pollution, the Board would be able to spend that money for remedial purposes to control environmental degradation or damage that has taken place as a result of such default. Both these purposes would squarely fall within the framework of law and the powers and functions of the Board.... Besides preventing and controlling the pollution, the Board is commanded by the Legislature to ensure that the conditions of the consent order are satisfied and are enforced. These conditions would obviously relate to the twin objects of ensuring emissions as per prescribed standards and prevention of damage to the environment. This is the paramount duty of the

Board. The intention of the Legislature to ensure implementation of these facets is further elucidated by the language of Section 31A of the Air Act where the Board can issue directions as afore-mentioned in exercise of its powers and performance of its functions under the Act. Thus, there has to be a direct nexus between the directions contemplated under Section 31A of the Air Act and the powers and functions of the Board as contemplated under Sections 16, 17 and other relevant provisions of the Air Act. Once these Sections are read co-jointly, then it becomes clear that a direction which would ensure compliance of the conditions of the consent order and further the cause of prevention and control of pollution would be a direction permissible under law.

33.   The procedure normally adopted by the Board is to permit the industrial operations for a definite period upon furnishing of Bank Guarantee for compliance and compensation, if required, and during integrin permitting the industry to comply with the various directions and the conditions stated in the consent order including installation of anti-pollution devices. This helps the sustainable development as industrial activity is not straightaway closed or prohibited but is permitted to carry on subject to compliance with the conditions imposed. Thus, it clearly falls in the domain of regulatory regime as opposed to prohibitory or closure regime.

39.   … It is the responsibility of the Board to ensure prevention and control of pollution on the one hand and compliance and implementation of the conditions imposed under Section 21 of the Air Act. While imposing these conditions and dealing with them, particularly their non-compliance, the Board has to keep in mind the three basic and fundamental principles which are now statutorily stated in the Indian Environmental jurisprudence, i.e. sustainable development, polluter pays principle and precautionary principle….

40.   … Striking a balance between environmental interest and sustainable development would require the expert bodies like the Boards to follow a path which would permit industrial growth and still protect the environment without allowing any irretrievable injury to the environment. In view of that, it will certainly be permissible in law for an expert body to provide an opportunity to a unit to attain the prescribed standards of emission or effluent discharge before it is directed to be closed in exercise of the powers vested in the Board…

42.   … In the case in hand, the regulatory regime under the Air Act permits taking of harsher steps in the nature of closure and prohibitory directions.

Therefore, permitting a unit to operate for a limited period upon furnishing a Bank Guarantee for compliance of the conditions/directions imposed in the consent order, being an order of lesser gravity and consequences, would be permissible. It is in the interest of sustainable development and is even beneficial to the industry itself. The Bank Guarantee asked for is for compliance, compensation for environmental restoration, if required, and is not punitive in nature.

55.   ... At this stage, we may also notice that there has to be a direct nexus between the directions issued within the ambit and scope of Sections 21 and 31A of the Air Act and the object sought to be achieved by issuing such directions. This nexus should be relatable to the functions and powers of the Board on the one hand and to the object of the Act on the other. Once this twin test is satisfied, then validity of such condition can hardly be questioned. We have already held that such nexus in the present case does exist. The purpose was to prevent and control pollution while permitting the industries to operate, as opposed to the closure of the industries and thus, obstructing the sustainable development. For these reasons, we hold that the plea of the respondent that the direction for furnishing of the bank guarantee was punitive or penal, is liable to be rejected.

* * *

NOTES AND QUESTIONS

1. The bank guarantee system is a noteworthy development in India's anti-pollution laws. Such a system could potentially improve the dismal levels of compliance ailing India's environmental norms. Are there any other changes that the environmental liability regime in India could incorporate to enhance compliance and introduce an element of deterrence?

2. The precedent that the judgment has set is of granting wide latitude to regulatory authorities in interpreting and invoking expansive principles such as sustainable development and polluter pays. The authorities need only to establish a link between the direction issued and the overarching objectives of the authority.

3. Is it appropriate to provide regulatory authorities with open-ended powers in the name of concepts such as sustainable development? Can such expansive concepts be kept open for interpretation by authorities? How likely are such arrangements to lead to abuse?

* * *

National Green Tribunal

(Principal Bench, New Delhi)

M.P. PATIL V. UNION OF INDIA

[Appeal No. 12 of 2012, Judgment Dated 13 March 2014]

Swatanter Kumar J. (Chairperson);

U.D. Salvi J. (Judicial Member);

Dr. D.K. Agrawal (Expert Member);

Prof. A.R. Yousuf (Expert Member);

Dr. R.C.Trivedi (Expert Member)

*   *   *

Relevant Extracts:

2.   The appellant claims to be a public spirited citizen and… has a property in the said village and the project proposed by the respondents is feared to have devastating effects – both long term and short term – in the region…. The project proponent, the National Thermal Power Corporation Limited (for short the "NTPC") on or around 28th January, 2009 submitted a proposal for seeking EC for setting up a 3x800 MW Stage-I project of ultimate capacity of 4000 MW. On the basis of this project proposal, the MoEF stated the Terms of Reference (for short the "TOR") vide letter dated 30th March, 2009. According to the applicant, while seeking the EC, the NTPC had stated that the land is mostly barren & rocky and partly agricultural with single crop cultivation. In its 36th meeting held on 14th–15th November, 2011, the Expert Appraisal Committee (for short the "EAC") recommended the project for EC subject to certain stipulations and specific conditions stated by it. On the basis of the recommendations of EAC, MoEF, which is the Regulatory Authority, accorded EC for the project under the provisions of the Environmental Clearance Regulations dated 14th September, 2006 (for short the "EIA Notification")….

4.   The NTPC had made available the Draft Environmental Impact Assessment Report (for short the "DEIAR") and summary reports in English and Kannada for the information of the public to enable them to participate in the Public Hearing which was arranged on 25th March, 2010. However, the facts in the DEIAR were not discussed and there was concealment of facts or submission of false, misleading and incomplete information/data. The DEIAR did not comply with the TOR, particularly, on the issue of alternative sites….

9.   From the above narrated averments, it is clear that the appellant is challenging the EC granted to the NTPC on, inter alia, the following grounds:

(i)   The EC was obtained from MoEF by making misrepresentation with regard to the land use/land cover of the project area and nature and categorisation of the land, claimed to be mostly barren and rocky, as opposed to mostly agricultural and fertile land.

(ii)   The 'public hearing' was not held in accordance with the prescribed procedure. Material information was withheld from the public and the objections raised during the public hearing have not been considered by the EAC. It has completely frustrated the advantages of the public hearing, as contemplated under the EIA Notification.

(iii)   Various terms of the TOR have not been adhered to. Even the AAQ data collected for grant of EC was not from proper locations, as required under the TOR. Monitoring stations have not been set up to check pollution levels from the downward wind direction, as contemplated under the TOR/EC.

(iv)   The EC had been granted without R&R plan being in place. The R&R plan was not put up before the public during the public hearing thus depriving a fair opportunity to the affected parties to examine objectively the pros and cons for establishment of the thermal power project even though prescribed at TOR Stage by MoEF. The R&R plan, in fact, was not ready at the relevant time and was not prepared covering all aspects even at the time of grant of EC to the NTPC. This has entirely vitiated the process of grant of EC.

(v)   The coal source and its quality were changed several times including at the stage of EAC recommendations as also at the stage of EC. This factor was also ignored by different authorities at the relevant time. Thus, the authorities have taken into consideration irrelevant materials while ignoring the relevant considerations.

WHETHER ANY MISREPRESENTATION HAS BEEN MADE BY THE NTPC IN REGARD TO THE NATURE AND CATEGORISATION OF THE LAND REQUIRED FOR THE PURPOSE OF THE PROJECT IN QUESTION:

27.   According to the NTPC, the site comprises of mostly barren and rocky land.... This statement appears to be doubtful as it is clear from the proceedings of the public hearing held on 25th March, 2010 that Kudgi is well known for its betel leaf crop for more than the last 100 years. In addition, onion, grapes,

banana, and other crops including other horticultural products are grown in the area. The major occupation of most of the families whose land is being acquired is agriculture and horticulture … It is seen from the R&R plan (July 2012) presented by NTPC that the land under acquisition includes 3500 acres of private land and approximately 20 acres of Government land. As mainly the private land being acquired belongs to the farmers, who are basically dependant on agricultural activities for their livelihood, they are the affected persons who will be ultimately forced to migrate to other places in search of their livelihood due to acquisition of their lands. It is pertinent to observe that the EC was granted on 25th January, 2012 whereas the R&R Plan was prepared by the NTPC in July 2012, which is about 6 months after the grant of EC. Even in the EC given by MoEF on 25th January, 2012, it is stated that the land to be acquired for the project was comprising of mostly barren and rocky land with some areas under agricultural land. There is a mismatch in the figures of actual land required for the project, as in the EC, it is written that 2440 acres of land will be acquired whereas in the R&R Plan prepared by NTPC in 2012 and submitted to MoEF, it indicates that about 3500 acres of private land and approximately 20 acres of Government land is under acquisition. During the public hearing, the farmers have opposed the proposed power plant on their agricultural land on which their livelihood is based but it appears that no satisfactory answer was given by the NTPC during the public hearing except mentioning that proper compensation, as applicable, would be paid to them. In fact, the MoEF should have looked critically into the aspect of land acquisition, primarily concerning agricultural land and not mostly barren and rocky, as has been stated in the documents submitted to the MoEF by the NTPC. In fact, it amounts to concealment of facts/suppression of factual information regarding the type and the nature of land proposed to be acquired by the NTPC.

37. … From this documentary evidence consisting of Government documentation, it is clear that the NTPC had not correctly filled in the above columns and these have been so relied upon by the authorities, particularly MoEF without any verification. Besides that, land in excess of the stated land is being used for the project in question. It, thus, further shows that it is largely agricultural land, which is sought to be acquired and is intended to be used for the project.

39. From the above discussion, it can safely be concluded that the land in question is primarily not barren and rocky land, as informed by NTPC and there appears to be improper disclosure of facts on the part of the NTPC which remained unverified even till the stage of issuance of the EC.

ISSUE WITH REGARD TO REHABILITATION AND
RESETTLEMENT POLICY WITH REFERENCE TO THE FACTS
OF THE PRESENT CASE:

40. R & R is an essential feature of any project which comes up for consideration
before the competent authorities in accordance with the EIA Notification.

41. If one examines the scheme of the EIA Notification, it becomes evident that
at the time of preparation of the TOR, the NTPC had to place all relevant
material before the EAC. The EAC is required to address all relevant concerns
for the preparation of EIA Report in respect of the project or activity for which
clearance is sought. Besides the information with regard to undeveloped
or agricultural land, as contemplated in Appendix I, Form I, the NTPC is
also expected to disclose the effect on the welfare of the people, vulnerable
group of people, who could be affected by the project along with such other
information, the disclosure of which would be significant for the purposes
of fair consideration of the project. Furthermore, the NTPC is required to
provide full information and, wherever necessary, attach explanatory notes
with the Form in relation to land environment, water environment, aesthetics
and socio-economic aspects besides environmental management plan.

42. The concept of sustainable development is to drive a balance between
environment on the one hand and development on the other. One of
the essential facets of this balancing approach is to find out the impact of
development upon civilization, particularly with reference to human beings.
If as a result of establishment and operation of any project, a large chunk of
land belonging to a large number of persons is expected to be acquired and
they are likely to be displaced in one form or the other from their livelihood,
R & R scheme would be one of the most pertinent aspects to be considered
by the EAC. This would be a matter which must be elaborately deliberated
upon and the general public must be heard on such an issue during the public
hearing. Formulating an R&R scheme would be necessary not only in the
interest of the project but also in the interest of the public at large.

45. Particularly in the facts of the present case, we may notice that the TOR given
by MoEF required for preparation of R&R plan, which was an integral part
of the DEIAR, which in turn, was the basis for organising public hearing, as
required under EIA Notification. But the DEIAR did not contain a detailed
R&R plan at the time of the public hearing, and as such, it amounts to non-
compliance of TOR. Even the EAC, while considering the project, has noted
that the R&R plan is too general but the EAC recommended the project for
EC and in fact R&R plan was submitted to MoEF only a few months (5 to 6
months) after the EC was granted to the project....

58. Thus, from the above discussion, it can be concluded that there was no comprehensive R&R as required under EIA Notification, and other policies even though the project entails acquisition of large private land.

GENERAL DISCUSSION

69. Under the environmental jurisprudence, sustainable development is a widely accepted principle. In India, it finds statutory recognition in terms of Section 20 of the National Green Tribunal Act, 2010. One of the most significant precepts to examine sustainable development in the facts of a given case is the application of the balancing principle or the principle of proportionality. The Tribunal has to drive a balance between the rival factors, the risks associated with environmental and ecological damage and impact on livelihood of project-displaced or affected persons on the one hand and economic and other benefits for the public at large on the other, upon establishment of the project. A number of factors need to be considered in this regard. In the framework of Indian economy, there is a relation between poverty and environment. Poverty and degraded environment are closely inter-related, especially where people depend primarily on natural resources based on their immediate environment for their livelihood. Restoring natural systems and improving natural resource management practices at the grass root level are central to a strategy to eliminate poverty. If we examine, in the light of the above facts of the present case, then it becomes evident that the establishment of the thermal power plant at Kudgi would squarely satisfy the requisites of the doctrine of proportionality or the balancing principle and thus would fall within the ambit of permissible sustainable development.

71. According to the NTPC, it has already spent a considerable amount on acquisition of land and initial establishment of the project. An amount of Rs.134 crores was allocated for R&R and a major part of it has been distributed.

72. The economists have reported a systematic relationship between income changes and environmental quality, the relationship known as the Environmental Kuznets Curve (for short the "EKC"). The EKC has become standard fare in technical conversations about environmental policy. Pollution often appears first to worsen and later to improve as countries' incomes grow. Because of its resemblance to the pattern of inequality and income described by Simon Kuznets, this pattern of pollution and income has been labelled as Environmental Kuznets Curve. The logic of the EKC relationship is intuitively appealing. At the low level of per capita income found in pre-industrial and agrarian economies, where most economic activity is subsistence farming, one might expect rather pristine environmental conditions, relatively unaffected

by economic activities, at least for those pollutants associated with industrial activity. Once income increases, they prefer to pay for better and cleaner water quality, better air quality, better sanitation, etc. including services like sewage and garbage management. Cleaner technology furthers this cause.

73. Upon a cogent analysis of the above, it becomes evident that the present case is not one where the only alternative available with the Tribunal is to cancel the EC and direct complete cancellation of the project. NTPC itself is a public undertaking and it is the public money, which is at stake. The principle of balancing would persuade the Tribunal to take an approach where environmental interests can be protected by taking certain reasonable and stringent measures and still ensure that the huge public investment is not permitted to go waste....

74. ... At this stage, we may usefully refer to a very recent judgment of the Supreme Court in the case of G. Sundararjan v. Union of India & Ors. Civil Appeal No. 4440 of 2013 ... the Court, while referring to the principles of balance inbuilt in the concept of sustainable development, elaborated the principles as follows:

> "228. ... The trend of authorities is that a delicate balance has to be struck between the ecological impact and development. The other principle that has been ingrained is that if a project is beneficial for the larger public, inconvenience to smaller number of people is to be accepted. It has to be respectfully accepted as a proposition of law that individual interest or, for that matter, smaller public interest must yield to the larger public interest. Inconvenience of some should be bypassed for a larger interest or cause of the society. But, the present case really does not fall within the four corners of that principle. It is not a case of the land oustees. It is not a case of "some inconvenience". It is not comparable to the loss caused to property. I have already emphasized upon the concept of living with the borrowed time of the future generation which essentially means not to ignore the inter-generational interests. Needless to emphasize, the dire need of the present society has to be treated with urgency, but, the said urgency cannot be conferred with absolute supremacy over life. Ouster from land or deprivation of some benefit of different nature relatively would come within the compartment of smaller public interest or certain inconveniences. But when it touches the very atom of life, which is the dearest and noblest possession of every person, it becomes the obligation of the constitutional courts to see how the delicate balance has been struck and can remain in a continuum in a sustained position. To elaborate, unless adequate care, caution and monitoring at every stage is taken and

there is constant vigil, life of "some" can be in danger. That will be totally shattering of the constitutional guarantee enshrined under Article 21 of the Constitution."

76. To an extent, there is a right to development. However, even this right is not free of limitations and regulations. It is not an unfettered right so as to completely give a go-by to the issues of environment. Development may be carried out to satisfy the need of a developing society but it has to be regulated so as to satisfy the requirement of preservation and nurturing of the natural resources, which are the real assets of the society.

77. In light of the above principles, we have to ensure that the establishment of thermal power plant does not unduly hamper the means of livelihood of the residents. Wherever acquisition of land and displacement is an inevitable factor in the establishment and operationisation of the project, there it must be supported by an appropriate compensatory and R&R scheme. It must provide reasonable chances of employment and earnings to the displaced persons becoming unemployed as a result of acquisition of the land and establishment of the project.

93. The above discussion on the various legal and factual aspects of the present case brings us to the last issue as to what relief can the Tribunal grant in the facts and circumstances of the present case. The defects in the process of grant of EC crept in right at the initial stages and have proceeded till the end. We have already held that there was an improper declaration in regard to the nature and category of the land acquired for the project. Furthermore, during the public hearing, there was non-declaration and non-disclosure of material factors like R&R scheme, source and quality of coal and location of AAQ monitoring stations. It had adversely affected the interests of the persons likely to be affected by the project. The EAC, while recommending the establishment of the project, did not seriously dwell upon these very material issues and even permitted that the R&R scheme could be declared within four months of the recommendation. Despite this, R&R scheme was not presented even after the passing of the order of the EC. Thus there has been violation of the provisions of the EIA Notification and violation of the prescribed procedure. As opposed to this, the Tribunal cannot ignore the fact that huge public money has already been invested in the project, large scale acquisition has been completed and even majority of the land owners have been paid compensation. The basic development has taken place and contracts for establishment for the project have been awarded. Cancellation of the project and setting aside of EC in its entirety may result in wastage of substantial public funds as well as rendering the entire development

project ineffective. The project, if properly completed with due protection in regard to environmental issues and the rehabilitation schemes, would help in improvement of socio-economic conditions of the area in question and the people living therein. It would also help in increasing the per capita income, as already noticed. The project would go a long way in uplifting the economy, the ecology and the environmental conditions of the area as well as providing adequate R&R scheme to the project-affected and displaced persons. Economic growth has a direct nexus with the improvement in environmental measures.

94. While keeping in mind the precautionary principle and principle of sustainable development, we have to pass directions which will ensure compliance with all the conditions that may be imposed for protection of environment, ecology and prevention of pollution in the proposed order granting the EC. There has to be a definite and unambiguous R&R scheme in place before the project can be permitted to be fully established and completely made operational. Thus, while partially allowing this main application, we pass the following order & directions for their strict compliance by all concerned in the given facts and circumstances:

a) The order dated 25th January, 2012 is hereby remanded to the MoEF to pass an order granting or declining environmental clearance to the project proponent afresh in accordance with law and this judgment. Till then, the said order shall be kept in abeyance.

b) MoEF, in turn, shall refer the matter to EAC for its re-scrutiny and imposition of such conditions, as the expert body may deem fit and proper, inter-alia but primarily, in relation to R&R scheme, effects of improper disclosure in relation to nature and categorization of the land in question, providing of AAQ monitoring stations keeping in view the downward wind direction to ensure continuous adherence to the prescribed standards of emission and providing of early warning system near the human settlements…

e) The EAC shall visit the site in question, give public notice and hear the project-affected or displaced persons individually or in a representative capacity and then proceed to record its findings….

i) During this period or till fresh order is passed by the MoEF, whichever is earlier, the project proponent shall maintain status quo as of today in relation to the project in question.

* * *

NOTES AND QUESTIONS

1. The clearance process for the project in the instant case was marred by numerous procedural and substantive irregularities, ranging from deliberate misrepresentation of facts to alteration of the expected emission levels at different points in the process. Despite such a heavily flawed process, the Tribunal did not set aside the entire environmental clearance or cancel the project, supposedly because of the involvement of "public funds". This has been a recurring reason for the Tribunal not taking strict action against environmental violations by governmental projects.

2. Is such a heightened sensitivity for the use of public funds and the consequential condonation of environmental violations conducive to sustainable development?

3. Given the Tribunal's reluctance to act strictly against such projects, is the present system encouraging public authorities to commence projects where following due procedure would have not allowed doing so? Given that the Tribunal will not cancel the project, is there any real risk faced by authorities by not complying with environmental norms?

4. The Tribunal alluded to the *G. Sundararajan Case*, in which the Supreme Court evinced an acceptance of utilitarian ethics within environmental law. Given the immense scientific uncertainty that can revolve around the long-term environmental impacts of developmental decisions, can we ever truly understand the "greatest good" in environmental matters?

5. Can the utilitarian axiom of "greatest good of the greatest number" be reconciled with the concept of sustainable development? Would a utilitarian perspective on sustainability be overly anthropocentric? Can such a view accommodate the interests of the environment as an entity in itself?

* * *

3.2 PRECAUTIONARY PRINCIPLE

3.2.1 INTRODUCTION TO THE PRECAUTIONARY PRINCIPLE

Age-old adages such as "better safe than sorry!" or "prevention is better than cure" reflect the central idea behind the precautionary principle. These adages posit that it is prudent to err on the side of caution rather than retrospectively lamenting a loss. Accordingly, the precautionary principle states that, in the absence of clear and compelling proof of harm, states should take precautions and measures to protect the environment and public health. In other words, the principle asserts that regulators and policymakers should act in anticipation of environmental harm even if there is no scientific certainty or consensus regarding the harm.[185]

Thus, according to the precautionary principle, if there is a strong suspicion that an activity can adversely impact the environment, then this activity should be controlled immediately, and the state should not wait for concrete evidence before taking precautions. The reasoning behind the requirement of a strong suspicion, as opposed to concrete evidence, to halt an activity is that the absence of concrete evidence has been frequently cited as a reason for inaction when it comes to preventing environmental damage.

As discussed in the previous section on sustainable development, there were several alarms raised prior to the Bhopal Gas Tragedy. While the exact chemical composition of the gas and the exact potential harm to human health were not known, there was a strong suspicion indicating the hazardous impact on life. Since the state and Union Carbide failed to act on these warnings and suspicions in the absence of incontrovertible proof, thousands lost their lives and many more became handicapped in some form of prolonged illnesses. As we will explore, there are many such instances wherein having a precautionary approach has averted significant environmental damage and has saved many lives.

The precautionary principle is also a recognition of the fact that there are many variables involved in environmental decision-making such as scientific and technological constraints, evidence gathering, and testing. The multiplicity of variables makes it extremely unlikely that concrete evidence will be discovered within the necessary time, if at all. Moreover, having complete scientific consensus is usually impossible as there will always be scientific opinions to the contrary. For instance, even something as conspicuous as the adverse effects of global warming is scientifically countered by some people (yes, there are "Climate Deniers"!). Thus, the principle acknowledges that the harm arising out of potential environmental damage to the environment outweighs harm arising out of halting a particular activity.

Let us understand this through an illustration. Compound X is a new chemical that has made it easier to do several industrial processes. Due to this advantage, the cost of manufacturing for several industries has come down substantially. Accordingly, there is an increase in the popularity and use of the chemical. The waste generated, however, as a result of the chemical's use is suspected to severely damage the environment due to several sporadic complaints. In response, several scientific studies are undertaken to ascertain whether this suspicion is true. About 60 per cent of the studies conducted confirm that this suspicion is warranted as there is serious environmental damage caused. However, the remaining 40 per cent of the studies do not indicate that the waste generated from the use of Compound X harms the environment.

Since there is no conclusive proof that Compound X is harmful to the environment, the government decides to wait for concrete evidence before banning the chemical. Due to the increase in industrial efficiency, Compound X quickly replaces other chemicals and becomes an important part of industrial processes. Two years later, new scientific research is done which demonstrates that the initial suspicion with respect to the environmental harm caused by the chemical was correct. This new research heavily tilts the scientific consensus in favour of banning the chemical (now 75 per cent of studies agree with the new findings). Due to the new scientific research, several human deaths and illnesses are traced back to the use of the chemical. In addition, serious groundwater contamination and destruction of microorganisms within the soil are linked to the chemical's use. In the light of this, the government finally decides to ban Compound X.

From this illustration, the benefits or a precautionary approach towards the environment and human health are evident. Had the government not waited for the scientific consensus to tilt in favour of the notion that there is environmental harm from the use of Compound X, many lives could have been saved and serious environmental degradation prevented. It is such a situation that the precautionary principle tries to avert by requiring states to not wait for concrete proof before taking precautionary measures.

However, while the principle states that states ought to take precaution in the absence of concrete proof of environmental harm, it does not mandate when this obligation begins. In other words, the precautionary principle does not give guidance on the threshold beyond which precaution should be exercised. For instance, in the above illustration, the principle does not guide us with respect to whether a precautionary approach should be taken given that 60 per cent of the scientific reports suggest that there is environmental harm caused by the use of Compound X. Accordingly, the threshold at which the state intends to apply precautionary measures depends on how prudent it wants to be in a situation.

Thus, there can be a weak, moderate, and strong application of the precautionary principle. For instance, if the state would have applied precautionary measures only when three-fourths (75 per cent) of all scientific studies confirmed the environmental harm, it would be a weak application of the principle as the threshold for applying the principle is very high. Correspondingly, if the state would have enacted precautionary measures proactively if around 40 per cent (below half) of the scientific studies confirmed the environmental harm, it would be a strong application of the principle. Likewise, if the state would have taken precautionary measures when 51 per cent or more scientific studies confirmed the environmental harm, it would be deemed to be adopting a moderate approach.

Thus, the application of the precautionary principle lies in a spectrum from weak to strong. Depending on how different jurisdictions define the principle, many variations of the principle exist.[186] As noted, these variations of the principle exist as the precautionary principle does not prescribe an exact standard or threshold that warrants intervention by the state in the form of precautionary measures. Before delving into the different variations of the principle in detail, however, it is important to trace the genesis and evolution of the precautionary principle.

As noted in the previous section, this principle forms a part of the overarching principle of sustainable development, and its underlying logic was explained in the Bergen Conference on Sustainable Development in 1990:[187]

> It is better to be roughly right in due time, bearing in mind the consequences of being very wrong, than to be precisely right too late.

In his address to the Parliamentary Earth Summit of the United Nations Conference on Environment and Development in Rio de Janeiro (1992), the Dalai Lama stated that the people of Tibet had enacted measures to protect the environment as early as the seventeenth century.[188] A precautionary approach towards the environment was inherent to the Buddhist principles that were instilled in Tibetans as children.[189] For instance, the Theravada Buddhist scriptures teach people to refrain from "unwholesome action" wherein monks are prohibited from injuring plants and trees unnecessarily.[190]

This demonstrates that a precautionary approach, just like the concept of sustainable development (discussed previously), is not a new concept. In fact, several civilizations in history have adopted a precautionary approach towards the environment, which was deemed sacred.[191] However, given the extreme environmental exploitation that accompanied the Industrial Revolution and the colonial period – wherein natural resources were seen as inexhaustible – a more cogent, transboundary legal principle was required.

The historic roots of the precautionary principle can be broadly traced to a push towards adopting in "safe minimum standard of conservation" by environmental economists during the 1950s.[192] A decade later, concerns relating to the uninhibited use of pesticides without adequate scientific knowledge regarding the actual harm came to light. In particular, concerns regarding the use of dichloro-diphenyl-trichloroethane (DDT) led environmentalists and policymakers to take more precaution.[193] In her book titled *Silent Spring* (1962), Rachel Carson put forth arguments that conform to the spirit of the precautionary principle, though the term did not exist at that time.[194]

While she attempted to highlight the problems with the uninhibited use of pesticides, her main contention was that federal agencies had proceeded with massive aerial spraying of these pesticides at a large scale without adequate knowledge about the actual extent of harm being caused. She highlighted how the research budget allocated to governmental labs was abysmally low and that due to the pesticide corporate lobby's influence not much research had been done. Given that most of the research on the possible harms caused by certain pesticides was done in small private labs, the book helped uncover several stories of people and farmers who had been adversely affected. However, this came too late, and it was later found that many people had already lost their lives.[195]

Gradually, learning from this experience, several countries including the US and the UK had incorporated a precautionary paradigm into their environmental policies to varying degrees.[196] However, it was Germany that developed this approach into broader environmental philosophy.[197] In the early 1980s, Germany developed the legal principle of *Vorsorgeprinzip* – which means "foresight" or "precaution" – as a response to the growing concerns of environmental degradation.[198] In particular, this was used to tackle environmental issues such as acid rain, global warming, and pollution in the North Sea through the enactment of stringent policies.[199] At the core of the idea of *Vorsorge* is the implied belief that governmental authorities should have the foresight to minimize and, if possible, prevent environmental harm.[200]

It gradually was incorporated into other jurisdictions[201] and first appeared in the international sphere in 1982 through the United Nations World Charter for Nature,[202] which stated that when "potential adverse effects [of activities likely to pose significant risks to nature] are not fully understood, the activities should not proceed". This was an implicit acknowledgement of the precautionary principle. However, it was a decade later in 1992 when the precautionary principle was explicitly mentioned and adopted for the first time in the Rio Declaration on the Environment and Development. The Rio Declaration emphasized the need for the adoption of a precautionary approach and held:[203]

> In order to protect the environment, the precautionary approach shall be widely applied by States *according to their capabilities*. Where there are threats of *serious or irreversible damage*, lack of full scientific certainty shall not be used as a reason for postponing *cost-effective measures* to prevent environmental degradation. (Emphasis supplied)

However, it is important to note that the strength of the precautionary principle was weakened considerably with the addition of the phrases "according to their capabilities", "serious or irreversible damage", and "cost-effective measures". These phrases granted considerable leeway to states in their interpretation and application of the principle. This considerably weakened the domestic application of the principle as states could claim that banning or regulating a particular activity which was harming the environment was not within their capability or they could not do so in a cost-effective manner. Moreover, states could justify the delay in the adoption of precautionary measures by stating that they did not consider the threat as amounting to serious or irreversible.

The Rio Declaration, thus, is an example of the weak model of the precautionary principle as it seeks to only prevent serious and irreversible damage, as long as it is within the capacity of the state to reasonably foresee and prevent it. A similar version of the principle was subsequently incorporated by other international bodies such as the United Nations Framework Convention on Climate Change[204]; the Convention on the Protection and Use of Transboundary Watercourses and International Lakes[205]; and the Convention on Biological Diversity.[206]

It was in 1998, however, that the Wingspread Conference on the Precautionary Principle provided a stronger application through the Wingspread Statement,[207] which defined the principle as:

> When an activity *raises threats* of harm to human health or the environment, precautionary measures should be taken *even if some cause and effect relationships are not established scientifically*. In this context the proponent of the activity, rather than the public, should bear the burden of proof. (Emphasis supplied)

This definition has come to be recognized as one of the strongest versions of the principle and is deemed to reflect the principle's strong model. Significantly, this version of the principle reverses the burden of proof by placing the burden on the proponent of the activity to prove that the activity is harmless (usually the burden of proof is placed on the party that alleges environmental harm). Further, the phrases that diluted the application of the principle in the Rio Declaration – "according to their capabilities", "serious or irreversible damage", and "cost-effective measures" – are missing from this definition. Accordingly, the definition simply states that where an activity "raises threats" of harm to human health or the environment, precautionary measures should be adopted. Further, while the Rio Declaration stated that "lack of full scientific certainty" should not be a reason for not taking precautionary measures, the Wingspread Conference lowers the threshold considerably by stating that precautionary measures should be taken "even if some cause-and-effect relationships are not established scientifically".

While this reversal of the burden of proof is gradually gaining traction internationally, it has not yet crystallized into the overarching norm of the precautionary principle.[208] The rationale behind this reversal of the burden of proof is partly that the burden must be borne by the party that is in the best position to procure the evidence. Given that the project proponent is likely to be the party that is best equipped with the information and knowledge of the consequences of its activity, the burden is sought to be imposed on it.[209]

The reversal of the burden of proof was acknowledged by Justice Weeramantry at the ICJ, in his dissenting opinion in the *Nuclear Test Case*.[210] The proceedings were instituted by New Zealand and Australia expressing concerns regarding France's tests which were proposed to be carried out in the atmosphere in the South Pacific Region. While France stated that the ICJ lacked jurisdiction, the Court ordered several interim measures requiring France to refrain from conducting the proposed tests pending the judgment as it would cause radioactive fall-out on New Zealand and Australian territory. However, subsequently, the Court held that the applications filed were no longer necessary as France had, through various public statements, expressed its intention to not carry out the proposed nuclear tests. In relation to the application of the precautionary principle in the case, Justice Weeramantry stated the following:[211]

> There are two ways of approaching this question. The first is to place the burden of proof fairly and squarely upon New Zealand, and to ask whether a prima facie case has been made out of the presence of such dangers as New Zealand complains of.
>
> The second approach is to apply the principle of environmental law under which, where environmental damage of any sort is threatened, the burden of proving that it will not produce the damaging consequences complained of is placed upon the author of that damage. In this view of the matter, the Court would hold that the environmental damage New Zealand complains of is prima facie established in the absence of proof by France that the proposed nuclear tests are environmentally safe.
>
> It will be noted in this connection that all the information bearing upon this matter is in the possession of the Respondent. The Applicant has only indirect or secondary

information, but has endeavoured to place before the Court such information as it has been able, to the best of its ability, to marshal for the purposes of this application.

The second approach is sufficiently well established in international law for the Court to act upon it. Yet, it is sufficient for present purposes to act upon the first approach, throwing the burden of proof upon New Zealand.

Thus, this dissenting opinion recognizes the importance of placing the burden of proof on the party initiating an activity that is likely to disturb the environmental *status quo*. This is required as the party initiating such an action is likely to possess more information about the consequences of its actions. Moreover, Justice Weeramantry states that such a strong application of the precautionary principle is "well established" in international law. This approach with respect to the burden of proof, as we will discuss in the subsequent section, has been accepted by the Indian Supreme Court.

Notwithstanding the noble premise of the strong model of the precautionary principle, it has been criticized for its lack of practicality as in the vast majority of cases, producing absolute evidence of the innocuousness of a particular activity is not possible without considerable effort and cost.[212] This in turn runs the risk of curtailing important industrial or technological advancements since in their nascent stage they may not be able to prove completely harmless.[213]

However, as we will see though several cases in the next two sections, the application of such an approach yields desirable results. This is because the strong model of the principle does not require the project proponent to discharge the burden of proof to an unreasonable extent. Several regulatory mechanisms such as the EIA already require the project proponent to demonstrate that its activity is not polluting in excess of permissible limits prior to obtaining an environmental clearance. Given that the project proponent is in the best position to explain the consequences of its activity, the overall economic cost is reduced (as other persons are likely to spend more time and resources explaining the possible harms of the concerned activity).

Nevertheless, given the different issues highlighted in the weak and strong models of the precautionary principle, it was felt that a middle ground was needed. Due to this, the moderate model of the principle emerged. A good example of the moderate model can be seen in the European Union Commission's Communication on the Precautionary Principle, which came out at the beginning of the twentieth century.[214] It required that the regulation of an activity needed to be proportional to the level of risk involved to avoid "potentially dangerous effects"[215] on the environment.

This went a step further than the weak model by not allowing states to easily delay or disregard precautionary measures on grounds of incapability or unfeasibility. On the other hand, it ameliorated the requirement of the strong model to show the absolute innocuousness of the activity, thereby making the moderate model more practical for states to implement. The key differences between the weak, moderate, and strong models of the precautionary principle have been summarized in Table 3.1.[216]

Table 3.1   Interpreting the Strength of Application of the Precautionary Principle

Attributes used to assess the strength of application of the precautionary principle	Weak precaution: "uncertainty does not justify inaction"	Moderate precaution: "uncertainty justifies action"	Strong precaution: "uncertainty justifies shifting the burden and standard of proof"
Severity of potential harm prompting precautionary action as referenced in international legislation and regulation	Rio Declaration suggests that regulation is permitted to avoid "serious and irreversible damage"	The Commission Communication on the precautionary principle suggests the use of regulation proportional to the risk level, following preliminary objective scientific evaluation to avoid "potentially dangerous effects"	The Wingspread Statement conveys that clear responsibility lies with the proponent in proving an activity is safe even if the cause and effect relationship cannot be determined scientifically to avoid "threats of harm"
Degree of epistemic uncertainty/quality of evidence prompting precautionary action	Regulation is permitted in the absence of full scientific certainty; significant precautionary action may be invoked under uncertainty	Research is needed to establish cause and effect (reduce uncertainty) upon which regulatory decisions are based; until then, precautionary action includes setting regulatory standards with large margins of safety built in through application of uncertainty factors	Uncertainty necessitates forbidding the potentially risky activity until the proponent of the activity demonstrates that it poses no (or acceptable) risk, and is sufficiently safe
Nature of precautionary action/measures taken and provision for review	Presumption of risk management; banning very rare	Underlying presumption of risk management; banning possible, but is a last resort; measures are provisional or subject to review when new information or scientific evidence emerges	Presumption of risk avoidance; banning is likely

Source: Kenisha Garnett and David J Parsons, "Multi Case Review of the Application of the Precautionary Principle in European Union Law and Case Law", *Risk Analysis* 37, no. 3 (2017): 502–16.

There is considerable debate at the international level as to whether the precautionary principle has crystallized into a part of customary international law.[217] Nevertheless, it has been deployed various times by international courts like the ICJ in the *Gabcikovo-Nagymaros Case*[218] and the International Tribunal for the Law of the Sea in the *Southern Bluefin Tuna Case*.[219] While these international adjudicatory bodies used the principle, they stopped short of holding that it is a part of customary international law.

As noted previously, the status and degree of application of the precautionary principle vary from jurisdiction to jurisdiction. Let us now look at the application of the principle in the Indian context. We will first examine the interpretation and application of the principle by the Indian Supreme Court, before assessing the NGT's use of the principle.

3.2.2   THE INDIAN SUPREME COURT AND THE PRECAUTIONARY PRINCIPLE

The recognition of the precautionary principle in Indian law stems from the constitutional mandate provided in articles 21, 48A, and 51A(g) of the Constitution.[220] The right to a healthy and safe environment has been recognized as a part of the fundamental right to life under Article 21.[221] Article 48A of the Constitution directs the government to protect and improve the environment and to safeguard the forests and wildlife of India. Further, Article 51A(g) prescribes a fundamental duty for every citizen to promote and improve the natural environment.

Though these are generic obligations and prescriptions contained in the Constitution, they have played an important role in the evolution of Indian environmental jurisprudence and the application of international principles in the Indian context. While these constitutional provisions are unambiguous, the Supreme Court has not been entirely consistent in terms of the model of the precautionary principle that it chooses to follow. Rather, as we will see in this section, the Court's approach varies on a case-by-case basis. To appreciate this, let us look at the history of the Supreme Court's interpretation and application of the precautionary principle.

The Supreme Court's first explicit interaction with the precautionary principle occurred in *Vellore Citizens Welfare Forum v. Union of India*.[222] The Court derived the principle from the broader concept of sustainable development (for further details, refer to the previous section on sustainable development) and the aforementioned constitutional provisions. In the context of municipal law, the Court broadly laid down the following characteristics of the precautionary principle:[223]

(i)   Environmental measures by the state government and the statutory authorities must anticipate, prevent, and attack the causes of environmental degradation.

(ii)   Where there are threats of serious and irreversible damage, lack of scientific certainty should not be used as a reason for postponing measures to prevent environmental degradation.

(iii) The "onus of proof" is on the actor or the developer/industrialist to show that his action is environmentally benign.

If we attempt to place this approach of the Supreme Court within the larger spectrum (weak to strong) of the precautionary principle, we see that it has elements of both the weak and the strong ends of the spectrum. This is because, on the one hand, the Court reinstates the weak standard prescribed by the Rio Declaration (1992) by stating that the precautionary measures are only warranted when there is a risk of serious or irreversible damage and, on the other, the Court adopts the reversed burden of proof (placing the onus on the project proponent, which is in line with the Wingspread Statement).

Though the strength of the application of the principle was considerably lowered by the high threshold required for the initiation of precautionary measures, the reversed burden of proof ensured that the hazardous tanneries were closed in Vellore by the Court. This decision has been lauded for its strong application of the precautionary principle and its placement of a high burden on the government to ensure that no environmental damage occurs and identify potential risks.

Following the *Vellore Case,*[224] the Supreme Court applied the precautionary principle in the *Lakes Case.*[225] In brief, the case was about construction activity adjacent to the green belt of the Surajkund and Badhkal lakes. There were concerns that the proposed construction could disturb the rainwater drains, thereby adversely impacting the water bodies and hydrology of the area. These concerns were based on research rendered by scientific agencies such as the National Environment Engineering Research Institute (NEERI).

The Court, on examination of the reports, held that there was a clear indication that the proposed construction could potentially adversely impact the water bodies and the storm drains. Accordingly, it applied the precautionary principle and placed restrictive conditions on the construction activity. The application of the principle in this instance is closer to the moderate model of the principle as the Court relied on scientific expert opinion from specialized agencies and did not direct the complete closure of the construction activity (refer to Table 3.1). Rather, it placed restrictions on the proposed construction. This was a more proportional response on the part of the Court as it attempted to balance environmental concerns with developmental concerns.

Subsequently, the Court employed a similar moderate model of the precautionary principle by placing reliance on expert scientific data and introducing a regulatory mechanism. This was exemplified in *Bittu Sehgal v. Union of India*[226] and *M.C. Mehta v. Union of India* (popularly known as the *Groundwater Case*).[227] In these cases, the Court placed reliance on scientific material that demonstrated a possibility of environmental harm on account of the concerned activity and directed the establishment of a regulatory body. The establishment of a regulatory body, in both cases, to monitor and check environmental damage is a creative deployment of the precautionary principle as it crystallizes the duty of the state to prevent and mitigate environmental damage. This demonstrates the flexibility and robustness in the adoption of the principle by the Court.

This robustness in the application of the principle is further evidenced by the *Taj Trapezium Case,*[228] wherein the Supreme Court clearly demonstrated that it could use the strong model of the principle when required by the facts of a case. The Taj Trapezium is the 10,400 square kilometre area around the Taj Mahal – one of the greatest architectural marvels in India – that underwent rapid industrialization over the past few decades. Several factories were set up in the area. These factories were powered by coal, which produced toxic fumes that resulted in acid rain. It was alleged that over time this acid rain was responsible for causing the discolouration of the Taj Mahal's pristine white exterior.

The Court relied on scientific reports[229] to ascertain the propensity of damage to the environment and the monument as a direct result of the industrial emissions. Significantly, the Court reiterated that the burden of proof was on the industries operating in the Taj Trapezium as they were disturbing the environmental "status quo". The industries provided scientific evidence as well to support their claim that their emissions were not leading to the Taj Mahal's discolouration. Nevertheless, given that there was an adequate threat posed by the industrial activity in the region, the Court mandated the industries switch from coal to cleaner fuels such as natural gas. This approach of the Court is in line with the strong model as it effectively banned industries that did not switch from coal to cleaner fuels.

We have previously noted that one of the justifications for the strong model of the principle is that the person initiating any activity is likely to have more information and knowledge about the consequences of his or her activity. For instance, in the Bhopal Gas Tragedy, thousands of lives could have been saved had the burden of proof been placed on Union Carbide to explain how their chemical composition is environmentally benign. As discussed earlier, Union Carbide intentionally used deceptive tactics to protect the trade secret of its chemical composition even when revealing it would have saved thousands of lives. In fact, even to this day the exact composition of the chemical used is unknown.

Interestingly, in addition to the aforementioned justification for the strong model of the principle, the Court takes a principle-based ecocentric approach. It holds that the imposition of the burden of proof on the person initiating an activity is justified on the grounds that he or she is changing the "environmental *status quo*".[230] This approach underpins the importance of preserving the present environmental condition and places the burden of proof on the person whose activity threatens to disturb this condition. In this regard, the Court has held that the larger public interest behind the reversal of burden of proof outweighs the practical challenges that come with such a reversal.[231] This approach is ecocentric in nature as it values ecological balance in terms of itself and is not based on human needs or wants.

Further, the Court has significantly reduced the threshold required for the application of precautionary measures when there are competing scientific opinions. It has held that a reasonable person's test is applicable while interpreting the likelihood of damage to the environment from scientific reports.[232] This is a significant move as it does away with the cumbersome requirement under the weak model that warrants a high degree of probability. According to the Court, if a reasonable person, upon reading the scientific reports, feels that there is a possibility of environmental harm then precautionary measures should be initiated. This standard can be seen as being similar to the standard of balance of probabilities in civil cases.[233] The Court has used this approach to invalidate a governmental direction that stated that a class of industries would not be required to prove that their actions were environmentally benign.[234]

Till now we have looked at cases wherein the Court has applied a moderate to strong model of the precautionary principle. However, in *Narmada Bachao Andolan v. Union of India*,[235] the Court deviated from this trend. The Sardar Sarovar Dam – Asia's second largest hydroelectric dam – was proposed to be constructed on the Narmada River. The main motivation for its creation was that it would enable the generation of large amounts of hydroelectric power as well as ensure a reservoir of water during the drought season. As discussed in the section on sustainable development, however, several social and environmental groups came out in fierce protest against this project as scientific reports indicated that there would be massive damage to the environment.

Several thousand acres of forest land needed to be cleared for its construction, thereby altering the natural flow of the river. The loss of natural habitat and flora and fauna was so great that the World Bank withdrew its support for the project just a few years after lending its support.[236] The concerns were further compounded by the fact that several tribal communities would have been displaced as a result of the project and thousands of tribal people would lose their way of life. Additionally, there were concerns over inadequate compensation and loss of livelihood for these displaced people.

The project was halted due to the protests and a long legal battle ensued. The concerned social and environmental groups petitioned the Supreme Court to halt the construction of the dam by applying the precautionary principle as there was a risk of serious and irreversible harm. The Court, however, approached the matter in an inconceivable manner. It held that the precautionary principle, and the reversal of the burden of proof, would be applicable only where the actual extent of damage of an activity is "unknown".[237] Since the government had indicated in its report to the Court that it had adequately assessed the extent of environmental and social damage, the Court deferred to the executive and held that the extent of damage was known, and that the precautionary principle was not applicable.

It is unclear why such deference to the executive was necessary. After all, in several cases where the Court has applied the strong model of the precautionary principle, the project proponent almost always would state that it has adequately assessed all possible environmental harm before beginning the project. Such reasoning did not stop the Court from employing the precautionary principle and should not have stopped the Court from doing the same in this case. As noted, the Court's only basis for claiming that the extent of damage was "known" was that the government had asserted that it was fully aware of the extent of possible damage. Due to this, the Court held that the right approach would be to not apply the precautionary principle but to use mitigative steps to offset the damage.

Further, the court went on to state that there was no need to presume that an ecological disaster was likely to occur in all instances. By stating this the Court impliedly drew a distinction between the tangible benefits of the project and the possible or speculative harm caused by the project. This is ironic as the serious damage being caused was apparent on the face of the record and was acknowledged by the Court. This is problematic since if this line of reasoning is taken to its logical end, in every case where the damage is claimed to be adequately known the precautionary principle would not be applicable and precautionary measures would not be undertaken irrespective of the extent of the damage.

This case demonstrates a significant departure from the earlier application of the precautionary principle. Effectively, it is weaker than the weak model of the principle as the Court holds that the principle is not applicable. Ironically, the Court holds that the principle of sustainable development is applicable in the case and provides mitigative directions to uphold the same – not realizing that the precautionary principle is a part of sustainable development. In addition, this approach of the Court is at odds with the basic premise of the precautionary principle, which recognizes that there are limits to the level of scientific certainty that can be achieved. As noted previously, it is internationally acknowledged that it is improbable that the full extent of ecological damage can be ascertained prior to an activity of the scale of the proposed dam. Hence, it seems improbable that the extent of the impact can be "known" fully as the court assumed in this case. This is a considerable dilution of the principle's application.

Similarly, in relation to the construction of the Tehri Dam, the Supreme Court, in *N.D. Jayal v. Union of India,*[238] once again restrained itself from blocking or curtailing the project despite there being a possibility of serious environmental and social harm. In fact, unlike the *Narmada Dam Case* discussed previously, the EIA carried out in relation to the Tehri Dam was far less rigorous. The majority opinion of the Court held that the precautionary principle was not applicable due to similar reasons stated in the *Narmada Dam Case* and held that the right approach would be to prescribe mitigative measures as the extent of damage was known.

Interestingly, however, Justice Dharmadhikari – in his dissenting opinion in the case – held that the precautionary principle was applicable to the construction of the Tehri Dam. He reiterated for the entire bench the environmental and social harms that were likely to ensue post the construction of the dam:[239]

87. … The dam area will cover 45 kms. Bhagirathi valley and 25 kms. Bhilangana valley with water spread over an area of 42.5 sq. kms. which will submerge nearly 100 villages including the town Tehri as many as 90,000 families will be relocated as the result of the dam project… Human Rights and environment activists have approached this Court to protect the interest of general public and particularly the people living in Tehri town and in surrounding areas of Garhwal who are likely to be displaced for completion of the Project. They have also raised issues of great importance such as the safety of the Dam and the likely devastation and loss of properties and lives of the people in the down stream, if the Dam, being situated in a highly earth quake prone area, bursts or leaks. It is stated that structurally the dam may be incapable of withstanding earthquake of above seven on Richter scale. It is submitted that great danger is posed to down stream cities and population particularly the holy Pilgrim centers like Haridwar and Rishikesh

which are in danger lone. The structural flaws of the dam and rehabilitation policies provoked public agitation and international attention.

Due to these serious environmental and social concerns, Justice Dharmadhikari held that the quantum of damage could not be fully known, and that the precautionary principle was applicable. Based on this reasoning, he opined that several precautionary measures were necessary to prevent possible grave damage. He opined that the Expert Committee created under the EIA process should monitor the situation regularly and submit a status report every three months with respect to whether the conditions stipulated in the environmental clearance were being met. Significantly, he stated that this report would cover the progress of resettlement and rehabilitation measures, and that no impoundment of the dam reservoir would be done until resettlement and rehabilitation work was fully completed.[240]

In conclusion, the approach of the Indian Supreme Court with respect to the precautionary principle has been mixed. As discussed, the Court started out on a strong footing in initial cases such as the *Vellore Case* and the *Taj Trapezium Case*. While it retained the words of the Rio Declaration (1992) such as "serious or irreversible damage", it reversed the burden of proof by placing the burden on any person that threatened to change the environmental *status quo*. This interpretation and application of the principle by the Court was in line with the strong model.

However, this approach became more moderate over time through the Court's adoption of creative solutions such as the establishment of regulatory bodies to ensure that environmental damage was mitigated. While the *Vellore Case* and the *Taj Trapezium Case* were examples where the Court outright banned the pollutive activity on account of the principle, cases such as *Bittu Sehgal v. Union of India*[241] and the *Groundwater Case*[242] demonstrated the Court's preference for precautionary measures that did not include banning of the concerned activity. Finally, cases such as the *Narmada Dam Case* and the *Tehri Dam Case* demonstrate the Court's reluctance to interfere with large governmental projects and not apply the precautionary principle on extraneous considerations.

Given this context and the mixed approach of the Court in relation to the precautionary principle, let us now examine the NGT's jurisprudence with respect to the principle.

3.2.3 THE NGT AND THE PRECAUTIONARY PRINCIPLE: INTERPRETATION AND APPLICATION

As we have noted previously, while Section 20 of the NGT Act mandatorily requires the Tribunal to apply the precautionary principle, it accords ample discretion to the NGT with respect to the interpretation and application of the principle. Given the mixed, and sometimes incompatible, precedents that the Supreme Court has given by employing the precautionary principle in a strong or weak manner depending on the case at hand, the NGT has had to navigate the contours of the principle in a practical manner. Equipped with ample discretion, guidance from international conventions to which India is a party, and the previously discussed approaches of the Supreme Court, one would assume that the NGT has been able to interpret and apply the principle pragmatically. Let us now analyse and explore how the NGT has developed its own jurisprudence with respect to the precautionary principle to confirm this assertion.

The initial cases in the NGT primarily dealt with issues relating to the application of the precautionary principle to adjudge the validity of allegedly defective environmental clearances.[243] A landmark case in this regard is *Goa Foundation v. Union of India*.[244] In this case, one of the questions that arose was whether the NGT could entertain a matter that dealt with inaction and the manner of discharge of statutory duties on the part of governmental authorities. Answering in the affirmative, the Tribunal stated that the "applicability of the precautionary principle is a statutory command" and that the non-application of the principle was actionable. This is because the principle casts an obligation on the state to anticipate and prevent environmental damage, and non-compliance with this prescription is reason enough to seek relief before the Tribunal.

This demonstrates the crucial difference between the Supreme Court's approach and the NGT's approach to the principle. Unlike the Court, the Tribunal is statutorily mandated to apply the precautionary principle. Given this predisposition, the Tribunal has conferred *locus standi* on parties that are apprehensive of the fact that the precautionary principle is not being applied in a particular EIA, and who want to spur complacent authorities into action to prevent irreversible environmental damage.

In *Rayons-Enlightening Humanity v. MoEF*,[245] a waste processing plant was constructed in the immediate vicinity of a residential area. The plant was disposing of solid waste in violation of laid down regulations. Noting the deficiency of the EIA undertaken, the Tribunal held that the project proponent ought to have conducted a technical analysis of the plant's impact on the environment before beginning operations. Further, it noted that the environmental clearance had been granted without performing the basic checks as stipulated in the relevant rules. Highlighting the possible risks that the plant posed to the environment and to the health of people living in the vicinity, the Tribunal invoked the precautionary principle to order the closure of the plant.

Through this, the NGT reaffirmed the burden that the principle casts upon the state to pre-empt environmental harm and act against potential environmental hazards. This robust application of the precautionary principle by the NGT underpins the value of having a statutory obligation to consider the principle while adjudicating the validity of environmental clearances. The deployment of the principle in this case is in line with the strong model of the principle. This is because not only did the NGT order the closure of an activity that could potentially harm the environment, but it also demanded that further studies be conducted to prove that the activity was indeed benign.

In fact, the NGT has unequivocally held that the environmental regulatory authorities such as State Pollution Control Boards must apply the three basic environmental principles – sustainable development, precautionary principle, and the polluter pays principle. [246] Accordingly, it has held that the non-application of these principles provides ample ground to challenge the decision-making process of these authorities.[247] However, the Tribunal has held that authorities cannot claim to adhere to the precautionary principle without relying on any scientific evidence.

This was clearly seen in *Sterlite Industries (India) Ltd. v. Tamil Nadu Pollution Control Board*.[248] The case involved a challenge to an order of the Tamil Nadu Pollution Control Board directing the closure of Vedanta's copper smelting plant. The Board had ordered this closure as there were reports of people suffering from eye irritation and throat issues in the vicinity of the plant. Based on these reports, authorities visited the factory suspecting its emissions to be the reason for the health hazard. However, the emissions were found to be within prescribed limits, with the exception of a few alleged technical deficiencies on the part of the plant. Consequently, the industry received a closure notice from the Board, which mainly relied on the precautionary principle with respect to the health-related complaints received previously.

The NGT, however, upheld the appeal and set aside the Board's order for the closure of the plant. It stated that since no scientific evidence whatsoever had been supplied by the Board in relation to the allegations, the precautionary principle was not applicable. In this regard, the NGT held:[249]

> There is no cogent or reliable evidence or reasonable scientific data, even by necessary implication, to contribute the leakage of SO_2 in excess of the prescribed parameters to the plant of the appellant-company. Nothing on record justifies the invocation of precautionary principle. In fact, it is a punitive action in the garb of a preventive measure.

The NGT held that no causal link had been established between the emissions of the plant and the alleged health conditions. In fact, there were allegations of political motives behind shutting down the plant. In this case, the Tribunal made the crucial distinction between precautionary and punitive measures. After revisiting the previous interpretations of the precautionary principle rendered by the Supreme Court, the Tribunal proceeded to state that the following conditions need to be fulfilled for the invocation of the precautionary principle:[250]

a) There should be an *imminent environmental or ecological threat* in regard to carrying out of an activity or development.
b) Such threat should be supported by *reasonable scientific data*.
c) Taking precautionary, preventive, or prohibitory steps would serve the *larger public and environmental interest*.

With reference to these ingredients, the Tribunal held that a decision-making authority, upon taking an objective approach, could take recourse to and pass directives under the precautionary and preventive principles if these conditions were fulfilled. However, the Tribunal held that these conditions in the impugned case were not fulfilled as there was no "reasonable scientific data" produced by the petitioners that demonstrated any causal link between the health conditions and the alleged emissions. While no scientific data whatsoever is a plausible ground for the non-application of the precautionary principle – as even the strong model of the principle requires at least some scientific data – given the serious health conditions and illnesses that the workers of the factory were alleging, it would have been better to order a more detailed study rather than reopening the plant directly.

Significantly, the Tribunal reiterated that its scope of "merit review" was not confined to Wednesbury's principles of reasonableness and proportionality.[251] This becomes significant as this marks an important departure from the earlier approach of the Supreme Court. As noted in the section on sustainable development, the Court, in *Sterlite Industries (India) Ltd. v. Union of India*,[252] acknowledged restraints on the application of the principle of sustainable development. Overturning a High Court decision that had quashed an environmental clearance, the Court held that its scope of review of the decision-making process was limited to procedural grounds such as patent illegality, irrationality, and procedural impropriety. Adopting a hyper-technical approach, the Court held that it was bound by the Wednesbury's principles of reasonableness and proportionality,[253] which set a very high standard for interference by the Court.

This departure of the NGT is welcome as it unshackles the Tribunal from the self-imposed restraints of the Supreme Court. Though Section 19 of the NGT Act accords significant discretion to the Tribunal with respect to procedural matters, an unequivocal holding by the Tribunal that it is not bound by the Wednesbury's principles – despite a contrary precedent by the Supreme Court – is significant. Rather than deferring to the executive by holding that the scope of review is limited to procedural matters, the NGT has expressly held that it can review decisions on merit. Further, as noted previously, it has held that governmental authorities ought to apply the principle of sustainable development, the precautionary principle, and the polluter pays principle during the decision-making process.[254]

Moreover, the NGT upheld the reversal of burden of proof as being an important component of the precautionary principle. It explained how the reversal of burden of proof would play out practically during legal proceedings before the Tribunal:[255]

Once an applicant approaches the Tribunal with a complaint of environmental injury or environmental degradation or health hazards resulting from negligence, or incidental occurrence of emission or discharge of gases or effluents in violation of the prescribed standards, then such an applicant discharges the primary onus by instituting a petition in the prescribed form, supported by an affidavit, which then shifts upon the industrial unit, developer or the person carrying out the activity complained of, to establish by cogent and reliable evidence that it has not caused pollution or health hazards by carrying out its activities; all the expected norms of discharge have been strictly adhered to by that unit; and any harm, if caused, was neither the result of any negligence nor violation of prescribed standards. Upon discharge of such onus, which is certainly much heavier, by the developer/industrial unit, it will then again be for the applicant to establish to the contrary. In other words, heavy onus lies upon the industrial unit or the developer to show by cogent and reliable evidence that it is non-polluting and non-hazardous or is not likely to have caused the accident complained of.

In adopting such a procedure, the Tribunal confirmed its adherence to the strong version of the precautionary principle. Nevertheless, it held that the narrative of the Tamil Nadu Pollution Control Board "was not reliable, trust-worthy and in any case, could not be the foundation for passing such a punitive direction".[256] It held that the project proponent had effectively discharged its burden by demonstrating that the emissions were within the prescribed legal standards. On the contrary, the Board was not able to provide any evidence to substantiate its claims. It held:[257]

> [T]he decision-making authority is expected to have before it some reliable and cogent evidence. An inquiry into the incident or accident of breach by the industrial company should be relatable to some reasonable scientific data. There should be a direct nexus between the leakage of gas, the source of leakage and its effect/impact on ambient air quality and public health.

Noting the absence of such evidence in the case, the Tribunal conclusively held that the order passed by the Board was not based on the precautionary principle but was, rather, a punitive direction. This case is significant as it propounds important and beneficial concepts that help demarcate the contours of the application of the precautionary principle. In summary, while it is important for governmental authorities to base their decisions on the precautionary principle, there needs to be at least some scientific evidence supporting their claims. Though this case was later overruled by the Supreme Court on procedural grounds[258] – as the NGT had exercised leapfrog jurisdiction (discussed in more detail in the previous chapter under the scope of judicial review) – these holdings on the precautionary principle remain pertinent.

In relation to the burden of proof, the NGT in *Krishan Kant Singh v. Triveni Engg. Industries Ltd. and Ors.*[259] has substantiated that the onus to show that the activity is being carried out with the consent of the competent governmental authority and is within the legally permissible limits is upon the project proponent. This is the reversed burden of proof. Nevertheless, the primary burden of proof is still on the person who brings the case before the Tribunal alleging environmental harm, such as the person needs to clearly state the allegations in the prescribed format accompanied by an affidavit. This primary burden will be tested at a level of preponderance of probabilities and the petitioner will simply have to show that the violations alleged are capable of making an environmental offence.[260]

Once this primary burden is fulfilled, the substantive burden shifts onto the project proponent to prove that his or her actions are environmentally benign. Thus, the concept of reversed evidentiary burden does not mean that this reversal would operate as soon as the person approaching the Tribunal makes some allegations. There is a certain minimum threshold that the applicant would have to meet before the opposite party can be called upon to tender an explanation. Additionally, the opposite party need not provide proof of absolute harmlessness but only "show that it has complied with the statutory requirements and is operating within the prescribed norms."[261]

In *Indian Council for Enviro-Legal Action v. MoEF*,[262] the Tribunal was concerned with the emission of HFC-23, a chemical compound produced as a by-product during the industrial production of HCFC-22. The Tribunal considered the scientific evidence pertaining to the potential harm of the compound. There was a lack of conclusive data about the exact magnitude of the chemical's emission and this, in turn, meant that the chemical could not be outright classified as a "pollutant". The Tribunal, invoking the precautionary principle, directed authorities to undertake in-depth scientific studies investigating the impacts of the compound on global warming before allowing its commercial use.

In *S.P. Muthuraman v. Union of India*,[263] the NGT was concerned with, inter alia, an office memorandum of the MoEF that sought to issue *post-facto* clearance to certain projects. It was contended, on behalf of the respondent, that the provision in the EIA Notification, 2006, that required the clearance process to be concluded prior to the construction of the project was not mandatory. In response, the Tribunal noted that such an *ex-post-facto* EIA report would suffer from a lack of diligence and would foreclose the opportunity to explore alternatives. It held that such a measure would invariably go against the fundamental tenets of the precautionary principle as irreversible environmental damage would have already been caused. (The new EIA Draft Notification, 2020, seeks to foster an *ex-post-facto* clearance mechanism and is analysed in the next chapter as one of the challenges faced by the NGT.) Due to this, the Tribunal quashed the office memorandum of the MoEF and ordered the project proponents of the illegally constructed projects to pay environmental compensation.

In *Ramdas Janardan Koli v. Secretary, Ministry of Environment and Forests*,[264] the Tribunal was concerned with certain construction activities undertaken by the Jawaharlal Nehru Port Trust, Mumbai. The activities had allegedly destroyed mangroves, which were the main breeding grounds for fish populations in the area, thereby leading to a loss of livelihood for the local fishermen. The Tribunal noted several deficiencies in the overall EIA process undertaken by the building corporations. It held that several conditions laid down in the clearance process had not been complied with and that no attention was given to the possible impacts of the project on the mangroves and the surrounding ecology.

Interestingly, the Tribunal held that adherence to the precautionary principle for corporations was a part of their CSR initiatives. To give effect to this and to practically implement the precautionary principle, the Tribunal directed corporations to prepare environmental policies, standard operating procedures, and an appropriate hierarchical system to deal with reporting and compliance with environmental issues. It further held:[265]

In the present era of sustainable development, there cannot be any dis-agreement on the need and necessity of putting such a system in place in large corporate like JNPT,

ONGC and CIDCO, which will be truly reflective of the precautionary principle embedded in corporate planning, project execution and operation stages. We could not see any such environmental responsibility and reporting system in the Respondent's affidavit which otherwise could have identified and addressed some or many of the issues raised in the Application. We are, therefore, of the opinion that such an integral system independently reporting to the top management is required to safeguard the environmental and social aspects of a project and Corporate. We expect the Respondents to take suitable steps in this regard.

Finally, the Tribunal noted that the construction activities of the concerned corporations had blatantly deviated from the precautionary principle and ordered the recovery of INR 95 crore from the corporations as environmental compensation for the affected fishermen, and INR 50 lakh as environmental restoration costs.

Similarly, in *Amit Upadhaya v. State Level Environmental Impact Assessment Authority,*[266] twelve mining projects had been given environmental clearance based on a single Regional Environmental Impact Assessment (REIA) Report. Excerpts from the regional report had simply been copied and pasted into the individual reports without application of mind. In other words, there was no EIA done individually for each project. Adding to this, the regional EIA had numerous defects. Therefore, the Tribunal held that solely relying on the regional EIA could not possibly capture the individual environmental impacts of each project. At most, the regional EIA would reflect the macro issues in the area. However, to assess the actual micro impact of each project it was necessary that individual EIAs be done for each project. This was necessary as each project, albeit similar in scope, would invariably have different risks and environmental impact. If the environmental clearances would be allowed on the basis of the regional EIA, the NGT held that it would result in a situation where the "environment [would be] the net looser ... which cannot be permitted in terms of the tenets of precautionary principle".[267] Consequently, the environmental clearances given to the projects were quashed by the Tribunal.

Based on our discussion, the NGT's use of the precautionary principle can be said to be overall in line with the strong model of the principle. However, the Tribunal has had a different approach with respect to large-scale developmental projects. Much like the Supreme Court in the *Narmada Dam Case*[268] and the *Tehri Dam Case,*[269] the NGT has refrained from outright banning the activity despite pleas to stop construction until the project is proven to be environmentally benign.[270] Akin to the Court, the NGT in these cases has preferred to add conditions that the project proponent must fulfil to mitigate and, if possible, prevent adverse environmental harm.[271] Due to this reason, the overall approach of the NGT can be said to be in between the moderate and the strong model of the precautionary principle.

In conclusion, the NGT's use of the precautionary principle has been much more consistent than the Supreme Court's. It has been able to successfully navigate between the mixed precedents provided by the Court and has created its own jurisprudence with respect to the principle. It has upheld the reversed burden of proof and has held that the three environmental principles – sustainable development, the precautionary principle, and polluter pays principle – are required to be considered by governmental authorities in their decision-making process.[272]

Unlike the Court's approach to the principle in the *Narmada Dam Case*[273] and the *Tehri Dame Case*[274] where the Court deferred to the executive and held that the precautionary principle is not applicable as the extent of damage was "fully known", the NGT has applied the principle consistently. It has acknowledged that though governmental authorities claim that they have assessed the full extent of possible environmental damage, it is practically impossible to do so. Further, unlike the Court, which had held that its scope of review of the decision-making process was limited to procedural correctness, the NGT has asserted that it can review the decision-making process on merit.

Partly, this assertiveness of the Tribunal can be traced to the fact that it is statutorily bound to apply the precautionary principle. Further, given that the Tribunal has the added advantage of having expert members on the bench, the assessment of scientific data becomes easier, and the application of the precautionary principle becomes more pragmatic. However, as noted previously, the NGT has also fallen short of halting large-scale public projects.[275] It has, instead, preferred to stipulate more conditions to mitigate and prevent environmental damage.

Overall, the NGT has produced a far more uniform jurisprudence of the precautionary principle than the Supreme Court, and this application has tended to be between the moderate and strong versions of the principle. Let us now analyse some important cases of the NGT in relation to the precautionary principle in detail.

3.2.4   PRECAUTIONARY PRINCIPLE – CASE EXCERPTS AND ANALYSIS

National Green Tribunal

(Principal Bench, New Delhi)

Indian Council for Enviro-legal Action v. MOEF

[Original Application No. 170 of 2014, Judgment Dated 10 December 2015]

Swatanter Kumar, J. (Chairperson)

*   *   *

Relevant Extracts:

1.   The applicant, a registered voluntary organisation working in protection of environment, rivers and lakes has filed the present application with the following prayers.

"A) Direct all the companies producing HCFC-22 to stop immediately venting HFC-23 by product and incinerate/destroy the same under the supervision of Respondent 1, 2 and Independent experts/body as deemed fit and proper by this Hon'ble Tribunal.

B) Direct respondent number 1 and 2 to immediately inspect the above said chemical Companies manufacturing HCFC-22 and thereby producing HFC-23 by product and file a status report of production, storing/venting. Incinerating the same by using the state of art and technology…."

2. According to the applicant, the above directions need to be issued as HFC-23 is being produced as a by-product while manufacturing of HCFC-22 and that it has serious climatic impacts, particularly, air pollution. The emission of this by-product is 14,800 times more global warming potential (being a greenhouse gas) compared to Carbon dioxide. The various companies who have been impleaded as respondents No. 5 to 9 are manufacturing HCFC-22 from their refrigerant production units resulting in the by-product of HFC-23 which is seriously dangerous to store in comparison to destroying the same through scientific methods. There is a need of having state of art destruction method/incineration of this by-product….

3. HFC-23, according to the applicant, is one of the most potent Greenhouse Gas under methodology 0001 of Clean Development Mechanism (CDM) of United Nations Framework Convention on Climate Change (UNFCCC).… HFC-23 is primarily a waste product that if vented/emitted into the atmosphere, will make a significant contribution to atmospheric gas concentrations, given the extra ordinary potency of HFC-23 with a GWP of 14,800 in comparison to CO2.

4. Respondent No. 5 is India's largest HCFC producer, so are the other respondents the 5 Indian fluoro chemical companies have made a cumulative revenue from HFC-23 destruction of Rs. 5000 crores (almost 1 billion US$), since 2007.

5. The producers of HFC-22 in all developed countries incinerate rate HFC-23 generated at the cost of doing business. So, the companies in India should be required to take similar steps. Rather than fulfilling the obligation of destroying HFC-23 emissions, the Indian CDM plants are continuing to demand that they be paid to destroy their HFC emissions. In absence of transparency, there is every likelihood that these companies may set off a climate bomb and vent all their HFC-23 amounting to 1000 tonnes of Carbon dioxide by 2020 into the atmosphere unless rest of the world pays them not to do so.…

6.   ... It is also averred by the applicant that the service industry in India is not regulated and most of the workers working in the service industries have no proper workshop facilities and are unqualified.... [I]nstead of storing or taking out gas, a large quantity of gas is released into the air resulting damage to the environment and health of the workers by inhaling such gases. Thus, there is a dire need to regulate the service sector in this direction. The applicant has relied upon Articles 47, 48 A and 51 A (g) of the Constitution of India, along-with the provisions of the Environment (Protection) Act, 1986 (for short the 'Act of 1986'). On these facts, the applicant has claimed the above prayers before this Tribunal.

7.   MoEF, the main respondent in this case has filed an affidavit raising a preliminary issue, that the application does not fall within the ambit of the powers conferred upon this Tribunal under Schedule 1 of the National Green Tribunal Act, 2010 (for short 'NGT Act, 2010'). On merit, it is stated that the HCFC-22 and HFC-23 is already regulated internationally by the Montreal Protocol. Emissive HFC-22 shall be phased out by 2030 in accordance with the said Protocol. It is also stated that there is no domestic law/rules regulating this aspect and in regard to regulating HFC-23 destruction, new rules need to be framed. It is deemed that the subject matter of the application is a matter of global concern and a policy that is constantly evolving to suit the needs of the hour is required to be framed. It is stated that the contribution of HFC-23 in the overall Global Warming is miniscule, at less than 1 per cent of the warming, which is mostly caused by other gases such as CO_2, methane, NO_2, HFCs, PFCs and SF-6. It is also stated by this respondent that the application is not supported by any statistics and therefore, the averments cannot be relied upon. MoEF states that it has already devised a HCFC phase-out Management Plan. Stage-I of this plan comprises of the combination of interventions such as technology, policies and regulation, technical assistance, training, awareness, coordination and monitoring in HCFC consuming sectors which is being implemented under the direct supervision of the Ozone Cell of the Ministry. It is stated that there is no scientific basis whatsoever for isolating HFC-23 selectively from the basket of 6 Greenhouse Gases, identified and regulated by the UNFCCC.

8.   ... It is also stated that HFC-23 is a by-product of HCFC-22, which is still used in refrigeration and Air Conditioning processes. HCFC-22 for emissive use such as refrigerants is regulated under the Montreal Protocol. It has been further submitted that HCFC-22 used for feed/stock is not controlled under Montreal Protocol since it is a non-emissive use of the same.... The answering respondent submits that issue of HFC-23 release into atmosphere

is not severe or life threatening and is already regulated by UNFCC. Finally, it is submitted on behalf of the Ministry that there are no administrative laws/rules regulating greenhouse Gases or HFC-23 destruction in the Country....

10. Respondent No. 5 has filed another affidavit on 9th April, 2015.... On merits it is stated that manufacture of HCFC-22 cannot be possibly stopped as it is a intermediate product for manufacturing Polytetrafluorethylene by the answering Respondent and it has wide use in industrial and domestic sectors as a refrigerant. HFC-23 is a by-product accounting for roughly 1–3% of HCFC-22.... This respondent also states that there is no law prohibiting emission. It is denied that they are violating any environmental laws including the Act of 1986....

15. First of all, we may deal with preliminary objection raised by most of the respondents stating that the present application is not maintainable as the application falls beyond the purview and scope of the provisions of the National Green Tribunal Act, 2010 (for short, "NGT Act"). The objection is that release or dealing with the by-product HFC-23 does not fall within any of the Acts specified in Schedule-I of the NGT Act and therefore, the Tribunal should not entertain this application.

16. According to the applicant, HFC-23 is polluting the air and in any case, this is a greenhouse gas leading to impact on global warming thus, finally affecting the environment/atmosphere. There is no specific Indian Legislation or law in force to deal with incinerator emission or otherwise with HFC-23 but it would be squarely covered under the Act of 1986 and therefore, the Tribunal would have jurisdiction.... [T]he scope of Act of 1986, does not relate only to air and water but even pollution of environment and atmosphere.

21. In light of what has been referred above, it is clear that the Tribunal exercised its jurisdiction within the provisions of the statutes under which it is constituted. The Tribunal is a creation of statutes and has to work within the confines of this statutes. But what is more significant is that language of the Act of 1986 and NGT Act, 2010 have to be given its correct interpretation which would help in protecting, conserving and improving the environment and particularly with the application of the provision of Section 20 which not only imposes upon the Tribunal an obligation to decide the cases on the strength of precautionary principles but even the inter-generational equity has to be kept in mind. HFC-23 may or may not be a pollutant per se but even if it is not still it will not be correct to contend that mostly on that ground alone the Tribunal would have no jurisdiction. Once it is a part of the greenhouse gases which admittedly are responsible for causing global warming there

appears to be no reason as to why the Tribunal will not exercise its jurisdiction on the principles stated in section 20 of the NGT Act, 2010 read with section 2(a) of the Act of 1986.

23. Coming to the merits of this case, let us notice some undisputed facts. It is not in dispute that there is no domestic law regulation in place to regulate any of the facets of HFC-23 in the country. The approach adopted by the Ministry of the concerned authorities is merely administrative in content and application both. Presently, this aspect is entirely governed internationally by the UNFCCC with reference to Montreal and Kyoto Protocol at the UNCCC.

24. It is also not in dispute that the HFC-23 forms a part of the basket of greenhouse gases which have an impact on depletion of ozone layer and global warming. Of course, there is some concern with regard to the extent and degree thereof.

25. There is dispute if HFC-23 emissions per se are a pollutant. According to the respondents, including MoEF and CPCB, it is nontoxic and non-pollutant. However, according to the applicant, the emission of HFC-23 in the air causes air pollution and has adverse impacts on human health and environment. The UNFCC itself had noticed that there are uncertainties in prediction of climate change particularly with regard to timing, magnitude and original pattern thereof…

27. In our considered view, we have no hesitation to say that contents of the application are a matter of global policy and therefore there would be a very little role for the statutory authorities within the country to take appropriate measures. The international convention and treaties have to provide a path for domestic legislation and in any case it has failed and it has to be regulated without further delay. At present, there is no detailed study placed before us to finally determine whether HFC-23 can have pollutant or toxic impacts on the air per se or not. Suffice is it to note that undisputedly HFC-23 has an effect on global warming being part of greenhouse gases. According to the Ministry, the Stage-I phase-out management plan comprising of a combination of interventions such as technology, conversions, policies and regulations, technical assistance, training, awareness, coordination and monitoring in selected HCFC consuming sectors implemented under the direct supervision of ozone cell by the ministry. This itself shows that there are concerns about the impacts on HFC-23 particularly in relation to global warming which would have adverse consequences in relation to agriculture, atmosphere and even social economic life of country, it will also have noticeable impact on atmosphere and environment. Corollary to this case is to travel into the field

of specifying regulatory and technological regime that should be enforced till proper legislation is enacted by the competent legislature. In our considered view, since it is a part of policy of Government of India at the global level, it not only has environment concerns but has also socio economic and wide range implications in the country and it may not be advisable for us to provide for bridging gaps in policy particularly at this stage. It is a field having vacuum but at the same time it is a field which cannot be ignored as well any further. The concerned quarters have to apply their mind and create some regulatory regime and appropriate guidelines till the legislative pillars of the country decide to enact some law in the direction.

28. We expect MoEF & CC and CPCB along with other concerned Ministries or expert bodies to carry out complete and comprehensive data base study in relation to all the units which are manufacturing HCFC-22 which results in by-product of HFC-23. The study should relate to the mechanism of storage, handling incinerators and emission standards of HFC-23. There should be a definite study on the question of HFC-23 being a pollutant and the extent of its impact on global warming being part of greenhouse gases. Let the study be conducted expeditiously. However, in the meanwhile, authorities should also issue appropriate interim and long term measures in terms of section 3 of the Act of 1986.

29. For the reasons afore-stated, we dispose of this application with a direction to MoEF & CC and CPCB to examine the entire regulatory regime in relation to HFC-23 a by-product of HCFC-22 and issue appropriate guidelines in all aspects thereof. We also direct them to issue interim and long term measures in terms of section 3 of the Act of 1986.

* * *

NOTES AND QUESTIONS

1. The case concluded with the Tribunal ordering comprehensive studies to be undertaken so as to remove scientific uncertainty surrounding HCF 23. Nearly ten months later, in October 2016, an executive order was issued wherein it was decided that HFC 23 would be eliminated and existing stocks of the chemical would be destroyed. This action was in stark contrast to the MoEF's submissions in the instant case, which projected the chemical as not warranting separate regulatory attention since its cumulative effect on the environment was "miniscule". Quite logically, it can be inferred that the NGT's decision of directing study into the effects of HFC 23 was well placed and must have played an important role in bringing about the final order.

2. Although the precautionary principle is a part of the law of the land, the instant case shows how judicial scrutiny is in fact the main factor enforcing the principle, without which regulatory authorities would fail to observe the principle in spirit. Should the Tribunal take a proactive approach in all cases involving scientific uncertainty, or should latitude be allowed to regulatory authorities to respond to the uncertainty themselves?

3. The priority of the Tribunal in the instant case was to remove scientific uncertainty to the maximum extent possible and not ban the chemical straightaway. Would it be proper to seek to achieve maximum scientific certainty, if it is realistically viable to acquire more data, in all cases involving the precautionary principle, or can there occasionally be situations where more stringent actions could be taken without trying to achieve maximum certainty, even though data required to do so can be viably acquired?

* * *

National Green Tribunal

(Western Zone Bench, Pune)

Satara Municipal Council v. MOEF and Others

[M.A. No.19/2015 (WZ) in Application No.135 (THC)/2013(WZ), Judgment Dated 9 February 2017]

Dr. Justice Jawad Rahim, (Judicial Member)
Dr. Ajay A. Deshpande (Expert Member)

* * *

Relevant Extracts:

1. This is a unique case where this Tribunal was required to invoke its inquisitive jurisdiction in order to reassert the well settled principles of environmental jurisprudence namely; 'precautionary principle' and 'Doctrine of public trust' to adequately address issues related to environmental sustainability of proposed reconstruction of Kas dam, located in close proximity of 'World Heritage site of Kas plateau' which is also an environmentally eco-sensitive zone (ESZ).

4. The Applicant's contention is that presently the drinking water supply to Satara city is provided from the existing Kas water storage reservoir which is about 35 km. away from Satara city.... [I]t is necessary to augment the water storage at the Kas dam to cater to the long term water requirement of Satara

city. The Applicant has therefore proposed that the height of the existing Kas dam be increased by 12.45m to enhance the water storing capacity of the dam from 107 Mcft to 500 Mcft. Applicant's further contention is for this augmentation project, they will need additional 23.63 Ha. of non-forest land as well as 2.67 Ha. of forest land at village Kas, Taluka Jaoli, District Satara. That both these land areas are covered in proposed ESA as per the draft notification by Ministry of Environment, Forest (MoEF) on 10th March 2014 regarding eco-sensitive area in the Western Ghats.

5.   The Applicant claims it has obtained all necessary permissions for this project, including in-principle forest clearance vide MoEF letter dated 19/12/2014. On that basis they have submitted their Application for EC to SEAC Maharashtra and vide order dated 21st March 2013, the said project was appraised for grant of TOR by SEAC. Thereafter, the SEIAA, Maharashtra has also appraised the project and sought clarification of MoEF regarding permissibility of such project in ESA area. The Applicant contends that MoEF vide letter dated 13th November 2013 informed SEIAA that the drinking water projects as well as hydro power projects are not prohibited in ESAs. Thereafter SEIAA, Maharashtra in its 25th meeting has considered the Communications from MoEF regarding non-applicability of Environment Clearance Regulations 2006 for the drinking water projects and agreed with the clarifications received from MoEF.... The Applicant has therefore, approached this Tribunal for grant of leave to go ahead with the project and also to cut the 675 trees as identified by the Forest Department, in compliance to the condition stipulated in the in-principle Forest Clearance granted to the project.

7.   ...Considering the proximity of the proposed project to the 'World Heritage site' of Kas plateau which incidentally is also an ecologically sensitive area, this Tribunal had to be more cautious while dealing with this particular Application.

8.   ... [T]he Tribunal was constrained to appoint a two Members Expert Committee... The Committee finalised the Terms of reference in consultation with the authorities and submitted the final report....

9.   The report of this Expert Committee is quite elaborate and has explicitly recorded its findings in the clear terms as under:

> "... [T]he Committee is of considered opinion that the proposal should not be accepted at all nor it is desirable in the vicinity of World Heritage Site (Kas Plateau)".

10.   ... The Committee has also noted that neither there are any efforts reportedly made to identify alternate sources of drinking water for the city of Satara

nor any alternative measures for augmentation of local water supplies are proposed. The Committee has also recorded that total 3375 trees are required to be cut for the construction of the project as against 675 trees as reported by the Applicant....

15. And finally, the MoEF has not offered any comment or opinion on the said report of the Expert Committee, on various technical issues flagged by the committee raising serious apprehension of environmental degradation and effect on the eco-sensitive area of Kas plateau.

20. The sum and substance of all the above factual matrix, would lead to a critical issue which the Tribunal has to decide: "Whether any project which may not require Environment Clearance as per EIA Notification, 2006 but is likely to have adverse impacts on environment, is not amenable to environmental Regulations and statutory supervision?"

27. ... [T]he Environmental Clearance Regulation 2006, in no case, restricts the responsibility and supervisory powers and control of the Central Government in terms of Section 3 and Section 5, as listed above, to protect the environment. The Central Government has full powers and more importantly, responsibility over and above, as notified by Environment Clearance Regulations 2006, under the provisions of Environment (Protection) Act, 1986 to take suitable measures to protect the environment. The Environment (Protection) Act, 1986 essentially aims at covering such gaps in environmental governance and the language of Section 3 of the Act would clearly demonstrate the legislative intent to empower MoEF in all such scenarios where environmental protection and conservation issues are raised or contemplated.

32. Another important aspect of environmental litigations is related to uncertainty of event, particularly, the impact on the environment. The environment is evolving science and many of the anticipated impacts and scenario cannot be assessed beforehand due to complexity and dependency of such predictions on innumerable attributes which are primarily dynamic in nature. The Hon'ble Supreme Court has therefore expanded the precautionary approach to even consider such uncertainty in the environmental matters and has held that the uncertainty is an accepted norm but the same has to be weighed and balanced towards environmental protection. In the instant case, the Tribunal is faced with a controversy where certain level of uncertainty is involved as far as environmental impacts of the proposed project on the unique and fragile eco-system of Kas plateau. We are conscious of the fact that in case of such uncertainty, the environmental protection and conservation of local eco-system needs to be the cardinal principle on which the Tribunal has to adjudicate....

34. The Public Trust Doctrine in the environment governance is a well settled legal proposition. Coupled with the precautionary principle, the public trust doctrine would envisage that the Central and State Government have the statutory responsibility to exercise sovereign supervisory and regulatory control and have an affirmative duty to ensure environmental protection while planning and executing such projects. In view of all the above facts and circumstances, we are not inclined to accept the stand of the MoEF or the Environment Department, State of Maharashtra that as the project of reconstruction of Kas dam do not attract the Environment Clearance Regulations, they are not legally obliged to ensure Environmental sustainability of this project.

40. ... [T]he Tribunal is required to consider the present application for grant of leave to cut the trees. The Tribunal is a statutory body and has to function within the framework of NGT Act, 2010, and do not have plenary powers as available with constitutional courts. The Hon'ble Supreme Court in Sachidanand Pandey Vrs. State of West Bengal, in A.I.R. 1987 S.C. 1109, 1114-15 has held that:

> "Whenever a problem of ecology is brought before the Court, the Court is bound to bear in mind Art.48A of the Constitution ... and Art.51A(g). When the Court is called upon to give effect to the Directive Principle and the fundamental duty, the Court is not to shrug its shoulders and say that priorities are a matter of policy and so it is a matter for the policy making authority. The least that the Court may do is to examine whether appropriate considerations are borne in mind and irrelevancies excluded. In appropriate cases, the Court may go further, but how much further will depend on the circumstances of the case. The Court may always give necessary directions. However the Court will not attempt to nicely balance relevant consideration. When the question involves the nice balancing of relevant considerations the Court may feel justified in resigning itself to acceptance of the decision of the concerned authority."

41. In view of above discussions, while holding that preservation, conservation and protection of pristine and fragile eco system of Kas plateau is the statutory duty and responsibility of the State and Central Government under the provisions of the Environment (Protection) Act, 1986 we are inclined to grant leave to cut 675 trees for proposed reconstruction of Kas dam, with following directions which we issue under Section 20 of the National Green Tribunal Act, 2010, based on the principles of sustainable development and precautionary principle:

1) The Central and/or State Government shall appraise and formulate environmental safeguard measures / management plan to be implemented by Satara Municipal Council and Irrigation department, prior to execution of the project.

2) The Central and State Government shall ensure the timely and effectively implementation of such EMP plans by regular monitoring and inspections.

3) In any event, if the project activities are found to be or apprehended to be detrimental to the eco-system of Kas plateau, the project proponent and also the Central and State Government shall immediately stop the construction activities of the project till necessary corrective actions are taken.

*   *   *

NOTES AND QUESTIONS

1. One of the primary strengths of the precautionary principle is that it emphasizes the consideration of alternative approaches when a certain approach is realized to be environmentally unsound. In the instant case, the Expert Committee pointed out that no efforts had been made to "identify alternate sources of drinking water for the city of Satara nor any alternative measures for augmentation of local water supplies are proposed". In this sense, the authorities' decision of tapping the Kas reservoir, which would inevitably have an ecological impact, was, in fact, not guided by the precautionary principle, which is the law of the land. This is just an instance of the general tendency of regulatory authorities failing to fully appreciate environmental principles.

2. The Tribunal, despite the Committee's decision against the proposed project, allowed the authorities to go ahead with the project, subject simply to an Environmental Management Plan and corrective actions being put in place. By citing the *Sachidanand Pandey Case*, the Tribunal indicated its reluctance to go into judging the propriety of the authorities' decision, even though the Expert Committee had pointed out the failure of the authorities to include relevant considerations. Even the number of trees required to be cut for the project had been miscalculated by the authorities. Given such apparent errors, was the Tribunal's reluctance well founded, or should the Tribunal have probed deeper into the decision?

3. The case highlighted the failure of the authorities to factor in relevant environmental considerations into their decisions, and their observance of only the bare minimum legal requirements while checking the environmental sustainability of the project.

This raises serious doubts about the effectiveness of principles such as public trust and the precautionary principle, which are mainly supposed to be enforced through the decisions of statutory authorities. Is there a need for better incorporation of these principles into the standard operating procedures of authorities that perform work related to environment and development?

* * *

National Green Tribunal

(Principal Bench, New Delhi)

Pandalaneni Shrimannarayana v. State of Andhra Pradesh and Others

[Original Application No. 171 of 2015, Judgment Dated 17 November 2017]

Swatanter Kumar, Chairperson,
Raghuvendra S. Rathore, Judicial Member
Bikram Singh Sajwan, Expert Member

* * *

Relevant Extracts:

1.   The applicant/appellants have raised a common question in respect to the formation of a new capital city for State of Andhra Pradesh....

3.   The applicant/appellants have now invoked the jurisdiction of this Tribunal ... to draw its attention to the Plan of State of Andhra Pradesh to build a Green Field New Capital namely; Amravati as it poses a serious threat to the environment and a large population. Therefore, the applicant has sought directions against State of Andhra Pradesh and Andhra Pradesh Capital Region Development Authority not to undertake any developmental activities, including urbanization or raising infrastructure on river flood plain, wet land and fertile agricultural lands which are part of the river catchment area. Further, directions have been sought against the Ministry of Environment, Forest and Climate Change (MoEF& CC) to constitute an Expert Committee consisting of independent experts from reputed institutions holding expertise on river ecology and hydrology, to undertake a comprehensive Environmental Impact Assessment due to large scale urbanization as well as infrastructure development in the region and also assess the social and livelihood impact of the said activities on people including the farmers and fishing communities. It has also been requested that all the respondents be directed to delineate hundred years flood line on

both the banks of river Krishna before undertaking any development in the region.

4.   The appellants … have prayed for quashing of the environmental clearance granted to the project….

6.   … [A]n Expert Committee was appointed by Government of India, Ministry of Home Affairs on 28.03.2014 to study various alternatives regarding new capital city. As per the terms of reference, the Committee was asked to consider issues like the least possible dislocation to existing agricultural system, preservation of local ecology, promoting environmentally sustainable growth, minimizing the cost of construction and acquisition of land, etc. The said Committee had submitted its report on 28.08.2014….

7.   The State Government had thereafter issued order dated 30.12.2014 identifying location of the capital city between Vijaywada and Guntur on the banks of river Krishna. Under the Notification, the Government has notified an area of about 7068 sq. km for capital region and 122 sq. km as Andhra Pradesh capital city…. [T]he State Government issued order dated 01.01.2015 notifying the Andhra Pradesh Capital City Land Pooling Scheme (Formation and Implementation) Rules, 2015. Under the Scheme, Andhra Pradesh Capital Region Development Authority is to procure land by signing agreement with land owners and farmers for minimal prices.

8.   The case of the applicant/appellant is that in the areas like Tullur Mandal of district Guntur, acquisition of some of the best fertile land is taking place. The land pooling scheme is facing opposition by the farmers as it would bring to an end the agricultural sector in the region.

10. According to the applicant/appellants, the State Government is in the process of acquiring about 1 lakhs acres of land along the banks and catchment areas of river Krishna for undertaking large scale urbanization without there being any EIA of the same and it poses serious threat to the environment of the catchment area of river Krishna….

35. Another issue raised in the application is the requirement of Comprehensive Environment Impact Assessment studies for development of the new capital city of Andhra Pradesh. Unless there is a proper study undertaken about the cumulative impact assessment of all proposed development activities, Cost-Benefit Analysis and Social Impact Assessment of the same on people and their livelihood is being undertaken, the State cannot even go ahead with the process of procuring lands. It is submitted by the applicants that they have filed the application for implementation of the precautionary principle to prevent loss of public money, agricultural land, destruction to

floodplains and wetlands which would be affected by the said development proposal.

48. ... It has been further submitted that since the State is at the initial stage of creating a new capital city and is having substantial period of time, it should take into consideration a comprehensive environment impact assessment scheme.

49. The land pooling scheme is completely against the provisions of the Environment Protection Act 1986 and there are various orders and directions of the Hon'ble Supreme Court and this Tribunal, pertaining to the same. Under the land pooling scheme the State Government is acquiring some of the best fertile land for agriculture in the country. Till date no assessment has been made of the negative consequence which would be caused due to conversion of agricultural land for urbanization, on such a large scale....

61. It has been argued by the respondents that the land pooling scheme has been adopted to ensure land owner participation and partnership in the process of development; to reduce the cost of building capital; avoiding the vexatious litigation and undue time constrains....

77. As per Section 6 of the Act of 2014, Central Government was to constitute an expert Committee to study various alternatives regarding the new capital for Successor State of Andhra Pradesh and make recommendations in a period not exceeding six months from the date of enactment of the re-organization Act. On 28th March, 2014 the Central Government had appointed an Expert Committee....

78. The Committee, on the review of the experiences of some other capital city development projects in India and abroad, identified the criteria that were to be used to decide on particular location. The criteria adopted by the Committee, in order of significance, are as under

    (i)   Availability of water

    (ii)   Connectivity

    (iii)   Favourable climate

    (iv)   Proximity to existing large urban Centre capital Land availability, suitability and cost an ease of construction

    (v)   Cost of ease of construction

    (vi)   Topography

    (vii) Centrality

(viii) Defence and security concern

(ix) Historical significance

130. The Sivarama Krishnan Committee has in its report clearly mentioned that the decision regarding location of the capital city is the prerogative of Government of Andhra Pradesh.

131. The Committee has not given any specific recommendation as to the location of the capital city which is clear from perusal of part VI of the report titled "Summary and Conclusion". The Committee has only identified "Potential Capital Zone Location" based on District and Capital Zone Suitability Index, wherein Vijyawada–Guntur region has come out to be the best among other zones.

205. In the instant case, the natural resources are being distributed in a fair, just and non-arbitrary manner for the benefit of the public at large. The distribution of land, the development of the Lanka islands, regulation of natural resources of water, etc. are being done in good faith, for the public good and in their interest which may in some manner result in encroaching upon such natural resources. Moreover, the public resources in the present case are not being diverted for commercial/private interest but for a project which will be for larger public good and serve interest of the State. Therefore, in our considered opinion, the Doctrine of Public Trust is not attracted in the present case.

216. … [T]he government had spent a substantial amount, running in crores. Besides, an amount of Rs, 128.92 crores had been spent by the State Government as annuity for loss of crops, to the farmers. Another instalment of Rs. 141 crores had also been released in the next year, for the same purpose. Before this, the State Government had to spend a huge amount for the farmers of Lanka islands who had to be rehabilitated and payments made for the land pooling scheme as they had volunteered for the same.

217. In view of the aforesaid development of new capital city for the State of Andhra Pradesh which has taken place with expedition because of the time frame, given for coming up of the new capital under the statute, substantial progress have already taken place. In such a situation, the Doctrine of Fait Accompli is attracted. A stage has now been reached where the position can be reversed only at a huge cost not only in financial terns but even environmental and human costs if the infrastructure already created were ordered to be demolished. In such circumstances the judicial Courts and Tribunals had been adopting a just and balancing approach by permitting the remaining work of the project to be completed. However, they have also provided stringent safeguards in the interest of environment.

220. Before parting with this case, we consider it appropriate to make certain observations with regard to Precautionary Principle. Though steps have already been taken in respect of establishing the capital for new State of Andhra Pradesh, but still much more remains to be done in future. Therefore, it is imperative for the State Government to adhere to the Precautionary principle. It may be required in the present situation and also in the times to come because the project of capital city would carry on for a sufficiently long period. Needless to say that it is more appropriate to take steps at this stage as delay may render them absolutely impracticable and even otherwise, prevention is better than cure.… In the present case which a big project and is a multifaceted one, we are of the view that this Principle should be applied with greater rigour, particularly when faults or acts of omission or/commission are attributable to the project Proponents.

221. It is with this purpose that we consider it just and proper to impose certain additional conditions, as would be mentioned hereafter, to the environment clearance. In view of the peculiar facts of this case a more detailed study on hydromorphology of the area needs to be undertaken to plan for adopting methods for water retention with the purpose of optimising water conservation. Similarly, before altering any flood plain, a study is required to be done. Likewise, the project proponent should not be permitted to alter the river course or that of natural storm water which can increase soil erosion and decrease ground water recharge. The existing embankments should not be altered, except for the purpose of flood protection. In order to have effective and proper implementation of the condition laid down by the Tribunal, it is deemed proper to have a proper committee constituted. Such committee would not only ensure the execution of the conditions in a time bound manner but also inspect the project to see that all environmental safeguards are in order. Above all, such committee shall submit its report to the Tribunal from time to time.

222. Even the Principle of Sustainable Development, by necessary implication, requires due compliance of Precautionary principle as well as the doctrine of Balancing. Such an approach can only protect the interest of environment and ecology in the capital city area of the new State of Andhra Pradesh. Therefore, efforts to be made by the project proponent, in furtherance of the aforesaid directions by way of additional conditions in the EC, formation of the committee for regulation for the projects yet to come up in future as much would be forthcoming in this big multifacet project of the capital of Andhra Pradesh, it is essential to prevent environmental problems which may arise in the coming times.

230. ... We have already held that the execution of present project, if carried out with due care, precaution and in consonance with the conditions imposed for environmental and ecological protection, would not be prejudicial to environment and ecology. The Tribunal has to balance the various factors which itself is an essential feature of Principle of Sustainable Development. The city project is being undertaken as a necessity of executive and legislative decisions taken by the respective competent forums. The State has to have its capital and as already discussed, no better site than the present one has been brought on record of the Tribunal. Large scale works of the project have already been executed at huge public expense and any prohibitory directions at this stage would not only jeopardize the financial interest of the State but would even become a serious environmental issue, capable of degrading the environment and ecology of the area to disadvantage of the public interest as well.

231. Thus we issue the following order and directions:

    I.   While declining to set aside the environmental clearance dated 9th October 2015, granted to the project, we hold and declare that the project, subject matter of the present application, falls under category B of the EIA Notification of 2006 and thus imposition of additional conditions would be necessary. They shall be applied *mutatis mutandi* to the conditions mentioned in the environmental clearance already granted to the project by the competent authority.

    II.   We direct that the following conditions shall be read as part of the environment clearance:

    ... 2) Any alteration of the flood plains by construction of storm water drains, retention ponds and related development within the capital city should be done only after conducting a study.

    3) No alteration of the river or natural storm water morphology, flow pattern and location by way of straightening shall be permitted, as such alteration may result in increase of soil erosion, sediment transport due to raised velocity and decrease in ground water recharge which may reduce base flow during the dry season.

    4) No alteration to the pre-existing embankments if any should be permitted except as may be required for its strengthening for flood protection of the proposed Capital City. Even such

exercise should be undertaken after detailed study of the flood pattern and hydraulics of the river or the storm water drains.

... 8) All the hills and hillocks in the catchment area of Kondaveeti Vagu, its tributaries and other storm water drains/channels should be treated with intensive soil and water conservation measures including afforestation so as to minimize surface run off and improve ground water recharge.

9) The capital city has about 251 acres of forest land which should be preserved as green lungs of the City and not to be diverted for non-forestry uses or even for uses like parks or recreational activities as that will alter its natural characteristics and deprive the capital of the ecosystem services which a natural forests provides, as opposed to a plantation forests.

III. In order to ensure proper implementation and compliance of the directions contained in this judgment and also to have requisite regulatory and supervisory control over the performance of the project proponent in the interest of environment and ecology, we constitute the following committees with the functions stated there-under:

I.   Supervisory Committee....
II.   Implementation Committee....

* * *

NOTES AND QUESTIONS

1. The instant case involved a major project, the construction of a capital city, which was initially decided to be located in the Vijayawada region, but was later relocated to the Amravati region, a region which was more environmentally sensitive, due to which litigation ensued. News articles and interviews highlighted how the initial behaviour of the government was environmentally inconsiderate and changed only after the intervention of the NGT. Even after the NGT ruling, detailed reports have come out highlighting deficiencies in the environmental credentials of the project as well as the process of environmental clearance followed.

2. Given the deficiencies and omissions that have been reported, do we need a stricter regime where the project proponent is actually deterred from ignoring important aspects of the EIA process? Does the EIA regime sufficiently incorporate the precautionary principle?

3. The NGT's application of the precautionary principle is considerably diluted due to the emphasis it lays on not letting used public funds go to waste. The Tribunal, therefore, leans towards a weak application of the principle. Would such a favourable treatment for public-funded projects be proper in all circumstances, or should the Tribunal be willing to take stricter action in some cases?

*   *   *

VEDANTA LIMITED v. STATE OF TAMIL NADU & ORS.

National Green Tribunal

Appeal No. 87/2018

(M.A. No. 1741/2018 & M.A. No. 1747/2018)

December 15, 2018

1. This appeal under Section 16 of the National Green Tribunal Act, 2010 … has been preferred against the orders dated 09.04.2018, 12.04.2018 and 23.05.2018 passed by the Tamil Nadu Pollution Control Board (hereinafter referred to as "TNPCB") and order dated 28.05.2018 of Government of Tamil Nadu under … [Water Act and Air Act]. The appeal was originally filed before this Tribunal on 22.06.2018. Subsequently, order dated 28.05.2018 passed by the TNPCB to permanently seal the appellant's unit was filed with an affidavit on 17.07.2018 to bring on record and challenge to the said order.

2. Case of the appellant is that it is engaged in extracting and processing minerals, including copper. It has a copper smelter plant at State Industries Promotion Corporation of Tamil Nadu Limited (SIPCOT), Industrial Complex, Thoothukudi, Tamil Nadu. In the said plant, the appellant manufactures copper cathodes, copper rods, sulphuric acid, phosphoric acid and other by-products in the process of smelting copper concentrate. The project was approved by the Government of Tamil Nadu on 13.05.1987 at 1083 acres, in Thoothukudi, Tamil Nadu, at an estimated cost of Rs. 938 lacs…, Environmental Clearance granted to the appellant was quashed by the Madras High Court and the unit was directed to be closed down in a petition filed by the MDMK a political party and CITU, a trade union organization. The order of the High Court was stayed and later set aside and reversed by the Hon'ble Supreme Court on 02.04.2013 in *Sterlite Industries (India) Limited and Ors. v. Union of India and Ors.*

4. … The Consent to Operate granted to the appellant's company was valid till 31.03.2018 under the Air Act and the Water Act. The appellant applied for

renewal on 31.01.2018 under the Air Act and the Water Act i.e. 60 days before expiry of the Consent to Operate. On 27.02.2018, inspection was carried out by a team of the TNPCB and the TNPCB found the appellant to be compliant of requisite standards.

5. On 24.03.2018, a protest was organized by certain persons against proposed expansion, which had been sought by the appellant. The appellant filed W.P. (MD) No. 7313/2018 seeking police protection....

6. On 09.04.2018, the impugned order was passed by the TNPCB. On 12.04.2018, the appellant filed an appeal before the Appellate Authority against the order dated 09.04.2018. The appellant also represented to the TNPCB to reconsider the consent renewal application on 13.04.2018.... In the meanwhile, on 12.04.2018, the TNPCB passed further order under Sections 33A of the Water Act and 31A of the Air Act directing that the unit shall not resume its production/operation without prior approval/renewal from the TNPCB.

8. Since the agitation against the unit of the appellant was continuing, the appellant filed W.P. (MD) No. 11190/2018 before the Madras High Court, seeking imposition of 144 of the Cr. P.C. to handle the agitation. The petition was disposed of on 18.05.2018 with the observation that the matter be considered by the authorities. Accordingly, order under Section 144 of the Cr. P.C. was issued but the agitation continued. On 22.05.2018, there was a police firing on the agitators, resulting in death of 13 persons.

11. On 28.05.2018, the State of Tamil Nadu endorsed the order of the TNPCB and directed TNPCB under Section 18(1)(b) of the Water Act to seal the unit and close it permanently.

[The Tribunal discusses the proceedings before it and the Supreme Court, along with the contentions of the appellant and the respondent.]

*   *   *

MAINTAINABILITY

44. It is undisputed that this Tribunal is an Appellate Authority as far as orders of closure under the Air Act and the Water Act are concerned. The impugned orders dated 12.04.2018, 23.05.2018 and 28.05.2018 are such orders. Mere fact that an appeal against the order declining renewal of Consent to Operate is provided for and was filed cannot be in the facts and circumstances of the present case, be a bar to exercise of powers of the Appellate Authority by this Tribunal. As already noted, the Appellate Authority has declined to proceed with the matter. The grounds in the impugned orders dated 09.04.2018, 12.04.2018, 23.05.2018 and 28.05.2018 are identical. If the appeals are held

to be not maintainable, the appellant will be without any remedy against the order of closure. Order of the Appellate Authority is also appealable before this Tribunal under Section 16(f) of the NGT Act, 2010. We, thus, do not find any merit in this case in the objections of the respondent.

45. Mere fact that the State of Tamil Nadu also endorsed the order of the TNPCB and that order of the State is not appealable to this Tribunal, does not deviate from the legal position that order of TNPCB is appealable to this Tribunal. Moreover, order of the State of Tamil Nadu is not a policy matter but mere endorsement of order of the TNPCB.

48. The order of the Government of Tamil Nadu issued under Section 18(1)(b) of the Water Act also cannot be said to be an independent order but relied on and endorsing the views of the TNPCB which is under challenge and that are not sufficient for ordering closure or refusal to grant even consent. If there are no other materials for the Government of Tamil Nadu to arrive at conclusion of closure on the ground of irreversible pollution being caused to the environment allowing the unit to function, then it cannot be said to be a policy decision to close down the industry permanently and if any order was passed based on the order by the Pollution Control Board, without independent application of mind and arbitrarily, then that can also be incidentally considered by the Tribunal for the purpose of deciding the question of legality of that order. So, under the present circumstances, it is not a case of this Tribunal entertaining the appeals where there is inherent lack of jurisdiction to entertain the same.

49. ... [T]here is no ground to reject the appeal on the ground of maintainability so as to deprive the appellant any judicial remedy in the matter.

*   *   *

ON MERITS

50. As already noted, the reasons for refusal to grant consent and thereafter to close the unit of the appellant are:

    i. Not furnishing groundwater analysis report;

    ii. Not removing copper slag stored along the River Uppar and not constructing physical barrier between the river and the slag.

    iii. The unit did not have authorization to generate and dispose hazardous waste;

    iv. The unit has not analyzed parameters of heavy metals in the ambient air quality;

    v. The unit has failed to construct gypsum pond as per CPCB guidelines.

51. The grounds in the impugned orders can hardly be sustainable to justify the impugned orders. With regard to (i), we find that the ground water analysis reports are available with the TNPCB. If anything was still required to be done in that regard by the appellant, this could not be a ground for rejecting consent for renewal or for closing the unit without opportunity of hearing to the appellant. Even if there is a technical breach as contended on behalf of the respondents, the breach is trivial in nature causing no prejudice to anyone.

52. With regard to (ii), copper slag is not found to be hazardous nor has been found to be obstructing the flow even on visit of the site by the Committee. Physical barrier could be directed to be constructed for the entire area. The fact remains that there was no opportunity given in this regard to the appellant to comply with any such requirement. On this ground, refusal of consent to a running unit and its closure could not be justified.

53. With regard to (iii), expiry of authorization under the Hazardous Wastes (Management, Handling and Trans boundary Movement) Rules, 2016 could not be a plea against the appellant as it had already submitted the requisite application. It was TNPCB itself which was sitting over the matter. Moreover, no harm has been caused by such technical breach.

54. As regards the fourth ground of failure to analyse parameters in the ambient air quality, there is nothing to show that the appellant caused any violation of air quality norms. The appellant had conducted analysis and there was no requirement of analysis to be done in a particular laboratory in absence of TNPCB not having its own lab as stated in the impugned order itself.

55. The fifth ground, of not constructing gypsum pond as per the CPCB revised guidelines, is unfounded as time to do so is still available and pond had been earlier constructed as per guidelines then applicable.

56. Once it is so, the impugned orders are liable to be quashed.

57. … In the present case, the TNPCB has adopted hyper technical approach unmindful of object of law. So long as establishment is complying with the Pollution Control norms and is willing to take further precautionary steps, the Pollution Control Boards cannot arbitrarily close such establishments on hyper technicalities, as has been done in the present case. We expect TNPCB to have more focused and professional approach in performing its regulatory functions.

58. … The Madras High Court had directed closure of the appellant unit which was set aside by the Hon'ble Supreme Court in [*Sterlite Industries (India) Limited and Ors. v. UOI*]. The approach adopted was that the closure should

be ordered only if it is necessary for protection of environment and the unit cannot be made compliant even after taking steps. In this context, reference may be made to the following observations:

> "142. The action taken by the Board on 29th March, 2013 directing closure of the appellant-company's unit was not as much of a preventive direction with reference to precautionary principle as it was a punitive measure.... The parameters for taking punitive action are entirely different to the ones that may be required for passing directions as per precautionary principle. Since there was no reasonable scientific data and the Respondent Board itself did not even care to collect stack and ambient air quality samples post-23rd March, 2013, we fail to understand as to how such an order could be passed, particularly in view of the admitted position that there are large number of industries in SIPCOT and out of which quite a few industries are heavy and 'red' category industries in relation to causing pollution.... In the case of punitive action, it should be tested on the touchstone of validly proved action while in a preventive order, it could be done as per a reasonable apprehension of a prudent person. Stringent proof and specific scientific data is the very crux for passing such direction and absence thereof would vitiate the action taken."

60. Though the learned Senior Counsel appearing for the Government of Tamil Nadu and for the TNPCB relied on certain opinions made by certain experts in their articles regarding the possible pollution being caused by gypsum waste as well as copper slag, there is no scientific evidence to accept that as such. Further these opinions were formed by the authors of those articles based on the technology available in dealing with those factories during 1950 and prior to that. Technology has changed, and the reduction of the impact of by products on environment could be reduced to a larger extent on account of the new scientific methods available in manufacturing the main project by the industry. Further it is seen from the documents produced by both the parties that the base value of TDS level in and around Tuticorin is more than 4000 (Four Thousand) i.e., far higher than the standard prescribed by the authorities. Further even as per the reports of CPCB and TNPCB is clear that copper slag as well as gypsum waste are not leachable and non-hazardous. It was recommended for even land filling, road formation, manufacture of cement, etc. If it is a material causing pollution, then this would not have been recommended by the authorities for these purposes as well. Further there is no evidence to show that even assuming that certain components in the water are higher than the standard provided, it has caused any health hazards in the locality and the pollution caused on account of the same to the environment is irreversible and irremediable. Unless such things are satisfied by the

authorities by scientific data, it cannot be a ground for refusal to grant consent or permanently close an industry. There is a duty cast on the SPCB as well as CPCB to provide remedial measures to prevent environmental pollution by the industries in such circumstances and without adopting those remedial measures refusing the consent and direct closure on that ground is illegal and not sustainable in law.

61.   The documents produced by the appellant shows that there was no possibility of Joint Inspection being conducted on 18.05.2018 and 19.05.2018 as claimed by the Board authorities to pass the order of closure and seal the unit. There is no evidence produced on the side of the respondents to prove that any notice of such inspection was given and copy of the report has been furnished to the appellant to remedy the shortcoming if any noticed at the time of inspection as contemplated under Section 26 of the Air Act and Section 27 of the Water Act, and by virtue of Section 26 (2) of the Air Act, such report if violates Section 26 (3) and (4) of that Act is not admissible in evidence. So, relying on such inadmissible document by the authority without giving an opportunity to the appellant to meet the same is arbitrary and order based on that is illegal and liable to be set aside.

75.   ... we are of the view that the appellant may, on 'Precautionary Principle', take following steps in the larger interest of safeguarding environment:

(i).   The appellant unit to create a dedicated and interactive website with participatory Public Forum wherein the affected stakeholders can lodge their environmental related grievance for the time bound redressal and disposal by unit....

(ii).   The appellant unit to regularly monitor the ground water quality as mandated by TNPCB and upload the data in comprehensible form without fail on the website....

(iii).   The appellant unit shall also deposit a sum of Rs. 2.5 Crores as a token amount for their failures for Extended Procedures Liability for inappropriate handling 3.5 lakhs M.T of Copper Slag on patta lands with the State Legal Services Authority for creating and maintaining the environmental awareness in the area through the District Legal Services Authority by preparing a comprehensive action plan.

...

(v).   The appellant unit shall ensure effective and environmentally safe management of Copper Concentrate, Sulphuric Acid including its leakage, leachate management of Gypsum Pond leachate and stored Copper Sulphate electrolyte etc.

(vi). In addition to above, the safe handling of effluents and emissions including solid waste should be done by a monitoring group comprising of TNPCB, CPCB, and representative of District Administration at regular intervals and have the same uploaded on the said website in comprehensible form for creating awareness on functioning and environmental performance of appellant unit.

*   *   *

NOTES AND QUESTIONS

1. This case portrays how the state governments and the Pollution Control Boards can be politically motivated to act in a certain manner. The role of the Tribunal becomes crucial in such situations as it has to not only look after the interest of the people and the environment but also act as a neutral arbiter and uphold the due process rights of the industrialists. Do you think that the Tribunal has due consideration of the interests of all the stakeholders?

2. The Tribunal found no evidence on record of pollution from the industrial premises and therefore had to set aside the order for shut down. However, the local population were still protesting against the functioning of the plant. In the light of these circumstances, this case probably portrays how even though an industry might be in compliance with the environmental regulations, its operations might still be harming the local populace. Can we blame the environmental regulations for not being strict enough or for not being in line with the current science?

3.3   POLLUTER PAYS PRINCIPLE

3.3.1   INTRODUCTION TO THE POLLUTER PAYS PRINCIPLE

The polluter pays principle is one of the oldest and, perhaps, the most intuitive of all environmental principles. Ensuring that the polluter adequately bears the cost of pollution makes both practical and moral sense. While the term "polluter pays" is fairly recent, the idea behind it has deep historical roots. Around 400 BCE, Plato stated:[276]

If anyone intentionally spoils the water of another ... let him not only pay damages, but purify the stream or cistern which contains the water.

Thus, it was understood that the polluter should not only make amends for the environmental wrong done by restoring the environment to its original condition, but also compensate the victims of pollution. It was expected that the payment of damages in addition to restoring the environment would act as a deterrent for potential polluters. Similar justifications for ensuring that the polluter bears the cost of pollution are found in the policies and works of Kautiliya (around 300 BCE) – the prime minister of the Magadh Empire during the reign of Chandragupta Maurya – for the protection of commons. [277]

However, as noted previously, the quantum and intensity of environmental pollution substantially changed with the advent of the Industrial Revolution in Europe. Workers worked in hazardous conditions and spent their lives in dingy and filthy hovels. Entire cities were covered in a thick black smog for several months on end due to the coal-driven furnaces.[278] Despite these apparently deleterious effects, there were no environmental regulations during the Industrial Revolution. The uninhibited discharge of gasses and waste into the air and water bodies was legitimized by the dominant paradigm that saw the environment as a large "sink" to be used for the fulfilment of human desires.[279]

It was only much later during the early twentieth century that some regulations began to surface in Europe, after the impact of pollution on human health was more directly visible.[280] It was, however, economists who took the lead in determining solutions to environmental costs. The primary concern of economists during this period was how to make a polluter accountable to bear the costs of pollution. This stemmed from the fact that the costs associated with pollution were borne by the society in terms of loss of natural habitat, species, and human health. This social and environmental cost was external to the private cost of the polluter. Due to this external nature, these costs were called "externalities" in economic literature.[281]

Since the costs of these negative externalities were frequently borne by governments and people at large, the genesis of the polluter pays principle came from the notion that the polluter must internalize the costs of his or her negative externalities and pollution.[282] A. C. Pigou, the famous English economist, provided a classic example of negative externalities.[283] As noted, during the early twentieth century, pollution in England on account of burning coal ensured that major cities were covered in black smoke. In fact, pollution levels were so high that laundered clothes would become dirty by just being hung outside to dry.

The Manchester Air Pollution Advisory Board conducted a study wherein it highlighted the extra costs that the residents of Manchester had to bear due to the pollution. The Board concluded that the total loss to the city, including costs for washing material and fuel, was over GBP290,000 in a year. Therefore, in economic terms, one economic activity (coal industry) had a negative impact on another (laundry). This economic understanding of the polluter internalizing costs of negative externalities would later play an integral role in the formulation of the polluter pays principle at the international level.

Causes of environmental degradation were, however, far more complex and could not completely fit in Pigou's simple illustration. For instance, while it was easy to state that the polluter must internalize the costs of pollution, such internalization would become difficult due to practical reasons such as transboundary environmental harm. This was demonstrated in the *Trail Smelter Case*.[284] The case involved a smelter run by a corporation in Trail – a small town in southern British Columbia, Canada. The smelter used to process lead and zinc, and was vital to the economy of the town as it generated substantial employment.

The smoke produced by the smelter, however, was laden with sulphur dioxide. Over time, this smoke made its way south through the river valley and settled in north Washington after crossing the international border between Canada and the US. Several forests and farmlands were negatively impacted in the northern parts of Washington, and the US sued Canada for the harm done to its environment and farmers. The arbitration lasted several years, and a decision was finally arrived at in 1941. The arbitral tribunal held that Canada was responsible for paying damages and compensating the farmers in the US that had suffered on account of the pollution caused in Canadian territory.[285] By navigating through the clash of sovereignties, the *Trail Smelter Case* helped develop its jurisprudential legacy that came to be known as the Trail Smelter principles:[286]

(1) The state has a duty to prevent transboundary harm
(2) The polluting state should pay compensation for the transboundary harm it has caused (later come to be known as the polluter pays principle)

When the arbitral tribunal decided the case, there was a dearth of international law dealing with disputes regarding air pollution between states. In fact, this was the first time that the polluter pays principle had been applied in an international context.[287] Several years later, in 1968, the Committee of Ministers of the Council of Europe issued a Draft Declaration of Principles on Air Pollution. The impact of the *Trail Smelter Case* is apparent in this declaration as under Article 6 the declaration states:[288]

The cost incurred in preventing or abating pollution should be borne by whoever causes the pollution....

Shortly thereafter, in 1971, the Organization for Economic Co-operation and Development (OECD) held a seminar in Paris where the polluter pays principle was discussed in detail. This was the first time that the principle was discussed internationally between major developed states. This was a significant step in the recognition of the principle as the member states of the OECD were also the major contributors to environmental pollution.[289] Finally, in 1972, the OECD formally recommended the adoption of the polluter pays principle as the "Guiding Principle Concerning the International Economic Aspects of Environmental Policies".[290] Significantly, the OECD recommended:[291]

The principle to be used for allocating costs of pollution prevention and control measures to encourage rationale use of scarce environmental resources and to avoid distortions in international trade and investment is the so-called "Polluter Pays Principle". This principle means that the polluter should bear the expenses of the above-mentioned measures (that is; pollution prevention and control measures) decided by the public authorities to ensure that the environment is in an acceptable state. In other words, the cost of these measures should be reflected in the cost of goods and services which causes pollution in production and/or consumption. Such measures should not be accompanied by subsidies that would create significant distortions in international trade and investment.

This marked the first time that principle was explicitly incorporated, and the definition focused primarily on ensuring that states ensure that polluters in their respective jurisdictions internalize the costs of pollution. To achieve this, the OECD countries recommended that the cost of pollution control and prevention should be reflected in the final cost of goods and services produced by the polluter, rather than the costs being borne by governments through subsidies. This was important as subsidies by states would indirectly result in the internalization of costs by the taxpayer instead of the polluter. These were, however, general recommendations and the OECD left the application of the principle to individual states.

The OECD continued to build upon the polluter pays principle in subsequent recommendations,[292] thereby continuing to expand the contours of the principle and calling for its application among member countries. In this regard, the Recommendation on the Application of the Polluter-Pays Principle to Accidental Pollution[293] is particularly significant as it marked the first time that the doctrine of strict liability[294] was incorporated at the international level with respect to environmental pollution. The Recommendation stated:[295]

4. In matters of accidental pollution risks, the Polluter-Pays Principle implies that the operator of a hazardous installation should bear the cost of reasonable measures to prevent and control accidental pollution from that installation which are introduced by public authorities in Member countries in conformity with domestic law prior to the occurrence of an accident in order to protect human health or the environment.

5. Domestic law which provides that the cost of reasonable measures to control accidental pollution after an accident should be collected as expeditiously as possible from the legal or natural person who is at the origin of the accident, is consistent with the Polluter-Pays Principle.

6. In most instances and notwithstanding issues concerning the origin of the accident, the cost of such reasonable measures taken by the authorities is initially borne by the

operator for administrative convenience or for other reasons[3]. When a third party is liable for the accident, that party reimburses to the operator the cost of reasonable measures to control accidental pollution taken after an accident.

Although the OECD Recommendation limited the scope of the application of strict liability to jurisdictions where it was already accepted, it was an important step towards the proliferation of strict liability as a key measure under the polluter pays principle. Further, the recommendation highlights certain important philosophical notions relating to the ownership of the environment. The polluter pays principle is premised on the idea that the state or the community owns the natural resources and the environment and forces the polluter to essentially pay damages for causing harm to its property. In contrast, if the state or the community bears to costs of pollution, the implicit notion is that the polluter owns the natural resources and the environment and can pollute with impunity.[296]

Further, the OECD identified four types of costs that could be imposed on polluters: (a) pollution prevention and control costs; (b) costs of administrative measures; (c) the cost of damage to individuals; and (d) costs of accidental pollution.[297] However, in its guidelines, the OECD recognized that there might be situations where a less stringent application of the principle may be needed as the costs imposed on a polluter might lead to grave economic consequences for the general public.[298]

For instance, let us assume that there is a thermal electricity power plant that is located in a generally underdeveloped area. Its emissions are usually controlled and environmentally benign. It is the only source of electricity within the region and provides substantial employment to the people living in the vicinity. Due to its presence, the region has been able to initiate various developmental activities. By accident, however, the plant releases a cloud of chemically toxic fumes which severely damages the health of a few people. The compensatory costs under the polluter pays principle payable to the people, however, are so large that it would cause the plant to go bankrupt and would result in its closure. As a result, numerous workers would lose employment. The region would lose access to electricity and ongoing developmental works would be halted.

In such a situation, the OECD recommended that an exception should be created, and the application of the principle should be relaxed. While this relaxation accords practicality to the application of the principle by states, it provides considerable leeway to states determine what constitutes economic dependency to a certain project in an underdeveloped region. Further, while it seeks to balance environmental concerns with economic needs, it dilutes the deterrence effect of the principle.

In the early 1990s, the polluter pays principle gained further prominence through its recognition and incorporation in several transnational agreements,[299] the most prominent of which was the Rio Declaration on Environment and Development in 1992.[300] Principle 16 of the Rio Declaration recognized the principle and stated:[301]

National authorities should endeavor to promote the internalization of environmental costs and the use of economic instruments, taking into account the approach that the polluter should, in principle, bear the cost of pollution, with due regard to the public interest and without distorting international trade and investment.

Emphasis was placed on the preservation of international trade and investment by ensuring accountability for polluting parties. Given this added impetus, shortly thereafter the principle was incorporated into several international conventions such as the Helsinki Convention,[302] Bamako Convention on Hazardous Waste,[303] Protocol to the London Dumping Convention,[304] and the Convention for the Protection and Development of the Marine Environment of the Wider Caribbean Region.[305]

In the international legal sphere, the principle has gained significant recognition. It has been applied in several international cases.[306] However, like the principle of sustainable development and the precautionary principle,[307] there has been no formal recognition of the principle as being a part of customary international law. In this regard, it is important to take note of the *Nuclear Tests* Case before the ICJ[308] and, in particular, Justice Weeramantry's dissenting opinion. Alluding to, inter alia, the principles of sustainable development, the precautionary principle, and the polluter pays principle, Justice Weeramantry held that these principles are a part of customary international law. Further, he stated that these principles did not depend on treaty provisions for their validity as they are a "part of the *sine qua non* for human survival".[309]

As we will discuss in the next section, the Indian Supreme Court has upheld the aforementioned dissenting opinion of Justice Weeramantry and concluded that the principle is a part of customary international law. However, there is still considerable ambiguity in relation to the principle's international status despite its adoption by numerous States. While the principle has played an integral role in ensuring that the costs of pollution are internalized by the polluter, there remain some key challenges. These challenges include:[310]

a) There exists significant ambiguity with respect to who is a polluter. For instance, if a car is found to be polluting in excess of the prescribed limits, then then the owner is identified as a polluter. However, the manufacturer can also be said to pollute indirectly. Further, the government can also be said to contribute to the pollution due to the bad roads that led to excess pressure on the engine of the car. Thus, based on various policy considerations, different jurisdictions define who is a polluter differently.

b) Given that the principle requires the costs of pollution to be internalized by the polluter, this results in a general increase in prices for the goods or services sold by the polluter. Thus, the cost is eventually passed onto the consumer who bears the burden of pollution indirectly. In several developing countries, this becomes problematic as the increase in costs is not feasible for the poor population and the government is forced to intervene through subsidies.

c) Due to the elasticity of demand and excess competition, exporters from developing countries find it difficult to pass on higher prices to their customers abroad. Likewise, small producers in developing countries who cater to the home country find it difficult to increase prices as their customers are unlikely to be able to pay for their goods and services. These situations again warrant the intervention of the State through subsidies and mitigative measures.

Despite these issues, the principle has played an integral role in holding polluters accountable. It remains one of the foundational principles of international and domestic environmental law. To understand the domestic interpretation and application of the polluter pays principle, let us now study its use by the Supreme Court of India.

3.3.2   THE INDIAN SUPREME COURT AND THE POLLUTER PAYS PRINCIPLE

The Supreme Court has utilized the polluter pays principle for more than thirty years to hold polluters accountable for their actions by ensuring that polluters internalize the costs of pollution. The interpretation and application of the polluter pays principle by the Supreme Court was initially strong. However, lately, the application of the principle has become more moderate due to a few cases in which the Court has awarded environmental compensation as a percentage of the annual turnover of polluters with little regard to the actual environmental damage. We will now trace the evolution of the Supreme Court's use of the polluter pays principle and its impact on Indian environmental jurisprudence.

While the first explicit utilization of the polluter pays principle by the Court in India was in 1996,[311] the Court had been previously using the principle implicitly. For instance, while the Court did not expressly rely on the polluter pays principle while delivering its judgment in the *Oleum Gas Leak Case*,[312] the Court's decision in the case is widely regarded as one of the strongest applications of the principle in the world. This is because, in response to a hazardous gas leak from the premises of Shriram Industries, the Court created the principle of absolute liability which disregarded the previous exceptions available under the strict liability doctrine.[313]

The Court held that the previous tortious standard of strict liability derived from *Rylands v. Fletcher*[314] was outdated as it was made in the early nineteenth century when industrial developments were at a nascent stage. Accordingly, it held that a stronger standard was required which did not accord the exceptions available to a polluter under the old standard. The Court held:[315]

An enterprise which is engaged in a hazardous or inherently dangerous industry which poses a potential threat to the health and safety of the persons working in the factory and residing in the surrounding areas owes an absolute and non-delegable duty to the community to ensure that no harm results to anyone on account of hazardous or inherently dangerous nature of the activity which it has undertaken... if *any harm* results on account of such activity, the enterprise must be *absolutely liable to compensate for such harm* and it should be no answer to the enterprise to say that it had taken all reasonable care and that the harm occurred without any negligence on its part. (Emphasis supplied)

The development of the absolute liability doctrine is regarded as one of the strongest expressions of the polluter pays principle as it holds the polluter absolutely liable for any environmental or health-related harm resulting from an inherently hazardous activity. In the introductory section to the principle, we discussed how the OECD's Recommendation on the Application of the Polluter-Pays Principle to Accidental Pollution was particularly significant as it incorporated the doctrine of strict liability.[316] The Indian Supreme Court, however, took this a step further and held that the usual exceptions available to a polluter under the strict liability doctrine[317] such as act of god, plaintiff's own fault, and plaintiff's consent would not be applicable under the absolute liability doctrine.

Following the *Oleum Gas Leak Case*, the Supreme Court made the first express reference to the polluter pays principle in *Indian Council for Enviro-Legal Action v. Union of India*.[318] The case concerned certain industries that had discharged untreated toxic wastewater and sludge into the nearby areas. This, in turn, had led to severe deterioration of the soil and groundwater in the region. The local agricultural communities were adversely affected by the industrial effluents and demanded compensation.

The Court considered the polluter pays principle as a "universally accepted principle",[319] and highlighted the principle's growing international relevance. After adjudging that the rule of absolute liability laid down in the *Oleum Gas Leak Case*[320] was applicable, it invoked the polluter pays principle in conjunction with the doctrine of absolute liability to hold polluting industries accountable. This was significant as had the strict liability standard been applicable, the polluters in the case would have likely escaped liability citing that they had taken all reasonable care. Thus, in practice, this strong application of the polluter pays principle goes well beyond the standard suggested by the OECD and the Rio Declaration (1992).

Shortly thereafter, in *Vellore Citizens' Welfare Forum v. Union of India,*[321] the Court was concerned with the discharge of toxic effluents into water bodies and adjoining soil by tanneries in Vellore. This seriously contaminated the groundwater and made the land barren and infertile. In response, similar to the *Oleum Gas Leak Case*, the Court applied the polluter pays principle in conjunction with the absolute liability doctrine to hold polluters accountable.

In arriving at its decision, the Court referred to developments at the international level (such as the Stockholm Conference of 1972 and the Rio Declaration of 1992), which had brought environmental concerns to the centre of international lawmaking. Significantly, the Court held that international environmental principles such as the polluter pays principle, precautionary principle, and sustainable development were a part of customary international law.[322] Thus, where the ICJ had stopped short of declaring these principles as a part of customary international law, the Indian Supreme Court emphatically upheld Justice Weeramantry's dissenting opinion in the *Nuclear Tests Case*[323] discussed previously. The Court went on to state that these principles would be applicable in the Indian domestic context if they were not in conflict with Indian municipal law.

To this effect, the Court cited various provisions of Indian environmental legislations such as the Water Act, 1974, the Air Act, 1981, and the Environment (Protection) Act, 1985, and held that the polluter pays principle formed an integral part of the scheme of these legislations. Further, the Court located the principle as being necessary for giving effect to the constitutional provisions contained under Articles 21, 48A and 51(A)(g). Thus, the Court rightly concluded that the principle was already a part of the Indian constitutional and legal framework, though it had not been expressly mentioned.

This trend was carried forward in other significant decisions in subsequent environmental cases.[324] During this period, strong environmental precedents and deterrents were set by the Court to effectively deal with industrial pollution. In *M.C. Mehta v. Union of India* (popularly known as the *Aravalli Hills Mining Case*),[325] the Court held:[326]

> Where the regulatory authorities, either connive or act negligently by not taking prompt action to prevent, avoid or control the damage to environment, natural resources and people's life, health and property, the principles of accountability for restoration and compensation have to be applied.

Such an extension of the principle to hold authorities accountable was also observed in a case dealing with illegally operated industries in Delhi's residential areas.[327] In effect, the Court held that governmental authorities who blatantly ignore their duties and disregard environmental harm can also be held accountable under the polluter pays principle. This is because these authorities had an affirmative duty to ensure that the environment is not damaged, and a dereliction of this duty would mean that they are enabling pollution.

The Supreme Court has also voiced strong disapproval of measures taken to abuse the process of law. In *Indian Council for Enviro-Legal Action v. Union of India*,[328] attempts were made by the respondent polluters to file frivolous interlocutory applications to delay payments ordered by the Court under the polluter pays principle. In response, the Court imposed a significant penalty of INR 10 lakh on each polluter. This was a significant step by the Court to ensure that future polluters would take environmental compensations more seriously as this would dis-incentivize them from using such delay tactics.

In *M.C. Mehta v. Kamal Nath*,[329] the Court was concerned with the illegal construction of a motel. The construction had encroached upon forest lands located on the banks of

River Beas and, as a result, had artificially altered the path of the river. This caused serious environmental issues to the surrounding ecosystem.

The Court found the construction to be illegal and ordered the remediation of the damaged lands.[330] Subsequently, applying the polluter pays principle, the Court held:[331]

In the matter of enforcement of Fundamental Rights under Article 21, under Public Law domain, the Court, in exercise of its powers under Article 32 of the Constitution, has awarded damages against those who have been responsible for disturbing the ecological balance either by running the industries or any other activity which has the effect of causing pollution in the environment. The Court while awarding damages also enforces the "POLLUTER PAYS PRINCIPLE" which is widely accepted as a means of paying for the cost of pollution and control. To put in other words, the wrongdoer, the polluter, is under an obligation to make good the damage caused to the environment.

... Pollution is a civil wrong. By its very nature, it is a Tort committed against the community as a whole. A person, therefore, who is guilty of causing pollution has to pay damages (compensation) for restoration of the environment and ecology. He has also to pay damages to those who have suffered loss on account of the act of the offender. The powers of this Court under Article 32 are not restricted and it can award damages in a PIL or a Writ Petition as has been held in a series of decisions. In addition to damages aforesaid, the person guilty of causing pollution can also be held liable to pay exemplary damages so that it may act as a deterrent for others not to cause pollution in any manner.

Through this, the Court highlighted the scope of damages under the polluter pays principle. In addition to compensating for ecological restoration and paying damages to the victims of pollution, the Court clarified that the polluter can be held liable for exemplary damages. This would, the Court held, act as a deterrent for potential polluters.

So far, we have discussed the strong interpretation and application of the polluter pays principle by the Court. However, more recently, the Court has diluted this strong approach to the principle. This is exemplified in *Deepak Nitrite Ltd. v. State of Gujarat*.[332] The case involved certain industries that had been directed to pay compensation for causing environmental damage as their emissions were, admittedly, beyond prescribed limits. Nevertheless, the fact that the emissions were beyond the legal limit was not enough to hold the polluters accountable as per the Court. It held:[333]

The fact that the industrial units in question have not conformed with the standards prescribed by GPCB cannot be seriously disputed in these cases. But the question is whether that circumstance by itself can lead to the conclusion that such lapse has caused damage to environment. No finding is given on that aspect which is necessary to be ascertained because compensation to be awarded must have some broad co-relation not only with the magnitude and capacity of the enterprise but also with the harm caused by it. May be, in a given case the percentage of the turnover itself may be a proper measure because the method to be adopted in awarding damages on the basis of "polluter to pay" principle has got to be practical, simple and easy in application.... However, *to say that mere violation of the law in not observing the norms would result in degradation of environment would not be correct.* (Emphasis supplied)

This marks a surprising departure from the Court's earlier application of the polluter pays principle. Effectively, the Court held that environmental damages under the principle were only payable when tangible evidence of damage could be demonstrated. The fact that there was a legal harm did not feature in the Court's reasoning. Moreover, the prescribed legal limits, with due regard to the legislative wisdom, were put in place as any pollution beyond those limits would result in unreasonable environmental harm. The Court, however, did not consider this and held that environmental compensation was not payable.

If the Court's reasoning in this is taken to its logical conclusion, any polluter can escape liability, even if the pollution is admittedly beyond the prescribed legal limits, as long as there is no tangible proof of environmental degradation. Further, in another case,[334] the Supreme Court had upheld that the effect of environmental degradation has far-reaching effects, which are well beyond the local area. For instance, the destruction of forests is a leading cause of global warming but does not have tangible physical effects that are immediately observable. Thus, if the Court's reasoning in the *Deepak Nitrite Case* is applied in this context, polluters can continue to cut trees beyond the permissible limit till tangible environmental harm is observed.

Industrial effluents, by their very composition and nature, are pollutive. If the effluents discharged are within the legal limits prescribed, it does not mean that the environment is not being harmed. It simply means that the amount of environmental harm is legally tolerable. Thus, to begin with, the question as to whether there is actual environmental harm should not arise.

The High Court in this case had imposed a meagre compensation of 1 per cent of the annual turnover of the polluting corporation. Even this paltry amount was stayed by the Court. However, as is evident, this amount was not stayed due to its inadequacy or due to the problems associated with having a percentage of the turnover as compensation. Rather, it was stayed as the Court did not think the excess emissions warranted any environmental compensation.

In arriving at a compensation amount of 1 per cent, the High Court had relied on an earlier decision of the Supreme Court in *Pravinbhai Jashbhai Patel v. State of Gujarat*[335] wherein a similar compensation of 1 per cent of the annual turnover had been awarded. As discussed in the section on environmental compensation in Chapter 2, pegging environmental compensation to an economic variable such as turnover or sale proceeds has two significant challenges.

First, such compensation is not based on actual costs required to remediate and rehabilitate the lost natural resources and the environment. Accordingly, basing the compensation on a percentage of the annual turnover is likely to underestimate or overestimate the actual remediation costs. Second, when this trend becomes fixed and the percentage of annual turnover to be awarded as environmental compensation can be reasonably estimated given the precedents, it is likely to lose its deterrence. This is because a potential polluter is likely to proceed with a polluting project if it is expected to be reasonably profitable after taking into account the environmental compensation percentage to be paid. Thus, potential polluters are likely to treat this environmental compensation as an additional business cost, and this has the potential to convert the polluter pays principle into "pay and pollute" principle.

Subsequently, in *Goa Foundation v. Union of India*,[336] the Supreme Court was faced with the issue of determining the environmental damage caused due to certain illegal mining in Goa. In arriving at the compensation amount, the Court held that the project proponents would have to pay 10 per cent of the sale proceeds to a public fund – Goan Iron Ore Permanent Fund – as compensation.[337] The Court felt that this was an appropriate compensation given that mining could not be completely stopped due to its contribution towards employment and revenue generation for the state of Goa.[338] As we have discussed in Chapter 2 and as we will again reiterate in the next section, this case has been used by the NGT as a precedent for awarding environmental compensation as a percentage of an economic variable. For the reasons mentioned earlier, this trend has seriously diluted the application of the polluter pays principle.

In conclusion, the Supreme Court has, for the most part, effectively used the polluter pays principle to ensure that the polluter internalizes the costs of pollution. Significantly, the Court has formulated one of the strongest expressions of the polluter pays principle through its use of the absolute liability doctrine. Further, by holding that exemplary costs are necessary to ensure adequate deterrence the Court has upheld the punitive aspect of the principle. However, as we have discussed, lately the Court has diluted this strong approach through the calculation of environmental compensation as a percentage of an economic variable. If this trend continues, it is less likely to deter a potential polluter and is expected to convert the polluter pays principle into the principle of pay and pollute.

Given this context, let us now analyse the NGT's interpretation and application of the polluter pays principle.

3.3.3   THE NGT AND THE POLLUTER PAYS PRINCIPLE: INTERPRETATION AND APPLICATION

As we have noted in our previous discussions on sustainable development and the precautionary principle, the key difference between the Tribunal and the Supreme Court is that the Tribunal is bound to consider the polluter pays principle while passing an order under Section 20 of the NGT Act. In addition, Section 17(3) of the NGT specifically adopts the Supreme Court's standard of absolute liability developed in the *Oleum Gas Leak*

Case[339] (refer to the previous section) by stating that the Tribunal shall apply the principle of "no-fault" in the event of an accident.

Being armed with these statutory prescriptions in its arsenal, one would assume that the NGT would have applied the polluter pays principle in a robust manner. Indeed, in certain cases it has done so. However, as we will demonstrate through an analysis of case law, the NGT's application of the principle has been mixed. While in some cases it has held governmental authorities adequately accountable through the imposition of exemplary costs, in other cases it has allowed the same authorities to get off scot-free despite complete dereliction of their duties. Likewise, while in some cases the NGT has imposed significant costs on polluters, in many cases the imposition of environmental compensation is inadequate. As we have also highlighted in Chapter 2, this is due to the Tribunal's trend of pegging compensation to a percentage of an economic variable, irrespective of the actual environmental damage. Let us now explore these trends through an analysis of case law.

An important step towards ensuring that polluters internalize the costs of pollution has been the NGT's use of the pollute pays principle in relation to the masses. In *Manoj Mishra v. Union of India*,[340] the Tribunal was concerned with widespread pollution across different stretches of the River Yamuna. It came to light that nearly 400 to 500 tons of waste debris per month was being dumped on the banks of the river in Geeta Colony. Applying the polluter pays principle, the Tribunal held that any person who is found dumping debris on the riverbank at any place on River Yamuna will be liable for paying INR 5 lakh for causing pollution. Similar orders were later passed in relation to pollution in River Beas.[341]

Similarly, in *Jagat Narayan Vishwakarma v. Union of India*,[342] the Tribunal was faced with widespread pollution of water bodies on account of industrial discharge in the states of Uttar Pradesh and Madhya Pradesh. The reservoirs that had been polluted were the main source of drinking water for the adjoining villages. In response, the NGT directed the Chief Secretaries of these two states to direct all large industries operating in the concerned regions to install RO (reverse osmosis) water treatment plants and ensure the supply of uncontaminated drinking water to all the affected villages. This direction was given over and above the compensation liable to be paid by the polluters. This, the Tribunal ensured that all concerned industries effectively internalized the cost of their pollution.

In a creative application of the polluter pays principle, the NGT has held individuals and corporations liable to pay fees for the establishment of a solid waste management system under the principle. In *Kamal Anand v. State of Punjab*,[343] the Tribunal was concerned with the implementation of the Municipal Solid Waste Management Rules, 2000, in Punjab. In particular, it was concerned with the lack of solid waste management in the area. Upholding the model action plan submitted by the State Government, the Tribunal held:[344]

On the basis of polluter pays principle, the corporation will charge every household, shop, hotel, or any industrial building to pay specific amount along with the property tax payable for the property, or on monthly basis, whichever is permitted by the concerned authorities. The amount shall be notified and duly publicised before implementing the same. Such payment at the specific rate would be applicable with effect from 1st January, 2015. The amount collected as afore-directed shall only be used for effective collection and disposal of MSW [Municipal Solid Wastes] in accordance with the rules and for educating masses in relation to the need for helping bodies/ authorities concerned to collect the MSW in appropriate manner.

Thus, the Tribunal held that households and corporations could be required to pay specific amounts as a fee by authorities to mitigate environmental degradation, in furtherance of the polluter pays principle. This crystallized the application of the principle as being applicable to individual citizens by requiring them to comply with municipal rules to ensure protection of the environment.

The Tribunal has also applied the polluter pays principle to hold polluters accountable even when a petitioner is unable to establish the extent of environmental damage. In *Ashok Gabaji Kajale v. Godhavari Bio-Refineries Ltd.*,[345] certain agriculturists alleged that emissions from an industrial unit were causing groundwater pollution, leading to a loss of agricultural produce. The agriculturalists, however, had not advanced any specific evidence to prove that degradation of the agricultural land had actually occurred. The Tribunal noted:[346]

> There is no escape from the conclusion that Godavari Bio-Refineries Ltd., i.e. Respondent No. 1 is required to pay damages caused due to operation of the industrial unit. Though, the Applicants have claimed that their agricultural lands are damaged in terms of its fertility and the yield, no such report has been placed on record. MPCB had directed the industry to engage the agricultural university but no such report is placed on record. In view of that though presently it may not be possible to decide the exact scope and quantum of such loss/damages, however, we may consider an approximate area within 2 km radius of the industry that can be assessed and verified by a Committee, constituted for such purpose. We hold that the Respondent No. 1-industry is also liable to pay the damages for the loss caused to the land-owners, to bear costs of remediation and to ensure the zero discharge.

Clearly, the appellants in the case were unable to provide evidence of damage to their farmlands in terms of loss of fertility and yield. Nevertheless, the Tribunal relaxed requirements of evidence from the appellant and concluded that since there was environmental damage generally, the farmlands must have been damaged as well.

This decision of the Tribunal assumes significance when it is juxtaposed with the Supreme Court's holding in the *Deepak Nitrite Case*[347] (discussed in the last section). In that case, the Court had held that the fact that the pollution was beyond prescribed legal limits was not enough to make the polluter liable for compensation. It held that the appellant had to demonstrate tangible or physical environmental harm to receive compensation. As noted, this seriously diluted the Court's otherwise strong approach to the principle. The NGT, through the aforementioned case, upheld the strong application of the principle by requiring the polluter to pay compensation even though the appellant was not able to provide evidence of physical harm.

One of the most robust and stringent applications of the polluter pays principle by the NGT was seen in *Gurpreet Singh Bagga v. Ministry of Environment and Forests.*[348] The Tribunal was concerned with rampant illegal mining in the Saharanpur region in Uttar Pradesh. The mining units were operating in complete violation of all relevant environmental norms. The judgment is noteworthy for its deliberation on the issue of scientific exactitude in damage assessment. The Tribunal stated:[349]

> Once the nexus between the activity, particularly illegal activities, and the consequential damage to the environment and ecology is established, the liability in terms of Section 15 and 17 of the NGT Act arises. There could be cases where it is not possible to determine such liability with exactitude but that by itself would not be a ground for absolving the defaulting parties from their liability. On reasonable basis, such defaulters could be called upon to pay the environmental compensation. In the present case, the parties opted not to lead any evidence except the documents and affidavit that they had filed in support of their respective cases. It is also evident that over exploitation of the sources has been done by the private respondents and the noticees to the extent that it is likely to cause environmental threats. Restoration thereof would be a long-drawn process and the private parties would be required to pay compensation even for restorative purposes. At present, we are dealing with the damage caused on approximate basis for continuous defaults and violation of the laws and specific terms and conditions of the EC and for their operation without consent of the concerned authorities including the State Pollution Control Boards.... They have carried on excessive unauthorized mining in a manner that has caused substantial damage and degradation of environment, ecology and biodiversity. Thus, a compensation of Rs. 50 Crores is to be paid by each of the private respondents/notices who are carrying on the extraction of minor minerals and Rs. 2.5 Crores respectively by each of the stone crushers/screening plants which had been running illegally, in an unauthorized manner, without consent of the concerned Pollution Control Board.

This judgment is significant in two aspects. First, the NGT held that though the actual extent of environmental damage was not ascertainable with exactitude, the polluter would be held liable for the costs associated with the overall restitution of the environment. Second, the NGT adequately held the polluters liable for their blatant disregard for environmental norms by imposing exemplary costs to the tune of INR 50 crore, which were to be paid individually by each polluter. Decisions like these are likely to deter potential polluters who completely disregard environmental concerns.

The NGT has used the polluter pays principle in a similar manner to award unprecedented sums of environmental compensation in a few other cases. For instance, in February 2016, the NGT ordered companies involved in illegal mining along the River Yamuna to pay INR 252.5 crore as environmental compensation.[350] More recently, in February 2018, the NGT awarded INR 195 crore as compensation payable to compensate for the environmental damage caused by M/s Goel Ganga Developers India Pvt. Ltd. due to illegal construction activities.[351] While these high compensation amounts are a much-needed change, further scrutiny through analysis of case law reveals that they are an exception and not the norm.

As noted in Chapter 2, the recent trend of the NGT with respect to determining environmental compensation in cases involving a lack of consent to operate seems to be to make the project proponent pay between 5 and 10 per cent of the project cost.[352] This trend started in 2014 when the NGT arbitrarily adopted[353] the Supreme Court's approach to determining compensation in *Goa Foundation v. Union of India & Ors.*[354]

(For the benefit of the reader, we will reproduce some analytical excerpts from Chapter 2 below.)

In the *Goa Foundation Case*, the Supreme Court was faced with the issue of determining the environmental damage caused due to certain illegal mining in Goa. In arriving at the compensation amount, the Court held that the project proponents would have to pay 10 per cent of the "sale proceeds" to a public fund – Goan Iron Ore Permanent Fund – as compensation.[355] The Court felt that this was an appropriate compensation given that mining could not be completely stopped due to its contribution towards employment and revenue generation for the state.[356] Accordingly, it held that if mining had to continue, determining compensation on the basis of sale proceeds would be apt as it would directly impact the profitability of the project.[357]

This approach adopted by the Supreme Court, however, was not intended to be a precedent for determining environmental compensation in all cases. This is evident from the fact that the Court had specifically based its decision on the special considerations prevalent in the case due to the economic significance of mining in Goa. In fact, to arrive at the compensation amount as 10 per cent of the sale proceeds, the Court had relied on its earlier decision in *Samaj Parivartana Samudaya v. State of Karnataka,*[358] wherein it had held that 10 per cent of the sale proceeds from the sale of iron ore should be used as compensation.

Thus, the approach, at best, can be a precedent for cases involving illegal mining in regions such as Goa. Clearly, considerations of the state's dependency on mining for revenue and employment generation had gone into arriving at the compensation. Thus, had the considerations been different – in that the Supreme Court was concerned with an activity which did not contribute largely to the sState's overall economic development – and had the Supreme Court banned mining altogether, it is very likely that the approach to determine compensation would have been significantly different.

However, without paying heed to the different considerations and factual context in *Goa Foundation*, the NGT has co-opted this approach in several cases that have had very different factual and legal considerations.[359] This was first exemplified in *Forward Foundation v. State of Karnataka*.[360] The case dealt with illegal construction by two companies in a Special Economic Zone without receiving the requisite environmental clearance.[361] Upon being granted conditional environmental clearance, the companies continued to flout the conditions stipulated therein.[362] The NGT noted that the project was a threat to the entire ecosystem in the area as it fell under the ecologically sensitive zone between the Agara and Bellandur lakes. In particular, the Tribunal noted that the project had a significant negative impact on the surrounding wetlands and stormwater drains.[363] Despite the serious environmental damage involved, the NGT unduly co-opted the Supreme Court's approach in *Goa Foundation* and imposed an environmental penalty amounting to a mere 5 per cent of the project cost.[364]

Further, while the NGT overtly based its assessment of compensation on the Court's approach in *Goa Foundation*, it significantly differed in two aspects. First, the NGT reduced the compensation amount from 10 per cent to 5 per cent without providing any reasoning for the reduction. It simply stated that "10 per cent of the project cost may be somewhat on the higher side", and that it was necessary to lower the compensation percentage to 5 per cent so as to "maintain the equitable balance between the default and the consequential liability". [365] However, an equitable balance between the default and the consequential liability can only be maintained when the extent of environmental damage can be reasonably estimated. Since the NGT did not engage in such an endeavour, it is not clear how the compensation levied would strike such a balance.

Second, instead of basing compensation on a percentage of the sale proceeds like the Court, the NGT based its compensation on a percentage of the project cost. The Court had used sale proceeds as it thought that this would be the most effective way of impacting the profitability of the project proponent. This is because in most mining operations, the mining site is leased from the government and the total project cost is significantly less than the sale generated. Likewise, in infrastructural projects such as the construction project in *Forward Foundation*, it is common practice – especially in Special Economic Zones – that the cost of the project is substantially lower than the eventual price at which the projects are sold. This is because of tax exemptions and the low cost of land allotted by the government to develop the area. For instance, if a developer constructs a shopping complex for INR 100 crore, he or she is likely to sell it further for five or six times the cost to prospective buyers. Thus, the NGT's decision to determine compensation as a percentage of the project cost does not affect the profitability of the project proponent as much as basing it on a percentage of sale proceeds.

What emerges from this discussion is a trend of the NGT to award compensation without paying heed to the actual amount of environmental damage. The compensation is not based on any scientific methodology or quantitative assessment. Rather, it is pegged arbitrarily on an economic variable which has no conspicuous nexus with the underlying environmental damage. In fact, even the high amount of compensation – totalling to INR 195 crore – mentioned at the beginning of this section was a result of this trend. While awarding the compensation, the NGT stated:[366]

> Goel Ganga Developers India Private Limited shall pay environmental compensation cost of ₹190 crore or 5% (five per cent) of the total cost of project to be assessed by State Expert Appraisal Committee (SEAC), whichever is more, for restoration and restitution of environment damage and degradation caused by the project proponent by carrying out the construction activities without the necessary prior environmental clearance within a period of one month. In addition to this, it shall also pay a sum of ₹5 crore for contravening mandatory provision of several environment laws in carrying out the construction activities in addition to and exceeding limit of the available environment clearance and for not obtaining the consent from the Board.

The case involved grave environmental damage on account of illegal construction of 12 buildings including 552 residential flats, 50 shops, and 34 offices. M/s Goel Ganga Developers India Pvt. Ltd. had flouted several conditions stipulated in the environmental clearance and had intentionally violated several municipal laws. Further, there was intentional suppression of material facts by the company and several governmental officers of the Pune Municipal Corporation.[367]

Despite noting the disastrous effects on the local environment due to the construction activities, the NGT did not conduct a scientific analysis of the extent of environmental damage. Rather, it based its compensation on the trend we have highlighted and pegged the compensation at 5 per cent of the project cost or INR 190 crore, whichever is higher. Thus, while the total compensation of INR 195 crore seems significant when viewed in isolation, it is possible that it could be inadequate for the restitution of the environment given that the actual amount of environmental damage was not determined.

In fact, on appeal to the Supreme Court, one of the main contentions of M/s Goel Ganga Developers India Pvt. Ltd. was that the NGT had not based its assessment on any scientific methodology.[368] The project proponent, on appeal, contended that the NGT ought to have determined the compensation on a "scientific basis" according to the actual "damage caused to the environment". It submitted that the calculation of the amount should have been based on the project's "carbon footprints" rather than being pegged at a percentage of the project cost. In response, the Supreme Court unequivocally stated that it was "totally unequipped" to deal with the matter due to the absence of details in the submission.[369]

Further, the Court opined that determining environmental compensation on the basis of carbon footprints was not appropriate as no expert evidence was led in this regard and the concept was not based on well-established principles of law. However, it clarified that this did not bar determining of compensation on carbon footprints in successive cases.

In relation to the calculation of the compensation by the NGT, the Court held that the trend of awarding 5 per cent of the project cost as environmental compensation amounted to "general law", as the Court had used this in several cases. However, given that the project proponent had intentionally suppressed material facts and had manipulated official authorities, the Court held that the correct assessment of compensation would be 10 per cent of the project cost.

Ironically, however, the Court reduced the compensation from INR 190 crore (awarded by the NGT) to INR 100 crore or 10 per cent of the project costs, whichever would be higher. No reasons were presented for the reduction in the amount. As noted previously, the issue with this approach of the Court and the Tribunal is that it disregards actual environmental damage. In other words, there is no nexus between the compensation levied and the actual amount needed to restore the environment to its original condition. This was acknowledged by the Court when it held:[370]

> We cannot assess the impact in actual terms and, therefore, we can only impose damages or costs on principles which have been well settled by law.

While the Court acknowledged this, it equally emphasized how the current trend was appropriate and was a part of the general law. However, it remains unclear why the Court would not order a scientific assessment of the environmental impact and why the current trend is preferable.

This trend is problematic as it allows a potential polluter to do a cost–benefit analysis before undertaking a project. Given that the environmental compensation, irrespective of the level of pollution, is likely to be pegged between 5 and 10 per cent of the project cost, it is likely to incentivise a potential polluter to proceed with the project if the project can still be reasonably profitable. In other words, instead of acting as a deterrent, the environmental compensation, in its current form, is likely to be viewed as an environmental fee or cess by a potential polluter which becomes a part of the calculation of the cost of the project. Therefore, this trend has effectively converted the polluter pays principle into "pay and pollute" principle.

This is ironic as in *Tanaji Balasaheb Gambhire v. Union of India and Ors.,*[371] the NGT has expressly acknowledged:[372]

> We are conscious of the fact that Polluter pays Principle shall not be construed as '*pay and pollute principle*', and the *payment has therefore to be exemplary and deterrent in order*

to pass a clear message that environmental compliance is supreme and the party which is non-complying the environmental standards shall be at economic disadvantage. (Emphasis supplied)

In fact, even in this case, the NGT awarded a compensation based on this trend. It held that the environmental compensation due would be the lesser of INR 100 crore or 5 per cent of the total cost of the project. While this might seem to be high when seen in isolation, it was very inadequate when compared to the colossal environmental damage involved and the huge size of the impugned project. This was noted by the Supreme Court on appeal, which overturned the NGT's compensation order and increased the compensation to INR 100 crore or 10 per cent of the project cost, whichever was higher.

We believe that this trend should be discouraged and the NGT should, instead of having a blanket practice of awarding a certain percentage of the project cost, determine compensation on a case-by-case basis as per the actual amount of environmental damage. This will not only disincentivise a potential polluter from polluting, but also allow the Tribunal to award stringent and appropriate compensation in cases where the pollution is more significant.

Additionally, this reflects the NGT's inability to use its technical expertise to scientifically quantify environmental damage. In fact, despite holding that there is significant environmental damage in some cases, the NGT has unequivocally relied on "guesswork" to compute environmental compensation.[373]

For instance, in *T.N. Godavarman Thirumulpad v. Union of India*[374] (yes, this is a part of the larger *T.N. Godavarman Thirumulpad Case* before the Supreme Court which has lasted more than two decades as discussed in Chapter 1!), the Tribunal was concerned with the illegal construction of a hotel-cum-bus stand complex. The construction had been undertaken in complete violation of clearance procedures. In response, the NGT ordered the demolition of the illegally constructed structures and imposed an environmental compensation to be paid by the project proponent. Notably, with respect to the polluter pays principle, the Tribunal held:[375]

Even the case where Polluter Pays Principle is invoked does not in any way grant legitimacy to an illegal or unauthorized act merely because the polluter is directed to pay compensation. *In cases where pollution is caused or environment or ecology is damaged, the status co-ante must be restored, and all efforts should be made simultaneously to reestablish the environment and ecology to its original pristine form.* This would be besides the fact that the polluter is held liable to pay the compensation.... *The Polluter Pays Principle takes in its ambit absolute liability for harm to the environment which extends not only to compensate the victim of the pollution but also cost of recovering the degradation of environment.* The polluter will be the person responsible who has to bear the cost of preventing or dealing with any pollution that such process has caused. The polluter does not get a right to pollute and pay.... Exact calculation of damages in this case is not possible. It has been settled that in such cases some *guess work* can be applied. (Emphasis supplied)

Thus, we see that the NGT has acknowledged the importance of requiring the polluter to pay costs for rehabilitating and restoring the environment in addition to compensating the victims of the pollution. In fact, the NGT unequivocally holds that the environmental "status quo ante must be restored" and that "all efforts should be made simultaneously to reestablish the environment and ecology to its original pristine form." However, as noted in Chapter 2, this is only possible if the baseline condition of the environment that existed prior to the alleged damage is determined – which the NGT does not do.

The reason that the NGT has to explicitly resort to the use of "guesswork"[376] is that while the Tribunal acknowledges the need to restore the environment to its original condition, it does not scientifically determine the original condition of the environment in practice. For instance, in the *Art of Living Case*,[377] the compensation eventually levied was very different from the initial estimate. The case dealt with the alleged damage to the Yamuna Floodplains due to the Art of Living Foundation's World Cultural Festival.

The initial estimate of the Expert Committee, based on a simple "visual assessment" was approximately INR 120 crore.[378] This estimate was later changed to INR 28.73 crore.[379] Finally, the Tribunal asked the Art of Living Foundation to deposit INR 5 crore (not as a penalty[380]), out of which only INR 25 lakh was required as a condition precedent for going ahead with the event. This substantial reduction in estimated compensation was a result of non-scientific estimation of the environmental damage (for a detailed analysis, refer to the section 2.4.2, titled "Case Study: Lack of Scientific Determination of Environmental Compensation – The *Art of Living Case*", in Chapter 2).

Not only had the chairperson of the Expert Committee denounced the report of the Committee for not being "based on any scientific assessment",[381] the NGT had itself admitted to not conducting a scientific analysis. To this effect, the Tribunal had held that the primary reason for not scientifically quantifying damage was that[382]:

> Estimate of the costs of restoration requires the preparation of a Detailed Project Report that may take several months to a year besides financial resources.

Accordingly, the NGT unscientifically levied a penalty without quantifying the environmental damage, if any, due to paucity of time and lack of financial resources. This substantial reduction in the estimated penalty from INR 120 crore to INR 5 crore caused substantial public embarrassment to the NGT as several media houses claimed that the reduction was due to political reasons.[383] However, as we have discussed, the reduction stemmed from an inherently unscientific assessment of actual environmental damage and resulting compensation.

This trend, in several cases,[384] has significantly diluted the application of the polluter pays principle. While the NGT in *Krishan Kant Singh v. National Ganga River Basin Authority*[385] has held that the Tribunal should be concerned with the "capacity and prosperity" of the project proponent while determining environmental compensation, in practice this trend has resulted in a situation where the profitability of the project proponent is hardly impacted. In fact, the cases analysed with respect to the pollution caused by sugar distilleries highlight that the compensation was between 0.012 and 0.07 per cent of the annual turnover of the project proponents.[386] Several polluting companies that had annual turnovers of several thousand crores were liable to pay only a few hundred thousand rupees.[387]

In addition to this trend of unscientifically calculating environmental damage and the resulting compensation, the NGT's application of the polluter pays principle has been mixed. While in some cases the Tribunal has explicitly recognized the need to hold governmental authorities accountable under the principle and has imposed exemplary costs, in many cases it has failed to adequately hold these authorities liable. Let us look at cases that demonstrate this.

The NGT has unequivocally recognized the application of the polluter pays principle to hold public authorities accountable for dereliction of their duties in *Vivek Tyagi v. State of Uttar Pradesh*.[388] The issue for consideration was non-compliance with the Solid Waste Management Rules, 2016, and the lack of preventive steps taken by public authorities in relation to the discharge of untreated sewage in water bodies around Ghaziabad. The Tribunal, taking note of the non-complacence on the part of the authorities, stated:[389]

> To uphold the Rule of Law and accountability of those who are *trustees for protection of environment*, it is necessary that the *State machinery is required to compensate for their negligence and failure* which may act as deterrent against the officers who neglected their basic duty of protecting the environment or colluded with the polluters and law violators. This is required not only as a part of principle of 'polluter pays' which applies not only to actual polluters but *also to those who collude with polluters or enable pollution to be caused and also for the negligence of public duties, adversely affecting the citizens.* (Emphasis supplied)

Thus, in addition to holding the state machinery responsible, the NGT highlighted the need for such measures as they act as a deterrent against officers who collude with polluters and violators of the law. Accordingly, the NGT imposed an environmental compensation of INR 25 lakh on the state government of Uttar Pradesh and directed the Urban Development Ministry to deposit a performance guarantee of INR 35 lakh.

While the NGT has upheld the imposition of environmental compensation and penalty on regulatory authorities, the amount imposed in several cases is negligible.

For instance, in *Rohit Choudhury v. Union of India*,[390] the Tribunal held that there was massive environmental damage on account of illegal mining activities in and around the "Ecologically Sensitive Zone" of the Kaziranga National Park. However, despite noting the complete failure of the MoEF and the state government of Assam in preventing the setting up of these industries in the "No Development Zone", the Tribunal imposed a paltry sum of INR 1 lakh on each of them.

In fact, in the judgment, the Tribunal had held that there was "a clear case of infringement of law"[391] by the MoEF and the state government as they completely disregarded environmental concerns by allowing the construction to take place in a prohibited and ecologically sensitive area. Thus, while the NGT has stressed the importance of awarding adequate environmental compensation to deter officials who neglect their duties, the practice speaks otherwise. It is unclear how awarding such an inadequate and disproportionate penalty will deter potential violations by regulators.

Similarly, in *Ajay Kumar Negi*, the Tribunal had held that the Forest Department had not performed its duties and could not explain the discrepancy between the number of trees allegedly damaged by the project proponent (398 trees) and its estimate (4,815 trees).[392] Furthermore, the project proponent in the case had been regularly paying environmental fines as and when required, but the Forest Department failed to utilize the amounts paid for environmental restoration for several years.[393] Despite noting such gross negligence on the part of the Forest Department, the Tribunal did not impose any monetary penalty on it.

Likewise, in the *Art of Living Case*,[394] despite holding that the Delhi Development Authority had wrongfully granted the permission to the Art of Living Foundation for holding the cultural event and that the Delhi Pollution Control Committee was negligent in performing its duties, the Tribunal did not impose any costs on the former and levied a mere penalty of INR 1 lakh on the latter.[395]

Additionally, prior to the event, the Art of Living Foundation had also taken permissions from, inter alia, the Ministry of Environment, Forest and Climate Change (MoEFCC), the Uttar Pradesh Irrigation Committee (UPIC), Delhi Disaster Management Authority (DDMA), and the Irrigation and Flood Control Department of Delhi (IFCD). However, despite holding that these departments had wrongly granted the permission, the NGT did not impose any penalty on them and did not hold them accountable in any manner.

However, recently this trend seems to be changing. In January 2019, the Tribunal held the state government of Meghalaya responsible for failing to curb illegal coal mining in the state and imposed a fine of INR 100 crore on it.[396] This amount was ordered to be deposited by the state government with the Central Pollution Control Board within two months.[397] This high amount was imposed to act as a deterrent as the state government had not performed its duties despite data showing that a majority of the 24,000 mines in Meghalaya were being operated illegally, that is, without a license or environmental clearance.[398]

On similar lines, the Tribunal, in *Indian Council for Enviro-Legal Action & Ors. v. Jammu and Kashmir State Pollution Control Board & Ors.*,[399] imposed an environmental compensation of INR 5 crore on the State Industrial Development Corporation for failing to prevent pollution by the industrial centre established by it. Additionally, a compensation of INR 10 lakh was also imposed on the concerned municipal council for the past failures in installing a sewage treatment plant and for allowing the discharge of untreated sewage in the river.

Likewise, the NGT recently imposed a fine of INR 25 crore[400] on the state government of Delhi for failing to curb air pollution and imposed a fine of INR 50 crore on the state government of Punjab for polluting the Rivers Sutlej and Beas due to uncontrolled industrial discharge.[401]

In addition to a lack of scientific methodology for calculating environmental compensation and frequently not holding regulators adequately accountable, there are concerns with respect to the implementation of the NGT's orders. The NGT, in *Manoj Mishra v. Union of India*,[402] has acknowledged the important role played by regulatory authorities in implementing the polluter pays principle:[403]

> We have already noted that 'Polluter Pays' principle can be applied by every regulatory authority and compensation can be and must be recovered from every polluter and the amount which is to be recovered spent for the restoration of the environment. *Mere passing of orders by the Tribunal is of no value unless the same are faithfully executed. Execution is in the hands of the authority.* As executing court, it is not only the right but also the duty of this Tribunal to take such measures as may ensure compliance. Mode of execution is laid down in CPC (Section 51), i.e., arrest and detention, appointment of a receiver or in such manner as nature of relief may require. (Emphasis supplied)

While the NGT has reiterated the need for regulators to implement its decisions and orders to give effect to the polluter pays principle, frequently these orders are not executed on the ground. For instance, the NGT's order dated 10 November 2016 with respect to air pollution in Delhi – wherein clear directions were given with respect to the next steps to be taken to combat long-term and short-term air pollution – remains completely unimplemented.[404] In fact, the PM 2.5 level (the metric relied on by the Tribunal for measuring the pollution level) was around 600 when the order was given.[405] This PM 2.5 level pales in comparison to the PM 2.5 level of 999+ reached during Diwali in 2019.[406] The NGT, while delivering the impugned order, had categorically reprimanded the government officials and had stated that "the right to life has been infringed with impunity by the authorities and other stakeholders who have been mere spectators to such crisis".[407] However, a year later when the orders were not complied with and the pollution was worse, the Tribunal admitted that the orders remained unimplemented and that it could find "no plausible explanation".[408] In fact, most of the significant cases involving illegal mining and solid waste management continue to remain unenforced.[409]

Furthermore, Section 24(1) of the NGT Act requires that any amount of money received as compensation or relief under an award made by the Tribunal for environmental damage shall be credited to the Environmental Relief Fund (ERF). Further, Rule 35(1) of the National Green Tribunal (Practices and Procedure) Rules, 2011, states that the amount must be credited to the ERF within thirty days of the order or as otherwise directed by the Tribunal.

In effect, the ERF is the primary means by which environmental restoration and rejuvenation are enabled. However, despite this provision, the NGT does not direct payment to the ERF in all cases.[410] A recent study shows that in nearly 40 per cent of all cases the payments are directed to state pollution control boards, in 17 per cent of cases to state forest departments, and only in 12 per cent of cases to the ERF. Moreover, even in the few cases in which the NGT directs that compensation should be deposited into the ERF, there have only been two deposits actually made to date.[411] These trends are problematic as they dilute the polluter pays principle entirely.

In conclusion, the NGT has upheld the robust and strong interpretation of the polluter pays principle developed by the Supreme Court. It has applied this strong interpretation in a few cases to hold both polluters and regulators accountable through the imposition of exemplary costs. However, as we have discussed in this section, there are some disconcerting trends in the NGT's adjudication.

First, there is no scientific assessment or quantification of environmental damage in most cases. Due to this, environmental compensation is frequently not based on the actual costs required for restoring the environment to its original position. Arbitrarily, the compensation is usually pegged at 5 per cent of the project costs and, in most cases, is extremely inadequate. Further, studies have shown that while the NGT aims to deter potential polluters by impacting their profitability, the final compensation levied is negligible when compared to the annual turnover of polluters. Given this trend, as discussed, potential polluters are likely to go ahead with a polluting project if it can be reasonably profitable after accounting for a 5 per cent increase in project cost on account of the environmental compensation that will likely be levied if they are caught. This has effectively converted the polluter pays principle into the pay and pollute principle.

Second, while the NGT has reiterated the importance of holding regulators and public authorities accountable for not performing their duties, the penalties and compensation levied on them are usually disproportionate with respect to their dereliction of duty. As discussed, the amounts levied are very low and are inadequate to deter officials and regulators. Third, the NGT's decisions and orders are frequently not implemented on the ground. Studies show that polluters have only deposited compensation in the ERF in two cases to date. These are worrying trends and have the potential to make the NGT's adjudication ineffective.

Let us now analyse some key judgments of the NGT with respect to the polluter pays principle in more detail.

3.3.4   POLLUTER PAYS – CASE EXCERPTS AND ANALYSIS

SRINAGAR BANDH AAPDA SANGHARSH SAMITI AND ORS. v. ALAKNANDA HYDRO POWER CO. LTD. AND ORS.

National Green Tribunal

Original Application No. 03 OF 2014

December 19, 2016

1.   An organization of the residents of Srinagar District Pauri, Uttarakhand and one Vimal Bhai … have filed this application for directions to the respondent no.1 Alaknanda Hydro Power co. ltd. to pay compensation for the damage suffered by the members of the Srinagar Bandh Aapda Sangharsh Samiti in terms of loss of life and property and for restoration of effected area in Srinagar due to the floods that hit the area between 16th June, 2013 and 17th June, 2013.

3.   The applicants have described Srinagar Hydroelectric Project as a run of the river scheme on Alaknanda River involving construction of 63meters high dam across the river Alaknanda, 800 meters long diversion tunnel as well as 4.8 meters long power channel for generating 200 MW of power (50MW x4 Units) causing submergence of 300ha. of land including 250ha. of forest land. This project was granted clearance vide letter dated 3rd May, 1985 issued by Director and Member Secretary Environmental Appraisal Committee on certain conditions....

4.   It is the case of the applicants that the respondent no. 1 – Alaknanda Hydro Power co. Ltd-the project proponent, dumped large quantity of muck generated from the construction of the said project just after the gates of the dams inappropriately on designated or non-designated sites without taking necessary or prescribed measures to secure such muck from the floods. According to the applicants due to heavy rains between 16th June, 2013 to 17th June, 2013 the reservoir of Srinagar Hydroelectric project was filled and the dam gates being kept closed led to creation of huge reservoir of water and opening of the gates resulted in massive flow of water suddenly sweeping away the muck dumped on the river body and carrying it to the villages and the area flooded by the floods.... According to the applicants, the area affected was filled with the muck at least 8 feet high causing loss to the property as well as life. The applicants are claiming damages to the tune of Rs. 9,26,42,795/- suffered by its members and other residents of Srinagar on account of expenses incurred in removal of the muck and restoration of the property and general loss to the property....

6.   … According to the respondent no. 1 [Alaknanda Hydro Power Co. Ltd.] the victims of the tragedy caused by the Kedarnath catastrophe on 16th and 17th June, 2013 have already been duly compensated by the State of Uttarakhand. Furthermore the respondent no.1 submits that the alleged loss caused by the floods between 16th and 17th June, 2013-Kedarnath catastrophe is due to act of God – *vis major* and as such the project proponent which itself suffered heavy loss and damages cannot be held liable for the damages claimed by the applicants.

9.   Respondent no. 1 in its reply referred to [the Expert Committee's report appointed by the MoEF] … stating that the project proponent was complying with Muck Management Plan prepared by IIT Roorkee and approved by the Forest Department of State of Uttarakhand…. [Further] … Mr. A.D.N. Rao was appointed [by the Tribunal] to conduct a site visit and submit a report which again showed the project proponent as fully compliant.

12.   According to the project proponent, the highest flood (12,610 cumecs) occurred on 17th June, 2013 and it was almost three times greater than the highest flood level (4500 cumecs) which occurred in August, 2012, the highest ever in the history of Uttarakhand.

14.   According to the project proponent … at no point of time during the floods the gates were closed so as to lead to the filling up of the reservoir but the flood water was allowed to pass over the dam spillway and it is for this reason the huge velocity of water in Dhari Devi Temple was noticed on 16th June, 2013…. The Project proponent in its reply gave account of muck disposal sites as approved by State Forest Department of Uttarakhand.

16.   Respondent no.1 revealed in its reply that even in the heaviest rain falls witnessed by Uttarakhand no muck was eroded from the muck sites other than the sites no 6 and 9. The project proponent confirming that the river had changed the course towards right sites at location no. 9 in spite of the deflectors installed by Central Water Commission for protection of the bank and the river course hit the site no. 9 overtopping the toe wall and part of the original land mass situate on the right bank of the river got eroded during the heavy flow of flood water which took way the muck from site no. 9.

17.   … the reservoir dead storage up to spillway level of dam is 28million Cum; and during the monsoon 2012 the reservoir bed level arose to 560 meters corresponding to the silt deposition of 2 million cubic meters; and during the floods of June 2013, the reservoir bed level rose to 585 meters corresponding to silt deposition of 26 million cubic meters. The Respondent No. 1 submits that this shows the severity of flood and silt carried by it and without the Srinagar dam this silt could have entered Srinagar town and completely buried it.

20. ... Applicant explained that the issue before the Hon'ble Apex Court was whether hydroelectric project had impact on environment and it contributed to the Uttrakhand disaster and not the issue of assessment of damage in the project area and fixing responsibility of the same as per 'Polluters Pay Principle'. Referring to the observations made by the Hon'ble Supreme Court in *Alakhnanda Hydro Power Co. Ltd v. Anuj Joshi and Ors.* that the total muck utilization to be 44%, the Applicant pointed out that the amount of muck lying at different muck disposal sites having been moved from the said sites due to floods caused damage downstream areas as referred to in the Application.... Significantly, the rejoinder maintained silence about the Respondent No. 1's contentions that the residential area suffered due to muck and silt deposition in the floods of 2013 as they were located below the flood levels.

22. ... [Applicants] argued that the Respondent No. 1- Alakhnanda Hydro Power Co. Ltd cannot seek shelter under specious plea of "Act of God – *Vis Major*" and avoid responsibility to pay the compensation. He further submitted that under section 17(3) of the National Green Tribunal Act, 2010, this Tribunal can invoke the principle of No Fault and saddle the Respondent No. 1 with the liability to pay the compensation for the damages incurred as a result of the floods caused even assuming the same to be an accident involving a fortuitous or sudden or unintended occurrence.

25. ... [Respondent 3] argued that the Principle of "No Fault Liability" under section 17(3) of the National Green Tribunal Act, 2010 cannot be invoked in the present case as the alleged loss incurred is not the consequence of accident or the adverse impact of an activity or operations or process; and if the unfortunate happening were to be viewed as merely an accident the same also do not fall within the meaning of the definition of the accident under section 2 of the National Green Tribunal Act 2010 ... whatever had happened may be sudden or unintended occurrence but the same had not taken place while handling any hazardous substance within the meaning of Section '2' (e) of the Environment (Protection) Act 1986 ... the muck generated due to excavation of the earth cannot be called as "hazardous substance" as nothing can be attributed chemically or by physicochemical property or by way of handling of such muck in any way would cause harm to life, property or the environment.

[The Tribunal discusses various expert committee reports favouring both sides.]

39. ... [We] quote the words of the Hon'ble Apex Court at para 9 of the Judgment in Divisional Controller, KSRTC's case (Supra) hereunder:

"9. The expression "Act of God" signifies the operation of natural forces free from human intervention, such as lightning, storm etc.... But every unexpected wind and storm does not operate as an excuse from liability, if there is a reasonable possibility of anticipating their happening. An act of God provides no excuse unless it is so unexpected that no reasonable human foresight could be presumed to anticipate the occurrence, having regard to the conditions of time and place known to be prevailing."

40. It is undisputed that June, 2013 floods were due to cloud burst in upper reaches of River Alaknanda near Kedarnath.... However, it was within the knowledge of the respondent no.1- Alaknanda Hydro Power Co. Ltd that the project is situated in Geologically Sensitive area of Himalaya, where cloud burst is not a rare phenomena and though the EC did not mandate plan for muck disposal the MoEF has sounded an alarm as regards the muck disposal vide direction dated 30th June, 2011. Having regard to these known conditions, human foresight could have reasonably anticipated that laxity in taking timely protective measures such as slope dressing, terracing, toe walls covering the top soil at the permanent muck disposal sites would prove disastrous to the environment, particularly, to the human beings who are the components of environment. Material before us points out the laxity on the part of the respondent no. 1-Alaknada Hydro Power Co. Ltd in relation to taking adequate safety measures for muck disposal sites.

41. We, therefore, reject the plea of the respondent no. 1 that the damage caused to the residential area was the result of "Act of God-Vis. Major".

42. Even if it was an "Act of God" a question remains to be examined as to whether the Principle of "No Fault Liability" as given under Section 17 (3) of the NGT Act, 2010 can be invoked in the present case.... It is correct that muck is not per se a hazardous substance as defined under Section 2 (e) of the Environment (Protection) Act, 1986.... It is not the case of anyone that the muck as such has chemical or physico-chemical properties which would *per se* or by handling would cause harm to human beings, other living creatures, micro-organisms, property or the environment. However, it will be necessary to examine whether the hydro electricity power project of the respondent no.1- Alaknanda Hydro Power Co. Ltd. can be regarded as a "plant" in order to call fortuitous or sudden or unintended occurrence of the floods of 2013 and the injury caused by it as the one caused by an accident within the meaning of Section 2 (a) of the NGT Act, 2010.

44. Oxford Dictionary of English 3rd Edition gives meaning of the word 'plant' as follows:- Plant – place where an industrial or manufacturing process takes

place. This dictionary further gives meaning of the word 'process' as follows:-
Process – a series of actions or steps taken in order to achieve a particular end.
In the present case the respondent no. 1- Alaknanda Hydro Power Co. Ltd. has
undertaken the construction and commenced of the project of manufacturing
Hydro Electric Power following the environmental clearance granted for
carrying out construction development and commencement of such project in
May, 1985…. Thus, the safeguards prescribed from time to time for execution
of the said project were inseparable constituents of the series of action or steps
taken in order to achieve the commencement of the said project…. Entire
place of the project therefore and the activities have to be regarded as a "Plant"
as understood in simple language.

46.   Even assuming the disaster of June, 2013 as the one involving fortuitous or
      sudden or unintended occurrence the injury that has resulted from such
      occurrence, to the human habitation needs to be regarded as the one resulted
      while handling the said plant or the process leading to manufacturing
      of power and, therefore, it is an "accident" within the meaning of said
      definition under Section 2 (a) of the NGT Act, 2010. In the given facts and
      circumstances, therefore, the principle of No Fault Liability under Section
      17(3) of the NGT Act, 2010 makes the respondent no.1- Alaknanda Hydro
      Power Co. Ltd. liable to pay compensation for the injury caused to the
      human habitation.

47.   The applicant have claimed an amount of Rs. 9,26,42,795/- as a compensation
      for the injury sustained by the members of applicant no.1 and the residents of
      Srinagar city…. Going by the Geochemical analysis the muck that was found
      was about 30 percent. This certainly is a footprint of the involvement of the
      respondent no. 1 in the occurrence resulting in damage caused as aforesaid.
      However, we also cannot turn a blind eye to the fact that the applicants did
      not specifically deny that the structure affected were located below the flood
      levels – para 14-C of the reply of respondent no.1. On the other hand there
      is material to suggest that the Government of Uttarakhand has yet to define
      the flood plain zone as per the provision of Uttarakhand Flood Plain Zoning
      Act, 2012…. There is nothing before us to suggest that these structures were
      affected in floods previously. In such circumstances, there can be no escape
      from the liability incurred as aforesaid. We, therefore, pass the following
      order:-

      1.   Respondent no.1- Alaknanda Hydro Power Co. Ltd. shall deposit an
           amount of Rs 9,26,42,795/- by way of compensation to the victims of
           the June, 2013 floods in city of Srinagar with the Environmental Relief
           Fund Authority established under Section 7 (a) of Public Liability

Insurance Act, 1991 within a period of 30 days from the date of this order.

...

3. The respondent no. 3- State of Uttarakhand shall issue necessary directions to the District Magistrate of District Pauri to depute any senior Sub-Divisional Magistrate to call for the claims from the persons as per list annexed as annexure A-5 with necessary proof in support of their claims. The SDM so deputed shall verify the claims made in light of the proofs produced and remit the amount due to such person/s after deduction therefrom the proportionate 1% amount of Court fees payable.... No Claim filed after 90 days of publication of such notice shall be entertained by the District Magistrate.

*   *   *

NOTES AND QUESTIONS

1. Hydroelectric power has historically been significant in India. Post-independence, large dams were built to provide electricity to disconnected villages, and such dams came to be seen as a symbol of development. Accordingly, in many instances, the Supreme Court has sided with the need for hydroelectric power despite the displacement of large communities and environmental damage. In this context, this case assumes importance as it is the first time that the NGT held hydro power projects responsible for environmental damage caused.

2. The Uttarakhand floods of 2013 killed nearly 6,000 people and had been termed by the Supreme Court as a "natural tragedy" in a 2013 petition. The applicant seeks to rely on this and claims the defence of *vis major*. Moreover, it argues that since Section 17(3) r/w Section 2(a) of the NGT Act, 2010, envisages the imposition of no-fault liability only in cases of accidents involving "hazardous substances", the application should be dismissed given that muck is per se not hazardous. The NGT counters this by holding that this is not a case fit for the defence of *vis major* as the respondent, being situated in a geologically sensitive area where cloud bursts are not rare, could have reasonably anticipated that taking adequate safety measures would have averted environmental damage. Furthermore, it holds that while muck is not a hazardous substance, the respondent's project can be deemed to be a "plant" within Section 2(a). In addition, it holds that even if it were an act of god, no-fault liability would still be attracted. Do you think that the Tribunal was right in coming to this conclusion given that Section

2(a) defines an "accident" in relation to a plant as that which results in "continuous or intermittent or repeated ... injury to any person or damage to any property or environment"? What does the holding of the NGT tell us about the judicial paradigm shift in relation to hydroelectric power projects being viewed as causing environmental damage under this definition?

3. The polluter pays principle envisages a reversal of the burden of proof wherein the project proponent has to demonstrate that its actions are environmentally benign. What does this decision say about the standard of such proof that needs to be discharged by the project proponent?

4. Historically, environmental adjudication to a large extent has been anthropocentric. In the present case, the NGT states, "human foresight could have reasonably anticipated that laxity in taking timely protective measures ... would prove disastrous to the environment, particularly to the *human beings who are the components of environment*". This suggests that the NGT, at least in this particular case, envisages a shift from anthropocentrism to ecocentrism. Do you think this is a welcome approach?

*   *   *

National Green Tribunal

(Western Zone) Bench, Pune

Tanaji Balasaheb Gambhire v. Union of India

[Original Application No. 184 of 2015, Judgment Dated 27 September 2016]

Dr. Jawad Rahim, Judicial Member
Dr. Ajay A. Deshpande, Expert Member

*   *   *

Relevant Extracts:

1. ... The Applicant Tanaji Balasaheb Gambhire has sought certain directions against the 9th Respondent – Project Proponent (PP) M/s Goel Ganga Developers India Private Limited who is said to have envisaged construction venture to construct a commercial and residential complex.

2. In the Application, the Applicant has sought following directions:

    A. Direct the Respondents to demolish the illegal structures at the site in question and restore the area to its original position.

    B. Direct the State Level Impact Assessment Authority and the Maharashtra State Pollution Control Board to initiate appropriate action against the project proponent for violation of the provisions of EIA notification, 2006 and other applicable laws....

E. Having regard to the damage to the public health, property and environment, principles of sustainable development and polluter pays principles and direct the Respondent No.9 to deposit a heavy amount of compensation to the environment relief fund.

3. In support of the reliefs so sought, he has averred factual and legal aspects to which we shall refer briefly now.

a. The 9th Respondent obtained Environmental Clearance (for short 'EC') for its project at Survey Nos. 35 to 40 in Village Vadgaon Budruk, Sinhagad Road, Pune. The project conceived and approved by said EC is to construct 12 buildings with stilt, basement plus 11 floors vertically for 552 flats, 50 shops and 34 offices. The total plot area is 79,100 sq.mts while the total built-up area is to 57,658.42 sq.mtrs.

b. The EC was obtained by the 9th Respondent-PP on 4th April, 2008 and thereafter, PP has commenced construction activity. The Applicant has not brought in question the EC dated 4th April, 2008 but has other serious grievances.

c. ...The Minutes of the Meeting held on 31st August, 2015 show that the Regional Officer of the MPCB had reported non compliance of the terms on which EC was granted to the 9th Respondent. In that, there is clear statement that though the EC was for construction of 12 buildings but the Respondent No.9-PP has built 15 buildings and increased number of flats from 552 to 738 as also the number of shops was increased from 84 to 111.

d. The Minutes of the Meeting further show that the representative of PP had accepted the non-compliance to the conditions of EC in increasing the construction of number of buildings, number of flats, offices and shops.

e. The Minutes of the Meeting would also record that consent for additional building of Ground plus 30 Floor was not taken though the civil work of its construction was in progress.

4. The Applicant relies on such material information recorded in the Meeting to contend that there was clear finding on inspection by the competent authority i.e. MPCB that the Respondent No.9-PP had not complied with the conditions of the EC granted. Reference is also made to the fact that MPCB having noticed such non-compliance had directed the Respondent No.9-PP to voluntarily stop construction activity till modified EC is obtained....

6. Amongst other issues raised he points out to the fact that building plan for construction activity of the project was revised by Respondent No.9-PP nine times. This, according to him, illustrates the significant modification in the scale of construction in terms of area, plinth area and floor heights, besides change in lay-out scheme. Referring to condition No.5 of the EC. It is alleged that the scope of the project in terms of built up area has changed. Moreover, the project lay-out as well as number of buildings also has substantially changed. Thus, the Respondent No.9-PP was obliged to obtain modified EC before undertaking such activity which is in total deviation to the original EC. Citing numerous statistical data, the Applicant would further claim that the construction activity carried out by the Repsondent-9 PP has grossly exceeded the scope of the project as approved by EC in terms of built up area and configuration of project.

7. Based on these facts, he would contend that the project activity is not as per the proposal which was considered and approved by Ministry of Environment and Forest while granting the original EC on 4th April, 2008 and therefore there is gross violation of EC condition.

8. The other contention urged by the Applicant is to indicate failure on the part of the Statutory Authorities like Pune Municipal Corporation (PMC), State Level Environment Impact Assessment Authority (SEIAA), Department of Environment, State of Maharashtra (DoE) in discharge of its statutory functions. In this regard, he contends that Pune Municipal Corporation (for short 'PMC') was well aware of such violations but granted Completion Certificate....

9. In this regard he would refer to the order passed by PMC imposing fine of Rs. 1,57,00,000/- for illegal occupancy of part of the project building which Respondent No.9-PP without remorse has accepted and deposited on 23rd October, 2015.

33. Though, much has been claimed by Respondent No.9-PP ... we do not find any confusion or contradiction in definition of terms BUA and FSI. The Respondent No.9-PP is a major developer and must be well versed with these terminologies.

34. From the material referred to above, it leaves no scope for doubt that F.S.I. and BUA are two terms which apply with a distinction defining different extent of area.

35. It will shake the conscious of all concerned when we see a deliberate attempt on the part of DoE, SEAC and SEIAA to confuse the issue virtually falling in line with misleading statements of Respondent No.9-PP and Deputy

Engineer, PMC. It is astonishing that both Respondent No.9-PP and Deputy Engineer, PMC refer to BUA as F.S.I. Despite such clear distinction in definitions and interpretations of BUA and FSI, they had attempted to mislead DoE, SEAC and SEIAA in believing that BUA and F.S.I are same. We expect an officer conferred with professional duty as an engineer in the Department of Building Permission of PMC to be very meticulous in at least understanding the terms which make lot of difference to the fact of construction. We least expected him as to know the distinction between BUA and FSI, as administration of Corporation would depend upon his professional advice and technical expertise to take action against the erring parties who contravene the mandate of law for safeguarding the interest of citizens which the Corporation is required to protect. We are also constrained to observe that the higher authorities of Building permission department had closed their eyes even when such incorrect affidavits are filed before the Tribunal and such misleading reports are sent to state authorities like DoE, SEAC and SEIAA.

36. Therefore, un-hesitatingly we could observe that the report dated 19th December, 2015 of the Deputy Engineer is a compromised statement to paint a wrong picture of the project firstly to suppress deviation and secondly to create ambiguity in definition of the terms of F.S.I. and BUA to help Respondent No.9-PP to obtain orders from the other authorities….

40. The prime issue that arises for consideration in this case is as to whether the construction activity of Respondent No.9-PP, is exceeding the sanction accorded by the EC. Could the Respondent No.9-PP proceed with construction without obtaining modified EC. The answer is obviously No.

41. For the reasons aforesaid, we answer the above issue in the negative hold that the construction activity of Respondent No.9-PP to the extent it exceeds the permissible limits as per EC cannot be saved and shall stop, subject to the grant of modified EC by competent authority.

45. With these findings, it is now necessary to consider the reliefs sought by the Applicant in this Application. He has sought demolition of the illegal structures and other consequential reliefs….

46. It is now a matter of record that the construction of the project in question is near completion and even the occupancy certificate is granted partially. We need to consider the fact that the project in question is primarily a residential project and many individuals have invested their money in the project for meeting need for residential accommodation by having a house in city like Pune. Any order to demolish structure would also adversely affect them. The

Respondent-9 has already created 3rd party rights. Though the Respondent-9 has blatantly violated the conditions of EC, we also note the total lack of supervision and enforcement at PMC level has resulted in such illegal activity.

47. The Tribunal is expected to apart on the principles of Sustainable Development and Polluter pays principle. We are conscious of the fact that Polluter pays Principle shall not be construed as 'pay and pollute principle', and the payment has therefore to be exemplary and deterrent in order to pass a clear message that environmental compliance is supreme and the party which is non-complying the environmental standards shall be at economic disadvantage.

49. We also refer to the judgment of Hon'ble Principal Bench in the matter of Krishnlal Gera Vrs. State of Haryana (Appeal No.22 of 2015 dated 25th August 2015) wherein the Tribunal has dealt with a matter regarding construction activities without the necessary prior environmental clearance. In para 58 and 59 of the judgment after discussing the legal framework, the Tribunal has imposed environmental compensation cost of 5 % (percent) of the total cost for restoration and restitution of the environment, in addition to payment of Rs.5 crores for violating the Law and starting and completing the project without obtaining environmental clearance, on the project proponent....

50. The Principal Bench in "Appeal No.7/2015 in the matter of *Jalbiradari* v. *MoEF*" pronounced on 31st May 2016, has also considered the legal consequences in case of quashing the environmental clearance for construction project, particularly with regard to the "fate accompli" situation.

> 16. ...*The inevitable consequence could be the Tribunal has dealt with quashing of the Environmental Clearance and set the project at in or they be directed to maintain status quo as on the date of determination. The Tribunal has dealt with large number of cases filing under the category "fate-accompli situation". There are large numbers of projects which have started their construction activity or other activities without even complying Environmental Clearance and the projects were largely completed and then either Environmental Clearance was granted or their cases for granting Environmental Clearance were delisted. In those cases following the principle of Sustainable Development and Polluter Pays Principle, the Tribunal imposed Environmental Compensation on the project proponent for degrading/damaging the environment for starting the project without complying with the provisions of law and for violating the orders and directions. The works of those projects were stopped and a Committee was appointed to revisit for grant/consideration of the Environmental*

Clearance and fresh Environmental Clearance orders were issued. Even where demolition was required the same was directed.… Largely, the 90 per cent of the projects were has already been completed except some other parts of the project. There can be proper regulations on these projects, as otherwise it will only lead to colossal waste of public funds. It will result in dual disadvantage, firstly, wastage of public funds and secondly, and more importantly the demolition of the project itself would generate so much of waste and other materials that this will become a huge environmental hazard itself. The cases are not one, which are incapable of reprisal or re-appreciation. Damage to the environment and ecology to some extent has already been caused. It will be more useful to take remedial and restorative steps.…"

51. We are also inclined to adopt the approach taken by the Bench in the interest of justice and fair play and based on the facts and circumstances of the case. The construction activity is not a prohibited activity in the subject, but a regulated activity. We also take a judicial note of the fact that the demolition of structures in question would also result in further environmental damage and generation of construction waste. Other option which could have been explored is asking the government to take over the additional construction and use it for public purpose but as noted above, already third party rights have been created, may be partially.

52. The purpose and object of the law including Environmental Clearance is to strictly regulate the development so as to prevent causing of damage of the environment and ecology. Though in the present case substantial damage has been caused to the environment and ecology, it will be more useful to take remedial and restorative steps.

53. The Respondent-9 is a defaulting entity which has not complied with law and has adopted a most careless and reckless attitude in relation to protecting the environment. The other Respondents, particularly the PMC and DoE have been the either the mute spectator or have not performed their statutory duties.…

54. For the aforesaid reasons, the Applicant succeeds in his legal pursuit to challenge the noncompliance of EC conditions by the Respondent-9 and obtain certain directions. Hence the Application is allowed and we issue following directions:

    1. The Respondent No.9-PP shall pay environmental compensation cost of Rs.100 crores or 5 % (Five percent) of the total cost of project to be assessed by SEAC whichever is less for restoration and restitution

of environment.... In addition to this, it shall also pay a sum of Rs. 5 crores for contravening mandatory provision of several Environment Laws in carrying out the construction activities in addition to and exceeding limit of the available environment clearance and for not obtaining the consent from the Board.

2. In view of our finding that there has been manifest, deliberate or otherwise suppression of facts of illegality in the project activity of Respondent No.9-PP by the officer of PMC, we impose fine of Rs.5 Lakhs upon the PMC and direct Commissioner PMC to take appropriate action against the erring officers. The amount of Rs. 5 Lakh shall be paid within one month....

*   *   *

NOTES AND QUESTIONS

1. The case presents the extent to which regulatory authorities can abet and aid environmental violations. The Pune Municipal Corporation, in the above case, was found to have actively misrepresented technical figures to allow the project proponent to continue. The Tribunal itself mentions the considerable extent to which the Corporation colluded with the violators. Despite having such a major role to play in the violations, the authority was fined a paltry sum of INR 5 lakhs, whereas the project proponent was ordered to pay INR 100 crores.

2. Should the Tribunal have imposed a greater liability on the Pune Municipal Corporation, and the other authorities involved, considering their collusion? Should there be a uniform framework for imposing liabilities on conniving and colluding authorities so as to introduce accountability and transparency in their workings?

3. The Tribunal imposed an environmental compensation of INR 100 crores or 5 per cent of the total project cost, whichever is less. This measure deviates from the Supreme Court's approach in the *Goa Foundation Case*, where compensation was equal to 10 per cent of the annual turnover of the project proponent. This was confirmed by the fact that upon appeal in this case, the Supreme Court imposed a compensation of "Rs 100 crores or 10% of the project cost, whichever is higher". Thus, although the NGT professes to follow the ratio of the *Goa Foundation Case*, in reality the NGT has significantly diluted the approach to assessing environmental compensation. Is such a diluted approach in line with the NGT's objective and the goal of upholding environmental norms?

*   *   *

National Green Tribunal

(Western Zone) Bench, Pune

Hazira Machhimar Samiti v. Union of India

[Appeal No. 79 of 2013, Judgment Dated 8 January 2016]

J. Kingaonkar, Judicial Member

Dr. Ajay A. Deshpande, Expert Member

*   *   *

Relevant Extracts:

1.   By filing this Appeal, Appellants named above, seek to challenge
      Environmental Clearance (EC) dated May 3rd ,2013, granted by Respondent
      No.2- Ministry of Environment and Forests (MoEF) for further development
      of Port activities at Hajira, district Surat. Chief bone of contention of their
      objection, is that such Port activities, amounting to expansion, in accordance
      with the (J) Appeal No. 79/2013 Page 5 of 21 impugned EC, would hinder
      appropriate, safe and proper access to seawater for the traditional fishermen
      of village Hajira, to undertake traditional fishing in inter-tidal zone. The
      Appellants are traditional fishermen folks and are likely to be put to loss due to
      contemplated expansion of the Port activities, if EC in question is implemented
      by the Respondent No.6. They further allege that the Respondent No.6,
      namely, Adani-Hajaria Port Pvt. Ltd (for short, AHPPL), has already caused
      massive destruction of Mangroves, in order to construct Port Berths as well as
      for the purpose of reclamation of land in the area for which the impugned EC
      is granted by Respondent No.2- MoEF. They allege that grant of impugned
      EC dated May 26.6.2003, is issued, without verification of compliances of
      conditions stipulated in the EC, which was previously issued to AHPPL,
      dated 3rd May, 2013 by the MoEF. They, therefore, along with certain other
      reasons, which are elaborated in the memorandum of Appeal, seek to quash
      the impugned E.C.

2.   According to the Appellants, inter-tidal zone of Hajira Peninsula, called
      "Pagariya" is fishing area in addition to fishing area alongside coastal area of
      Arabian Sea, adjacent to boundary of village Hajira. There are about eighty
      (80) fishing families in village Hajira. They are doing traditional fishing
      business of catching stock of fishes from the seawater by using traditional
      boats, which are sailed through a creek at the opening of Hajira Port.…
      The AHPPL, applied for CRZ permission. That was granted in 2003, under

certain conditions viz. afforestation of Mangroves in area of 550Ha at Kadia Bet in the vicinity of project site. This condition was later on got modified at instance of AHPPL and M/s Nikko Resources Ltd to undertake compensatory afforestation over 200Ha as per the communication dated 19.2.2007, issued by the Additional Director of MoEF.

3. The Appellants allege that … AHPPL commenced construction work in 2010, reclaiming Port backup area, in addition to construction of Berths without transfer of EC or seeking fresh CRZ permission. The validity period of previous clearance had lapsed. There are white back vultures and long billed vultures at the vulture feeding site designated towards conservation efforts. At least, two species f vultures are declared as critically endangered Bird species. There is a component of Railway network, HT transmission line, and internal roads etc., which are not considered while granting the impugned EC. The impugned EC was granted on basis of 'Ex-post Facto' hearing based upon Office Memorandum (O.M) dated 3rd November, 2009, issued by the MoEF. The procedure to grant such an 'Ex-post Facto' hearing, is itself bad in Law, because, it does not give prior opportunity of hearing, which is called 'public consultation', to know objections of members of the public and issues, including R&R, impact of proposed project on life of the objectors, impact of proposed project in the area, including ecology, flora and fauna etc. The impugned EC is, therefore, illegal, improper and liable to be quashed with directions to the Respondent Nos.6 and 7 to deposit restoration cost as well as cost of environmental damage caused by them.

5. Points which arise for determination of this Appeal, are as follows: i) Whether the impugned order of Environmental Clearance (EC) dated May 3rd, 2013, suffers from any illegality, impropriety or irregularities, which makes it liable to be quashed? ii) Whether it is necessary to direct Adani Hazira Port Pvt. Ltd (AHPPL) and M/s Hazira Infrastructures Pvt. Ltd (HIPL), to pay amount of restoration cost or cost for damage caused to environment due to destruction of Mangroves, illegal expansion of the Port or activities like reclamation without valid EC? (J) Appeal No. 79/2013 Page 10 of 21 iii) Whether the creek at mouth of the Port area of Hazira, is narrowed down/ constricted/ infracted due to Port activity of the Respondent Nos.6 and 7, which impede fishing activities of the Appellants and hence they had and have suffered financial loss? If yes, what order is required to be passed?

8. We have carefully perused the maps, which are placed on record by the Appellants.… The maps filed on record go to show that most of Mangroves

area, is destructed. The creek situated in north-east corner is narrowed down due to reclamation of land, as a result of port/cargo activities and Port expansion activities. What we find from the record is that instead of expanding Port work in phase-out manner, expansion was already practically done almost without obtaining EC and CRZ clearance. Obviously, AHPPL labored under impression that it can manage with the authorities to alleviate the problems.... It is evident from the affidavit of Deputy Conservator of Forest date 6.1.2015, that this area, which once had abundance of Mangroves stretches as per MoEF's own record, presently do not have any Mangrove vegetation, clearly indicating the environmental degradation and damage.... The Office Memorandum shows that the State-Govt. shall identify Eco-Sensitive Area (ESA) or areas, categorize them as CRZ-I and water bodies with high biodiversity, shall not be considered for locating Ports and Harbours. The communication reveals that fishing facilities for local communities could be set up with an Environment Impact Assessment (EIA) as per EIA Notification, 2006. It is but obvious that, the Port activities in CRZ-I, area could not have been permitted without following due process of Law....

11. The record shows that hazardous products/material is likely to be brought to the Port and will be stored in storage facility which is shown in the maps. The Hazardous Chemical (Storage & Handling) Rules, 2000, ought to be duly complied with and for such purpose, Pollution Control Board (PCB), is required to certify due 'consent to establish' the hazardous material storage and various facilities, to avoid any future mishap besides specific disaster management plan. This care is not taken by the MoEF, while issuing the impugned EC.

13. ... The fact, however, remains that undaunted by absence of EC and absence of CRZ clearance, the AHPPL proceeded with expansion work after 2007 and did not care for any adverse order or adverse impact on environment. Such irresponsible attitude of the AHPPL, must be deprecated. In this view of the matter, we are of the opinion that the Respondent Nos. 6 and 7, shall be made liable to pay amount of Rs.25 Crore (Rs. Twenty five Crore), as an amount of penalty for restoration as well as shall be restrained from closing/narrowing down mouth of the creek or narrowing down access of the boats of traditional (J) Appeal No. 79/2013 Page 20 of 21 fishermen in the seawater through mouth of the creek, which is situated in north-east corner of the Port area. It follows, therefore, that the impugned EC, is illegal and must be set aside...

*   *   *

NOTES AND QUESTIONS

1. The case presents another instance where the environmental clearance process was heavily flawed, and the project proponent proceeded in blatant violation of the law. Despite this, the Tribunal arrived at an arbitrary figure of INR 25 crores as environmental compensation. A subsequent report by CSE India highlighted that the project cost was INR 1,800 crores. As such, the NGT diluted the approach to even below 5 per cent of the project cost. This goes to evidence the haphazard, inconsistent, and illogical manner in which the Tribunal has applied the polluter pays principle.

2. In 2018, the Supreme Court struck down the INR 25 crore compensation and declared the impugned clearance legal while hearing the appeal against the NGT decision. The Supreme Court's order stated:

> The counsel for the parties state that the matter has been settled for the satisfaction of the fishermen who have also been paid adequate compensation. We are also informed that mangroves have been planted at some other place. In view thereof, since the order of the tribunal has been worked out, the embargo placed in the judgment stands removed and is set aside.

3. Essentially, the project proponent was let off scot-free despite the fact that he had initially deviated from the conditions in the environmental clearance and had shown a blatant disregard for environmental concerns. Although the affected communities had been compensated, the environmental damage remained unaccounted for. Compensatory afforestation was taken to exonerate the project proponent for illegally destroying the mangroves in the first place. Is the Supreme Court's decision tantamount to establishing a "pay and pollute" regime?

*   *   *

COURT ON ITS OWN MOTION v. STATE OF HIMACHAL PRADESH

National Green Tribunal

Application No. 237 (THC)/2013 (CWPIL No.15 of 2010)

6 February 2014

3. … [Rohtang Pass] is termed as the 'Crown Jewel' of Himachal Pradesh. It attracts a large number of tourists. Heavy tourism, besides being a boon to the economy of Himachal Pradesh, is also the cause for adverse impacts on ecology and environment of the State. Diverse and devastating impacts are attributable to unregulated and heavy tourism, overcrowding, misuse of natural resources, construction of buildings and infrastructure, littering of

waste and other activities associated with tourism.... As per the report of the Expert Committee constituted by the High Court of Himachal Pradesh, vide order dated 12th October, 2010, nearly 10,000 persons visit this tourist spot and nearly 3600 (75% taxis) go to the Rohtang Pass per day in the months of May and June, every year, which number is continuously increasing. The available amenities and facilities for tourists within the township are becoming insufficient and thus, the carrying capacity of these amenities and facilities have virtually crossed its physical and ecological limits. Over-construction, increased vehicular traffic and associated air pollution and its impact on snow caps owing to unregulated tourism remain the notable impact.... It has also been reported that nearly 87.3 per cent of the total vehicles plying on Rohtang Pass belong to tourists.... Such natural picnic spots being connected by roads in the Himalayan region lead to these areas being over-pressurized. The ambient air quality, due to high number of vehicles on the top of these mountains, also gets polluted and traffic congestion adds to it.... The snow cover is a source of recreation for the visitors. However, as an adverse impact of heavy tourism, there has been a considerable fall in the amount of snowfall received by the region. Based on another study conducted by the Indian Institute of Technology, Kanpur ... suggests that 40% of the glacial retreat could be attributed to Black Carbon impact....

7.   ... The air pollution problem has aggravated in the recent years due to tremendous increase in the number of trucks and other vehicles for tourists and local population, being plied on these routes. Another serious impact of increased vehicular traffic in these areas is on the wild animals living along the traffic routes. These include walking or running away from vehicles. Many wild animals including birds show "high response" to vehicles. Increase in number of vehicles coincides with decrease in walking activity and vice versa. The vehicles are interfering with the animal activity and their mobility in particular. In some sections, even survival of the animals is affected.

*   *   *

[The Tribunal discusses the right to wholesome and decent environment and the significant aspects of importance of development and protection of environment]

19.   ... The Polluter Pays principle, the Precautionary Principle and the Principle of Proportionality could be applied as facets of the said balanced approach. Irretrievable damage to the environment is not acceptable. The legislative intent behind the Act of 1986 evidently demonstrates this principle. It is a general legislation for environmental protection, as there were uncovered gaps in areas of major environmental aspects and hazards in the existing laws. The

Act contains regulatory, prohibitory and punitive provisions and are aimed at preservation of environment.

*   *   *

DISCUSSION ON POLLUTANT-CONTENTS AND REMEDIES:

20. It is indisputable that the glacier of Rohtang Pass is facing serious pollution issues and with the passage of time, is being degraded environmentally, ecologically and aesthetically. The time has come when not only the State Government, the authorities concerned but even the citizens must realize their responsibility towards restoring the degraded environment of one of the most beautiful zones of the country as well as preventing further damage.

22. ... At present, Bharat Stage-III norms are applicable in Himachal Pradesh whereas BS-IV norms have been implemented in 20 cities in the country. Introduction of more stringent norms in that area, thus, would be desirable. The vehicular traffic has to be restricted as well as regulated. BS-IV compliant fuel should be provided. Preferably, CNG or electrical vehicles should be used for tourism purposes, at least at the initial stage. Only these vehicles should be plying on those roads and more particularly the vehicles going to the glacier for tourism or commercial purposes should be subjected to regular pollution checks. There should be free flow of traffic and over-loading of vehicles should be prohibited. The vehicles which are unworthy of plying on such terrain, should not be permitted to ply, particularly the vehicles which are more than 10 years' old. Regulated tourism for source point control of dust and BC emission should be done. Roads for vehicular traffic should be maintained in a good condition to achieve the desired results of curbing vehicular pollution.

Thus, with this object in mind, we proceed to pass the following directions, particularly in relation to vehicular pollution:

(i) The State Government shall also introduce and install computerized weigh-in-motion systems to check over-loading of the vehicles.

(ii) There should be regular pollution check of vehicles plying on that route.

(iii) If any vehicle is not adhering to the prescribed emission norms, it shall not be permitted to ply on that road. This will equally apply to Government and private vehicles.

(iv) No heavy vehicle – public or private – more particularly trucks will be permitted to cross the barrier to ply on that road if such vehicles or trucks exceed the prescribed permissible load. In other words, no over-loaded vehicle would be permitted to ply on that road, as recorded by the weigh-in-motion systems.

(v) CNG or electricity operated buses or other vehicles of any kind, which would provide incentive to tourism are permitted to ply from Vashishta onwards…. No other vehicle – public or private or Government, including two wheelers – shall be permitted to ply between Vashishta and Rohtang Pass for tourism purposes.

(vi) The petrol driven vehicles plying in Manali and other surrounding areas of Rohtang Pass should have catalytic convertors in all types of vehicles. Preferably even the diesel driven vehicles should be provided with soot collector system to reduce carbon soot pollution. This could be checked at the time of issuing of PUC.

(vii) The vehicles which are more than 10 years' old and plying on this route, shall be phased out and should not be permitted to operate or ply on the route to Rohtang Pass from Vashishta.

(viii) The State Government of Himachal Pradesh is further hereby directed to take appropriate steps in accordance with law to introduce BS-IV norms…

(ix) The Government of Himachal Pradesh should explore the possibility of providing ropeway from Vashishta to Rohtang Pass….

… [The Tribunal also passed ancillary directions in this regard for the complete and effective implementation of the above directions.]

* * *

CLEANLINESS AND PUBLIC AMENITIES

26. … Providing of public amenities and absolute cleanliness at Rohtang Pass and even *en route* is absolutely essential in the interest of environment…. Thus, it is imperative for the Tribunal to issue directions even in this regard, which are as follows :-

(i) Carrying and/or use of any kind of plastic bags, packaging material of food or other items at Rohtang Pass is strictly prohibited. Littering of any kind in, around and also en route Rohtang Pass is also strictly prohibited.

(ii) The Government of Himachal Pradesh may develop a small market at Marhi, which will be entirely eco-friendly and would not be a permanent structure. This small market shall provide eatables, medicines or such other goods of necessities of day-to-day life for the tourists.

(iii) The Government shall also provide eco-friendly toilets at Marhi. Collection of municipal solid wastes and other wastes shall be the responsibility of the State Government and it shall be ensured that these places and the toilets so provided are kept clean and hygienic. The wastes so collected shall be taken to the nearest Municipal Solid Waste (for short the 'MSW') plant and/or the prescribed dumping ground....

(iv) There shall be public toilets provided at Rohtang Pass which should be eco-friendly, the cleanliness of which is to be strictly maintained. These public toilets should be the ones which are removable during non-tourism season. Urinating in open space should be prohibited.

(v) To ensure hygiene, cleanliness and natural beauty of the glacier, it is essential that no commercial activity of any kind is permitted at Rohtang Pass Glacier. Thus, we direct that no commercial activity of any kind would be carried on in, around and en route to Rohtang Pass without any exception.

*   *   *

FORERSTS [*sic*], DEFORESTATION, THEIR IMPACT ON ENVIRONMENT AND REMEDIES

28. ... The solution lies in the urgent need to ensure that tourism industry in the State is environmentally benign and the benefits of decentralization are equally distributed, particularly to rural and local households. High density of traffic in the forest area should be controlled. There is a dire need for carrying out reforestation activity rapidly and at a massive scale. Taking adequate and effective measures for prevention and control of forest fires is also another need of the hour....

... [W]e issue the following directions:

(i) The State Government and all authorities concerned shall take immediate and effective measures for reforestation of the area of Kothi, Gulaba and Marhi. Reforestation shall be taken up as a top priority project and all possible efforts would be made for commencing and completing the plantation in this area.

(ii) As a first step in this direction, the State Government agencies should identify areas that can be brought under reforestation, using latest available remote sensing data coupled with ground verification by the Forest Department.

(iii)   Such species may be used for afforestation as the forest authorities in the State of Himachal Pradesh consider appropriate....

[The Tribunal passed further directions in this regard.]

*   *   *

33.   Global warming has its impacts in other parts of the world, as in the Indian sub-continent. It is likely to affect the glaciers. There will be early and untimely melting of ice resulting in various environmental issues. Rohtang Pass being one of the eco-sensitive and fragile areas of the glacier, is likely to get affected more than other areas. Thus, there is a need for evolving schemes and mechanism to take greater care of the glacier in the interest of environmental and ecological balance.

34.   The other relevant principle is the 'Polluter Pays' principle which can be applied to prevent as well as control further environmental damage in the area. The 'Polluter Pays' principle is one which is aimed at ensuring that the costs of environmental damage caused by the polluting activities are borne in full by the person responsible for such pollution. It is said that this principle means that the polluter should pay for the administration of the pollution control system and for the consequences of the pollution, for example, compensation and clean up. Under this principle, the Government alone cannot be held responsible for preventing and controlling the environmental pollution. If this fiscal incident in its entirety is shifted to the Government, then it would amount to unduly burdening the common tax payer, for none of his fault, for taking anti-pollution, preventive and remedial measures. The actual polluter, thus must be held liable for the damage done. This doctrine has been accepted in larger parts of the world as the fundamental principle on environmental matters and has been one of the underlying principles for action programme on the environment.

The liability of the polluter is absolute for the harm done to the environment which extends not only to compensate the victims of pollution but is also aimed to meet the cost of restoring environment and also to remove the sludge and other pollutants. [Ref: Indian Council for EnviroLegal Action and Ors. Vs. Union of India and Ors. supra].... A large number of tourists and vehicles which are using the roads and are carrying on such other activities for their enjoyment, pleasure or commercial benefits must be made to pay on the strength of the 'Polluter Pays' principle. It will be entirely uncalled for and unjustified if the tax payers' money is spent on taking preventive and control measures to protect the environment. One who pollutes must pay. We have already discussed at some length that the high tourist activity, vehicular pollution and deforestation attributable to acts of emission require to be compensated, restored and maintained in a manner that there is minimum damage and degradation of the environment. Such an approach can even be justified with reference to the doctrine of sustainable development.

38.   ... We would also issue the following general directions:

    (i)   ... The persons who are travelling by public or private vehicles to the glacier of Rohtang Pass must pay a very reasonable sum of money as contribution on the principle of 'Polluter Pays'. Thus, we direct that every truck, bus and vehicle of any kind which passes through the route ahead of Vashishta and Rohtang Pass shall be liable to pay a sum of Rs.100/- for heavy vehicles and Rs.50/- for light vehicles. The passengers travelling through the CNG or electric buses to Rohtang Pass as tourists shall be liable to pay a sum of Rs. 20/- per head, which shall form part of the ticket for the bus.

    (ii)   The funds so collected shall be kept by the State Government under the existing head of Green Tax Fund. The amounts so collected shall be used exclusively for development of this area i.e. from Vashishta to Rohtang Pass and five kilometers ahead of Rohtang Pass.

    (x)   To start with, the State Government shall provide all requisite funds for commencement and progress of the various projects that are to be commenced by it under these directions. These funds shall be provided on top priority basis.

    (xi)   The State Government and all its authorities, municipalities and all private organizations are directed to fully co-operate, co-ordinate and ensure that these directions are complied with, without default or demur.

    (xii)   We hereby constitute a Monitoring Committee consisting of Secretary (Environment), State Govt. of Himachal Pradesh; Conservator of Forests concerned of Kullu Division....

    (xiii)   The above Monitoring Committee shall submit quarterly reports to the NGT, clearly stating non-compliances with the directions, if any, the persons responsible for such default(s) and also suggestions, if any, as it may consider appropriate in order to make further improvements and catalyze the prevention and control of pollution in that area more effectively.

(xiv) The State Government of Himachal Pradesh has already taken a definite stand and made a statement that it shall follow the 'Madhya Pradesh Model' for prevention and control of forest fires. Thus, we direct that an extra effort should be made by the State Government of Himachal Pradesh, for ensuring prevention and control of forest fires, particularly in the Himalayan region, as they are the direct source of deposition of Black Carbon and suspended particulate matter on the glacier.

* * *

NOTES AND QUESTIONS

1. This case portrays an expansion of the polluter pays principle. One of the most important questions under the principle is: who is a "polluter"? Traditionally, the definition was understood in a narrow sense to include industrial polluters and other entities but not the ordinary public and consumers of goods and services. The judgment portrays a partial implementation of the "user pays" principle – a further development of the polluter pays principle. The user pays principle directs the users of a natural resource to bear the costs of the environmental harm. As the tourists in Rohtang Pass are consuming petrol and diesel to ply their cars and are consequently harming the environment, they are being made to pay for the same.

2. The Court took up the case on its own motion (*suo motu*). Do you think that there is any statutory basis for the invocation of such jurisdiction? Do you believe that a quasi-judicial body like the NGT must possess such wide-ranging powers?

3. Article 243W of the Indian Constitution requires the state legislatures to enact laws to confer powers on the municipalities so that they are able to carry out responsibilities laid down in the Twelfth Schedule of the Constitution. The Schedule specifies matters such as the provision of public and urban amenities, public health, sanitation conservancy, and solid waste management. In pursuance of this obligation, the state legislature of Himachal Pradesh enacted the Himachal Pradesh Municipal Corporation Act, 1994, and delegated such powers under it. However, contrary to the above constitutional and legislative scheme, in the case, the Tribunal ruled that the state government will bear the responsibility of collecting municipal waste and other solids in the area in question. Have the courts and tribunals come to have such distrust in the local governments that they have to go against the constitutional mandate? Is this move legitimate? If the obligation of waste collection and management were not to be displaced, could Section 26 of the NGT Act (penalty for failure to comply with the Tribunal's order) be helpful to ensure compliance from the municipality?

NOTES

1. "Report of the United Nations Conference on Environment and Development", United Nations Conference on Environment and Development (Rio De Janeiro 3 June–14 June 1992) (12 August 1992) UN Doc A/CONF.151/26 Rev.1 (Vol. 1); see also "Report of the United Nations Conference on the Human Environment", United Nations Conference on the Human Environment (Stockholm 5–16 June 1972) (15 December 1972) UN Doc A/CONF.48/14/Rev. 1.

2. Armin Rosencranz, Shubham Janghu and Pratheek Reddy, "The Evolution and Influence of International Environmental Norms", *ELR* 49, no. 2 (2019): 125–33.

3. See generally *Vellore Citizens Welfare Forum v. Union of India*, (1996) 5 SCC 647 (Supreme Court of India); *M.C. Mehta v. Union of India*, (1997) 3 SCC 715 (*Lakes Case*) (Supreme Court of India); *Delhi Transport Department Case*, (1998) 9 SCC 250 (Supreme Court of India).

4. See generally Oxford Academic (Oxford University Press), "Sustainability: A History Jeremy L. Caradonna" (YouTube Video, 28 August 2014), https://www.youtube.com/watch?v=hho1h7OR6l8 (accessed 20 December 2022).

5. John Evelyn, *Sylva or a Discourse of Forest-Trees and the Propagation of Timber in His Majesty's Dominions, London 1664* (London: J. Martyn and J. Allestry, 1664).

6. Oxford Academic (Oxford University Press), "Sustainability: A History Jeremy L. Caradonna".

7. Evelyn, *Sylva or a Discourse of Forest-Trees.*

8. T. R. Malthus, *An Essay on the Principle of Population* (London: J. Johnson, 1798), http://www.esp.org/books/malthus/population/malthus.pdf (accessed 22 December 2021).

9. Ibid.

10. Malthus, *An Essay on the Principle of Population.*

11. Adam Smith, *An Inquiry into the Nature and Causes of the Wealth of Nations* (London: Strahan, 1776).

12. Julia Martinez, "Great Smog of London", *Encyclopedia Britannica* (updated 28 November 2021), https://www.britannica.com/event/Great-Smog-of-London (accessed 22 December 2021).

13. H. C. von Carlowitz, *Sylvicultura oeconomica – Anweisung zur wilden Baumzucht* (Leipzig, 1713) (reprint, bearb. von K. Immer u. A. Kiessling, mit einer Einleitung von U. Grober, Freiberg, 2000), 84.

14. Evelyn, *Sylva or a Discourse of Forest-Trees.*

15. Ibid.

16. Ibid.

17. John-Stuart Mill, *Principles of Political Economy* (7th ed., London: Longmans, Green, Reader and Dyer, 1871).

18. Ibid.

19. John Muir, *The Writings of John Muir by John Muir* (Boston: Houghton Mifflin 1916).

20. Ben Purvis, Yong Mao, and Darren Robinson, "Three Pillars of Sustainability: In Search of Conceptual Origins", *Sustainable Science* 14 (2018): 681–685, https://link.springer.com/article/10.1007/s11625-018-0627-5 (accessed 22 December 2021).

21. Dennis Meadows, Donella Meadows, Jorgen Randers, and William Behrens III, *The Limits to Growth* (New York: Potomac Associates-Universe Books, 1972), 158.

22. Mill, *Principles of Political Economy*.

23. Herman E. Daly, "U.N. Conferences on Environment and Development: Retrospect on Stockholm and Prospects for Rio", *Ecological Economics: The Journal of the International Society for Ecological Economics* 5, no. 1 (1992): 9–14.

24. "Report of the United Nations Conference on the Human Environment", United Nations Conference on the Human Environment, Principle 2.

25. "Report of the United Nations Conference on Environment and Development", United Nations Conference on Environment and Development; "Report of the World Summit on Sustainable Development", United Nations World Summit on Sustainable Development (Johannesburg 26 August–4 September 2002) UN Doc A/CONF.199/20; "Report of the United Nations Conference on Sustainable Development", United Nations Conference on Sustainable Development (20 June–22 June 2012) (13 August 2012) UN Doc A/CONF.216/16.

26. Brundtland Commission, *Our Common Future* (New York: Oxford University Press, 1987).

27. Ibid.

28. J. Tobin, "What Is Permanent Endowment Income?", *The American Economic Review* 64, no. 2 (May 1974): 427–432.

29. Ibid.

30. Edith Brown Weiss, "Intergenerational Equity", *Max Planck Encyclopedia of International Law* (2021), https://opil.ouplaw.com/view/10.1093/law:epil/9780199231690/law-9780199231690 -e1421 (accessed 23 December 2021).

31. "Report of the United Nations Conference on Environment and Development", United Nations Conference on Environment and Development.

32. Ibid., Principle 3.

33. Ibid., Principles 7, 12, and 14.

34. Ibid.

35. Ibid., Principle 5.

36. Ibid., Principle 7.

37. Satish C. Shastri, "Environmental Ethics Anthropocentric to Eco-Centric Approach: A Paradigm Shift", *Journal of the Indian Law Institute* 55, no. 4 (October–December 2013): 522–530, http://www.jstor.com/stable/43953654 (accessed 23 December 2021).

38. Ibid.

39. UNGA Res 66/288 (27 July 2010) UN Doc A/RES/66/288.

40. UNGA United Nations Framework Convention on Climate Change (adopted on 9 May 1992, opened for signature on 4 June 1992) 31 I.L.M. 849 (1992).

41. United Nations Convention to Combat Desertification and Drought (entered into force 26 December 1994) 1954 UNTS 3 (1996).

42. FAO The International Treaty on Plant and Genetic Resources for Food and Agriculture (approved on 3 November 2001, entered into force 29 June 2004) 2400 UNTS 303 (2006).

43. Luis A. Avilés, "Sustainable Development and the Legal Protection of the Environment in Europe", *Sustainable Development Law and Policy* 12, no. 3 (2012): 29–44, 30, https://digitalcommons.wcl.american.edu/cgi/viewcontent.cgi?article=1536&context=sdlp (accessed 23 December 2021).

44. Ibid.

45. Hans H. Vedder, "The Treaty of Lisbon and European Environmental Law and Policy", *Journal of Environmental Law* 22, no. 2 (2010): 285–299.

46. Ibid.

47. Ibid.

48. John Martin Gillroy, "Adjudication Norms, Dispute Settlement Regimes, and International Tribunals: The Status of 'Environmental Sustainability' in International Jurisprudence", *Stan. J. Int'l L.* 42, no. 1 (2006): 1–52, 13.

49. Ibid.

50. Ibid.; see also Rosencranz, Janghu, and Reddy, "The Evolution and Influence of International Environmental Norms".

51. See World Trade Organization, *United States – Import Prohibition of Certain Shrimp and Shrimp Products* (12 October 1998) WT/DS58/AB/R [127]–[131].

52. Robert Howse, "The Appellate Body Rulings in the Shrimp/Turtle Case: A New Legal Baseline for the Trade and Environment Debate", *Colum. J. Environmental. L.* 27 (2002): 491–519, http://www.worldtradelaw.net/articles/howseshrimp.pdf.download (accessed on 23 December 2021).

53. Ibid.

54. World Trade Organization, *United States – Import Prohibition of Certain Shrimp and Shrimp Products*.

55. *Legality of the Use by a State of Nuclear Weapons in an Armed Conflict* (Advisory Opinion) [1996] ICJ Rep 66 (8 July 1996).

56. *Gabčíkovo-Nagymaros Project (Hungary v. Slovakia)* (Judgment) [1997] ICJ Rep 7 [140].

57. Prue Taylor, "Case Concerning the Gabcikovo-Nagymaros Project: A Message from the Hague on Sustainable Development", *N.Z. J. Envtl. L.* 3 (1999): 109–26, 114.

58. *Gabčíkovo-Nagymaros Project (Hungary v. Slovakia)*.

59. Ibid.

60. *Case Concerning Pulp Mills on the River Uruguay (Argentina v. Uruguay)* [2010] ICJ Rep 14.

61. Vaughan Lowe, "Sustainable Development and Unsustainable Arguments", in *International Law and Sustainable Development: Past Achievements and Future Challenges*, ed. A. Boyle and D. Freestone, 19–37 (Oxford: Oxford University Press, 1999).

62. Ibid.

63. Ibid.

64. Ibid.

65. Business Standard, "What Was Bhopal Gas Tragedy" ("About" section in *Business Standard*), https://www.business-standard.com/about/what-is-bhopal-gas-tragedy (accessed on 24 December 2021).

66. Ibid.

67. Ibid.

68. Ibid.

69. Ibid.

70. Ibid.

71. Anjali Dhingra, "Bhopal Gas Tragedy and the Development of Environmental Law" (blog, 2 June 2019), https://blog.ipleaders.in/bhopal-gas-tragedy/ (accessed 24 December 2021).

72. Kim Fortun, *Advocacy after Bhopal: Environmentalism, Disaster, New Global Orders* (Chicago: University of Chicago Press, 2001).

73. Edward Broughton, "The Bhopal Disaster and Its aftermath: A Review", *Environ Health Article* 4 (2005): art. 6, https://ehjournal.biomedcentral.com/articles/10.1186/1476-069X-4-6 (accessed 24 December 2021).

74. Japnam Bindra, "Bhopal Gas Tragedy: New SC Bench to Hear Compensation Case", *Mint* (29 January 2020), https://www.livemint.com/news/india/bhopal-gas-tragedy-new-sc-bench -to-hear-compensation-case-11580279138703.html (accessed 20 December 2021).

75. Ibid.

76. Ibid.

77. Narain and Bhushan, "30 Years of Bhopal Gas Tragedy".

78. Ibid.

79. Ibid.

80. Ibid.

81. Arup Poddar, "Indian Supreme Court and Sustainable Development: A Tool for Delivering Environmental Justice" (9 March 2017), https://papers.ssrn.com/sol3/papers.cfm?abstract_ id=3421354 (accessed 24 December 2021).

82. See generally *M.C. Mehta v. Union of India*, (1997) 2 SCC 353 (*Taj Trapezium Case*) (Supreme Court of India); *S. Jagannath v. Union of India*, (1997) 2 SCC 87 (Supreme Court of India); *State of Himachal Pradesh v. Ganesh Wood Products* (1995) 6 SCC 363 (Supreme Court of India); *Karnataka Industrial Areas Development Board v. C. Kenchappa* (2006) 6 SCC 371 (Supreme Court of India).

83. *State of Himachal Pradesh v. Ganesh Wood Products.*

84. Scientific name: *Senegalia catechu.*

85. Extract of the heartwood of the *khair* tree, used as an ingredient in *paan.*

86. Brundtland Commission, *Our Common Future.*

87. *State of Himachal Pradesh v. Ganesh Wood Products* (n 583).

88. *Vellore Citizens Welfare Forum v. Union of India.*

89. Ibid.

90. *Gabčíkovo-Nagymaros Project (Hungary v. Slovakia).*

91. Martin Gillroy, "Adjudication Norms, Dispute Settlement Regimes, and International Tribunals".

92. *Lakes Case.*

93. *In Re: Delhi Transport Department Case.*

94. *S. Jagannath v. Union of India.*
95. *Taj Trapezium Case.*
96. In general terms, "carrying capacity" can be defined as the maximum capacity or capability of the ecosystem to sustain a set of population or biological species in the specified area without any social, economic, or natural repercussions or damage to the environment.
97. *Taj Trapezium Case.*
98. *Vellore Citizens Welfare Forum v. Union of India. Lakes Case*; *T.N. Godavarman v. Union of India*, (2010) 13 SCC 740 (Supreme Court of India).
99. Govt. of India, Ministry of Environment and Forests, Environmental Impact Assessment S.O. 1533(E) (14 September 2006).
100. Gitanjali Nain Gill, *Environmental Justice in India: The National Green Tribunal* (London: Routledge, 2016).
101. Nupur Chowdhary, "Sustainable Development as Environmental Justice: Exploring Judicial Discourse in India", *Economic and Political Weekly* 51, nos. 21–27 (June 2016); see also Sumita Bhowmik, "Sustainable Development and Indian Judiciary" (2 August 2012), https://papers.ssrn.com/sol3/papers.cfm?abstract_id=2122825 (accessed 24 December 2021).
102. *Consumer Education & Research Society v. Union of India*, (2000) 2 SCC 599 (Supreme Court of India).
103. *S. Jagannath v. Union of India.*
104. *Taj Trapezium Case.*
105. *S. Jagannath v. Union of India*, para 7.
106. Ibid.; *M.C. Mehta v. Union of India*, (1997) 2 SCC 353.
107. *Narmada Bachao Andolan v. Union of India*, (2000) 10 SCC 664 (Supreme Court of India).
108. India Today Web Desk, "9 Facts about the Sardar Sarovar Dam, the Second Largest Dam in the World", *India Today* (New Delhi, 18 September 2017) https://www.indiatoday.in/education-today/gk-current-affairs/story/modi-inaugurates-sardar-sarovar-dam-1047031-2017-09-18 (accessed 24 December 2021).
109. Nikhil Eapen, "Narmada Bachao Andolan, Movements are Not Like Governments That Come and Go: 34 Years of the Narmada Protests", *The Caravan* (14 October 2019), https://caravanmagazine.in/communities/narmada-bacaho-andolan-sardar-sarovar-dam (accessed 24 December 2021).
110. Ibid.
111. Climate Diplomacy, "Sardar Sarovar Dam Conflict in India" (Case Study on Climate Diplomacy), https://library.ecc-platform.org/conflicts/sardar-sarovar-dam-conflict-india#:~:text=Villages%20and%20productive%20land%20suffered,the%20river%20bed%2C%20and%20deforestation (accessed 24 December 2021).
112. Ibid.
113. Ibid.
114. Ibid.
115. *Narmada Bachao Andolan v. Union of India*, para 229.
116. Ibid., paras 89–90.

117. Ibid., para 123.

118. *Taj Trapezium Case.*

119. *N.D. Jayal v. Union of India*, (2004) 9 SCC 362 (Supreme Court of India); *Narmada Bachao Andolan v. Union of India.*

120. *N.D. Jayal v. Union of India.*

121. *State of Himachal Pradesh v. Ganesh Wood Products.*

122. *M.C. Mehta v. Kamal Nath*, (1997) 1 SCC 388 (Supreme Court of India).

123. *Vellore Citizens Welfare Forum v. Union of India .*

124. *Narmada Bachao Andolan v. Union of India.*

125. *Karnataka Industrial Areas Development Board v. C. Kenchappa.*

126. Ibid., para 102.

127. Ibid., paras 30 and 100.

128. *Lafarge Umiam Mining (P) Ltd. v. Union of India*, (2011) 7 SCC 338 (Supreme Court of India).

129. Ibid., para 119.

130. Ibid., para 119.

131. Ibid., para 119.

132. Ibid., para 119.

133. Ibid., para 119.

134. *Narmada Bachao Andolan v. Union of India.*

135. *N.D. Jayal v. Union of India.*

136. Ibid., para 19.

137. *Sterlite Industries (India) Ltd. v. Union of India*, (2013) 4 SCC 575 (Supreme Court of India).

138. Ibid., paras 30–33.

139. Utkarsh Sharma, "Five examples of Judicial Overreach" (blog, 30 January 2018), https://blog.ipleaders.in/judicial-overreach-india/ (accessed 24 December 2021).

140. Ibid.

141. Nain Gill, *Environmental Justice in India.*

142. See generally *Vimal Bhai v. Ministry of Environment & Forests*, 2011 SCC OnLine NGT 16 (National Green Tribunal, India); *Bhalachandra Bhikaji Nalwade v. Ministry of Environment & Forests, Government of India*, 2011 SCC OnLine NGT 8 (National Green Tribunal, India); *Krishi Vigyan Arogya Sanstha v. Ministry of Environment & Forests*, 2011 SCC OnLine NGT 18 (National Green Tribunal, India); *Jan Chetna v. Ministry of Environment & Forests*, 2012 SCC OnLine NGT 81 (National Green Tribunal, India).

143. *T. Murugandam v. Ministry of Environment & Forests*, 2012 SCC OnLine NGT 18 (National Green Tribunal, India); *Adivasi Majdoor Kisan Ekta Sangthan v. Ministry of Environment and Forests*, 2012 SCC OnLine NGT 51 (National Green Tribunal, India); *Samata and Forum of Sustainable Development v. Union of India & Ors.*, Judgment dated 13 December 2013 in Appeal No. 9 of 2011 (Southern Zone, National Green Tribunal, India).

144. *Adivasi Majdoor Kisan Ekta Sangthan v. Ministry of Environment and Forests.*

145. UNEP Convention on Environmental Impact Assessment in a Transboundary Context (signed 25 February 1991, entered into force 10 September 1997), 1989 UNTS 309 (1997),

http://sedac.ciesin.org/pidb/texts/environmental.impact.assessment.1991.html (accessed 26 December 2021).

146. *M.C. Mehta v. Kamal Nath*, (2000) INSC 334 (Supreme Court of India); *Taj Trapezium Case*; *Suo Motu Proceedings In Re: Delhi Transport Department Case*.

147. *K.G. Mathew v. State of Kerala*, 2012 SCC OnLine NGT 46 (National Green Tribunal, India).

148. Ibid.

149. *Rohit Choudhury v. Union of India*, 2012 SCC OnLine NGT 66 (National Green Tribunal, India).

150. *Sterlite Industries (India) Ltd. v. Tamil Nadu Pollution Control Board*, 2013 SCC OnLine NGT 68 (National Green Tribunal, India).

151. Ibid., para 114.

152. *Sterlite Industries (India) Ltd. v. Tamil Nadu Pollution Control Board*, para 116. In addition, in applying the principle of proportionality, the Tribunal relies on the following: *Research Foundation for Science and Technology and Natural Resource Policy v. Union of India*, (2007) 9 SCR 906. *Narmada Bachao Andolan v. Union of India*; Charmian Barton, "The Status of the Precautionary Principle in Australia", *Harv. Envtl. L. Rev.* 22, no. 2 (1998): 509–558, 549-A as in *A.P. Pollution Control Board v. M.V. Nayudu (I)*, (1999) 2 SCC 718 (Supreme Court of India) and *M.C. Mehta v. Union of India* (1997) 2 SCC 353 (Supreme Court of India).

153. *N.D. Jayal v. Union of India*; *Narmada Bachao Andolan v. Union of India*.

154. *Sterlite Industries (India) Ltd. v. Tamil Nadu Pollution Control Board*, para 146.

155. *Vellore Citizens Welfare Forum v. Union of India*; *Lakes Case*; *T.N Godavarman v. Union of India*.

156. The Constitution of India.

157. *Gaur Green City Residents Welfare Association v. State of U.P.*, 2013 SCC OnLine NGT 79 (National Green Tribunal, India).

158. Ibid., para 26.

159. Ibid., para 36.

160. Ibid., para 45.

161. *Sarang Yadwadkar v. Commissioner, Pune Municipal Corporation*, 2013 SCC OnLine NGT 4485 (National Green Tribunal, India).

162. Ibid., para 30.

163. See generally *Lafarge Umiam Mining (P) Ltd. v. Union of India*, (2011) 7 SCC 338 (Supreme Court of India); Sterlite Industries (India) Ltd..

164. *Laxmi Suiting v. State of Rajasthan*, 2014 SCC OnLine NGT 1419 (National Green Tribunal, India).

165. *Goa Foundation v. Union of India*, (2014) 6 SCC 590 (Supreme Court of India).

166. *Laxmi Suiting v. State of Rajasthan*, para 58.

167. *Vellore Citizens Welfare Forum v. Union of India*.

168. *State Pollution Control Board v. Swastik Ispat Pvt. Ltd.*, 2014 SCC OnLine NGT 13 (National Green Tribunal, India).

169. Ibid., para 7.

170. *State Pollution Control Board v. Swastik Ispat Pvt. Ltd.*, para 40.

171. *Save Mon Region Federation v. Union of India*, Judgment dated 7th April 2016 in Appeal No.39 of 2012, (Principal Bench, National Green Tribunal, India).

172. Ibid., para 22.

173. *Suo Motu Uttarakhand Human Rights Commission v. Chief Secretary, Govt. of Uttarakhand*, 2016 SCC OnLine NGT 1436 (National Green Tribunal, India); *Tribunal on Its Own Motion v. State of Haryana & Ors.*, 2014 SCC OnLine NGT 1478 (National Green Tribunal, India); *Sonya Ghosh v. State of Haryana*, 2016 SCC OnLine NGT 1608 (National Green Tribunal, India).

174. *Court on Its Own Motion v. State of Himachal Pradesh*, 2014 SCC OnLine NGT 1 (National Green Tribunal, India).

175. *Ramdas Janardan Koli v. Secretary, Ministry of Environment and Forests,* 2015 SCC OnLine NGT 4 (National Green Tribunal, India).

176. Ibid., para 45.

177. United Nations Industrial Development Organization, "What Is CSR" (United Nations Industrial Development Organization), https://www.unido.org/our-focus/advancing-economic -competitiveness/competitive-trade-capacities-and-corporate-responsibility/corporate-social-responsibility-market-integration/what-csr (accessed 27 December 2021).

178. See generally *Shailesh Singh v. Sheela Hospital & Trauma Centre, Shahjhanpur & Ors.*, 2019 SCC OnLine NGT 1360 (*National Green Tribunal, India*); *Sandplast (India) Ltd. & Anr. v. Ministry of Environment and Forest & Ors.*, Order in Original Application No. 102 of 2014 (National Green Tribunal, India).

179. *T.N. Godavarman Thirumulpad v. Union of India & Ors.* 2016 SCC OnLine NGT 1196, Para 32 (National Green Tribunal, India).

180. *Sarang Yadwadkar v. Commissioner, Pune Municipal Corporation.*

181. *Vellore Citizens Welfare Forum v. Union of India*; *Lakes Case*; *T.N. Godavarman v. Union of India*, (2010) 13 SCC 740 (Supreme Court of India).

182. *Ajay Khera v. Container Corporation of India Limited and Others*, 2018 SCC OnLine NGT 2188 (National Green Tribunal, India).

183. Ibid.

184. Ibid.

185. Gregory D. Fullem, "The Precautionary Principle: Environmental Protection in the Face of Scientific Uncertainty", *WILLAMETTE L. Rev.* 31, no. 2 (1995): 495, 497–98.

186. Agne Sirinskiene, "The Status of Precautionary Principle: Moving Towards a Rule of Customary Law", *Jurisprudence* 4, no. 118 (2009): 349–64, https:// www.mruni.eu/upload/ iblock/b27/20sirinskiene.pdf (accessed 26 December 2021).

187. "Action for a Common Future: Report of the Economic Commission for Europe on the Bergen Conference", Economic Commission for Europe (8–-16 May 1990) (6 August 1990) UN Doc A/CONF.151/PC/10.

188. Dalai Lama, "Universal Responsibility and the Global Environment – Address by His Holiness the Dalai Lama at the Rio Earth Summit on June 7th, 1992" (Speech at United Nations

Conference on Environment and Development, Rio De Janeiro Summit on 7 June 1992), https://www.dalailama.com/messages/environment/global-environment (accessed 26 December 2021).

189. Ibid.

190. David N. Snyder, *The Complete Book of Buddha's Lists – Explained* (Las Vegas: Vipassana Foundation, 2009), https://www.thedhamma.com/buddhaslists.pdf (accessed 27 December 2021).

191. See generally Benudhar Patra, "Environment in Early India: A Historical Perspective", *Environment: Traditional & Scientific Research* 1, no. 1 (January–June 2016): 39–56, 42.

192. See generally Sigfried von Ciriacy-Wantrup, *Resource Conservation: Economics and Policies* (Los Angeles: University of California Press, 1952).

193. See generally Samuel P. Hays, *Beauty, Health, and Permanence: Environmental Politics in the United States, 1955–1985* (New York: Cambridge University Press, 1987).

194. Rachel Carson, *Silent Spring* (Cambridge, MA: Houghton Mifflin, 1962).

195. See generally Hays, *Beauty, Health, and Permanence:*.

196. Marco Martuzzi and Joel A. Tuckner (eds), *The Precautionary Principle: Protecting Public Health, the Environment, and the Future of Our Children* (Copenhagen: World Health Organization, 2004), 33.

197. Ibid.

198. Jonathan H. Adler, "More Sorry than Safe: Assessing the Precautionary Principle and the Proposed International Biosafety Protocol", *Texas International Law Journal* 35 (2000): 173–205.

199. Martuzzi and Tuckner, *The Precautionary Principle.*

200. Ibid.

201. Ibid.

202. "World Charter for Nature" UNGA Res 37/7 (28 October 1982) UN Doc A/RES/37/7.

203. "Report of the United Nations Conference on Environment and Development", UN Conference on Environment and Development.

204. UNGA Res 48/189 (20 January 1994) UN Doc A/RES/48/189.

205. United Nations Economic Commission of Europe Convention on the Protection and Use of Transboundary Watercourses and International Lakes (opened for signature on 17 March 1992, entered into force 6 October 1996) 1936 UNTS 269 (1996).

206. United Nations Environmental Programme Convention on Biological Diversity (opened for signatures on 5 June 1992, entered into force 29 December 1993) 1760 UNTS 79 (1993).

207. Science and Environment Health Network, "Wingspread Conference on the Precautionary Principle" (blog on Science and Environment Health Network detailing Wingspread Conference held on 26 January 1998, 5 August 2013).

208. Philippe Sands, *Principles of International Environmental Law* (Cambridge, UK: Cambridge University Press 2003), 273.

209. Arie Trouwborst, *Evolution and Status of the Precautionary Principle* (Springer Netherlands, 2002), ch. 8.

210. *Request for an Examination of the Situation in Accordance with Paragraph 63 of the Court's Judgment of 20 December 1974 in the Nuclear Tests (New Zealand v. France) Case* (Order dated 22 September 1995) [1995] ICJ Rep. 288, 348.

211. Ibid.

212. Trouwborst, *Evolution and Status of the Precautionary Principle*, ch. 8.

213. Ibid; also see Frank B. Cross, "Paradoxical Perils of the Precautionary Principles", *Washington and Lee Law Review* 53, no. 3 (1996): 851–925, https://scholarlycommons.law.wlu.edu/cgi/viewcontent.cgi?article=1656&context=wlulr (accessed 27 December 2021).

214. Commission of the European Communities, "Communication from Commission on the Precautionary Principle", COM (2000) 1 final.

215. Ibid.

216. Kenisha Garnett and David J Parsons, "Multi Case Review of the Application of the Precautionary Principle in European Union Law and Case Law", *Risk Analysis* 37, no. 3 (2017): 502–16; also see Douglas Crawford-Brown and Sean Crawford-Brown, "The Precautionary Principle in Environmental Regulations for Drinking Water", *Environmental Science and Policy* 14, no. 4 (2011): 379–387; J. Zander, *The Application of the Precautionary Principle in Practice: Comparative Dimensions* (Cambridge: Cambridge University Press, 2010); N. Sachs, "Rescuing the Strong Precautionary Principle from Its Critics", *University of Illinois L. Rev.* 4 (2011): 1285–1338; R. Lofstedt, "The Precautionary Principle: Risk, Regulation and Politics", *Process Safety and Environment Protection* 81, no. 1 (2003): 36–43; United Kingdom Interdepartmental Liaison Group on Risk Assessment, "The Precautionary Principle: Policy and Application – The Need for Consistent Approach" (UK-ILGRA, 2002).

217. Supporting the proposition that the precautionary principle was a part of customary international law –Sands, *Principles of International Environmental Law*; also see James Cameron and Juli Abouchar, "The Status of the Precautionary Principle in International Law", in *The Precautionary Principle and International Law: The Challenge of Implementation*, ed. D. Freestone and E. Hey, 29–52 (The Hague, London, Boston: Kluwer Law International, 1996). Against the proposition that the precautionary principle was a part of customary international law – Patricia Birnie, Alan Boyle, and Catherine Redgwell, *International Law and the Environment* (3rd edn., Oxford: Oxford University Press, 2009). See also Jonathan B. Wiener, "Precaution", in *International Environmental Law*, ed. Daniel Bodansky, JuttaBrunee and Ellen Hey, 597–612 (Oxford: Oxford University Press, 2007).

218. *Gabčíkovo-Nagymaros Project (Hungary v. Slovakia)* (Order dated 5 February 1997) [1997] ICJ Rep 3.

219. *Southern Bluefin Tuna cases (New Zealand v. Japan)* ITLOS Case No. 3.

220. The Constitution of India.

221. See generally *Subhash Kumar v. State of Bihar*, (1991) 1 SCC 598 (Supreme Court of India); *Shanti Star Builders v. Narayan Totame*, (1990) 1 SCC 520 (Supreme Court of India).

222. *Vellore Citizens Welfare Forum v. Union of India*.

223. Ibid., para 11.

224. Ibid.,.

225. *Lakes Case.*

226. *Bittu Sehgal v. Union of India*, (2001) 9 SCC 181 (Supreme Court of India).

227. *Lakes Case.*

228. *Taj Trapezium Case.*

229. Vardharajan Committee, "Report on Environmental Impact of Mathura Refinery" (National Environment Engineering Research Institute [NEERI] Overview Report, 1990).

230. *A.P. Pollution Control Board v. M.V. Nayudu (I).*

231. Ibid.

232. *A.P. Pollution Control Board v. Prof M V Nayudu (II),* (2001) 2 SCC 62 (Supreme Court of India).

233. *Narayan Ganesh Dastane v. Sucheta Narayan Dastane,* AIR 1975 SC 1534 (Supreme Court of India).

234. *A.P. Pollution Control Board v. M.V. Nayudu (II).*

235. *Narmada Bachao Andolan v. Union of India.*

236. Climate Diplomacy, "Sardar Sarovar Dam Conflict in India".

237. *Narmada Bachao Andolan v. Union of India,* para 103.

238. *N.D. Jayal v. Union of India.*

239. Ibid.

240. Ibid.

241. *Bittu Sehgal v. Union of India.*

242. *Lakes Case.*

243. See generally*The Sarpanch, Grampanchayat Tiroda, Tal. Sawantwadi, District Sindhudurg, Maharashtra v. Secy, MoEF,* 2011 SCC OnLine NGT 10 (National Green Tribunal, India); *Krishi Vigyan Arogya Sanstha v. Ministry of Environment & Forests; T. Murugandam v. Ministry of Environment & Forests; Jeet Singh Kanwar v. Union of India,* 2013 SCC OnLine NGT 1 (National Green Tribunal, India).

244. *Goa Foundation v. Union of India,* 2013 SCC OnLine NGT 86 (National Green Tribunal, India).

245. *Rayons-Enlighting Humanity v. Ministry of Environment and Forests,* 2013 SCC OnLine NGT 48 (National Green Tribunal, India).

246. *State Pollution Control Board v. Swastik Ispat Pvt. Ltd.*

247. Ibid.

248. *Sterlite Industries (India) Ltd. v. Tamil Nadu Pollution Control Board.*

249. Ibid., para 146.

250. Ibid., para 122.

251. *Associated Provincial Picture Houses Ltd v. Wednesbury Corporation* [1947] EWCA Civ 1, [1948] 1 KB 223.

252. *Sterlite Industries (India) Ltd. v. Tamil Nadu Pollution Control Board.*

253. The Wednesbury Principle was laid down in the *Associated Provincial Picture Houses Ltd. v. Wednesbury Corporation* and was meant to set a certain standard for the courts to justify

interference. It was held that courts of authority could interfere in the judgment or decision of a court as long as the decision was such that no reasonable authority could have reached such erroneous conclusion.

254. *State Pollution Control Board v. Swastik Ispat Pvt. Ltd.*

255. *Sterlite Industries (India) Ltd. v. Union of India,* para 136.

256. Ibid., para 139.

257. Ibid., para 140.

258. *Tamil Nadu Pollution Control Board v. Sterlite Industries Ltd*, (2019) 19 SCC 479 (Supreme Court of India).

259. *Krishan Kant Singh v. Triveni Engg. Industries Ltd.*, Judgment dated 10th December 2015 in Original Application No. 317 of 2014 (National Green Tribunal, India).

260. Ibid., para 20.

261. Ibid., para 18.

262. *Indian Council for Enviro-Legal Action v. MoEF*, Judgement dated 10 December 2015 in Original Application 170 of 2014 (National Green Tribunal, India).

263. *S.P. Muthuraman v. Union of India* 2015 SCC OnLine NGT 169 (National Green Tribunal, India).

264. *Ramdas Janardan Koli v. Secretary, Ministry of Environment and Forests.*

265. Ibid., para 72.

266. *Amit Upadhyaya v. State Level Environmental Impact Assessment Authority*, 2019 SCC OnLine NGT 865 (National Green Tribunal, India).

267. Ibid., para 56.

268. *Narmada Bachao Andolan v. Union of India.*

269. *N.D. Jayal v. Union of India.*

270. See generally *Sreeranganathan K.P. v. Union of India*, 2014 SCC OnLine NGT 15 (National Green Tribunal, India); *Sarang Yadwadkar v. Commissioner, Pune Municipal Corporation.*

271. Ibid.

272. Section 20, The National Green Tribunal Act, 2010 (Act 19 of 2010) (India).

273. *Narmada Bachao Andolan v. Union of India.*

274. *N.D. Jayal v. Union of India.*

275. *Narmada Bachao Andolan v. Union of India.*

276. Plato, *The Dialogues of Plato: The Laws* (vol. 4, 4th edn, tr Benjamin Jowett, London: Clarendon Press 1953).

277. R. P. Kangle, *Kautiliya Arthasastra* (Part II, tr R. P. Kangle, Delhi: Motilal Banarsidass Publishers, 1986).

278. Muhammad Munir, "History and Evolution of the Polluter Pays Principle: How an Economic Idea Became a Legal Principle?" (8 September 2013), SSRN, https://papers.ssrn.com/sol3/papers.cfm?abstract_id=2322485 (accessed 28 December 2021.

279. Ibid.

280. See generally Council of Europe Committee of Ministers, Resolution (68)4 adopting the Declaration of Principles on Air Pollution Control (Adopted by the Ministers' Deputies

on 8 March 1968); William J. Baumol and Wallace E. Oates, "The Use of Standards and Prices for Protection of the Environment", *The Swedish Journal of Economics* 73, no. 1 (1971): 42–54, 51.

281. O. A. Davis and Andrew Whinston, "Externalities, Welfare and the Theory of Games", *Journal of Political Economy* 70, no. 3 (1962): 241–262.

282. Jean-Philippe Birde, "Studies in International Environmental Economics", in *International Economics of Pollution*, ed. Ingo Walter (New York: Halstead Press, 1976), 138.

283. A. C. Pigou, *The Economics of Welfare* (London: Macmillan & Co., 1920); see also Munir, "History and Evolution of the Polluter Pays Principle" .

284. *Trail Smelter Case (USA, Canada)* (Arbitration Tribunal) (16 April 1938 and 11 March 1941) 3 UN Rep. Int'l Arb. Awards 1905 (1941), https://legal.un.org/riaa/cases/vol_III/1905-1982.pdf (accessed 28 December 2021).

285. *Trail Smelter Case.*

286. Russel A. Miller and Rebecca M. Bratspies (eds.), *Transboundary Harm in International Law: Lessons from the Trail Smelter Arbitration* (Cambridge: Cambridge University Press, 2006), 3.

287. Jaye Ellis, "Has International Law Outgrown *Trail Smelter*?" in *Transboundary Harm in International Law: Lessons from the Trail Smelter Arbitration*, ed. Russel A. Miller and Rebecca M. Bratspies, 56–65 (Cambridge, UK: Cambridge University Press, 2006).

288. Council of Europe Committee of Ministers, Resolution (68)4 adopting the Declaration of Principles on Air Pollution Control.

289. Organization for Economic Co-operation and Development, "Statistics on Emissions of Air Pollutants" (Statistics, last updated on September 2001), https://stats.oecd.org/Index.aspx?DataSetCode=AIR_EMISSIONS (accessed 29 December 2021).

290. "Recommendation of the Guiding Principles Concerning International Economic Aspects of Environmental Policies", OECD Environment Policy Committee (adopted on 26 May 1972) C(72)128.

291. Ibid.

292. "The Polluter-Pays Principle: OECD Analyses and Recommendations", Organization for Economic Co-operation and Development' Environment Directorate, Organization for Economic Co-operation and Development (1994) OCDE/GD (92)81.

293. "OECD Recommendation on the Application of the Polluter-Pays Principle", OECD Council (adopted 7 July 1989) C(97)132, https://legalinstruments.oecd.org/en/instruments/OECD-LEGAL-0251 (accessed 28 December 2021).

294. *Rylands v. Fletcher*, [1868] L.R. 3 H.L. 330.

295. OECD Council (n 795) Point 4, https://legalinstruments.oecd.org/en/instruments/OECD-LEGAL-0251 (accessed 28 December 2021).

296. J. Moffet and F. Bregha, "The Role of Law in the Promotion of Sustainable Development", *Journal of Environmental Law and Practice* 6, no. 3 (1996): 3, 8.

297. "The Polluter-Pays Principle: OECD Analyses and Recommendations", Organization for Economic Co-operation and Development.

298. Ibid.

299. The Alpine Convention (opened for signature on 9 November 1991); United Nations Economic Commission of Europe Convention on the Protection and Use of Transboundary Watercourses and International Lakes; Convention for the Protection of the Marine Environment of the North-East Atlantic (opened for signature 22 September 1992, entered into force 25 March 1998) 2354 UNTS 67 (2006); Convention on the Protection of the Marine Environment of the Baltic Sea Area (Helsinki Convention) (entered into force 3 May 1980) 1507 UNTS 166 (1988).

300. "Report of the United Nations Conference on Environment and Development", United Nations Conference on Environment and Development.

301. Ibid., Principle 16.

302. Convention on the Protection of the Marine Environment of the Baltic Sea Area.

303. Bamako Convention on the Ban of the Import into Africa and Control of Transboundary Movement and Management of Hazardous Waste Within Africa (entered into force 22 April 1998) 2101 UNTS 177 (2000) Article 12.

304. Convention on the Prevention of Marine Pollution by Dumping of Wastes and Other Matter (adopted 29 December 1972, entered into force 30 August 1975) 1046 UNTS 120 (1977).

305. Convention for the Protection and Development of the Marine Environment of the Wider Caribbean Region (adopted 24 March 1983, entered into force 11 October 1986) 1506 UNTS 177 (1988) Article 14.

306. See generally *Case Concerning the Auditing of Accounts (The Netherlands/France)* (Award) Permanent Court of Arbitration Case No. 2000-02 (12 March 2004). Also see *Trail Smelter Case*.

307. See *New Zealand v. France*.

308. Ibid.

309. Ibid.

310. Abu Hena Mostofa Kamal, "Polluter Pays Principle and Its Limitations", *Daily Star*, Law & Our Rights (January 2007) (No. 4), https://www.thedailystar.net/law/2007/january/04/depth.htm (accessed 28 December 2021).

311. *Indian Council for Enviro-Legal Action v. Union of India*, (1996) 3 SCC 212 (Supreme Court of India).

312. *M.C. Mehta v. Union of India*, (1987) 1 SCC 395 (Supreme Court of India).

313. Ibid.

314. *Rylands v. Fletcher*.

315. *M.C. Mehta v. Union of India*, (1987) 1 SCC 395, para 31.

316. "OECD Recommendation on the Application of the Polluter-Pays Principle", OECD Council.

317. *Rylands v. Fletcher*.

318. *Indian Council for Enviro-Legal Action v. Union of India*.

319. Ibid., para 67.

320. *M.C. Mehta v. Union of India*, (1987) 1 SCC 395.

321. *Vellore Citizens Welfare Forum v. Union of India*.

322. Ibid., paras 10–11.

323. *New Zealand v. France.*

324. See generally *Taj Trapezium Case*; *M.C. Mehta v. Union of India*, (1997) 2 SCC 411 (Calcutta Tanneries Case) (Supreme Court of India); *S. Jagannath v. Union of India*.

325. *M.C. Mehta v. Union of India*, (2004) 12 SCC 118 (Supreme Court of India).

326. Ibid., para 47.

327. *M.C. Mehta v. Union of India*, (2006) 3 SCC 399 (Supreme Court of India).

328. *Indian Council for Enviro-Legal Action v. Union of India*, (2011) 8 SCC 161 (Supreme Court of India).

329. *M.C. Mehta v. Kamal Nath*, (2000) INSC 334 (Supreme Court of India).

330. Ibid., para 39.

331. Ibid., paras 10 and 24.

332. *Deepak Nitrite Ltd. v. State of Gujarat*, (2004) 6 SCC 402 (Supreme Court of India).

333. Ibid., para 6.

334. *Vedanta Alumina Ltd. v. Prafulla Samantra & Ors.*, LPA No.277 of 2009.

335. *Pravinbhai Jashbhai Patel v. State of Gujarat*, (1995) 36 Guj LR 1210 (Gujarat High Court, India).

336. *Goa Foundation v. Union of India.*

337. Ibid., para 63.

338. Ibid.

339. *M.C. Mehta v. Union of India*, (1987) 1 SCC 395.

340. *Manoj Mishra v. Union of India*, Judgment/Order in O.A. No. 6 of 2012 (National Green Tribunal, India).

341. *Abhishek Rai v. State of HP*, 2013 SCC OnLine NGT 3617 (National Green Tribunal, India).

342. *Jagat Narayan Vishwakarma v. Union of India*, 2014 SCC OnLine NGT 2685 (National Green Tribunal, India).

343. *Kamal Anand v. State of Punjab*, 2014 SCC OnLine NGT 6893 (National Green Tribunal, India).

344. Ibid., para 15.

345. *Ashok Gabaji Kajale v. Godhavari Bio-Refineries Ltd.*, 2015 SCC OnLine NGT 127 (National Green Tribunal, India).

346. Ibid., para 57.

347. *Deepak Nitrite Ltd. v. State of Gujarat* (Supreme Court of India).

348. *Gurpreet Singh Bagga v. Ministry of Environment and Forests*, 2016 SCC OnLine NGT 92 (National Green Tribunal, India).

349. Ibid., para 92.

350. Aniruddha Ghosal and Sowmiya Ashok, "Inside the NGT as It Turns Seven", *Indian Express* (New Delhi, 26 June 2018), https://indianexpress.com/article/india/ngt-national-green-tribunal-delhi-smog-pollution-swatanter-kumar-inside-the-ngt-as-it-turns-seven-4943859/ (accessed 29 December 2021).

351. HT Correspondent, "NGT Slaps ₹195 Cr. fine on Pune's Goel Ganga Developers for Environmental Damage", *Hindustan Times* (Pune, 9 January 2018), https://www.hindustantimes.

com/pune-news/ngt-slaps-195-cr-fine-onpune-s-goel-ganga-developers-for-environmental-damage/story-eHVl8micvPT7X3Bp58ZEcO.html (accessed 29 December 2021).

352. See generally Raghuveer Nath and Armin Rosecranz, "Determination of Environmental Compensation: The Art of Living Case", *NUJS L. REV.* 12, no. 1 (2019): 1–19; also see Chandra Bhushan, Srestha Banerjee, and Ikshaku Bezbaroa, *Green Tribunal, Green Approach: The Need for Better Implementation of the Polluter Pays Principle* (New Delhi: Centre for Science and Environment, 2018).

353. *Forward Foundation v. State of Karnataka*, 2015 SCC OnLine NGT 5 (National Green Tribunal, India).

354. *Goa Foundation v. Union of India and Ors.*, Order dated 21 April 2014 in Writ Petition (Civil) No. 435 of 2012 (Supreme Court of India).

355. Ibid., para 63.

356. Ibid.*Goa Foundation*, para 63.

357. Ibid., para 66.

358. *Samaj Parivartana Samudaya v. State of Karnataka*, Writ Petition No. (C) 562 of 2009 (Supreme Court of India).

359. See generally *S.P. Muthuraman v. Union of India*, Original Application No, 37 of 2015 (National Green Tribunal, India); *Manoj Misra v. Union of India*, Original Application No. 65 of 2016 (National Green Tribunal, India); *Krishan Lal Gera v. State of Haryana*, Appeal No. 22 of 2015 (National Green Tribunal, India); *Sunil Kumar Chugh v. Secretary Environment Department*, Appeal No. 66 of 2014 (National Green Tribunal, India). Also see Bhushan, Banerjee, and Bezbaroa, *Green Tribunal, Green Approach*, 8.

360. *Forward Foundation v. State of Karnataka*.

361. Ibid., para 2.

362. Ibid., para 43.

363. Ibid., para 4.

364. Ibid., para 84.

365. Ibid., para 84.

366. *Mr. Tanaji Balasaheb Gambhire v. Union of India*, Application No. 184 of 2015 (National Green Tribunal, India). Also see HT Correspondent, "NGT Slaps ₹195 Cr. Fine on Pune's Goel Ganga Developers for Environmental Damage".

367. Ibid.

368. *Goel Ganga Developers Private Limited v. Union of India*, (2018) 18 SCC 257 (Supreme Court of India).

369. Ibid.

370. *Goel Ganga Developers Private Limited v. Union of India*, para 61.

371. *Tanaji Balasaheb Gambhire v. Union of India and Ors.*, 2016 SCC OnLine NGT 4213 (National Green Tribunal, India).

372. Ibid., para 47.

373. *Krishan Kant Singh v. Triveni Engineering Industries Ltd.*, Miscellaneous Application No. 1099 of 2015 (National Green Tribunal, India).

374. *T.N. Godavarman Thirumulpad v. Union of India*, 2016 SCC OnLine NGT 1196 (National Green Tribunal, India).

375. Ibid., para 29.

376. *M/s. DSM Sugar Distillery Division v. Shailesh Singh & Ors.*, Order/Judgment dated 10 December 2015 in Review application no. 13 of 2015 in Original Application No. 35 of 2015 (National Green Tribunal, India); *Krishan Kant Singh v. Triveni Engineering Industries Ltd.*

377. *Manoj Mishra v. Delhi Development Authority & Ors.*, Judgment/Order in Original Application No. 65 of 2016 (National Green Tribunal, India).

378. Ibid., para 34.

379. Ibid., para 39.

380. In order dated 11 March 2016, the Tribunal clarifies that INR 5 crore is not a penalty in terms of Section 26 of the NGT Act, 2010. See also ibid.

381. Letter dated 3 March 2016 from Mr Shashi Shekhar to the National Green Tribunal, D.O. No. 5 (UIR, RD 1 GR)/ Misc./2016.

382. Ibid., 57 and 61.

383. Debobrat Ghose, "NGT v AOL: How the Green Tribunal Flouted Its Own Order against Sri Sri's Organisation", *FirstPost India* (New Delhi, 11 March 2016), https://www.firstpost.com/india/ngt-vs-aol-how-the-green-tribunal-flouted-its-own-order-against-sri-sris-organisation-2670494.html (accessed 29 December 2021); Express News Service, "Maybe Someone Called Up NGT to Clear Sri Sri Event: Cong Leader Jairam Ramesh", *Indian Express* (18 March 2016), https://indianexpress.com/article/india/india-news-india/wcf-ngt-aol-sri-sri-jairam-ramesh/ (accessed 20 December 2021); SCOI Report, "How Art of Living Managed to Circumvent the NGT Ruling", *Legally India* (12 March 2016), https://www.legallyindia.com/the-bench-and-the-bar/how-art-of-living-managed-to-circumvent-the-ngt-ruling-and-get-away-paying-only-rs-2-5-cr-despite-its-open-defiance-20160312-7312 (accessed 21 December 2021).

384. Bhushan, Banerjee, and Bezbaroa, *Green Tribunal, Green Approach*, 39.

385. *Krishan Kant Singh v. National Ganga River Basin Authority*, 2014 SCC OnLine NGT 5640, Para 51 (National Green Tribunal, India).

386. Bhushan, Banerjee, and Bezbaroa, *Green Tribunal, Green Approach*, 12.

387. Ibid., 12.

388. *Vivek Tyagi v. State of U.P.*, 2019 SCC OnLine NGT 1034 (National Green Tribunal, India).

389. Ibid., para 13.

390. *Rohit Choudhury v. Union of India.*

391. Ibid., para 35.

392. Ibid., para 17.

393. Ibid., para 15.

394. *Manoj Mishra v. Delhi Development Authority*, 2016 SCC OnLine NGT 114 (National Green Tribunal, India).

395. Ibid., para 4.

396. *Threat to Life Arising out of Coal Mining in South Garo Hills v. State of Meghalaya*, 2019 SCC OnLine NGT 105 (National Green Tribunal, India); also see Public Trust of India, "NGT Imposes Rs. 100 Crore Fine on Meghalaya Govt for Failing to Curb Illegal Mining", *Economic Times* (New Delhi, 4 January 2019), https://economictimes.indiatimes.com/news/politics-and-nation/ngt-imposes-rs-100-crore-fine-on-meghalaya-govt-for-failing-to-curb-illegal-mining/articleshow/67388967.cms (accessed 29 December 2021).

397. Ibid.

398. *Threat to Life Arising out of Coal Mining in South Garo Hills v. State of Meghalaya*; Public Trust of India, "NGT Imposes Rs. 100 Crore Fine on Meghalaya Govt for Failing to Curb Illegal Mining".

399. *Indian Council for Enviro-Legal Action & Ors v. Jammu and Kashmir State Pollution Control Board*, 2018 SCC OnLine NGT 393 (National Green Tribunal, India).

400. *Satish Kumar v. Union of India & Ors.*, Order dated 03 December 2018 in Original Application No. 56 (THC) of 2013 (National Green Tribunal, India).

401. *Mayank Manohar & Anr. v. Govt. of NCT of Delhi & Ors.*, Order dated 24 January 2019 in Original Application No. 601 of 2018 (National Green Tribunal, India).

402. *Manoj Mishra v. Union of India,* 2019 SCC OnLine NGT 644 (National Green Tribunal, India).

403. Ibid.

404. *Vardhaman Kaushik v. Union of India & Ors.*, 2017 SCC OnLine NGT 758, Para 5 (National Green Tribunal, India).

405. Ibid.

406. Dipu Rai, "Air Pollution in Delhi Was 16 Times Worse than Prescribed Limit on Diwali Night", *India Today* (28 October 2019), https://www.indiatoday.in/diu/story/delhi-air-pollution-16-times-worse-prescribed-limit-diwali-night-1613477-2019-10-28 (accessed 29 December 2021).

407. Public Trust of India, "Delhi Pollution: NGT Bans Construction, Industrial Activities till 14 November", *Live Mint* (New Delhi, 9 November 2017), https://www.livemint.com/Politics/MHVjYfmyoaZVnnYKg2mFzK/Delhi-air-pollution-NGT-imposes-ban-on-industrial-construc.html (accessed 29 December 2021).

408. Ibid.

409. Geetanjoy Sahu, "Wither the National Green Tribunal?" *Down To Earth* (23 September 2019) https://www.downtoearth.org.in/blog/environment/whither-the-national-green-tribunal--66879 (accessed 29 December 2021).

410. Bhushan, Banerjee, and Bezbaroa, *Green Tribunal, Green Approach,* 18.

411. Ibid., 19.

4

EVALUATING THE NATIONAL GREEN TRIBUNAL AFTER A DECADE

CHALLENGES TO OVERCOME

It has been a decade since the NGT Act was enacted by the parliament.[1] As discussed in Chapter 1, however, this enactment was primarily a result of judicial assertion rather than legislative will. The Supreme Court, throughout the 1980s up till the early 2000s, tackled environmental degradation and pollution through the process of public interest litigation. This process allowed the Court to provide wider remedies by way of procedural innovations such as the expansion of *locus standi* through the introduction of epistolary jurisdiction,[2] introduction of a non-adversarial procedure,[3] and ensuring monitoring and implementation of orders through *continuing mandamus*.[4] While most of the present environmental jurisprudence came from this, the Court found it increasingly difficult to adjudicate complex scientific and technical issues involved in environmental cases.[5] In addition, the Court found itself increasingly indulging in fact-finding and evidence collection since writ petitions under the expanded *locus standi* were accepted without the requirement of much proof.[6] Frequently, the Court would overstep its constitutional boundaries and enter into regulatory, administrative, and policymaking domains to meet the ends of justice.[7]

Accordingly, as discussed previously, the Supreme Court, through four major decisions, called for the creation of the NGT by voicing the urgent need for a "green tribunal".[8] Further, the 186th Report of the Law Commission of India recommended the establishment of "environmental courts" in every state, which would be composed of judges as well as experts and would have both original and appellate jurisdiction.[9]

However, the lack of legislative will in this regard was evident from the failures of the NGT's predecessors – the NET and the NEAA. These tribunals were made toothless due to a lack of appointments and funding.[10] The NET remained on paper as the NET Act, 1995, was never notified, and the NEAA remained without a chairperson for almost a decade. In fact, at one point in time, the NEAA had only one member who was also its chairperson.[11] Nevertheless, due to the concern voiced by the Supreme Court and the Law Commission, coupled with the need to give effect to India's obligations under the Stockholm[12] and Rio[13] Declarations, the Indian legislature enacted the NGT Act.

Given this context, it is clear that the raison d'être of the NGT is to tackle "substantial questions relating to environment" replete with complex scientific and technical issues in an effective and expeditious manner. In Chapter 2, we have discussed the Tribunal's interpretation and application of various provisions contained in the NGT Act. We have, inter alia, analysed the NGT's expansive interpretation of its jurisdiction through a broad reading of an aggrieved person, the assumption of *suo motu* jurisdiction, the compensation regime, and the scope of judicial review. Further, in Chapter 3 we have analysed the NGT's interpretation and application of three international environmental principles – sustainable development, the precautionary principle, and the polluter pays principle – to further environmental justice.

In its existence of more than a decade, the establishment of the NGT has certainly been a progressive step when compared to the environmental adjudication regime that existed before. Its expertise has allowed for more expeditious disposal of environmental cases. For instance, between 2010 and 2017, out of a total of 23,626 cases that were filed, 19,066 cases were disposed of.[14] However, there are significant challenges that the NGT still needs to overcome.

Through this chapter, we will explore these challenges. While some are more serious than others, they all have the potential to seriously affect the NGT's functioning and its ability to provide effective environmental justice. Some of these issues have been discussed in detail in previous chapters. Nevertheless, this chapter consolidates the issues and highlights ten significant challenges that the NGT has faced in its first decade of existence.

4.1   LACK OF ACCESS TO JUSTICE

At present, in addition to the Principal Bench in New Delhi, the NGT has four other zonal benches in metropolitan cities. These are located in Pune (Western Zone Bench), Chennai (Southern Zone Bench), Kolkata (Eastern Zone Bench), and Bhopal (Central Zone Bench). Given that most industries, forests, mines, and ecologically sensitive areas are located away from these cities, access to environmental justice for those affected by environmental damage becomes challenging.

In fact, during the parliamentary debate prior to the enactment of the NGT Act, concerns relating to access to justice were expressed.[15] The NGT Bill was referred to the Standing Committee on Science and Technology, Environment, and Forests. In its report,[16] the Standing Committee expressed particular concern for the lack of access to justice. Since the Bill proposed to accord the NGT exclusive jurisdiction over all civil cases where a substantial question relating to the environment was involved, the Committee opined that this would seriously hamper access to justice:[17]

> The Committee feels that the National Green Tribunal which claims itself to be a mechanism aimed at effective and expeditious disposal of civil cases relating to environmental protection and conservation of forests does not exude much confidence given its infrastructural framework, particularly in view of the geographical vastness of our country.... Thus, the poor and the tribal people living in remote areas will be deprived of the opportunity to approach civil courts for redressal of their grievances on substantial question relating to environment.

Thus, it was thought that as the Tribunal would take over the powers of the lower courts with respect to environmental cases, many people would not have local access to justice.[18] Particularly, this would affect the economically weaker sections of society the most as they rely on more than 13,000 district and subordinate courts for environmental litigation and relief.[19] Unfortunately, this is exactly what happened. After the enactment of the NGT Act, these lower courts were barred from taking up environmental cases.[20] This meant that the economically weaker and the most affected communities living in remote parts of the country had to approach their respective zonal bench for seeking justice.[21]

A good example of this is in Jharkhand's Chaibasa district where the Bindrai Institute for Research and Action (BIRSA) along with the Occupation Health and Safety Centre (OHSC) approached the NGT to address environmental damage caused due to abandoned asbestos mines.[22] In doing so, the convener of BIRSA pointed out:[23]

> We do not have much knowledge about NGT. For a tribal activist based in a remote location, it is extremely difficult to travel to Kolkata and find accommodation there.

This demonstrates how the socio-economic inequalities do not allow tribal activists to access the NGT. Another tribal activist, Dayamani Barla, who has worked to curb illegal mining and displacement, has said that she does not know about the NGT and questions why she would be required to travel to Kolkata to address a local environmental issue. She has further opined:[24]

> A green tribunal should have been based in a place that has the highest forest cover or large mineral deposit. That is where the extremely poor live.

This highlights the lack of access to environmental justice for the poor and the marginalized. The setting up of the NGT's zonal benches in metropolitan cities is contrary to the logic of establishing environmental tribunals in places that are likely to have more environmental litigation, such as areas with high forest covers and mineral deposits. While the NGT has opened further circuit benches in Shimla, Shillong, Jodhpur, and Kochi, these are still inadequate to fill the void cast by the absence of 13,000 local courts for addressing environmental issues locally.

Moreover, there remain concerns with respect to the functioning of all zonal and circuit benches. As noted previously, due to the non-appointment of several judicial and expert members, the four zonal benches have been completely shut for over two years[25] (much before the outbreak of COVID-19). In effect, this means that only the Principal Bench of the NGT at New Delhi is physically available to provide environmental justice for the entire country.

The Tribunal has tried to address this by allowing "e-filing" of cases over the internet and commencing online hearing of cases.[26] However, this still does not remedy the lack of access to people in remote and tribal areas, where internet connectivity is a serious issue. Additionally, many lawyers practising in the Tribunal have expressed their discomfort with respect to video conferencing as it increases the cost of procuring adequate infrastructure to host a prolonged video-based hearing.[27] As Sahu highlights, hearings are often adjourned or listed in an unhelpful manner without adequate notice to the parties to prepare their case.[28] Moreover, lawyers complain about not getting adequate chances to mention new matters via video conferencing. Accordingly, the majority of the cases take longer than the stipulated six-month period for resolving an issue.[29]

Aruna Chandrasekhar, in her brilliant article titled "Scorched Earth: The Suffocation of the National Green Tribunal", published in the August 2019 issue of *The Caravan*,[30] vividly captures the struggles faced by Shivpal Bhagat – an Adivasi activist – to access environmental justice at the NGT. We have produced the article below for the benefit of the reader.

Scorched Earth

The suffocation of the National Green Tribunal

ARUNA CHANDRASEKHAR

01 August 2019

(Published in the August 2019 issue of *The Caravan*)

At first light one day in July last year, Shivpal Bhagat packed his modest holdall and caught the first bus out of Kosampali – an Adivasi village in Chhattisgarh's Raigarh district, fragmented by three coal mines and two power plants. After two hours of trailing coal trucks through patches of sal forest, Bhagat alighted at the Raigarh railway station, and boarded a cramped train to Bilaspur, another two hours away. With afternoon wearing on, he caught the Chhattisgarh Express to Bhopal. The next morning, having crossed the state border into Madhya Pradesh, the train approached Bhopal. Bhagat changed into a white shirt as the train pulled into the city, then squeezed into a shared auto for the last stretch of his journey. Finally, more than a full day after he left home, he arrived at the Bhopal branch of the National Green Tribunal, the country's only court dedicated to environmental issues.

Bhagat, the sarpanch of Kosampali and an Adivasi himself, is no stranger to the courts. For years, Raigarh's residents have resisted the exploitation of the area's massive coal reserves by public and private companies given permission to mine and generate power here by the central government. Getting at the coal often means stripping away forests, farmland and homes, with devastating environmental consequences even before the pollution from the coal dust, fly ash and contaminated runoff that accompanies mines and power plants. Bhagat has long been part of the resistance, in court and on the ground, and has had to fight multiple cases filed against him by the companies, as well as state authorities. This court date, however, was unusual. For the first time, Bhagat would be appearing not before a judge of the NGT in Bhopal, but on camera, via videoconference, before the NGT's principal bench in Delhi.

The case in question, filed by Bhagat and several co-petitioners, involved the Gare Pelma IV/2&3 mining complex. The complex was operated by Jindal Steel and Power, but, in the aftermath of a 2014 ruling by the Supreme Court that cancelled all prior coal-block allocations, the government handed custody of it to a public company, Coal

Image 4.1   The people of Kosampali are reeling under the impact of three coal mines and two power plants in the village

Source: Ishan Tankha.

India. During the video hearing, the Delhi bench accepted that mining at the complex had devastating health effects. It noted that the project did not have the consent of affected villagers, and that in many cases mines had encroached to barely ten metres from their homes. Earlier, the NGT had directed a joint committee with representatives from the coal and environment ministries to prepare a report on the matter. Now, the bench accepted the report's recommendation for measures to contain pollution, as well as the recommendation that JSPL and Coal India be fined Rs 5 crore each. It ordered "that the recommendations be given effect to in letter and spirit and in a time bound manner," but it did not specify any deadline, leaving the companies free to act at their own pace while the mining continued.

Environmental justice has always been dauntingly remote for Bhagat and his village, both figuratively and physically. "We went wearing chappals," Bhagat said, but the lawyer for JSPL was wearing suits worth many thousands of rupees. "Everything he was wearing was special." The villagers "don't have the money to pay a lawyer's fees, or the money to cover our costs up and down." Since the case began, in 2014, Bhagat had travelled the eight-hundred-plus kilometres to Bhopal four times, supported by community collections towards the case in Raigarh. There is no closer option – the Bhopal branch of the NGT has jurisdiction over all of Chhattisgarh, Madhya Pradesh and Rajasthan, host to many of the country's most polluting mines and industrial facilities. At the Bhopal bench, Bhagat appeared before a live court until, in October 2017, the last judge to sit there was transferred to Delhi. Now petitioners from the three states address themselves remotely to a judge in the national capital.

Videoconferencing has become a feature of many Indian courts in recent years. The Supreme Court, for example, allows witnesses to testify on live camera in a growing variety of cases. But while this is seen as a welcome innovation in some courts – cutting down delays from waiting for witnesses to appear in person – in the environmental courts, it papers over a festering crisis. The NGT has been crippled by a lack of judicial appointments by the Modi government. Its regional benches have been rendered defunct, and the system of environmental justice has come to a near-complete halt. Videoconferencing with Delhi has kept some cases limping along, but most proceedings are inordinately delayed, and the list of pending cases is getting longer and longer. By its own count, at the end of this May, the NGT had 2,821 cases pending before it. Meanwhile, in most instances, the environmental destruction these cases are meant to address continues unhindered.

The National Green Tribunal Act, which created the NGT in 2010, stipulates that the tribunal must have, at any given time, between ten and twenty full-time judicial members, and between ten and twenty full-time expert members, "as the Central government, may, from time to time, notify." To improve access, on paper the NGT has four regional benches – in Bhopal, Chennai, Kolkata and Pune – as well as four circuit benches – in Shimla, Shillong, Jodhpur and Kochi. For a bench to function, it needs at least one dedicated judicial member and an expert member. The Bhopal bench currently has a judge assigned to it, who sits in Delhi, but has no dedicated expert.

In August 2017, the NGT had only eight judicial members, including its chairperson, and just six expert members. When an advocate alerted the Delhi High Court to the shortage, it asked the central government, "Would you like to wind up the National Green Tribunal?" When the NGT's chairperson stepped down in December 2017, the tribunal was left headless. The NGT Bar Association petitioned the Supreme Court for remedy, and after the top court's intervention the government appointed an acting chairperson, in March 2018. A real replacement arrived that July, in the form of the former Supreme Court judge AK Goel, six months after the last permanent chairperson departed. The tribunal's work slowed even more drastically in the interim, exacerbating the logjam of cases.

Petitioners, lawyers and activists were relieved to see the post filled, and hoped for some restoration of order. But though the NGT resumed function, its staffing, and its backlog, did not improve after Goel arrived. Today, the NGT has only five judicial members, and two expert members – both forest officers. The only new appointees have been judicial members, all to the principal bench. The NGT Act suggests that the body also include experts on such things as pollution control, environmental-impact assessment and climate-change management, but none of them currently feature. This March, in another hearing on the NGT Bar Association's petition, the Supreme Court noted, "We find that the vacancy position in respect of both the categories" – judicial and expert members – "is quite staggering. Resultantly, some Benches of the NGT have virtually become dysfunctional, thereby causing severe inconvenience to the litigating public."

The solicitor general reassured the Supreme Court that the "process of selection of eight Expert Members is already at an advanced stage and the selection process for six Judicial Members has also commenced." Last year, the lawyer Gitanjali Sreedhar filed a right-to-information application with the environment ministry, asking whether it had formed a committee to select appointees, how many times it had met in the last six months, how many applications it had received and how many interviews it had conducted. The ministry responded that this information "prejudicially affect strategic interest of the state," and so was confidential. Sreedhar appealed, but has not received a fresh response.

Regional benches have been allotted specific, limited days for hearing via video. Cases from Bhopal, for example, are heard only on Tuesdays and Thursdays. "This should be a short-term crisis measure, not a long-term solution," the environmental lawyer Ritwick Dutta told me, yet it has been the practice for well over a year.

Bhagat and his co-petitioners' case dragged on because of the hobbling of the NGT. Rinchin, a Raigarh-based filmmaker and one of the co-petitioners, pointed out that between January and July 2018 there was no Bhopal bench. "*Tareeq pe tareeq*, we waited," she said, "and finally asked for a transfer petition to Delhi." The transfer was accepted, but the case was then sent back to Bhopal because the principal bench in Delhi was overloaded. Finally, the NGT delivered its verdict.

But at Kosampali, Coal India was in no rush to see that the recommendations of the joint committee were effected "in a time bound manner." Mine fires continued to rage despite an explicit recommendation that they be put out, and the boundaries of open-cast mines drew ever closer to locals' doorsteps, ignoring the recommendation that they be kept at least five hundred metres from any villages. "What good does it do for us?" Rinchin said of the NGT order. "The environmental damage, if it's still happening, then there's no point."

With the Bhopal bench inoperative, Bhagat, Rinchin and residents of six villages in Raigarh approached the Delhi bench asking for orders to enforce the recommendations on the ground. They also asked the bench to order a comprehensive clean-up, examine the carrying capacity of the district – that is, the number of mines and other industrial installations it can safely sustain – and declare a moratorium on mining in the meantime. JSPL later took the matter to the Supreme Court, where it remains. The case will now require the petitioners to travel to Delhi – over a thousand kilometres overland.

While hearing the matter, Goel ordered that petitioners seeking action on unfulfilled recommendations must first approach government authorities, and give them 15 days to respond before appealing to the courts. Activists saw this as a dangerous precedent. For one, it could give authorities and companies lead time to cover up violations. For another, it could put complainants at risk of intimidation and retaliation to forestall a case.

As cases against environmental violators languish, the environment minister, Prakash Javadekar, announced recently that environment clearances will be processed in no more than 80 days, down from an already sped-up 108 days. One ministry expert told me that his colleagues already barely get time to read project reports before they are forced to approve them. The environment ministry has rejected fewer than one percent of project proposals under the Modi administration.

Last month, Bhagat, Rinchin and their co-petitioners finally received an action report on their new case, from the Chhattisgarh Environment Conservation Board. Shweta Narayan, a public-health researcher who helped to empirically establish the contamination of the area's air, soil and water, found it flawed. "For their study, they've taken only air and water samples from two villages, Sarasmal and Kosampali," she said. "But we had talked about the whole of Tamnar block, which has nine mines and 21 power plants." Narayan's report showed, among other things, heavy-metal contamination of soil and water – and an alarming frequency of musculoskeletal disorders among local teenagers. The conservation board's report, even with its limited sample, corroborated heavy-metal contamination, the mismanagement of fly ash and the presence of particulate matter in excess of safe limits – all pointing to coal mining as the root cause of the pollution.

The report's authors, Narayan said, had "tried to lessen the impact of their own findings – something you don't expect scientists to do. When scientists put out statements like 'slightly polluted,' that's where one starts using kid gloves to communicate problems of very serious concern. That's when you are compromising on your scientific integrity and making it political and biased." The remedial measures suggested by the conservation board were aimed at only one polluter in the area, Coal India, and again left to the company to implement at its pleasure. Other mine and power-plant operators were let off. When the petitioners complained about the report's shortcomings, the court agreed that it did not adequately address the concerns they had raised. As of late July, the petitioners were awaiting further hearings.

Coal India sent Bhagat legal notices in August 2018, threatening to sue him and a fellow activist for Rs 73 crore of damages that it estimates were caused by strikes that the two had been part of. Bhagat has court dates coming up everywhere from Raigarh to Delhi. He still has faith in the judiciary. "In the beginning, we didn't even have an idea that we could fight in a court somewhere and get our rights," he said. "But as soon as we started getting orders from the high courts, from the NGT, we realised that there's a lot that the law can save. At the district level and the block level, unless there's a kick from the higher courts, no work happens here. We've learned that for any kind of justice to arrive here, whether it's for rehabilitation or the environment, it has to come this way."

New mines continue to come up in Raigarh, threatening the region's last remaining forests. "The new Adani-operated one has started, Ambuja started, Coal India is starting," Rinchin said. "You can't just open up eight or nine mines at one go. You have to think about cumulative impact, especially if you're taking away the green cover. They have to rethink the whole mining plan and impose a moratorium. In the US, they'd evacuate people with this kind of pollution." But this is India. "They fought so hard because their lives are precarious," Rinchin said. "How much are people going to fight?"

*   *   *

Therefore, there is an alarming lack of access to justice faced by the majority of the population in the country. It is the need of the hour that more benches be opened in strategically significant areas involving more environmental issues. While conducting hearings via video conferencing is a welcome step, it needs to be augmented by ensuring local infrastructure in remote areas for people to avail themselves of the video conferencing facility. We suggest that in designated local courts, facilities providing video conferencing with the principal and zonal benches should be installed. This will ensure that many people will have access to the NGT.

*   *   *

4.2   FREQUENT APPEALS TO HIGH COURTS

Section 22 of the NGT Act states that any person aggrieved by any award, decision, or order of the NGT "may" file an appeal directly to the Supreme Court within ninety days of its communication to the person. The Act does not provide for an appeal to the High Courts. This is understandable given that the preamble of the Act states that the Tribunal is being constituted for the effective and expeditious disposal of cases.[31] Invariably, an appeal to the High Courts is likely to be time-consuming and can potentially defeat the aim of providing expeditious disposal of cases by adding another stage of appeals.

Nevertheless, this legislative intention has been disregarded by a few High Courts.[32] For instance, the Madras High Court has held that the NGT Act does not exclude the right to appeal to the High Courts despite expressly providing for an appeal to the Supreme Court.[33] It has opined that the bar on jurisdiction envisaged by the Act, if any, is applicable only to lower courts. It arrived at this conclusion by relying on the Supreme Court's reasoning in *L. Chandra Kumar v. Union of India*.[34] In this case, the Supreme Court had held that the powers of judicial review under Articles 226 and 227 of the Constitution were a part of the "basic structure" of the Constitution and could not be ousted or abridged even by a constitutional amendment.[35] However, unlike the NGT Act, which expressly provides that the appeal from the Tribunal should lie with the Supreme Court, the Administrative Tribunal Act, 1985, in question before the Supreme Court in *L. Chandra Kumar* expressly excluded the jurisdiction of all courts apart from labour courts and the Supreme Court.[36]

In contrast to the Madras High Court, the Bombay High Court, in view of the legislative intent of the NGT Act, has declined to hear appeals from the NGT and has directed appellants to approach the Supreme Court under Section 22 of the Act.[37] While the Bombay High Court agreed with *L. Chandra Kumar* to the extent that the jurisdiction of the High Courts could not be excluded, it held that the writ jurisdiction of the High Courts under Articles 226 and 227 of the Constitution has to be sparingly used, such as in situations of gross breach of principles of natural justice or issues of jurisdiction.[38] An appeal from the NGT was not one of those rare occasions, because the NGT Act provided for an "effective alternate remedy".[39] To this effect, the Bombay High Court relied on the Supreme Court's reasoning in *United Bank of India v. Satyawati Tondon*, wherein it was held:[40]

Unfortunately, the High Court overlooked the settled law that the High Court will ordinarily not entertain a petition under Article 226 of the Constitution if an effective remedy is available to the aggrieved person. (Emphasis supplied)

Thus, the High Court rightly held that Section 22 of the NGT Act provides an effective alternate remedy, and in line with the legislative intent behind the Act, the appeals from decisions of the Tribunal should ideally be directed to the Supreme Court.[41]

In furtherance of this line of reasoning, the Telangana High Court initially refused to hear an appeal from an order of the NGT on the pretext that the statutory appeals from the NGT lie with the Supreme Court.[42] However, it subsequently agreed to hear the appeal as one of the primary contentions was with respect to the breach of principles of natural justice.[43] This is the correct approach and is in line with the reasoning of the Supreme Court. Moreover, it is in consonance with the underlying legislative intent to enable expeditious disposal of cases by the Tribunal. It is recommended that all High Courts adopt the Bombay High Court's reasoning and not entertain appeals under Articles 226 and 227 of the Constitution unless grave issues of jurisdiction or violation of the principles of natural justice are involved. This will ensure that environmental adjudication of the NGT is both effective and expeditious.

*   *   *

4.3   NON-SCIENTIFIC DETERMINATION OF COMPENSATION

The NGT Act does not prescribe any minimum or maximum amount of compensation that may be imposed by the Tribunal. Accordingly, the NGT Act accords wide discretion to the Tribunal with respect to the amount of compensation and the methodology used to arrive at such an amount. This is evident from the fact that the only guidance with respect to the determination of compensation in the Act is under Section 20, which states that the NGT is required to apply the principle of sustainable development, polluter pays principle, and the precautionary principle while passing an award or order.[44] While the Tribunal has this wide discretion, the recent trend in its adjudication highlights the lack of use of any methodology for the calculation of environmental compensation in several cases. The trend in many cases seems to be to award a compensation between 5 and 10 per cent of the project cost.[45] This was started in 2014 when the NGT arbitrarily adopted the Supreme Court's approach to determining compensation in *Goa Foundation v. Union of India*.[46]

Goa Foundation dealt with the issue of environmental damage due to illegal mining in Goa. In arriving at the compensation amount, the Court held that the project proponents would have to pay 10 per cent of the sale proceeds.[47] However, this method to compute compensation was not intended to be a precedent for determining compensation in all cases. In fact, it was deemed appropriate in this case only because the Court felt that mining could not be completely banned due to its economic benefits to the state of Goa in terms of revenue and employment generation.[48] Thus, in light of the peculiar considerations in the case, the Court held that determining compensation as a percentage of sale proceeds would be appropriate as it would directly affect the profitability of the project proponent.[49]

Accordingly, at most, the approach to determine compensation can be deemed as a precedent for cases involving illegal mining in regions such as Goa which are heavily dependent on it for revenue and employment. Thus, in all other cases where such peculiar considerations are absent, the approach taken ought to be different as the impugned approach is not based on the extent of actual environmental damage.

However, the NGT has disregarded these peculiar considerations in *Goa Foundation* and has co-opted this approach in several cases that have very different considerations.[50] This trend of unduly relying on the Supreme Court's approach in *Goa Foundation* was started in 2014 by the Tribunal in *Forward Foundation v. State of Karnataka*.[51] The case dealt with unauthorized construction by two companies, prior to receiving an environmental clearance. Despite holding that the illegal construction had severely damaged the entire ecosystem of the adjacent lakes, wetlands, and storm water drains, the NGT arbitrarily relied on *Goa Foundation* and awarded an environmental compensation amounting to a mere 5 per cent of the project cost.[52]

While the NGT claimed to rely on the Supreme Court's approach, it differed in two significant ways. First, it arbitrarily reduced the compensation percentage from 10 per cent to 5 per cent by simply stating that "10 percent of the project cost *may be somewhat on the higher side*" (emphasis supplied).[53] Second, instead of using a percentage of sale proceeds – as was used by the Supreme Court – the NGT used a percentage of the project cost. The Tribunal did not provide any reason for this departure. Thus, while the NGT overtly relied on *Goa Foundation* for determining compensation, it departed materially in terms of the quantum of compensation and the approach adopted.

Nevertheless, in co-opting this approach the NGT was focused on impacting the profitability of the project proponent instead of primarily being concerned with the quantum of environmental damage. This is evident from the Tribunal's reliance on its earlier decision in *Krishan Kant Singh v. National Ganga River Basin Authority*,[54] wherein the Tribunal was concerned with the "magnitude, capacity, and prosperity of the unit". [55]

However, these concerns of the Tribunal with respect to impacting the profitability of the project proponent do not materialize into action. In several cases, the compensation levied is extremely low in comparison to the project proponent's annual revenue/turnover, as also concluded by a recent study of the Centre for Science and Environment (refer to Table 2.2 in Chapter 2).[56] In fact, the cases analysed with respect to the pollution caused by sugar distilleries highlight that the compensation was between 0.012 and 0.07 per cent of the annual turnover of the project proponents.[57] Several polluting companies which had annual turnovers of several thousand crores were liable to pay only a few hundred thousand rupees.[58]

In addition to the compensation amount being extremely low, the certainty of the compensation amount is likely to allow potential polluters to do a cost–benefit analysis before undertaking a project. Given that the initial compensation, irrespective of the level of pollution, is expected to be pegged at a mere 5 per cent of the project cost, it is likely to incentivize the potential polluter to proceed with the project if the project can be reasonably profitable after accounting for this amount. Accordingly, this trend is likely to result in the environmental compensation being viewed as a business cost and convert the polluter pays principle into "pay and pollute".

This trend has led to an embarrassing situation for the NGT, wherein due to non-scientific assessment of the compensation, it has had to retract the penalty initially levied. For instance, in *Ajay Kumar Negi v. Union of India*,[59] the Tribunal had initially levied a compensation of INR 5 crore due to the violations of the conditions contained in the environmental clearance with respect to clearing forest areas.[60] However, a few months later, the Tribunal changed its stance and held that "the stage is not yet ready for relief as … damage to environment, if any, arising out of the project activity is yet to be completely assessed".[61] The reason for this change was that the Expert Committee, which had recommended the levy of the initial compensation, subsequently held that the livelihood of the people was "least likely to be affected by the project operation" and that there was no apparent threat of irreversible damage to the forest cover.[62] Thus, the NGT went from levying an initial compensation of INR 5 crore to not levying a compensation at all.

Similarly, in *Manoj Mishra v. Delhi Development Authority & Ors.*,[63] popularly known as the *Art of Living Case*, the compensation eventually levied was very different from the initial estimate. The case dealt with the alleged damage to the Yamuna floodplains due to the Art of Living Foundation's World Cultural Festival. The initial estimate of the Expert Committee, based on a simple "visual assessment", was approximately INR 120 crore.[64] This estimate was later changed to INR 28.73 crore.[65] Finally, the Tribunal asked the Art of Living Foundation to deposit INR 5 crore (not as penalty[66]), out of which only INR 25 lakh was required as a condition precedent for going ahead with the event. This substantial reduction in estimated compensation was a result of non-scientific estimation of the environmental damage (for a detailed analysis, refer to the section titled "Case Study: Lack of Scientific Determination of Environmental Compensation – The *Art of Living Case*" in Chapter 2).

Not only had the chairperson of the Expert Committee denounced the report of the Committee for not being "based on any scientific assessment",[67] the NGT itself had also admitted to not conducting a scientific analysis. To this effect, the Tribunal had held that the primary reason for not scientifically quantifying damage was as follows:[68]

> Estimate of the costs of restoration requires the preparation of a Detailed Project Report that may take several months to a year besides financial resources.

Accordingly, the NGT unscientifically levied a penalty without quantifying the environmental damage, if any, due to paucity of time and lack of financial resources.

This trend should be discouraged, and the NGT should calculate compensation based on actual environmental damage and the actual costs required for the rehabilitation of the environment. As suggested in Chapter 2, the NGT should adopt the resource equivalency approach, whereby compensation should be based on any deviations from the baseline condition of the environment that existed prior to the alleged damage. Such a compensation mechanism will impact the profitability of the project proponent and will dis-incentivize a potential polluter.

*   *   *

4.4   TREND OF NOT ADEQUATELY PENALIZING GOVERNMENTAL AUTHORITIES

In addition to the lack of methodology followed and the lack of scientific analysis undertaken by the NGT while determining compensation, the NGT has failed to impose significant monetary penalties on governmental authorities. Even in cases where the Tribunal has unequivocally held that governmental agencies have completely disregarded the environment and have not performed their duties, the NGT has only awarded negligible sums as compensation, if at all.

For instance, in the aforementioned case of *Ajay Kumar Negi*, the Tribunal had held that the Forest Department had not performed its duties and could not explain the discrepancy between the number of trees allegedly damaged by the project proponent (398 trees) and its estimate (4,815 trees).[69] Furthermore, the project proponent in the case had been regularly paying environmental fines as and when required, but the Forest Department failed to utilize the amounts paid for environmental restoration for several years.[70] Despite noting such gross negligence on the part of the Forest Department, the Tribunal did not impose any monetary penalty on it.

Likewise, in the *Art of Living Case*, despite holding that the Delhi Development Authority had wrongfully granted the permission to Art of Living Foundation for holding the cultural event and that the Delhi Pollution Control Committee was negligent in performing its duties, the Tribunal did not impose any costs on the former and levied a mere penalty of INR 1 lakh on the latter.[71]

Additionally, prior to the event, the Art of Living Foundation had also taken permissions from, inter alia, the Ministry of Environment, Forest and Climate Change (MoEFCC), the Uttar Pradesh Irrigation Committee (UPIC), Delhi Disaster Management Authority (DDMA), and the Irrigation and Flood Control Department of Delhi (IFCD). However, despite holding that these departments had wrongly granted the permission, the NGT did not impose any penalty on them and did not hold them accountable in any manner.

However, at present this trend seems to be changing. In January 2019, the Tribunal held the state government of Meghalaya responsible for failing to curb illegal coal mining in the state and imposed a fine of INR 100 crore on it.[72] This amount was ordered to be deposited by the state government with the Central Pollution Control Board within two months.[73] This high amount was imposed to act as a deterrent as the state government had not performed its duties despite data showing that a majority of the 24,000 mines in Meghalaya were being operated illegally, that is, without a license or environmental clearance.[74]

Similarly, the NGT recently imposed a fine of INR 25 crore[75] on the state government of Delhi for failing to curb air pollution and a fine of INR 50 crore on the state government of Punjab for polluting Rivers Sutlej and Beas with uncontrolled industrial discharge.[76]

Accordingly, it is recommended that this recent trend continues, and the NGT continues to not only hold governmental authorities accountable for environmental pollution but also impose heavy monetary costs on them for disregarding their duties. This will act as a much-needed deterrent.

4.5 INADEQUATE IMPLEMENTATION OF DECISIONS

In addition to recommending the setting up of environmental courts, the Law Commission of India, in its 186th Report, had further recommended that these courts must have contempt jurisdiction.[77] It noted that the trial of ordinary criminal cases was very time-consuming and that the proposed environmental courts ought to have contempt jurisdiction to ensure effective and efficient implementation of their orders.[78] However, this recommendation was not accepted, and the NGT Act does not have any provision that accords contempt jurisdiction to the Tribunal. While Section 26 of the Act provides that if a person fails to comply with the orders of the Tribunal, he or she may be punished with imprisonment up to three years or with a up to INR 10 crore; this offence is triable only by ordinary criminal courts.[79]

Nevertheless, in a case where a petitioner filed contempt applications before the Tribunal, the NGT held that it had the "inherent powers" to enforce its orders.[80] However, the Tribunal failed to elaborate on the source of such inherent powers. Despite such bold moves on the part of the Tribunal, there exists a serious challenge with respect to the enforcement of directions and orders. In many landmark cases, either the directions of the Tribunal are not implemented on the ground or the compensation awards are not complied with on time.

For instance, the NGT's order dated 10 November 2016 with respect to air pollution in Delhi – wherein clear directions were given with respect to the next steps to be taken to combat long-term and short-term air pollution – remains completely unimplemented.[81] In fact, the PM 2.5 level (the metric relied on by the Tribunal for measuring the pollution level) was around 600 when the order was given.[82] This pales into comparison with the PM 2.5 level of 999+ reached during Diwali in 2019.[83] The NGT, while delivering the impugned order, had categorically reprimanded the government officials and had stated that "the right to life has been infringed with impunity by the authorities and other stakeholders who have been mere spectators to such crisis".[84] However, a year later when the orders were not complied with and the pollution was worse, the Tribunal admitted that the orders remained unimplemented and that it could find "no plausible explanation".[85] In fact, most of the significant cases involving illegal mining and solid waste management continue to remain unenforced.[86]

Furthermore, Section 24(1) of the NGT Act requires that any amount of money received as compensation or relief under an award made by the Tribunal for environmental damage shall be credited to the Environmental Relief Fund ("ERF"). Further, Rule 35(1) of the National Green Tribunal (Practices and Procedure) Rules, 2011, states that the amount must be credited to the ERF within thirty days of the order or as otherwise directed by the Tribunal. In effect, the ERF is the primary means by which environmental restoration and rejuvenation are enabled. However, despite this provision, the NGT does not direct payment to the ERF in all cases.[87] A recent study shows that in nearly 40 per cent of all cases the payments are directed to state pollution control boards, in 17 per cent of cases to state forest departments, and only in 12 per cent of cases to the ERF.

Moreover, even in the few cases in which the NGT directs that compensation should be deposited into the ERF, there have only been two deposits actually made to date.[88] Additionally, there is a general tendency, in cases involving high amounts as a penalty, to challenge the NGT's decisions in the Supreme Court.[89] In contrast, in cases where the payments are relatively negligible when compared to the turnover of the company involved, the payments are usually made.[90] Despite this worrisome trend, as discussed, the NGT continues to not hold the governmental authorities accountable in several cases. For instance, as previously noted, in *Ajay Kumar Negi*, even though the Tribunal held that the Forest Department had not performed its duties and had not utilized the funds deposited by the project proponent for environmental restoration for several years, it did not penalize the Forest Department.[91]

At present, there exists no systematic monitoring of payments made to the ERF. Further, given that the NGT lacks contempt jurisdiction, it is very difficult for it to consistently keep track of whether directions have been complied with. Thus, we suggest that the legislature either grants the Tribunal contempt jurisdiction or provides for an effective mechanism which ensures that the directions of the Tribunal are complied with.

* * *

4.6   LACK OF BASIC AMENITIES AND INFRASTRUCTURE

Since the NGT's inception, it has faced hurdles in its functioning due to a lack of basic amenities and infrastructural support. In fact, the Principal Bench started operating in a temporary office and a makeshift courtroom in Delhi's Van Vigyan Bhavan, which is a building used for housing guests of the MoEF.[92] As Shrivastava highlights, these quarters lacked basic amenities such as a kitchen, and the members of the Tribunal – who were retired High Court judges – could not afford to rent a house and live with their families because of their meagre salary.[93]

Due to this, three judicial members – Justices C. V. Ramulu, Amit Talukdar, and A. S. Naidu – resigned from their posts in the Tribunal.[94] Furthermore, while a minimum of ten expert and judicial members were required for the NGT to be functional, due to the poor infrastructure, lack of basic amenities, and inadequate salary, there were few responses when the positions were initially opened, and the Tribunal was made functional with only three expert members and three judicial members.[95] There was a period when four benches of the NGT were being run by a total of five members, which of course meant that only the Principal Bench was operational.[96]

Gopal Subramanium, a senior counsel, informed the Supreme Court that the NGT's functioning was in a "very sorry state of affairs".[97] He highlighted that even after three years of the enactment of the NGT Act, the government had not sanctioned the INR 22 lakh rent that the NGT had to pay to the government to use its premises.[98] Further, the initial budget of INR 32 crore was slashed to INR 6 crore. Moreover, he highlighted that the judicial and expert members had to pay from their own pockets for their commute to and from the Tribunal and that they were compelled to eat food from the canteen.[99]

The lack of governmental will to rectify the issue is evident from the fact that the state government filed an affidavit claiming that the Bhopal Bench was functioning smoothly despite the fact that no infrastructure was provided for its functioning and it had to function out of a basement in a building.[100] Similarly, while the Pune Bench was inaugurated on 17 March 2012, due to a lack of governmental support it was made functional only after a year.[101] The case with the Kolkata Bench was worse, and a report submitted by the NGT to the Supreme Court stated that the chairperson found the accommodation offered to be "shabby, uninhabitable and without a toilet".[102] The Supreme Court went to the extent to state that it was possible that the Kolkata Bench was set up due to "political reasons", and it requested the Central government to consider shifting the Tribunal to Guwahati or Ranchi due to the inaction of the West Bengal government.[103]

Akin to how the push for the enactment of the NGT Act came from the Supreme Court and not the legislature, it was the Supreme Court that had to eventually push for better amenities and infrastructure for the different benches of the NGT. A Supreme Court bench consisting of Justices G. S. Singhvi and S. J. Mukhopadhaya referred to the affidavit filed by the Madhya Pradesh state government as "false" and "misleading".[104] The bench further held that all members of the NGT "must function with dignity" and ordered the state governments to provide adequate facilities and amenities.[105]

While the infrastructure and amenities have improved gradually over the past few years, it is still not adequate to ensure effective adjudication. As of today, all four zonal benches have completely shut down over the past year.[106] The hearing of cases of these zonal benches happens over video conferencing, which lasts only for one or two hours a day.[107] Ironically, in 2019, while the Environment Ministry's budget was increased by 20.27 per cent from INR 2,586 crore to INR 3,111 crore, the budgetary allocation for the NGT and pollution abatement was reduced by 44 per cent and 50 per cent, respectively.[108]

These trends highlight the lack of legislative will to effectively deal with the issue of inadequate infrastructural facilities by both the Central and the state governments. There is a conflict of interest between promoting the NGT and the ambitious developmental projects that the state governments intend to undertake. The apathetic response of the state governments of West Bengal and Madhya Pradesh stems from this conflict of interest. To retain power in the next elections, the ruling parties of these states need to demonstrate developmental work to win votes. Due to this, the NGT, due to its expanding influence, is seen as an impediment as several state projects are often delayed or halted by the Tribunal.

We suggest that the Central government should undertake a study that demonstrates how much expenditure is required to maintain the dignity of the members of the Tribunal as well as to enable the effective functioning of all zonal and circuit benches of the NGT. This will help provide a baseline for the Tribunal's budget, which should be mandatorily maintained. It will ensure that the NGT's functioning is not dependent on the whims of different governments or different political priorities.

4.7 DELAYS, CONFLICTS OF INTEREST, AND DILUTION OF EXPERTISE IN APPOINTMENTS OF EXPERT MEMBERS

As discussed in Chapter 2, despite the enactment of the NGT Act in 2010, political apathy, in terms of providing amenities and facilities to the Tribunal, resulted in a delay of nearly three years before the NGT became fully functional.[109] This was made possible only after the intervention of the Supreme Court.[110] However, since then, the apathetic attitude of the government has not abated. This has resulted in a situation where although Section 4 of the NGT Act states that, in addition to a chairperson, the Tribunal shall consist of a minimum of ten judicial members and ten expert members, the NGT did not have the basic quorum for the first decade of its existence.

As of late 2020, there were just six members in the NGT.[111] These included three judicial members and three expert members. It is only recently, in early 2022, that the number of members has been increased to twelve (five judicial members and seven expert members).[112] Evidently, the Tribunal continues to operate below its minimum statutory quorum. As highlighted previously, all zonal benches of the Tribunal have shut down, and their cases are heard over video conferencing at the Principal Bench in New Delhi.[113] Moreover, given that the NGT has taken away the jurisdiction with respect to environmental cases from more than 13,000 local courts, in effect, the six members are responsible for the adjudication of all environmental cases in the country.

Due to this, thousands of legal proceedings relating to compensation owed to victims and the environment on account of illegal deforestation and large projects such as dams, mining, and power plants are pending across the different zonal benches.[114] In addition to the non-appointment of expert and judicial members, the litigating parties have to suffer constant shuffling of benches, resulting in increased litigation costs as they have to brief the new members and, in some cases, repeat arguments, leading to further delays.[115] Moreover, as previously highlighted, the lack of appointments has hurt those living in remote and vulnerable areas the most.

In response to the Tribunal's pleas for filling the vacancies, the MoEF preferred to instead pass an amendment to the National Green Tribunal (Practices and Procedure) Rules on 1 December 2017, allowing the NGT's chairperson to constitute a single-member bench under "exceptional circumstances".[116] While the Supreme Court stayed the notification on 31 January 2018, this demonstrates the intention of the government to halt the functioning of the Tribunal.[117] In fact, while hearing a petition with respect to the lack of appointment of members, the Delhi High Court asked the Central government whether it wanted to wind up the NGT.[118]

Moreover, the Ministry of Personnel, Public Grievances and Pension issued an order dated 2 September 2019 stating that two serving officers of the MoEF had been approved for appointment as expert members of the NGT.[119] This is problematic on two grounds. First, there is a clear conflict of interest. With the inclusion of these two expert members to the existing three expert members, all five expert members of the NGT will be from the Indian Forest Service.[120] The Director General of Forests chairs the Forest Advisory Committee, which recommends the diversion of forest land for non-forest uses. Often, the NGT adjudicates petitions involving forest clearances.[121] Therefore, in effect, the personnel of the NGT who was earlier responsible for granting clearances will now be adjudicating its validity and impact.

Second, this trend of appointing erstwhile bureaucrats as expert members has diluted the expertise of the Tribunal. As highlighted earlier, the NGT was created to enable effective adjudication of environmental matters involving complex scientific and technical issues. However, given the ongoing dilution of the Tribunal's membership, the effectiveness of its adjudication is at risk. When the NGT was initially established, the expert members consisted of environmental scientists and professors with expertise in different domains.[122] Their expertise ensured that the Supreme Court rarely overruled their decisions.[123] However, after 2014 only personnel of the Indian Forest Service have been appointed as expert members. Apart from raising issues of conflict, this is likely to diminish the quality of NGT's decision-making. Environmental issues often require adjudication on issues involving pollution with respect to air, water, noise, mining, and hazardous substances. Their effective adjudication requires domain expertise in areas other than just forests.

Thus, the present trend with respect to appointments can potentially cripple the NGT's adjudication and independence. It is recommended that instead of bureaucrats, expert members are appointed based on their domain expertise in varied environmental subjects that enable them to not only deal with scientific complexities in a wholesome manner but also keep the independence of the Tribunal intact.

4.8 TUSSLE WITH THE MOEF AND THE PROPOSED DILUTION OF ENVIRONMENTAL IMPACT ASSESSMENT (2020)

While India has consistently been improving its ranking in the global index for ease of doing business due to its economically conducive laws, recently it was ranked among the bottom five countries worldwide in terms of environmental performance.[124] In fact, in 2018, as per the global Environmental Performance Index, India ranked 177 out of 180 countries in terms of environmental health.[125] Despite the irreparable environmental harm indicated by this index, the MoEF has dismissed the indicators as "just rankings".[126] Given this apathetic attitude of the government coupled with the fact that India leads the world in environmental conflicts, a strong NGT is a necessity.

Nevertheless, as highlighted previously, the Supreme Court – and not the government – had to push for the creation of the Tribunal. Moreover, the Court has been primarily responsible for ensuring the functioning of the Tribunal after the enactment of the NGT Act by ordering the respective state governments to provide the basic amenities and facilities.[127] On the other hand, the MoEF and the government have consistently attempted to clip the powers of the NGT since its inception.

Several amendments to the Environmental Impact Assessment Act, 2006, by the Central government and the MoEF have severely diluted the process for environmental clearance. For instance, in January 2019, the MoEF standardized the procedure for granting an environmental clearance for two sectors – infrastructure and construction projects – that presently see the highest investment.[128] The process of granting an environmental clearance under the EIA Act was not intended to be standardized as different projects have different complexities and need different assessments of environmental and social costs. Moreover, the time for assessing the environmental cost of a project has been substantially reduced from 600 days to 190 days.[129] In addition, the Environment Minister, Prakash Javadekar, in 2017 released a statement that the number of days required for granting an environmental clearance would be further reduced to 100 days.[130] The result of this shortening of the environmental assessment process was that over 1,500 projects were cleared after July 2014.[131] These amendments demonstrate the governmental paradigm with respect to the NGT, the EIA process, and the environment in general. This paradigm views the latter as obstacles to development.

Despite this, the NGT has, in several cases, challenged the decisions of the MoEF with respect to environmental clearances. For instance, in *Prafulla Samantray v. Union of India*,[132] the NGT asked the Environment Ministry to review the environmental clearance granted after some local villages refused to consent to the project under the Forest Rights Act, 2006. In *M.P. Patil v. Union of India*,[133] upon examination, the NGT held that the environmental clearance had been granted to the National Thermal Power Corporation Ltd. (a governmental public utility undertaking) by misrepresentation of facts. In another case, the NGT held that the public consultation process had not been carried out properly by the project proponent and the executive summary of the EIA report in the vernacular language of the area and the full report had not been made available to the public prior to the public hearing within the stipulated time.[134] Despite the fact that these preconditions had not been fulfilled, the MoEF had granted the environmental clearance. The NGT held that as per the precautionary principle, the environmental clearance was wrongly granted and quashed the environmental clearance granted by the MoEF.[135]

Such a position of the NGT vis-à-vis infrastructure projects is a significant departure from the earlier decisions of the Supreme Court relating to large-scale projects such as big dams and power plants.[136] With respect to those large projects, as noted in Chapter 3, the Supreme Court had followed a more conservative approach and had supported the environmental clearance decisions of the government.[137] Thus, the NGT's lack of deference to the government is a welcome change. However, this is not viewed favourably by the government and the MoEF. As highlighted, the NGT's growing influence has only met governmental hurdles in the form of a lack of funding and infrastructural facilities, a lack of appointments of members, and dilution of the Tribunal's independence.

However, unfortunately, the main dilution is yet to come and has already been proposed at the time of writing this book. This is the dilution through the draft Environment Impact Assessment (EIA) Notification, 2020. As we have noted in Chapter 3, the environmental clearances granted under the EIA process are fundamental to the NGT's adjudication. In fact, a large part of the Tribunal's jurisprudence has come from holding polluters accountable for not meeting the conditions stipulated under the environmental clearance. For instance, the NGT has been able to uphold the application of the precautionary principle by requiring the EIA process to assess all possible environmental and social risks associated with a project before its commencement. However, if the proposed EIA Draft Notification, 2020, is passed, it will severely weaken the EIA process and will have a deleterious impact on the Indian environment.

This is due to several reasons. First, and perhaps the most dangerous, is the proposal of granting *ex-post facto* environmental clearances. This betrays the fundamental logic of having a "clearance", which is given after assessing and mitigating the environmental risk of a particular project. This proposal is antithetical to all three environmental principles that the NGT is bound to statutorily consider. It runs against the precautionary principle which requires governmental authorities to take preventive measures and not proceed with a project if there is a reasonable likelihood of environmental harm even in the absence of scientific proof. By allowing projects to commence without requiring any risk assessment, it makes the application of preventive measures practically impossible.

Granting of an *ex-post facto* environmental clearance is also antithetical to the polluter pays principle. Requiring a polluter to pay a fine after environmental damage has already been done to obtain the clearance is likely to propagate the notion of "pay and pollute". Further, this puts the environment on sale and normalizes pollution by pegging an economic value on it. Accordingly, the proposal also runs counter to the principle of sustainable development by completely removing the term "sustainable" from the principle. It is impossible to ensure a balance between developmental goals and environmental concerns if projects are allowed without any assessment of environmental damage. Since there is no assessment of any kind prior to the commencement of projects, most of the irreversible environmental damage is likely to take place by the time the clearance is granted or revoked. Hence, this proposal eradicates intergenerational equity by removing all environmental safeguards that have been painstakingly evolved over the years.

The proposal to grant *ex-post facto* environmental clearance, therefore, is extremely regressive and dismantles all environmental principles that have evolved over several years through trial and error. Invariably, this runs counter to India's international obligations under several treaties we have discussed in this book. Moreover, it runs counter to the guarantee of a safe and healthy environment that has been upheld by the Supreme Court as being part of the fundamental right to life under Article 21 of the Constitution.[138]

The Supreme Court has unequivocally held that "[t]he concept of an ex post facto EC is in derogation of the fundamental principles of environmental jurisprudence and is an anathema to the EIA notification...."[139] Additionally, the Court has also held that such clearances are inherently unsustainable and patently illegal.[140] Moreover, the Court has held that the commencement of a project without obtaining prior environmental clearance is a violation of the fundamental right to life guaranteed under Article 21 of the Constitution.[141]

These holdings of the Supreme Court are not surprising given the important role that the EIA process and environmental clearances play in protecting the environment. Several processes such as screening, scoping, public hearing, and appraisal form an integral part of the overall EIA process. These processes assess the likely environmental and socio-economic impacts of the proposed industrial activity and scientifically prescribe mitigative measures. Projects are only granted an environmental clearance once all risks have been assessed, mitigative measures applied, and the environmental impact of a project has been found to be within legally permissible limits. Thus, allowing *ex-post facto* clearance would essentially disregard all of this and would normalize irreversible environmental harm. Given India's international obligations and the Supreme Court's decisions in this regard, we are hopeful that even if the legislature passes the proposed EIA Draft Notification, 2020, it will be held unconstitutional by the Court.

Second, and perhaps most pernicious, provisions of the proposed amendments seek to take away the right of citizens to report and challenge environmental violations in respect of projects. Apart from the fact that this is *prima facie* unconstitutional, it highlights the mentality of the government with respect to suffocating environmental justice. The developmental agenda has blinded the decision-makers to such an extent that they have chosen to disenfranchise the very citizens that have elected them to office.

Adding insult to injury, the right to challenge an environmental clearance or report an environmental violation has been accorded only to the project proponent and governmental authorities. Not only is this ironical, it also makes a mockery of the evolution of Indian environmental jurisprudence and justice. Have not the thousands of reported environmental cases demonstrated that polluters go to lengthy extents to deliberately conceal their violations and that governmental authorities often look the other way? Why are project proponents being trusted to disclose their wrongdoings *suo motu*, while the public is not being trusted to raise environmental concerns? Could we have trusted Union Carbide – which has to date refused to disclose the exact composition of the chemical that killed thousands on account of trade secrecy – to report its own violations? Such blatant disregard for fundamental rights is uncharacteristic at best and dangerous at worst.

Third, the EIA Draft Notification, 2020, has significantly expanded the list of projects that do not require public consultation before seeking *ex-post facto* environmental clearance along with laying down conditions that would allow for public hearings to be circumvented in their entirety. In addition to heavily limiting public hearings to a small class of cases, the proposal seeks to reduce the number of days from thirty days (at present) to twenty days. The Supreme Court and the NGT have repeatedly emphasized the need for having a public hearing by holding that they represent the concerns of the people most affected and that such hearings are not a mere formality that can be dispensed with.[142]

In furtherance of this disregard for hearing the public, the EIA Draft Notification, 2020, was made into only three languages as opposed to the twenty-two official languages recognized by the Constitution. This has severely hampered the ability of communities with alternate languages and dialects to understand and effectively voice their concerns. In fact, even the EIA Act, 2006, mandates that summaries and all related information contained in the EIA report must be prepared in the local language in which the project is being propounded as has been held by the Supreme Court.[143] On 13 August 2020, the Supreme Court rejected the Central government's petition challenging a Delhi High Court order that had directed the publishing of the Draft Notification in twenty-two languages officially recognized in the Constitution.[144]

Fourth, the EIA Draft Notification, 2020, provides that the government can classify any project or a class of projects as being important for national security, defence, or strategic considerations. Once a project or a class of projects are classified as such, all EIA-related documents of these projects will be removed from the public domain. The vagueness of this provision is particularly problematic as it provides no threshold with respect to what is a "strategic consideration". This phrase can be used as a catch-all phrase to conveniently demarcate any developmental project as strategic to avoid accountability and public scrutiny.

In addition to the four reasons highlighted, there are other significant issues with the proposed draft. The proposed notification permits land fencing and levelling prior to the grant of an environmental clearance, which is problematic as fencing and levelling usually involve harm to the environment. Additionally, the Draft Notification has failed to incorporate a system for assessing possible transboundary environmental harm stemming from projects undertaken within India. The obligation to prevent transboundary harm is one of the foremost principles of customary international law, originating from the landmark *Trail Smelter Case*[145] (discussed in Chapter 3). Thus, the proposed EIA regime has failed to account for these developments in the international sphere and is in violation of customary international law.

Further, the EIA Draft Notification, 2020, fails to consider environmental changes due to changes in seasons. The draft requires baseline data to be collected from only one season for almost all projects. As demonstrated in the section titled "Case Study: Lack of Scientific Determination of Environmental Compensation – The *Art of Living Case*" in Chapter 2, changes in seasons can have a significant impact on environmental decisions. This proposal is likely to allow the creation of misleading EIA reports as the baseline data is likely to be hand-picked from a season in which environmental disruptions are minimal. For reference, the present EIA regime measures the environmental baseline at least for a minimum of three seasons to fully appreciate the actual environmental impact of the proposed activity. Furthermore, the proposed draft seeks to establish an ineffective and lax monitoring mechanism by extending the mandated time for reporting from every six months to once a year. The reporting needs to be more frequent so as to prevent long-lasting damage to the environment.

The legislative intent to completely dilute environmental impact assessment in India is apparent. However, the legislature's disregard for the environment and public concerns is even more apparent through this proposed draft. As of August 2020, a record-breaking 17,00,000+ public comments have been submitted to the MoEF expressing disapproval of the proposed changes.[146] Despite this, when R. P. Gupta, the secretary of the MoEF, was asked why he thought there was such a huge public outcry against the EIA Draft Notification, 2020, he stated:[147]

> I don't think there is anything disturbing in the clauses … maybe it has nothing to do with an environmental agenda, but more to do with a political agenda.

Well, at least Mr R. P. Gupta was half right. There is clearly a political motive behind the proposal that disregards environmental concerns. Next, he was asked about why the MoEF sees the Draft Notification as an important regulation. He replied:[148]

> We must see it in an overall context rather than looking at it in isolation. We are a country that takes a lot of time in issuing environmental clearances. We have poor enforcement and monitoring of projects. No amount of scrutiny can substitute for the monitoring. You can scrutinize a project for 5 to 6 years and delay it but if you don't monitor it, then it will remain environmentally unfriendly. We need to switch

this equation. We should be quick in giving clearances. There should be very strict and regular monitoring and we should come down heavily on non-compliance. This notification is only the first part. We are developing a monitoring mechanism, which will be the second part. To discourage violations, the best way is to ensure fast tracking of clearances.

Next, he was categorically asked, "But the draft is talking about regularizing these violations?" In response, he stated:[149]

Post-facto scenario happens when someone has started a project without taking prior approval, which is the norm. So if an industry is in violation, what is the punishment? There is nothing in law which says you will not appraise it on merit. After appraisal, if you find a project cannot be approved then you close it down. If it can be approved, approval will be effective from the date we give approval. For the past period which is a violation, a penalty is to be imposed as per law.

This response is reflective of the MoEF's paradigm with respect to the environment. It highlights an underlying assumption that the environment can be readily valued in economic terms and that the license to damage the environment can be purchased. Further, the response demonstrates that there is absolutely no intention to prevent environmental damage. Subsequently, when Mr R. P. Gupta was asked whether there would be any space for discussion on the EIA Draft Notification, 2020, he retorted:[150]

Concerns will be considered on merit. There is no requirement for discussion. That will open another Pandora's Box. Then nothing will happen in future. Everything can be stifled.

This statement highlights the fear of the MoEF to open a discussion on the issue. It clearly says that there will be no discussion as it is not deemed necessary by the government. This fear of public opinion and lack of trust in the general masses is evident through the draft proposal as well. As discussed, public hearings have been greatly curtailed, and citizens have been debarred from reporting violations in the EIA process.

Based on our discussion above, we believe that the EIA Draft Notification, 2020, is regressive, dangerous, and has the potential to completely dilute all Indian environmental jurisprudence. Moreover, it has the potential to lead to irreversible and deleterious environmental damage. For the reasons provided, we believe that the draft proposal is unconstitutional and conspicuously violates India's international commitments. Thus, even if the notification is passed, it is unlikely to stand the constitutional scrutiny of the Supreme Court.

*   *   *

NOTES

1. This section contains portions from a previously published article by the authors of the book. See Raghuveer Nath and Armin Rosencranz, "Evaluating the National Green Tribunal after Nearly a Decade: 10 Challenges to Overcome", *National Law Institute University L. Rev.* 9, no. 1 (2019): 1–39.

2. *P. S. R. Sadhanantham v. Arunachalam & Anr.*, AIR 1980 SC 856 (Supreme Court of India).

3. *Kannanaikil v. State of Bihar*, Writ Petition No. 8136 of 1983; *Bandhua Mukti Morcha v. Union of India*, AIR 1984 SC 802 (Supreme Court of India).

4. *T.N. Godavarman Thirumulpad v. Union of India*, Writ Petition (Civil) No. 202 of 1995 (Supreme Court of India).

5. *A.P. Pollution Control Board v. Prof. M.V. Nayudu (I)*, (1999) 2 SCC 718 (Supreme Court of India). Here the Court states:

   > In such a situation, considerable difficulty is experienced by this Court or the High Courts in adjudicating upon the correctness of the technological and scientific opinions presented to the courts or in regard to the efficacy of the technology proposed to be adopted by the industry or in regard to the need for alternative technology or modifications as suggested by the Pollution Control Board or other bodies.

6. For instance, in *T.N. Godavarman Thirumulpad v. Union of India*. The Supreme Court constituted an expert body called the Central Empowered Committee (CEC) in May 2002 to investigate and dispose of interim applications based on the directions of the Court.

7. Ibid.

8. The four decisions are *M.C. Mehta v. Union of India*, (1986) 2 SCC 176 (Supreme Court of India), *Indian Council for Enviro-Legal Action v. Union of India*, (1996) 3 SCC 212 (Supreme Court of India), *A.P. Pollution Control Board v. Prof. M.V. Nayudu (I)*, and *A.P. Pollution Control Board v. Prof. M.V. Nayudu (II)*, (2001) 2 SCC 62 (Supreme Court of India).

9. Law Commission of India, "Proposal to Constitute Environmental Courts" (17th Law Commission, 186th Report, 2003).

10. ET Bureau, "Environmental Activist Ramesh Agrawal: We Need Compliance, Not More Environmental Laws", *Economic Times* (1 June 2014), https://economictimes.indiatimes.com/opinion/interviews/environmental-activist-ramesh-agrawal-we-need-compliance-not-more-environmental-laws/articleshow/35855007.cms?from=mdr (accessed 29 December 2021).

11. Ibid.

12. "Report of the United Nations Conference on the Human Environment", United Nations Conference on the Human Environment (Stockholm 5–16 June 1972) (15 December 1972), UN Doc A/CONF.48/14/Rev. 1.

13. "Report of the United Nations Conference on Environment and Development", United Nations Conference on Environment and Development (Rio De Janeiro 3 June–14 June 1992) (12 August 1992), UN Doc A/CONF.151/26 (Vol. 1).

14. PTI, "NGT Disposed of Over 19,000 Cases from 2011–2017", *Economic Times* (New Delhi, 11 April 2017), https://economictimes.indiatimes.com/news/politics-and-nation/ngt-disposed-of-over-19000-cases-from-2011-17/articleshow/58128891.cms (accessed 30 December 2021).

15. Yukti Choudhary, "Tribunal on Trial", *Down to Earth* (30 November 2014), https://www.downtoearth.org.in/coverage/tribunal-on-trial-47400 (accessed 29 December 2021).

16. Department-Related Parliamentary Standing Committee on Science and Technology, Environment and Forests, "Report on the National Green Tribunal Bill, 2009 presented in Parliament of India – Rajya Sabha" (203rd Report, November 2009), //164.100.47.5/newcommittee/reports/EnglishCommittees/Committee%20on%20S%20and%20T,%20Env.%20and%20Forests/For%20Net.htm (accessed 29 December 2021).

17. Ibid., Point 8.8.

18. Department-Related Parliamentary Standing Committee on Science and Technology, "Report on the National Green Tribunal Bill, 2009 presented in Parliament of India – Rajya Sabha".

19. Ibid.

20. Justice D.Y. Chandrachud, "Indian Environmentalism", *National Green Tribunal International Journal on Environment* 2 (2017): 6.

21. Ibid.

22. Choudhary, "Tribunal on Trial".

23. Ibid.

24. Ibid.

25. Debayan Roy, "NGT Working with Just 6 Members Instead of at Least 21, Zonal Benches Vacant for 2 Years Now", *The Print* (New Delhi 4 November 2019), https://theprint.in/environment/ngt-working-with-6-members-instead-of-at-least-21-zonal-benches-vacant-for-2-yrs-now/314616/ (accessed 29 December 2021).

26. Ranu Purohit, "NGT Goes Online: Now You Can Approach NGT from Any Part of India without Your Physical Presence", *Live Law* (21 September 2019), https://www.livelaw.in/top-stories/ngt-goes-online-148310 (accessed 29 December 2021).

27. Ibid.

28. Ibid.

29. Ibid.

30. Aruna Chandrasekhar, "Scorched Earth: The Suffocation of the National Green Tribunal", *The Caravan* (1 August 2019), https://caravanmagazine.in/law/suffocation-national-green-tribunal (accessed 29 December 2021).

31. Preamble, The National Green Tribunal Act, 2010 (Act 19 of 2010) (India).

32. For instance, see generally *Kollidam Aaru Pathukappu Nala Sangam v. Union of India*, 2014 SCC OnLine Mad 4928 (Madras High Court, India); *State of Telangana v. Md. Hayath Uddinand*, (2007) 2 SCC 1 (Supreme Court of India).

33. *Kollidam Aaru Pathukappu Nala Sangam v. Union of India*.

34. *L. Chandra Kumar v. Union of India*, (1997) 3 SCC 261 (Supreme Court of India).

35. Ibid., para 76.

36. Ibid., para 11.
37. *Shri Anil Hoble v. Kashinath Jairam Shetye*, 2015 SCC OnLine Bom 3699 (Bombay High Court, India).
38. Ibid., para 16.
39. Ibid.
40. *United Bank of India v. Satyawati Tondon*, (2010) 8 SCC 110, Para 43 (Supreme Court of India).
41. Ibid., para 17.
42. Special Correspondent, "High Court to Hear Appeal against NGT Order", *The Hindu* (Hyderabad 1 March 2019), https://www.thehindu.com/news/cities/Hyderabad/high-court-to-hear-appeal-against-ngt order/article26401062.ece (accessed 30 December 2021).
43. Ibid.
44. This section of the paper contains paraphrases from authors' previous work titled Raghuveer Nath and Armin Rosencranz, "Determining Environmental Compensation: The Art of Living Case", *NUJS L. Rev.* 12, no. 1 (2019): 1–19.
45. See generally *S.P. Muthuraman v. Union of India*, Original Application No. 37 of 2015 (National Green Tribunal, India); *Manoj Misra v. Union of India*, Original Application No. 177 of 2015 (National Green Tribunal, India); *Krishan Lal Gera v. State of Haryana*, Appeal No. 22 of 2015 (National Green Tribunal, India); *Sunil Kumar Chugh v. Secretary Environment Department*, Appeal No. 66 of 2014 (National Green Tribunal, India); see also Chandra Bhushan, Srestha Banerjee, and Ikshaku Bezbaroa, *Green Tribunal, Green Approach: The Need for Better Implementation of the Polluter Pays Principle* (New Delhi: Centre for Science and Environment, 2018), 8.
46. *Goa Foundation v. Union of India and Ors.*, Judgment/Order dated 21 April 2014 in Writ Petition (Civil) No. 435 of 2012 (Supreme Court of India).
47. Ibid., para 63.
48. Ibid., para 63.
49. Ibid., para 63.
50. *Goa Foundation v. Union of India and Ors.*, (2014) 6 SCC 590 (Supreme Court of India).
51. *The Forward Foundation v. State of Karnataka*, 2015 SCC OnLine NGT 5 (National Green Tribunal, India).
52. Ibid., para 14.
53. Ibid., para 84.
54. *Krishan Kant Singh v. National Ganga River Basin Authority*, Judgment in October 2014 in Original Application No. 299 of 2013 (National Green Tribunal, India).
55. Ibid., para 51.
56. Bhushan, Banerjee, and Bezbaroa, *Green Tribunal, Green Approach*, 12.
57. Ibid.
58. Ibid..
59. *Ajay Kumar Negi v. Union of India*, Judgment dated 7 July 2015 in Original Application No. 183 (THC) of 2013 (National Green Tribunal, India).
60. Ibid., para 22.

61. Ibid., para 29.
62. Ibid., para 25.
63. *Manoj Mishra v. Delhi Development Authority & Ors.*, Original Application No. 65 of 2016 (National Green Tribunal, India).
64. *Manoj Misra v. Delhi Development Authority*, 2017 SCC OnLine NGT 966, para 42 (Principal Bench, NGT, India).
65. Ibid.
66. Ibid., para 24 (National Green Tribunal, India).
67. Letter dated 3 March 2016 from Mr Shashi Shekhar to the National Green Tribunal, D.O. No. 5 (UIR, RD 1 GR)/ Misc./2016.
68. Ibid., 57 and 61.
69. *Ajay Kumar Negi v. Union of India*, para 17.
70. Ibid., para 15.
71. *Manoj Misra v. Delhi Development Authority*, para 22.
72. *Sandeep Kumar v. Ministry of Environment and Forests and Climate Change*, Order dated 2 January 2019 in Original Application No. 517 of 2015 (National Green Tribunal, India); see also *Economic Times*, "NGT Imposes Rs. 100 Crore Fine on Meghalaya Govt for Failing to Curb Illegal Mining"(New Delhi, 4 January 2019), https://economictimes.indiatimes.com/news/politics-and-nation/ngt-imposes-rs-100-crore-fine-on-meghalaya-govt-for-failing-to-curb-illegal-mining/articleshow/67388967.cms (accessed 31 December 2021).
73. Ibid.
74. *Sandeep Kumar v. Ministry of Environment and Forests and Climate Change*; see also Public Trust of India, "NGT Imposes Rs. 100 Crore Fine on Meghalaya Govt for Failing to Curb Illegal Mining".
75. *Satish Kumar v. Union of India & Ors.*, Order dated 03 December 2018 in Original Application No. 56 (THC)/2013.
76. *Mayank Manohar & Anr. v. Govt. of NCT of Delhi & Ors.*, Order dated 24 January 2019 in Original Application No. 601 of 2018 (National Green Tribunal, India).
77. Law Commission of India, "Proposal to constitute Environmental Courts", 151.
78. Ibid., 151.
79. While Section 25 of the NGT Act accords the NGT with execution jurisdiction by vesting in it all powers of a civil court, it is distinct from contempt jurisdiction. Moreover, it remains to be seen how the NGT will interpret the powers under this section in practice.
80. *The Braj Foundation v. Govt of U.P.*, Order/Judgment in Original Application No. 278 of 2013 and M.A. No. 110 of 2014 (National Green Tribunal, India).
81. *Vardhaman Kaushik v. Union of India & Ors.*, 2017 SCC OnLine NGT 758 (National Green Tribunal, India).
82. Ibid.
83. Dipu Rai, "Air Pollution in Delhi Was 16 Times Worse than Prescribed Limit on Diwali Night", *India Today* (28 October 2019), https://www.indiatoday.in/diu/story/delhi-air

-pollution-16-times-worse-prescribed-limit-diwali-night-1613477-2019-10-28   (accessed   31 December 2021).

84. Press Trust of India, "Delhi Pollution: NGT Bans Construction, Industrial Activities till 14 November", *Live Mint* (New Delhi, 9 November 2017), https://www.livemint.com/Politics/ MHVjYfmyoaZVnnYKg2mFzK/Delhi-air-pollution-NGT-imposes-ban-on-industrial-construc.html (accessed 31 December 2021).

85. Ibid.

86. Geetanjoy Sahu, "Wither the National Green Tribunal?" *Down To Earth* (23 September 2019), https://www.downtoearth.org.in/blog/environment/whither-the-national-green-tribunal --66879 (accessed 31 December 2021).

87. Bhushan, Banerjee, and Bezbaroa, *Green Tribunal, Green Approach*, 18.

88. Ibid., 19.

89. Ibid..

90. Ibid..

91. *Ajay Kumar Negi v. Union of India.*

92. Kumar Sambhav Shrivastava, "Green Tribunal Gets Short Shrift", *Down to Earth* (30 June 2012), https://www.downtoearth.org.in/news/green-tribunal-gets-short-shrift-38426 (accessed 30 September 2020).

93. Ibid.

94. Geetanjoy Sahu, "Ecocide by Design? Under Modi, Vacancies at National Green Tribunal Reach 70%", *The Wire* (15 February 2018), https://thewire.in/politics/ngt-political-apathy-vacancies (accessed 30 September 2020).

95. Shrivastava, "Green Tribunal Gets Short Shrift".

96. Ibid.

97. Utkarsh Anand, "NGT Member Quits Citing Lack of Facilities", *Indian Express* (New Delhi, 30 January 2013), http://archive.indianexpress.com/news/ngt-member-quits-citing-lack-of-facilities/1066585/ (accessed 31 December 2021).

98. ibid.

99. Anand, "NGT Member Quits Citing Lack of Facilities" .

100. Legally India Admin, "SC Slams Poor Facilities for Green Tribunal", *Legally India* (20 September 2013), https://www.legalindia.com/news/sc-slams-poor-facilities-for-green-tribunal (accessed 31 December 2021).

101. Ibid.

102. Dhananjay Mahapatra, "Kolkata May Lose Green Tribunal Bench to Guwahati or Ranchi", *Times of India* (New Delhi, 10 July 2013), https://timesofindia.indiatimes.com/city/kolkata/ Kolkata-may-lose-green-tribunal-bench-to-Guwahati-or-Ranchi/articleshow/20996616.cms (accessed 31 December 2021).

103. Ibid.

104. Legally India Admin, "SC Slams Poor Facilities for Green Tribunal".

105. Ibid.

106. Bhushan, Banerjee, and Bezbaroa, *Green Tribunal, Green Approach*, 18.

107. Ibid., 18.

108. Press Trust of India, "Environment Ministry Gets Rs. 3,111 Crore in Budget – a 20 Per cent Increase", *Economic Times* (New Delhi, 1 February 2019) <https://economictimes.indiatimes.com/news/economy/policy/environment-ministry-gets-rs-3111-crore-in-budget-a-20-per-cent-increase/articleshow/67794117.cms?from=mdr> accessed 31 December 2021; see also Nityanand Jayaraman, "Environmentally, There Is No Talk to Walk in Budget 2019", *News Minute* (7 July 2019), https://www.thenewsminute.com/article/environmentally-there-no-talk-walk-budget-2019-104995 (accessed 31 December 2021).

109. Shrivastava, "Green Tribunal Gets Short Shrift".

110. Legally India Admin, "SC Slams Poor Facilities for Green Tribunal".

111. Members of the NGT, available at http://www.greentribunal.gov.in/members.aspx (accessed 30 September 2020). As on 9 September 2020 there are only three judicial members, namely Justice Sonam Phintso Wangdi, Justice K. Ramakrishan, Justice S. K. Singh, and three expert members, namely Dr S.S. Garbayal, Dr Nagin Nanda, and Dr Saibal Dasgupta.

112. Members of the NGT as of March 2022, available at greentribunal.gov.in: Judicial Members are Justice K. Ramakrishnan, Justice S.K. Singh, Justice Sudhir Agarwal, Justice B. Amit Sthalekar, Justice Brijesh Sethi and Expert Members are Dr Nagin Nanda, Mr. Saibal Dasgupta, Dr Arun Kumar Verma, Dr Satyagopal Korlapati, Dr Vijay Kulkarni, Dr A Senthil Vel and Dr Afroz Ahmed.

113. Bhushan, Banerjee, and Bezbaroa, *Green Tribunal, Green Approach*, 18.

114. Shrivastava, "Green Tribunal Gets Short Shrift".

115. Ibid.

116. Ibid.

117. Ibid.

118. Scroll Staff, "Do You Want to Shut Down the National Green Tribunal, Delhi High Court Asks Centre", *Scroll* (25 August 2017), https://scroll.in/latest/848499/do-you-want-to-shut-down-the-national-green-tribunal-delhi-high-court-asks-centre (accessed 31 December 2021).

119. Ritwick Dutta, "Woes of the National Green Tribunal: Are the Recent Appointments Unconstitutional?" *Bar & Bench* (9 October 2019), https://barandbench.com/new-appointments-national-green-tribunal-unconstitutional-judicial-independence/ (accessed 31 December 2021).

120. Ibid.

121. Ibid.

122. Ibid.

123. Ibid.

124. Malavika Vyawahare, "India Among 5 Worst Countries in Terms of Environmental Health", *Hindustan Times* (24 January 2018, New Delhi), https://www.hindustantimes.com/india-news/india-4th-worst-country-in-curbing-environmental-pollution/story

-VWjWupzHcy8H5VdNGbp32J.html (31 December 2021); see also Ishan Kukreti, "Ease of Doing Business Comes at an Environmental Cost", *Down To Earth* (2 November 2017), https://www.downtoearth.org.in/news/governance/the-environmental-cost-of-making-business-easy-59001 (accessed 31 December 2021).

125. Ibid.

126. Kukreti, "Ease of Doing Business Comes at an Environmental Cost".

127. Legally India Admin, "SC Slams Poor Facilities for Green Tribunal".

128. Digvijay Singh Bisht, "How the Centre Is Diluting Green Clearance Norms", *Down To Earth* (15 January 2019), https://www.downtoearth.org.in/blog/urbanisation/how-the-centre-isdiluting-green-clearance-norms-62828 (accessed on 18 December 2021).

129. Ibid.

130. Bisht, "How the Centre Is Diluting Green Clearance Norms".

131. Ibid.

132. *Prafulla Samantray v. Union of India*, Judgment dated 30 March 2012 in Appeal No. 8 of 2011 (National Green Tribunal, India).

133. *M.P. Patil v. Union of India*, Judgment/Order dated 13 March 2014 in Appeal No. 12 of 2012 (National Green Tribunal, India).

134. *Jeet Singh Kanwar v. Union of India*, Judgment dated 16 April 2013 in Appeal No. 10 of 2011 (National Green Tribunal, India).

135. Ibid.

136. For instance, the Supreme Court deferred to the government's developmental agenda unequivocally in *Narmada Bachao Andolan v. Union of India*, (2000) 10 SCC 664 (Supreme Court of India).

137. Ibid.

138. See generally *Subhash Kumar v. State of Bihar*, (1991) 1 SCC 598 (Supreme Court of India).

139. *Alembic Pharmaceuticals Ltd. v. Rohit Prajapati*, Judgment dated 1 April 2020 in Civil Appeal No. 1526 of 2016, Para 23 (Supreme Court of India).

140. *Common Cause v. Union of India*, (2017) 9 SCC 499 (Supreme Court of India).

141. *Association for Environmental Protection v. Union of India*, (2013) 7 SCC 226 (Supreme Court of India).

142. *Electrotherm (India) v. Patel Vipulkumar Ramjibhai*, (2016) 9 SCC 300 (Supreme Court of India).

143. *The Forward Foundation v. State of Karnataka*.

144. Ishan Kukreti, "Draft EIA: SC Rejects Centre Challenge to Delhi HC Translation Order", *Down To Earth* (13 August 2020), https://www.downtoearth.org.in/news/environment/draft-eia-sc-rejects-centre-challenge-to-delhi-hc-translation-order-72803 (accessed 31 December 2021).

145. *Trail Smelter Case (USA, Canada)* (Arbitration Tribunal) (16 April 1938 and 11 March 1941) 3 UN Rep. Int'l Arb. Awards 1905 (1941), https://legal.un.org/riaa/cases/vol_III/1905-1982.pdf (accessed 31 December 2021).

146. Asmita Bakshi, "EIA Draft 2020: 'Violation of Environmental Law Is Seen as Development'", *Mint* (17 August 2020), https://www.livemint.com/mint-lounge/features/eia-draft-2020 -violation-of-environmental-law-is-seen-as-development-11597593043757.html (accessed 31 December 2021).

147. Jayshree Nandi, "'Nothing Disturbing in the Clauses of Draft EIA 2020' Says RP Gupta" (17 August 2020), https://www.hindustantimes.com/india-news/nothing-disturbing-in- the-clauses-of-draft-eia-2020-says-rp-gupta/story-FclDTDbTKIeIMB73tAD10H.html (accessed 31 December 2021).

148. Ibid.

149. Ibid.

150. Ibid.

INTERVIEW WITH JUSTICE SWATANTER KUMAR (RETIRED SUPREME COURT JUDGE; EX-CHAIRPERSON OF THE NGT FROM DECEMBER 2012 TO DECEMBER 2017)

Authors: The impetus for the creation of the NGT was primarily led by the Supreme Court through a series of cases. This is because it was felt that ordinary courts lacked the scientific expertise required to handle complex and technical environmental matters. One can say that the need to effectively deal with scientific complexities and uncertainty in such cases formed the raison d'être of the NGT. Do you think that the Tribunal has been able to fulfil its role as a scientifically oriented adjudicatory forum?

Justice Swatanter Kumar: I think it's not totally correct to say that the higher judiciary in India was not able to handle environmental cases because of a lack of technical knowledge or for other reasons. The NGT, to my mind, was enacted primarily because of the international conventions, whether it be Rio (1992), Montreal (1987), or Stockholm (1972), which called for specialized environmental justice systems. So it was done more in terms of India's international commitments with the aid of Article 253 of the Constitution.

In the meanwhile, the Supreme Court pronounced judgments tilting the balance in favour of establishing specialized courts. This was not limited to the environment but happened even in other fields like taxation and company law. So, there was a general emphasis on creating specialized tribunals. Moreover, all the landmark environmental cases, whether it be the *Kamal Nath Case*[1] or the *Bhopal Tragedy Case*,[2] were dealt with directly by the Supreme Court in a very efficient manner. I do not think there has ever been a more expeditious disposal of cases in our history.

So, if I were to take a balanced view, I would say that the impetus for the NGT's formation came from collective wisdom. This consisted of the government's appreciation of India's international commitments and the judiciary's consciousness of the fact that increasing litigation and modern developments in jurisprudence, all over the world, required the formation of specialized tribunals. That, I think, is the right approach to understanding the impetus.

Even when you talk of the technical aspect, ultimately, the judges were aided by the scientific reports that used to come. So, in the NGT, all that has changed is that the experts are on the bench and are part of the adjudicatory process. That, of course, is a very big addition. I do not deny that. But their absence, by itself, did not incapacitate the justice system.

Authors: This impetus that we are talking about led to the formation of two tribunals – the NEAA and the NET. However, these predecessors of the NGT were viewed as mostly dysfunctional due to the limited jurisdiction and lack of appointments by the government. They are not viewed in the same light as the NGT. Our question is – do you ever feel, due to several attempts to curtail the NGT's independence, it might be headed towards the same fate as its predecessors? What do you think sets the NGT apart from its predecessors?

Justice Swatanter Kumar: See, these predecessors of the NGT were administrative tribunals. They were not quasi-judicial tribunals like the NGT. That is a marked difference between them. And secondly, maybe they did not approach the functions provided to them creatively. They just remained what they were. Their contribution was minimal, and I would say that ineffectiveness became the cause of their demise.

But I do not see the NGT going the same way. The NGT has established itself so prominently that there's no possibility of travelling down that sad path. The functions of the NGT are under a statute, and now we have judgments which highlight the NGT's role. Additionally, we have the Supreme Court overseeing the NGT's functioning. So, it's a very positive setup. That's why I think it won't go that way.

Authors: You have adjudicated environmental disputes at both the NGT and the Supreme Court. Given the NGT's different structure – having expert members as a part of the adjudicatory process – did you feel any prominent differences in adjudicating at these two places? Do you think the NGT is better equipped to deal with environmental matters?

Justice Swatanter Kumar: See, this is like comparing two incomparable things. Ultimately, the Supreme Court is the apex court of the country. So, we cannot really equate it to the NGT or determine which is better. But, yes, they operate in different ways. The Supreme Court, by statute, remains the appellate body for the NGT's decisions. This means that the finality of NGT's decisions comes from the Supreme Court in cases of appeal. But yes, the addition of expert members is certainly a wise idea. At the same time, I don't think the Court suffers from any infirmity. But a very important consideration is the kind of expert members you pick up because it is not the institution itself but the persons that make up the institution that matters.

I will narrate a very interesting example. When I was heading the NGT, I had members who were outstanding. Professor Trivedi, for instance, had researched on the Ganga, from Gangotri to Kolkata, as a scientist. So, you can imagine how rich his knowledge must be. He was a professor from IIT. Then he became a secretary on a scientific board, and then he took his place in the NGT. So, we had some really outstanding experts. We had people from various fields such as forests, industries, and chairpersons of pollution control boards. So, they had that calibre. The purpose was to get proper technical input on the industrial development systems, as well as to check the prospective impacts of our judgments. So, if we asked someone to add filtration plants somewhere, what effect would that have? The experts were able to analyse this very well. We had very fair discussions.

So, I think adding experts – IITians, professors, scientists, or environmentalists – was right. But the selection of these people is really important. If you appoint a person who is only an environmentalist, you are likely to lose the balance. What you need to do is appoint an expert member who has a holistic view of the environment and who can really think in terms of sustainability.

Authors: There has been a general view that the MoEF and the NGT are at odds with each other, and that the former views the latter as an opponent. Even when the NGT had just been formed, very little infrastructural support was extended by the government to the NGT. Many judicial members quit citing uninhabitable accommodation provided and low salaries. We have had judges who were not given adequate kitchen and washroom facilities, and who could not afford the commute to the tribunal premises due to the meagre allowances. In many zonal benches, the NGT has not been provided with the necessary infrastructure to start functioning.

As of today, all zonal benches have been shut down in the last two years due to a lack of appointments. What are your views on such treatment of the NGT? And does this indicate that the NGT is not viewed favourably by the government or the MoEF?

Justice Swatanter Kumar: I'll be very honest while answering this. The general view appears to be what you narrated, but you know, after I had taken over as the chairperson, I did not have any conflicts. People do not usually believe that, but it is the truth. I must thank the Supreme Court during that time. It passed very positive judgments for the infrastructure of the NGT. But, more importantly, I did not see any opposition from the two governments. I found both the governments that I encountered very compatible. Of course, you must know how to deal with them.

We had infrastructure, amenities, and everything. An interesting fact is that before any other courts in India went digital, the NGT did. My members did not have any problems either, even in the zonal benches. The Madras Bench of the NGT was actually given a location in one of the heritage buildings of Chennai. So, I would not say that there is some perennial conflict. The government is entitled to have its own point of view. You can tell them that their demand is not reasonable. You can tell them that in black and white.

So, I do not really subscribe to this narrative of opposition. I have had deliberations with senior government officials. But there was no acrimony. The head of the institution plays a very big role. If some unavoidable conflict arises, then go to Court, why not?

The Supreme Court and even the High Courts, under Article 227, are superintending courts. So how do they superintend? When I was in Mumbai, I opened up a number of courts all across the state. The High Court's budget was about INR 32 crore per annum. I put up a budget of INR 378 crore and the chief minister approved it in a minute. You should be able to convince other people. Where I was right, people conceded. Where they were right, I did the same. So, it was a positive environment.

Authors: The next question we have has to do with access to justice. Aruna Chandrasekhar, an environmental journalist, wrote a wonderful piece in *The Caravan* where she narrated the plight of an Adivasi worker to reach the NGT. She highlighted that since the NGT's zonal benches had shut down and given that the NGT has taken away the jurisdiction from 13,000 civil courts to hear environmental matters, the people in remote and rural areas have very little access to justice. A major reason that the zonal benches have shut down is that the government simply did not appoint members. What are your thoughts on this issue?

Justice Swatanter Kumar: You're very right in bringing up the issue of access to justice. Under our Constitution, we talk of economic and social justice. That can be provided only when the access to justice is unimpeded and easy. In Mumbai, I always preferred physical hearings in judicial processes instead of digital media. See, we are a very diverse country. We are highly populated, and people are located even in the most remote areas. There are very few places where you won't find people. So, you have to establish a physical court system to ensure access to judicial remedies. That should be the right approach.

Let's take an example of a case involving Adivasis. I was in Mumbai at that time; I went to inspect a site where I saw Adivasis who were naked. I asked people where they come from, and I was informed that Chagroli in Maharashtra was home to an entire colony of Adivasis. The people also told me that they were offered clothes to wear, but they simply refused; they want to stay like that. The point I'm trying to make is that I had to take notice of these facts. Despite our diversity, access to justice is fundamental; there is no exception to it. You must do everything in your power to ensure that access is provided.

If we read the NGT Act, we see that it is a very inexpensive act. The cost of access to justice is negligible. An ordinary man can afford it. Moreover, one thing that I personally feel good about is that letters were being treated as applications. So, we could take *suo motu* action. It's a long debate whether we could or could not. I do not know about the latest developments on this front, but I personally think that the Tribunal has *suo motu* jurisdiction.

These powers were tools for environmental justice. So, one must make sure that irrespective of the structure or the limitations of the NGT, the Tribunal is accessible to all, and anybody can reach it. The presence of zonal benches, therefore, is very important. I had opened every bench during my tenure, and I can tell you that whether it was the Bhopal or the Madras Bench, they had no dearth of infrastructure. They were sound establishments, and I think they should operate in full swing.

Finally, on the point that the Delhi Bench is now hearing environmental cases from all over the country, I think the government and the Tribunal should put their heads into it, and definitely not make people run to Delhi. How many people know of e-filing? The people sitting in the remote areas do not even know the names of the places.

Authors: The next question has to do with Section 22 of the NGT Act, 2010. The section prescribes that an appeal from the NGT's decisions may lie to the Supreme Court. Different High Courts have interpreted this very differently. We have the Delhi High Court, which, in accordance with the spirit of the NGT Act, has refused to entertain appeals from the NGT's decisions. On the other hand, we have the Madras High Court, which has accepted appeals from the NGT, citing *L. Chandra Kumar's*[3] ratio, while reasoning that the High Court's jurisdiction cannot be ousted. In the middle, we have the Bombay High Court, which although accepting the *L. Chandra Kumar* ratio, adds the caveat that the High Court's jurisdiction under Article 226 must be used sparingly, also considering that the appeal to the Supreme Court is an efficacious alternative remedy. So, there is an entire spectrum of views. What would be your advice to High Courts on this issue? What would be the right approach?

Justice Swatanter Kumar: I think we must understand the clear distinction between Article 226 of the Constitution and appellate jurisdiction. Jurisdiction under Article 226 simply cannot be divested. But we must understand the scope of Article 226. You cannot bring appellate jurisdiction into Article 226. The article must be invoked only to correct errors of jurisdiction, patent errors, etc. The High Courts must realize this. The statutory appeal to the Supreme Court is pretty broad, and all forums must be allowed to operate in their respective fields.

Authors: The next question has to do with the NGT's manner of assessing environmental compensation. We saw in *Forward Foundation v. Union of India*[4] that the NGT adopted the Supreme Court's ratio from the *Goa Foundation Case,*[5] which was a case specific to mining in Goa. What has now become a trend is that irrespective of the actual quantum of damage, the NGT awards 5 per cent of the project cost as environmental compensation. In a lot of cases, this is being seen as just an additional environmental fee. This virtually means that the polluter pays principle is becoming "pay and pollute" principle, simply because potential polluters can factor in the 5 per cent compensation into their calculations beforehand. What are your thoughts on this trend?

Justice Swatanter Kumar: See, the NGT Act does not provide any formula for the computation of the environmental compensation. It must depend on the facts of the specific case. But what I strongly feel is that there should be at least some evidence on record that logically leads you to grant a compensation of one rupee or one crore rupees. It cannot be entirely irrational.

For example, in water pollution cases, you should be able to show what is the cost of restoration, what is the cost of invoking the precautionary principle, and what are the general damages to be imposed, which may have a punitive character. So, you can have restorative costs, precautionary costs, and also punitive costs. Punitive costs obviously cannot have a rationale. It's just a discretionary matter. So, I think the overall award granted should have some rational basis.

Authors: In this regard, we have highlighted in this book that environmental courts in other jurisdictions such as the United Kingdom and the United States determine environmental compensation differently. These courts follow an approach called the resource equivalency analysis (REA). This involves determining a baseline condition – basically the state in which the environment was before the alleged damage occurred. Then, they see the deviation from this baseline condition to assess the extent of damage that has been caused. Thereafter, the compensation imposed is assessed on the costs required to restore the damaged environment back to the baseline condition. Do you think that perhaps the NGT could adopt such an approach instead of the arbitrary 5 per cent figure in all cases? Would you say that assessing baseline conditions should be made an important part of the computation of environmental compensation?

Justice Swatanter Kumar: I think that assessing baseline conditions is very important. However, a general system might not be practically possible in India. This is because the variety and quantum of litigation we have here are totally different than what we see in foreign jurisdictions. I remember that I used to handle thirty–thirty-five cases a day when I was heading the NGT. In the United States, judges probably deal with these many cases over a period of six months. Having said this, I agree with you to the extent that in a certain class of cases the NGT should necessarily determine the environmental baseline condition before quantifying environmental compensation. For instance, in cases dealing with forest clearances, I should have a broader baseline that will define the characteristics of the area and the natural life there at the time of the alleged damage. So there has to be some reference point to compute damage and compensation.

Also, in relation to the 5 per cent figure, it is very important to have a case-by-case analysis of compensation and not a blanket calculation. For instance, a small industrial plant using electroplating can cause significantly more environmental damage than many bigger plants put together.

Authors: This question is in relation to the implementation of the NGT's orders. The 186th Report of the Law Commission of India recommended that the proposed environmental court be vested with contempt jurisdiction. The Parliamentary Standing Committee, to which the Bill was referred, also suggested similarly. The NGT Act, however, did not incorporate this. We only have Section 26, which, although providing for fines and imprisonment for non-compliance of orders, is only enforceable by ordinary criminal courts given that the NGT does not have criminal jurisdiction. However, in the case of *Braj Foundation v. State of Uttar Pradesh*,[6] the NGT proclaimed that the Tribunal has the inherent power to enforce its own decisions. But the Tribunal did not elaborate on the source of this power. So, on the ground, we see that even landmark orders remain unimplemented. Given this lack of statutory power to the NGT to try for contempt, I would like to hear your thoughts on this issue.

Justice Swatanter Kumar: See, the Act clearly doesn't have contempt powers. But there are a lot of grey areas in the Act. Non-compliance with the NGT's directions was made a criminal offence, even though the NGT was specifically not provided criminal jurisdiction. So, there are multiple judicial processes contemplated under the Act. I think these issues need clarity. Secondly, see, the NGT has the powers of a civil court. Even though it cannot punish contempt itself, it can always recommend that contempt proceedings be initiated. But there is no judgment clarifying this issue. The ideal thing would be that the Tribunal should be able to invoke the powers under Order 21 of CPC [Code of Civil Procedure], 1908. That has all the necessary powers for enforcement – you can impose civil imprisonment and you can attach his property, so that violators can be dealt with expeditiously.

Authors: The next question is in relation to Section 24, which deals with the Environmental Relief Fund (ERF). The provision states that any award made by the Tribunal must mandatorily be credited into the ERF. Even Rule 35 of the NGT (Practice and Procedure) Rules, 2011, states that the amount must be credited to the ERF within thirty days. A recent report[7] by the Centre for Science and Environment highlights that 40 per cent of the judgments directed payment to be made to the State Pollution Control Boards, 17 per cent to the State Forest Department, and only 12 per cent to the ERF. Even out of these limited cases, where payments were directed to the ERF, to date, only two polluters have actually deposited the money in the ERF. So, firstly, considering that directing payment into the ERF is a mandatory provision, is it right for the NGT to direct payment elsewhere? Secondly, given that the Act does not really give the NGT the power to oversee the operations of the ERF, how can we tackle the issue of non-payment?

Justice Swatanter Kumar: See, the problem that I see is that it does not matter to whom the payment is directed. Technically, it should be sent to the ERF, but in the orders and awards I have passed, I was more concerned about how the money is to be used. In some orders, we asked the State Pollution Control Board to submit a proposal for estimated restoration costs. And that proved to be more effective. For instance, if somebody had polluted a water body, spending money on restoring it was more useful than seeing where it was deposited. If you direct payment without further directions, then that money just goes into some account of the authority. So, any order must aim at removing the pollution against which the complaint is made.

On the point of only two violators making payment into the ERF, I think the Registry must actively put up instances where the fine has not been paid. It is their obligation to make sure that the money is paid.

Authors: The amendments sought to be introduced by the Finance Act, 2017, which thankfully has been stayed by the Supreme Court, are seen by many as being an attempt to destroy the independence of the NGT, as far as the selection process of judges and experts is concerned. The amendments expanded the Central government's control over the Tribunal. A certain provision even allowed a person with no judicial experience to head the NGT. This has raised a lot of alarm bells. What are your thoughts on this proposed dilution of the NGT's independence?

Justice Swatanter Kumar: Well, as you mentioned, the changes have been stayed by the Supreme Court. And I believe that some directions were also passed by the Court on the appointment and tenure of members. So, I think the Finance Act, 2017, did not have much effect and was rendered ineffective by the Supreme Court. But I do think that, if the NGT has to carry on as a judicial or a quasi-judicial body, it is appropriate that a judge heads it. And I'm saying that because if you look at the current environmental jurisprudence in India, the Supreme Court and the High Courts are taking up a lot of environmental matters. They are mainly the bodies dealing with a plethora of environmental matters, rather than the Tribunal.

So, I think that judges familiar with environmental jurisprudence should be taken up to head the Tribunal. That would be in the interests of the objective of the NGT Act. These objects of the Act have remained firmly enshrined in the preamble and nobody has tried to meddle with it before. Some have tried to dilute the substantive and material provisions of the NGT. But if you want to keep the objects and reasons for the enactment of the NGT intact, then you need a judicial mind heading the Tribunal.

Second, you asked me about the appointment of members. I think the earlier system (before the proposed amendments under the Finance Act, 2017) was a very robust system. It had the participation of the government too. The secretary of the Ministry of Environment of Forests was a member of the Appointment Committee, a sitting judge of the Supreme Court was the chairman, the chairperson of the NGT was also a member, and then we had a few government-nominated expert members on the Committee as well. Although the government had a big part in the process, I remember that we used to have deliberations on selections. It was not an empty formality; we used to discuss why or why not to select someone. There was marking; there was analysis of the candidate's qualifications, contributions, etc. They should not dilute that process. If they do, that will certainly have a major impact on the working of the Tribunal. If you exclude any party from the process, it will become an unfair process. Moreover, the stakes before the NGT are definitely very high. The economic consequences of the Tribunal's decisions are very serious. So, you need very strong-minded people as adjudicators.

Authors: The proposed EIA Draft Notification, 2020, is widely regarded as one of the most regressive environmental legislative proposals to date. The five major concerns with respect to the draft are

a) ex-post-facto clearance;
b) any project can be categorized as "strategic", and there will be no public disclosure regarding these projects;
c) construction projects up to 150,000 square metres are exempted from the EIA process;
d) violations can only be reported by the project or a government representative; and
e) time for a public hearing is reduced from thirty days to twenty days.

Given these regressive proposals, what are your thoughts on the EIA Draft Notification, 2020?

Justice Swatanter Kumar: There is no second opinion that the new notification has certain drawbacks; there are negative points. There are certain points that are not advantageous. There has to be judicial review of this, which only the Supreme Court will be in a position to do. I am not so sure what will be the result. There are certain matters which raise concern. But the notification has not yet been notified, I believe.

Authors: We have seen, due in part to your efforts, that environmental clearances have played a really big part in the NGT's jurisprudence, whether it be to uphold the precautionary principle or the polluter pays principle. This Draft Notification dismantles all that by providing for *post facto* clearances – which are totally antithetical to the precautionary principle. I would like to know your opinion on this specific provision of *ex-post facto* clearances. Also, what are your thoughts on the fact that citizens cannot report violations under the proposed EIA process?

Justice Swatanter Kumar: Yes, the latter point seems to be the basic matter of concern. I think people have filed objections. I do not think you can deny a citizen the right to object, because under our Constitution, access to justice is simply not deniable. When we have environmental laws talking about any "aggrieved person", how can you deprive him of the right to object by a subordinate legislation? To me, this is a very fundamental issue.

About the change of instituting an *ex-post facto* clearance, I remember delivering a judgment in the NGT on this issue. In 2016, a Notification was brought out giving a similar kind of relief. You can refer to the judgment; it represents exactly my views on this issue. To me, it is these two issues, the denial of access to justice and a universal provision for *ex-post facto* clearances. Occasionally, an *ex-post facto* clearance might be all right. We did it when the matter involved a canal project in Rajasthan. We allowed it, even after thirty years. It differs from case to case. But a blanket provision is not right.

[The case Justice Swatanter Kumar is referring to is *S.P. Muthuraman v. Union of India*.[8] As discussed in Chapter 3, in this case, the NGT was concerned with, inter alia, an office memorandum of the MoEF that sought to issue *post-facto* clearance to certain projects. It was contended, on behalf of the respondent, that the provision in the EIA Notification, 2006, that required the clearance process to be concluded prior to the construction of the project was not mandatory. In response, the Tribunal noted that such an *ex-post facto* EIA report would suffer from a lack of diligence and would foreclose the opportunity to explore alternatives. It held that such a measure would invariably go against the fundamental tenets of the precautionary principle as irreversible environmental damage would have already been caused.]

*   *   *

NOTES

1. *M.C. Mehta v. Kamal Nath*, (2000) INSC 334 (Supreme Court of India).
2. *Union Carbide Corporation v. Union of India*, (1989) 2 SCC 540 (Supreme Court of India).
3. *Kollidam Aaru Pathukappu Nala Sangam v. Union of India*, 2014 SCC OnLine Mad 4928 (Madras High Court, India); *State of Telangana v. Md. Hayath Uddinand*, (2007) 2 SCC 1 (Supreme Court of India).
4. *The Forward Foundation v. State of Karnataka*, 2015 SCC OnLine NGT 5 (National Green Tribunal, India) .
5. *Goa Foundation v. Union of India and Ors.*, Judgment/Order dated 21 April 2014 in Writ Petition (Civil) No. 435 of 2012 (Supreme Court of India) .
6. *The Braj Foundation v. Govt of U.P.*, Order/Judgment in Original Application No. 278 of 2013 and M.A. No. 110 of 2014 (National Green Tribunal, India).
7. Chandra Bhushan, Srestha Banerjee, and Ikshaku Bezbaroa, *Green Tribunal, Green Approach: The Need for Better Implementation of the Polluter Pays Principle* (New Delhi: Centre for Science and Environment, 2018), 12.
8. *S.P. Muthuraman v. Union of India*, 2015 SCC OnLine NGT 169 (National Green Tribunal, India).

INTERVIEW WITH VIMAL BHAI
(ENVIRONMENTAL ACTIVIST)

Having heard the thoughts of Justice Swatanter Kumar on several issues faced by the NGT, we would like to feature a discussion with an environmental activist to understand and appreciate issues at the grassroots level. Vimal Bhai is an environmental activist who has successfully raised several important environmental concerns before the Supreme Court, the NGT, and even the NEAA. He has attended more than 200 public hearings which are an integral part of the present EIA process. We engage him in a discussion to understand general environmental concerns with respect to the public hearing process as well as challenges that the NGT can overcome.

Authors: What are some concerns that you have about the present direction of this discourse?

Vimal Bhai: I think we can't ever talk about the environment in isolation. We have to acknowledge that the environment is very closely linked to the people. This means that it has a major relation to the way people live, the expectations of the people, and their religious understandings; it is all linked with the environment. The initial stage of environmental activism was prominently marked with concerns about the River Ganga, and other similar concerns brought together a lot of like-minded people.

Another problem in these movements is that people often think of various concerns in a totally disjunctive manner. In my opinion, change cannot transpire this way. You cannot advocate one stance for an issue, and a totally opposite stance for another closely related issue. But this is happening. Let's take the issue of the displacement of people due to developmental projects. You cannot go on fighting for the environment without thinking about the closely related problem of displacement of affected communities. These are intricately connected problems, not separate ones. The plight of these displaced people is miserable. For years on, they remain ousted without any fixed home.

One can take the example of the Bhakra-Nangal Dam, one of the first major hydro projects of India. I visited Bhakra village sometime around 2001, and I saw that the displaced have yet not been rehabilitated. New problems arise for them every day. The same is the case for the thousands that are displaced from their homes because of developmental projects around the country. So, the inherent value of human life cannot be seen to be detached from the environment.

Authors: The next question that I would like to pose to you is with regard to your participation in the public hearing process of various projects. As somebody who has been a part of numerous such hearings, and as somebody who has been very vocal about these hearings being a sham, how has your experience been? The NGT has stated that environmental clearances will not be invalidated unless the defects in the public hearing process are of a very serious nature. What do you feel about the public hearings process in developmental projects and the efficacy of this process?

Vimal Bhai: I started participating in public hearings in 2003. I can modestly claim that, in the state of Uttarakhand, barring two or three instances, I have been a part of almost every public hearing since then. In 99 per cent of the hearings that I participated in, the first public hearing had to be cancelled. The public hearing at the Pala Maneri Project on the Bhagirathi River was our first experience with this process. It was also the first time that the authorities witnessed opposition at a public hearing. Hitherto, they had been oblivious to the possibility of protest at a public hearing.

In another instance, at a project site located near the Sutlej River, I remember reaching the area and having to actually locate and find the people who would have been affected by the project, and then convincing them to voice protest against a project that would have affected them the most. After much deliberation, I was able to persuade them to ask for documents containing details of the project from the authorities so that a letter citing the main concerns about the project could be drafted and sent to higher authorities.

When we approached the authorities for acquiring these documents, the authorities were reluctant to comply with our request. Now the (Draft) EIA Notification clearly prescribes that concerned parties can ask the authorities to provide documents containing relevant information about the project. Realizing this, the authorities finally provided the 400-page-long EIA report and asked us to get it photocopied. It felt like a major victory to get that report. Nowadays, reports can be accessed online.

We conveyed to the district administration that the local people hardly had any knowledge about the hearing process which was scheduled for the 28th of the month. I reached the area on the 25th and procured the EIA report just two days prior to the scheduled hearing. The next day, on the 27th, the SDMs [sub-divisional magistrates] visited every village and notified people to attend the hearing the next day but the notification should have been given thirty days prior to the date of the hearing per the law. We again raised concerns about the lack of time to assess the report before the hearing. On the 28th, the newspaper revealed that the hearing had been cancelled. We felt that this was another achievement for us.

Anyway, about the Sutlej incident, after the hearing got cancelled the first time, it was rescheduled a few months later. I went again, and we undertook a planned campaign. We went to villages, met people, and explained to them the whole process.

The hearings were organized at two places, where the actual dam was to be built and where the water was being discharged. We first went to the former and started explaining our concerns about the project. I asked the officials seated there, with due respect, to introduce themselves. I was instead asked to provide my credentials. When I asked the officials if they had been through the documents and the EIA report of the project, the authorities had no answer. It was an interesting experience. Seeing the authorities dumbfounded, the attendees started sloganeering "Bina jaankari jan sunvaayi radd karo!" ("Due to inadequate information, invalidate the hearing!"), and the hearing got disrupted. The officials tried to placate the crowd by offering refreshments but were met with refusal. The attendees asserted that the authorities should provide them comprehensible information instead of food. Therefore, another hearing was cancelled in such a fashion. Another concern that came to the fore due to the people's agitation was that the EIA report and other documents were in English and, therefore, incomprehensible to most.

The third public hearing was scheduled a few months later. But even then the EIA report was not translated into Hindi. All that changed was that events like these started a discourse about the need to provide a summary of the report in Hindi. Earlier, no such provision was there. Also, another concern we raised was that only the draft EIA report was made available to the public for consultation, the final EIA was not. This virtually meant that there was no guarantee that the concerns forwarded by the public were incorporated into the planning process. There was a lot of opacity, but before 2006, we could at least walk out of the hearing and get it cancelled. Since the 2006 Notification, the need for quorum in hearings has been done away with, so the authorities now have an easy way out. Another concern we raised was that people were never notified about the hearing thirty days before the scheduled date, as required by the law. Actually, the notion that previously existed amongst the people in authority was that hearings are a remote occurrence and should be wrapped up with the least effort.

Now, let me come to the Pala Maneri hearing which was scheduled for September 2004. The day of the hearing saw people providing strong opposition to the process. Basically, it came to everybody's knowledge, even the authorities, that I was the reason behind the strong opposition of the people. Everybody knows these things in most hearings. There is an entire nexus of people who have reasons to threaten the activist – the politicians, and the authorities, the project proponents. They try to sabotage the process.

The law mandates that the summary has to be provided in the local language, but a twenty-page summary is gravely inadequate for a 500-page EIA report. The summary also contains very basic details like "What is a Dam?", and "What are the benefits of a Dam?", with undue emphasis being laid on the pecuniary benefits of a dam, so as to sway public opinion in the project's favour. No mention is made of the technical details and risks of the project. The summary, in essence, is a redundant document, more of a sham. I raised this concern at the Pancheswar Dam hearings in front of three District Magistrates. I explained how expecting illiterate village folk to comprehend a 700-page report was unreasonable. All my grievances were met with an apathetic reply – "We are proceeding according to the law."

The first characteristic of public hearings is that the people rarely know the details of the process. A small notice is put in the newspapers in a miniscule font size, in complex language unlikely to be understood by common folk, something that has always been ignored by the government. So, the authorities fulfil all the formalities, whereas, in fact, nothing has been done that will actually allow the people to understand the details.

When a public hearing was conducted for the Jaghol Dam, I went to Jaghol, a remote village. The village chief told me that he had received some incredibly bulky documents, written in English, and was instructed to explain their contents to the villagers, obviously an impossible task. Apart from hollow preliminary formalities, the authorities employ certain tactics to get through the hearing process without much effort.

This was the usual state of hearings at that time. We participated in public hearings for other projects around that time as well. For example, Kotlibel-1A, Kotlibel-1B, and Kotlibel 2. Kotlibel-1A was on the Bhagirathi River, Kotlibel-1B on the Alaknanda River, and Kotlibel 2 at Kodiala. Almost every hearing brought a new unanticipated challenge, challenging characters, and new issues.

Firstly, let's talk about the Kotlibel-1B public hearing. The main effort is put in much before the actual hearing. One has to inform, educate, and mobilize the people. At the aforementioned hearing, we gathered a crowd of around 500 to attend the hearing. This was an unprecedented scale. I was accused of instigating people and was ejected from the hearing premises. I was even arrested later. But before that, we continued our protest outside the hearing premises. Sometime later, we approached an official to voice our grievance and explained to him that the public was notified of the hearing a mere ten days before the hearing, unlike the prescribed thirty-day period. So, to counter that, the authorities afterward began a comprehensive propaganda campaign in the name of notifying the public. All advertisements about the hearing highlighted the generic benefits of having a dam.

Authors: During the public hearings process there was no mention of the risks involved with the project?

Vimal Bhai: Discussion about risks was a redundant exercise for the authorities. The people were mostly led to believe that the project would mean direct pecuniary benefit to them. The Kotlibel EIA was challenged in court. And during the adjudication, the minutes of the hearing were adduced as evidence, which clearly mentioned that the notification of the hearing came just ten days before the date of hearing. We challenged the EIAs of all three Kotlibel projects at the NEAA. The matter ended with the adjudicators reluctantly agreeing on visiting the dam sites and assessing the veracity of the concerns.

Although the NEAA's final order was a very light (mild) order, it acknowledged the people's grievances, and consequently, cancelled the environmental clearance. But the order has been challenged in the Supreme Court, and litigation is going on for the past ten years.

At the second Devasari public hearing, I was arrested for instigating the crowds. I was taken to the police station. Somehow, some companions of mine were able to capture photographs of the arrest to keep a record. They kept me in lockup for a day. The villagers visited me in the evening, bailed me out, and thanked me.

Another instance worth mentioning is the last hearing for the Pancheshwar Dam project. A lot of effort was going on behind the scenes – preparing representations, writing letters, etc. We reached the public hearing, but I was not allowed to enter the premises at first. We were later stopped from taking banners and placards into the premises. So, we had to put up an elaborate ruse to sneak in important documents and the EIA report into the hearing.

In my conversation later with a District Magistrate, who was supposedly a part of the hearing process, it came to my knowledge that the District Magistrate was not even aware of the contents of the EIA report, so hollow is the whole process of public hearings. This is my main grievance; we need to have a robust process as only then can it lead to some productive deliberation.

Another phenomenon that I have noticed is that before every public hearing, the electricity in the area, or the network mysteriously shuts down. At the first Jaghol Saakri hearing, the area did not have electricity for two days before the hearing. My attempts to attend the second hearing were sabotaged as well.

At the time of the first Pancheshwar hearing, the stage was occupied mostly by political figures, whom people were anxious not to irk. For some reason, in the name of ensuring security of the hearing, policemen with heavy weaponry were posted all around. It was really an intimidating experience and doused any hopes of the hearing witnessing any protest by the people. The whole setup was designed to curb any dissent from the people. I was hardly given any time to speak. As soon as I started making contentious points, the mic was cut off. My views were also reflected in a distorted manner in the minutes of the hearing.

Authors: What do you think about the "employment argument" that is often forwarded in favour of dams and other projects? Political figures often waylay the people by simply talking about how much employment the project, if allowed to materialize, would generate, and how much benefit will accrue to the people.

Vimal Bhai: My counterargument to such propaganda mostly consists of the same two points, mainly because I have not yet received a satisfactory response to my points. First of all, I ask about the amount of employment generated by previous dams. Through an RTI, we once discovered that an enormous project that submerged nearly 125 villages created employment for just about 600 people. The second point that I make is that the nature of employment generated is not stable. They do not provide permanent employment to most, plus the kind of jobs provided is such that the villagers come in clash with each other. A person from one village is hired to demolish houses of the same village, and thus, conflict is bred.

In fact, these kinds of jobs lead to people losing out on other better opportunities because the time for those has passed. The private construction companies which hire the affected people often exploit them. In the end, these "employment" opportunities end up hurting the people more than they benefit them. But it is human nature to be allured by the prospect of immediate gain even if it ultimately leads to your loss. The villages affected by these projects lack the most basic amenities. They are mostly underdeveloped, and the people keep clamouring for employment opportunities. So, it is a vicious circle that has been created by false assurances of employment.

Authors: Do the authorities concerned with the projects adequately reply to the queries that are forwarded to them by the people?

Vimal Bhai: Who are we to seek replies? In our democracy, a citizen's role ends with the casting of the vote. He should endeavour to meddle no further. If a citizen affected by the project raises his voice, then they create problems in his rehabilitation.

This is exactly why public hearings are so important. Each and every citizen must get a chance to put forth his grievance and his or her view. If due process is followed, if the people are explained the whole matter in a language they can comprehend, and then asked their views, that counts as a real public hearing. At Devasari, we once conducted a "People's Public Hearing", organized by ourselves. Around 2,000 people arrived, without any pecuniary incentive. And what a conventional public hearing would have done was to provide all these people with complex information in a language they cannot understand.

So, a public hearing, if done correctly, can become a really effective way of knowing people's aspirations. And I think if hearings were conducted sincerely, no dam would ever be cleared, because in reality, almost all projects are environmentally unsound. In fact, if one randomly picks up the EIA report of any four dams, one will see an overwhelmingly repetitive pattern. The only explanation for this is that the government simply does not have the inclination to respect environmental safeguards. They do not want the people to really know, so they conceal and deceive.

Authors: What are your views about the Draft EIA Notification, 2020, which has been put out for public consultation?

Vimal Bhai: Till now, the system that the government had put in place was a total ruse in the name of the EIA process. The theory of it all was commendable, and it appeared like a breakthrough in the beginning, a result of many campaigns and efforts. The 2006 Notification weakened the regime set up under the 1994 Notification. More importantly, the textual law was followed neither in letter nor in spirit.

The new EIA Draft which has come out is symbolic of the MoEF letting go of even the pretence of environmental sensitivity. They have made their stance very clear. Till now, the sham of EIAs was used to show that the people's concerns had been considered before the Ministry arbitrarily and inevitably gave clearance to the projects. The public consultation process was totally flawed in the past as well. The notifications, the document delivery, the timelines, everything was flawed. It was a sham. The people were asked to put forth their demands, even though nothing was done to ensure that the common folk understood what they were involved in. They did not know of the possible effects, risks of the dam, mitigation strategies, etc. But despite all these flaws, there was some purpose to participating in the hearing. There was, at the least, some productive outcome, howsoever small, because of the hearing. What the new EIA does is completely remove the people from the process.

Authors: What we have also seen is a constant effort to minimize the EIA process. For example, the prescribed duration of the screening process was initially 600 days. This was then reduced to 300 days, and then to 180 days. Even the provision of *ex-post facto* clearances has been made for industries currently operating without due clearances. Why do you think the government has adopted this consistent agenda of diluting the EIA process? How does the government get the confidence to bring out changes like these?

Vimal Bhai: About the issue of where the government derives its confidence from, I will again refer to the Bagpiper's story. I think that environmental activism in India, which started with the Chipko Movement, the Narmada Bachao Andolan, etc., led to legal "breakthroughs" like the EIA regime. I personally believe that this "breakthrough" was a ploy by the government, which thinks that it can easily deceive the public. Innumerable industries, in the meanwhile and even currently, started operations without any clearances. At places that are beyond the reach of environmental activists, we have no idea of what goes on there. And that is when people, to get justice that they were denied by the authorities, approach forums like the NGT. Adjudication, on the other hand, is an incredibly tardy process. The system of appeals often kicks in, and it can take years before you get the relief you are entitled to. Few have the patience, the money, and the strength to fight it out in the courts. The government now sees this. They realize that once the clearance is granted, a common man is virtually left without any practical remedies. So, the new EIA Notification is sort of an open challenge by the government to those affected by their projects.

Authors: Another question that comes to our mind is about the NGT's comparison with its predecessors. You were one of the persons whose campaign and litigation in the Supreme Court led to the establishment of the NGT. You have also actively litigated before the NGT several times. What do you perceive as the main differences between the NGT and the NEAA? And what are your views about the present state of functioning of the NGT?

Vimal Bhai: Under the NEAA, the state of adjudication was really poor. The premises consisted of a room inside the Jawaharlal Nehru Stadium. There was only one member occupying a bench, which ideally should have been occupied by two judicial and three expert members. The single judge had only one task – to dismiss applications. The Loharinag Pala appeal was dismissed on the technical ground that we did not file it within the prescribed ninety-day period. A judge sitting in a room in Delhi would have little idea about the time and effort required to collect evidence related to an EIA process. To explain the problem to illiterate witnesses, to persuade them to be a part of the case, to get a single affidavit signed, it all takes an incredible amount of time. But the NEAA overlooked all this and dismissed the case.

So, obviously, we went to the Delhi High Court. The judge at the High Court also took up the matter of the poor state of functioning of the NEAA, the problem of inadequate appointments, etc. There was a whole series of problems that the government refused to cooperate on. They were paying something around INR 20,000 to the members; why would anyone want to be appointed? This went on for long, and finally the Delhi High Court imposed a penalty of INR 20,000 on the Ministry for not acting on its directions. The final stand taken by the Ministry was that since the NGT was in the process of being established, it was pointless to appoint new members to the NEAA. And soon, the NEAA was shut down. But the NGT was not functional yet. So, in the meanwhile, there was a period when there was virtually no remedy available for environmental grievances.

We went to the Supreme Court to highlight this. Our advocates even suggested the kinds of facilities that the NGT and its members must be provided to avoid an NEAA-like debacle. But when the government finally announced its plans for the NGT, we were taken aback. The state of the infrastructure that was provided to the NGT and its members was nothing less than humiliating. If the state of the NGT in the nation's capital was so poor, one can easily imagine the plight of the regional benches.

I really must give credit to Justice Ashok Kumar Ganguly, who ordered the establishment of the NGT. He was a visionary who understood and appreciated the role that the NGT had to play in protecting the country's environment. The NGT was a game-changer for environmental litigants. Previously at the NEAA, we had only a few lawyers, but the NGT saw numerous lawyers of great repute argue before it. Sometimes, they also argued against us. But Justice Swatanter Kumar was a really progressive judge, and it was his good sense that led to the imposition of heavy liability on the Tehri Hydrodevelopment Corporation for disposing of muck from the dam construction directly into the river.

Most importantly, the people became aware of environmental issues. The people's expression of environment-related grievances got emboldened, so did their aspirations for securing justice. The NGT's name reached every village, and this was probably the most positive development of all. The NGT also was clearly a decisive tribunal.

This was a predicament for the government. They had themselves created an agency that was, in fact, doing its job of protecting the environment. This was obviously inconvenient for those in power. So, something had to be done to detract from the NGT's authority and effectiveness. They did this by totally diluting the EIA process first. *Na rahega baans, na bajegi bansuri* (when the bamboo won't be there, then the flute won't play). So, now what will the people challenge in court when there's very little scope to challenge? So, they reduced the legal grounds available for challenging a clearance.

Secondly, engineered sabotage of the regional benches of the NGT was initiated. In this lockdown, they have now completely brought things to a halt. Who do you think from within India's remote villages will be able to manage video conferencing? Moreover, in our appearances before the NGT, the judges were benign and often gave us laymen time to explain our concerns, much to the chagrin of opposing lawyers and despite their best efforts to snub us. In video conferencing, which is a digital man's arena, do you think that simple folk will get a chance to adequately put their point across?

Authors: Could you tell us about how the EIA and environmental clearance regime are interlinked with the NGT's jurisprudence and their importance in litigating before the NGT? It is seen that in nearly half of the cases before the NGT, it is the environmental clearance that is being challenged.

Vimal Bhai: Definitely. In fact, it is the environmental clearance which becomes the basis for approaching the NGT. The whole thing being done to the EIA regime is a kind of a planned conspiracy. The whole of the EIA Draft, 2020, is aimed at suppressing or turning silent the voices of those aggrieved by projects. Secondly, it is also aimed at weakening the institution of the NGT. But I'll also add here that this Draft will not silence the voices of the thousands that toil for environmental justice. We have resisted in the past, and we will continue to voice our protest till we are alive.

Authors: What do you think are the three biggest challenges that the NGT would have to overcome in the coming times? It has been more than ten years since the NGT was formed. What do you see as the main challenges in the next ten years which must necessarily be tackled for the NGT to meet the people's aspirations?

Vimal Bhai: It is very tough to answer this question, given that the government is hell-bent on destroying the NGT itself. But firstly, I do believe that if the new Draft EIA is prevented from taking effect, if the NGT takes a stand against it, it will mean a lot.

Secondly, I think that it is crucial to have such judges at the NGT who adjudicate effectively. The appointment of the judges and expert members is the pivot around which the NGT's story will revolve. Then, we have to see which agency is responsible for appointing them, and the process by which they are appointed. We believe that there must be a People's Commission to appoint judges to the NGT. This Commission should be occupied by people who have genuine credentials in the field of environmental activism. This Commission should be responsible even for the appointment of expert members. Previously, we have seen people with hardly any actual expertise in environmental matters occupying the position of expert members. We have many genuinely qualified experts in India, and it is not tough to find such people to occupy these positions.

Thirdly, I feel there is an immediate need to increase the number of benches of the NGT. In the past, at most, we have had probably four benches working at once. These benches had jurisdiction over regions, and the regions were too large. Take the Southern Zone, for example, which has to deal with matters from such a vast range of states – Kerala, Tamil Nadu, Maharashtra, Karnataka, etc. I think that there should be sub-regional benches too, with jurisdiction over, at most, two or three states.

I also have a personal opinion that others might find seriously disagreeable, which is that there must also be some issue-based classification of the benches. This is because the kind of environmental issues that arise in the Himalayas are very different from those that arise in Tamil Nadu. So, for the Himalayan zone, there should be a special bench. Another opinion that I hold is that in such benches there must be a jury along with the judge and the expert members.

Authors: We would like to explore the idea of a People's Commission that you mentioned. Who do you think should be responsible for appointing persons to the People's Commission?

Vimal Bhai: See, this again finally boils down to the government's decision. It's very tough to totally disassociate the government from the process. But I feel that representatives from various political parties should be part of the People's Commission, which will then approve the appointments to the NGT.

Another challenge that the NGT needs to, and can, overcome is that it must be very particular about ensuring the sanctity of the public hearing process. Just like the Supreme Court, which often sends Commissions for on-ground inquiry, the NGT must use this measure more often and really assess these hearings at the grassroots level. This subaltern approach would be the right path for the NGT.

Also, there must be measures to promote transparency and efficiency in environmental adjudication. Time-bound judgments are extremely essential. Otherwise, the process becomes fictitious, because while the case goes on, the project construction also goes on, and then finally, it is claimed that now it is unviable to stop the project. Only in very few cases, the NGT has stayed the project during the course of the litigation. Usually, as time goes on, the NGT says that whatever damage was apprehended has already been done, and then usually asks the proponent to pay a fine. This is another important point. The value of human lives cannot be weighed in money.

Another crucial point is the issue of monitoring. It should be the biggest concern of the NGT. There is hardly any monitoring. If there is, the concerned party is usually asked to self-evaluate and then send a report created by themselves – as patent a conflict of interest as there can be. And the court relies on such documents created by the project proponent. Projects should be monitored by neutral parties. The MoEF and the SPCBs are often understaffed and do not have enough manpower to adequately play their role. I have, in my informal conversations with officials, been told that the manpower available to these authorities is gravely inadequate for the scope of their duties. When they simply do not have staff, how will they monitor? This was also an argument given to us by MoEF officials, albeit in a repulsive tone.

*   *   *

INDEX OF CASES

www.ingramcontent.com/pod-product-compliance
Ingram Content Group UK Ltd.
Pitfield, Milton Keynes, MK11 3LW, UK
UKHW050151060325
455824UK00009B/79